Smith B. Goodenow

Bible Chronology

carefully unfolded

Smith B. Goodenow

Bible Chronology
carefully unfolded

ISBN/EAN: 9783337099817

Printed in Europe, USA, Canada, Australia, Japan

Cover: Foto ©Lupo / pixelio.de

More available books at **www.hansebooks.com**

BIBLE CHRONOLOGY

CAREFULLY UNFOLDED.

SHOWING:

I.—That there is a Bible Chronology, which is strikingly definite and evident to the searcher after truth.

II.—That there is no outside Chronology, at all reliable, to set aside the Bible Chronology.

III.—That therefore the Scriptures are historically truthful, giving a correct account of ancient events and dates.

TO WHICH IS ADDED A
RESTORATION OF JOSEPHUS.

BY REV. SMITH B. GOODENOW, A. M.,

Author of "The Pilgrim Faith Maintained;" "Immortality and the Doom of Sin;" "Inspired Truthfulness of the Original Scriptures," etc

FLEMING H. REVELL COMPANY,
NEW YORK,   CHICAGO,   TORONTO.
1896.

SOME OTHER TREATISES
Auxiliary to this work, by
the same author.

The Classic Chronology.

The Early Christian Chronicles.

The History of the Christian Era.

The Adjustment of Eras.

Cycles, Epacts, Equinoxes, etc.

Copyright, 1896, by Smith B. Goodenow, Battle Creek, Iowa.

INTRODUCTION.

There is a measure of truth in the sentiment of Horace Bushnell, that "Every man's life is a plan of God." At least to any one who has from youth devoted himself to the service of his Maker there is a consolation in feeling, that everything down to old age, however mysterious the Providence, has ministered to the achievement of that service.

The present writer was led from his boyhood, at 14 years of age, in the City of Providence, Rhode Island, under the venerated Charles G. Finney, in A. D. 1831, to consecrate himself, soul and body, for life, to the work of the Master, and the vindication of his truth. Being beset with opposition, frequent lone hours of devotion on the neighboring hills were solaced by gazing into the stars and repeating all through that wonderful hymn (then just produced):

> "Jesus, I my cross have taken,
> All to leave and follow thee;
> Naked, poor, despised, forsaken,
> Thou from hence my all shalt be.
> * * * * * *
> Go, then, earthly fame and treasure !
> Come, disaster, scorn and pain !
> In thy service pain is pleasure,
> With thy favor loss is gain."

Has the omen proved true?

He forthwith found himself engaged with a corps of S. S. workers and others in various Old Testament studies connected with Moses and the Jewish kings. The chronological investigations and manuscripts then evolved, before the age of 15 and 16, have been of service to this day. And the result was a ladies' education society formed in the church and the youthful investigator started by them through a course for the ministry.

Never did the fervor of that first zeal for God's truth abate. And the boy thus set apart by hallowed sanctions for the search and defense of God's word, has never forgotten to use all his natural faculty and acquired scholarship in elucidating and magnifying the Book Divine. Whatever vicissitudes and disappointments have attended the ministerial work in general, an unseen hand has led; and most of the unspent energy which others gave to vacation pastimes and promiscuous literature, was for fifty years spent in delving in remote libraries, copying voluminous masses of material from different languages, and searching out abstruse and difficult points. Thus the youthful bent was pushed into the enthusiastic work of a life-time;

and what was represented by most as a very uncertain and unprofitable study, was found to develop into a research of untold interest and value.

The writer was early impressed very strongly with the fact that the coming contest over the Bible would center about the question of its historical truthfulness: and he could not fail to see, that the question of truthfulness would turn largely upon the chronological certitude of the dates given. To that point he has bent his energies, and he has reached the most convincing conclusions. Today, when the onset has really come, and the Old Testament veracity is on all hands assailed, the chronological results here reached find their use, and serve as a breast-work against the tide of archæological assault, which threatens to make havoc of the Old Testament history. As the New Testament has signally won in the chronological struggle, so the Old Scriptures are destined to win. The research thus begun in boyhood, is thus proving the sure determiner of faith in old age. Was it not in the plan?

When we pushed with zest into the datings of Scripture, we were surprised to find almost everybody casting reproach upon the study, as trivial and of little account. From the little interest taken in the subject, and from the vague and irrational methods of inquiry adopted, it came to pass, that very defective results were reached, and this led to reproach upon the whole investigation. A vast variety of different results were claimed, where sober sense should have shown but a single interpretation possible; and Bible datings were represented as a matter of very great uncertainty. As long ago as in the Bibliotheca Sacra of 1858 (p. 289), there was such a representation of Bible Chronology, as if it were a perfect bank of fog. Since then, various similar articles have been published: and within a few years latterly, there have appeared labored treatises (by men otherwise sound in the faith), vainly trying to make the chronology of Gen. v and xi, to be no chronology at all, but only undated genealogical tables! (See the Bib. Sacra, 1873, p. 323, and 1890, p. 285.)

One aim and result of our work is, to scatter all these illusory notions concerning the uncertainty of Bible datings, (which in general arise from very superficial study of the subject), and to convince the Bible student, how sure and determinate a matter Scripture chronology is. As a basis for all, the date of Christ's death, as on Friday, April 7th, A. D. 30, is found to be sure and unmistakable, and now generally agreed upon: instead of being assigned to almost every other year but that, as was the case when this work was undertaken. The nativity, as near the beginning of B. C. 4, together with all the other N. T. dates, we have here taking their definite position,—in place of the multiplied, vague and erroneous figures commonly given fifty years ago.

Then follows the Old Testament dating, assuredly started with B. C. 587, as the time of Nebuchednezzar's capture of Jerusalem (not 588, as put by Usher); whence the Jewish kings are easily seen to date back, first 133 years to B. C. 720 at the capture of Samaria—and then 254 years more to the death of Solomon in B. C. 974—and 37 years more to the founding of the temple in the 4th year of Solomon, B. C. 1011; a total of (133+254+37=) 424 years from the capture of Jerusalem back to the founding of the temple, or (67+133+254+37=) 491 years from the second temple in B. C. 520, back to the first temple in B. C. 1011, just as given by Josephus as well as the Scriptures.

All this is made so plain and sure, by the many unmistakable dates and cross dates given, interlocking in every way, that by this simple and certain method of self-adjustment, the Bible Chronology is made indisputable back to the founding of the temple in the 4th year of Solomon, as being in B. C. 1011 (not 1012, as Usher's B. C. 588 instead of 587 for Jerusalem's destruction makes it.) This date for Solomon's Temple may be considered as perfectly assured in the Bible. And the attempt of archæologists to construct from the Assyrian Eponym Canon another chronology of the kings, 40 or 50 years later than that of Scripture, is thus shown to leave Bible Chronology itself untouched. The true Bible Chronology of human history back to the founding of Solomon's Temple, as in B. C. 1011, is fixed and assured.

The time from Solomon's Temple back to the Exodus, is the first interval where we come to any scriptural doubt; but careful study shows the uncertainty to be much less than supposed. The I Kings vi: 1, probably covers "the 480th year" of *actual reign*, excluding 100 years of foreign subjugation deemed unworthy of recognition. This is made probable by *the 580 years* reckoning of the New Testament, (Acts xiii: 17-21); and it reaches almost a certainty, when we find Josephus and all the early fathers, both Jewish and Christian, giving only the longer interval, with no allusion to the shorter now found in I Ki. vi: 1.

Most likely, the "480th" is a copyist's variation or addition to the previous reading, taken from the margin as an explanation of the original value intended, which was "580 years" (expressed or more probably understood). *

---

* There might be a *single* copyist's error here or there in Scripture; and indeed we know for a certainty, that there is *occasionally* a corruption of a date or number. But there could not be any such *wholesale* corruption of the dates generally as the Assyriologists ascribe to the history of the Jewish kings. What they call *harmonizing* Scripture with Assyriology, is rather a demolition of the Bible to make way for alleged Assyriology. If the Scripture is *so* corrupt as they make it, (*i. e.*, in most of its dates), then it is no true history, and is not to be believed at all.

Thus Scripture is made consistent with itself (in Acts and Judges as compared with I Ki. vi: 1); and the Exodus is carried to B. C. 1591 (instead of Usher's 1491). This is more consistent with the monuments, than are the anti-scriptural theories of the Egyptologists at present current, which put down the Exodus to about B. C. 1300.

The interval from the Exodus back to the birth of Abram is very plainly (430+75—) 505 years; making the birth of Abram to be in B. C. 2096, in place of Usher's 1996. Thus far back Bible Chronology is remarkably simple and sure. The preceding Diluvian Chronology (post- and pre-diluvian), adds to this, either in the Hebrew (+352+1656), making 4104 B. C. for the creation, or in the Greek of Josephus (+992+2256), making the creation B. C. 5344. With the Hebrew B. C. 4104, the human race is *six thousand years old* in A. D. 1897, but with the Greek, the human race was *seven thousand years old*, somewhere from A. D. 1471 to 1721, according to variations of the Septuagint.

This great divergence in the copies as to the full age of the world, may have been providentially allowed (by the corrupt copying either of the Hebrew or of the Greek text), for the very purpose of preventing any sure fixing prematurely of prophetic "times and seasons" (purposely hidden, though told, Acts i: 7); while at the same time giving that exactness of dating so characteristic of the Bible, which vouches for the history as truthful and leaves the total assured within a few hundred years.

This work is intended to supply

A LONG EXISTING WANT.

—to furnish

A BIBLE TEXT-BOOK,

indispensable to every thorough student of Scripture.*

---

* "With nearly all existing books in this department, the weakest part is the treatment of the Old Testament data. Men put in their best work for deciphering some obscure inscription that has been dug up somewhere, and in deciding what inferences may, and what may not, be drawn from it; but they fancy that they know without much study what the Old Testament says. So they heedlessly accept some crude traditional interpretation of an Old Testament statement, instead of looking freshly and keenly to find out what the statement actually is. The extent to which existing criticism is vitiated by this process is appalling. * * * In the department of Old Testament study, such (thorough) work is now more needed than work of any other kind." (*Sunday School Times, Sep. 28, 1895, p. 620.*)

CONTENTS.

Bible Chronology may, for convenience, be divided into seven portions, denoted by the letters A, B, C, D, E, F, G, as follows:

- A. From Creation to the Flood.
- B. From the Flood to the Birth of Abram.
- C. From the Birth of Abram to the Exodus.
- D. From the Exodus to the Founding of Solomon's Temple.
- E. From the Founding to the Burning of the Temple.
- F. From the Burning of the Temple to the Christian Era.
- G. From the Christian Era to the Close of the New Testament.

In our examination of the subject, we work *backward*, from the most obvious to the most obscure, beginning with the Crucifixion and ending with the Creation, as follows:

Period G. *The New Testament.*

PART I. The Date of Christ's Death, historically and astronomically fixed, on Friday, April 7th, A. D. 30. § 1.

 Chap. I. Historical Review, § 4.
  1. Historical Age, § 4.
  2. Equinoctial Cycle Age, § 11.
  3. Later Theory Age, etc., § 17.

 Chap. II. Astronomical Demonstration, § 18.
  1. The State of the Case, § 18.
  2. The Means of Adjustment; Lunar Cycles, § 23.
  3. The Lunar Calculations; Corrections, § 33.
  4. The Data Combined, § 39; The True Date, § 44.
  5. Important Results, § 48.

APPENDIX.

- A. Christ's Resurrection on Sunday, § 56; Crucifixion on Friday, § 57.
- B. The Jewish Months were Lunar, § 67.
- C. Ancient Lunar Cycles Exhibited, § 73.
- D. Was the Crucifixion on the 14th or 15th Nisan ? § 80.
- E. Corrected Reckoning of the N. T. Lunar Dates, § 90.

PART II. Sundry New Testament Dates, § 95.

 Chap. I. Christ's Baptism, § 95; the Nativity, § 96.
  Cyrenius Governor, § 99; Day of Nativity, § 101.
  Pauline Dates, § 102; N. T. Events, § 106.
  Roman Emperors, § 107; Jerusalem Taken, A. D. 70, § 109; Local Rulers, § 110.

 Chap. II. Women at the Tomb; a Harmony of the Resurrection, § 111.

  TABLE OF BIBLE DATES, § 120.

Old Testament Chronology; the certainty and importance of it, p. 102. Assyriology and Egyptology, p. 104.

Period F. The Exile and After.

From the Captivity to the Christian Era.

PART I. The Intervening Dates, § 1; Ptolemy's Canon, § 1; Josephus and the Maccabees, § 3; The Year B. C. 163, § 5; The Detailed Reigns, § 9; Corroborations, § 12; Back to the Captivity, § 14.

PART II. Jerusalem Destroyed by Nebuchadnezzar B. C. 587, not 588, § 15; Corrected View of Jer., lii: 28-30, § 20; Scripture Evidence, § 26; The Sabbatic Year, § 29; Further Confirmation, § 32; Origin of the Error, § 36.

Period E. The Kings.

PART I. From Solomon's Temple to the Captivity, § 1.
  Chap. I. The Capture of Samaria, § 2.
  Chap. II. Hezekiah's 14th year; Harmony of Isa. xxxvi: 1, § 7; Assyrian Assaults, § 11; Isaiah, ch. 20, 21, § 15; Senacherib's Account, § 18.

PART II. Bible Chronology of the Kings.
  Chap. I. The Bible Dates, § 21; Table of Synchronisms, § 25; Explanations, § 27.
  Chap. II. The Bible Method, § 34; But One Bible Method, § 42; Corroborations, § 45.
  Chap. III. Jubilee Reckonings, § 49; Given Jubilee Years, § 56; Given Sabbatic Years, § 65.
  Chap. IV. Unfounded Theorizings, § 75-80.

PART III. Assyriology and the Jewish Kings, § 81; First Division, Pul and Ahaz.
  Chap. I. Who was "Pul" of Assyria? § 82.
    (1) Vul-nirari, § 86.
    (2) Assur-daan, § 89.
    (3) Tiglath-pileser, § 93.
  Chap. II. "This is that king Ahaz," § 100; Interregnum in Israel, § 109; Second Division, Ahab and Jehu.
  Chap. III. The Inscriptions, § 111.
    (*a*) As to Jehu, § 114; (*b*) as to Ahab, § 115.
  Chap. IV. The Surroundings, § 120;
    The Ahab and Jehu Interval, § 126;
    The Course of Events, § 128.
    Conclusion, § 132.

PART IV. Comparative Reliability of the Jewish and the Pagan Chronology, § 133.
  Chap. *I.* Assyriology and the Bible, § 133.
      1. As to Consecutiveness, § 138.
      2. As to Accuracy of Reporting, § 143.
      3. As to Certainty of Interpretation, § 149.
  Chap. II. Tyrian History and the Bible, § 151.
  Chap. III. Egyptian History and the Jewish Kings, § 159; The Olympic Era, § 164; Astronomical Allusions, § 168.

Period D. The Judges.

PART I. From the Exodus to Solomon's Temple, § 1.
  Chap. I. The Interval of 580 years, § 1; The Period of "450 years," § 2; Period of the Judges, § 5; Confirmation, § 8; Ancient Authorities, § 14; The Church Fathers,
  Chap. II. Attempted Defenses of the "480th year," § 21; Overlapping the Reigns, § 24; The Text of Acts xiii: 20, § 27; "Twenty Years," 1 Sam. vii: 2, § 32; Other Points, § 35.

APPENDIX.
  A. The "4th year" of Solomon, § 41.
  B. The Astronomical Date, § 44.
  C. Attempts to make "480" years, § 47.
  D. That "Canonical Formula," § 54.

PART II. Origin of the "480th year" Reading, § 58; The "612" in Josephus, § 63; The Original 980, § 65; The "440th" of the Septuagint, § 71; The "480th" of the Hebrew, § 78.

APPENDIX.
  A. Josephus and the Priest Record, § 85.
  B. Independence Era of Ehud, § 88.
  C. Israel's Stay in Haran, § 96.
  D. Corruption of the Scripture Text, § 99.
  E. Reliability of Josephus, § 100.

PART III. The Pharaoh of the Exodus, § 101.
  Chap. I. Egyptian Chronology, § 101.
  Chap. II. Theories of the Exodus, § 109; The 18th Dynasty, § 113; Probable Exodus Date, § 117.
  Chap. III. Meneptah as Pharaoh of the Exodus, § 120.
  Chap. IV. Thotmes IV, the Pharaoh of the Exodus, § 130-149.

Period C.—The Patriarchs.

PART I. From the Birth of Abram to the Exodus, § 1.
    The "400 years," § 3; Generations, § 9.
    The Census of Israel, § 14.

PART II. When Was Joseph Sold? § 19.
    Order of Events, § 20; Argument, § 22; Results, § 25.

Periods A, B.—Diluvian Chronology.

PART I. The Differing Texts, § 1.
  Chap. I. Is the Hebrew Corrupt? § 9.
  Chap. II. Process of Corruption, § 21.
  Chap. III. Is the Septuagint Correct? § 29.
  Chap. IV. Net Result, § 38.
PART II. Chronology of Gen. v and xi, § 44.
    The Non-Chronology Theories, § 48.
    Gen. v and xi are Genuine Chronology, § 58.
PART III. Primeval Man, § 61.
    Two Periods of Creation, § 64; The First Man, § 70.
PART IV. History and Prophecy, § 72.
  Chap. I. Age of the World, § 72.
    End of 6000 Years, § 78.
  Chap. II. Prophetic Datings, § 84; "Trodden Under Foot," § 89; The "2300 days" or years, § 94.

Restoration of Josephus.

PART I. The Primary Mistake, § 4; The Occasion of it, § 10; Correction of the 57 years, § 14; Chronology of the "War," § 16.
PART II. Jewish Datings Expounded, § 21; The "70 years" Captivity, § 25; The Priest Record's "414 years," § 31; Its "466 years," § 37; Its "612 years," § 44.
PART III. Josephus' One Consistent System, § 48; Josephus' "470 years," § 54; The Caption Datings, § 62; Josephus' Whole Chronology, § 69.

SUPPLEMENTARY NOTE.

APPENDIX.

A. Reliability of Josephus, § 74 (Period D, § 100.)
B. The View of Jacob Schwartz, § 75.
C. Scripture and Josephus Compared, § 80.
D. The Numbers in the "Jewish War," § 83.
E. The Finished Capturing, § 87.
F. How the Critics Differ, § 89.
G. Josephus' "592 years," § 90.
H. The Davidic Era, § 95.
I. The Captions Amended, § 97.
J. Josephus' One Consistent System, § 101-103.

PERIOD G THE NEW TESTAMENT.

PART I.

THE DATE OF CHRIST'S DEATH

HISTORICALLY AND ASTRONOMICALLY FIXED ON FRIDAY, APRIL 7TH, A. D. 30.

§ 1. "I determined," says Paul, "not to know anything among you, save Jesus Christ, and Him crucified." And that death scene of Calvary is still the great central theme of all our thoughts and teachings. How important that we be able to speak of it, not as a story located at *about* such a time in the world's progress, but as an actual event, of assured occurrence, at its own proper and unmistakable date. That crucifixion day was a day by itself, the like of which this fallen world has never beheld. It was in the counsels of God marked out from eternal ages for this particular transaction, and to eternal ages it will be commemorated as the birthday of human redemption.

§ 2. To treat the Messiah's passion only as belonging *somewhere* within a space of four or five years, as the church so long has been doing,* savors too much of mythologic tradition for this scientific and sceptical age, when "many run to and fro, and *knowledge is increased.*" God has suffered darkness, in this as in other matters, to creep over His Zion during the long ages of her wilderness wandering; but now, as the new day of her triumph begins to dawn, the better light of her earlier days may be expected again to break forth.

§ 3. Moved by these considerations, over forty years ago we set about this investigation; and here is the result then reached (now recopied).† Soon after that date, Weisler's like result in Germany reached this country, that being the first promulgation of A. D. 30; but this investigation was made in entire ignorance of that. Their independent concurrence is a confirmation of the agreeing date found, April 7th, A. D. 30.

---

* Now (in A. D. 1855), the Vulgar Chronology of Usher makes it April 3, A. D. 33. The great system of Hales puts it March 27, A. D. 31. The elaborate work of Clinton sets it April 15, A. D. 29. All dates but the true one have been confounding the minds of men.

† This treatise was a revision made in A. D. 1855, by request of Prof. Edwards A. Park, D. D., editor, for the purpose of publication in the Bibliotheca Sacra.

We will first give an Historical Review of New Testament dating; to be followed by an Astronomical Demonstration of the crucifixion date.

CHAPTER I.

Historical Review.

§ 4. Our examination of history* has developed the following facts:

(I.) *The Historical Age.* The earliest historical dating of the crucifixion which has come down to us, outside the New Testament, is the testimony of Clemens of Alexandria (A. D. 189-205), concerning the teachings of Basilides† (A. D. 134). Clemens tells us, that some of Basilides' disciples "assign the passion of Christ to the 16th year of Tiberius,—some putting it on the 25th day of Pharmonti." This "16th year of Tiberius," reckoned from the death of Augustus (on Aug. 19, A. D. 14), fixes the crucifixion in the spring of A. D. 30; and "the 25th of Pharmonti" in the Egyptian rotary year was then April 7th Julian‡, which was a *Friday*, and was at the *Paschal full moon* that year, as we shall prove astronomically.

---

* Fully given in a preliminary essay.

† Basilides was a Gnostic Christian, and therefore not considered thoroughly orthodox; but his testimony as to facts is unimpeached.

‡ The language of Clemens is this: "The passion of Christ some of them, (the followers of Basilides) assign to the 16th year of Tiberius, the 25th day of Phamenoth, some put it the 25th of Pharmonti (*pharmontiké*), others the 19th, some say the 24th or 25th." (*Clem. Strom., I, P. 340.*)

Now in the 16th of Tiberius (A. D. 30) the rotary 1 Thoth or new-year day of the Egyptians came on the 16th day of August, Julian, (having moved from Aug. 20 in the 16 years since Augustus' death, and from Aug. 29 in the 52 years since his introduction of the *fixed* year, Aug. 29, B. C. 23). And as the Egyptian year consisted of 12 thirty-day months with 5 days added at the end, therefore, its rotary months now began at the Julian Aug. 16, July 12, June 12, May 13, April 13, March 14; and the 25th of this 8th month "Pharmonti" was (March 14+24= 38—31=) April 7th.

It would not thus come on 16 Tib. after A. D. 30, nor on April 7 in any year after A. D. 31; for the next year (A. D. 32 bissextile) 1 Thoth changed to Aug. 15th. And it could not thus come on *Friday*, April 7th, except in the year 30, the 16th year of Tiberius after the death of Augustus,—as Clemens here gives the early tradition derived through Basilides. So that, in this number he is evidently giving the passion-date originally assigned; it being (as he adds) by some called "the 24th or 25th" (April 6th or 7th), according as they dated "the passion" from the crucifixion Friday, or (like Theophilus Caes., A. D. 196) from the betrayal by Judas the day before.

We therefore suppose all these day-dates named to have originated

§ 5. Here then we have a dating of our Lord's passion historically on April 7th, A. D. 30, in accordance with the facts. This A. D. 30, while the 16th year of Tiberius (after Augustus) was the year 78 of the Cæsars, from the close of B. C. 49, when Julius Cæsar, having crossed the Rubicon, gained possession of Rome. The Christian fathers generally until the 4th century adhered to this reckoning of Christ's death, as in the 16th year after Augustus, or the year 78 of the Cæsars, which means A. D. 30.

§ 6. Eusebius Pamphilus (A. D. 308-340) tells a story which fixes the same date.* The day-date April 7th (or Egyptian " Pharmonti

---

from that as the first and true tradition, somewhat as follows:

The rotary year having fully given way to the fixed year of Egypt, —it seems from Clemens that the passion-day dating had become misunderstood and perverted. For, as the 1 Thoth was stopped and fixed by Augustus when it was at Aug. 29, soon after his conquest of Egypt, by the insertion of the Julian leap-day then recently established, (by means of which the 5 extra days preceding each Thoth were properly increased to 6 every 4th year),—therefore, this *fixed year* beginning Aug. 29, was after 52 years 13 days later than the rotary year, beginning Aug. 16, A. D. 30. And the passion-date, April 6, 7, (or Pharmonti 24, 25, *rotary*), was thought by "some" to mean 13 days later, April 19, 20, (or Pharmonti 24, 25, *fixed*.)

This mistake made by some was in forgetfulness of the old rotary year; which, although ended by authority in Egypt just before the Christian era, as we saw, yet had still continued to be used among Jews and others, as appears in this passion-date, in Censorinus, etc. For the Jews, so soon afterward dispersed, had not yet worked out of the 365 day reckoning long since borrowed from their Egyptian neighbors, into the Julian 365¼-day reckoning so lately imposed upon the world by their Roman conquerors.

But after the Alexandrines with their long-fixed year had vitiated the Palestine passion-date, as if meaning April 19, 20, (instead of April 6, 7)—then some (it seems) thinking that altogether too late, put back the passion by conjecture a month earlier, *i. e.*, at March 21 (or "Phamenoth 25" instead of "Pharmonti 25"); just as it is afterward given by Epiphanius (A. D. 400), also Proterius (A. D. 457), and Victor (A. D. 566). Others, finding (by the lunar cycle then in use) that in the 16th of Tib. (A. D. 30), the April 19, 20, (as well as Mar. 20, 21), came on the wrong day of the week, moved back the passion-date to Friday, April 14, (or "Pharmonti 19" instead of "25"). Those days were loosely assigned a century after the event, without calculation as to lunar requirements, in that age of rude cycle knowledge.

Such was the state of things as Clemens found them after Basilides, in the second century, reporting them to us as above— not as his own speculations, but as traditions handed down from those before him. And thus was the true passion-day confounded and lost, its substitutes leading on to the confusing and losing afterward of the true year-date also. For, the dates, April 14 and March 21, as being (according to the same lunar cycle) near the full moon of 15 Tib. (A. D. 29) and 17 Tib. (A. D. 31) respectively, encouraged the subsequent cycle assignment of the passion to those respective years.

* The legend is this: "After Christ's resurrection from the dead,

25"), was soon lost through a confounding of the fixed with the rotary years of Egypt, as seen in the note just given. And the year itself after a time became confused in ways which we proceed to notice. At first the Christians had the nativity rightly 33 years before A. D. 30, or 4 years before our Christian era, and the baptism at the beginning of A. D. 27;* which was "the 15th year of Tiberius" (Lu. iii: 1) reckoned from his joint reign with Augustus.† But afterwards, mistaking Luke's "15th year of Tiberius" as if meaning the 15th year after Augustus' death, the fathers put the baptism along to A. D. 29, which threw along the nativity also to be only 2 years before our A. D., reducing the ministry of our Lord to but little over a year,‡ and his whole life to only 31 years.‖

―――――

Judas called also Thomas, moved thereto by Divine impulse, sent Thaddeus to Edessa to be a preacher and evangelist of the doctrine of Christ. * * * The written evidence of this matter we have out of the Office of Records within the princely city of Edessa, in which Agbarus then was governor. It is there preserved to this day as follows [the citation ends]: 'These things were done in the 340th year.' Which also we have translated word for word out of the Syriac tongue." (*Euseb. Eccle. Hist., B. I., ch. 13.*) As the Edessenes used the Seleucic Era, making their year 1 equivalent to our B. C. 311 (as shown in the previous essay), therefore, this year 340 closed at our A. D. 30, where, consequently, they must have assigned the crucifixion. Whatever may be thought of the *story* here related, these remote traditions and records do show the dates early assigned to New Testament events; thus corroborating the astronomical demonstration which we afterward give. (See the comments of Valerius on this passage of Eusebius, *Edit. Val. Paris, 1659, Camb., 1683.*)

* Ignatius, bishop of Antioch (A. D. 90–115), the second in succession from Peter, and himself a disciple of John, says: "God the Word * * * having lived in the world *three decades* of years was baptized, and having preached the gospel *three years* was crucified." (*Cotelerinus, Patres Apost.*) This is called spurious by Clinton. "Melito, who flourished about A. D. 160–172, calls the ministry *three years. En te trietia meta to baptisma.*" (*Apud Routh. Relig. Patrum, Tom, I, p. 115.*) Hippolytus (A. D. 220-226) places it within three years." (*Id. p. 136.* See Clinton's *Fas. Rom.* Vol. II, p. 227.) So Origen.

† Luke may have simply *antedated* the reign of Tiberius to the previous new year, as was the way of Ptolemy's Canon and other ancient Chronicles: and he may then have numbered *inclusively*, reckoning in as years the fractions at both ends, according to Jewish custom—so virtually covering a joint reign. For such a joint reign there is ample testimony in Roman historians, as given here, in § 95.

‡ No one in view of the Scripture narrative, could ever have given so short a ministry, except *under constraint* of the already assigned "16 Tib." for the crucifixion (compared with Lu. iii: 1), both taken as after the death of Augustus. So that, this traditional "16 Tib." could be made no later, but *had* to adhere to A. D. 30.

‖ "Irenius (A. D. 197) and Tertullian (A. D. 214) put the nativity in U. C. 751 or [end of] B. C. 3." (*Hales' Tech. Chron. on Eras.*) So

§ 7. Not only Clemens Alex. *, but also Africanus, the first great Christian chronologist† (A. D. 200), and others, kept the year to the 16th of Tiberius (or A. D. 30). The shortened life of Christ was afterward amended by Eusebius and Jerome in the 4th century; so as to make the ministry over 3 years and the life of Christ over 32; with the baptism and passion at the originally assigned places, A. D. 27 and 30, and the nativity 3 years before our A. D.‡

§ 8. With Julius Africanus (A. D. 221) was fully established the *vernal* reckoning of reigns, as beginning with the March *after* their

---

afterward Photius (A. D. 860) "Veterum multorum opinio fuit, Christum uno tantum anno praedicasse, eoque passum fuisse. Ex eorum numero fuit Africanus, ut testatur Hieronymus in ix Dan. Quem recte ex auctoritate evangelica Georgius [Syncellus] redarguit." (*Petavius, De Gracc. Eris, Cap. II, p. 1410.*) "Eusebius makes the nativity by Africanus to be 2 years before A. D." (*Dissert. of Bredov. in Syncel. Vol. II, p. 6.*) In his work *Peri Archon*, Origen has the ministry "a year and a few months." But in his *Com. in Lucam*, he departs from that view; and in his *Adv. Cel.*, he reckons the ministry between 2 and 3 years, confirming the same in his *Com. in Mat*. "If he began the years of Tiberius, as was the custom of the ancient Christians and others, from the paschal month *preceding*, the same year would be thought the 16th of Tib, which otherwise was the 15th." (*Petavius.*) "Gaudentius (A. D. 387) allowed only 1 year to the ministry." (*Clinton, Fas. Rom. Vol., II, Art. V.*)

* Clemens' Alex. not only gave the crucifixion date "16 Tib." as derived from Basilides (see before), but he adhered to it himself, putting the Baptism at the "15th Tib." (A. D. 29) and even antedating *vernally* the 15th Tib., to carry back the baptism to the spring of A. D. 28 (with the nativity 2 years B. C. as in Africanus), and thus allow 2 years of ministry; expressly saying that from this *baptism* to the capture of Jerusalem (in A. D. 70) "was 42 years and 3 months." All these express statements of Clemens (*Strom. I, p. 310, 340*), are cited in full in the previous essay. Jerome afterward spoke of the same "42 years" of preaching and warning for the Jews, from the baptism of Christ to the overthrow of Jerusalem. The notion of some, that it was the 16th Tib. (or the crucifixion) which Clemens and his cotemporaries were putting in A. D. 28, is too palpably wrong to need refutation.

† Africanus (A. D. 221) says of the crucifixion: "*Hos een olumpiados sb' etos deuteron Tiberiou de Kaisaros heegemonias etos ek-kaidekaton,*" [Olym. 202: 2, the 16th of Tiberius.] *Chronograph. lib. 5 in Euseb. Demonst. VII, p. 389, 390.* Compare *Routh, Vol. II, p. 187-190.* So cited in Syncellus, p. 323. "*Christon chronon . . . mechris hektou kai dekatou Tiberion Kaisaros hoper een Olumpiados sb' etos deuteron*;" "until" (the beginning of the) 16th Tib. *postdated* vernally, and Olym. 202: 2, *antedated* vernally, as both beginning with 1 Nisan in March, A. D. 30. This vernal chronology of Africanus is fully shown in the previous essay.

‡ One year was lost to the life of Christ by the reckoning of Lu. iii: 23, as meaning "the 30th year" (*ton triakonta eniauton.*) *Athanasins, tom. I, p. 586.* So Bede seems to explain Dionysius; and so Clin-

real start.* So that, he had Augustus as beginning March, B. C. 43, and Tiberius March, A. D. 15, and Vespasian March, A. D. 70. He thus had the crucifixion of A. D. 30, at the *beginning* of his "16th Tiberius," with the baptism a year before, and the nativity 31 years before, at 2 full years B. C., where he placed his A. M. 5500.† And the capture of Jerusalem in the 2nd of Vespasian, he thus had in A. D. 71 (instead of the true 70); making it the 42nd year after the *crucifixion* (not after the *baptism* as Clemens had it).‡ This vernal chronology of Africanus was followed by his cotemporaries, Tertullian (A. D. 214), Hippolytus (A. D. 227), Origen (A. D. 253), and many afterward.

§ 9. It has been supposed that Tertullian has an earlier crucifixion date than Africanus. But, using a suggestion of Petavius, we find a substantial agreement between them. Tertullian, having the same vernal reckoning as Africanus, locates the crucifixion as at the old Equinox March 25 (of A. D. 30), the very *end* of "15th Tiberius" and the "two Gemini" consuls thus *vernally reckoned* as reaching to the Equinox;‖ while Africanus calls it the beginning of the "16th Tibe-

---

ton seems to teach. (*Fas. Rom., A. D. 29.*) That the chronology of Eusebius was as here stated, not the different reckoning often ascribed to him, we fully show in the previous essay.

* The well-assured Vernal Chronology of the Christian fathers is fully set forth and demonstrated in the previous essay. (Contrast Ptolemy's Canon, here § 108.)

† Africanus "commenced his years A. M. from the paschal month," yet "makes the baptism to be in the consulship of the two Gemini, when by Luke it was the 15th of Tiberius." So says Petavius (*Dissert. de Graec. Eris., c. ii: in op. Euseb. i. p. 1402*). Syncellus cites Africanus as "by agreeing apostolical tradition putting the incarnation in 5501 A. M. [beginning], while numbering the passion 5531 A. M. [ending], and having about 31 years to Christ, an error of 2 years too little." (See in *Syncell., p. 609, 614, Vol. xii: Hist. Byzant.*, and in *Petavius, Graec. Eris, ii: p. 1402, and iv: p. 1410.*) The "about 31 years" cover 5501-5531 *inclusive*, with a few days allowable on 5500 and also on 5532 (from Nisan 1 to 14 of A. D. 30). Hippolytus has about the same reckoning.

‡ Origen (A. D. 253), who was no chronologist, having been a student of Clemens Alex., either misconstrued his remark, or applied it to the new *post-vernal* reckoning, and called the destruction of Jerusalem "42 years" (or the 42nd year) after the *crucifixion*, viz., from April 7, A. D. 30, to September of A. D. 71, in the 42nd year by his post-vernal reckoning. Others in later times (such as Clinton and Schwartz) have misunderstood the "42 years" and "42nd year" datings of the fathers, as if they were intended to change the crucifixion year from A. D. 30; and thus have they sadly confounded the Bible Chronology, and the history of it, as we show in the previous essay.

‖ The "15th Tib." or A. D. 29 was by Tertullian made to end at March 25, A. D. 30; so that the "2 Gemini," the consuls of that pre-

rius," as being on the 14th Nisan, with the year vernally reckoned as starting from the *1st Nisan*. And thus they have *the same date* with *different new-year start*. This reconciles all Tertullian's dates of the baptism and of the nativity as well as the crucifixion, with those of his cotemporary Africanus. The peculiar vernal reckoning, as applied to the consuls by Tertullian, and followed by many subsequent writers, has led to great errors in chronology.* But the true understanding of Tertullian,† and especially of Africanus, clears up all doubt as to the real crucifixion date, A. D. 30.

---

vious year, were represented as continuing till the crucifixion. Thus the "15 Tib." and the "2 Gemini" of A. D. 29, became associated with the crucifixion, instead of the baptism as formerly. And afterward, many Latin authors followed the Latin Tertullian in this respect; such as retained his vernal reckoning meaning of course (like him), to designate the *end* of that chronal year, in March, A. D. 30, as the passion-date. The following writers thus assign the "two Gemini" to the crucifixion; Lactantius (A. D. 317), Sulpicius (400), Augustine (438), Idatius (461), Victorius (457); also, the *Catalogus Pont. Rom. Apud Pasch. Chron., tom. ii: p. 198* (616); and the *Fasti apud Noris*. The full citations we give in the previous essay.

* It is *seeming* divergence between Tertullian and Africanus as to their vernal reckoning, the one having the crucifixion of A. D. 30 as the end of the "15th Tib," the other as the beginning of "16th Tib." (so creating a confusion as to the Gemini consuls, as if in different years, A. D. 29-31),—it is this, and mistake in regard to this, that has given rise to the two rival errors of modern crucifixion-dating; that of Hales, putting it in A. D. 31, and that of Clinton, putting it in A. D. 29. To these we subsequently revert, when we come to give " Modern Views." (This whole history and origin of errors is fully treated in the course of our investigation.)

† Tertullian puts the baptism as well as the crucifixion in the same " 15th Tiberius;" which he must have believed to mean fourteen full years *after Augustus' death*, or else he could not have allowed so short a ministry. So that, like Africanus, he had the baptism at A. D. 29, and the nativity 30 years before that, at full 2 years B. C. His language is: "Christ was born in the 41st year of the Emperor Augustus after the death of (Julius); and Augustus survived fifteen years [and over] afterwards. Anno xv, *Tiberii Christus Jesus de coelo manere dignatus, spiritus salutaris* [etc., at his baptism]. In the 15th year of Tiberius he suffered [*i. e.*, he suffered through the 15th year], having about thirty years (*annos habens quasi* xxx), when he suffered (or while suffering). * * * The passion was *perfected* [by crucifixion] under Tiberius Cæsar, the consuls being the two Gemini [*i. e.*, put as then ending] in the month of March, at the time of the passover, the VIII Kal. Apl." (*Tertullian, Adv. Jud., c. 8.*)

It is here plain, that Tertullian (like Africanus) dates *post-vernally*, viz., from March, B. C. 43, *after* the death of Julius, 41 years to March, B. C. 2, as near the nativity: then fifteen (and over) to the death of Augustus (Aug. 19, A. D. 14); or +30 from the beginning of B. C. 2 to the beginning of B. C. 29, as the baptism, with the crucifixion in A. D. 30, as at the end of " 15th Tib." reckoned post-

§ 10. Concerning Africanus, Petavius says: "On this perplexing point my view is this: That in the opinion of Africanus the incarnation was 2 years before the common era,* at his 5501 A. M. [beginning,—its latter part would be only 1 year B. C.]; the baptism was in the 15th Tib., the two Gemini being consuls, at his 5530 A. M. *ending* [*i. e.* at beginning of A. D. 29, Christ being 30 years of age]; and the passion was at *the end* of 5531 A. M., 5532 beginning from that passover, *i. e.*, in *April* of our vulgar *A. D. 30*, [actually April 7], *the 16th of Tiberius*, and the 2nd year of the 202nd Olympiad, *not yet begun from the summer months*, but by prolœpsis *anticipated* (from Jan. or some other time),—for such things were done   *   *   *   Africanus makes the baptism to be in the consulate of the 2 Gemini, when by Luke it was the 15th of Tiberius, allowing a solid year for the ministry [evidently from first of the 15th to first of the 16th]; whereas, if he meant to put the passion also in the early part of the Gemini consulate [A. D. 29], he could have only 3 or 5 months to the ministry; which I do not believe was the opinion of Africanus." (*Petavius De Graec. Eris, ch. II, in Patrilog. Migne, Paris, p. 1395.*)

Clinton also agrees (with writers generally) that "the passion was in the year A. D. 30, according to Africanus," quoting from him as we do above. (*Clinton Fas. Rom., vol. I, year 30.*)

---

vernally from March, A. D. 15. This is just like Africanus' dating. And Clemens Alex. also (another cotemporary) has the same, as we saw; only that he reduces Christ's "30 years," at baptism to "30th" (or about 29, *i. e.* 30 from *conception*), in order to get the years of Tiberius *antedated*, with the baptism at A. D. 28, and so a longer ministry of two years. Thus the fathers of that generation *agreed* in this thirty-one year reckoning of Christ's life from two years before Christ to A. D. 30.

Jerome (A. D. 400) undertook to show the agreement of Tertullian with Africanus, by citing the latter *mutilated* into accord with the former, thus: He quotes the very passage of Africanus which we have already cited (note to § 7), yet makes it read, "the 15th of Tib. about the 31st year of Christ," at the crucifixion, instead of "the 16th Tib.", as it is in the Greek. (*Hieron. Com. Daniel.*) Syncellus (A. D. 800) quoting from Jerome, perpetuates this alteration of Africanus. And so also does Bede (A. D. 700), saying: "Africanus believed the passion to be at the 15th of Tib." (*De Temp., Rat. ix, p. 334.*) They seemed to suppose that Africanus was not consistent with himself without this change. But by the vernal chronology we find that he was consistent, meaning by "the 16th of Tib." the very beginning of it at 14 Nisan, A. D. 30, which Tertullian calls the end of "the 15th Tib." On the other hand, in later years, Clinton (and so Schwartz) has assiduously taught, that Tertullian (and others following him) were putting *the crucifixion earlier*, he says in A. D. 29. But Petavius has lucidly shown, that no such amending of Africanus is needed; whence we see that his A. D. 30 is equally applicable to Tertullian.

* Just as Bredovius says that Eusebius puts him. But the Encyc. Brittan. wrongfully says, that "Jul. Africanus put the nativity *three years* before our era, so that A. D. began in 5503 of Africanus." This error has led Schwartz and many others astray.

§ 11. (II). *The Equinox Cycle Age.* It was Theophilus, Bishop of Cæsarea, and his Council there held (A. D. 196), under the sanction of Victor, Bishop of Rome, that first promulgated the new and fanciful *theory* of Christ's resurrection, as most fitly to be located on the Equinox, supposed to be then March 25; because that must have been the first day of Creation, when light begins to prevail over darkness, and because it was *fitting*, that He, the Author of light should then rise to the light of the new creation, on that very day when He first created light!* Thus was the age of historical day-dating passed, the true April 7th being now lost: and the age of theory and idle speculation had dawned.

§ 12. This equinoctial theory was the root of that methodical dividing of the year which afterward came into vogue, whereby Dec. 25, March 25, June 25, and September 25, were set apart for special commemorations. (See § 101.) These quarter-days of the old Julian year, we all know, have no basis either of astronomy or of well attached historical events; and they are not essential to a "Christian year," which properly begins from "the 14th of Nisan," not from any supposed equinoctial day.

§ 13. Theophilus thus set March 25 as the original *Resurrection Sunday;* but Tertullian a few years later made March 25 the original *Crucifixion* Friday.† This divergence of theory at the very start shows how purely fanciful and theoretical this whole equinoctial scheme was, without any basis of historical fact. These two methods of applying the theory were widely disseminated and reiterated by the writers of subsequent ages,‡ the true crucifixion date being entirely buried out of sight. Some portions of the Christian world (the churches of Gaul, for instance), escaped from the prevailing *quartadeciman* controversy (as to whether the 14 Nisan or the Sunday following it should be Easter), by taking neither side, but settling down upon the fixed March 25 of the equinoctial theory.

§ 14. The new theoretical assignment of the *day-date* of crucifixion was not intended as any change in the *year-date* always called A. D. 30 (or 16 Tiberius). For, we have already seen Tertullian virtually retaining that *year* assignment of Africanus and Clemens Alex., although he gives the *day* as March 25. It is true that this day and this year will not agree together, either in lunar or week-day reckoning: and how (it may be asked) could such a date be set forth in face

---

* Theophilus *in Consil. Caesareae, apud Bede. De Ord. Pasch., vol. I. p. 607.* Also *Petav. De Graec. Eris. Chap. III, p. 1406.*

†Tertullian, Adv. Jud. ch. viii. See citation given before §9, note.

‡ See list of writers in preceding essay.

of such an incongruity?* The answer is simple. The true cycle reckoning of the moon and of the week (backward over 200 years) was in that age but little understood;† and when it was looked into the intervening chronology was so little fixed that a year or two of the reigns between Titus and Diocletian was overlapped or interjected as occasion required.‡ And so they made the cycles reach back with seeming fitness to the New Testament times, without disturbing the long-fixed year-date of crucifixion as "the 16th year of Tiberius" after Augustus' death, the year 78 of the Cæsars.

§ 15. When the more satisfactory lunar cycles of 19 years (as at the Council of Nice) came in, then there were made such applications of those cycles in reference to the times long past, as to be deceptive concerning old-time dates. Particularly the misleading cycles of Anatolius (A. D. 279) and of Victorius (A. D. 451), seem to have been arranged as if purposely to accommodate the current equinoctial dating of crucifixion as at March 23 or 25, and to fit those *day-dates* to certain *year-dates* finally devised, A. D. 29, 28, 31, etc. ‖

§ 16. Thus were new year-dates of crucifixion at length brought in, not by any historical data, but by theoretical day-dates applied to misleading cycles. By these means, such writers as Theophilus and Tertullian, and the many who followed their equinoctial theory, were made to *seem* as if meaning to date the passion in A. D. 31, 29, and

---

*This query has led Schwartz to doubt whether these church fathers believed the Bible "14 Nisan" to have had any reference to the stage of *the moon*. But this idea is entirely inconsistent with the fact that these very fathers were themselves carefully adjusting their Easters to the lunations of their day.

† Schwartz himself has shown what a strange medley of erroneous cycle reckoning was made out by the *ogdoad* cycles of Hippolytus (A. D. 236), whereby the lunations were set many days out of place.

‡ Every one knows what confusion exists in the Early Christian chronicles as to the length of those reigns; one reign being shortened a year or two, and another lengthened a year or two, as the exigencies of their reckoning required. So, that, it has been found difficult to reconstruct the true chronology of those times. Thus great was the evil of being without an established era such as we now have.

‖ Those cycle adjustments are fully discussed in a separate essay. Clinton and others have been led astray by theoretical assignments into the adopting of A. D. 29 for the crucifixion year, as if so taught by Tertullian and his successors. But Tertullian, like Africanus, meant A. D. 30; just as asserted in a note to Tacitus (*Delph. London, 1823*): "*Tradit que, his coss (Gem. et Gem.) Christum Salvatorem passum, id est, Tiberii 16* (A. D. 30)."

even 28.* Whereas, upon examination, we find no *intentional* departure, for some 400 years, from the original assignment of the crucifixion, as "Tiberius 16th," or A. D. 30.

§ 17. (III.) The *Later-Theory Age*. We have seen (§ 8), that Africanus had the life of Christ but 31 years, from two whole years B. C. to A. D. 30, the ministry being put as only one year, A. D. 29-30. We have further seen (§ 16) that the Alexandrine cycle, dating from the time of Epiphanius (A. D. 400) got the thirty-one years as reaching from one whole year B. C. to A. D. 31, for the crucifixion.† We here only add, that afterwards, the life of Christ was lengthened from the 31 to its proper 33 years; which carried the crucifixion to A. D. 33. Dionysius Exiguus (A. D. 525) had the *incarnation* thus at B. C. 1, and proposed this date for the Christian Era. But the Venerable Bede (A. D. 700) misunderstood him as meaning that the *nativity* was at the

---

* Augustine, *C. D. 18, 54*. Sulpicius, *S. H. 240*. *Descript. Con.*, *p. 891, Vol. LI. Migne Patrolog. Catalog. Pont. Rom. apud Pasch. Chron., tom. II, p. 198, Narrat. 18 Tib.* Refer also to Gaudentius, Apollinarius, Chrysostom, etc. Victorius (A. D. 451, *Can. Pasch., p. 8, 9, 15*), got the passion at A. D. 28. But before him, the Alexandrines (who had most to do with the cycles) had judged the equinoctial theory of passion to require A. D. 31. For, that year alone gave the passover on Friday, according to the 19-year cycle, with the resurrection coming on Sunday, March 25, as they understood the equinoctial theory to demand.

This A. D. 31 then became the Alexandrine or current dating, from Epiphanius at the end of the 4th century (See Clinton. *Fas. Rom., p. 31*), down to the Paschal Chronicle at the beginning of the 7th century. (*Corp. Hist. Byzant., Vol. 16;* down to A. D. 616.) Hales has wrongly followed this A. D. 31 as if the true historical dating: just as Clinton has wrongly followed the A. D. 29. The truth is between them, at A. D. 30. This A. D. 31 dating increased the life of Christ again to its full and proper 33 years (as reckoned by Eusebius) from 3 years before our A. D. to A. D. 31. (Cassiodorus *Chron. Migne, Vol. 69, p. 1214*.) But as reckoned by many from 2 years before A. D., it made only 32 years. (Anianus *in Syncel., Vol. 5, p. 82*.)

And indeed, those who followed the 31-year reckoning of Africanus, now reduced the nativity to only 1 year before our A. D. This was the method of Panadorus (A. D. 400 *in Syncel. Hist. Byzant., Vol. XII, p. 614*), and of Dionysius Exiguus, (A. D. 523. *Epis. in Petav. De Doct. Temp. App.*) And from the latter our Vulgar Era was afterward erroneously deduced, as 1 year later still. But every date of the crucifixion except A. D. 30 was purely theoretical, derived from later *cycles* as applied to the *equinoctial* theory, without any basis of historical fact.

† With this review of the early history of the crucifixion date, here brought down to A. D. 400, we may suspend for the present our history of opinion (which we have carried down to the present day) in order to give next our Astronomical Demonstration of the crucifixion date as unmistakably A. D. 30, Friday April 7th Julian.

end of 1 B. C. (or beginning of 1 A. D.), and so established the Christian Era as it now is, four years too late; which made the life of Christ, 33¼ years (as he rightly reckoned it), extend to A. D. 34.

(IV.) *The Astronomical Age*. At length, science showed that the long-followed passion date of Bede, A. D. 34, was astronomically impracticable; and Roger Bacon (A. D. 1250) fell back upon A. D. 33, April 3, Friday, as the crucifixion date, because more in harmony with the lunar reckoning for the passover. And this reckoning, A. D. 33, has ever since, down to the present century, been the currently received date for the death of Christ.

CHAPTER II.

Astronomical Demonstration.

I. The State of the Case.

§ 18. When the date A. D. 33 for the crucifixion, as assigned by Roger Bacon and Archbishop Usher, was abandoned at the beginning of the present century, instead of a return to the original and correct date, A. D. 30, there was a two-fold wandering to A. D. 31 and A. D. 29. Hales in his great work (A. D. 1812) set forth A. D. 31, and Clinton (A. D. 1845) elaborated A. D. 29, as the crucifixion date. The difficulties of each of these systems arise largely from the neglect of both to make a strict astronomical verification of the result; which, if introduced would at once disprove both theories, and reveal the true date as A. D. 30.

Thus Clinton finds that according to Cunninghame it was full moon on Friday, March 18, A. D. 29, at 9 P. M., and that he and Browne regard that as the paschal day, *five days before* the actual, and nine before the standard equinox of those times! contrary to all acknowledged modes of puschal reckoning. But Clinton also finds that, by adding 14¾ and 29½ days, he gets a new moon April 2 at 3 P. M., (five hours earlier than Benson), with a full moon on April 17 at 9 A. M., that is, on Sunday. So he concludes to assign the passion to the previous Friday, two days before the full moon! making the lunar month commence over a day before the change of the moon!

§ 19. A similar difficulty in the case of Hales is thus described by him: "If the year of crucifixion was A. D. 31, as is most likely, it follows from an eclipse of the moon in Pingrè's tables, April 25 at 9 P. M. [of that year], that the paschal full moon [a month earlier taken as the crucifixion date] fell on the 27th of March; which, in the calculation of Newton, Ferguson, Lang, and the compilation of Bacon, is reckoned Tuesday." But Christ died on Friday. This formidable difficulty

Hales surmounts by adding: "But there is *sometimes an error of a day or two* in these computations of the days of the week; so that, it [the full moon] might have happened on Thursday. On the other hand, Scaliger, Dodwell, and Manne reckon the paschal full moon a day earlier, the 26th of March, and Petavius the 23d day of March. * *This shows the uncertainty of the precise day of full moon* (!) and how little stress can be laid on such calculations, as Petavius says."

Indeed! we may well exclaim, what "uncertainty" can there be about the age of the moon at the time of an eclipse, accurately calculated and recorded in the astronomical tables? And what uncertainty can there be about the length of time back to the full moon before? And what can all these guesses of theorists, made to carry their point, weigh against the scientifically established place of a heavenly body? Such random assertions of "uncertainty" do but serve to cover the weakness of a favorite but untenable hypothesis.

§ 20. It is not strange, perhaps, that with such vague theories, we find Clinton speaking thus: "It can not be determined from their [Jewish] computation, in what year the paschal sacrifice fell on the 6th day of the week. So also says Giesler, Vol. I, P. 38. Benson justly condemns those who take for granted that the time may be known * * * We can not fix it by astronomy." †

Of course not, by such astronomy as here displayed. In like manner, Hales gives his theory as only a thing "most likely," an hypothesis dependent upon some imaginable error of all the scientific men, concerning the days of the week and of the moon!

How idle thus to speculate on such a matter, when these data may be so readily and so exactly verified. For, it surely can be no more difficult, to ascertain beyond a possibility of error, the particular day of the week on which any new moon or full moon fell, at any point of past history,—than it has been to calculate to a minute the eclipses occurring at them, and indeed to fix, as is done, every eclipse ever recorded, at any full moon and new moon since the beginning of history!

§ 21. Hear the distinguished Herschel on this point: "Now that the lunar theory is fully understood, remarkable eclipses [and of course the new and full moon] can be calculated back for several thousands of years, *without the possibility of mistaking* the days of their occurrence. And whenever any such eclipse [or lunar phenomenon] is so interwoven with the account given by an ancient author, of some historical event, as to indicate precisely the interval of time between the

---

* Hurrying up the moon, to accommodate the preceding Friday! What a farce does this make of science!

† Fas. Rom., Vol. II, P. 241. Farrar also, in his Life of Christ, says, "The date of our Lord's crucifixion cannot be depended on."

eclipse and the event, and at the same time completely to identify the eclipse, *that date is recovered and fixed forever.*" (Outlines of Astron. by Sir F. W. Herschel, Bart, K. H., London, 1851. 8 Vo., P I, Ch. vi, § 933.)

§ 22. It is by astronomical determination, therefore, that the original and historical date of the crucifixion is at length to be restored. * And this determination is a practicable one, imposing no uncertainties. If, in the calculations of Newton, Bacon, and others, there may have been found, as Hales asserts, some misprints or mispennings of one or two days, the whole Gospel need not and should not be left hanging on such trivial possibilities, but should be verified by new and unmistakable reckoning. It is a wonder that Hales, and Clinton, with all their research and thoroughness in other respects, should have left this matter thus loose. It may be a want of astronomical taste or mathematical skill, that allows men to propagate (with excusable zeal) such dates as *the figures* will not sanction.

And is it not time, that, amid all the advance of modern science, throwing its light upon Bible scenes and events, conflicting theories should be set at rest, by a simple *demonstration of the crucifixion date in astronomical as well as historical facts?* As no one else undertakes this, we venture upon the attempt. The wish is, to give all the principal steps of the abstruse calculation, yet so simplified as to be within the grasp of any average scholar, *to judge for himself* the accuracy of the result.

II. THE MEANS OF ADJUSTMENT.

§ 23. There is in the Gospel History the fortunate and providential concurrence of two chronological determinations, namely, the *age of the moon* and the *day of the week* when our Lord suffered; and these data, truly and astronomically calculated, should determine the day of the passion. That the day of the week was FRIDAY few have undertaken to call in question; and there is so little to sustain any different view, that we need not dwell upon the matter here.† In regard to the age of the moon at the crucifixion passover, we lay down the following as the true and incontrovertible statement: *The time for slaying the Jewish passover was within a few hours after the full of the moon which next followed the vernal equinox.* Here are three points to be noticed:

---

* "These astronomical observations, being *mathematically sure and reliable*, instituted upon the occurrence of important events, * * * because none of these planetary configurations can occur twice in history, * * * do determine the dates of the events connected with them *with mathematical certainty.*" (Seyffarth, Recent Discov., p. 22,)

† We have fully discussed the week-date of crucifixion and of resurrection, in Appendix A, § 51.

§ 24. (1) The passover always followed the *vernal equinox.** This the Jewish appointments concerning first-fruits and Pentecost required; this the "Jewish Calendar," continued to this day, demonstrates; this the writers of all ages have confirmed and settled. † The Jews must have had a rule upon this point; and no other can be assigned but this, which they now employ; while the referring of the date by Josephus to "the sign of Aries" shows that this was indeed their rule. ‡

(2) The passover was at the *full moon.* That is, in being fixed to the close of the 14th day of the 1st Jewish month, it was a *lunar month* referred to, and such were always, as now, the months of the Jews. The Mosaic appointments and history show this fact, and it has been conceded by about all writers. ‖

§ 25. (3) The passover in the New Testament times was immediately *after* rather than before the full moon. For, the new month and new year was not reckoned till the moon was about two days old.

---

* That is, the Jewish New-year began with the new moon nearest to the equinox. Dodwell, Petavius, and all others reckon thus, making the passover never later than our April 18, or earlier than our March 21. "When the passover would fall before the equinox, they put in a month." (*Encyc. Brit. Art. Chronol.*) It came "about that full moon which fell upon or next after the day of the vernal equinox." (*Hales' Anal., P. 65.*) So the *Jewish Calendar, De Sola, Montreal 5614=1854.* "The paschal term or 14th of the Easter moon can fall only on 29 different days, from March 21 to April 18 inclusive." (*Nicholas' Chronol. of Hist.*)

† Clinton alone, at this late day has attempted to throw doubt upon this point; but he does not succeed. (*Clin. Fas. Rom., Vol. II, P. 240, 242.*) He says, "Benson properly remarks, that in the Mosaic law there is no injunction which refers to the equinox at all." But that law did require a certain state of the grain, which *necessitated* the adoption of this rule. (Lev. xxiii: 5-16.) "In order to secure the proper reduction of the lunar to the solar year, Moses obliged the priests to present the first-fruits on the 16th day of the 1st month. So they had to put in an intercalary, usually in the 3d year." (*Jahn's Arch.*) For this purpose, "the 19-year cycle was divinely revealed through Moses," says *De Arg. Lun., P. 723 in Bede.* In like manner, "the Greek Olympiads were begun at the full moon of that month whose new moon fell nearest to the summer solstice." (*Note to Hieron., P. 351.*) "The Mosaic ordinance decrees, that the passover is not to be observed before the day of the equinox. So Anatolius (A.D. 279) attests; so Philo evidently teaches, and Josephus, and before them Agathabulus, and also Aristobulus, one of the Lxx. So says Eusebius, and we say the same." (*Bede, Cap. xxx, P. 426.*) So, "the council of Nice established the Easter full moon to follow the vernal equinox, from xii Kal. April, to xiv Kal. May." (*Epistle Dionys. Exig., A. D. 525.*) In this all the fathers were agreed.

‡ He says that was the time which "the law ordained." (Jos. Antiq., 3, x, 5.) So Philo.

‖ This matter of Lunar Months we discuss in Appendix B., § 67.

From the early times the Jews began the month with the signal of trumpets, (Psa. lxxxi: 3), not sounded by the priests till the new moon was seen. Nor was the new moon inaugurated without the further delay of signaling by watch-fires over all the land. * By these means, the 14th or paschal day of the month was prevented from coming till the full moon had arrived; the average time of which full moon being near 15 days after the moon's conjunction with the sun, included nearly 2 days before the month, with 13 days of the month, until the beginning of "14 Nisan," the average date of the full moon.

§ 26. When, from clouds or other reason, the moon did not appear till 30 days from its last appearance, they knew that its time had fully come, and began the new month accordingly. † Philo tells us (as in Hales), that in that clear climate, they *sometimes* saw the moon when only about a day old. But the witnesses had then to be examined, the decree of the Sanhedrim issued, ‡ the signal fires lighted, and the tidings fully spread; so that the month could hardly commence under two days after the moon. †† This view is confirmed by Robinson, Horne, Jahn, and Jewish and Christian writers generally.∥

---

* "Formerly, fires were lighted on the tops of the mountains, to announce the appearance of the new moon. They lighted the flaming brands, and kept them moving to and fro, until they could perceive the same repeated by another person on the next mountain," etc. "But when the Samaritans led the nation into error, by lighting these mountain beacons at wrong times, to mock and mislead the Jews, it was ordained that messengers should be sent out." "At Nisan and Tisri they went as far as Syria." (*Mishna, Rosh Hashanah, ch. II, § 2, 3. Trans. of DeSola & Raphael, p. 157.*) † Id.

‡ "Formerly, evidence as to the appearance of the new moon was received from any one; but afterward, all the witnesses met and were examined in a large court at Jerusalem, called Beth Yanzek, as to the form of the moon, the direction of the horns, her elevation, etc. The chief of the tribunal then gave decree." (*Mishna, § 1, 6, 7.*)

†† "When the moon is in perigee and her motion quickest, she does not usually appear until the 2d day; nor in apogee when slowest, until the 4th." (*Old Greek Astron. Geminus, B. C. 60. See Hales, p. 67.*) "After the moon's conjunction, it is generally 2 days or more before any part of her enlightened surface is visible." (*Dick's Solar Sys., II. 5, p. 51.*)

∥ "They did not begin it [the month] from that point of time when the moon was in conjunction with the sun, but from the time at which she first became visible after that conjunction: and the beginning of the month was proclaimed by sound of trumpet." (*Robinson's Calmet, at Month.*)

"The Jewish months being lunar, were originally calculated from the first appearance of the moon, on which the feast of the new moon, or beginning of the month was celebrated. It was proclaimed by the sound of trumpets." (*Horne's Introd. Antiq., P. III. Ch. iv: § 2.*)

"The days of the new moon were not obtained by astronomical cal-

§ 27. The process we have been describing answered for the Hebrews in determining their months, only while they continued in their own land. So that, when scattered abroad, as they were at an early day, they had to resort to some more scientific method, and no doubt some such improvement was introduced into their own land. For this purpose, they made use of a LUNAR CYCLE, probably the same 19-year cycle which the Greeks employed for a like end, and which is still used (in adapted forms) by the Jews as the "Jewish Lunar Cycle" in our almanacs, and by Christians as the "Golden Number." These cycles show with great accuracy the date of returning new moons in successive years for generations and even centuries continuously; but every such 19-year cycle has a slight fractional excess, by which in a very long lapse of time it little by little overlaps the moon's lunations, carrying the *new moon date* gradually later and later after the *new moon itself*, to the total amount of 1 whole day in 310 years. *

§ 28. Take, for example, the old Greek cycle of 19 years established by Meton, B. C. 433, and readjusted by Calippus in B. C. 330; which was probably used, more or less, by the Jews in the subsequent

---

culation, as the Rabbin's assert, but when the moon was seen, as maintained by the Caraites. It is evident, that neither Josephus nor Philo knew the difference of the astronomical and the apparent new moon." (*Jahn's Archæology.*)

"The beginning of the month was determined only by sight. When a new moon became visible, a new month began. When the 15th of Nisan would have occurred before the vernal equinox, an intercalary month was inserted." (*Encyc. Brittan. Art. Chronology.*)

"The moment of conjunction can only be known through an amount of astronomical knowledge and calculation, which there is no evidence to show that the Israelites possessed so soon after their departure from Egypt. The commencement of the new moon festival can only be understood, therefore, of the first phases or appearance of the moon, which God ordered as a season that they were fully able to determine themselves by their own observation." "The reader will please remember, that the beginning of the Jewish months was not reckoned from the moon's conjunction with the sun, but from the time the former emerges from the latter, and is first visible in the west after sunset." (*Jewish Calendar, Montreal, p. 12.*)

The contrary view of Hales cannot be sustained, as the Jewish Calendar ably shows. "Theophilus planned, that on the 14th of the moon it be seen to rise in the heavens with full orb at that moment when the sun sets." (*Cyril, Prologue in Petav. Doc. Temp.*)

* The 19 years taken as Julian, with 365 days each and an extra day allowed every 4 years (or 19 in every 76 years, as arranged by Calippus), contain 6939d.75 each on an average. But the 235 lunations therein, each being 29d.5305885, come to 6939d.68829, which is less by .0617 of a day. This fraction multiplied by 16¼ cycles (amounting to 310 years) will give a whole day of excess to the cycle in that length of time. That is, the cycle's Julian years exceed by that much its total lunations during that time.

centuries, even as used by them now.* As adjusted by Calippus, this cycle had its year 1 at B. C. 330, and at every repetition of 19 years from that time downward; viz, at 311, 292, etc.—at B. C. 45, 26, 7, and A. D. 13, 32, etc. Every year 1 of that cycle had Epact 0, year 2 had Epact 11, year 3 had Epact 22, year 4 had Epact (33—30=) 3, and so on through; each Epact increasing by 11 days, with a whole lunation of 30 days dropped whenever reached.†

§ 29. The several Epacts showed *the age of the new moon* commencing the successive years, at the return of a fixed annual date, the standard point of the solar year. Thus, year 1 of Calippus' cycle (viz, B. C. 330, A. D. 32, or the like), had Epact 0; that is, the new moon had no age, occurring upon the standard day itself, namely, the day of the *Summer Solstice.* The year 2 (namely, B. C. 329, A. D. 33, or the like), had Epact 11, that is, the new moon, was 11 days old on the standard day of the Summer Solstice; so that the 15th day of the first lunar month, or full moon day, when the Olymphic Games were to be celebrated (viz, always at the first full moon after the Summer Solstice, as the first month of their year), would that year be (15 —11=) 4 days after the Solstice. And so of every new year and its full moon festival; all were exactly regulated as to their date by the revolving cycle.

§ 30. Now the Standard Day of Calippus and the Greeks was June 28 Julian (or its equivalent) as the supposed Solstice day of those times,‡ and to that day the Epacts were applied. But they would ap-

---

* "Employed by the Jews even from the time of Alexander," says Dr. Hales. (*Tech. Chron., Vol. I, p. 66.*) He even says; "It has been suspected, and not without foundation, that this celebrated cycle was borrowed by Meton from the ancient Jewish tables. This was the opinion of the learned Anatolius, Bishop of Laodicaea, about A. D. 270." So also teaches the Jewish Calendar; "The 19-year cycle was divinely revealed through Moses." (*De Arg. Lun., p. 723 in Bede.*)

† The Epacts of the cycle are as follows:
Cycle Yr. 1, 2, 3, 4, 5, 6, 7, 8, 9, 10, 11, 12, 13, 14, 15, 16, 17, 18, 19.
Epact, 0, 11, 22, 3, 14, 25, 6, 17, 28, 9, 20, 1, 12, 23, 4, 15, 26, 7, 18.

‡ Meton had it more correctly on June 27, (says Prideaux, Vol. II, p. 409), *i. e.* on "Phamenoth 21" in B. C. 432; and the Solstice was indeed that year on that very day, June 27, at 11½ A. M. in Greece, as we find by our exact calculation. But, because the exact length of the solar year was then unknown, and until Calippus, leap-days were not always inserted regularly to adapt the rotary Egyptian year to the Solstice, therefore Calippus wandered to June 28 in beginning his cycle, the very day of new moon in B. C. 330, at 3¼ P. M. in Greece, by our mean reckoning.

"The Calippic cycle began June 28, B. C. 330. M. Biot has shown that the Solstice and new moon not only coincided on the day here set down as the commencement of the Calippic cycle, but that by a happy coincidence a bare possibility existed of seeing the crescent moon at Athens within that day, reckoned from midnight to midnight." (*Herschel, Outlines of Astron., London, 1851.*) More correctly, the Solstice was then June 26th, 27th.

ply equally well to March 31, just 3 lunations before; so that the Jews could easily use those Greek Epacts for the adjustment of their years. For instance, the year A. D. 30 was cycle year 18, having epact 7: that is, by the cycle the new year month was 7 days old on June 28 or on March 31 (ending at sunset); * so that the 15th of the 1st month Nisan or Abib by the cycle began on April 7 at sunset, before which the paschal lambs must be slain. And the 1st month began the new year at sunset of March 24; which was near 2 days after the actual new moon in the night of March 22–23.

§ 31. This tardiness of the cycle in beginning the month and year arose (as we have seen) from its accumulation of excess in the lapse of about 400 years, amounting to 1 day and several hours, added to part of a day's overlap at the very beginning. Thus every cycle year in the New Testament times would be near two days later than the moon.† So that, whether reckoning by an old cycle like that of the Greeks, ‡ or by their still more ancient method of observation concerning the moon's reappearance, the Jews would naturally have their months and years, beginning about two days after the moon's conjunction with the sun, and their slaughter of the lambs (near the close of the 14th Nisan) coming just *after* rather than before the full moon.

§ 32. In view of the foregoing well-established principles, see now the certainty of error in the dates of crucifixion assigned by Hales and by Clinton. Astronomical calculation, according to their own state-

---

* The Jewish days thus began, as we learn from Gen. i: 5, etc., Lev. xxiii: 32. So all authors agree.

† Herschel remarks (*Astron.,* § 926), that the cycle of Meton itself was begun at "the earliest possible visibility" of the moon, and was, therefore, 1 day too late for astronomical accuracy. So, also, Clinton (F. R., ii, p. 242, and F. H., ii, p. 338). So, in A. D. 1856, the new moon came April 4, while the Jewish 1st month Nisan did not begin till April 6. See Amer. Almanac. "The new moon occurs 1, 2 or 3 days before the day marked by the epact, rarely falling on the day indicated." (*Lardner's Nich. Chron.*) Compare II Ki. xxv: 27, with Jer. lii: 31. So the modern Jews have an 18-hour rule," and a duplicate new moon day, to adjust visibility with conjunction. (*Jewish Calendar p. 24, 15.*) "According to Newton, the phasis occurs when the moon is 18h. old; but the month is sometimes delayed till the moon is 1d. 17h. old." (Clinton, F. R., ii: *p. 240.*) "If the conjunction is after sunset, it is not the 1st but the 30th day of the month. In the 19th year, the moon might be even 2 days before the cycle." (*Bede.*)

‡ When the Jews applied the epacts to the equinox (as the Greeks applied them to the Solstice), they had to reduce them each by 3, for the 3 days from March 31 down to the old equinox, March 28, or by 6, for the 6 days down to Julius Cæsar's equinox, March 25. How they changed their Lunar Cycle along 9 years to its present order, is shown in Appendix C, § 73.

ments, has determined that the paschal full moon of A. D. 31, was on the 27th of March, being *Tuesday*, the 3d day of the week, and that of A. D. 29, was April 17th, being *Sunday*, the 1st day of the week.* But the Gospel history tells us that Christ was crucified at the passover, and therefore, *at the full moon* on FRIDAY, the 6th day of the week. Of course, it could not have been in either of those years, A. D. 29 or 31, unless, indeed, these astronomical calculations are false, and unless the full moon and the Friday can somehow be brought together. This divinely recorded and purely natural concurrence of the moon's aspect with the day of the week, a matter fixed and umistakable and capable of existing in only one particular year out of several, this must settle the true date, or else the Gospel History is not true to nature and is false!

III. THE LUNAR CALCULATIONS.

§ 33. A re-calculation, therefore, of the astronomical facts, set forth with clearness and certainty, is what every inquirer needs, in order to determine for himself beyond a doubt the date of crucifixion.† This calculation requires, that we enter somewhat into the complicated phenomena of the moon's motions, which are so numerous and intricate, that nearly fifty particulars have to be minutely adjusted in the reckoning of an eclipse.‡ However, it will not be necessary here to exhibit in full any but the *mean* reckoning (with the two largest corrections), which will settle the days and hours in question, and which may be comprehended by all. We will first take the mean time of new moon in our day, and by mean reckoning will find our way back to the new moon or new year preceding the Saviour's death.

§ 34. We find by the Astronomical Tables,†† that at the time of this writing, in A. D. 1855, the mean new moon fell on the 18th of January, at 6h. 3m. A. M., Greenwich time,‖ which in the longitude of Palestine was 2¼ hours later, at 8¼ A. M.¶ If we restore the twelve days of

---

* Hales' New Anal., *in Loco*. Clinton's Fas. Rom. Vol. ii. p. 242.

† "If we could determine in what year, between A. D. 28 and A. D. 37, the passover occurred on Thursday or Friday, we might ascertain the year of our Savior's crucifixion." (*Prof. Packard Bib. Soc., 1858, p. 289.*) This is the candid confession of an article, which finds and leaves all chronology as but a bank of fog. It reveals the want and the craving of many minds.

‡ Dick's *Celestial Scenery*, ch. iv, p. 113.

†† Gummere's *Astron.* Table xviii. Robinson's *University Astronomy*, Table xi, etc.

‖ See Nautical Almanac, 1855.

¶ This date is a convenient starting point. For, being so near to the earth's *perihelion*, which in the present generation is January 1 (See Naut. Al.), the true new moon is made by the shape of the earth's

Gregorian correction which have been omitted (10 in the 16th century,* one at 1700, and one at 1800), we have our January 18th equivalent to January 6 of *Old Style* Julian reckoning, which it is necessary to use in these old time calculations. Thus have we the time O. S. of the mean new moon in our own day (viz., 1855. January 6, O. S., at 8¼ A. M., in Palestine); and we are prepared to trace our way back from this to any new moon in the ancient time.

§ 35. Take, for instance, the new moon of March. A. D. 31†. We say, A. D. 1855—A. D. 31=1824 years×365¼=666,216 days from January 6, O. S. 1855, back to January 6, A. D. 31. As this carries us farther back than we wish, we take out thirty-one days to February 6, and twenty-eight days to March 6, leaving 666,157 days back to March 6, A. D. 31. This number of days is found to contain 22,558 lunations of the moon, or waxings and wanings of 29½ days from new moon to new. Each of which lunations being reckoned at the exact *present* length of a lunation,‡ the whole amount to 666,151 days, with a decimal (.015) which gives ½ hour over. But as, by reason of the moon's *acceleration* of motion, its present lunations are slightly shorter than of old, making nearly three hours difference in the past twenty-six centuries,‖ therefore we must add to the lunations of eighteen centuries

orbit but 1¼ hour later than the mean. And being only fifteen hours before the moon's mean *perigee*, (which was January 18, at 9 P. M., at Greenwich, See Appendix E), it is made by the shape of the moon's orbit, but 1¼ hour later than the mean. So that, between the two corrections, the time of true new moon is only 2½ hours later than the mean, viz., January 18, 1855, 8½ A. M., at Greenwich. (See *Naut. Al.*)

* Oct. 5, A. D. 1582, by order of Pope Gregory; adopted in England, Sept. 3, A. D. 1752, when the 10 days had become 11. See *Herschel*, § 926.

† We take this rather than another year, because, compared with our starting point, it gives an even number of 4's or leap days, enabling us to multiply by 365¼.

‡ That is, 29d. 5305885. Hales and others give 29d. 12h. 44m. 2.8; yet his figuring makes the last decimal figures 89. Olmstead says 28.8; yet he makes the last decimal figures 87. So the Astronomy of Hind. Lyon's Jewish Calendar has 28.8283, which brings the last decimal figures 83. But the decimal now in use has 85, as we here use it, for the nicety of which we are indebted to the courtesy of S. H. Wright, Astronomer of the American Almanac. All these differences, however, can not affect the result more than the small fraction of an hour.

‖ It is found that the moon's present motion and length of lunations are a little too quick and short, to reach the hour of an eclipse recorded by the Chaldeans in B. C. 720, but carry us to a point when the moon was nearly 1½ degree past the sun. (*Olmstead's Astron.*) And as the moon (moving daily 13°.17640, while the sun moves 0°.98565), gains on the sun over 12° every day, or ½ a degree in an hour, therefore the phases of the moon were nearly three hours earlier in B. C. 721, than our present lunations give them.

about two hours, making the whole amount to 666,151 days 2½ hours. This lunar amount taken from the above Julian amount (666,157 days), leaves a remainder of 5 days 21½ hours; the lunations falling that much short of filling up the Julian years.

As therefore the time of mean new moon was in A. D. 1855 on January 6 O. S. at 8¼ A. M. in Palestine, therefore its time in the year A.D. 31, by our mean reckoning was 5 days 21½ hours later than that hour of March 6, namely, March 12 at 5¾ A. M., as the mean new moon in Palestine, A. D. 31.

§ 36. How was it in the adjacent years? If we multiply 29d. 53 by 12, we find that the 12 lunations in a year by mean reckoning, amount to 254d. 36; and if we subtract this amount from 365 days, we have left 10d. 63, or 10 days 15 hours; showing that the mean new moom in any ordinary year comes so much earlier than the year before, and in a leap year, when there are 366 days, it will come 1 day earlier still.

Therefore, as the year A. D. 32 was leap year, if we substract 11 days 15 hours from March 12 (A. D. 31), at 5¾ A. M., we find that the mean new moon was in A. D. 32, February 29 at 2¾ P. M.; as well as 29d. 12¾ h (29d. 53) afterward, March 30 at 3½ A. M. If we next subtract 10 days 15 hours, we find that the mean new moon was, in A. D. 33, March 19 at ½ P. M. And substracting yet again, we find it, in A. D. 34, March 8 at 9½ P. M., or 29d. 12¾ h. afterward, April 7 at 10¼ A. M. So, on the other hand, if to the hour in A. D. 31 we *add* the 10 days 15 hours, we find that the mean new moon was in A. D. 30, March 22 at 8¾ P. M.; and adding again we find it in A. D. 29. April 2 at 11¼ A. M.

Thus we have the mean dates of those *new moons*. And we shall arrive at the subsequent mean *full moons* of the several years, by adding to each the half of a full mean lunation, or 14 days 18¼ hours.

§ 37. To all these *mean* dates, there are two considerable corrections to be applied, in order to have the approximate *true time* of new moon and full moon in each case. These corrections are made with reference to the position, (I) of the earth's *perihelion*, (II) of the moon's *perigee*, as relatively situated at the respective dates. But these allowances made for eccentricity of orbit affect only the hours of our calculation, never amounting to a day. And we need not here give the particulars determining their respective values, but will only give their results; referring the reader for the details to our examination of them elsewhere.* Nor need we trouble ourselves in this investigation with the nicety of minutes and seconds, a certainty of *the day and hour* being sufficient for our present purpose.

§ 38. Summing up, therefore, all our calculations, we obtain as follows:

---

* The full complicated process is given in Appendix E, § 90.

TRUE NEW MOON.

Year	Mean		Corrections		True	
A. D.	New	Moon.	I	II	New	Moon.
29	Apl. 2	11¾+A. M.	+3¼h	+4¼h	7¼+ P. M.	Apl. 2
30	Mar. 22	8¾ P. M.	+4	−5¼	7½ P. M.	Mar. 22
31	Mar. 12	5¾ A. M.	+4	−9¾	0 A. M.	Mar. 12
32	Mar. 30	3½ A. M.	+3½	−9¼	9¾ P. M.	Mar. 29
33	Mar. 19	½ P. M.	+4	−3¼	11¾ A. M.	Mar. 19
34	Apl. 7	10¼ A. M.	+3½	+ ¾	2½ P. M.	Apl. 7

TRUE FULL MOON.

Year	Mean		Corrections		True	
A. D.	Full	Moon.	I	II	Full	Moon.
29	Apl. 17	6 A. M.	+2¾h	−5¼h	3½ A. M.	Apl. 17
30	Apl. 6	3 P. M.	+3½	+2½	9 P. M.	Apl. 6
31	Mar. 27	0 A. M.	+3	+8¾	11¾ A. M.	Mar. 27
32	Apl. 13	9¾ P. M.	+3	+9¾	10½ A. M.	Apl. 14
33	Apl. 3	6¾ A. M.	+3½	+6	4¼ P. M.	Apl. 3
34	Apl. 22*	4½ A. M.	+2½	+1½	8½ A. M.	Apl. 22

* Or, Mar. 23, the very day of the true equinox then.

NOTE.

VERIFICATION. In A. D. 31, the mean full moon Mar. 27 at 0 A. M. +29d. 12½h.—Apl. 25 at ½ P. M.+corrections 2¼+6¼=9 P. M. of Apl. 25; and Pingre's Tables give an eclipse of the moon as occurring in "A. D. 31, Apl. 25 at 9 P. M." (See here § 19.) This proves to a certainty that our reckoning is correct.

Again, Benson gives the full moon as "at the *beginning* of Apl. 17, A. D. 29, (here 3½ A. M., Clinton says 10 A. M.); and he puts the preceding new-moon as "Apl. 2 at 8 P. M.", (here about 7½ P. M., Clinton says 3 P. M.). This is close agreement with our result.

Our list above also proves Cunninghame's statement that the full moon in A. D. 29 was Mar. 18, correcting Greswell's Apl. 16. It further confirms Usher (*annals* yr. 4036) and Hales, in saying that the paschal full moon of A. D. 33 was Apl. 3, of A. D. 32 was Apl. 14, and of A. D. 31 was Mar. 27. At the same time, it shows the inaccuracy of Dodwell and Manne in calling the latter Mar. 26; and the random notion of Petavius, setting it at Mar. 23. (See Hales' as before cited, §19.)

Our dates will be found in accord with the noted eclipses calculated for ancient times; that near Augustus' death, Sep. 27, A. D. 14 (*Hales I, p. 76*, also *Edin. Cyclo.*); that near Herod's death, March 13, B. C. 4, at ⅔ A. M. (*Hales' Anal.*, *Whiston in Jos. Antiq.*, 17, vi: 4, *Edinburgh Cyclo.*, etc. See calculation of this eclipse at end of *Ast. Lect. Latin ed.* p. 451, 2.) Exact agreement will also be found with the "Eclipse of Thales," as demonstrated in the Philosophical Transactions of the Royal Society of London, (Vol. C. I., 1811, p. 220); namely, Sep. 30, B. C. 610 at 8¼ A. M., conjunction at Greenwich. Usher and Prideaux give this as the eclipse of Sep. 20, B. C. 601; Bayer and Hales, as that of May 18, B. C. 603.

Being thus in agreement with all the data laid down by astronomers, there cannot be any possible mistake about these our dates here set forth. (Bowyer has also given tables of the time of the paschal full moons, in his "Conjectures on the N. T." note on John vi.) Thurman says the new moon of A. D. 30 was Mar. 22 at 7⅔ P. M. in agreement with our 7½ P. M.

IV.—THE DATA COMBINED.

§ 39. It only remains to ascertain the *days of the week* on which the respective full moons and passovers fell. As the days of the week change 1 in every ordinary year, they would return to the same place every 7 years but for the intervention of a leap-day every 4 years. This prevents a sychronism until 4 times 7 or 28 years; at which time the order returns precisely as before. The days of the week are, therefore, the same at an interval of any number of times 28 years, say 65 times 28 or 1820 years. That is, the days of the week are at the same place in the Julian Year A. D. 1854 (O. S., without the Gregorian correction), as they were 1820 years before, in A. D. 34.

§ 40. But in A. D. 1854, by the Almanacs, March 12, N. S., which is equivalent to O. S. March 0 (7, 14, 21, 28,) was *Sunday*. Therefore, March 0, (7, 14, 21, 28), A. D. 34, being 1820 years before, was also *Sunday*. And since, in any ordinary year having 365 days, one more than even weeks (52×7=364), any Julian date comes one day later in the week than it did the year before, while after a leap-day it comes two days later than before; therefore, March 0 (7, 14, 21, 28) in A. D. 34 being Sunday, in A. D. 33 it was Saturday, in A. D. 32 Friday, in A. D. 31 (passing a leap-day) it was Wednesday, in A. D. 30 Tuesday, in A. D. 29 Monday, and in A. D. 28, Sunday.*

---

*Remember this FACT: Julian dating gives SUNDAY, March 0 (7, 14, 21, 28) in A. D. 0 (28, 56, etc.). Therefore we have this useful

RULE.—Divide the year A. D. by 28, and the remainder by 7, and to the second remainder add 1 for every 4 contained in the first remainder: the result shows the days to be added to Sunday on March, 0 (7, 14, 21, 28) of the given year A. D. Then, if necessary, reduce to the N. S. or Gregorian date.

Note.—It will be already N. S. if we reckon the A. D. as so many years after 1700 for the 18th century, after 1796 for the 19th century, after 1892 for the 20th century. Always number Jan. and Feb. in the previous year. With a B. C. date, take 1 less than the year and *subtract* the result (increased by 1 if there be a remainder when dividing by the 4) from Sunday.

Examples.—A. D. 34 ÷ 28 leaves 6, which ÷ 7 leaves 6 with + 1 (in the previous 6) = 7, *i. e.*, 0 days after Sunday, giving us SUNDAY, March 0 (7, 14, 21, 28), in A. D. 34.

Again, A. D. 1854–1796 = 58 years ÷ 28 leaves 2 which ÷ 7 leaves 2 with + 0 (in the previous 2) = 2, *i. e.*, 2 days after Sunday, viz. TUESDAY, March 0 (7, 14, 21, 28) A. D. 1854. So that the N. S. March 12, A. D. 1854, was Sunday as seen above.

Again, on what day of the week will July 4, 1894 fall? The 1894–1796 = 98 yrs ÷ 28 leaves 14, which ÷ 7 leaves 0 with + 3 (in the previous 14) = 3, *i. e.*, 3 days added to Sunday, viz. WEDNESDAY, March 0,

From these determinations for March 0, (7, 14, 21, 28) in each year, we easily find the day of the week at the succeeding full moon and passover of each year. And the combined results of all our reckoning are exhibited in the following table:

§ 41. TABLE OF THE PASSOVERS, FROM A. D. 29 TO A. D. 34.

Anno Domini.	Vernal New Moon.	Paschal Full Moon.	March 0, 7, 14, 21, 28, came on	Lunar Cycle. No. of Cycle Year.	Lunar Cycle. Epact Mo. age at sunset Mar. 31.	New Year 1 Nisan began at sunset.	Passover sunset, end of 14 Nisan.
29	Apl. 2, 7¼ P. M.	Apl. 17, 3½ A. M.	Sunday	17	26	April 4	Mon. April 18
30	Mar. 22, 7½ P. M.	Apl. 6, 9 P. M.	Thursday	18	7	Mar. 24	Fri. April 7
31	Mar. 12, 0 A. M.	Mar. 27, 11¾ A. M.	Tuesday	19	18	Mar. 13	Tues. Mar. 27
32	Mar. 29, 9¾ P. M.	Apl. 14, 10½ A. M.	Monday	1	0	Mar. 31	Mon. Apl. 14
33	Mar. 19, 11¾ A. M.	Apl. 3, 4¼ P. M.	Friday	2	11	Mar. 20	Fri. Apl. 3
34	Apl. 7, 2½ P. M.	Apl. 22, 8½ A. M.	Saturday	3	22	Apl. 8	Tues. Apl. 22

NOTE: These Julian dates are of course Old Style, the N. S. Gregorian dates being (correction 14—12 =) 2 days less.

A. D. 1894, with (Mar. 31, April 30, May 31, June 30 to July 4 = 126 days ÷ 7 leaves) 0 change, giving WEDNESDAY, July 4, A. D. 1894.

Once more, on what day of the week will fall *inauguration day* in A. D. 1901? The 1901—1892 = 9 yrs, which ÷ 28 leaves 9, which ÷ 7 leaves 2 with + 2 (in the previous 9) = 4, *i. e.*, 4 days after Sunday, viz. THURSDAY, March 0, A. D. 1901. So that we have MONDAY March 4, A. D. 1901.

§ 42. We have a striking proof from archæology, that our astronomical calculations here are accurate. "An inscription of the year A. D. 26 has been found at Berenike in Egypt, in which the last day of the feast of tabernacles (observed by the Jews) is said to have occurred on the Egyptian Paophi 25th, which was the Julian October 22d." (*J. Schwartz, archæologist, New York, 1890.* See his letter Jan. 11, '90.) The last day of the feast of tabernacles was at the sunset ending the 21st day of the 7th Jewish month; so that, as this was in that year on Oct. 22, the 1st day of that 7th month began on the 1st day of October. Take out the 6 previous lunar months (alternating 29 and 30 days) *i. e.*, 177 days, and we are brought to April 7 as the beginning of 1 Nisan that year. But by the Lunar Cycle of those times (as in the table here), A. D. 26 was cycle year 14, having Epact 23 (see before § 28 note); that is, the month was 23 days old on March 31, and 1 of the next month Nisan would be after 7 days, viz.: on April 7, just as the inscription makes it.

§ 43. This is a perfect demonstration, not only that the Jewish months were certainly lunar months, but also that those lunar months began about two days after the moon's conjunction with the sun, as we have shown; and that the Greek Lunar Cycle of those times gave the very date of Jewish new year then, showing correctly the Jewish dating then, as given in the table. Our tabular exhibit is thus shown to be accurate beyond a question.*

The table proves the utter impossibility of Hales' and Clinton's theories, that our Lord was crucified in one or the other of those years, A. D. 29 or 31.† From this table it moreover appears that the only years in which the crucifixion date is *astronomically possible* are A. D. 30 and 33; and that the former, A. D. 30, is the only year astronomically *probable*, as alone having the full moon on the Thursday night

---

* Our table agrees exactly with "Ferguson's Astronomy, where there is a calculation of the exact time of full moon in A. D. 30, viz., as being Apl. 6." (*J. Schwartz*, as above.) The table shows that Clinton is right in calling Apl. 17 A. D. 29, *Sunday;* and that the computation which Hales cites from Newton, Bacon, etc., is correct, in making the paschal Mar. 27, A. D. 31, to be on *Tuesday;* and it thereby shows the fallacy of Hales' surmise, that this might have been later in the week. The table also agrees with the tables in *Nicholas' Chron. Hist.* in Lardner's series; for these give the year A. D. 29 with O. S. Dominical Letter B, which puts March 1 on *Tuesday*, as above. The whole matter is fully exhibited in my essay on "Cycles and Epacts."

† Hales' argument for A. D. 31, that the early passover of Mar. 27 agrees with the statement of John xviii: 18, that "they had made a fire of coals," is of little weight; since the difference of 10 days later would make but a small difference in the weather, and a little fire was needed in the *night air* all along through the spring.

wherein Christ ate the supper, and having the Jews' passover on the *Friday* wherein he suffered.*

THE TRUE DATE.

§ 44. This A. D. 30, therefore, must have been the true date. For, by astronomical demonstration, the only infallible method, it is settled, that the crucifixion *could not* be either in A. D. 31 or in A. D. 29, where the systems of Hales and of Clinton assign it; while A. D. 33, the only possible alternative for A. D. 30, is proved to be astronomically improbable, as well as historically false, according to Chap. I of this discussion.

There remains, therefore, a moral certainty, that CHRIST'S DEATH OCCURRED IN THE YEAR A. D. 30, FRIDAY, APRIL 7TH, the 16th year after Augustus' death, and the 33d year after Herod's death, *just where the early Christians and fathers had it down to the 4th century of the church.*

§ 45. All cycle theories of the intermediate ages being dropped, this last or astronomical age comes into harmony with the first or historical age; and what might well have been supposed is verified—the people of that very age knew their own times best. By return to their reckoning, we find everything reconciled,—the evident 33 years of Christ's life, the 30 years at his baptism and the 3 of his ministry; while the imagined difficulty concerning the "15th year of Tiberius," is found to be (as the 15th year from his partnership with Augustus) no difficulty at all. And so, as the Saviour's birth and baptism have

---

*The crucifixion was certainly *as late as* the 14th of the 1st month; and as the 14th, therefore, could not end later than Friday at sunset, the month and year could not commence later than Friday also, two weeks before. This in A. D. 33 was Mar. 20, when the moon was only 1¼ day old, less than seems requisite, whether they began the month by sight or by the cycle. On the other hand, in A. D. 30, this Friday night of New Year came March 24, when the moon was nearly 2 days old, as required by either mode of commencing the months.

If any one chooses to maintain (as some do), that Christ died on the 15th of Nisan instead of the 14th, or on Thursday instead of Friday, he will only be compelled the more decisively to renounce A. D. 33, and accept A. D. 30 as the year. But to claim (as some 7th day "Sabbatarians" now do), that the 15th Nisan ended as early as Thursday, is to violate entirely the astronomical data,—putting the new month and new year before the occurrence of the new moon.

"Roger Bacon found by computation, that the paschal full moon of A. D. 33 fell on Friday; and this circumstance led him and several others, Scaliger, Usher, etc., to conclude, that this was the year of the crucifixion. But, admitting the computation to be exact, as afterwards verified by Scaliger, Newton, Maunc and Lang, this very circumstance proves that this was not the year of the crucifixion; for the true paschal full moon then was the day before, on Thursday, when Christ celebrated the passover." (*Hales I, p. 99.*)

been by degrees restored, from their wrong calculation in the old vulgar chronology, back to the place where the first Christians assigned them,—in like manner is the crucifixion, by the harmony of history and astronomy, now at length restored. *

§ 46. This conclusion of our calculations is corroborated by John ii: 20, where the Jews observe, at Christ's first passover, "forty and six years was this temple in building;" or we may read, "forty-six years this temple *has been built upon*." † Now Herod began this new construction, ‡ as Josephus definitely tells us, in "the 18th year" of his reign, ‡‡ and died when he had reigned 34 years; ‖ and so, as his death was in B. C. 4, his 18th year was in B. C. 20.¶ To this add 46 years, †† and we are carried to A. D. 27, the very time of Christ's first

---

* "Ferguson, in his Astronomy, has shown that in A. D. 30, there was a paschal full moon on Thursday, April 6, which Bengel thought was the true date" of passion. (*Prof. Packard, in Bib. Sac.*, *1858*, p. 299.) Why has Bengel been so long alone in this correct identification of *the year* of passion as A. D. 30?
Postcript. When this treatise was written (in A. D. 1855), we could find no writer adopting A. D. 30. Soon afterward came from Germany Weisler's acceptance of that year; and in 1869, Thurman was found adopting it in America. Now (in 1893) A. D. 30 is very commonly accepted as the date. So Dr. Simon of England gives it from Gaspari, in the Bib. Sacra, July, 1871, p. 469.

† "'This temple *hath been* six and forty years building.' Dr. Lightfoot has well shown that the original word may signify as we here render it." (*Doddridge, Expos. Jn., ii: 20.*) The facts "amend our English translation to read, '46 years hath been building.'" (*Hales, So Calmet, Scott, David Brown, etc.*)

‡ He did not *finish* it, but the Jews kept adding to and adorning it. For, Josephus, as late as A. D. 65, (Antiq. 20, ix: 7), speaks of its being then at length finished, and the workmen dismissed. (Compare John viii: 59, and x: 31.) So Whiston's translation, '46 years hath this temple been built,' is not only inapplicable but unnecessary; as well as Fleming's reference of this passage to the times of Nehemiah.

‡‡ Antiq. 15, xi: 1, 5, 6. ‖ Antiq. 17, viii: 1.

¶ Josephus says expressly (in Bk. 16), that Herod's 28th year, when he held the dedication, 10 years after he began to build, was in the 192d Olympiad. This ended in B. C. 8; therefore, his 18th year, when he began to build, was as soon as B. C. 18. He also tells us (14, xii: 5, comp. with 17, viii: 1), that three years before Herod began to reign was the 184th Olympiad. This ended in B. C. 40; so that, his reign could not begin later than B. C. 37 (as all agree), or his 18th year later than B. C. 20, as above.

†† Doddridge thus dates from B. C. 20, but reckons 47 years (47th) to A. D. 28, so as to agree with the delayed view of Christ's death, as A. D. 31. While Hales himself (Vol. II, p. 601) reckons only 45 years (46th) from B. C. 17 (!) to A. D. 28, (by mistake of adding), this being really but 44 years. So Calmet dates from B. C. 17, presuming to say that two years after Herod's 18th year were consumed in preparation.

passover, three years before his death in A. D. 30, as our demonstration shows.

§ 47. The same conclusion is still further corroborated by "the sign of Jonas," given by Christ not long before his death. To the Pharisees demanding a sign, he answered: "A wicked and adulterous generation seeketh after a sign; and no sign shall be given unto it, but the sign of the prophet Jonas. And he left them and departed." * The sign did not now, as on a former occasion, † mention his resurrection, but referred rather to the Ninevites, who, to save their city from destruction, "repented at the preaching of Jonas," ‡ —a fit sign of present duty (Jesus would teach) in view of the impending danger which some of "this generation" should live to see. Jonah came crying: "Yet 40 days [prophetic form of 40 years ‖] and Nineveh shall be overthrown."¶ Such was the sign to the Ninevites; and the same belonged to "this generation." For Christ was now *by this sign* proclaiming: "Yet 40 years and Jerusalem shall be overthrown." And, according to our determination, it was just 40 years from the death of Christ in A. D. 30, when he finished his warning, to A. D. 70, when Jerusalem was destroyed. ††

And thus is the year A. D. 30 confirmed as the year of Christ's death, by references backward and forward, both historic and prophetic; while itself absolutely determined as the year by historical and astronomical demonstration.

V. Important Results.

§ 48. From this demonstration of the time at which Christ died, we not only arrive at this fact so important in itself, but we also derive therefrom other highly valuable results, which we elsewhere more fully discuss.

1. We help to settle the long-mooted controversy concerning the

---

Doddridge countenances the same idea, reckoning 47 years to A. D. 30, so as to make out the Usher view of Christ's death as in A. D. 33. Whereas, all such preparing by Herod came *before*, from his 16th to his 18th year, as we learn from Josephus (War. 1, xxi: 1); and he expressly tells us (Ant. 15, xi: 5, 6) that the main temple was *done* (not prepared for) in a year and a half after the beginning in the 18th year, and the cloisters in eight years more, so that all his erecting was finished in the 10th year after, viz.: in his 28th year. The falsity of those datings of the "46 years" by different writers, appears at once from the simple reckoning above.

* Mat. xvi: 4; Mark viii: 13.　† Mat. xii: 40.
‡ Lu. xi: 29–32.　‖ Ezek. iv: 6, etc.　¶ Jonah iii: 4.
†† The generally acknowledged date.

post-paschal theory of the crucifixion,* and the double passover of Jesus and the Jews. †

2. We adjust all the dates of our Saviour's ministry; fixing the time of his tabernacle sermon, of his dedication discourse, and of his closing labors with many other like interesting determinations.

3. We fix still more certainly the year of Herod's death; and we establish the date of Christ's *nativity* beyond all reasonable doubt; at the same time bringing to light the true history and basis of our vulgar Christian Era. In fact, we have thus a fixed and sure *starting point* for the whole Bible Chronology.

4. We settle the accuracy of Daniel's "70 weeks," as reckoned by Usher, Prideaux and others (from the 7th of Artaxerxes, B. C. 437, to A. D. 34=490 years); by finding the crucifixion, A. D. 30, at the very middle of the 70th week, as required by Daniel's vision. (Dan. ix: 27.) And thus we have a more certain basis for the hitherto uncertain calculation of prophetic dates.‡

5. But chiefly, we furnish a most convincing demonstration of the historical truth of Christianity, such as infidels must find it impossible to gainsay. THE SCIENTIFIC ACCURACY OF THE RECORDED DATE, PROVES THE GENUINE ACCURACY OF THE NARRATED FACT. And the determinate time of crucifixion cuts off the sceptical query, whether there was any such event as the crucifixion of Christ.

§ 49. *No event can be historically assigned to a particular day, with a correct indication of the moon's age or aspect on that day, except in one*

---

* This post-paschal theory, that the crucifixion was not on the 14th, but on the 15th Nisan, after the passover had been eaten by the Jews, we fully discuss in Appendix D, § 80. (See also a full discussion by Rauch in the *Bib. Repository* for 1834, p. 108.)

† It seems as if Thursday, April 6th, A. D. 30, could not have ended the 14th Nisan; because it was *before* the full moon, in contravention of all we have here shown. (See § 31.) Therefore, we acknowledge a *double paschal observance*, Thursday night by Christ, and Friday night by the Jews. Hales agrees with this, and thinks it arose from the double reckoning of months, by *sight* and by *cycle*; seen also in the *duplicate* new moon day of the modern Jews. (§ 80.)

‡ Josephus (Antiq. 11: v. 1, 2) wrongly puts the decree or "commandment" given to Ezra, as in "the 7th year of Xerxes" (B. C. 478, instead of the correct B. C. 457). This shows a common error of those New Testament times, by which the "70 weeks" of Daniel (or 490 years) "FROM the going forth of the commandments to restore and build Jerusalem UNTO the Messiah the Prince," would expire about (B. C. 578—490 yrs.=) A. D. 13. So that then, in the very middle of Christ's life, the Jewish people were set upon a discussion about the expected Messiah living then, in the mood we find them at Christ's public appearing, of questioning expectancy and wonderment. This throws a remarkable light on many incidents and utterances of the Saviour's ministry.

of two ways, either (1) *by being so assigned artlessly, at the very time of occurrence, by the witnesses of the actual event then taking place;* or else (2) by being laboriously calculated in later times, by the precise developments of astronomy. But,

(I) The great event of the Gospel *is* assigned by its writers to a particular day of a particular year, with a statement of the paschal or lunar aspect for that day; and the correctness of that assignment, as being at the only possible point of agreement between the narrative and the moon's position, is now at length proved, after the lapse of 18 centuries, by this second mode of assignment, a full astronomical calculation, with all the modern data.

(II) That Gospel assignment was made long before this exact reckoning of modern astronomy was possible in making the assignment, or even imaginable as a future test of it. And it was so evidently without calculation or design, that the year itself is not stated by any of the Gospel writers, but is made sure only from incidental allusions gathered from them all. These allusions, such as Matthew's mention of Herod's slaughter, Luke's mention of 30 years later, John's mention of three passovers later still—these allusions exhibit not even an attempt at the dating of Christ's death; and yet, when combined, they do all point unmistakably to the 33d year after Herod's death, that is to A. D. 30, the very year required by astronomy, as the crucifixion date.

§ 50. (III) Therefore this incidental assignment in the Gospel, given with accuracy yet unquestionably without calculation, could have been made only in the other method, namely at the very time mentioned, by witnesses of the actual event then occurring before them.* Let any one attempt, without exact data, in a fictitious narrative, to name an eclipse or a full moon on a definite day, even no longer than five years ago; and lo! how certainly will astronomy expose the fiction. And so, by astronomy superadded to history, the Gospel is proved to be no after invention, but a genuine and authentic narrative, originating in the very times and among the very events described on its pages.

Upon this basis of scientific facts rests the story of Jesus. And thus is the historic origin of Christianity determined, beyond the peril of assault!

---

* "All such configurations were real perceptions of the human eye, not at all results of astronomical calculations. For, without the Copernican system and astronomical tables, which were denied to the ancient world, nobody was able to determine what places of the heaven were at a certain time occupied," etc. (*Seyfforth Recent Discov.* p. 151.) Cycles were not yet applied to measure large intervals, and if so applied, being inaccurate, they would only lead astray, as we see was afterward the case.

APPENDIX A.

(For § 23.)

Christ's Resurrection on Sunday.

And His Crucifixion on Friday.

§ 51. That Christ's Resurrection was on Sunday morning early, was never called in question, so far as we know, until now (in A. D. 1892), some 7th-day "Sabbatarians" think it necessary, for the furtherance of their *ism*, to claim with strenuous argument, drawn solely from Mat. xxviii: 1-6, that Christ rose before sunset on Saturday. A complete and overwhelming refutal of this notion is Luke xxiv: 21: "To-day (Sunday P. M.) *is the third day* since these things were done," *i. e., the very day when Christ promised to rise*. Nothing more than this really needs to be said against the absurd Saturday scheme. But that no claim, however unreasonable, may seem to be slighted, we give the following exhibit:

§ 52. (I) As to Mat. xxviii: 1. The best scholars think this verse expresses the time as *very early Sunday morning*, in harmony with Mark xvi: 2; Luke xxiv: 1; John xx: 1, (so conceded by all). But it is no matter whether Matt.xxviii: 1, means Sunday morning early or Saturday at sunset; if it means the latter, still that will not remove the resurrection from its assured place on Sunday morning. For, if the statement here is, that the women came to the tomb Saturday evening, then the order of events in ver. 1-6 is chronological, and the descent of the angel, and opening of the tomb, and resurrection of Christ, were *after* the women had come and gone, they having "come *to see* the sepulchre," and left it till morning because they found it sealed up.

The only way in which a Saturday resurrection is loosely *inferred* from a Saturday night coming of women, is by interpolating the word "had" into verse 2, so making it read, "and behold there *had been* a great earthquake," etc., that is, *before* the women came. And Mr. Reihl in arguing the case actually quotes the Scripture as reading in that way,—"an angel *had* descended" and "Jesus *had* risen," he reads it. Now, it is true, that if ver. 1 means (as commonly supposed) early in the morning, then a *previous* idea must be implied (not expressed) in ver. 2, as if it read "had." But this cannot be claimed if the time of ver. 1 is Saturday P. M. In that case, to put in "had" is a plain falsification of the text. Hence, this being the only argument for a Saturday resurrection, the theory at once and forever perishes.

§ 53. (II) The allied facts stated in the history all instantly crush the notion of a Saturday resurrection.

1. In their morning coming, the women were troubled "and they said among themselves, Who shall roll us away the stone from the door of the sepulchre." (Mark xvi: 2, 3.) Of course, then, the tomb had not been found open the night before.

2. Their morning visit was "bringing the spices which they had prepared" *to anoint the body*. (Lu. xxiv: 1.) Of course, then, no one had heard that the tomb was open and the body gone the night before.

3. Mary Magdalene in the morning was astonished to find the tomb open and Jesus gone, and "she runneth and cometh to Simon Peter" and John to tell the news; whereupon they quickly "ran both together" to see if it was indeed so. (Jn. xx: 1-4.) Of course, then, nobody had visited an opened and emptied tomb the night before; for if so, the news would have spread like wild-fire, and Peter and John would not have been coolly delaying a visit to the tomb.

4. Mat. xxviii: 9, says: "And as they went to tell His disciples behold Jesus met them, saying, All hail," etc. This could not be Saturday evening, because Mark xvi: 9, tells us: "Now when He was risen early on the first day of the week, *he appeared first* to Mary Magdalene," *i. e.*, first to her *alone* (Jno. xx: 14) on her *second* visit Sunday morning, says Mr. Reihl himself. Therefore, as Mat. xxviii: ver. 9, belongs to Sunday morning, the preceding verses, 2-8, also belong to Sunday morning, even if ver. 1 does not.

5. No report of an open tomb was carried to the city and to the chief priests by the guards until the women had fled from the tomb in the morning, and then the soldiers were hired to say, "His disciples came *by night and stole him away while we slept*." (Mat. xxviii: 11-13.) Of course, then, they could not tell any such story if Jesus arose on Saturday, nor could they delay their tidings till Sunday morning. Luke xxiv: 22, shows the same.

§ 54. (III) The testimony of the two disciples going to Emmaus Sunday p. m. (Lu. xxiv: 21, revision): "It is now the third day since these things came to pass," is perfectly overwhelming and unanswerable. When presented to Mr. Reihl he attempted an answer by change of *translation*, and when this was shown to be impossible he attempted again an *evasion* of the language equally monstrous.

(1) He claimed that the Greek word rendered "is" should be rendered "brings," so giving as the statement "this day *brings* the third day," which means (he says) "this is the *fourth* day." (!)*

---

* Yet, strange to say, a writer in the Bib. Sacra, (July, 1894, p. 510) reiterates this folly. He says: "The day on which Cleopas spake was the fourth, but *it brought with it* the third day *as already past*." (!) Was ever such senseless utterance in so respectable a publication? See its folly shown in the same volume of the Bib. Sacra, p. 339.

Only smiling at the absurdity of this, we gave these comments on the Greek word.

The passage in Greek is idiomatic, and somewhat difficult for an uncritical reader to translate into smooth English. For this reason variations of the Greek have crept in. But they all agree in meaning with our English Bible, and with all versions ever made into any language. The Latin reads (*tertiam diem hodie agit*) "To-day it leads along or carries through [more simply IS] the third day." The Greek of the revision is (*triteen tauteen hemeran agei*: "THIS THIRD DAY it carries" itself, or is going on, or simply IT IS. The pith of the statement is in the expression "THIS THIRD DAY"; and the question, how best to render the idiomatic *agei* into smooth English cannot change the assertion made of *this Sunday* (the time of speaking) as being *the third day*.

§ 55. This verb (*agei*) ordinarily means *carry*, *bring* or *lead*, as Mr. Reihl says. But hardly any word is confined to a single shade of meaning. And this word, tho' usually thus transitive, often becomes intransitive or reflexive, meaning *to carry one's self, i. e.*, to *go* or *pass along;* as translated at Matt. xxvi: 46; Mark i; 38, and xiv: 42;Jn. xi: 7, 15, 16, and xiv: 31. Winer, in his N. T. Grammar (§ 38, 1), states this principle concerning many Greek verbs, giving this verb *agein* as his first example, "let us carry ourselves," *i. e.*, "let us go."

So also in Mat. xiv: 6, "Herod's birthday feast *going on*," common version, "was kept," revised version "came." Also Ac. xix: 38, "the courts are *going on*," common version "the law is open," revised version "the courts are open," margin "court-days are kept." All these are correct renderings of the word *agei*, whether in Latin or Greek, and the only question is, which is the smoothest way of saying it in English.

In the passage before us, the *agei* is impersonal (without a nominative), and means as in the other passages, "it carries itself," or "it is going on." The verse reads literally, "And besides all this *it carries itself* (or is going on) THIS THIRD DAY since these things were done; or to simplify the English, "it is now the third day since" those events, as the Revision correctly puts it.

Winer (§ 66, 3, note) says of this Lu. xxiv: 21," "in Greek the *numeral* was considered simply as a predicate adjunct"; so that he translates the verse thus: "To-day it is *going on the third* day since" these events. No translator ever gave the passage any other meaning, and no critical scholar can discover any other sense. To say that it means "it is now the fourth day" is—what? Let the candid reader say what.

§ 56. (2) The final device was, to say the statement means, "This is the third day since" *the tomb was sealed* on "the next day," after the crucifixion (Matt. xxvii: 62)! But what had the remark of the two disciples to do with the sealing of the tomb? They said expressly, "to-day is the third day since *these things* were done, *of which they were speaking*, namely, the 'delivering' and 'crucifying' of their Master (ver. 20). Why did they emphasize the fact and the expression "the third day?" Because that was the expression their Master had repeatedly used in promise to them (as in this very chapter, ver. 7 and 46), of *what should next occur to him after his death;* so that, it was time for them to expect the rising he spake of. It was *his words* and his promise they were tenderly calling to mind; and to suppose that, instead of this, their language only referred to an intervening freak of the officials, which had no bearing on the promise, and which yet they were trying exactly to date for no possible reason, such an assumption is simply monstrous. Plainly, it is a mere get-off. There is no excuse whatever for such attempts to mutilate the Word of God, as is this theory of a Saturday resurrection.

The lately discovered apocryphal "Gospel of Peter," understood to have been written about A. D. 150, very distinctly puts the resurrection on Sunday, repeatedly calling it "the Lord's Day;" which shows how certainly that designation of John in Revelation (1:10) was from the first established as the name of the Christian sacred day. For instance, Tertullian (A. D. 190) customarily calls Sunday "*solo die dominico resurrectionis.*" (*Neander, Vol. I, p. 296, 301.**

II. CHRIST'S CRUCIFIXION ON FRIDAY.

§ 57. Those "Sabbatarians" who try to get the resurrection on Saturday, at the same time attempt to make the crucifixion on Wednesday. This scheme is so unreasonable, that we do not need to waste many

---

* "In the Catholic Epistle ascribed to Barnabas (companion of Paul as some think) Sunday is designated as the day of Jubilee in remembrance of Christ's resurrection." *Neander, Vol. I, p. 295.*) In our copy it is at Chap. xiii: 10. Barnabas here puts resurrection and ascension together, as if occurring on one and the same Sunday. Neander notices this view of the ascension; and Prof. Bush (*Resur., p. 157*), adopts it. See John xx: 17.

Dr. Wm. De Loss Love, in his treatise on the Sabbath (Bib. Sacra, October, 1880, p. 662) shows, that the Lord's Day resurrection as on Sunday is set forth by Barnabas in the first century, by Pliny the Younger (A. D. 112), by Justin Martyr (A. D. 140), by the Epistle to the Magnesians (A. D. 150), by Dionysius, Bishop of Corinth (A. D. 170), by Melito, Bishop of Sardis (A. D. 170), by Ireneus (A. D. 178), by Clement of Alexandria (A. D. 189), by Bardesanes (A. D. 190), by Tertullian (A. D. 195), by Minucius Felix (A. D. 198); and he adds (p. 671): "In the first century after the apostle John's death, we find *eleven* thoroughly credible witnesses concurring in the fact that the Christians of that era regarded and observed the first or 'Lord's Day' as the chief of all days (the day of Christ's resurrection); and we find no contemporary testimony to the contrary."

words upon it. We simply allude to the evident erroneousness of this Wednesday theory, in its professed "harmony" (given in the monthly "*Truth*," Chicago, April, 1892); wherein all the working and noisy events of Matt. xx: 29 to xxi: 17, the travel from Jericho finished, the triumphal entry to Jerusalem, the casting out of profaners from the temple (all five days before the passover, as seen from Jn. xii: 1, 12)—these all are made to come on Saturday, the Jewish Sabbath, about which the Jews were so scrupulous. We only note further, the fatuity of putting between the burial and the resurrection two whole *Sabbath* days, with a third whole day (Friday) between them! Whereby the Saviour is kept "three days and *four* nights" in the tomb, in violation of His own words!

But there are some good Christian people who have doubted, whether the crucifixion was not really on Thursday instead of Friday.* And for their sake we give the following exhibit.

§ 58. (1) The crucifixion was on "the preparation of the passover," "that is the day before the Sabbath" occuring at the passover, "for that Sabbath-day was a high-day." John xix: 14, 31, 42, with Mark xv: 42.)† And no subsequent Sabbath is anywhere referred to besides that Sabbath which thus immediately followed the crucifixion. In fact, no other day was called "the Sabbath" among the Jews, besides the weekly Sabbath and the solemn day of atonement. See Lev. xxiii: 3, 32, 38; (also xvi: 31). In verses 24, 39, it is a different Hebrew word, *shabatone* (not *shabat*), translated "solemn rest" by the Revisers.

In this 23d of Leviticus, "the morrow after the Sabbath, at vers. 11, 15, 16, means "the morrow after the *weekly Sabbath* occurring within the seven days of unleavened bread; that is, as the weekly

---

* Thus taught Seyffarth (*Rec. Discov.*, p. 184). He not only put the crucifixion on Thursday, but he also had it before the equinox, at the new instead of the full moon, and in the year A. D. 33. Thurman, in A. D. 1868, advocated Thursday as the day of crucifixion. And Rev. J. K. Aldrich argued the same, in the *Bibliotheca Sacra* (July, 1870, p. 401), and afterward in a book.

† Mark xv: 42, "It was the preparation, that is, the day before the Sabbath." Some say there was no "preparation" for the weekly Sabbath. But certainly, there was from the very first commanded a *preparation of food;* see Ex. xvi: 22-26. The apocryphal Gospel of Nicodemus, which was in use in some of the churches 200 years after the apostles, says, that Joseph of Arimathea was imprisoned after his burial of Jesus "on the day of preparation" (Nic. xi: 19), which was "before the Sabbath" (ix: 7)—and that "after the Sabbath" (ver. 8, 13), and then after "the 40th day" (xi:25), and then "on the morrow, *being a preparation day*" (ver. 17), Joseph came again before the authorities; that is, after forty-two days, or just six weeks from the crucifixion, Friday, was again a "preparation" Friday. This shows, that the "preparation" was understood to be simply a Friday or 6th day of the week, before any weekly Sabbath.

Sabbath came any day from Nisan 14 to 20 inclusive, so the first-fruit offering came any day from Nisan 15 to 21 inclusive, the days when the great "convocation" were together (ver. 7, 8). Many wrongly suppose the meaning to be "the morrow after the festival-rest day," or 15th of Nisan, so as to bring the first-fruit offering always on the 16th of Nisan, as it was when our Lord rose from the dead.* But the wrongfulness of this view is easily seen, as follows:

The strict order (in ver. 14) was, "ye shall eat neither bread, nor parched corn, nor green ears—until the self-same day that ye have brought an offering unto your God." But the very first offering and eating of first-fruits that ever occurred, upon the entering into Canaan, we are told in Josh. v: 10, 11, was "on the morrow after the passover," which had been kept "on the 14th day of the month at even." And this "morrow after the passover," Num. xxxiii: 3, exactly defines as "the 15th day of the first month." (See D, § 12.)

§ 59. These passages prove two things: (1.) That the term "passover" was applied only to "the 14th day at even," and the daytime of the 15th was called "the morrow after the passover," so that in John xviii: 28, the 15th Nisan could not have arrived. (2.) That, as that first occurrence of the first-fruit offering was of course in accordance with the law just established for it, its being on the 15th Nisan is a complete overthrow, from the start, of the uniform 16th day theory; while showing that "the Sabbath" referred to in the law was a weekly Sabbath (that year on the 14th),† not a feast Sabbath (taken as the 15th Nisan).

§ 60. It is true that in the latest days of the temple, a Rabbinical reckoning came into use, for some reason, putting the first-fruit offering as regularly on the 16th Nisan. The first mention we have of this is by Philo, the Jew, in A. D. 40 to 50, and Josephus also gives it in A. D. 90 (Antiq. 3, x: 4). Dr. Lightfoot, the learned Hebraist (followed by most commentators since) takes this late Rabbinical reckoning as if the true meaning of the Levitical law. But we have here proved the contrary. (See it also proved in the Bib. Sacra., April, 1894, p., 339; also July, 1880, p. 426.)

Even the late Jews, in setting the first-fruit offering as "the 16th

---

* "The morrow after the seventh Sabbath" (ver. 16) can mean nothing but the first day of the week as always Pentecost. The 16th of the 1st month, plus 49, to the 6th of the 3d month, could not be the constant reckoning. "If this were the true meaning, why was not the date given by the day of the month, as in the case of all the other annual feasts mentioned in this chapter, rather than by such a misleading expression?" (Bib. Sacra., April, 1894, p. 340.)

† The slaying of the paschal lambs was not regarded as a breach of the Sabbath, even as the "daily sacrifice was slain every Sabbath." (Ex. xxix: 38-42.)

of Nisan," did not call the 15th Nisan a "Sabbath." Josephus himself says (Antiq. 13, vi: 1): "That festival which we call Pentecost did then (that year) fall out to be next day after the Sabbath (*meta to sabbaton*); nor is it lawful for us to journey, either on the Sabbath day or a festival day." Hence it is made plain that when a weekly Sabbath came next to a festival day, they were not both called Sabbath.*

§ 61. (2) To speak of the 15th Nisan as itself a Sabbath is not Scripture usage. When it fell upon a weekly Sabbath, that was what made it (as in the year of Crucifixion) specially "a high day." (John xix: 31.) "The Jews therefore, because it was the preparation, that the bodies should not remain upon the cross ON THE SABBATH, for the day of THAT SABBATH was high (or great), besought Pilate," etc. Here Sabbath is twice over emphasized as "*the* Sabbath," "*that* Sabbath;" and the conviction can not be avoided that it is the special weekly Sabbath of complete rest that is referred to. Thus only was it possible to speak of *resting on that day following the crucifixion as* THE VERY SABBATH *spent in waiting for* "*the first-day* of the week" when the Sabbath was past. Thus exactly is the matter presented in Mark xv: 42, to xvi: 2, and Luke xxiii: 54, to xxiv: 1; and it is impossible to make that account tally with more than one intervening "Sabbath," or with any Sabbath but that immediately following the crucifixion.

No sane man like Mark could mean by "Sabbath" in xvi: 1, a different day from the Sabbath just named in xv: 42; and the Sabbath that "drew on," during which they "rested," was not merely a Sabbath, or simple Sabbattic time, but was the "Sabbath-day," that is, the special day of that name. This record in Mark and Luke, of one single continuous Sabbath between "the preparation" day and the "first day of the week," is proof positive that the crucifixion was on Friday, and by no means on Thursday, much less on Wednesday, as claimed by some.

DIFFICULTIES DISPOSED OF.

§ 62. (1) It was only about "the 9th hour" (Matt. xxvii: 46) or 3 p. m. when Jesus died—that is, "when the even was come" (ver. 57) or last quarter of the day, in which Joseph intervened; and when the

---

* See this, our view, proved by Prof. Murphy in the Bib. Sacra, Jan., 1872, p. 77. If the Pentecost mentioned by Josephus was in the year after Hyrcanus' accession, as Josephus seems to make it, *i. e.*, in B. C. 134, then the 16th Nisan that year was Sunday, April 10, by the Greek Cycle of Calippus (see here § 81, 83). But if that Pentecost was in the year before Antiochus' death, as Rollins puts it (Vol. vii: p. 248), *i. e.*, in B. C. 131, then the 16th Nisan that year was Sunday, April 6, by one day earlier observation of the moon. But in either case, this occurrence of "first-fruits" on the 16th Nisan (as in the year of Christ's death) does not prove that it was on that same 16th Nisan every year, even in those last Rabbinical years, much less that it was so in the original law and custom of Moses.

burial was finished, it was still "the preparation, and the Sabbath *drew on*" simply (Luke xxiii: 54), as sunset had not yet arrived, "for the sepulcher was nigh at hand," John xix: 42). So that the women had time to run into the city before sunset, and they "bought sweet spices" (Mark xvi: 1) ; and thus beginning to prepare them, they "rested the Sabbath day according to the commandment," (Luke xxiii: 56), evidently *the fourth commandment*. At sunset of Saturday they doubtless renewed their preparations, and very early in the morning they came unto the sepulcher bringing the spices which they had prepared," (xxiv: 1). Spices might be bought after the Sabbath or before. So that no extra day need be interposed for their preparations as some allege.

§ 63. (2) The only other objection offered against Friday as the crucifixion date, is, that this does not furnish an interval of "three days and three nights" before the resurrection. But the usual expression is "on the third day," and thirteen times over this expression is used. Matt. xvi: 21, and xvii: 23, and xx: 19, and xxvii: 64; Mark ix: 31, and x: 34; Luke ix: 22, and xviii: 33, and xxiv: 7, 21, 46; Acts x: 40, I Cor. xv: 4). It is certain that this was the Jewish mode of counting (as from Friday to Sunday), *i. e.* inclusively, beginning with the day or object started from. So Luke xiii: 32; Acts xxvii: 18, 19; Ex. xix: 10, 11; Lev. vii: 16, 17; and xix: 6; John xx: 26-30; and so I Sam. iv: 7, marg. ("Woe unto us! for there hath not been such a thing *yesterday nor the day before*") literally ("nor the third day"). Like II Sam. iii: 17; II Ki. xiii: 5; II Chron. xi: 2; Ex. iv: 10; Deut. xix: 4, 6; Josh. iii: 4. So also Lev. xxv: 8-10, etc. See particularly II Chron. x: 5-12. *

Jesus said (John ii: 19), "Destroy this temple, and *in three days* I will raise it up;" that is, "within three days," as his revilers reported it (Mark xiv: 58, and xv: 29; Mat. xxvii: 40). The Jewish rulers expressed it as "after three days" (Mat. xxvii: 63); but they immedi-

---

* "The expression *meta treis hemeras* always means *three days after* [*i. e.*, the third day], and not as usually rendered. So Josephus in his Jewish War (1, xiii: 1) says 'two years after,' but in his Antiq. (14, xiii: 3) he gives it as 'the second year.' This is according to classical usage. Theophrastus says of the Egyptian thorn, 'When it is cut down, *meta triton etos* it sprouts again,' which Pliny (N. H., xiii: 9) renders, '*cæsa anno tertio resurgit*.' Demosthenes uses *meth' hemeras duo* in the sense of 'two days after.' Cicero adopts it. Speaking to Anthony of the Ides of March, on which Cæsar was assassinated, he says: 'I neither saw you that day, nor the day after, but *post diem tertium* (the third day after) I came into the Temple of Tellus.' (Philippic, ii: 35.) Some learned commentators, such as Beza, Grotius, Campbell, Newcome, render such phrases, 'within three days,' etc., which certainly conveys the meaning, but is not the literal translation of the preposition *meta*, after." (Hales, Vol. I, p. 21.)

For further proofs, see Horne's Introd., Vol. II, P. 77.

ately explained this as meaning only "the third day" (ver, 64) "That deceiver said while he was yet alive, *after three days* I will rise again; command, therefore, that the sepulcher be made sure *until the third day*." (So Gen. xlii: 17, 18.) Jesus himself once said (Mark viii:31), he would "after three days rise again." But we have just seen that with the Jews "after three days" or "three days after" meant the same as "the third day after." This further appears from I Kings xii: 5,12: II Chron. x:5,12: "Come again unto me *after three days*," said the king: "*so they came on the third day as the king bade*." Can anything be more certain than this determination of the case before us?

But see also Luke ii:31, with Lev. xii:3, where "eight days were accomplished" when it was only "the eighth day." (Compare Gen. xvii: 12.) See also John xx:26, where one week or "the eighth day after," is expressed as "after eight days." And see Lev. xxiii:16, where "fifty days" means "the fiftieth day" or Pentecost; while "the fiftieth year" (xxv:10,11) has but forty-eight full years between its successive occurrences,—just as in the case before us, "the third day" has but one full day between its extreme days.

§ 64. In Matt. xii:40, Christ says: "For as Jonah was three days and three nights in the belly of the sea-monster, so shall the Son of Man be *three days and three nights* in the heart of the earth." This is the one great stumbling block of those, who (in view of it) try to be rid of Friday as the crucifixion date. There were parts of "three days" after the crucifixion, as we have seen; but where are the "three nights?" it is asked. Answer: "Three days and three nights" was only a colloquial phrase equivalent to three diurnal periods, and the word nights contained in it had no special significance. So in Esther iv: 16, and v: 1. "Fast ye for me, and neither eat nor drink *three days night or day*, I also and my maidens will fast likewise." And "*on the third day* she put on her royal apparel," having finished the fast.

So also in I Sam. xxx:12,13, "He had eaten no bread nor drunk any water *three days and three nights*," yet he immediately says, "*the third day ago* I fell sick," and was left thus to famish; (so the Hebrew should be rendered, as Scott observes). Here we find used the very expression before us, "three days and three nights," applied to an affair which was only "on the third day" inclusive, as the Jews counted. They spoke in round numbers, of the third day as counting three day-night units.

§ 65. But further: The Council of Caesarea, in A. D. 196, with its renowned leader, Bishop Theophilus, thus decreed: "*Passus namque Dominus ab 11 Kal. Apl., qua nocte a Judaeis traditus est et ab 8 Kal resurrexit, quomodo ergo hi tres dies * * * intra termanum inducantur,*' etc. "For our Lord suffered from the 11th Kal. of Apl., in which night he was betrayed, and rose the 8th Kal.; therefore those three days (from betrayal to resurrection) must be included within the limit', of allowable Easter days. We here see that the ancient fathers, (though getting the month-date wrong) spoke of the "three days" of Christ's passion as reaching from the Thursday "night on which he was betrayed;" they seeming to understand thus the "three days and three nights" during which he was "in the heart of the earth," or under the dominion of death, as they appear to have interpreted it. Why is not this a plausible explanation of Christ's fuller meaning? Not that he was to be entombed just so long, (the tomb was not even underground); but that he was to be overwhelmed under the world's will and the sway of death for "three days and three nights" from Gethsemane to Resurrection—just as expressed in the typical swallowing up of Jonah.

§ 66. But at any rate, this citation from the fathers proves that the tradition of Friday as the crucifixion date, instead of being imposed upon us by the later Romanism (as some allege), was the well-established view of those earlier times (in the second century)—since they reckoned *but three days from the betrayal to the resurrection*, thus fixing the crucifixion on Friday. And other like testimonies might be brought from the fathers.* There is no excuse whatever for disturbing the time honored fact, so fully demonstrated that our Lord died on Friday, the sixth day of the Jewish week.

The surest proof of all is the *astronomical demonstration*. It is now known beyond doubt (and generally agreed), that the year of Christ's death was A. D. 30. Astronomy proves to us that the New Moon of A. D. 30 was March 22nd at 7:30 P. M. Consequently, the New Moon could not be observed and reported and the New Year or 1st Nisan made to begin before the sunset of March 24. This makes the 14th Nisan to be on FRIDAY, April 7th. And this lunar assignment of the New Year must hold, whether it were made by *observation* of the moon, or by a lunar cycle, which after use for some time would necessarily (by aggregation of slight deficiency in all such cycles) give later reckoning than the moon itself. (See § 31.) And

---

* Justin Martyr (A. D. 140) expressly names Friday as the crucifixion day. (*Schwartz*.) His language is: "Sunday is the day on which we all hold our common assembly, because it is the first day, on which God, having wrought a change in the darkness and matter, made the world; and Jesus Christ our Saviour on the same day rose from the dead. For he was crucified on the day before that of Saturn [Saturday]; and on the day after that of Saturn, which is the day of the sun, he appeared to his apostles." (*Ant. Nic. Lib., Vol. II. p. 65, 66. See Bib. Sac., Oct. 1880, p. 665.*) So early and so general an establishment of Friday and Sunday as the dates (see § 56, note) must be correct.

thus it is, that the Friday reckoning is the key to the whole New Testament chronology.

To assign the crucifixion as Wednesday, would put it on the 12th of Nisan, three days before the passover festival! To ascribe it to Thursday, is nearly as bad. Nothing can be plainer than that our Lord was crucified on FRIDAY, April 7th (Julian), and rose on SUNDAY, April 9th A. D. 30.

APPENDIX B.
(For § 24.)

THE JEWISH MONTHS WERE LUNAR.

§ 67. Seyffarth was one of the very few who have ventured to deny that the Jewish months were lunar. (*Rec. Discov.*, p. 166.) How little account we can make of his view, will appear from the fact, that he makes the same denial concerning the Greeks, and substitutes Julian reckoning in the Jewish Calendar! Following in the same line, Jacob Schwartz, the learned librarian in New York City, comes forward (A. D. 1889), denying that the Jews had lunar months; and substituting therefor a novel Calendar of his own device, to throw the crucifixion (conceded to be in A. D. 30) upon the old Julian Equinox, March 25! In disproof of these theories, see the full evidence of Lunar reckoning in the *Encyc. Brit.*, Art. *Chronology*.

The use of 30 day months at the flood, and in prophecy, is no disproof of lunar months (alternating 29 and 30 days) in the practical system of the Jewish code. This lunar system was evidently based upon the commanded observance of "new-moon" festivals, so obvious throughout the Jewish scriptures. Lev. xxiii: 24; I Sam. xx: 5, 18; II Ki. iv: 23; I Chron. xxiii: 31; II Chron. ii: 4, and xxxi: 3; Ezra iii: 5; Neh. x: 33; Psa. lxxxi: 3; Isa. i: 13, 14, and lxvi: 23; Ezek. xxxxv: 17, and xxxxvi: 1, 3, 6; Amos viii: 5; Hos. iii: 11; Col. ii: 16. Hear also the ancient writers:

§ 68. "Our fathers left Egypt on the 15th day of *the lunar month*" *tessara kai dekatee kata seleeneen, en Ario* (in Aries) *tou heeliou kathestotos*. (*Josephus, Antiq. 2. xv: 2, and 3. x: 5.*) The months certainly were lunar in the times of Josephus and the New Testament.

"The passover, a public feast, was to be celebrated on the 14th day, the moon's circle coming to be full-shining," *tessara kai dekatee heemera, mellontos tou seleeniakou kuklou genesthai pleesiphaous*. (*Philo, De Vita Mosis, p. 530.*) Could anything be plainer than such testimony? So also, *Noumeenia gar orchetai photizein oistheeto to phezzi ho heelios seleeneen*, "for at the new month the sun starts to enlighten the moon," etc. (*id.*)

So the Council of Cæsarea, A. D. 196. So also Anatolius, A. D. 287. (See in Bede, and Hales.) "The law commands the passover to be slain on the 14th by the moon." (*Bede, cap. 47, p. 491.*) So Proterius, A. D. 457. "He rose on the 17th of the moon." (*Migne, vol. 67, p. 507.*)

"The Greek Olympiads commenced at the full moon." (*Jerome.*) "The Greeks and other ancients proposed to have the months lunar and the years solar, that the sacrifices might come always about the same time of year, as more acceptable to the gods." (*Geminus, the great astronomer, about 240 B. C., in Euseb. II, p. 747.*) "In proof that the Greeks counted the days accurately according to the moon's age, note that the solar eclipses always happened on the 30th day of their month, and the lunar at its middle." (*Hales I, p. 24.*) As the Greeks then had lunar months, why not also the Jews?

To make plain the certainty that the Jewish months were lunar, we here bring forward several express cases, all but the first cited by Schwartz himself.

(1) April 7, A. D. 30, *at the full moon*, was certainly the crucifixion passover, as assigned at an early date, being called "Pharmonti 25" of the rotary Egyptian year. See here, § 3.

§ 69. (2) "In A. D. 26, there was an inscription at Berenike in Egypt, in which the last day of the feast of Tabernacles is said to have occurred on Paophi 25. The fixed Alexandrian Paophi begins Sep. 28 [the fixed Thoth 1 being Aug. 29]; so that the 25th is Oct. 22, hence 1 Tisri was Oct. 1." (*J. Schwartz, Letter, Jan. 11, 1890.*)

As the 7th month Tisri 1 began at sunset of Oct. 1, the 1st month Nisan 1 began 6 lunar months or ($29\frac{1}{2} \times 6 =$) 177 days before, at sunset of April 7. This agrees exactly with the Greek Lunar Cycle (as applied by the Jews,—see here, at § 28 note); thus, A. D. 26=Cy. yr. 14 (from B. C. 330 as yr. 1), epact or age of the moon 23 on (June 28 and) March 31; giving 1 Nisan as beginning (30—23=) 7 days later on April 7,—the moon's conjunction itself being about two days before that.

The only question that can be raised is, whether "the last day of the feast" on the inscription meant Tisri 21 or 22. The "Paophi 25" = Oct. 22 was Tisri 21 till sunset, after that Tisri 22. In any case, Tisri 1 was Oct. 1 at sunset (as Schwartz concedes), till the sunset of Oct. 2.

The "last day of the feast of tabernacles" was really Tisri 21: for over and over we are told it was to last "seven days," viz., 15-21 inclusive. (Lev. xxiii: 6, 8, 34, 36, 39, 40, 41, 42.) The "8th day" mentioned in ver. 39 (and II Chron. vii: 8, 9, 10) was not considered a day of the feast. "The feast of tabernacles, strictly so-called, is supposed to have continued only 7 days, during which all the Israelites dwelt in booths. The '8th day' is thought to have been an additional festival—of thanksgiving—celebrated in their own houses." (*Scott's Com.*) This extra 8th day (the 22nd) Solomon lengthened (on the 23d) into *full 7 days extra* in dedication of the temple. (II Chron. vii: 9, 10.) At any rate, "the 8th day" as Tisri 22 *began* in the year A. D. 26 on "Paophi 25" or Oct. 22, in agreement with the inscription. It may even have begun at the sunset before, if observation instead of the cycle were then in use. In either case, the months are proved to have been *certainly lunar*.

§ 70. (3) "In A. D. 70, Josephus says, the temple was burnt on Lous 8 (= Sat. Aug. 5)—the 5th Macedonian month;—and the city was captured on Gorpieus 8, the 6th Macedonian month. The tradition of the Jews and the express testimony of Roman historians (Dio for one) make them both *Saturdays*." (*Schwartz' Letter.*)

As Josephus calls the 5th Jewish month Ab by its Macedonian name Lous, on what Roman date does he here put its 8th day? That year A. D. 70 was (like the year 32) year 1 of the Lunar Cycle (from B. C. 330), with epact 0 on March 31, June 28, and August 26. Therefore, the 6th lunar month began at sunset of August 26, and the 5th lunar month began at sunset of July 27; so that, the 8th day of the 5th month ended at sunset on August 4 of that year, A. D. 70; which was *Saturday*, as the tradition requires (not Saturday, August 5, as Schwartz has it).

For, by the week-day rule (at § 40 note),—A. D. 70+28 leaves 14, wh. ÷ 7 leaves 0 + 3 (in the previous 14)= 3 days to be added to Sun. —Wed. Mar. 0, A. D. 70 + (Mar. 31 + 30 + 31 + 30 + 31 + Aug. 4 =) 157 days ÷ 7 leaves 3d + Wed. = *Saturday*, Aug. 4, A. D. 70.

We thus see, that the Jewish reckoning was certainly by the *lunar months;* and that the Jewish tradition rightly has the burning of the temple on the Jewish Sabbath (Saturday, Lous or Ab 8, A. D. 70). But the destruction of the city could not be also on the Sabbath, if the "Gorpieus 8" is correct; for the intervening *whole month* cannot thus be reduced to even weeks.

§ 71. (4) "Pompey captured the city in the 3d ecclesiastical month, Sivan 23, a fast day, and a *Saturday*, as Dio testifies, in 64 B. C." (*Schwartz' Letter.*) He adds, "In a lunar year the 23d day of Sivan would fall on June 21, in B. C. 64." That is right. For, this B. C. 64 and the A. D. 70 (just considered) are exactly 133 years apart, or 7 lunar cycles; so that, by the cycle, 1 Nisan began in both years alike. That is, in this year 1 of the cycle, with epact 0 on Mar. 31, the 1 Nisan began at sunset on March 31. Therefore, 1 Sivan, 59 days later, began May 29, and 23 Sivan ended at sunset on *Saturday* June 21, B. C. 64, as "the fast day."

We find it to be *Saturday* by the rule (at § 40 note), thus: B. C. 64 − 1 = 63 + 28 leaves 7, which + 7 leaves 0, to which we add 1 (for the

1 four in the 7), and add 1 more (for the rest of the 7), making 2 days *before Sunday, i. e.* Friday, March 0, B. C. 64. Then, March 31 + April 30 + May 31 + June 21 = 113 days + 7 leaves 1 *after Friday*, Mar. 0, making *Saturday, June 21, B. C. 64.* The Jewish months are thus proved to have been *lunar*.

(5) "Judas' defeat of Nicanor on Adar 13 (1 Mac. vii: 43) = March 12, B. C. 161; which was a *Sunday*, as plainly appears by 2 Mac. xv: 1, 37." (*Schwartz' Letter*.) It was at least soon after the Saturday Sabbath, in the 152d year Seleucic (see 1 Mac. vii: 1) *i. e.* in B. C. 160 (not 161), when Adar 13 was Feb. 24 by the Lunar Cycle. For, that was cycle year 19, epact 18 on March 31: *i. e.*, 1 Nisan beginning Mar. 13 = Adar 30, so that Adar, 13 = Feb. 24,—which was *Sunday*.

We know it was *Sunday* thus: B. C. 160−1 = 159 ÷ 28 leaves 19, which ÷7 leaves 5 + 4 + 1 more, making 10 or 3 days *before Sunday, i. e.*, Thursday, Mar. 0, B. C. 160. So that we have *Sunday, Feb. 24, B. C. 160.* Thus the months were *lunar*.

§ 72. (6) "The capture of the first temple by Nebuchadnezzar was on Ab 8, according to the Jewish traditions; and they claim that this was a *Saturday*." (*Schwartz' Letter*.) That is, it was supposed to be the day after the coming, 2 Ki. xxv: 8. We have elsewhere proved that it was in the year B. C. 587 (not 588 or 586 as often given). Josephus says, that Titus' burning of the temple was "the same month and day" as that of Nebuchadnezzar, viz. "Lous (or Ab) 8," when the burning began, (*War 6, iv: 1, 2, 8*) though the burning continued till "Lous or Ab 10," (§ 5).

B. C. 587 is 616 years before A. D. 30, or 8 years over 32 of the 19 year cycles. Those 8 years carry the months back two days; (see epact 0 or 30 changed to 28 after 8 years, 11 changed to 9, etc.,—in the list of epacts, § 28 note.) So that, 1 Nisan in B. C. 587 began by cycle March 22, instead of the March 24 (at sunset) in A. D. 30. But if the cycle when Meton put it forth (in B. C. 432) agreed nearly with the moon, it would in B. C. 587 be nearly a day before the new moon. Therefore, that year, instead of 1 Nisan begun on March 22, the new moon itself was not until March 23; and (going then only by observation) they began the new year, 1 Nisan, two days after, at sunset of March 25. This made the 8th of Ab (the 5th month) begin at sunset of *Friday*, July 28, and *Saturday*, July 29, B. C. 587, was the Ab 8, on which tradition puts the destruction of the temple.

We know it was Saturday thus: B. C. 587−1=586+28 leaves 26, which ÷7 leaves 5+6+1 more, making 12 or 5 days *before Sunday, i. e.*, Tuesday March 0, B. C. 587. Then March 31+April 30+May 31 +June 30+July 29=151÷7 leaves 4 days after Tuesday, Mar. 0, making Saturday, July 29, B. C. 587. Thus the months were *lunar*.

Indeed, B. C. 587+A. D. 30=616 years, which contain just 22 solar cycles of 28 years each. And July 29—March 25=126 days, or just even weeks after March 25. Therefore, as March 25, A. D. 30, was Saturday, so the July 29, B. C. 587, was Saturday also (on the 8th day of the 5th lunar month Ab).

And the tradition cited is thus found to be well grounded, that the temple was burned this time also upon the Jewish Sabbath; while the year date B. C. 587 is thus also verified, as the fundamental or starting date for the whole Old Testament Chronology.

All the foregoing dates, therefore, go to prove demonstratively, that the Jews employed *lunar months* all through their history. At the same time they show, that, in the later centuries at least, they had their months beginning about two days after the new moon conjunction; in accordance with the lunar cycle, confirming our demonstration of the crucifixion date as on the 14th Nisan, or Friday, April 7, A. D. 30.

APPENDIX C.

(For § 31.)

ANCIENT LUNAR CYCLES.

§ 73. Although Calippus used June 28 (or its equivalent) as his solstitial standard day for the lunar epacts, as we have seen, yet Meton before him had more correctly assigned June 27 (or its equivalent) as his standard summer solstice.

"Meton observed the summer solstice to be, in this year B. C. 432, on the 21st day of the Egyptian month Phamenoth, which reduced to the Julian year falls on the 27th of June. And therefore the Greeks having received the cycle from him, did, from this time forward, celebrate their Olympiads on the first full moon after the 27th day of our June; beginning their year from the new moon preceding." (*Prideaux, Connex, Vol. I. p. 409.*)

This was a correct placing of the solstice; since, by our exact reckoning, the solstice in B. C. 433 was on June 27 at 4 A. M. at Greenwich, or 5½ A. M. in Greece,—and in B. C. 432 it was on June 27 at 10 A. M. at Greenwich, or 11½ A. M. in Greece. Thenceforward, it was found necessary to add a day from time to time to the Egyptian date of the solstice, making the Phamenoth 21 to become Phamenoth 22, and then 23, etc., to keep their solstice day right in that rotary year of Egypt. But this was done irregularly, the exact length of a solar or equinoctial year not being then understood; so that a day was added sometimes in 3 years, sometimes in 5 years, two days being sometimes added when there was too long delay.

After 100 years, Calippus found that 25 days in all had been inserted, carrying the solstice to Pharmonti 16; therefore he judged that about 1 day in each 4 years was the right change required. And he deemed it expedient to establish *a rule* of change with his improved cycle, viz., that *at each return of the Olympic games* (in B. C. 332, 328, 324, etc.) the solstice should be considered as having moved 1 day later in the Egyptian year. He thus got in an extra day-change at B. C. 432, making 26 days added since Meton (instead of the correct 25), and carrying the solstice from Phamenoth 21 to Pharmonti 17 (instead of the right 16); which Pharmonti 17 in B. C. 330 (his cycle year 1) was June 28 Julian, instead of Meton's more correct solstice June 27.

§ 74. Thus the standard solstitial date of the Greeks became from that time equivalent to June 28 Julian, although June 27 had been started by Meton 100 years before, as the more correct solstice date. Calippus found the mean new moon of that B. C. 330 to be on that very Pharmonti 17 (= June 28 Julian) at $3\frac{1}{4}$ P. M. in Greece. And therefore, he called that B. C. 330 year 1 of his 76-year cycle (4 of the 19's), with epact 0, or no age of the month on June 28. (See here, § 30.)

Meton, having epact 0 on June 27 (as really year 1 of his 19-year cycle), while the new moon—by our exact mean reckoning—was June 26 at 2 P. M. at Greenwich, or $3\frac{1}{2}$ P. M. in Greece,—we see that he had the months, from the very start, beginning a day after the mean new moon, as if assigned by observation. The next year, B. C. 432, was really year 2 of his cycle, with epact 11, showing the month 11 days old on June 27; so that, another new month that year would begin after (30—11=) 19 days from June 27, viz., on July 16.

But most writers call this year, B. C. 432, the beginning of Meton's cycle, as if he had the epacts 11, 22, 3, &c., instead of the 0, 11, 22, &c., of Calippus. And they put its beginning at the new month July 16, B. C. 432, instead of the new month June 27, B. C. 433.* But this throws the Olympic full moon too long after the Solstice, or has an intercalary month at the very 1 of the cycle, which is not at all likely.

After 5 cycles of Meton, or 95 years from B. C. 433, the year B. C. 338 was a proper year 1 of Meton's cycle. But Calippus interposed an 8-year cycle, making his cycle year 1 to be B. C. 330. That inter-

---

*The *Edinburgh Encyc.* says: "The cycle of Meton was adopted July 16, B. C. 433 [432]." *Herschel's Astron.* tells us: "The Metonic cycle (astronomical epact) began July 15, B. C. 432. The civil epoch of it was 1 day later than the astronomical, the latter being the epoch of the absolute new moon, the former that of the earliest possible visibility of the lunar crescent in a tropical sky." The *Chronology of History* says: "The beginning of the Metonic cycle was July 15, B. C. 432."

posed 8-year cycle increased the epact of B. C. 330 by 2 days from 28 to 30 or 0; but being applied to June 28, instead of the previous June 27, it was really an increase of only 1 day in the age of the month, into nearer agreement with the actual age of the moon. And that was probably one reason why the Calippic change was introduced. For, in that year, B. C. 330, the mean new moon was on June 28, at $3\frac{1}{4}$ P. M. in Greece; *i. e.*, on the very day of epact 0, instead of a whole day before, as in the case of Meton.

§ 75. Assuming that, at or after the time of Meton and Calippus, the Jews used a 19-year cycle, they, of course, would apply it to the *equinox*, not (as did the Greeks) to the solstice. Considering Meton's solstice as correct (equivalent to June 27), and regarding the equinoxes as 91 days (or one-quarter of the year) before and after that date (equivalent to March 28 and Sep. 26), in applying the cycle at first (for fixing their *civil* year) to the *autumnal* equinox as Sep. 26, the Jews would have their epacts 2 larger than those of Calippus (1 larger in part of the cycle), because the 91 days (from June 27 to Sep. 26) were $1\frac{1}{2}$ day more than the three lunations ($89\frac{1}{2}$ days).

This was adding another 8-year cycle to Calippus, as he added an 8-year cycle to Meton. And now, calling epact 11 (instead of 9) the epact of the cycle year 1, the Jews had their year 1 (twice 8+1 or) 17 years later than that of Meton, as if in B. C. 416 (instead of 433). So that year 1 of their cycle was the same as year 18 of Meton. And in this shape they have it to this date. For, the "Jewish Lunar Cycle," as given in our Almanacs and as found in the Calendars of the Modern Jews, has year 1 as A. D. 1884, *i. e.*, B. C. 17, and A. D. 3, and 22, etc., with its year 9 at A. D. 30, etc. When the Jews used the cycle to assign the *vernal* new year, they had simply to take 5 from each autumnal epact, and apply the remainder to their vernal equinox, March 28; because the 182 days (or two 91's) from Sep. 26 back to March 28 were 5 days more than the 6 intervening lunations (6 times $29\frac{1}{2}$ or) 177 days.

Thus the epact 9 in year 10 of Calippus' cycle became autumnal epact 11 in year 1 of the Jewish cycle, or, used vernally (—5) epact 4 as the age of the month on March 28, with 1 Nisan consequently beginning at sunset of March 24 in A. D. 30. And so, by cycle reckoning (as well as by observation), whether the cycle were that of Calippus, applied at March 31, or a modified form of it, as the Jewish Lunar Cycle, handed down to our times with (+2—5—) 3 less epact applied to the old equinox, March 28, in either case, the Jews had 1 Nisan beginning about 2 days after the new moon; *i. e.*, at sunset of March 24 in A. D. 30, the year of crucifixion. (As to the lunar reckoning of Julius Cæsar, see afterwards, in Appendix D.)

§ 76. The Council of Nice (in A. D. 325) reduced the standard day for epacts from the old Greek, June 28, or Mar. 31 (as used by the Jews) down to March 22, as the day after the true equinox then (March 21), and as the earliest date allowable in the paschal term. This loss of nine days (from Mar. 31 to 22) in applying the epacts required a corresponding reduction of the epacts by 9. But the cycle error of two days (in the more than 600 years since Calippus) being allowed for, the reduction would be seven days. They in fact reduced the epacts but six days, and so over-corrected the cycle, carrying their new months *one day before* the new-moons. This they did, perhaps, in order to anticipate further error of the cycle—which they foresaw would accrue. But, in order to have year 1 of the cycle still at epact 0, this reduction of six days required them to move along the cycle six years; so that, its year 1 came where the year 7 of Calippus came, viz., at B. C. 1 instead of B. C. 7 (and before in B. C. 330). Thus the year 1, or "Golden Number" 1, of the Nicene cycle was A. D. 323, when the mean new moon was March 23.*

And thus have we the Nicene Lunar Cycle (still in use as the Golden Number, with year 1 at B. C. 1), three years earlier and greater than the Jewish Lunar Cycle (with year 1 at A. D. 3). And it had, at the start, its year 1 or A. D. 323, with epact 0 on March 22, *one day before* the mean new moon of March 23.

§ 77. In the lapse of time, the equinox so went down in the Julian year, that in the 17th century the standard March 22 (or day after the equinox) had reached March 12; and pope Gregory dropped ten days, throwing it back to be March 22 again: But meanwhile, the mean new-moon had moved along in the Julian year (at the rate of one day in 310 years) to be nearly five days earlier at cycle-year 1, viz., on March 18, Julian, instead of the March 23—*i. e.*, on March 28 of the new Gregorian dating. So that, if March 22 were still used for applying the epacts, they would now make the months begin (28 − 22=) six days too soon. Hence it was concluded, to apply the epacts no longer to March 22, but to March 30, or (what was the same thing) to January 1, the modern New Year, just three lunations before.

§ 78. But as the mean new moon of Cycle-year 1 was at March 28 (as just seen), this putting of its epact 0 as at March 30 (or January 1) was making the months begin with March 31, or three days after the mean new moon. However, the Gregorian loss of another day at

---

* For, A. D. 1855−323=1532 years × 365¼ =559,563 days and 18,948 lunations × 29d.5305885=559545d. 591 (or 14h+1¾ h acceleration=15¾ hours from the 559,563 days=17d 8¼ h+the mean new moon in A. D. 1855, viz., March 6, Julian, at 8½ A. M. at Rome=the mean new-moon in A. D. 323, on March 23, at 4¾ P. M. at Rome (G. N. 1, epact 0, on March 22).

A. D. 1700,† carried the new moon of March 28 (in Cycle-year 1) up to be March 29, making the last century to have the cycle months beginning but two days after the mean new-moon. And the loss of another day at A. D. 1800, carried the new moon (in cycle-year 1) up to be March 30, making the present century have the cycle months beginning but one day after the mean new moon. ‡ So that when, directly, A. D. 1900 shall have lost to us still another day, the next century will have the cycle months beginning just about with the mean new-moon.

In other words, the Gregorian loss of 12 days now reached offset by 5 full days correction of the lunar cycle (in 1873—325 = 1550 yrs + 310), has left 7 days change of epact needed, from the new moon of Mar. 23, A. D. 323, to the new moon of Mar. 30, now (in cycle yr. 1); so that our present putting of epact 0 (in cycle year 1) on Mar. 30 or Jan. 1, gives the lunar months as beginning but a single day after the mean new moon.

§ 79. Comparative View of Ancient Cycles and Epacts.

		Year B. C.	*						*							A. D.		*	
			15	14	13	12	11	10	9	8	7	6	5	4	3	2	1	1	2	3	4
Epacts.	Metonic, June 27	*0	11	22	3	14	25	6	17	28	9	20	1	12	23	4	15	26	7	18
	Callipic, June 28	1	12	23	4	15	26	7	18	*0	11	22	3	14	25	6	17	28	9	20
	Jewish, Sep. 26	3	14	25	6	17	28	9	20	1	12	23	4	15	26	7	18	0	*11	22
	Jewish, Mar. 28	28	9	20	1	12	23	4	15	26	7	18	0	11	22	3	14	25	*6	17
	Nicene { Mar. 22 / Jan. 1 }	25	6	17	28	9	20	1	12	23	4	15	26	7	18	*0	11	22	3	14
	Golden Number	6	7	8	9	10	11	12	13	14	15	16	17	18	19	*1	2	3	4	5

*Beginning of the cycles—Metonic, Callipic, Nicene, Jewish.

APPENDIX D.

(For § 48.)

Was the Crucifixion on the 14th or the 15th Nisan?

§ 80. There has always been going on an earnest and elaborate debate, as to the question, on which of the Jewish days Christ was crucified, on the 14th of Nisan, the day of slaughtering the paschal lambs, or on the 15th of Nisan, the first festival day of the passover. Centuries ago this question was agitated, and every year or two in this

---

† As England then dropped the eleven days just=a year's change of the lunar epacts, "the Gregorian epact for any year was the same with the Julian epact for the year preceding it." (*Chambers' Cyc*).

‡ Thus, in A. D. 1855, the Almanacs give the Golden Number (or Nicene cycle-year) as 13, with epact 12, *i. e.*, with the lunar month 12d old on January 1, making it 30d old (or epact 0) of the next lunar month on (30—12=) 18d after, or January 19; whereas, that mean new moon was January 18, at 6 A. M., as we saw.

century there appears a labored discussion and alleged determination of the matter one way or the other. This debate excites the more interest because the gospel of John seems to be all written in favor of the 14th day, and the other three gospels are thought to support the 15th day as the date of crucifixion.

Sceptical critics of Scripture love to harp upon these appearances of collision between the gospels, and to array the one against the others in alleged proof of the unreliability of the history. It is worth our while, therefore, to inquire if there is any plain and plausible explanation of the seeming discrepancy. A new elaboration of the subject, just appearing (from Prof. Whitford, Outlook, October, 1892), emboldens us to present the following view, which we have long entertained:

§ 81. The Jewish months were lunar, and they felt obliged by the Mosaic law carefully to conform their new year and their months to the successive returns of the new moon, so that the sacred festivals should come at the very times divinely appointed, and the passover feast and the feast of tabernacles should be at the full moon or 15th day of their respective months. Now, the 15th Nisan would not thus come correctly at the full moon, unless that first month should be started properly soon after the new moon of the new year appeared.

In order thus to start the year right, in all their earlier history, the rulers had an artless method of announcing annually the arrival of the new year's new moon, as seen by careful observation within a day or two after the change. Whoever first caught sight of the new moon was rewarded for reporting it to the authorities, and the order was at once issued by the Sanhedrim fixing and starting 1 Nisan on its way, while bonfires lighted on the hills spread at once the news of the new year begun. (See here § 25.) This was a rude method of early times, and would, of course, give way to simpler and surer ways of inaugurating the year, as knowledge of the movements of the heavenly bodies advanced.

In B. C. 432 Meton gave to the Greeks the wonderful Lunar Cycle of 19 years, each year having set to it an *Epact*, or moon's age, on a fixed starting or standard date (the day of the summer solstice). So that the commencement of each lunar year was known by the simple Epact number of that year, and after 19 years the same succession returns over again, with only a slight departure from perfect accuracy, there being only a deviation from the exact new moon of one day in 310 years.

This cycle of the Greeks was still further perfected by Calippus in B. C. 330, which was made year 1 of a 76-year period or four-fold return of the 19-year cycle. In that year B. C. 330 (cycle year 1) the mean new moon was June 28 at 3¼ P. M., and so that day, June 28, then taken as the day of the summer solstice (see Appendix C, § 74) was a suitable starting point for the Epact or age of the moon each year. Thus B. C. 330, as cycle year 1, had Epact 0, *i. e.*, no age of the moon on June 28; B. C. 329 as cycle year 2 had Epact 11, *i. e.*, moon 11 days old on June 28: next year 3, Epact 22, and so on, the Epact increasing 11 days each year, with 30 days dropped whenever reached; until the 20th year as again year 1 brought Epact 29, called 0 by a "saltus" here of 1 day to keep the cycle right.

§ 82. This Greek 19-year cycle proved such a convenience that Julius Cæsar, in reforming the Roman Calendar, B. C. 46, established his new year at Jan. 1, B. C. 45, purposely located on the day of the new moon; so that this year being year 1 of the cycle (because 15 times 19=285 years from B. C. 330—B. C. 45),—the Epact of this year should be 0, *i. e.*, no age of the moon on Jan. 1. The next year as cycle year 2 would thus have Epact 11 (or moon 11 days old on Jan. 1), the next year or cycle year 3, Epact 22: next year, Epact 33—30=3, etc.

In thus accurately fixing his Jan. 1, at the new moon, Julius had corrected out the 1 day of error, that had (in 310 years) accumulated in the Greek cycle. For the 178 days from their summer solstice reckoned as June 28, back to January 1, was one day more than the 6 lunations or 177 days that intervened. So that, changing the standard date for applying the Epacts from June 28, not to January 2 or 177 days earlier, but to January 1 or 178 days earlier, with the same Epacts applied:—was really increasing all the Epacts 1 day; which was just what the error of the Greek cycle after that length of time required.

§ 83. Now the Jewish nation could not escape from these improvements of their times, in the methods of determining the lunar new years. And they had their choice in our Savior's time, whether to use the original Greek cycle, or to use the later corrected Roman cycle of Julius. It is not at all likely that they would, after becoming intimate (as they were) with the Greek language and learning, and with the Roman government and control, and after seeing therefore the simple and sure method they had of knowing when the lunar year began,—it is not at all likely, that they would confine themselves to the old rude way of waiting for observation. But they would naturally learn how, by the cycle, to determine the new year beforehand, and have it known all over the land, without the need of bonfires to spread the news. But which would they follow, the Greek or the Roman reckoning, differing (we see) by one day?

A Jewish application of the cycles would work thus: The Greek Epacts applied to June 28, would apply with equal accuracy to March 31, just three lunations earlier. But the Roman Epacts (the same in value) applied to Jan. 1, would apply with equal accuracy to March 0 or March 30, just two or three lunations later. The question was, which should they do? Should they with the Greeks apply the Epacts to March 31, or should they with the Romans apply the same Epacts (o, 11, 22, 3, etc.) one day earlier at Mar. 30?

For instance, in A. D. 30, the year of Christ's crucifixion, which was the year 18 of the cycle, (because the year A. D. 32 is 361 years or just 19 times 19 years after B. C. 330, and therefore the same cycle year 1), the Epact was 7. Which, if applied Greek-wise to March 31, made 1 Nisan to be March 25, and *the 14th Nisan* to be Friday, April 7th as the crucifixion day; but if applied Roman-wise to March 30, the same Epact 7 made 1 Nisan to be March 24, and *the 15th Nisan* to be Friday, April 7th, as the crucifixion day. Which was it? Here is the whole question of the ages condensed before us.

§ 84. The Jewish rulers could but see that the Roman dating (having been corrected a day) was the more accurate, giving 1 Nisan as soon as the moon could anyway appear; while the Greek dating put 1 Nisan when the moon was two days old. But then the Greek method was the older and better known, perhaps long used by the Jews before Julius' method was known. And then again, the Jews had a prejudice against adopting the ways of their Roman conquerors, while the Greeks had a great influence over them. Says Neander, (Chh. Hist., Vol. I p. 50), concerning those times: "In the course of those centuries (from Alexander the Great) the peculiar asperity and stiffness of the Jewish character must have been considerably tempered by intercourse with the Greeks. * * * The Jews (in Alexandria), completely imbued with the elements of Hellenic culture, endeavored to find a mean betwixt these and the religion of their fathers." Of course, then, the Sanhedrim would more naturally follow the old Greek reckoning of the lunar year, even though not quite so exact as the more modern Roman way, especially as the later Greek dating agreed nearer with rough *observation* of the moon. And so they had their months and their passovers really one day too late.

And yet, this would not be without remonstrance of some among the people, of those most intelligent and least prejudiced against the Romans, and most anxious to conform to the strict time assignments of the law,—a characteristic of the Saducees, and of the later sect of Caraites. Perhaps there were disputes, when the new moon was sometimes so long before 1 Nisan was allowed to come,—questioning whether the new year and the passover ought not to be a day sooner. And, perhaps our Savior purposely allowed himself to sanction that earlier and more correct date for the passover (well understood, it may be, by the disciples), by celebrating his anti-typical passover on the evening beginning the Sanhedrim's 14th Nisan (which was really the true 15th Nisan, if rightly numbered), in order himself to be put to death as "the Lamb of God" next day, at the hour when they slaughtered the Lambs. (See §48, note.)

§ 85. The law allowed the keeping of the passover out of its regular time (in the 2nd month instead of the 1st) when necessity required (Num. ix: 10, 11); and Hezekiah availed himself of this privilege (2 Chron. xxx: 2, 3, 15). The present Jewish traditions allow a duplicate day in special cases for a new moon or other observance. And who shall say, that the slaying of paschal lambs "between the evenings" of the 14th Nisan (Ex. xii: 16) might not at times be construed as permitting such paschal observance in the *beginning* of 14th Nisan, between its own initial evening and the evening of the 15th following it?

There seems at Acts ii: 1, an intimation of such a double reckoning of the feast days that year. "When the Day of Pentecost was fully come," *Revis. marg.*, "was being fulfilled;" as if there had been an initial day claimed by some for the festival, but the official date was waited for.

The three first evangelists, writing earlier, when the dispute about days was in mind, and when most likely (as a result of the dispute) the newer and more correct cycle reckoning had come into use, took pains to say, that Christ commanded paschal preparations to be made on the *correct 14th Nisan* "when the passover must be killed," (ought to be killed, or was due to be killed, Lu. xxii: 7); so that it was really a true and legal passover that Christ observed, not a sham passover as some might claim. Whereas, John, writing long afterward, when such trifles were lost sight of, emphasized rather the fact, that Christ was sacrificed as "the Lamb of God," at the very hour of *the Jews' 14th Nisan* when they were slaying the lambs. (John i: 31, etc.)

§ 86. If we are asked, then, on which day Christ died, the 14th or the 15th Nisan of the movable lunar year, our answer is: He died on what everybody knew to be, and what he treated as being, the proper 15th Nisan,—but on what was by edict of the Sanhedrim the *official* (though incorrect) *14th Nisan* of the Jews that year, which thus has become the historical date of the crucifixion.

The work of Chs. Ed. Caspari (Hamburg, 1869), well proves this date, A. D. 30, April 7, *Friday, the 14th of Nisan.* (Bib. Sacra., July, 1871, p. 469.)

The lately discovered apocryphal "Gospel of Peter," understood to have been written about A. D. 150, testifies that the crucifixion was not on the feast day but on the day before. For it tells of Herod as speaking to Pilate about the burial of Jesus, and saying, "Already the Sabbath draws on; and it is written in the law, that the sun must not go down upon a person put to death on the day before their feast, the feast of unleavened bread." This shows the opinion entertained upon this subject in those early days.

"They crucified him on the day before the feast of the passover."
(*Babylonian Gemara, Tract. Sanhedrim, Fol. 43.* In Bib. Sac., Oct., 1868, p. 742.) "The Talmud places the crucifixion on Nisan 14th." (*Schwartz.*)

In Mark xv: 21, and Luke xxiii: 26, "Simon the Cyrenian" was "coming out of the *field*,"—so the word (agros) is commonly translated in other passages. And this would not be likely if that crucifixion day was the 15th Nisan, the day of festival *rest.* (So says Schwartz.)

That the supper which our Lord ate with his disciples, was in anticipation of the passover eaten by the Jews the next evening, and that this was probably occasioned by a diverse reckoning of the lunar date, has been suggested by several writers; though none have given the explicit form to the thought which we have exhibited above. Hales gives this view in general, and Farrar in his life of Christ mentions it. Cudworth gave a distinct form to the theory, saying: "If after [the later assigning of the new moon] reputable witnesses came from far, and testified that they had seen the new moon in its due time, the Senate [Sanhedrim] were bound to alter the beginning of the month, and reckon it a day sooner. As the Senate were very unwilling to be at the trouble of a second consecration when they had once fixed on a wrong day,....they afterwards made a statute to this effect, 'That whatever time the Senate should conclude on for the calends of the month, though it were certain that they were in the wrong, yet all were bound to order their feasts according to it.'" This is what Cudworth gathered from the Babylonish Talmud and from Maimonides; and he supposed that this was what actually took place in the time of our Lord; showing from Epiphanius, that there was contention (*thorubos*), a tumult among the Jews, about the passover that very year. (See Prof. Townsend's Notes on the Gospels, p. 158.)

§ 87. Rev. J. K. Aldrich (in the Bib. Sacra, July 1870, p. 418) adopts this view; but he errs (as we think) in making Christ's earlier 15th Nisan begin on *Wednesday* at sunset, with Christ crucified on Thursday as the 14th day of the Sanhedrim. His ground for it is the allegation of "Roger Bacon, Manne and Scaliger, Dodwell and Ferguson," that the paschal full moon that year, A. D. 30, was on *Wednesday*. We have shown the folly of such random astronomical assignments (here at § 17-22), and have demonstrated (at § 41) that the full moon was not till *Thursday night* at 9 P. M, of April 6 in A. D. 30. So that all this Wednesday reckoning of our Lord's supper falls to the ground; and with it the whole theory of a Thursday crucifixion.

The early churches of the 2nd century, divided on the question, whether the crucifixion and resurrection (or Easter) should be celebrated always on Friday and on Sunday, as they occurred in the *week,* or always on the 14th and 16th Nisan, as they occurred in the *lunar month*. The western churches contended for Friday and Sunday and at last prevailed, giving us Easter as we have it now; the eastern churches, more influenced by Jewish ideas, long adhered to the 14th and 16th of the Jewish month as their Easter dating. They were therefore called "quartadecimani," which shows that the later claims of the 15th Nisan as crucifixion day had not then arisen. Neander (Vol. I, p. 298,) finally comes to this conclusion.

As we have shown that the crucifixion was on Friday the 14th Nisan of the Jews, it follows that the day of "First Fruits" (the 16th Nisan "the morrow after the Sabbath" (Lev. xxiii: 11), was on Sunday, the morning of "first fruits" and of Christ's resurrection; verifying the words of Paul (I Cor. xv: 20, 23), that Christ rose as "the *first fruits* of them that slept"; even as he also says (I Cor. v: 7), "Christ *our passover* is sacrificed for us," having died at the very hour when the passover lambs were slain. There can be no doubt that the apostle in these passages is indicating how closely Christ the antitype occupied the place and the time of the types, as a paschal " Lamb " slain and as the " First Fruits " of harvest. So that here we have a convincing proof that our chronological reckoning, in agreement with all church tradition, is right.

Moreover, it follows that the day of Pentecost, just 7 weeks after the day of first fruits (on "the morrow after the 7th Sabbath," Lev. xxiii: 15, 16), was on Sunday, the first day of the week; thus, by the outpoured Spirit, sanctifying and affirming that, as the newly established " Lord's Day " of the Christian church. This is in accordance with all the early traditions. These valuable facts are lost to us by the theory that Friday was the 15th Nisan as the day before " first fruits," § 60, (the day of crucifixion as held by Weiseler, the day after crucifixion as held by Aldrich.)*

§ 88. It only remains to notice the passages, which are cited from the gospels as proving a discrepancy, in the opinion of Tholuch and others. John's gospel plainly assigns the Lord's Supper to the night before the Jews ate the passover. (John xiii: 1, 2, and xviii: 28, and xix: 14, 31, etc.) But the other three gospels (at Mat. xxvi: 17, Mark xiv: 12, Luke xxii: 7) *seem* as if teaching that the Lord's Supper was in the very night of the Jews' passover. The appearance of discrepancy, however, is unduly magnified. What Matthew says (xxvi: 20), when exactly rendered, is not that Jesus sat down with the twelve "when the even was come,' but simply "it being evening (*opsias genomenees*) he

---

*The Bib. Sacra, April, 1894 (p. 339), by rejecting the 16th day theory (§ 59), retains "Christ the *first fruits*" on Sunday as the 17th of Nisan; but, by thus putting the crucifixion Friday on the 15th of Nisan, it fails to make "Christ our *passover* sacrificed for us."

sat down with the twelve." (*Mark*, "in the evening he cometh;" *Luke*, "when the hour was come.") It was late in the evening; and the evening may have been going on all the while from the first mention of preparation till the sitting down.

Hence Luke xxii: 7, "Then came the day of unleavened bread, when the passover must be killed," need not mean (as usually assumed) "then come *the day-time* of the 14th Nisan," but rather, "Then came (or was coming on) the evening or first part of the Jews' 14th Nisan, during which day (usually in its last hours of sunlight) the passover would be killed." The disciples may have started at sunset of Thursday, and easily made ready in two or three hours; since Jesus had evidently arranged things beforehand, and told them they would find the room "furnished and prepared." Even a lamb killed early in the evening of the 14th Nisan would be "between the two evenings" of that day, and might be thought legal in emergency; or they may have dispensed with the lamb, making this only a *preparatory* supper, to be completed (the disciples thought) the next night. The message sent to the owner of the house shows a forestalling of the feast: "Say unto him, the Master saith, My time [for the passover] is at hand. I make it with thee." In this view of the case discrepancy disappears, and both Jesus and the Jews have the same 14th Nisan.

§ 89. Mark Christ's language at the table (Luke xxii: 15): "With desire I have desired to eat this passover with you before I suffer,"—not that I am actually eating the full passover, but I have earnestly *desired* to eat it. As if to say: "I have so earnestly desired this opportunity of establishing the Lord's Supper in place of the passover that I have taken pains by anticipation to get you around this table *before I die*, (as die I must to-morrow, though you know it not);—not indeed eating the full desired passover with the Jews, but substituting for it a better memorial of my death. My strong desire has led me thus to forestall my death." This passage, instead of showing that Jesus was eating the paschal lamb with the Jews (as often argued), indicates rather the contrary.

And all the three evangelists, Matthew, Mark and Luke, do themselves (like John) show, that the arrest, trial, and crucifixion of Christ, were not on the 15th but on the 14th Nisan. For they give the preliminary agreement of the rulers: "Not on the feast-day, lest there be an uproar among the people (Mat. xxvi: 2,5, Mark xiv: 1,2, Luke xxii: 1, 2, 6.) "The feast day" or day of holy *convocation*, when there was a great concourse of people, and might easily arise an "uproar," was the 15th Nisan. And after so prudently planning to avoid that day, they (and Judas) hurried up matters on the 14th. It is entirely unbelievable, that they went through all the hubbub of arrest, trial and crucifixion during that "feast day" which they had resolved to avoid; to say nothing of their scrupulosity not allowing such doings on a day wherein the law forbade them to do any servile work.

Thus the synoptists, instead of being in collision with John, as alleged, are confirmatory of him. The seeming discrepancy between the Evangelists is harmonized, and the historic accuracy of the Gospel is verified and assured.

[Appendix E left in manuscript.]

PART II.

Other New Testament Dates.

CHAPTER I.

Christ's Baptism, Etc.

§ 95. The Gospel of John enumerates *four passovers* in the ministry of Christ, viz.: (1) John ii: 13, (2) John v: 1, (3) John vi: 4, with vii: 11, (4) John xii: 1. The second of these is called simply "a feast," or, rather, "*the* feast," as given (from many ancient authorities by Tischendorf, last edition), and by the margin of the Revised Version. That it means the passover is shown by Robinson (*Harm. of the Gosp.* § 36, *note*).

The four passovers prove that Christ's ministry was *over three years*, so that his baptism must have been near the beginning of A. D. 27, just as was taught by the earliest fathers of the church. (See § 6.)

When John began his work, probably six months before, at thirty years of age, that is, in A. D. 26, it was "the 15th year of Tiberius Cæsar (Luke iii: 1, 2). So that Luke must have reckoned the reign of Tiberius, not from the death of his predecessor Augustus, Sep. 19, A. D, 14, but from the joint reign of the two, beginning A. D. 12. The certainty of this joint reign, as understood in the provinces, is shown by the ancient Roman historians, Velleius Paterculus, Tacitus, Suetonius and Dion Cassius, "who all agree that Tiberius was colleague of Augustus two or three years, and this was confirmed by decree of the senate." (*Hales*.)

. "Senatus populusque Romanus, postulante patre ejus, ut equum ei jus omnibus provinciis exercitibusque, quam erat ipsi decreto, complexus est." (*Velleius Paterculus, B.* II, c. 121, *speaking of Tib. and Aug.*)

"Lege per consules lata, ut provincias cum Augusto communiter administraret, simulque censum ageret, condito lustro in Illyricum profectus est." (*Suetonius in Tiberius*, c. 21.)

"*Simulque censum ageret*, i. e., during the time when a provincial census was being taken. This then was (B. C. 4 + 15 =) A. D. 12, as the beginning of *indiction one*." (Schwartz.)

The Nativity.

§ 96. Jesus was born before the death of Herod the Great. But when was his death? A *short time* before Herod died, there was an eclipse of the moon, which has been identified as occurring March 13th, B. C. 4. In June of that year B. C. 4 began the 34th year from Herod's conquest of Jerusalem, on "the fast of the 3d mo." (Antiq. 14, xvi: 4) *i. e.*, in June, B. C. 37. Josephus says that he reigned "34 years." (Antiq. 17, viii: 1; War 1, xxxiii: 8.) His death in the 34th year would, therefore, be some time between June, B. C. 4 and June, B. C. 3. And at the following passover, (Whiston says of B. C. 3, Jos. Antiq. 17, ix: 3), sedition was raised against Archelaus, before he was confirmed as successor by Rome.

The birth of Jesus will thus be somewhere near the beginning of B. C. 4, not far from the time of the eclipse occurring before Herod's death. (See the possibilities of the occasion depicted in my series on "The Setting up of a New Kingdom.") This agrees exactly with Luke iii: 21-23, "And Jesus himself began to be about 30 years of age" at his baptism early in A. D. 27, *i. e.*, 30 years after the beginning of B. C. 4. The nativity could hardly have been near the beginning of B. C. 3 (as Schwartz and others suppose), with only 29 years to the baptism; for this will put along the death of Herod in B. C. 3 too long after the eclipse of March 13, B. C. 4.*

§ 97. From June, B. C. 37 to Herod's death was strictly *the 34th year*, or only 33 full years. This appears evident thus: The year of Archelaus' banishment Josephus calls "the 10th year" of his government (Ant. 17, xiii: 2), at the *beginning* of "the 37th year of Cæsar's victory over Anthony at Actium" (18, ii: 1). Therefore, he cannot

---

* If, in order to have Herod's full "34 years" of reign to B. C. 4, as well as the full "107 years" given by Josephus, we should call the accession of Herod B. C. 38, instead of 37,—this would require us to use Josephus' "125 years" (instead of his "126"), reducing his "27 years" after Pompey to 26; and it would hardly comport with Herod's "7th year" at Actium. Or, this would require Pompey's capture of Jerusalem to be at B. C. 65, violating the Olympic dating, as well as other facts. Therefore, Herod's death *must* be B. C. 37. (Period F, § 3.)

here begin Archelaus over (37th—10th or 36—9—) 27 years after the battle of Actium; which (being Sep. 2, B. C. 31) he assigns to "the 7th year" of Herod, (15, v: 1, 2), whose first 6 years reached from June, B. C. 37 to June 31. Now, the 27 years after that date which he thus allows to Herod, carries Herod only to the summer of B. C. 4, (*i. e.*, 31–27), where he begins to reckon Archelaus. He here gives but (6+27—) 33 years to Herod, instead of 34.

The "34 years" for Herod's reign seems (as full years) to be reckoned to the accession of his successor Archelaus *by the Roman consent*,* which was not until B. C. 3, some time after Herod's death. (Antiq. 17, xi: 4.) From that date Josephus reckons "69 years" to the coming of Vespasian against Jerusalem in A. D. 67 (War, Book 2, title). This was early in A. D. 67. For, after Vespasian's arrival, Josephus recites all his campaigns, from early spring of A. D. 67 (War 3, iv: 2, and vii: 3, 29), through the autumn, (4, i: 10), to the next spring of A. D. 68, the 3d month Sivan or May, (at War 4, viii: 1.) Two or three months after this, in July or August, Vespasian was informed that "Nero was dead," (ix: 2),—he having died early in June, A. D. 68. (Chambers" Cyc. says "June 11, A. D. 68.") †

So then, the death of Herod was in B. C. 4 (not 3), and the birth of Christ was no doubt not far from the beginning of B. C. 4. (See § 101 note.)

§ 98. As Schwartz puts Herod's death too late (B. C. 3), so others set it too early, or only about 20 days after the eclipse of Mar. 13, B. C. 4. Thus, H. B. Tristam, D.D., L.L.D., F.R.S. in the S. S. Times, July 7, 1894, says: "Herod died about a week before the passover, which fell on the 12th of April, B. C. 4." Whereas, his death was probably not before summer of that year, when he had entered upon *his 34th year* from his conquest of Jerusalem, which cannot be removed from June, B. C. 37. (See § 96, note.) Josephus repeatedly says: "Herod reigned 34 years," *i. e.*, till Archelaus was acknowledged at Rome as his successor in the summer of B. C. 3. True, Archelaus started for Rome *just after a passover*, (Jos. War, 2, ii: 1, Antiq. 17, ix: 3); concerning which Whiston correctly says: " This passover

---

* See Restor. of Jos., § 21.

† That Josephus has Nero's death in June, A. D. 68, appears further thus: He makes the death of Vitellius and the full accession of Vespasian to be on " Casleu 3," *i. e.*, Nov., A. D. 69 (War 4, xi: 4); and he gives Vitellius "8 mo. 5 days" (*id.*) + Otho "3 mo. 2 days" (ix: 9) + Galba "7 mo. 7 days" (ix: 2);—total 18 mo. 14 days, reaching back from the 9th month (Casleu 3) to the 19th of the 3d month (June 11) in the year A. D. 68, for the death of Nero. Before which, in the spring of A. D. 67, Vespasian came to Jerusalem; whence Josephus' "69 years" carry us back to the *beginning* of B. C. 3 (or thereabouts) for the death of Herod (or rather the accession of Archelaus).

was not one but thirteen months after the eclipse of the moon, Mar. 13, B. C. 4." The mistake of Tristam and so many others, arises from calling the interval *but one month*, with only about 20 days from the eclipse to the death of Herod, and with only a week or 10 days from Herod's death to the passover; into neither of which spaces is it possible to crowd the events narrated by Josephus.

After the eclipse, Herod's malady increased, he consulted various physicians, journeyed beyond Jordan, visited the warm baths at Callirhoe, had oil baths administered, came again to Jericho, made murderous plots in view of his death, got letters from Rome about his son Antipater, whom he kept in prison awhile, and then ordered slain, and after five days more died himself; could all these things take place in 20 days after the eclipse of Mar. 13? No, they reached till June at least, as the time of his death. Then there was funeral pomp seven days, followed by many consultations with the people, resulting finally in bitter complaints against Archelaus, and at last a long insurrection, with violent abuse of him "on all occasions," delaying his intended visit to Rome, till at length at the next passover it broke out into war, and he slew 3,000 Jews, and then after the passover started for Rome; did all these events occupy but a week or ten days after Herod's death? No, they reached from the summer of B. C. 4 (at Herod's death) to the passover in April, B. C. 3.

"Cyrenius Governor of Syria."

§ 99. Christ's birth at Bethlehem was occasioned by an enrollment (for taxation), "the first enrollment made when Cyrenius was governor of Syria." (Luke ii: 2, Rev.) Now Josephus gives us an account of the enrollment and "taxing" referred to in Acts v: 37; which he says occurred in A. D. 8, the year after the banishment of Archelaus, telling us it was then that Cyrenius became governor of Syria. (Antiq. 17, xiii: 5 and 18. i: 1, and ii: 1.) Neither Josephus nor any other author mentions *Cyrenius* as governor of Syria at any previous time, and Tertullian says Christ was born when Saturninus was governor of Syria. The seeming difficulty is explained in several different ways, which are described in Lange's Commentary. The most probable explanations are these two: Either,

1. Read the "first" *adjectively*, as in the Revision, thus: "This was the first enrollment (made) with Cyrenius governing Syria." In which case Cyrenius is understood as having *twice ruled* there; either (a) both times as governor, for which some evidence is claimed by Zumpt, Momsen, and Schaff (in Lange); or (b) the first time in B. C. 4 as a mere census legate under another as governor of Syria,—so

taught by Browne in his *Ordo Seculorum* and by others. Or, Luke may be supposed to speak elliptically, meaning, "This was the first *of two* enrollments *finished up* when Cyrenius was governor of Syria." Or else, if preferred,

2. Read the "first" *adverbially*, with the common version and many writers, thus: " This enrollment or the enrollment *itself* (as read by Hales, Paulus, Langè, Van Oosterzee, etc.), was first made (or accomplished) when Cyrenius was governor of Syria," in A. D. 8; it having been only "decreed" and partially acted upon in B. C. 4, as in verse 1 and 3, 4—while verse 2 is parenthetic, alluding to the final result. This is substantially the view of Van Oosterzee, and is certainly reasonable. Did not the Jews, hearing of the decree, in their peculiar zeal for tribal genealogy, hasten (many of them) to their own tribe to register? And did not the main enrollment get postponed (perhaps by the death of Herod), and so become overlooked in history,— as indicated by Joseph's ready retreat to Egypt without waiting for the taxation *itself?*

§ 100. Concerning this subject Hales informs us (*Chron.* vol 3, p. 49):

" The enrollment was made by Cyrenius (called Quirinius by Tacitus), as we learn from Justin Martyr, Julius the Apostate and Eusebius, when Saturninius was president of Syria (as given by Tertullian), and in the 33d year of Herod's reign, as given by Eusebius [*i. e.* in B. C. 4]. After Archelaus, Cyrenius was again sent, this time as president of Syria. We may read 'the taxing *itself* was first made when Cyrenius was governor of Syria,' with the first word (*ante*) without aspiration."

We have further testimony, as follows:

"Zumpt has shown by an exhaustive analysis of all the facts in our possession, that Cyrenius was governor for the *first* time in the latter part of the year B. C. 4, Varus having preceded him in the early part of that year. But there is a more certain and much shorter method of demonstrating that Cyrenius was at a census in this year. The old cycle of Indictions, as Ideler has shown, simply indicated epochs of the *taxing of the provinces* (each 15 years). According to the *Chronicon paschale*, one of these epochs began on Sep. 1, B. C. 49, and this date is confirmed by the revival of the cycle by the Emperor Constantine on Sep. 1 of A. D. 312; for $311 + 49 = 360$, or 24 of such cycles. Hence, if an epoch began on Sep. 1 of B. C. 49, it follows that the indiction epoch that coincided with the birth of Christ must have begun on Sep. 1 of B. C. ($49-3$ times $15 =$) 4. Hence, our Lord was not born any earlier than Sep. 1, B. C. 4." (*Schwartz Chris. Chron. A*, § 3.) We should rather say: The period for the taxing was *to end* on Sep. 1, B. C. 4, so that Joseph hastened to Bethlehem early in B. C. 4, bringing the nativity there.

The Day of Nativity, Etc.

§ 101. The day-date of the nativity, as well as of the baptism of Jesus, is utterly beyond our knowledge. The assignment of Dec. 25 for the nativity, as well as of March 25 for the passion, was a part of that arbitrary arrangement of quarter-days in the calendar for religious observance, on the supposed dates of the equinoxes and solstices, Mar. 25, June 25, Sep. 25, Dec. 25; which scheme was at a later date made to apply to church festivals, and has no authority either from Scripture or the early fathers. (See § 12.) "Easter," or the resurrection Sunday, is known as at the *vernal equinox;* but all other dates of the "Christian year," (so-called) are mere random assignments agreed upon solely for convenience of co-operative worship. It is not at all likely that the birth of Jesus, with shepherds by night out on the hill-sides, took place in the cold weather of Dec. 25.*

Like other early writers, "Eusebius nowhere mentions the day. It was the common opinion of the Western churches that Christ was born on the 8th Kal. of Jan. [Dec. 25]; but the Eastern churches thought differently, that he was born on the 8th Ides of Jan. [Jan. 6], so much Valensius. The learned have found so great difficulty in assigning the day of our Saviour's birth that Scaliger said, 'unias Dei est non hominis definere.'" (*In Euseb. Eccle. Hist., I. 5; page 75.*)

"The Oriental Christians kept the memorial of the Saviour's birth and of his baptism on one and the same day, viz., the 6th of Jan., and this day they called Epiphany." (*Murd. Mosheim, Cen. iv: p. 2, ch. 4, § 5.*)

---

* Very likely the nativity was about the time of the lunar eclipse, March 13, B. C. 4; and 30 days afterwards with the crowds at the passover the "wise men" appeared at Jerusalem; and 10 days later (just after the paschal seven days were through) the 40 days to the purification ended; and it may have been in Jerusalem the very night after the presentation in the temple that Joseph was warned to flee to Egypt from the slaughter-edict which Herod was just then issuing. This flight to Egypt prevented immediate return to Nazareth, on their way to which they probably were in going to the temple, since, of course, they did not contemplate a return to continued residence at Bethlehem. Why should they go back there? The slaughter-edict probably meant infants of "the *second year* and under," as Horne's Introduction shows (Vol. II, p. 77), covering the 25 days that had passed since the spring new year, March 28, and the 15 or more days of the previous (or *second*) year, back to the date given by the wise men (as we are expressly told; so that, the 40 or 50 days covered would include but a very few infants born in so small a town as Bethlehem, and the non mention of the slaughter in outside history is thus accounted for. Herod died in the summer (§ 98), and some time after that Joseph returned from Egypt.

"From Clemens Alex. (Strom. I, page 340), the only passage of an ante-Nicene writer referring to any nativity festival: 'Some say the nativity was on the 5th Pachon [20th May]. Followers of Basilides say the baptism was on the 15th Tybi [Jan 10], some say the 16th.'" (*Coleman's Chris. Antiq.*)

"Not only was the day of nativity unknown, but for 300 years after the ascension no day was set apart for the commemoration of the birth of Christ. According to authorities given by Giesler, Julius, who was bishop of Rome, A. D. 337-352, first appointed the 25th of Dec. for the purpose. Then, it was not observed in Cyprus in the time of Epiphanius, A. D. 376, as learned from his silence in his elaborate arrangement of the ecclesiastical dates. Chrysostom, A, D. 387, attests that this day had been observed at Antioch less than 10 years. After this period we have notices of the day. In Egypt it was not yet acknowledged in A. D. 420; it was appointed in the episcopate of Cyril before A. D. 431." (*Clinton, Fas. Rom, Art. v: p. 233.*)

"The idea of a birthday festival was foreign to the Christians of the early period. * * * Besides, nothing definite was ascertained respecting the date of Christ's birth. * * * Clement Alex. seems to censure inquiry as to it as idle and unprofitable." (Neander, Vol. I, p. 301, 2.) "In the earlier ages there were several different determinations of the day of Christ's nativity." (II., p. 314.)

Pauline Dates.

§ 102. PAUL'S VOYAGE TO ROME was in the winter of A. D. 60-61 For, he arrived in Rome in spring, after wintering at Malta; and he sailed from Palestine at the beginning of the preceding autumn, and was in Crete in October, soon after the "Fast" (Acts xxvii: 9), which was on the 10th of Tisri. He was sent to Rome by Festus upon his appeal to Cæsar; and his hearing before Festus had taken place about a fortnight after the arrival of Festus in the province. (Acts xxiv: 27 to xxv: 6.) Hence, the arrival of Festus (and consequently the departure of Felix) took place in the summer preceding St. Paul's voyage, when Paul had been a prisoner two complete years (*dietias plerotheises*), since his confinement at pentecost. (Acts xx: 16, and xxiv: 27.) That summer when Festus took the place of Felix was A. D. 60, as fully proved in Conybeare & Howson. (*Life of St. Paul, Appendix C.*)

This A. D. 60, is the date given also by Spanheim, Pearson, Tillemont, Bertholdt, Winer, Koehler, Feilmoser, Wurm, Anger, Weiseler, Lechler, De Wette; Schaff says 60 or 61; (and 61 is given by Meyer, Hug, Schmidt, Schrader, Schott, and Ewald; see *Lange's Acts, Chron.*

Chart). So that, there is pretty general agreement upon A. D. 60, as the date of Paul's starting for Rome.

§ 103. THE COUNCIL OF JERUSALEM (Acts xv: 2) was held about A. D. 51. For, "reckoning backward from the ascertained epoch A. D. 60, when St. Paul was sent to Rome, we find that he must have begun his second missionary journey in A. D. 51, and that therefore the council must have been either 50 or 51. This calculation is based upon the history in Acts." (*Con. & How. Ch. 7 end.*) With this date, 51, agree also Tillemont, Koehler, Anger; De Wette says 51 or 50; (and 50 is given by Basanage, Schott, Wieseler, and Schaff.) Thus is there here also an extensive agreement.

§ 104. PAUL'S FIRST VISIT TO JERUSALEM after his conversion (Acts ix: 26) was about A. D. 37, the very year in which Aretas became supreme in Damascus.* (II Cor. xi: 32). For, in Gal. ii: 1, Paul says, "fourteen years after" that "I went up again to Jerusalem with Barnabas, and took Titus with me also," that is, to attend that council (as seen by Acts xv: 2). Now A. D. 51—14=A. D. 37, or A. D. 50—14=A. D. 36; and so Paul's first visit was in A. D. 37 (or possibly 36). It is set at A. D. 37 by Baronius and Tillemont, and at A. D. 36 by Petavius and Vogel, and still earlier by Bengel and Suskind. Conybeare and Howson, by calling the "14 years" only the 14th year or but 13 full years, get this first visit at A. D. 38; and there also Meyer, Usher, Pearson, Hug, Feilmoser, Olshausen, Sanclement, and Ideler have it. (And others have it later still.) But this later dating of it is because all these writers put Christ's crucifixion too late (viz., A. D. 31 or 33, instead of the right A. D. 30.)†

Not only have we the before-named six authors, who put Paul's first visit as early as 7 years after Christ's crucifixion (i. e., at A. D. 37 or before), but we have also Meyer, Bassanage, Heinrich, Hug, Schrader, and Schott, putting it just 7 years after, and Baronius, Petavius, Usher, Pearson, Tillemont, Bengel, Vogel, Suskind, Koehler, Feilmoser, and Olshausen, give it less than 7 years after. Indeed, a majority of authors give 7 years or less for the interval, rather than more. Therefore we are safe in saying that this first visit was 7 years after the crucifixion, i. e., in A. D. 37, as already found.

---

* This supremacy over Damascus of Aretas, king of Arabia, was occasioned, either by the emperor Caius on his accession to the throne in March, A. D. 37, or else by the withdrawal of Vitellius, governor of Syria, upon hearing of Tiberius' death in March, (as Con. & How. show in Chap. 3).

† Conybeare & Howson (Ch. 7, end) fully show, that the "14 years" must end at the Council, and not at any other visit to Jerusalem.

§ 105. THE CONVERSION OF PAUL, having been "three years" before his first visit to Jerusalem (Gal. i: 18), took place in A. D. 34 (possibly 33). Baronius and Tillemont agree with us on A. D. 34, and Jerome, Petavius and Vogel agree on A. D. 33. Moreover, Meyer, Bassonage, Michaelis, Heinrichs, Hug, Schrader, and Schott, all put the conversion just 4 years after the crucifixion, just as we do; while Jerome, Baronius, Petavius, Usher, Pearson, Tillemont, Bengel, Vogel, Suskind, Koehler, Feilmoser, and Olshausen, all put it less than 4 years. Indeed, a large majority of authors give 4 years or less from Christ's death to Paul's conversion. "Within three years of the death of Jesus, we see the principal and most zealous agent in the persecution, suddenly allying himself, body, soul and spirit, with the community against which he had 'breathed out threatenings and slaughter.'" (*Rev. Dr. D. W. Simon, Berlin*.) Bib. Sac., Oct., 1868, p. 746.

So that, as we prove the crucifixion to have been in A. D. 30, we are authorized in saying that Paul's conversion was in A. D. 34; which is just at the end of the "seventy weeks" or 490 years of Daniel, reaching from the 7th year of Artaxerxes, B. C. 457, to A. D. 34. The last of those weeks, or the final 7 years, began at the baptism, A. D. 26-27, the beginning of the Gospel to the Jews, and reached to the conversion of Paul and Cornelius, A. D. 33-34, the finished Gospel for the Gentiles.* Thus "he confirmed the covenant with many for one week" (Dan. ix: 27); while "in the midst of the week," i. e., in A. D. 30, Messiah "caused sacrifice and oblation to cease," nailing it to his cross when he was "cut off" (ver. 26).† And so, all our datings are confirmed, and the divine prophecy is proved true. (See period F, § 14, and E, § 68.)

§ 106. NEW TESTAMENT EVENTS.

Birth of Christ,	4 B. C.
Annas, H. P.,‡	8 to 15 A. D.
Caiaphas, H. P.,	25 to 34 A. D.

---

* "Paul was summoned to evangelize the heathen (Acts ix: 15), and Peter began this (with Cornelius) almost simultaneously. The great transaction of admitting the Gentiles to the church was already accomplished when the two apostles met at Jerusalem (A. D. 37, Gal. i: 18). The early chapters in the Acts are like the narrations in the Gospels; it is often hardly possible to learn how far the events related were contemporary or consecutive." (*Conybeare and Howson, ch. iv.*)

† Formerly, when Christ's death was supposed to be at A. D. 33 (or even 34; see § 17), the last week of the 70 was explained as covering John's ministry and Christ's ministry, each reckoned as half the week. But the true explanation is far more satisfactory.

‡ Annas, or Ananus, was father-in-law to Caiaphas, and officiated with him.

Baptism of Christ,	27 A. D., early.
Death of Christ,	30 A. D., April 7th, Fri.
Conversion of Saul,	34, and Cornelius.
Return to Jerusalem,	37, Acts ix: 26.
Death of Agrippa,	44, Acts xii: 23.
Council of Jerusalem,	51, Acts xv: 2.
Ananias, H. P.,	47 to 63, Acts xxiii: 2.
Voyage to Rome,	60, Acts xxvii: 1.
End of Acts,	62, Acts xxviii: 30.
War begins,	66, in May.
Jerusalem destroyed,	70, 6th mo., 8th d.

ROMAN EMPERORS.

§ 107. We have already seen (at § 97) that Josephus has the death of Nero at June (11) A. D. 68; so that, with Nero's reign given as in Josephus' present text, at "13 years 8 days," (War 4, xviii: 2), his 12th year of Nero would begin near the beginning of June, A. D. 66. But he himself says, (War 2, xiv: 4): " The war began in the 12th year of the reign of Nero, in the month of Artemisius [Jyar]," that is, in April, A. D. 66. So that Nero's 12th year must have begun earlier than his length of reign makes it; and that reign must have been longer than his present text gives it.

Most authorities give Nero's reign as 13 yrs. and 7 or 8 mo., making the 13th year begin the previous October. The months may have been dropped out from Josephus' value: or he may have written 8 mo. instead of the 8 d. now found in his text. Taking this last as Josephus' true reckoning,*— and also calling his 3 years 8 mo. for Caius as 3 years 10 mo., (so given by Schwartz and others),—we have the dates of Josephus as follows:

---

* This makes Nero's 12th year end Oct., A. D. 66, just where Josephus ends his Book 2 chap. xix of the War. The rest of that Book is spent upon the events of Nero's 13th year, until the early spring of A. D. 67, when Vespasian came to the army in Palestine, as related at the beginning of Book 3. For on arriving, he met his son Titus at Ptolemais (or Acre), who had arrived by a winter voyage "sooner than the winter season did usually permit." (War 3, iv: 2.) The previous "12th year of Nero," A. D. 66, was "the 17th year of Agrippa" (War 2, xiv: 4), and the 2d year of Florus" the ruler of Judea. (Antiq. 20, xi: 1.)

§ 108. Josephus' Dates

	War.	Antiq.		B. C.		Ptol. Can.
Julius Cæsar	1, xi: 1	14, xi: 1	3 yr. 7 mo.	— Aug. 9,	48	
				— Mar.	44	
Augustus	2, ix: 1	18, ii: 2	57 – 6 — 2d.			A. D.
				— Sep.	14	14
Tiberius	2, ix: 5	18, vi: 10	22 – 6 — 3			
				— Mar.	37	36
Caius	2, xi: 1	19, ii: 5	3 – 8 [10]			
				— Jan.	41	40
Claudius	2, xii: 8	20, viii: 1	3 – 8 — 20			
				— Oct.	54	54
Nero	4, ix: 2		13 – [8] – (8)			
				— June	68	
Galba	4, ix: 2		7 – 7			
				— Dec.	68	
Otho	4, ix: 9		3 – 2			
				— Mar.	69	
Vitellius	4, xi: 4	"3d Casleu"	8 – 5			
				— Nov.	69	
Vespasian	4, x: 1-5	July, 69		A. D.		68

From the death of Julius = 112 yr. 9m. 9d.

The 3 yrs. 7 mo. of Julius Cæsar are reckoned from the battle of Pharsalia, Aug. 9, B. C. 48 (*Cham. Cyc.*) to March, B. C. 44, the death of Julius Cæsar. Then five reigns carry the date 111 yrs. 2 mo. 25d. to early in June, A. D. 68, at the death of Nero. And then the short reigns cover 18 mo. 14d., to late in Nov., A. D. 69,—or 112 yrs. 9 mo. 9d. after the death of Julius Cæsar in March.

Ptolemy's Canon (in the last column, see Period F, § 2), dates by whole years, from the Thoth or Egyptian new-year (in Sep. or Aug.) *preceding* each king's accession; but reckons Tiberius from A. D. 14, because the transition (Sep. 19) was so near the Thoth (Sep. 20). Vespasian is reckoned from July 1, A. D. 69, when he was proclaimed emperor by the army in Syria (Jos. War 4, x: 4); so that the Canon puts his accession to the Thoth of A. D. 68, throwing the rest of the short reigns upon Nero. Although Josephus has the death of Vitellius in Nov. A. D. 69, yet reckoning Vespasian from the previous July 1, he has the destruction of Jerusalem in Aug. A. D. 70 as in the second year of Vespasian.

Jerusalem Taken A. D. 70.

§ 109. As we are showing the dates of Josephus backward from his own time to the distant epochs of the Old Testament, it is necessary for us to be assured concerning his starting point, the destruction of

Jerusalem by Titus, "in the 2d year of Vespasian," as he says. That this was fastened by him to the year A. D. 70 (not 69 as Schwartz asserts), is seen already by his datings from the Maccabees and from Herod downward. Particularly,

1. Josephus gives " 107 years" back to Herod's capture of the city in B. C. 37. This latter date is fixed and certain, as we show, (period F, § 4); and if we add the 107th year (*i. e.*, 106 full years), we are carried to A. D. 70.* The full "107 years" taken from A. D. 70 show B. C. 38; and thus it is impossible to get the terminal date any earlier than A. D. 70.

2. Josephus gives the exact length of reigns, in years, months, and days, for every emperor down to Vespasian: and the total of all his numbers (in his present text uncorrected) is 111 years, 11 months, 17 days from the accession of Augustus to the death of Vitellius. This (112 years) cannot begin earlier than March, B. C. 44, when Julius Cæsar was assassinated, and therefore reaches to A. D. 69. So that, the destruction of the city in "the 2d year o. Vespasian" must by Josephus be in A. D. 70.†

3. A. D. 70 is proved by the headings of Books in Josephus' War. The "167 years" heading Book 1 cannot begin before the spring of B. C. 170, since Josephus himself says (Antiq. 12, v: 3), that this taking of Jerusalem by Antiochus Epiphanes was in "the 143d year" Seleucic. The "167 years," therefore, cannot end earlier than the spring of B. C. 3 for the death of Herod. The "69 years" heading Book 2 extend thence to the spring of A. D. 67 for "Vespasian's coming." The time "about 1 year" heading both Book 3 and Book 4, more correctly amounts to 2 years and 9 months, (as seen at §97, 108); which carry us to the siege of Jerusalem at the end of A. D. 69. And then the 6 months and 1 month heading Books 5 and 6, end in August A. D. 70 for the fall of Jerusalem. No other date can be made out.‡

---

*In adding from any year A. D. to any year B. C. (and *vice versa*) *the number of years is reduced 1*, because A. D. 1 and B. C. 1 are adjoining years, without a year o between.

†The only variations needed in Josephus' numbers are, 2 mo. added to Caius, and 8 mo. substituted for 8 d. in the reign of Nero. And then we have the true reckoning, as universally accepted; which (as taken from Josephus) is here given at § 108.

‡Schwartz' attempt to make Josephus have A. D. 69 for Josephus' date of the destruction of Jerusalem, is part of his strange theory, that all the Roman dates of emperors, etc., should be shoved back 1 year earlier than they are universally put, Augustus' death at A. D. 13, Tiberius' death at A. D. 36, etc.

§ 110—Local Authorities.

JUDEAN RULER.		SYRIAN GOVERNOR.	OUTSIDE JUDEA.
Herod the Great,	— 3 B. C.		
Archelaus,	— 8 A. D.	Cyrenius,	
Copernius,	—11 "		
M. Ambianus,	—13 "		
Annius Rufus,	—15 "		
Valerius Gratus,	—26 "	Flaccus,	
Pontius Pilate,	—36 "	Vitellius,	
Marcellus,	—37 "	Petronius,	37 Agrippa I.
Murullus,	—41 "		
Agrippa I,	—44 "	Longinus,	44 Agrippa dies
Cuspius Fadus,	—46 "		
Tib. Alexander,	—49 "	Quadratus,	49 Agrippa II.
Cumanus,	—53* "		
Felix,	—60 "		
Festus,	—62 "		
Albinus,	—65 "	Cestius Gallus,	66 Agrippa's 17th yr.
Gessius Florus,			
Vespasian came,	—67 early		
Titus came.	—70 early		

CHAPTER II.

Women at the Tomb.

A HARMONY OF THE RESURRECTION ACCOUNTS. †

"The first day of the week . . . Mary Magdalene came, and told the disciples that she had seen the Lord."—JOHN xx: 1-18.

§ 111. The resurrection of Christ was a momentous event. Upon the certainty of it hangs our eternal hope. For He is the first-fruits; and if the first-fruits fail, no harvest can come of resurrection to us.

---

*Felix began at the "beginning of the 13th year of Claudius." (*Jos. Ant.*, *20, vii: 1.*) "Tacitus places the beginning of Felix earlier: but on such a question his authority is not to be compared with that of Josephus." See Weiseler (*Con. & How., Appen. 3.*)

† Reprint from the Andover Review, November, 1886. The editor of the Review, in volunteering a liberal reward for the article, said: "You are very thorough in this investigation. No scholar hereafter examining this subject, can afford to miss your exhaustive treatment of the matter."

Is the thing sure? There are four narrators of Christ's resurrection. And there is a seeming diversity in their accounts, especially in regard to the women at the tomb. Hence infidels cavil; and even Christians may have misgivings. How important that the history be harmonized in our minds!

Many harmonies have been offered; but none of them are perfectly satisfactory. Meyer says: "In no section of the evangelical history have harmonists, in their critical mosiac work, been compelled to expend more labor, and with less success, than in the section on the resurrection. The adjustment of the differences between John and the Synoptists, as also between the latter among themselves, is impossible." And Professor Westcott ("Gospels," p. 327) says: "The various narratives of the resurrection place the fragmentariness of the Gospel in the clearest light. They contain difficulties which it is impossible to explain with certainty. . . . In this point of view, we can dismiss without any minute inquiry the various schemes which have been proposed, for bringing the accounts, as they stand at present, into one connected narrative."

Notwithstanding this discouraging outlook, we have carefully gone over the ground, and have reached a more satisfactory result, which we give, as follows:

The guide to this whole narrative is to be found in John xx: 1-18. For, of all the four narrators, John was the only eye-witness, and was most likely to give the true order of events, as Doddridge well remarks. Let us therefore take him for our guide. We will divide off his account of the resurrection morning (contained in these 18 verses) into *seven* successive periods of time, putting into each the contemporaneous items mentioned by the other narrators.

§ 112. THE SEVEN PERIODS.

Period 1. (John, verse 1.) *Women at the Tomb.* (John, 1 verse; Luke, 2 verses; Matthew, 3 verses; Mark, 4 verses.) John mentions Mary Magdalene alone, (for reason see afterwards); Matthew mentions also the other Mary; Mark adds Salome; Luke adds Joanna and others.

Period 2. (John, ver. 2, 3.) *Mary gone; meanwhile a vision of one angel.* Matthew and Mark, through 8th verse; Luke, ver. 3, 5, 9, has it mixed in with a later scene.

Period 3. (John, ver. 4-10.) *Peter and John at the Tomb.* (Luke, ver. 12, 24.) The women meanwhile flying and silent (Mark, ver. 8), meet (it may be), and some of them return with Mary, between the two visions (Matthew and Mark, ver. 8; Luke, ver. 9).

Period 4. (John, ver. 11-13.) *Mary and the women together again at the tomb; a vision of two angels.* John speaks of Mary as if alone (for reason see afterwards). She was not alone (Luke, ver. 3 5, 10). *Two* angels were now seen by them all.

Period 5. (John, ver. 14-16.) *Mary turns aside and sees Jesus* (she "first," Mark, ver. 9). Meanwhile the other women are still in the angel-vision in the tomb (Luke, ver. 5-8).

Period 6. (John, ver. 17.) *Other women coming out from the tomb see Jesus with Mary*, and fall at his feet; He says, "Touch me not" (Matthew, ver. 9, 10; Luke, ver. 9). *Some* of the women, hurrying out and scattering, get no sight of Jesus, but run and tell of angels only (Luke, ver. 9, 22, 23).

Period 7. (John, ver. 18.) *The sight of Jesus reported*, by Mary (Mark, ver. 10), and by those with her (Luke, ver. 9, 10). But they are perhaps *delayed* about it, by being met and questioned by the authorities (Matthew, ver. 11); so that the two disciples had started for Emmaus before this last message arrived (Luke, ver. 22, 23). Their tidings were hardly believed (Mark and Luke, ver. 11). "But Peter arose" (Luke, ver. 12). West, White, and Doddridge favor the regarding of this as a second visit of Peter, connected with this sight of Jesus (ver. 34).

RECAPITULATION.

Period	1	2	3	4	5	6	7
John xx:	1,	2, 3,	4-10,	11-13,	14-16,	17,	18.

Thus the narrative of John is seen to be exact and consecutive; Matthew and Mark having the same order, only filling in different details (with some left out which were best known to John). Luke alone seems somewhat to mix the two visions of angels; and *he*, throughout his Gospel, is notoriously less exact than the rest in regard to dates—his account being supervised by Paul, who was not an eye-witness.

We here see that there were *two visions* of angels (instead of one or three, as some make out). These were (1) the *one-angel* vision, seen by others in absence of Mary; (2) the *two-angel* vision, afterwards seen by Mary with the rest (not by them separately in two visions, as usually taught). The errors and perplexities of the harmonists are thus happily resolved; and the whole story becomes luminous, consistent, and beautiful.

§ 113. ERRONEOUS VIEWS CONSIDERED.

Let us now look more particularly at the errors committed, and the way we are led to escape them.

Matthew and Mark (first eight verses) narrate only a one-angel vision of the women; and Luke (first eight verses) narrates only a two-angel vision of the women; while John seems to give no angel-vision of the *women* at all, but only a two-angel vision of Mary alone. The whole trouble is in locating the women's two visions of the first three Gospels into harmony with Mary's vision in John. So that the two great questions are, with the errors concerning them:—

I. Where in this account of John does the one-angel vision of Matthew and Mark belong?

Error 1, putting the one-angel vision *too early;* error 2, putting it *too late;* error 3, having *no* one-angel vision at all till the close.

II. Where does the two-angel vision of Luke belong?

Error 4, putting the two-angel vision *too late;* error 5, putting it *too early;* error 6, *mixing* together the one-angel and the two-angel vision.

One-angel Vision.

1. Where does the one-angel vision of Matthew and Mark belong? Here three errors are committed:—

Error 1. Putting the one-angel vision *too early*, that is, before Mary ran to tell Peter (in John ver. 1, at our period 1). This is the error of Calmet and White, of Guyse and Clarke; and it is open to these objections: (1.) It does not comport with Mary's meagre seeing, as in John, ver. 1; nor with her meagre tidings to Peter (Meyer), as in ver. 2. Nor would she have said to him and afterwards to Jesus, "we know not where they have laid" our missing Lord, if she had already received angelic assurance that He was risen. (2.) This view leaves the women unaccounted for, during all Mary's flight and Peter's visit to the tomb, or even longer. (3.) As Calmet and White have both the women's visions here mixed together, they thus incur all the additional objections of that view, as seen directly (at error 6).

Error 2. Putting the one-angel vision *too late*, that is, not until after Peter and John left the tomb (in ver. 10, at our period 4; see Doddridge). This might seem a plausible plan between other extremes; but it is liable to these objections: (1) It leaves the women still unaccounted for, during all Mary's flight and Peter's visit (John ver. 2-10, periods 2 and 3). Or, if to obviate this Doddridge difficulty we adopt the amendment of President Edwards, Olshausen, Ebrard, and even Meyer, not having the women start for the tomb till some time after Mary,—then (2) not only does this contradict Matthew, Mark, and Luke (ver. 1), that they all started together very early; but it is also difficult to think of Mary, a lone female, going off to visit a sepulchre "while it was yet dark," without any company,—especially as in her report of it she says "we" (John, ver. 2).

Error 3. Having *no* one-angel vision till after Mary's visit (all being left till John ver. 18, at period 7). This is the error of Doddridge (with West) and President Edwards; and it is liable to these objections: (1.) It leaves the women unaccounted for from their arrival (ver. 1) through all Mary's adventures (John ver. 1-18, period 1-7). Doddridge and Dr. Clark are forced to say that they must have "fled to some retired place astounded!"—a statement certainly astounding. President Edwards delays even the *coming* of the women till this latest point, by which means Mary does not join them at all, contrary to Matthew, Mark, and Luke (ver. 1), who all put *them with her*, as starting very early in the morning, as it began to dawn. (2.) This view violates the order in Mark (ver. 9), which puts Mary's sight of Jesus as *after* a vision of the women. (3.) This view compels the putting of the women's two-angel vision also at this late point, with all the objections attending that *mixed* method, as directly seen (at error 6; also error 4).

Since, therefore, we have seen the place of the first angel-vision to be *too late* after the visit of Peter and John to the tomb, and *too early* before Mary ran to them from the tomb,—it follows that this first angel-vision belongs truly *between* those two points, namely, in the interim between Mary's leaving the tomb and Peter's reaching it, (that is, in period 2). Luke (ver. 12) puts Peter's starting for the tomb as "then," when an angel-vision had but just transpired. According to this, Mary, first coming to the tomb, and finding it open and empty, runs off at once to tell Peter and John; while the rest of the women stopping behind are addressed by an angel inside, (none but the keepers having seen the angel outside, Matthew ver. 2-4), contrary to Meyer; after which Peter and John come running up; and afterwards Mary returns with women to another vision of angels.

§ 114. This more correct view of the matter, advanced by Scott in his Commentary, 1788, and by White in his Diatessaron, 1799, as well as McKnight, has latterly been adopted by Robinson, in his English and Greek Harmonies; by Gardiner in his Greek Harmony; by Brown in the new British Commentary; by Olshausen, and Barnes, and Lange, and Meyer, in their Commentaries; and by Haley, Ebrard, Kitto, etc. And it may now be considered as settled that this is the true arrangement for the first or one-angel vision.

Two-angel Vision.

II. Where does the two-angel vision of Luke belong? Here also three errors are committed:—

Error 4. Putting the two-angel vision *too late*, that is, after Mary's interview with Jesus (at John ver. 18, in period 7). This is the error of Doddridge, with West. and Guyse, of President Edwards, and Scott, and White, and Lange, and it is open to these objections: (1.) It allows no tidings from *women* about a vision of *angels only* (more than one *without Christ seen*) to come to the disciples, before the two started for Emmaus, and before Mary came telling of *Jesus seen;* as required by Luke (ver. 22, 23); noted by Godet. (2.) After their first visit the women fled (Matthew and Mark, ver. 8); and there is in this arrangement no accounting for their being back (especially so soon) and after Mary had left a second time. Doddridge and Edwards try to escape this objection by mixing both visions of the women (thus delayed) into one, and so having *no return* of women after a flight. But they thus fall into all the other difficulties of this *mixed* method (at error 6, also 3).

Error 5. Putting the two-angel vision *too early*, that is, before Mary's return to the tomb. Thus Calmet, and White, and even Godet (seemingly), put the two-angel vision, mixed with the one-angel vision, as all seen by Mary before her running to tell Peter. They thus not only fall into the other objections (given at errors 1 and 6), but they add these: (1.) This leaves the women unaccounted for from Mary's leaving the tomb *until all her proceedings are through* (that is, all the six periods after John ver. 1, on to 18); when *after* appearing to Mary (Mark, ver. 9), Jesus met *them* as they went from the tomb (Matthew, ver. 9), although (according to this view) they left there with Mary at the first! (2.) This makes Mary have the two-angel vision twice over, which certainly cannot be.

We can not avoid the difficulty by putting the one-angel vision *before* Mary's leaving the tomb, and the two-angel vision *after* she had left. This would set the two visions *in immediate succession*, but (not exactly mixing them) would make actually *three* angel-visions instead of two. This is an impossible view; because objection (1) still remains in large part, and objection (2) of the previous error 4 is added; but especially a new objection (3) comes in, viz.: that after fleeing in fear from an angel-vision, the *same women* would not *immediately enter again* to a new vision of *multiplied* angels. Morison, Eddy, and even Godet may seem as if tending to this view. But certainly Robinson, Gardiner, Olshausen, Meyer, and Barnes *mix up* the two visions as both one and the same, occurring just after Mary ran from the tomb— the proper place of the one-angel vision only. This still leaves the objection (1) just given, with all the objections against *mixing* the two visions. Which latter we now proceed to give:—

Error 6, the most common of all. *Mixing together* the one-angel and the two-angel visions, as if they were the same. This is the error of Doddridge, Edwards, Calmet, White, Macknight, Robinson, Gardiner, Godet, Meyer, Olshausen, Barnes, Morison, Elliott, and Eddy; and indeed of nearly all the writers we have consulted. We can except only Guyse, West,* Scott, White, and Lange; all but the first of whom have the second women's vision at period 7, after Mary's sight of Jesus (as at error 4), making *three* angel-visions, instead of *two* as most reckon. Scott, White, and Lange have the first vision correctly at period 2; and Guyse (cited in Doddridge) has two visions at our periods 1 and 4.

§ 115. Mixing the Two Visions

Is exposed to the following grave objections: (1.) The sight of *two angels* and of *one angel only* do not harmonize as the same event. At the first visit to the tomb one angel alone sat inside the tomb (Mark, ver. 5), one angel having left the outside (Matthew ver. 2-5); but at the second visit two angels stood and spoke (Luke, ver. 3, 4), arising *in sight* from a reclining posture. (See Haley and Macknight; John, ver. 11.) (2.) The message of the two angels was quite different from that of the one angel, as shown by Godet. (Compare Luke and Mark, ver. 6-8. Luke mixes the two.) The one angel alarmed them (flying with fear) by saying, "Why seek ye the living among the dead? He is not here, but is risen—see where he laid—go tell—and meet him in Galilee." The two angels soothed them (retiring calmly) by tenderly inquiring of Mary, "Woman, why weepest thou?" and then (seemingly in view of her answer) continuously reminding them all how Jesus himself had foretold these very scenes of death and resurrection. (3.) The mixed view necessitates *two* separate visions of the *two* angels, one of them with Mary all alone, which is not likely; so that Kitto entirely ignores one of the two. (4.) Mary *did* return to a later two-angel vision, after leaving the tomb (John, ver. 2, 11); and others of the

---

* *The Resurrection of Christ.* By Gilbert West, Esq. London, 1747. 8vo. Highly commended in Horne's *Introd. Bib. Ind.*, p. 61. Doddridge in his *Expositor* cites and approves West; and he is nearly followed by Towson, 1793, and by White's Diatessaron, 1799 (says Horne as above). With the last named, Clarke nearly agrees.

women would be likely to meet her, and return also (as Macknight shows), they thus seeing the two angels when she did, not when, before, they had seen but one. (5.) If they did not thus, like Mary, return to the tomb after leaving it, what could they be about in all the interval of John (ver. 2-18, period 2-7)?—until after Mary's second visit and her interview with angels and with Jesus—not until *after* which did He appear to *them* also, "as they went" fleeing from the tomb. This can not mean their *fleeing* at first before even Peter was there, when even Mary had not seen Him; but it must teach (as Barnes insists) that they "went" away a second time.

Mark (ver. 2) indicates two arrivals at the tomb, mixed in the account—the one "very early" (Matthew, "as it began to dawn"); the other, "at the rising of the sun." (See Meyer.) Also ver. 8 indicates that after the first visit the women *in fear* reported nothing; whereas, the mixed account of Luke (ver. 9) gives their *joy* and their announcement after the second visit,—which Gardiner himself rightly shows must be different affairs. Doddridge, West, Scott, Lange, Haley, and Godet suggest a *second set* of women coming out—Joanna, etc. (Luke, ver. 10). Brown, in the British Commentary (at Mark, ver. 9), suggests *a return* of women with Mary; Barnes has them back without her; but neither has them see angels. What could they be about?

Robinson, Olshausen, and others, to meet the difficulty of Mark (ver. 9) in their mixed method without women again at the tomb, have to interpret the "first" appearing of Jesus to Mary as meaning, not the first appearing of all, *before* his appearing to the women, but only the *first-named* by Mark!—a very untenable idea. But they thus, by having an earlier appearing of Christ to the women, fall into the greater absurdity of having no party of women come telling of *angels alone seen* (with Christ not yet reported as seen), so late as the start to Emmaus, as required by Luke (ver. 22, 23). To Kitto this is inexplicable; but Doddridge, Lightfoot, Macknight, and Lange try to meet the difficulty by *denying the literal truth* of Matthew (ver. 9), that Jesus met *women* as they returned from the tomb. To such straits are expositors reduced to get along with their mixing of the two-angel with the one-angel vision.

§ 116. THE CORRECT VIEW.

Now, then, since we have found that the women's two visions can not be mixed, and that before Mary's vision is *too early* for their second vision, and after her vision is *too late*—therefore, we have to *regard the two-angel vision of the women as closely allied with the two-angel vision of Mary herself.* Doddridge does in fact make the women enter the tomb *while* Mary, near by but unseen, is conversing with Jesus. Rather, we say, they came out of the tomb, while she, unseen by *some* of them, was thus conversing; so that some ran to tell of the *angels seen*, while others lingering *saw Jesus* with Mary, and they with her *afterwards* brought this greater news.

This separation and double report of the women upon going away is testified to by Gardiner, Barnes, and other harmonists. Godet even tells us that the women's sight of Jesus in Matthew (ver. 9), is *the same* as Mary's sight of him in Mark (ver. 9), John (ver. 17); in confirmation of which he bids us compare "embraced his feet," and "tell my brethren," in the one account, with "touch me not," and "go to my brethren," in the other. Lange says: "The special experience of Mary [in seeing Jesus] is [at Mark, ver. 9] *incorporated* with the vision of the other women." Yes! the things were indeed "incorporated" together; for they are but parts of a single scene.

No view but this will harmonize Matthew (ver. 9) with John (ver. 17) and Mark (ver. 9). The fact, so inexplicable to Kitto and others, that *the women* "held Jesus by the feet," while yet he required of Mary "touch me not," is not explainable except in this view of a mingled scene. For they could have "held him by the feet" only just before his charge "touch me not." Matthew (ver. 9) shows *why* Jesus spoke as in John (ver. 17). That the women passed from the tomb just as Mary recognized the Saviour, appears from a trifling yet very suggestive phrase, noted by Meyer,—as Jesus said "Mary!" she "*turned herself* and saith unto him, 'Rabboni,'" showing that she had *turned around*, —I would say, at the rush of women. Did Providence leave *this little key* (unnoticed so long till Meyer) on purpose *now at last* to unlock this harmony of the resurrection story?

Of all the expositions to be found, the plan of Scott, White, West, and Lange alone seems to approach our view, in the separate locating of the one-angel and the two-angel vision. They have the first vision rightly in Mary's absence from the tomb; but they put the second *after* Mary's vision of angels, not in conjunction with it, as we alone do. Moreover, Lange strangely puts Matthew's one-angel vision as coincident with Luke's two-angel vision; somewhat as Guyse (cited in Doddridge), while rightly making two angel-visions, and even seeming to make one of them coincident with Mary's, yet strangely mixes up the accounts of them.

The now current view of most writers differs from ours chiefly in this: that it combines the women's sight of two angels with *the one-angel vision*, instead of combining it with *Mary's sight of two angels* (as is here done). Several writers come very near, but no one quite seizes this determining idea.

§ 117. According to the improved arrangement we have now established, the events at period 4 proceed as follows:—

Mary Magdalene, after starting out Peter and John, on *her* way back to the tomb takes with her some women not before starting ("Joanna and other women,"—Luke, ver. 1, 10; "several others," *Meyer*,— "bringing the spices," not named at the previous coming,—Mark, Matthew, John, ver. 1), with other returning women, perhaps, whom she meets (Mark ver. 8). Being arrived there the women (mostly a new set) enter the tomb; while Mary stands in the doorway stooping down, and sees "two angels sitting" (John, ver. 11, 12). The angels speak to Mary weeping in the doorway, and she answers them (ver. 13, 14). As the angels rise in presence of the women, just then Mary hears a footfall without, and turning she sees a stranger off a little one side. So stepping away from the tomb to ask him for help she, after a little conversation, discovers that it is Jesus himself whom she is addressing.

Meanwhile, the women in the tomb who, while Mary was addressed by the angels, were bowing down their faces to the earth in fear (Luke, ver. 5), as soon as Mary turned away were themselves addressed by the angels (now arisen plainly in view); whom they did not answer, as Mary had done (ver. 5-8),—no question being asked. But in timid joy (Matthew, ver. 8) over the comforting reminder of the angels, "they returned from the sepulchre" (Luke, ver. 9). Some of them hurry off for the city, to tell of *angels seen* (Luke, ver. 22, 23); while others, turning a little one side, run directly upon *Mary talking with Jesus himself,*— just as she "turned herself" from looking at them as they came up, and discovering who he was exclaimed, "Rabboni—Master!" As he salutes them all, they all fall in worship and embrace his feet (Matthew, ver. 10). Upon which he says to them all (including Mary), "Touch me not . . . but go to my brethren" (John, ver. 17); "Be not afraid: go tell my brethren" (Matthew, ver. 10).

They all start to go; but are met by the watchmen (ver. 11), who are preparing for an overhauling of the matter before the council; and being questioned and detained (perhaps) as witnesses, they do not reach the disciples with their message from Jesus till later in the day (Luke, ver. 9, 10; Mark, ver. 10; John, ver. 18). Meanwhile, the two disciples have started for Emmaus, not knowing that Jesus himself has been seen (Luke, ver. 22, 23). Peter's sight of Jesus does not come in till now, later in the day (ver. 33, 34).

Thus is the whole history beautifully harmonized, and made simple and consistent. And this is done by the now accepted method of putting the first-angel vision during Mary's absence from the tomb, together with this our newly-arranged method, of putting the two-angel vision afterward on the return of Mary, with her and the women all present in it, as one single two-angel vision.

§ 118. A SUMMARY ARGUMENT,

to show that Christ's appearing to Mary and to the other women was all really in one continuous event, as suggested by Godet :—

Three Evangelists have a mention of a woman-sight of Jesus, and each has *but one* such account ; Mark and John only saying that it occurred to Mary Magdalene, but Matthew saying that it occurred to the women promiscuously, *including Mary* (ver. 1, 9): " . . . came Mary Magdalene and the other Mary . . . and as *they* went Jesus met *them*." Therefore, as *each Evangelist has but one such event*, and as by Matthew *the plural case is made to include the singular*, it is plain that there were not two separate events to be distinguished by any one of the writers, but a single affair, to be told in full or in part by the writers, according as it was impressed on the mind of each. Nor does the word "first" (at Mark, ver. 9) make Mary's meeting of Jesus entirely separate from that of the women, but only the *first step* in it. Mary did "first" see Jesus, as there stated; but she was *not alone* in seeing him, for "the other Mary" joined her in it (Matthew, ver. 1, 9), and perhaps others too. Matthew expressly gives Mary Magdalene's sight of Jesus and the women's sight of Jesus as but one whole event, while Mark and John only state Mary's part in it as commencing "first."

There was a particular reason why John remembered Mary's vision and sight of Jesus more than that of the other women, all mention of which he entirely omits. It was *she* who came running to *him* and Peter, and first startled them with tidings from the tomb, which sent them hurrying thither themselves. (This reason Tholuck notes.) For the same reason, Peter also remembered chiefly Mary's part in the seeing of Jesus; and telling it to his amanuensis, Mark, he thus secured the insertion in that Gospel also, without mention of the other women. But Matthew, who had no such personal reason to fasten Mary indelibly in mind, has told the fact in its general form, "Jesus met *them*," —the women. And Luke, having only Paul's tuition, who was not present to be thrilled by the women's story of *seeing Jesus alive*, says nothing about it; and also mixes up the visions.

I need only say, in closing, that we find in this Harmony of the Resurrection (so happily adjusted at last) a wonderful confirmation of the inspired accuracy of the Evangelists. Substantial agreement, with varied selection of details, especially when that agreement is seen only by careful sifting of those details,—this is the very height of corroboration to the testimony of independent witnesses. The cavils of infidels upon this very point of alleged discrepancy in the narrations are here met by a demonstration of unpremeditated concurrence that sets all objection at rest.

At the same time, the dates at which the several Gospels were written, as well as the identity of their authors, receive here a striking illustration. The mention of Mary Magdalene, and of the personal meeting with Jesus that first-day morning, is in each writing just what the authorship calls for, as already seen. The story of the first three Evangelists, evidently unadjusted by any collusion, could hardly be put together into harmony; until the fourth Gospel comes in at a later date, and without any seeming reference to the previous accounts, by means of new details personally known by John, furnishes a key which in consecutive order reconciles together the whole seemingly diverse account.

How beautiful, how grand, is the Harmony of Divine Revelation!

NOTE.—The following harmony has been arranged as a Sacred Drama or Bible Reading exhibited by a Sunday School as an Easter Service; being set forth by five male and five female readers, personating the individuals concerned in the Gospel narrative.

MATTHEW XXVIII.	MARK XVI.	LUKE XXIV.
1 In the end of the sabbath, as it began to dawn toward the first *day* of the week, came Mary Magdalene and the other Mary to see the sepulchre. 2 And, behold, there was a great earthquake: for the angel of the Lord descended from heaven, and came and rolled back the stone from the door, and sat upon it. 3 His countenance was like lightning, and his raiment white as snow. 4 And for fear of him the keepers did shake, and became as dead *men*.	1 And when the sabbath was past, Mary Magdalene, and Mary the *mother* of James, and Salome, had bought sweet spices, that they might come and anoint him. 2 And very early in the morning, the first *day* of the week they came unto the sepulchre (at the rising of the sun). 3 And they said among themselves, Who shall roll us away the stone from the door of the sepulchre? 4 And when they looked, they saw that the stone was rolled away; for it was very great.	1 Now upon the first *day* of the week, very early in the morning, they came unto the sepulchre, bringing the spices which they had prepared, and certain *others* with them. 2 And they found the stone rolled away from the sepulchre.
5 And the angel answered and said unto the women, Fear not ye, for I know that ye seek Jesus, which was crucified. 6 He is not here: for he is risen, as he said. Come, see the place where the Lord lay. 7 And go quickly, and tell his disciples that he is risen from the dead; and, behold, he goeth before you into Galilee: there shall ye see him: lo, I have told you.	5 And entering into the sepulchre, they saw a young man sitting on the right side, clothed in a long white garment; and they were affrighted. 6 And he saith unto them, Be not affrighted: ye seek Jesus of Nazareth, which was crucified: he is risen; he is not here: behold the place where they laid him. 7 But go your way, tell his disciples and Peter that he goeth before you into Galilee: there shall ye see him, as he said unto you.	(3 And they entered in, and . . . 5 [*it was*] said unto them, Why seek ye the living among the dead? 6 He is not here, but is risen: remember how he spake unto you when he was yet in Galilee. . . . 9 And [*they*] returned from the sepulchre.)
8 And they departed quickly from the sepulchre with fear and great joy; and did run to bring his disciples word.	8 And they went out quickly, and fled from the sepulchre, for they trembled and were amazed: neither said they anything to any *man;* for they were afraid.	
(*Omitted.*)	*Omitted.*)	12 Then arose Peter, and ran unto the sepulchre; and stooping down, he beheld the linen clothes laid by themselves, and departed, wondering in himself at that which was come to pass. 24 And certain of them which were with us went to the sepulchre, and found *it* even so as the women had said: but him they saw not. (*Luke combines the second angel-vision after this period with the one before.*)

RESURRECTION.   91

JOHN XX. KEY	ORDER OF EVENTS.	PERIOD.

1 The first *day* of the week cometh Mary Magdalene early, when it was yet dark, unto the sepulchre, and seeth the stone taken away from the sepulchre.

At dawn there was an earthquake, and the stone was rolled away by an angel.

Mary Magdalene comes (the other Mary and Salome following her), and they find the stone rolled away. Thinking the tomb robbed, and not waiting for the others

1. Women at the tomb.

2 Then she runneth, and cometh to Simon Peter, and to the other disciple, whom Jesus loved, and saith unto them, They have taken away the Lord out of the sepulchre, and we know not where they have laid him.

Mary runs off to Peter and John, and they start for the tomb.

Meanwhile, the other women (left behind by Mary) venture into the tomb, and there listen to a single angel (the one who had sat on the stone). He assures them of Jesus' resurrection, and sends them off with a message to the disciples.

2. Mary gone: one-angel vision.

3 Peter therefore went forth, and that other disciple, and came to the sepulchre.
4 So they ran both together; and the other disciple did outrun Peter, and came first to the sepulchre.
5 And he stooping down, *and looking in*, saw the linen clothes lying; yet went he not in.
6 Then cometh Simon Peter following him, and went into the sepulchre, and seeth the linen clothes lie.
7 And the napkin that was about his head, not lying with the linen clothes, but wrapped together in a place by itself.
8 Then went in also that other disciple, which came first to the sepulchre, and he saw, and believed.
9 For as yet they knew not the Scripture, that he must rise again from the dead.
10 Then the disciples went away again unto their own home.

Just after their leaving, John arrives at the tomb.
Peter next comes up, and goes in. They find no body of Jesus, and no angel appears. But they see the grave-clothes lying. Presently they return home.
Meanwhile, Mary Magdelene is on her way back to the tomb, taking with her Joanna, and other women met by the way at sun-rise.

3. John and Peter at the tomb.

MATTHEW XXVIII.	MARK XVI.	LUKE XXIV.
(*Mary, with Joanna and others, returns to the sepulchre.*)	(2 . . . They came unto the sepulchre at the rising of the sun.)	3 And they entered in, and found not the body of the Lord Jesus. 4 And it came to pass, as they were much perplexed thereabout, behold, two men stood by them in shining garments:
		5 And as they were afraid, and bowed down *their* faces to the earth,
(*Women in the tomb.*)	9 Now when *Jesus* was risen early the first *day* of the week, he appeared first to' Mary Magdalene, out of whom he had cast seven devils.	they said unto them, Why seek ye the living among the dead? 6 He is not here, but is risen: remember how he spake unto you when he was yet in Galilee, 7 Saying, The Son of Man must be delivered into the hands of sinful men, and be crucified, and the third day rise again. 8 And they remembered his words, 9 And returned from the sepulchre.
9 And as they went to tell his disciples, behold, Jesus met them, saying, All hail. And they came and held him by the feet, and worshipped him. 10 Then said Jesus unto them, Be not afraid: go tell my brethren that they go into Galilee, and there shall they see me.	(*Two sets of women.*)	22 Yea, and certain women also of our company made us astonished, which were early at the sepulchre; 23 And when they found not his body, they came, saying, that they had also seen a vision of angels, which said that he was alive. (13 And, behold, two of them went that same day to a village called Emmaus. *Ver.* 22. 23.)
11 Now when they were going, behold, some of the watch came into the city, and shewed unto the chief priests all the things that were done. 12 And when they were assembled with the elders, and had taken counsel, they gave large money unto the soldiers.	10 *And* she went and told them that had been with him, as they mourned and wept. 11 And they, when they had heard that he was alive, and had been seen of her, believed not. 12 After that he appeared in another form unto two of them, as they walked, and went into the country.	9 . . . They returned from the sepulchre, and told all these things unto the eleven, and to all the rest. 10 It was Mary Magdalene, and Joanna, and Mary *the mother* of James, and other *women that were* with them, which told these things unto the apostles. 11 And their words seemed to them as idle tales, and they believed them not. (12 Now Peter *had* arisen, *&c.* 13. And behold two of them *had* gone that same day to a village, *&c.* *See the Gr. and the Rev. and Marg.*)

RESURRECTION (*concluded.*)

JOHN XX. (KEY).	ORDER OF EVENTS.	PERIOD.
11 But Mary stood without at the sepulchre weeping: and as she wept, she stooped down, *and looked* into the sepulchre, 12 And seeth two angels in white sitting, the one at the head, and the other at the feet, where the body of Jesus had lain. 13 And they say unto her, Woman, why weepest thou? She saith unto them, Because they have taken away my Lord, and I know not where they have laid him. 14 And when she had thus said, she turned herself back, and saw	The other women go right into the tomb; but Mary stands in the doorway, stooping. They all see a vision of two angels within. The angels speak to Mary weeping in the doorway, and she answers. Perceiving a shadow behind her, she turns, and stepping from the tomb,	4. Women's two-angel vision.
Jesus standing, and knew not that it was Jesus. 15 Jesus saith unto her, Woman, why weepest thou? whom seekest thou? She, supposing him to be the gardener, saith unto him, Sir, if thou have borne him hence, tell me where thou hast laid him, and I will take him away.	she beholds a man before her who kindly inquires her business. Him she addresses as the gardener. He simply responds in a familiar tone, "Mary!" Meanwhile, the women in the tomb are addressed by the two angels. They now leave the tomb.	5. Mary sees Jesus.
16 Jesus saith unto her, Mary.		
She turned herself, and saith unto him, Rabboni; which is to say, Master. 17 Jesus saith unto her, Touch me not; for I am not yet ascended to my Father: but go to my brethren, and say unto them, I ascend unto my Father, and your Father; and *to* my God, and your God.	Some of them, hurrying to the city, tell of *angels* seen: while others, turning one side, run directly upon Mary, just as she recognizes the voice of Jesus saying "Mary!" and exclaims, "Rabboni, Master!" They all at once fall to grasp his feet in worship. Whereupon he says, "Touch me not: I am soon to ascend. But go to my brethren, and then to Galilee, where I shall be seen."	6. Other women see Jesus.
18 Mary Magdalene came and told the disciples that she had seen the Lord, and *that* he had spoken these things unto her.	They start to go; but are met by the watchmen, who are preparing for an overhauling of the matter by the council. With this detention (perhaps used as witnesses), they do not reach the disciples with their message from Jesus himself, until later in the day, when the two have started for Emmaus, not knowing that *he* has been seen.	7. The story told to all.

ERRATA.

P. 39, end of § 46, insert (See also Period E, § 62, p. 159.)
P. 49, § 63, line 10, read 'Judges', not John.
P. 49, § 63, line 13, read 'I Chron.', not II Chron.
P. 50, line 11, read 'Lu. ii: 21', not 31.
P. 52, § 67, last line, read 'Hos. ii: 11,' not iii: 11.
P. 64, line 9, read (Ex. xii: 6), not 16.
P. 64, § 85, last line, read (John i: 29 etc.), not 31.
P. 72, § 100, line 9, read (*ante*), not (*ante*).
P. 73, par. 2, line 6, read ' unius ', not ' unias '.
P. 103, line 7, read 'Gen. v and xi', not v: 11.
P. 108, line 2, read 'kingdom', not king.
P. 124, § 30, line 1, read 'Zedekiah's 8th year', not 9th.
P. 126, line 5, read '515', not 575.
P. 136, line 4 from bot., read 'repeated', not repented.
P. 138, § 19, line 2, read 'sacked', not sucked.
P. 155, line 8 from bot., read '332', not 532.
P. 155, line 6 from bot., insert 'to' before 'the spurious'.
P. 187, line 8 from bot., read 'verses', not years.
P. 218, § 7, line 4, read '580,' not 585.
P. 221, line 5 from bot., read '1491', not 1493.
P. 231, line 3-5 from bot., read 'Astruc', and 'p 678' and '§ 19'.
P. 245, end of 2nd par., read 'Gal. iii: 17', not 7.
P. 245, line 6 from bot., read 'p 775', not 375.
P. 251, § 80, line 3, read '§ 1, 5'. not 4.
P. 255 line 12, after 'dedication' insert ')to the 9th of Darius('
P. 258, § 93, line 9, read 'vii: 13', not ix: 13.
P. 260, line 3 from bot., read '(xxx: 29)', not (ver. 29.)
P. 261, line 5 from bot., read 'ch. xxxvii', not xxvii.
P. 261, line 3 from bot., read 'xxxiv. xxxv', not 35.
P. 262, line 9, read 'xxxi: 41', not 40.
P. 278, § 129, line 7, read '§ 146', not 156.
P. 280, line 6, after 'Thotmes' insert (")
P. 282, par. 3, line 1, read (Jos. § 26), not 'here'.
P. 289, line 9 from bot., read 'xxi: 5', not 3.
P. 292, line 5, read 'Gen. xv', not xiii.
P. 292, line 9, read 'D. § 10', not 6.
P. 295, § 20, line 7, read (9-15), not ix: 15.
P. 297, § 23, line 7, 8, read 'ch. xxxiv. xxxvii', not xxiv. xxvii.
P. 298, line 5 from bot., read 'xxxiii: 19', not 11.
P. 304, § 10, line 3, read '1, vi: 5', not 3, vi: 5.
P. 305, §13, line 3, read 'Psa.', not Isa.
P. 313, § 33, line 6, read 'Jos 11', not II.
P. 335, § 72, line 6, read (A—F) not (A - E).
P. 335, § 72, line 14 from bot., read '1997', not 1977.

ERRATA

P. 337, line 6, read '5530' and '1470', not 5510 and 1490.
P. 341, § 84, line 10, read 'i: 12', not i: 2.
P. 343, line 11 from bot., read 'vision', not division.
P. 354, § 7, line 5, read 'here, § 4', not p. 3.
P. 360, line 4, read '1130½', not 1030½.
P. 367, line 8 from bot., read 'citation 1, § 4', not p. 3.
P. 368, § 36, line 2, read '646', not 649.
P. 370, § 41, line 1, read 'the year of Jozedek', not 'about'.
P. 373, § 47, line 3 from end, read '§ 23', not p. 13.

§ 120. TABLE OF BIBLE DATES.
By the Hebrew Text.

	B. C. Usher.	B. C. Correct.
Creation	4004	4104
Birth of Abel	3874	3974
" Enos	3769	3869
" Cainan	3679	3779
" Mahalael	3609	3709
" Jared	3544	3644
" Enoch	3382	3482
" Methuselah	3317	3417
" Lamech	3130	3230
" Noah	2948	3048
" Shem	2446	2546
The Flood	2348	2448
Birth of Arphaxed	2346	2446
" Saleh	2311	2411
" Eber	2281	2381
" Peleg	2247	2347
" Reu	2217	2317
" Serug	2185	2285
" Nahor	2155	2255
" Terah	2126	2226
" Abram	1996	2096
Abram to Canaan	1921	2021
Isaac born	1896	1996
Isaac offered	1884	1984
Jacob born	1836	1936
Jacob to Haran	1760	1880
Joseph born	1746	1846
Jacob to Canaan	1740	1840
Jacob to Egypt	1706	1806
Exodus from Egypt	1491	1591
Arrival in Canaan	1451	1551

TABLE OF BIBLE DATES—Continued.

By the Hebrew Text.	B. C. Usher.	B. C. Correct.	By the Hebrew Text.	B. C. Usher.	B. C. Correct.
Joshua's death,		1526	Manasseh ends,		642
Chushan ends,		1508	Amon ends,		640
Othniel ends,		1468	Josiah ends,		609
Eglon ends,		1450	Jehoiachin taken,		598
Ehud ends,		1370	Jerusalem destroyed, 588		587
Jabin ends,		1350	Capturing finished,		583
Barak and Deb. end,		1310	Jehoiachin ends,		561
Midian ends,		1303	Cyrus' Decree,		537
Gideon ends,		1263	Darius' Decree, 520		520
Abimelech ends,		1260	2nd Temple Jubilee,		513
Tola ends,		1237	Ezra Decree, 7 Art.,		457
Jair ends,		1215	Nehemiah Decree 20 Art.,		444
Ammon ends,		1197	Malachi, end of O. T.,		408
Jephthah ends,		1191	Alexander the Gr't ends,		323
Ibsan ends,		1184	Seleucic Era begins,		312
Elon ends,		1174	Ant. Epiph. pol'tes Temp.		168
Abdon ends,		1166	Judas Maccabeus begins,		163
Eli begins,		1146	Judas Aristobulus King,		106
Samson begins,		1126	Pompey takes Jerusalem,		64
Samuel begins,		1106	Julius Cæsar ends,		44
Saul begins,		1094	Herod takes Jerusalem,		37
David begins,	*	1054	Christ born,		4, 5
Solomon begins,		1014	Herod dies, B. C.		4, 3
Temple, 4th of Sol.,	1012	1011	Archelaus ends, A. D.		8
Temple, dedication,	1004	1003	Christ in the temple,		9
Solomon ends,		974	Tiberius' co-reign,		12
Rehoboam ends,		957	Augustus Cæsar ends,		14
Abijah ends,		954	Pilate begins,		26
Asa ends,		913	John Baptist begins,		26
Jehos. wi Jehoram,		896	Christ baptized,		27
Jehoshaphat ends,		888	Christ crucified,		30
Jehoram ends,		884	Saul, Cornelius, & Gentiles,		34
Ahaziah ends,		883	End of "70 weeks,"		
Athaliah ends,		877	Paul visits Jerusalem,		37
Jehoash ends,		838	Agrippa I begins,		41
Amaziah ends,		809	Council of Jerusalem,		51
Azariah ends,		757	Felix begins,		53
Jotham ends,		741	Festus begins,		60
Ahaz ends,		726	Paul sent to Rome,		60
Samaria captured,	721	720	Vespasian comes,		67
Hezekiah ends,		697	Jerusalem destroyed, A.D		70

*Josephus, by giving Solomon 1 year of joint-reign with David, has David's reign B. C. 1053-1013. Then, in the Antiq., he puts the temple building 1010-1003, offsetting by 1 year given to Shamgar. (See Period D, § 5, note, and Restor. Jos., § 18, 51.)

(Go to Page 101.)

OLD TESTAMENT CHRONOLOGY.

OLD TESTAMENT CHRONOLOGY.

Its Certainty and Importance.

The several intervals of Old Testament chronology are clear and determinable beyond reasonable dispute. Each interval may in its turn be called in question, and honestly discussed. But these occasional questionings do not combine to unsettle the several datings, or bring the whole chronology into uncertainty. On the contrary, the whole certainty is increased by the interplay of the several questionings. Thus,

1. The certainty of the scripture interval 254 years, from the death of Solomon to the capture of Samaria, B. C. 974 to 720, as the duration of the Ten Tribes, may be denied by some Assyriologists; but not denied as biblical (that were impossible), only denied as not in accordance with Assyriology. But this can throw no doubt on scripture chronology as such; it can only raise the question whether there is a possible rival to overturn it. The fact is, the interval 254 years is the only one that scripture gives or can give without self-contradiction. And whether that 254 is correct, is only a question whether the scriptural dating is *worth anything* or not? No question arises as to what date is *given by scripture;* it is only, what use can be made of it? (See Period E, § 34, 44.) Again,

2. The certainty of the scripture interval 580 years given by Paul (in Acts xiii: 18-22) and the book of Judges, reaching from the Exodus to the Temple, may be denied by some Egyptologists and others—denied as inconsistent with some other scripture (say I Kings vi: 1), or more likely denied as disagreeing with some late theory of Egyptology. But this unsettles nothing. The presumption is in favor of the Bible reckoning; and any uncertainty as to what that Bible reckoning is, research is fast clearing away. (Period D, § 1, 40.) Yet again,

3. Uncertainty as to the scripture interval 430 years of sojourning at Ex. xii: 40, may be brought forward. But the whole chronology viewed together keeps it quite sure that the entire sojourning in Canaan as well as in Egypt is included in the 430; and the harmony of the complete history is helped, not hindered, by the separate points raised. (Period C, § 1, 9.) Still further,

4. The certainty of Abraham's delay of sixty years in reaching Canaan, till "his father was dead" (Acts vii: 6), may be called in question. But it certainly is scripture teaching, and will probably stand as long as Bible datings are acknowledged at all. (Period A, B, § 58.) Once more,

5. The certainty of the diluvian periods $1656 + 352 = 2008$, given in Gen. v: 11 (Period A, B, § 72), may be questioned as more probably correct in the Septnagint ($2242 + 1172 = 3414$—see Period A, B, § 75). But the late attempts to make out here *no chronology at all*, must fail; and the doubt between the Hebrew and Greek texts will not always confound Bible chronology. (Period A, B, § 39, 40.)

These are all the great questions that disturb Old Testament dating as a whole. And the notable thing about them is, that they do not combine to make a chaos of the subject, as some would represent; but the combining of these different points reduces the difficulties of the whole. The one grand fact made apparent by the whole Old Testament considered together, is, that *the Bible has a chronology*, a clearly intended and plainly marked plan of dating, all its own. And the second thing apparent, is, that it has *no rival system of chronology*, Assyrian, Egyptian, Tyrian, or other, to set it authoritatively aside. The overwhelming result is, to set forth the scripture dating as *the one only universal chronology* of the world; which has the right of way, with full presumption in its favor; so that every opposing claim must bear the whole burden of proof, and only assert itself by proving the Bible false.

Hence the way many Bible apologists have, of telling over the many chronological difficulties of the Bible, as rendering the whole uncertain, like a mere bank of fog, is entirely to be deprecated. Says the *Sunday School Times* (October 27, 1894): "Is there anything in the Bible text that forbids the supposition that man was created ten thousand years before the Christian era? Is there any approximate agreement among the more strict interpreters of the letter of the Bible text as to the world's chronology, and that of the Bible? If so, the editor of the *Sunday School Times* is not aware of the fact. She (the writer referred to) is permitted to say her say on *that vague and unessential* subject." What we object to in this way (so common) of treating the subject, is not the pointing out of the things that are under discussion, but the representing of the points in dispute as more numerous and flagrant than they are, and especially turning off the whole matter of chronology (thus befogged in people's minds) as being "a vague and unessential subject."

The *certainty* of a true Bible chronology is what we wish emphatically to set forth. And the *importance* of it, we urge as being the fundamental historical basis of Bible truth. If God has kept the time-piece of the universe, and correctly adjusted his inspired word thereto, it is well for God's people to know and utilize the fact.

Assyriology and Egyptology.

During this last part of the nineteenth century, Assyrian excavations and decipherings have made great progress, and have thrown much light upon Bible manners and events. We duly appreciate the many illustrations and confirmations of scripture thus furnished; but are sorry to find among Assyrian scholars too much of a disposition to underrate the Bible chronology, and to bring Assyrian datings into collision with it, for which there is no occasion whatever.

The fragments of a supposed annual chronicle of Assyrian rulers have been found, which, when pieced together, give a seeming record of two hundred years during the time of the Jewish kings. This Assyriologists call the "Eponym Canon," and by it many undertake to prove, that the Bible chronology of the kings is forty or fifty years out of the way, in having the death of Solomon, B. C. 974, which they say should be about B. C. 929. (See Period E, § 79.) This theory can not be reconciled with scripture, except by a complete destruction of all the scores of Bible numbers given in the books of Kings and Chronicles, etc. So that this newly announced Assyrian chronology completely overturns the whole Bible dating, and can not escape with the plea, that some single passage of scripture is corrupted.

With the greatest confidence this anti-biblical chronology is being propagated as if the genuine and certain reckoning, in defiance of scripture. And it is put forward in many of our Sunday School Lesson Helps, without a note of warning that it is merely an unproved *theory*, by no means displacing the Bible dating. (For specimens of the bold assurance of leading Assyriologists in giving this innovation as the absolute truth, see Dr. McCurdy on "Oriental Research and the Bible," in *Sunday School Times*, May 11, 1895, and many similar articles in that and other quarters.)

Now, a little study shows the complete uncertainty of all this theorizing in Assyriology, and the fallaciousness of building any system of chronology on such a flimsy basis, in contradiction of the multiplied and assured assertions of the Bible. One great object of this present work is to show how sure is the Bible dating, especially through those times of the kings, and how impossible it is for Assyriological theory to overthrow it. Moreover, the late and present attempt to contradict by 200 years the Bible date of the Exodus, by means of Egyptology, is here shown to be equally futile. These archæological researches of our day are found to be greatly corroborative of the Bible history, and in no respect contradictory to it.

PERIOD F—EXILE AND AFTER.
PART I.

THE INTERVENING DATES.

§ 1. The standard of chronology, from the close of the scripture back to the Old Testament kingdom of Israel, is Ptolemy's Canon, whose datings we here give:

		Years.	Total.	B. C.	1 Thoth begins.
			0 +	747	Feb. 26, 747.
Babylonian, 209 years.	Nabonassar..................	14	14	733	
	[We omit]..................	108	122	625	
	Nabopolassar..................	21	143	604	
	Nebuchadnezzar..................	43	186	561	
	Evil Merodach..................	2	188	559	
	Neriglisar..................	4	192	555	
	Nabonadus..................	17	209	538	
Persian, 207 years.	Cyrus..................	9	218	529	
	Cambyses..................	8	226 +	521	Jan 1=747.
	Darius I..................	36	262 +	486	Dec. 31=748.
	Xerxes..................	21	283	465	
	Artaxerxes I..................	41	324	424	
	Darius II..................	19	343	405	
	Artaxerxes II..................	46	389	359	Nov.
	Ochus..................	21	410	338	
	Arogus..................	2	412	336	
	Darius III..................	4	416	332	
Egyptian and Macedonian, 302 years.	Alexander Mac..................	8	424	324	
	Philip Arid..................	7	431	317	
	Alexander Ægus..................	12	443	305	
	Ptolemy Lagus..................	20	463	285	
	Philadelphus..................	38	501	247	Oct.
	Euergetes I..................	25	526	222	
	Philopator..................	17	543	205	
	Epiphanes..................	24	567	181	
	Philometor..................	35	602	146	Sep.
	Euergetes II..................	29	631	117	
	Soter..................	36	667	81	
	Dionysius..................	29	696	52	
	Cleopatra..................	22	718 +	30	B. C.=748.
Roman, 189 years.	Augustus..................	43	761 =	14	A. D.+747.
	Tiberius..................	22	783	36	Aug.
	Caius Calig..................	4	787	40	
	Claudius..................	14	801	54	
	Nero..................	14	815	68	
	Vespasian..................	10	825	78	
	Titus..................	3	828	81	
	Domitian..................	15	843	96	July.
	Nerva..................	1	844	97	
	Trajan..................	19	863	116	
	Adrian..................	21	884	137	
	Antonius Pius..................	23	907 =	160	A. D.+747.

907 Nab. years total, from Feb. 747 B. C. to July, 160 A. D.

REMARKS.

Ptolemy, the author of the Canon, lived in the middle of the second century, and he gives (as above) the correct chronology of the reigns back from his own day to the beginning of the Nabonassan era in Babylon, B. C. 747. He employs the Nabonassan or Egyptian year of just 365 days.

This Nabonassan year was rotary, revolving about the seasons 1461 times in 1460 Julian years of 365¼ days each. Its year 1 began with 1 Thoth at Feb. 26, B. C. 747. In B. C. 521 (bissextile) 1 Thoth came on Jan. 1 and also on Dec. 31, two Canon years starting in the same Julian year. This makes the B. C. dating (in the table above) change one year at that point. But one year is also lost in passing from B. C. to A. D. or *vice versa* (because there is no year 0); so that from B. C. 1 to A. D. 1 is but one year, and from B. C 3 to A. D. 4 is but six years. In B. C. 1 or A. D. 0 to 3, the 1 Thoth came on August 23; in A. D. 12 to 15 it came August 20, and Augustus died August 19, A. D. 14.

Hales (following Dodwell) has shown conclusively that the Canon of Ptolemy *ante*-dates each reign; that is, it begins each reign (as a whole number of years) from the Nabonassan new year or first of the month, *Thoth* next *before* the accession of the king. The only exception was the case of Augustus, whose death (Aug. 19) was so near the 1 Thoth (then Aug. 20), that the succession was put there in the same year (A. D. 14). This rational view of the case exhibits a *natural courtesy* shown to the reigning monarch on the part of the court recorder of the time, in calling his first fractional year a whole year, it suiting a king's vanity to seem to have ruled not less but rather more than he had.

Hales says: "Alexander began at the battle of Arbela, Oct. 1, B. C. 331, but the Canon puts him at the preceding new year, Nov. 14, B. C. 332. The death of Alexander was May 22, B. C. 323, but his successor is set down in the Canon at the previous new year, Nov. 12, B. C. 324; which is confirmed by Censorinus, who reckons from thence 294 years to the beginning of Augustus (alone) in B. C. 30. Again, Tiberius died Mar. 16, A. D. 37; but his successor is put at the preceding new year, Aug. 14, A. D. 36. Vespasian began July 1, A. D. 69; but the Canon reckons him from the previous new year, Aug. 6, A. D. 68. Petavius had complained that Ptolemy often makes the *reigns begin a year too soon;* but this new year antedating explains it all." (Hales.) See all this confirmed at Period G, § 108.*

---

*§ 2. NOTE—Schwartz makes a desperate attempt to reverse this well-established law of Ptolemy's Canon, and to show that it *post*-dates each reign, instead of ante-dating as shown above. For this purpose he claims that the death of Alexander the Great in Olym. 114:1, was at

JOSEPHUS AND THE MACCABEES.

§ 3. To learn the Jewish dating for 170 years before the Christian era, Josephus is our best authority, together with the books of Maccabees in our O. T. Apocrapha.

Josephus' reckoning of those times is learned from the following citations:

1. "King Antiochus returning out of Egypt, for fear of the Romans,

---

the beginning of that Olympic year, not toward its close, in the spring of B. C. 523. The only argument he gives is that Plutarch puts the death of Alexander in the month "Daesius," which he (Schwartz) claims as "corresponding to the Athenian month Hecatombion" in August (B. C. 324, he says). This is very dubious, to say the least. The month "Daesius" must mean "Desius," which Josephus gives as the Macedonian name for the 3d Hebrew month "Sivan" (May). Whiston's Josephus (War., 3, vii: 29, 31, 32), gives it as "the month Desius [Sivan"]; and the context (§ 3, 39) gives before it "the 2d month Artemesius [Iyar]," and after it the 4th month Panemus [Tamuz]" or June.

Accordingly, all historians tell us, like Rollin, that Alexander "died in the middle of the spring, the first year of the 114th Olympiad. [Hales says May 22, B. C. 323]. He was 32 years and 8 months old." "He was born in the first year of the 106th Olympiad, when his father had just won in the Olympic games." (*Rollin* v, p. 192, and iv, p. 278). From the beginning of Olymp. 106: 1, the 32 years 8 mo. carry us to the spring ending Olymp. 114: 1, *i. e.*, May, B. C. 323. And Josephus tells us that "Hecateus, the philosopher, who was contemporary with Alexander, mentions the battle near Gaza, in the 11th year after the death of Alexander, and in the 117th Olympiad." (*Jos. vs. Ap.* I, § 22.) Now to reach Olym. 117: 1, the "11th year," must run back only 11 years to the *end* of Olym. 114: 1, as the time of Alexander's death, viz., in the spring of A. D. 323. Soon after this battle at Gaza, Seleucus entered Babylon, and then began the famous Seleucic era, B. C. 311-312 (+ the 11 years = the 323 B. C.)

Another fact proves the same. At Alexander's death he had been in Babylon "almost a year" (p. 189). But one of the first things he had done after entering Babylon was the writing of "a letter which was to be read publicly in the assembly of the Olympic games" (p. 186). This letter must have been written just before the games of Olym. 114, in July of B. C. 324, and his death, "almost a year" afterward, was in May, B. C. 323. It is not possible to disturb this well-established date.

Mr. Schwartz further claims (Letter July 28, '93), that "Augustus was emperor, so far as Egypt was concerned, Aug. 1, B. C. 30, but Ptolemy's Canon dates his first year from Aug. 31 of that year, *post*-dating again." To which we answer, not so. True, "Cæsar Augustus gained Anthony's fleet on the Kal. of August" (*Clinton*, B. C. 30); but he did not enter Alexandria till the last of August (*Clinton* at A. D. 14); and Cleopatra did not die till some time after, as all agree. The Egyptians could not reckon the reign of Augustus as beginning until their Queen Cleopatra was dead in September. So that Ptolemy's Canon certainly *ante*-dates in putting it at 1 Thoth or Aug. 31, B. C. 30. (*Note continued on next page.*)

made an expedition against the city of Jerusalem; and when he was there, in the hundred and forty-third year of the king of the Seleucidæ, he took the city without fighting, those of his party opening the gates to him." (Antiq. 12, v: 3.)

2. "The temple was made desolate by Antiochus (Epiphanes), and so continued for three years. This desolation happened to the temple in the hundred and forty-fifth year, on the twenty-fifth day of the month, Apelleus [Kisleu], and in the hundred fifty and third Olympiad: but it was dedicated anew, on the same day, the twenty-fifth of the month Appelleus, in the hundred and forty-eighth year, and in the hundred and fifty-fourth Olympiad." (Antiq. 12, vii: 6.)

3. "Then the fore-named Antiochus (Eupator) and Lysias, the general of his army, deprived Onias, who was also named Menelaus, of the high-priesthood, and slew him at Berea, and put Jacemus into the place of the high-priest." (Antiq. 20, x: 1.) "This was in the hundred and fiftieth year of the dominion of the Seleucidæ . . . . It was the seventh year, in which by our laws we are obliged to let it (the land) lie uncultivated. . . . So the king sent Menelaus to Berea, a city of Syria, and there had him put to death." (Antiq. 12, ix: 3, 5, 7.)

4. "The city was taken [by Pompey] in the third month, on the day of the fast [the 23d Sivan], in the one hundred seventy-ninth Olympiad, when Caius Antonius and Marcus Tullius Cicero were consuls." (Ant. 14, iv: 3.) "This destruction [by Herod] befell the city of

---

Schwartz also claims that Augustus died in A. D. 13, a year before Ptolemy's Canon has it (A. D. 14). And he gives Dio in evidence, with his 76 years only for the life of Augustus, and 56 years only for Augustus' reign, *i. e.* (he says) from B. C. 44 to A. D. 13. But this very "Dio tells us that Augustus reigned 44 years from the battle of Actium" (so says Usher), *i. e.* from Sept. 2, B. C. 31 to Aug. 19, A. D. 14. (His 56 years may have begun from B. C. 43, just as Appleton's Cyc. of Biog. and some other authors now put it; which will not change the terminus, A. D. 14). Schwatz himself says that Dio has the "Aug. 19" wrong for the death of Argustus; so his 56 and 76 may also be wrong.

Josephus, who was almost contemporary, is certainly better evidence than Dio 300 years afterward. And Josephus (Antiq. 18, ii: 2) says that Augustus "lived 77 years," and "reigned 57 years," *i. e.*, from B. C. 44 to A. D. 14. Ptolemy's Canon has 43 years for Augustus alone, from A. D. 14 back to the death of Cleopatra (its next reign) in September, B. C. 30 (not to the defeat of Anthony, Aug. 2, nor to Augustus' entrance into Alexadria the last of August, as alleged). Schwartz makes but 42 years, from B. C. 30 to A. D. 13. He decides that Augustus died, not on August 19 (as in Dio), but on Sept. 22 (which he works out from Velleius). This agrees better with Josephus and at the same time it more fully verifies Ptolemy's Canon, as always *ante*-dating an accession. The contrary theory can not by any possibility be maintained. See Period G, § 108, Period E, § 3, § 142.

Jerusalem when Marcus Agrippa and Caninius were consuls of Rome, in the hundred eighty and fifth Olympiad, in the third month, on the solemnity of the fast, as if a periodical revolution of calamities had returned, since that which befell the Jews under Pompey; for the Jews were taken by him on the same day, and this was twenty-seven years' time." (*Antiq. 14, xvi: 4.*)

5. "And thus did the government of the Asmoneans [or Maccabees] cease, a hundred and twenty-six years after it was set up." (*Ib.*) At 17, vi: 4, it is "125 years."

6. "The number of the high-priests from the days of Herod until the day when Titus took the temple and the city and burnt them, were in all twenty-eight; the time also that belonged to them was a hundred and seven years." (*Antiq. 20, x: 1.*)

7. "Herod died, having reigned since he had procured Antigonus to be slain [and took Jerusalem] thirty-four years; but since he had been declared king by the Romans, thirty-seven." (*Antiq. 17, viii: 1.*) "Herod died, having reigned thirty-four years since he had caused Antigonus to be slain, and obtained his kingdom; but thirty-seven years since he had been made king by the Romans." (*War, 1, xxxiii: 8.*) See further in Restor. of Jos., § 4.

§ 4. These several statements being collated, give the following as the intervals and dates of Josephus:

INTERVALS OF JOSEPHUS.

Jerusalem taken by Antiochus...... ....B. C. 170—"	2"	
Antiochus Ep. profanes the temple......B. C. 168—"	3"	
Judas Maccabeus cleanses it............B. C. 165—	2	
Ant. Eupator deposes Menelaus........B. C. 163—	57	
Judas Aristobulus puts on a crown......B. C. 106—	42	
Pompey conquers Jerusalem............B. C. 64—"	27"	"126th"
Herod conquers Jerusalem.............B. C. 37—"	34"	
Herod dies..........................B. C. 4–3—	40	"107th"
Josephus is born.....................A. D. 38—	32	"xxxth"
Titus destroys Jerusalem..............A. D. 70—	24	
Josephus writes his Antiquities........A. D. 94		

110 PERIOD F

DATES OF JOSEPHUS.

EVENTS.	B. C.	REIGNS.	Seleucic Year.	Olym. Year.	OLYMPIAD. Begins.	Jos.	Sabbatics Noted.
Jerusalem taken	170	" 2 "	" 143 "	609	713	" 153 "	
Ant. Eph. prof. temple	168	" 3 "	" 145 "	609	713	" 153 "	
Jud. Mac. purif. temple	165		" 148 "	612	733x	" 154 "	
Ant. Eup. begins reign	164		" 149 "	613x	733	" 184 "	
Ant. Eup. deposes Men	163	" 3 [1] "	" 150 "		737	" 185 "	"Sabbatic."
Alcimus killed	160	" 3 "	" 153 "		740	" 187 "	
Jud. Mac. slain	157	" 4 "	" 156 "		746		"Sabbatic."
Jonathan made H. P.	153	" 10 "	" 160 "		745		
Jonathan slain	143	" 8 " th	" 170 "				"Sabbatic."
Simon's death	136	" 30 [1] "	177	641 (645)		" 162 "	"Sabbatic."
Hyrcanus' 1st year	135	" 1 yr. "					
Aristobulus' reign	106	" 27th, 9 "					
Alexander's death	79	6			705	" 177-3 "	"Sabbatic."
Pompey captures Jeru	64	" 24 "			707		
Hyrcanus' end, Herod	40	" 3 "			713	" 179 "	
Herod captures Jeru	37	"34" th "27"			713		
Herod "7th year, Actium	31	8			737x	" 184 "	
" Herod's 13th, 14th "	23	13			740	" 185 "	"Sabbatic."
" Herod's 28th," Cæsarea	10	6			746	" 187 "	"Sabbatic."
Herod's death	4–3				767	" 192 "	"Sabbatic."

(See Period G, §§ 96–98.)

ITEMS AND SPECIFICATIONS.

The Year 163 B. C.

§ 5. (I.) The deposition of Menelaus from the high-priesthood by king Antiochus Eupator, as the era of substituted Maccabean rule, was in B. C. 163, and could not, in Josephus' reckoning, be any *earlier*.

Proof. Antiochus Epiphanes died in the Seleucic year 149, as stated by Josephus (Antiq. 12, ix: 2), and in the First Book of Maccabees (6:16). But in II Maccabees (10: 23, 33) the son, Antiochus Eupator, after his accession, dates his message to Lysias and to the Jews, on "the 15th of Xanthicus [Nisan] in the year 148." Whiston, in a note to Josephus (Antiq. 13, vi: 7), tells us that "the era of Seleucus is known to have begun in the 312th year before the Christian era, from its spring in the first book of Maccabees, and from its autumn in the second book of Maccabees; it did not begin at Babylon till the next spring, in the 311th year. See Prideaux at the year 312," where we find similar statements. Accordingly, the year 149 of I Mac. and Jos. began in the spring of B. C. 164; but the year 149 of II Mac. did not begin till the autumn of B. C. 164. Therefore, the Xanthicus or Nisan of its 148, when Ant. Eupator issued his message, was in April of B. C. 164; and he must have come to the throne just before that, within the same month. And the letter of Lysias, his general, dated "in the year 148, the 24th day of the month Dioscurus," or the *twin month* (II Mac. 11: 21, see in Lid. & Scott Gr. Lex.), may have been in Sivan or June, B. C. 164. These messages brought peace; "and when these covenants were made, Lysias went to the king, and the Jews gave themselves to husbandry." (II Mac. 12: 1.)

§ 6. But according to this chapter (II Mac. 12), Judas Mac. spent this year, B. C. 164, in various warlike operations, which I Mac. (Ch. 5) followed by Josephus (Ant. 12, Ch. viii), narrates before mentioning the death of Ant. Epiphanes, which preceded these things, in the spring. It was not till *the next spring*, of B. C. 163, that is, at the beginning of Josephus' Seleucic "year 150," that Judas attacked the foreign citadel in Jerusalem, as Josephus states (Antiq. 12, ix: 3). And thereupon, King Ant. Eupator being vexed changed his policy of peace, and with Lysias came against Judas; when the siege of Bethsura and of Jerusalem followed (Antiq. 12, ix: 2-5; I Mac. vi: 18-54; II Mac. xiii: 1-21). This was in the summer of B. C. 163, before the Seleucic year 149 of II Mac. ended in the autumn (II Mac. 13: 1). It was also (in September) the end of the Jews' *Sabbatic* year, causing great scarcity of food in the siege. (Antiq. 12, ix: 5; I Mac. vi: 49-54.)

A peace was finally concluded, and the enemy left that fall. It is here at the leaving of Ant. Eupator, toward the close of B. C. 163 (I Mac. vi: 55-63; II Mac. xiii: 22-26), that Josephus mentions his deposition of Menelaus, the high-priest, and having him put to death (Ant. 12, ix: 7). But in II Mac. (13: 3-8), whence the account comes, it is put in the early summer, at the coming of Ant. Eupator. At any rate, it was in B. C. 163; and *it can not be got any earlier*, because the attack of Judas upon the citadel, which preceded it, did not occur until this year 150 Sel., which began in March, B. C. 163. Moreover, the fact that that was the *Sabbatic year*, proves that it must be B. C. 163 to agree with the Sabbatics given at B. C. 135, 37 and 23. In the next spring, B. C. 162, Seleucic "151." beginning, Ant. Eupator was slain, as stated in I Mac. (vii: 1-3), having reigned just "two years," as Josephus says (Ant. 12, x: 1.)

§ 7. (II.) The deposition and death of Menelaus, as the era of established Maccabean rule, was in B. C. 163, and it could not, in Josephus' reckoning, be any *later*, for example in B. C. 162. This is not only proved by the above exhibit of the events and dates, but by the following demonstrations. (*See citations from Jos.*, § 3.)

(1.) CITATIONS 5 AND 6: The "126 years" + the "107 years." Here is given the time, from the Menelaus event, when fully "the Asmonean government was set up," to "the day when Titus took the temple" in A. D. 70—given as "126" + "107" = 233 years, or the 233d year, viz., from A. D. 70 back to B. C. 163, which is just 232 years or the 233d year. From A. D. 70 to B. C. 37 is 106 years or the "107"th year, and from B. C. 37 to 163 is just the "126 years" given. What could be a plainer demonstration, that we are correct in our reckoning of Josephus?

(2.) DOWN TO JOSEPHUS' DAY, the "471 years" + the "200 years."* Here (War. 1, iii: 1; Ant. 3, viii: 9) the time from the end of "the Babylonish slavery when our people came down into this country," until the date when Josephus "composed this book" of Antiquities, is given as "471" + "200" = 671 years, or the 671st year. But in Ant. 20, x: 1, the time from the end of the Babylonish captivity, "when they were returned home, "until King Ant. Eupator" when he "deprived Menelaus of the high-priesthood," is given as "414 years." So that, from the deposition of Menelaus to the date of Josephus' writing, he gives as 671—"414" = 257 years, or the 257th year. And in Jos. Life, § 1, he gives his own birth as "in the first year of the reign of Caius Cæsar," which was A. D. 38 (Tiberius having died March 16, A. D. 37); so that his 56 years (Ant. 20, xi: 3) reached into A. D. 94, where also ended "the 13th of Domitian who began in A. D. 81. And in that "56th year" of his life, or A. D. 94, he says he was writing.

§ 8. Hence, his "200th year before that must reach to B. C. 106, the year when "Aristobulus put on the diadem; and his 257th year just now found reaches 57 years farther, from B. C. 106 to 163, at the deposition of Menelaus. We thus find, that the two events, when "Aristobulus changed the government into a kingdom and was the first to put a diadem on his head" (War. 1, iii: 1), and when "the breast-plate (of the high-priest) left off shining, God having been displeased at the transgression of his laws (Ant. 3, viii: 9)—were synchronous events, both occurring at the year 106 B. C., just 57 years after the deposition of Menelaus. Could anything be plainer than this doubled demonstration of Josephus, by the combination of all his intervals, that we have him correct? But note,

---

* See Restor. of Jos., § 4, citations 2, 3.

The Detailed Reigns.

(3.) Take the detailed reigns from Antiochus to Herod, to see how they corroborate the "126 years" and all our reckoning.

§ 9. (a.) The Maccabean era. Josephus says (Ant. 20, x: 1), that after the captivity the Jews "until Ant. Eupator were under a democratic government 414 years,* and then "Menelaus was "deprived of the priesthood" or supremacy, giving full place for the new dynasty of Judas Maccabees and his successors. It is true, Judas gained great victories before that event, but he could not be officially recognized as the head of the government, so long as the high-priest Menelaus, was in power. And it is true, when Menelaus was deposed and killed, another man (Alcimus or Jacimus) was appointed in his place by the invader Eupator; but the *Jews* did not acknowledge him (II Mac. xiv: 3-7), and Judas was now recognized as their only sovereign. That year. B. C. 163, Seleucic 150, was the era of established Maccabean supremacy.

§ 10. (b.) The 57 years of Maccabean supremacy, until the "putting on of the diadem." This period is made up by Josephus as follows:

		B. C.	
		163	="150" (12, ix, 3)
Judas Mac. till Alcimus dth........	"3 yrs"—		
		160	(Ant. 20, x, 1)*
" after "	"3 yrs"—		
		157	(Ant. 12, xi, 2) ‡‡
Jonathan in the interim	"4 yrs"—	(Ant. 13, ii, 3)
		153	="160" (13, ii, 1)
" after "	10 yrs —		
		143	="170" (13, vi, 7)
Simon.............................	"8th—		
		136	(Ant. 13, vii, 4)‡
Hyrcanus I.........................	"30 yrs"—		
		·106	(Ant. 20, x, 1)†
	57 yrs		

*At 12, x: 6, it is wrongly "4 years."
†At 13, x: 7, it is wrongly "31 years."
‡It reads "in all 8 years," including Jonathan's *captivity* (13, vi: 2).
‡‡At 20, x: 1, this is made an interregnum *i. e.*, without high-priests "7 years." till B. C. 153, Jonathan being ruler "these seven years," and high-priest also 10 years more. Also 1 Mac. ix: 18, 56 makes Judas die before Alcimus.

---

*The citations 1, 2, 3, at §3 show, that the "414 years" date to Eupator was reduced by 2, by 5, and by 7 years, to give the several special dates of Eupator's predecessor, Epiphanes. For, the Seleucic "150, 148, 145, 143," were the years B. C. 163, 165, 168, 170: so that the desolating by Antiochus Epiphanes began in B. C. 170, or 7 years before the "414 years" expired, *i. e.*, after 407 years, called the "408th" year. (*See Restor. of Jos.*, §4 *cit. 1, 4, and §31-33*.)

§ 11. (c.) "The 126 years" of Maccabean supremacy until Herod. Besides the foregoing 57 years, there are contained 69 other years, thus:

		B. C.	
After Menelaus...............	57 yrs		
		——106	
Aristobulus, diadem...........	"1 year"—		(Ant. 13, xi, 3)
		105	
Alexander.....................	"27"th—		(Ant. 13, xv, 5)*
		79	
Alexandra....................	"9 yrs"—		(Ant. 13, xvi, 6)
		70	
Hyr. & Aristobulus.............	6 yrs—		(Ant. 20, x, 1)†
		64	
{ Hyrcanus II ("24 more")......	"24 yrs"—		(")
		40	
{ Antigonus....................	"3¼ yrs"—		(")
		——37	
	69 yrs		
After Menelaus, total..........	"126 yrs"—		(Ant. 14, xvi, 4)
Herod, ("37 after Hyr.")........	"34th"—		(Ant. 17, viii, 1)‡
	B. C. 4		

(left margin: "27"—Ant. 14, xvi, 4)

*It is given "27 years," but this includes the ignoble year of the brother Aristobulus before it.
†It reads "3 years and 6 months," which is plainly a corruption for 6 years (and 3 mo. of Hyrcanus? Ant. 14, i: 2.) See this correction in Prideaux. Pompey's conquest of Jerusalem thus comes B. C. 64, *i. e.*, at 99 years of the Maccabees, with 133 onward to Titus. (Prideaux calls it the early summer of B. C. 63.)
‡The full "34 years" and "37 years" given will bring Herod's death to B. C. 3; but it seems as though it could not be so long after the eclipse of Mar. 13, B. C. 4. (See Antiq. 17, vi: 4, note, and what follows. See also our period G, § 96-98.)

CORROBORATIONS.

§ 12. (4.) The *Olympic dates* of Josephus prove that our exhibit of his reckoning is correct, as above. Thus, examining his eight instances of such dating,‡‡ as shown in the table here (at §4), we find but one definite Olympic year specified, viz., Olym. 177: 3=707, which year must have begun in June, B. C. 70, since Olympic year 1 began in June, B. C. 776. Taking this, then, as the test of all his Olympic dates, we find six of the nine in agreement with his other dates (by Seleucic years, by reigns, and by Sabbatics); namely, at Olympic years 609, 707, 713, 740, 746, 767.

But at the Olympic year 641 he is plainly wrong, as Whiston has pointed out; Josephus' "Olympiad 162" beginning with year 645, should certainly read "Olympiad 161" beginning with year 641. Furthermore, the Olympic year 612 is *one year too small* for his "Olym. 154," and the Olympic year 737 is *one year too large* for his

---

‡‡He has a ninth instance, at Ap. I, 21, viz., the death of Alexander "in the 114th Olympiad, *i. e.*, May 22, B. C. 323. (Hales.)

"Olym. 184." These two cases of one year error in *opposite directions* prove, that we have him right, and that his three errors are either corruptions, or mistakes of a single unit in the number of the Olympiad in these two cases. On the whole, we may conclude from these nine uses of the Olympic dating, about the only ones occurring in Josephus, that he was not particularly an expert in the use of that Olympic era, which was not very familiar to the Jews. But he gives enough accurate dating of this sort, to demonstrate our exhibit of him as correct.

§ 13. (5.) The *Sabbatic Dates* of Josephus further corroborate all our adjustments of him as exact and accurate. He describes at least *four* Sabbatic years within 140 years' time, as seen in the table on page 5, with the hostile invasions invited by them, and the lack of food caused by them, under the judgment of heaven. And they all harmonize with the datings we assign him, as regular multiples of the returning 7 years' interval; from B. C. 163 to 135, to 37, to 23, and thence to A. D. 27, as each being (in September) the close of a Sabbatic year—and the last two being JUBILEE Sabbatics.* The correctness of this is indicated by the striking fact, that in the summer of A. D. 27 (the first year of His ministry), our Lord publicly read the *Jubilee selection* of scripture in the synagogue of Nazareth (Lu. iv: 16-21.) Nothing is wanting from the demonstration of our exhibit, as the assured and indisputable dating of Josephus.

BACK TO THE CAPTIVITY.

§ 14. From B. C. 170 backward, the dating of Josephus is very vague. Especially when he has passed by the Seleucic Era (B. C. 312), and has given the "12 years" of Alexander the Great (Ant. 12, ii: 1), who died in May or June, B. C. 323—beyond that he is all afloat. And we have to depend almost entirely on Ptolemy's Canon, to reach the dating of the captivity.

We thus find (by the Canon) that the 1st year of Cyrus begun in January B. C. 538 (Nabonassan), so that the conquest of Babylon may have been some months later than that. And since there follows a "first year of Darius the Mede" (Dan. ix: 1, and xi: 1), doubtless the decree in favor of the Jews "in the first year of Cyrus" (Ezra i: 1), was in B. C. 537.

The renewal of that decree in "the 2d year of Darius" Hystaspes (Ezra iv: 24), is fixed to the year B. C. 520; and the completion of the second temple in "the 6th year of Darius" (vi: 15), was in Adar

---

* Prideaux dates the rule of Judas Mac. from his father's death. Hales puts it (as we see Josephus does) from the death of Menelaus, when Judas was formally acknowledged by Ant. Eupator. And he also puts Hyrcanus I as beginning at B. C. 136, because of the Sabbatic years, which he says must come at 135 and 163 B. C., just as shown above.

(March) of B. C. 516 (or 515, if the Jews delayed the Babylonian year to their own new year in spring. § 33.

The 7th year of Artaxerxes (Ezra vii: 7), when the decree "to restore Jerusalem" was issued to Ezra, ended by the Canon in December B. C. 458; but probably some months later by the King's actual accession, namely, in B. C. 457. So that, no doubt it was in the spring of this Sabbatic year (ending B. C. 457), that Ezra received his commission. From this decree the "70 weeks" of Daniel are reckoned, reaching, the first "7 weeks" or 49 years of restoring to B. C. 408, the next "62 weeks" or 434 years to Christ's baptism in the early spring of A. D. 27 (Jubilee Sabbatic), the whole "70 weeks" or 490 years to A. D. 34, when the gospel was opened to the Gentiles. (See period G, § 105, and E, § 68.)

PART II.

Jerusalem Destroyed by Nebuchadnezzar in B. C. 587, not 588 as Generally Assigned.

Leading Evidence.

§ 15. All agree, that the reign of Nebuchadnezzar was (in accordance with Ptolemy's Canon) 43 years long, from the January *Thoth* (or Nabonassar New Year) of B. C. 604 to the January Thoth of B. C. 561.*

Now it was in summer, the middle of Nebuchadnezzar's eighteenth year, by this Ptolemaic-Babylonian reckoning, that Jerusalem was destroyed; which event must therefore be in B. C. 587, not in 588 as given in the vulgar (or Usher) chronology.

That it was in the summer of Nebuchadnezzar's eighteenth year by the Babylonian reckoning, is expressly declared by Josephus in *two* of his works, this being the only numbering which he gives. Antiq. 10. viii: 5. Versus Apion i: 21. He gives Nebuchadnezzar only 43 years of reign (Antiq. 10, xi: 1); thus following the Babylonian reckoning of Ptolemy's Canon, so that his eighteenth year of Neb. is Babylonian reckoning or B. C. 587.

Moreover, Josephus expressly tells us (Vs. Ap. i: 21), that "in our books (the O. T.) *it is written*, that Nebuchadnezzar in the eighteenth year of his reign laid our temple waste." Where in the Old Testament is this written? It is at Jer. lii: 29; and this statement of Josephus concerning it, proves that we have *here* the Babylonian reckoning of Nebuchadnezzar's reign—and that the capturing here spoken of is that connected with the destruction of Jerusalem (as given at II Ki. xxv: 9-11; II Chron. xxxvi: 19, 20; Jer. xxxix: 7-9; lii: 11-15).

That the destruction of the city was thus in the summer near the

---

*We have found only Schwartz calling this in question, and putting it B. C. 605 to 562. But he gives no proof, except his novel theory, that Ptolemy's Canon has all its dates from the Thoth *after* (not before) accession.

middle of the Babylonian year, appears not only from Josephus (as above), but also from scripture. (II Ki. xxv: 8-11; Jer. xxxix: 2; xli: 1; lii: 5-7, 12.)

FURTHER PROOF.

§ 16. Josephus (Antiq. 10, ix: 7) says, that "in the fifth year after the destruction of Jerusalem, which was the twenty-third of the reign of Nebuchadnezzar, he [by his captains] took captive those that were there (in Egypt—II Ki. xxv: 26), and led them away to Babylon." This is the very thing asserted of this "twenty-third year" of Babylonian reckoning, here at Jer. lii: 30. (See xliii: 7-12; xliv: 27, 28.)

Again, as Jerusalem was destroyed eleven years (of Zedekiah's reign) after the beginning of Jehoiachin's captivity, therefore, the twenty-fifth year of that captivity corresponds with the fourteenth year after the destruction of Jerusalem; just as it is declared in Ezek. xl: 1. Moreover, as thus Jehoiachin's captivity began eleven years before the eighteenth of Nebuchadnezzar, it began in the seventh of Nebuchadnezzar. And this is the very thing asserted of this "seventh year" of Babylonian reckoning, here at Jer. lii: 28. We have seen that Josephus expressly affirms this to be the correct view of this lii: 29. To escape it, Whiston most strangely says (Note in Jos., Ap. i: 21), "This number in Josephus, that Nebuchadnezzar destroyed the temple in the eighteenth year of his reign, *is a mistake* in the nicety of chronology; for it was in the nineteenth"—*i. e.*, by Jewish reckoning. But see the fallacy of this.

§ 17. (1.) Josephus does not follow that Jewish reckoning of Nebuchadnezzar, in any of his datings, and therefore could not rightly give the "nineteenth year." (2.) He gives it as in the "eighteenth of Nebuchadnezzar" not only here but also in his other work, as seen above, consistently adhering always to that Babylonian number. (3.) He found this "eighteenth Nebuchadnezzar" (he says) given in his Bible for the destruction of Jerusalem, viz., at this Jer. lii: 29. To say that Josephus here mistakes, is to say that he everywhere mistakes, and that the Bible itself mistakes, and that there was no Babylonian reckoning, but that the Jewish reckoning alone was correct. On the contrary, Josephus is right. He gives only the Babylonian reckoning (one year different from the Jewish); and he gives it correctly, taking it from the book of Jeremiah which has it correctly. Its "eighteenth Nebuchadnezzar" for the capturing of Jerusalem and its people is the true Babylonian date for its fall, which necessarily is B. C. 587.

Yet again, this true reckoning makes the thirty-seventh year of Jehoiachin's captivity correspond with the (7 + 37=) forty-fourth year of Nebuchadnezzar. But as Nebuchadnezzar reigned only forty-three years, his forty-fourth year was really the first year of his successor Evil Merodach, B. C. 561; just as asserted of this "thirty-seventh year of Jehoiachin's captivity" here in Jer. lii: 31, as taken from II Kings xxv: 27.

§ 18. Once more, this makes the twenty-seventh year of Jehoiachin's captivity correspond with the (7 + 27=) thirty-fourth year of Nebuchadnezzar, or B. C. 571, when he had just finished the thirteen years' seige of Tyre (Ezek. xxix: 17, 18), viz., at the end of B. C. 572. The correctness of this date is seen from the reckoning of Josephus (Vs. Ap., i: 21), where he says that "on the seventh year of Nebuchadnezzar he began to beseige Tyre for thirteen years." This makes the taking of Tyre (6 + 13) nineteen of Nebuchadnezzar (*i. e.*, of his career from his final invasion of all Syria, Judea, and Egypt, at the beginning of B. C. 590)—namely, at the close of B. C. 572, as here found.

The same is seen from Philostratus (in Josephus, Vs. Ap. i: 21, and Ant. 10, xi: 1), who says, "Nebuchadnezzar beseiged Tyre for thirteen years in the days of Ithobal their king; after him reigned Baal ten years (followed by reigns of) two months and ten months, and three months, and six years, and one year, and four years, then Hiram twenty years; under his reign Cyrus became king of Persia"—viz., in his "fourteenth year," adds Josephus. This fourteenth year of Hiram as the first of Cyrus, is here made to be the thirty-sixth after the taking of Tyre at the end of B. C. 572, viz., the beginning of B. C. 536; when, in the view of Josephus and the Jews, Cyrus issued his decree in his first year after the death of "Darius the Mede." "So that (adds Josephus) the whole interval is fifty-four years besides three months;" *i. e.* (35 + 13 + 2 years of Nebuchadnezzar), "fifty years" from the end of B. C. 537 back to 587 or (+ 4=) "fifty-four years" to the end of B. C. 591.

§ 19. Prideaux treats Josephus as if beginning Cyrus with the fall of Babylon in B. C. 538; and so he makes the thirty-sixth year preceding carry the fall of Tyre back to B. C. 583, and the fall of Jerusalem to B. C. 588. But that Josephus puts the Cyrus decree at the beginning of B. C. 36, appears from Vs. Ap. i: 21, where he says: "In the eighteenth year of Nebuchadnezzar's reign he laid our temple desolate, and so it laid in that state of obscurity *for fifty years;* but that in the second year of the reign of Cyrus *its foundations were laid,*" etc., *i. e.*, the decree for that purpose having been issued in the first year of Cyrus. (See Ezra i: 1, comp. with iii: 8-13.) This "fifty years" certainly begins with B. C. 587, and therefore ends with B. C. 537, as we have seen. The *decree* itself Josephus puts in "the first year of Cyrus" (Ant. 11, i: 1), *i. e.*, in B. C. 537, by no means so early as B. C. 538.

CORRECTED VIEW OF JER. lii: 28-30.

§ 20. Jeremiah proper ends with the 51st chapter, as seen by its last verse. The 52d chapter was added as a summary, being taken from II Kings xxiv: 18-25, 30; except that for ver. 22-26 in Kings is interpolated the summary of ver. 28-30 in Jeremiah. This interpolation is evidently a *Babylonian* enumeration of the captives, and therefore is expressed with Babylonian numbering of Nebuchadnezzar's years (7 and 18 and 23, for 8 and 19 and 24), instead of the Hebrew numbering found in the rest of the Bible.

The British Commentary (of Jamieson, Fausset and Brown) rightly assigns the seventh and eighteenth of Nebuchadnezzar as here given, to the beginning and end of Zedekiah's reign. But it fails to give the true reason why these numbers are here used in place of eighth and nineteenth employed elsewhere (See Ver. 12). Its explanation concerning the *fewness* of the captives here enumerated is in part correct. Ver. 28, 29, "Nebuchadnezzar carried away," give only the *official* captives, sent or coming to Nebuchadnezzar's headquarters, and by him *personally* taken to Babylon, as seen at II Kings xxiv: 12, 15, and II Chron. xxxvi: 10, and Jer. xxxix: 4-7, and lii: 7-11, with Josephus 10, viii: 2; not including the greater numbers carried off by means of his generals, as seen at II Kings xxiv: 14, 16, and xxv: 11, with Jer. xxxix: 9, and lii: 15 (also Ver. 30).

§ 21. From an oversight of the fact here brought out, that Jer. lii: 28, 30, is a later addendum drawn from Babylonian data, being the list of Nebuchadnezzar's own official captives, has arisen the error of Usher, Lowth and the vulgar chronology generally; which treats the "7th" and "18th" here given as the Hebrew numbering of years. So that they are thus made to refer to some unrelated capturings *one year before* the great capturings of the "8th" and "19th" years given in II Ki. xxiv: 12, and xxv: 8 (copied at Jer. lii: 12).

Thus Lowth (in Scott): "Archbishop Usher supposes that this Jer. lii: 28, 30, gives an account of the lesser captivities which the Jews suffered under Neb., whereas there were three others, viz: in the 1st year of his reign, in the 8th year, and in the 19th year when the city was destroyed." Prideaux even strangely calls this "7th year" (of ver. 28) the 7th of Jehoiakim instead of Neb.; although it is the latter alone referred to, and there is no allusion to the former in all the context. To such marvelous devices does a missing of the truth lead on.

Now note, on the contrary, that neither in the Bible nor in any other history have we the least hint of any such carrying away of captives in those extra imagined years; nor do the circumstances allow such suppositions. And above all it is impossible to regard the book of Jeremiah as here summing up the captives by announcing: "*This is the people* whom Neb. carried away captive," and then naming only three "lesser captivities" with the three principal (in fact the only real) capturings entirely unnoticed!! It is plain, that the capturings here given are at the closed reigns of Jehoiakim and Zedekiah, 11 years apart, together with the later deportations, at which three times occurred the only general capturings known; since that of Dan. i: 3, was only a selection of "children."

Josephus' "23d Neb."

§ 22. Although Josephus gives the final capturing of the Jews as "*on the 5th year* after the destruction of Jerusalem, which was the 23d year of the reign of Neb." by Babylonian reckoning; yet he probably thought of it as only *four full years*, or at the very beginning of the Babylonian 23d (or end of the Jewish 23d), putting the Babylonian year as closing along with the Jewish year (in September), only 1 year later. So he made the Babylonian 1st of Neb, parallel with the 5th of Jehoiakim, B. C. 605-4. (See Antiq.: 10, vi: 1.)

This "23d of Neb." as in the autumn of B. C. 583 for 4 years after the destruction of the city), was the time Jews *got through leaving Palestine* for Egypt, there to be captured and carried to Babylon. For the migration into Egypt, stated at II Ki. xxv: 26, Jer. xliii: 7, was doubtless in successive bands going to different localities (xliv: 1, 26) during four years; until a last flight at rumor of the new coming Babylonian invasion of 23d Neb. (See our Restor. of Jos., § 29.)

Hebrew Reckoning of Nebuchadnezzar.

§ 23. The Hebrews at Jerusalem began the reckoning of Neb.'s reign earlier, from his first coming to besiege Jerusalem before the death of his father; namely, in the summer of B. C. 606, over a year from the Babylonian beginning of his reign.

This Jewish beginning of Neb. was near the close of the 3d year of Jehoiakim, as stated in Dan. i: 1; II Ki. xxiv: 1. So that the years of Neb. were computed along with the Jewish civil years, the 4th of Jehoiakim being called the 1st of Nebuchadnezzar, as said at Jer. xxv: 1, and xlvi: 2, and beginning from September B. C. 606. (So *Prideaux connec.*) Thus Neb's reign was made over 44 (instead of 43) years; and from its beginning in B. C. 606 to the Cyrus decree (at the end of B. C. 537) there were 70 years of servitude, as foretold at its beginning. (Jer. xxv: 1, 9, 11.) The Bible is mostly written with this Hebrew reckoning of Neb., the only exception being Jer. lii: 28-30, as shown above —unless we add also Dan. ii: 1.

Study of Daniel ii: 1.

§ 24. Most expositors interpret "the 2d year of the reign of Nebuchadnezzar," in Dan ii: 1, as meaning his 2d Babylonian year, B. C. 603. But this seems hardly to comport with chapter 1, or with this chapter 2, verse 13, 25, 26, 48. How could Daniel, only 3 years after his boyhood of chapter 1, be regularly numbered among the wise *men* of Babylon? and yet so soon, within a few weeks after, i: 19, 20, be all unsought for by Neb. in his extremity? and so little known and understood by him? and how improbable, that a youth (not over 18) was then made a great *man* and ruler over the whole province of Babylon, and *chief* of the governors." Moreover, the complete supremacy of Neb. described in verses 37, 38, seems better to fit him after his later conquests.

§ 25. This dilemma is escaped by Josephus; who (in Antiq. 10, x. 3) renders it, as " two years after the destruction of Egypt," and he elsewhere (Vs. Ap. i, 21) dates the years of Neb. from B. C. 590. (See here §18.) The meaning might be (as in the LXX) "the second year of supremacy, that is, over Egypt, or over the nations generally, or over Jerusalem destroyed in B. C. 587. This would well fit Ezek. xiv: 12-20,* and Ezek. xxviii: 3.†

Scripture Evidence.

§ 26. The Hebrew reckoning of Nebuchadnezzar is seen at Jer. xxxii: 1, which says, "the 10th year of Zedekiah was the 18th year of Nebuchadnezzar"; also in Jer. xxv: 1, 3, which says, "the 4th year of Jehoiakim was the 1st year of Nebuchadnezzar," being "the three and twentieth year from the 13th year of Josiah." Now, Josiah's 31 years with 12 whole years taken out leave 19, and 3 whole years of his son Jehoiakim added make 22 whole years, giving the 4th of Jehoiakim as the 23d year from Josiah's 13th—just as here stated.

This made the 11th of Jehoiakim to be the 8th of Neb., at the close of which 11th year (in summer) Jehoiachin was taken captive, as stated

---

*Ezekiel's first reference to Daniel as already celebrated, is near or after the destruction of Jerusalem. For his first 15 chapters reach from the 5th year of Jehoiachin's captivity (i: 2), past the 6th year (viii: 1), on through the 11th (xii: 26-27), and still on after the destruction of Jerusalem (xiii: 1, 5, 10, 16). After which, at chap. xvi, a new series goes back to an earlier date, and forward again to the 7th year (xx: 1), and to the 9th year (xxiv: 1), and the 11th year (xxvi: 1), and afterward. So that chapter xiv may thus come after the destruction of Jerusalem, at about B. C. 585; as seen at verses 21-23, "When I send my judgments" *as I have*, "a remnant shall be brought—they shall come forth unto you [to Bablyon, as in Jer. lii: 30]—and ye shall be comforted concerning the evil that *I have brought* upon Jerusalem," and at xv: 5-7, "they shall go out from one fire, another fire shall devour them," viz: in Egypt (comp. Jer. xlii: 7:11, and xliv: 12-14).

†This comparing of Tyre with Daniel was made long after the destruction of Jerusalem, when the fame of Daniel was widely spread. (Dan. ii: 46-48.) For the prophecies of Ezekiel are in clusters. Those against Tyre begin with the 26th chapter: viz., in the 11th year of Jehoiachin's captivity and of Zedekiah's reign, Sep., B. C. 588; and they continue from time to time (xxvii: 1; xxviii: 1; xi: 20), until Tyre was taken (xxix: 17) just before the 27th year beginning Sep., B. C. 572. Then Egypt is treated from the 10th year (xxix: 1), with episode (ver. 17) to the 11th year (xxxi: 1), and the 12th year (xxxii: 1, 32): after which, chap. xxxiii-xl is general, beginning before the 12th year (xxxiii: 21.) As Ezek. xxix: 17 is at the 27th year," viz., B. C. 472, the reference to Daniel at xxviii : 3, may well be about B. C. 580, not 588 as Prideaux makes it.

in II Ki. xxiv: 12. So, 10 years afterward, the 10th of Zedekiah was the 18th of Neb., as given at Jer. xxxii: 1. And the next year, the destruction of Jerusalem (in summer) near the *close* of Zedekiah's 11th year (Jer. i: 3) was also the close of Neb.'s 19th year in this reckoning, just as given at II Ki. xxv: 8, and copied at Jer. lii: 12.

As the 1st year of Neb. by this reckoning began with the Hebrew civil year, Sep., B. C. 606, the 19th Neb. thus ended 19 years afterward, at Sep., B. C. 587; just before which, in the summer of that 587, Jerusalem was destroyed; for it was in the 5th Jewish month (or August), as stated at II Ki. xxv: 8.

And thus, by both reckonings alike, Jerusalem's destruction was in B. C. 587, not 588 as commonly said: which was 25½ years before Neb.'s ending at the Jan. Thoth of B. C. 561, and 17½ years after Neb.'s accession in B. C. 604; total 43 years.

Decisive Verification.

§ 27. There were 22 whole years from the destruction of Jerusalem back to the death of Josiah. For, Jehoiakim reigned 11 whole years (including 3 months interposed, II Ki. xxiii: 31, 36; II Chron. xxxvi: 2, 5): and then Zedekiah reigned 11 whole years (including 3 mo. 10 days interposed, II Ki. xxiv: 8, 18; II Chron. xxxvi: 9, 11; Jer. i: 3.) Now these 22 years back to Josiah added to the last 18 years of Josiah, give just 40 years from the destruction of Jerusalem back to the end of Josiah's 13th year, at which time Jeremiah's warning prophesy commenced. (Jer. i: 2.)

From the finished capturing 4½ years after the destruction of Jerusalem (Neb. 23d, Jer. lii: 30), there were also just 40 years back to Josiah's reformation, at the spring Passover of his 18th year, 4½ years after his 13th year ended, II Ki. xxii: 3, and xxiii: 21-23, II Chron. xxxiv: 8, and xxxv: 1, 17), from which 18th year Ezekiel's warning prophesy was dated. For, he says (i: 1, 2), his "30th year was the 5th year of Jehoiachin's captivity," *i. e.*, there were 25 years between his date and the capture of Jehoiachin, viz., the 11 years of Jehoiakim and 14 years of Josiah's 31 (II Ki. xxii: 1, 2; II Chron. xxxiv: 1), making his date to begin with Josiah's 18th year, from B. C. 623 to 583.

Now, Ezekiel (iv: 6) assigns just these 40 years for the "iniquity (or hardening) of the house of Judah," until the accomplished "siege of Jerusalem" (verse 7, 8). This proves our reckoning of the reigns to be correct.

§ 28. But we thus have 19 whole years from the destruction of Jerusalem back to the first invasion of Neb., which was near the close of 3 full years of Jehoiakim, as shown before. That invasion was in the summer, as Jerusalem was finally taken in the summer; so that there were even years. These 19 years were from B. C. 587 back to B. C. 606 in summer, at which time the 4th of Jehoiakim must commence, *i. e.*, with the Jewish civil year in September, called also by the Jews the 1st year of Neb., owing to his *then* invading the land. This brings the destruction of Jerusalem near the *end of Neb.'s 19th year* by the Hebrew reckoning (viz., in the summer of B. C. 587), just as declared in scripture, and even by Usher himself (at year 3416).

The Sabbatic Year.

§ 29. The destruction of Jerusalem being rightly assigned to B. C. 587, near the end of Zedekiah's 11th year, it follows that the commencement of the siege, in the 9th year in the 10th month (II Ki. xxv: 1; Jer. xxxix: 1, and lii: 4; Ezek. xxiv: 1), was in December, B. C. 590 (as set by Prideaux himself); just before which, in that year 590, Zedekiah had revolted. (II Ki. xxiv: 20; II Chron. xxxvi: 13; Jer. lii: 3.) So Josephus (Antiq. 10, vii: 3, 4, and viii: 1, 2, 5), "When Zedekiah had preserved the league *for 8 years*, he broke it * * * the king of Babylon made war * * * but departed from Jerusalem * * * the false prophets deceived Zedekiah * * * Jeremiah said they should serve Babylon seventy years * * * Jeremiah was imprisoned * * * Now in the 10th year of Zedekiah on the 10th day of the month, the king of Babylon made a second expedition against Jerusalem, and lay before it 18 months and besieged it * * * a famine and pestilence * * * siege 18 months * * * the city was taken on the 9th day of the 4th month in the 11th year of Zedekiah * * * in the 5th month, 1st day in the 11th year of Zedekiah, and the 18th of Neb., he also burnt the place."

§ 30. Now the Jewish *Sabbatic year* ended with Zedekiah's 9th year in September, B. C. 590. For, according to Josephus, the year B. C. 137 closed a Sabbatic, as also B. C. 163. (§ 13.) So 40 Sabbatics before that, or 280 years, at B. C. 443, ended a Sabbatic (see Neh. x: 31, that year): and so, 77 years before that, at B. C. 520; also 10 Sabbatics before that, at B. C. 590. At that time, Zedekiah, warned by the prophet, proclaimed liberty to Hebrews in servitude, in accordance with the Mosaic law (Jer. xxxiv: 8, 9); and also himself declared independence of Babylon. But when Nebuchadnezzar, after being thus brought upon him (ver. 1), had left for a time to meet the king of Egypt (ver. 21 and xxxvii: 11), Zedekiah grew arrogant, and again enslaved the freedmen; for which Jeremiah rebuked him (xxxiv: 11-22) in B. C. 589. (See period E, § 69-74.)

Then Neb. returned, just one year after his previous siege began, as Josephus states, viz., in Dec., B. C. 589, the 10th year of Zedekiah having begun in Sep. along with the 18th of Neb. by Jewish reckoning (Jer. xxxii: 1, 2); and after 18 months' siege he destroyed the city, in the 4th and 5th months, or summer of B. C. 587. So then, from Zedekiah's revolt and Neb.'s siege at the close of the Sabbatic, B. C. 590, there were just 70 years of *land-sabbath* (II Chron. xxxvi: 13, 20, 21), to the close of the Sabbatic, B. C. 520, the 2d of Darius, when his decree practically released the land.

§ 31. Now the fact of the Sabbatic in B.C. 590, fixing the arrival of Neb. and so the beginning of the 9th Zed. to that year, and aggravating the consequent famine (Jer. xxi: 2, 9), compels the ending of 11th Zed. and the destruction of the city (Jer. i: 3) to be in B. C. 587, over 30 months afterward. And when Prideaux makes the taking of the city only some 18 months afterward, he is confounding the *second* approach of Neb. after having gone to meet the Egyptians (which Josephus expressly says was 18 months before the conquest, viz., in 10th Zed. or Dec. 1, B.C. 589), with his *first* coming a year before, in the 9th Zed. 10th month, or Dec. B. C. 590. (This 10th month from spring must not be misunderstood, as the 10th month of the year's reign, which began in September. Confusion on this point has made much of the current mistaken reckoning.)

Further Confirmation.

§ 32. The destruction of Jerusalem being rightly assigned to B. C. 587, there are just 70 years of *fasting for the temple desolation*, from this time to the finishing of the second temple with the year B. C. 517, as stated in Zech. vii: 5. For it was at the beginning of B. C. 516 (as set by Hales) that the dedication of Ezra vi: 15-19, took place, not in B. C. 515, as set by the Usher Chronology.

The 1st year of Darius, by Ptolemy's Canon was the Nabonassan year of (365 days) from Jan. 1 to Dec. 31, B. C. 521 (Julian Bissextile), each of those dates being that year the Egyptian *Thoth* or new year's day. (§ 2.) We learn from Ezra iv: 24, etc., that the temple was recommenced in the second year of Darius (B. C. 520), and from Hag. i: 1-15, we learn that it was commenced in the sixth Jewish month of that year, viz., Elul (about September) Haggai prophesied in that month, and also in the seventh and ninth months (Hag. ii: 1, 10, 18, 20).

In the fourth year of Darius, "in the fourth day of the ninth month, even in Chisleu, (Zech. vii: 1-5), *i. e.*, in December, of B. C. 518, Zechariah received a Divine message concerning the *fasts*, which, had then been observed "these seventy years;" *i. e., seventy times annually* from the destruction of Jerusalem, B. C. 587-518 *inclusive*.

And in the sixth year of Darius, on the third day of the month Adar (the twelfth Jewish month), *i. e.*, about the end of February, the temple was finished; its dedication being closely connected with the following passover about the beginning of April. (Ezra vi: 15-22.) This was B. C. 516, the sixth of Darius having begun with the Babylonian year, December 30, before. So that the seventy years of temple ruin reached from the summer of B. C. 587 to the summer of B. C. 517, a few months before the new temple was dedicated.

§ 33. Prideaux and others in the vulgar chronology, make this dedication to be in the spring of B. C. 515, considering "the sixth year of Darius" here as *delayed* to end with the Jewish year at Nisan (or March). But this is not probable. For, although Zech. i: 1-7, looks like such a delay of the Babylonian year there is no other instance of such delayed reckoning; certainly not in Ezra. On the contrary, Jer. i: 3, is decisive that "the fifth month" was near "the end of the year" of a reigning king; and Nehemiah (i: 1 & 2: 1), makes the ninth Jewish month (December) and the following first Jewish month (April) to be both in the same 20th year of Artaxerxes at the Persian court; which therefore does not begin with the Jewish new year, but back as early as the Egyptian new year or *Thoth*, then at December 12th. This plainly settles it, that the reckoning of Ezra and Nehemiah, who lived at the Persian court, was the Persian reckoning, *not delayed*, but back as far as from Thoth to Thoth. Since, therefore, it is Ezra who says that the temple was finished in "the twelfth month which was in the sixth year of Darius," he must mean that twelfth Jewish month which came in the sixth Persian or actual year of Darius (as early as December, B. C. 517 to December, 516), namely, the March of B. C. 516, not of 515 as Prideaux alleges: which latter is over seventy-one and one-half years after the destruction of Jerusalem in B. C. 587.

Indeed, Prideaux himself (at year 561), bases his chronology on the fact, that the Jews reckoned the years of the Bab. kings as beginning *before* their own vernal new year; thus making the 37th year of their own king Jehoiachin to *end* in the first year of Evil Merodach. The Zech. i: 1-7, is very likely a relict of that Jewish *antedating* (not delay) of Babylonian regnal years as coincident with the Hebrew regnal or civil year (from September) which prevailed before (as we have seen) in the days of Nebudchadnezzar. Thus viewed, Zech. i: 1, is, in the last part of the actual first year of Darius, and verse 7 is near the beginning of the actual second of Darius, when as yet the temple was not recommenced (see vers. 12-16) of which there is no intimation till a later day (iv: 1-9).

§ 34. In September of this second year of Darius, B. C. 520, ended the Sabbatic year, just seventy years (as said in Zech i: 12) after the Sabbatic of B. C. 590, when Neb. invaded the land. And as then, it was followed by a famine. This was employed by Haggai (II: 6-11, and ii: 16-19) as an argument for recommencing the temple. That work was accordingly entered upon before this 2d of Darius expired (Hag. i: 1, 12-15, and ii: 1, 10, 18, 20); although some pleaded "the time is not come, the time that the Lord's house should be built," *i. e.*, the seventy years of its actual desolation (from B. C. 587) were not yet out. This would hardly have been said had the interval been longer, from B. C. 588 as commonly alleged.

After this, "in the 4th year of King Darius, in the fourth day of the ninth month, even in Chisleu," *i. e.*, in Nov., B. C. 518, Zech. (vii: 1-5), received a divine message concerning the *fasts* "in the fifth and seventh month" (as well as the fourth and tenth months, viii: 19), which had then been observed "these seventy years." Now the fasts of the fourth, fifth and seventh months were for the destruction of Jerusalem, and of the temple, and of the remnant under Gedaliah (II Ki. xxv: 2, 3, 8, 25), in July, August and October of B. C. 587; and the seventieth recurrence of these (including the events themselves) was in the year B. C. 518, when Zechariah (vii: 1-5) thus spoke of it. The fast of the tenth month (viii: 19) was for the assault of Neb. in December, B. C. 590 (II Ki. xxv: 1, etc.), and his renewed seige in December, B. C. 589 (Jer. xxxiv: 22, and xxxii: 1, 2), and had been observed just seventy years, in November, B. C. 518, when Zechariah (vii: 1-5) gave that duration of the fasts. Thus all the datings were reconciled by our corrected view.

§ 35. And so, reviewing our study here, we see that the captivity was *cumulative*, having not only a seventy years of *capture* from B. C. 606 to 536 the return; but then also a seventy years of *land-Sabbath* from the Sabbatic, B. C. 590 to the Sabbatic, B. C. 520, of recultivation; and still further a seventy years of *desolation* from the ruin to the rebuilding of the temple, B. C. 587 to 517-16. *

Origin of the Current Error.

Usher mistook the time of Neb's. first invasion of Judea, supposing (on account of Dan. i: 5, 18) that the Jewish pre-reckoning of his reign must be over two whole years before the Babylonian commencement of it; namely, in B. C. 607 (instead of B. C. 606, over one year before January, 604). So that nineteen years of Neb. from this invasion *thus reckoned* end in B. C. 588; and there he puts the destruction of Jerusalem in the vulgar chronology which has come down from him.

---

* Josephus makes out another seventy years, from the Sabbatic B. C. 583, which ended the *finished* capturing of 23d Neb., to the Sabbatic B. C. 513; not until which passover does he make the second temple to be really finished and re-dedicated, after seven years' progress from the Sabbatic B. C. 520. (Ant. 11: iv: 7). This gives him "seventy weeks," or 490 years or ten jubilee periods from the dedication of Solomon's temple at the jubilee passover of B. C. 1003 (the correct date as he has it, one year later than Usher) down to the jubilee passover of B. C. 513, as the rededication date. Such was the divine cycle as cherished by Jewish tradition, preliminary to the "seventy weeks" of Daniel ix: 24.

Thus we read in Usher: "A. M. 3467 (beginning October, 538 B. C.), last part of the first year of Darius the Mede (*i. e.*, of B. C. 538); here begins the seventieth year from the taking of the city at the first of Neb.," which is thus made to be in (538+69—) 607 B. C. Again he says: "A. M. 3416 (ending October, 588), Jerusalem taken, the last of Neb's. nineteenth year, the beginning of the first year of the 48th Olympiad year, 160 of Nabonassar." These data all make Neb. begin in B. C. 607.

Modified Form of Error.

§ 37. Usher's long antedating of Neb. was soon seen to be utterly untenable. For, according to Berosus in Josephus, Ant. 10, xi: 1, and Vs. Ap. I, 19, at his invasion of Judea Neb. was on his way to subdue Egypt; which was no sooner done in the very next year, than he at once took the throne at Babylon; his father having died before Egypt was left. Therefore, since a Babylonian reign was by the canon numbered only to the January *Thoth* or new year *before* its close, the first of Neb. by the canon *could not begin more than one whole year after the invasion into Judea.*

Consequently, Prideaux, Calmet, and others corrected back the invasion of Neb. to its true year, B. C. 606 (requiring the "three years" of Dan. i: 5, 18, to reach to the very end of B. C. 604, the "second year of Neb. in ii: 1). But they failed to correct back also the destruction of Jerusalem to its true year, B. C. 587, as required to make out the nineteen years for a certainty intervening. For, they still wrongly thought, that the Jewish antedating of Neb. was just two full years, or rather, was a regular Babylonian partnership of the throne, and not Jewish antedating. And by this means, they had B. C. 588 still *in* the Jewish nineteenth of Neb. though not ending at its close.

§ 38. See now the necessary results. (1.) The required nineteen years from the invasion to the destruction of Jerusalem are reduced to eighteen, and the interval back to Josiah is only twenty-one instead of the correct twenty-two years; and the reign of Zedekiah is reduced to ten years, in place of the assured eleven. This eleven is certain, not only from II Kings xxiv: 8, 18, and II Chron. xxxvi: 9, 11, before cited, but also from Ezek. xl: 1 ("25th year minus 14th year"— 11 years); and especially from Jer. i: 3 ("unto the end of the 11th year of Zedekiah"), and Ezek. xxxiii: 21, the news of Jerusalem's overthrow not reaching Ezekiel in Babylon until "the 12th year," viz, December, B. C. 587. Prideaux does indeed try to mend the matter, and to get the destruction of Jerusalem (at his B. C. 588) within the beginning of Zedekiah's 11th year, by putting back the beginning of the Jewish regnal years to the spring, in place of their true autumnal reckoning by the civil year. But this device is by no means allowable, as we show elsewhere; and this beginning of the 11th year by no means makes out eleven years as required.

§ 39. (2.) Moreover, the forty years of Ezek. iv: 6, from the 18th of Josiah to the completed capturing at 23d Neb., are reduced to thirty-nine, contrary to the claim of Prideaux himself (at year 584). Here note that, beyond Josiah the Usher reckoning is returned to by Prideaux, an extra year being gratuitously inserted after Amon, to make up for the one he has wrongfully left out from Zedekiah. Because, he remarks, "the chronology of *the ensuing history makes necessary* to be here *supposed* * * * certain odd months over and above"! Indeed! If he had only left the destruction of Jerusalem correctly at B. C. 587, he would have had all right and even, without need of *supposition* and "odd months" contrived.

(3.) Not only is all this falsity produced by this too-long antedating of Neb's invasion, but, moreover, the two years of co-reign is in itself unallowable. The testimony of Berosus, from whom alone the facts are learned, is, that the father "committed to his son, who was still but a youth, some part of his army, and sent them against the enemy." Not a word about "admitting him as partner in the empire," as Prideaux (year 607) and Rollin (Hist. Assyr.) put it. That theory is a pure assumption without authority. It was a *Jewish antedating* of Neb., and, therefore, must correspond with Jewish civil years, numbering Neb. along with their own regnal years from September to September. This was the very time of year when he attacked their city, as Prideaux himself testifies, saying he did not get possession of the city till November, B. C. 606.

§ 40. (4.) Still further, this putting of the 1st Neb. to begin back in the 3d of Jehoiakim, instead of having it correspond with the 4th of Jehoiakim, is directly contrary to Jer. xxv: 1, and xxxii: 1, and Jos. Ant. 10, vi: 1, and the testimony of Prideaux himself (at year 607). Moreover, thus to make the Jewish 19th Neb. expire in January of B. C. 587, before Zedekiah's eleven years are out in September, contrary to II Ki. xxiv: 18, with xxv: 8, this is to make the Jewish 8th Neb. expire in January, B. C. 598 before Jehoiakim's eleven years are out in September, contrary to II Ki. xxiii: 36, with xxiv: 12.

(5.) And yet again, this vulgar date, B. C. 588, for the destruction of Jerusalem, is only the 17th of Neb. by the Babylonian reckoning: whereas it was certainly the 18th of Neb., as given by Josephus, who evidently follows that forty-three-year reckoning of the reign, and as given also by Jeremiah (lii: 29). There is no authority whatever for putting this event back to the 17th of Neb., or $27\frac{1}{2}$ (instead of the correct $26\frac{1}{2}$) years before the end of his forty-three-year reign.

Important Conclusions.

§ 41. For these reasons, we pronounce the 588 assignment an evident mistake, and set down B. C. 587 as most clearly the date of Jerusalem's destruction.*

The wrong dating of this event has *put back the whole previous chronology of Usher one year too early.* And, since the Usher intervals can be shown to be otherwise correct back to the reign of Solomon, this vulgar chronology has the date of David's reign, and Solomon's temple, and all subsequent events down to the captivity, one year wrong.

Hence the present readjustment is important, as a basis for all the Old Testament dates.

---

* The theory of a still later assignment for Jerusalem's overthrow, as in B. C. 586, was early given by Syncellus, followed by Scaliger, then by Jackson, and finally by Hales within the present century. It was founded upon an attempted modification of Ptolemy's Canon, and is here passed by as entirely untenable. The strange theorizings of Seyffarth and Thurman, upon still later assignments, need not here be noticed.

PERIOD E—THE KINGS.

PART I.

FROM SOLOMON'S TEMPLE TO THE CAPTIVITY.

§ 1. Proceeding backward, the last division of the kings reaches back to the capture of Samaria; the middle division reaches thence to the death of Solomon; and the earlier division reaches thence to the founding of the Temple.

CHAPTER I.

THE CAPTURE OF JERUSALEM, ETC.

The capture of Jerusalem being fixed at B. C. 587, it follows that the capture of Samaria was 133 years before, at B. C. 720. For the intermediate reigns are certainly as follows: Hezekiah's 29—the 6 elapsed=23+Manasseh 55+Amon 2+Josiah 31+Jehoahaz and Jehoiakim 11+Jehoiachin and Zedekiah 11=total, 133 years. These numbers are assured to us by II Ki. xviii: 2, 10, and xxi: 1, 19, and xxi: 1, and xxiii: 31, 36, and xxiv: 8, 18; and the same numbers are doubly assured to us by II Chron. xxix: 1, and xxxiii: 1, 21, and xxxiv: 1, and xxxvi: 2, 5, 9, 11. There is no way to increase the total 133, so as to carry the capture of Samaria to 722 B. C.

§ 2. It has been fashionable of late, particularly among Assyriologists, to assign the capture of Samaria to B. C. 722; and the reason given is, that an Assyrian monument of King Sargon says, that in "his 13th year" he conquered Babylon, while Ptolemy's Canon "makes Sargon begin his reign over Babylon at B. C. 709." (*Dic. of Relig. Knowl., Art. Assyria.*) Hence, it is argued that Sargon must have begun in (B. C. 709+13=)722; and as one of his inscriptions says he conquered Samaria "in the beginning of his reign," therefore that event must have been in B. C. 722. But see how fallacious is this reckoning.

§ 3. As B. C. 709 was only "the 13th year" of Sargon, his first year began but twelve whole years before, in B. C. 721; and his conquest of Samaria near "the beginning of his reign" was naturally in B. C. 720 (during his first year), just as scripture makes it. Moreover, while one inscription of Sargon (K. 2688) thus makes his conquest of Babylon to be in his thirteenth year, another inscription of his (a tablet in the Louvre) calls it "the twelfth year of Sargon" (see *Eponym Canon*, p. 86), which certainly puts the capture of Samaria in B. C. 720. Still further observe, that since the canon of Ptolemy always dates a reign from the Thoth *before* it actually began (as shown conclusively by Hales and others)*, therefore, its assigning of Sargon to Babylon in B. C. 709, shows that his real conquest there was certainly as late as the *end* of B. C. 709, with his first year down to B. C. 720.†

§ 4. There is, therefore, no occasion to change the date of Samaria's overthrow away from its established location as in B. C. 720, where scripture assigns it. In B. C. 723, after three years of Hezekiah, Shalmaneser, King of Assyria, besieged Samaria, and after his death, his son, Sargon, took the city in B. C. 720, when Hezekiah had reigned six years. (II Ki. xviii: 9, 10.) The expression "*they* took it," indicates that it was not the same king ending the siege as the one who began it. There is no way to increase the total 133 years, so as to carry the capture of Samaria back to B. C. 722.

The Death of Solomon.

§ 5. The history of the Ten Tribes, or the time between Solomon's death and the capture of Samaria is the great modern battle-ground of scripture chronology. We shall presently proceed to demonstrate that this interval, covering the duration of the Kingdom of Israel, was by scripture put 254 years from B. C. 720 to 974, the date of Solomon's death (though Assyriologists are trying to reduce it over 40 years, to about B. C. 930). For the present take for granted the B. C. 974 as the true Bible date.

The Founding of the Temple.

§ 6. This was "in the 4th year of Solomon," and as Solomon reigned "40 years," it was (40—4th=) 37 years before his death, viz., in

---

*See Period F, § 2.

†Schwartz tells us that in its method "the canon of Ptolemy simply exemplifies the universal Semitic habit, as illustrated by the Eponym canon (of Assyria) and by the annals of Judah and Israel." So then, the canon's assignment of B. C. 709 for the beginning of Sargon at Babylon may indicate a real beginning of reign there in B. C. 708;—and "the 13th year" will carry us only to B. C. 720 as the real beginning of Sargon, which in like manner is antedated to the new year in B. C. 721 (not 722) by the Eponym Canon. Note also, that this accords better with the Eponym Canon itself, which has Sargon as Eponym in B. C. 719, making his accession (the usual two years before) to be in B. C. 721. "Prof. Hechler, in his address before the Oriental Congress in London on 'Assyriology and the Bible,' said, that the biblical statements and the results of scientific research unite in making 721 or 720 B. C. the date for the capture of Samaria." (*Boston Watchman*, Oct., 1892.)

(B. C. 974+37=) 1011 B. C. For a discussion of "The 4th year of Solomon," see Period D, Appendix A, § 41. This B. C. 1011 may be considered as the determinate scripture date for Solomon's Temple.

Usher has Nebuchadnezzer's destruction of Jerusalem in his A. M. 3416, B. C. 588, with the interval 133 years back to the fall of Samaria, as in B. C. 721, and 254 years back to the revolt of Jereboam as in B. C. 975, and 40 years back to the death of David as in B. C. 1015, or 427 years before the destruction of Jerusalem in B. C. 588. But we have shown conclusively (in Period F, § 15, etc.) that Nebuchadnezzar *took the city a year later*, in B. C. 587; and this throws down all those dates one year to B. C. 587, 720, 974, 1014, which last may be considered as the now-settled date of Solomon's accession to his "40 years'" reign.

There is one other subject belonging here, as introductory to our study of the Assyriological claims (which will presently come before us), viz:

CHAPTER II.

Hezekiah's "14th Year.

The Harmony of Isaiah, xxxvi: 1, with Assyrian Datings.

"Now it came to pass in the fourteenth year of King Hezekiah, that Sennacherib, King of Assyria, came up against all the defenced cities of Judah, and took them."

§ 7. By the scripture chronology, Hezekiah's 14th year of reign began B. C. 712. At which time Sargon was king of Assyria, reigning B. C. 721-705, followed by his son Sennacherib, who, on his inscriptions at B. C. 701-2 (we are told by Assyriologists), describes his *third campaign* as an invasion and plundering of Hezekiah's domain. This would be Hezekiah's 24th year, instead of the "14th;" and, therefore, some propose to consider the "14th" as a corruption of the text, as suggested by Dr. Geikie, in the *S. S. Times*, Jan. 9, 1892.

But this supposition involves a similar corruption at II Ki. xviii: 17; and worse still, it contradicts the subsequent history; which (at Isa. xxxviii: 1, and II Ki. xx: 1) gives Hezekiah's sickness as "in those days" (viz. of Sennacherib's coming). And as the sickness was "15 years" before the end of his 29 (ver. 5), its date must be in the *end* of his 14th year—the coming of Sennacherib having been near the *beginning* of that 14th year. Therefore, we can not suppose the "14th year" date to be a corruption; since Isa. xxxviii: 1, would in that case be without sense or truth.

§ 8. More probable is the suggestion drawn from Rollins in his Ancient History (Assyr. ch. 2), that scripture for some reason speaks of Sargon under the name of Sennecherib. Or, we may take suggestion from the British commentary of Fausset, which gives Sargon as ending B. C. 715, and Sennacherib as then commencing; who (it says) in his 3d year of service (B. C. 711-712) "overran Syria, took Sidon and other Phœnician cities, and then passed to southwestern Palestine, where he defeated the Egyptians and Ethiopians," as his inscriptions state.

§ 9. Our suggestion is, that Sennacherib may have become *viceroy* at about B. C. 712, going for his father on the campaign against Palestine *in the west*, while the father Sargon devoted himself *in the east* to those successive campaigns of B. C. 711-709, by which at last in 709 he conquered Babylon, as Sargon's inscriptions show. (See Dic. Relig. Knowl.) At about this same time (709) the son, Sennacherib, would be (in his 3d year of service) threatening Palestine and Egypt in the west, in the name of his father Sargon, who still lived till B. C. 705.* At any rate, the Jews seem to have come in contact with the son rather than the father, and so to have recorded him as the "King of Assyria"—at first *prospectively* and at last actually the king—who so threatened them and met with such a disastrous end.

We, therefore, propose to read the scripture passage before us as meaning, when properly rendered with an *italic* thought-word supplied, as follows:

"Now it came to pass in the fourteenth year of King Hezekiah, that Sennacherib, *future* king of Assyria, came up against all the defenced cities of Judah, and he took them," *in the course of time*. (See II Chron. xxxii: 1.)

There is, then, *no corruption* of the text; but only a slight hiatus of the thought, requiring the italic word inserted.

§ 10. The only remaining difficulty arises from the common understanding of Sennacherib's invasion of Palestine, as all occurring within a single season; so as to fit together Isa. xxxvi: 1, and xxxviii: 1, as at beginning and end of the same year. Whereas, in truth, there are given *three distinct campaigns*, evidently covering several years of time.

When the first campaign (at xxxvi: 1) is named, the writer thinks best to go on at once and describe the subsequent campaigns, even to the terrible death of the invader many years later; so as to show up the whole story of Sennacherib complete, in the graphic manner of

---

*This case is thus parallel to that of Nebuchadnezzar, whose reign was prereckoned by the Jews while his father still lived. (See period F, § 23.)

anticipation so common in writing history, and especially so common in scripture. Then (at xxxviii: 1) he returns to finish his account of "the 14th year of Hezekiah, begun at xxxvi: 1, the two intermediate chapters being passed over in thought as parenthetic.

THE ASSYRIAN ASSAULTS.

§ 11. Our Bibles ought to show a space or distinct paragraph notation, at Isa. xxxvi: 2, and at xxxvii: 9. For, at those points are probably commenced new and distinct campaigns, separated by years of time. At xxxvii: 9, the "he" does not mean "Rabshakeh," as sometimes thought, but "the king of Assyria," as shown by the "my" in Ver. 12.

There is here no "when" in the Hebrew, but it reads literally, "And he heard, and he sent." The meaning probably is (by *constructio pregnans*): "And he hearkened *and yielded*" (to the "rumor," *i. e.*, acted in view of it). "And *afterwards* he sent to Hezekiah." For, often this word "hear" implies thus fully an *obeying*, as here at Ver. 16, "*Hearken* not to Hezekiah"; where the Hebrew "hearken" is the same word "hear."

§ 12. Hence, the following "sent" may be (after a colon) a long time subsequently (see Scott's Com.), even after Sargon's death. For now (in ver. 11-13) he boasts, as not before, of "all lands" destroyed, naming the regions of "Eden" and all about Babylonia as now conquered by "my father," *i. e.*, by Sargon in the conquest of Babylon (B. C. 709), which had intervened since his former coming. It was "Samaria" most prominent before as overthrown (xxxvi: 19); but now it was "Babylon fallen," (as seen at xxi: 9.) A "rumor" of Tirhakah's approach (xxxvii: 7, 9) alarmed Sennacherib away from Judea; but the real onset against Tirhakah and Egypt may have been years after.

At xxxvi: 2, also, there is certainly a long preceding interval; for there is an omission here, supplied at II Kings xviii: 14-16. Hezekiah obtained terms from the invader at his first campaign, and bought him off by payment of a large price set by the invader himself, for a withdrawal or "return from" the land. Of course, a year or two (at least) must have elapsed, before a claim for more tribute would bring the invader back. See also II Chron. xxxii: 1-9; where other operations intervene, and "after this" the second campaign comes in.

THE INSCRIPTIONS.

§ 13. The Assyrian inscriptions tell us that "The Assyrian Sargon conquered Babylon, and announced himself as king of it, in the thirteenth year of his reign, B. C. 709." And again: "Sargon fought with Merodach-baladan of Babylon in 710 and in 709, becoming final victor in the latter year." (*Dic. Relig. Knowl.* art. *Assyriology*.) This was *at the east;* what was going on *at the west?*

"The inscriptions tell us, that Sargon received tribute from a Pharaoh of 'Egypt,' besides destroying in part the Ethiopian 'No-Ammon' or Thebes; also that he warred with the cities of Ashdod, Gaza," etc.—in harmony with Isa. xx: 1. (*British Com. of Fausset.*) This campaign "against Ashdod was B. C. 711" (says the *Dic. Relig. Knowl.*); and it was *followed* by the second campaigns against Hezekiah (at Isa. xxxvi: 2).

For, II Ki. xviii: 17, informs us that "the king of Assyria sent to King Hezekiah," the same "Tartan" whom "Sargon sent against Ashdod" (in Isa. xx: 1). Hence, the two affairs are closely connected. And the taking of Hezekiah's cities comes last (say in 710 or 709), because Sennacherib's inscription says he gave those cities when taken to the Philistines of "Ashdod," who must, therefore, have been previously subdued and brought into allegiance.

§ 14. We thus find, that the same years (B. C. 712–708), in which the *western* campaigns to Palestine and Egypt were going on, were also occupied with the *eastern* campaigns (B. C. 710, 709), in which Babylon was assailed and finally conquered. What more natural, then, than that Sargon himself should take charge of the eastern or home operations about Babylon, and should entrust the western or distant operations at Palestine to his son Sennacherib as viceroy? Indeed, how could the son, full-grown and warlike as we know he then was, help joining thus in the fight?*

The Assyrian army, after passing from Lachish to assault Libnah (Isa. xxxvii: 8), and after giving to the Philistine "Ashdod" the cities taken from Hezekiah (say in 709), went on south to attack Tirhakah and Egypt, stirring up all Arabia with fleeing hosts. But years afterward, when Sargon had died (B. C. 705), Sennacherib may have returned to the onset upon Tirhakah and Egypt, and may then again have threatened Hezekiah (as at Isa. xxxvii: 9). How else, if there be no gap at Isa. xxxvii: 9, can "the Egyptian prisoners and Ethiopian captives" after "three years," as told in Isa. xx: 3, 4, be brought in?

Isaiah Ch. xx: 21.

§ 15. The "Ashdod" account at Isa. xx: 1, shows that the scripture itself knew of "Sargon," and recognized him as really "king of Assyria" at the time of these Palestine invasions. So that its else-

---

*The revisers tell us that "Tartan," etc., are "the *titles* of Assyrian officers." Tartan being the first and leading officer named, its meaning to a Hebrew in the Chaldean idiom, as a contracted compound Tar'-tank, would be "the royal court repented," or the *second porte* (in the Turkish sense of *porte*). See Gesenius at ת ר ע or teray. And might not this be the title of Sennacherib himself, as the heir apparent, or viceroy of the king?

where attributing the invasions to the son Sennacherib as "king" must be only as *prospectively* king, or "king apparent" in his father's place and (to them especially) even more notable than his father.

That section of Isaiah (ch. xx: 21) is certainly connected with the campaigns against Hezekiah and belongs to his 14th to 18th years as B. C. 712-708 (see Scott's Bible)—not B. C. 701—as plainly shown by its contents.

In ch. xx, "in the year that Tartan came unto Ashdod" and Jerusalem (B. C. 712-710). Isaiah declares the folly of Palestine's dependence on Egypt for help, foretelling that during "three years" the "king of Assyria shall lead away the Egyptian prisoners" (ver. 3-4). Then in ch. xxi he gives "the burden of the desert" eastward to Euphrates, and prophecies "Babylon is fallen, is fallen" (ver. 9), *i. e.*, is taken by Sargon (B. C. 709) in anticipation of its final destruction by Cyrus. And he closes (at ver. 13) with "the burden upon Arabia," when "within a year" (from 709?) that country should be stirred up by the fleeing hosts from the Assyrian invasion through Palestine upon Egypt, when "they fled from the swords" (ver. 15-16).

§ 16. All centers about the year 709 B. C., when Sargon conquered Babylon and when Isaiah had "walked naked and barefoot *three years* for a sign and a wonder upon Egypt" (xx: 3), *i. e.*, from B. C. 712, the fourteenth year of Hezekiah, the first of Assyrian invasion. Our exposition here of the *Fall of Babylon*, in Isa. xxi: 9, as meaning *primarily* its conquest by Sargon in B. C. 709, is *new* and striking. Is it not more satisfactory than the view universally given which overlooks entirely that event?

§ 17. What, then, have we learned?

1. That "in the fourteenth year of Hezekiah" (B. C. 712) Sennacherib came (for his father, Sargon) against Judah, but was bought off and induced to return.

2. That afterward (say in three years, B. C. 709) Sennacherib again made invasion with Tartan and Rabshakeh and (in the name of his father, Sargon) having before taken Ashdod and other Philistine cities, as recorded in Isa. xx: 1-6, he now assailed Hezekiah again as in xxxvi: 2. And now, perhaps, he mostly did what is by anticipation in xxxvi: 1, "he took them," the defenced cities of Judah, giving them to the Philistines (as he says in his inscription).

3. Then, it may be long after, even after Sargon had died in B. C. 705, Sennacherib, going to fight Tirhakah and Egypt, again threatened Hezekiah (by letter), as told at xxxvii: 9, but miserably perished as at ver. 36-38. (In this view the mention of King "Sennacherib" in Isa. xxxvii: 17, 21, 37; II Ki. xix: 16, 20, 36; II Chron. xxxii: 9, 22, would be correct, and the mention of "Sennacherib" in Isa. xxxvi: 1, *might* be treated as the error of some ancient copyist writing the Hebrew

"Senherib" in place of the Assyrian "Sharukin" or "Shargina," that error finding its way to the parallel, II Ki. xviii, 13, and II Chron. xxxii: 1, 2.)

Sennacherib's Account.

§ 18. The inscription of Sennacherib "on the third column of his hexagonal clay cylinder, discovered in 1830 in the ruins of Nineveh," as translated by Professor Hilprecht (*S. S. Times*, Jan. 9, 1892), is a mixed up and pompous account of his various adventures above mentioned, as if all in a single "third campaign, B. C. 701, with plain intent to cover up his final disaster. When examined, it clearly confirms the orderly history of affairs in scripture as indicated above.

The invader concedes that Hezekiah "sent his envoy to pay over the tribute" to him when distant from Jerusalem. Which shows that this was what bought off the enemy for a time *at the beginning* of affairs, just as described in II Ki. xviii: 13-14, and was not money exacted *at the end*, as he tries to make it appear.

The many captives and much plunder he tells of carrying off, came also not at the close, as he would like to have it thought; but, doubtless these were largely "the Egyptian prisoners and Ethiopian captives" whom Isaiah foretold near the beginning (Isa. xx: 1-6) as doomed to be carried off, *i. e.*, after the second campaign (xxxvii: 8).

Sennacherib says: "The Arabs and Hezekiah's allies took fright." And so, Isaiah follows that prophecy of Egyptian capture (chap. 20) with a *flight*, as "the burden upon Arabia," to come "within a year," when he foresaw that they "fled from the swords." (xxi: 13, 15, 16.)

§ 19. Sennacherib's inscription says: "Hezekiah's cities that I had sucked, I separated from his country, and gave them to the king of Ashdod, of Ekron, and of Gaza, and thus reduced his country." This shows that *before* Hezekiah's "fenced cities" were taken, "Ashdod" and those other coast cities of Philistia had been subdued and brought into allegiance; as we have been explaining.

He also says: "I added *another* payment of tribute from Hezekiah," showing that there had been a period of rest after the tribute paid at II Ki. xviii: 15. All these circumstances prove that the procedures from that point onward do not occur in the 14th of Hezekiah, when invasion commenced, but a considerable time afterward; even reaching, it may be, into Sennacherib's sole reign, or to Hezekiah's 24th year, B. C. 701-2.

At that time, or some time after all was over, Sennacherib, undertaking to cover up his final disaster, jumbles the whole story of previous adventures together in a pompous display of conquest.

[It is not necessary here to notice the impossible scheme of destructive critics who try to reconstruct the whole reign of Hezekiah, to accommodate the Assyrian account. That is rending instead of harmonizing scripture.]

Result.

§ 20. In view of this exposition, we find the Assyrian inscriptions wonderfully corroborating the scripture history; indeed demonstrating its reality and accuracy beyond the need of dispute.

But we here learn, that there must be thorough sifting of the whole scripture, and critical analysis of its construction, as well as careful sifting of Assyrian datings themselves, before the harmony of the two appears.

So that, we are set upon the closest study of the Bible, along with archæologicial and critical research, to get at the whole truth, and learn the beautiful accord of true science and Divine Revelation.

PART II.

BIBLE CHRONOLOGY OF THE KINGS.

(Shown to be Remarkably Obvious, Simple and Certain.)

CHAPTER I.

THE BIBLE DATES.

§ 21. A well-settled starting-point for Old Testament chronology is the 2d year of Darius Hystaspes, King of Persia, at B. C. 520; when that king re-issued the decree of Cyrus for the rebuilding of the temple at Jerusalem. And from that time there are just 200 years back to the capture of Samaria and the exile of the ten tribes in B. C. 720.

These 200 years are made up as follows: From the 2d of Darius, B. C. 520, there are 67 years to the destruction of Jerusalem, B. C. 587, in the 19th of Nebuchadnezzar (II Ki. xxv: 8). Hence, the kings of Judah reach back 133 years, thus: Zedekiah and Jehoiachin 11+Jehoiakim and Jehoahaz 11+Josiah 31+Amon 2+Manasseh 55+23 of Hezekiah's 29=133 years to B. C. 720. (II Ki. xviii: 9, 10.) Ptolemy's Canon and the Bible carry us securely thus far.

§ 22. From the capture of Samaria in B. C. 720, the Bible gives 254 years back to the death of Solomon in B. C. 974, and then+40 to the beginning of Solomon in B. C. 1014. The current Usher chronology makes 1 year more, having David's death in B. C. 1015, and the destruction of Jerusalem in B. C. 588, leaving the reigns of the kings just the same length as here given. Usher's mistake of 1 year too early for the destruction of Jerusalem, and so for Solomon's temple and reign, we fully exhibit elsewhere.

THE KINGDOM OF ISRAEL.

The period from the death of Solomon to the capture of Samaria, though much called in question by recent critics in their attempts to satisfy supposed Assyrian dates, is very obviously 254 years by the scripture accounts: which have here the advantage of giving contemporaneous reigns, in the *two kingdoms* of Judah and Israel, which by their continual synchronisms generally confirm each other; with the

THE KINGS 141

extra advantage of a *double record* in the books of Kings and Chronicles, together with many corroborative datings found in the prophets. There could scarcely be more favorable and trustworthy data, or a more easily adjustable reckoning of dates, in any period of human history.

§ 23. As the Kings of Judah are a single hereditary line, without any break, while the kings of Israel are a broken series of usurpers, with anarchies or interregnums between, it is plainly the kings of Judah whose reigns in succession are to indicate the time. We proceed to give the reigns in both kingdoms, as filling up the 254 years.

TABLE OF REIGNS.

JUDAH.			ISRAEL.		
Rehoboam	17 yrs		Jeroboam	22 nd, *i. e.*, 21 yrs	
Abijah	3 yrs		Nadab	2 nd, *i. e.*, 1 yr	
			Baasha	24 th, *i. e.*, 23 yrs	
			Elah	2 nd, *i. e.*, 1 yr	
			Omri	12 th, *i. e.*, 11 yrs	
Asa	41 yrs		Ahab	22 nd, *i. e.*, 21 yrs	
	18 yrs		Ahaziah	2 nd, *i. e.*, 1 yr	
		79			79
Jehoshaphat, 25 yrs	4 yrs		Jehoram	12 yrs	
	3 yrs				
Jehoram, 8(th *i. e.*, 7 yrs)	4 yrs				
Ahaziah	1 yr				
		12			12
Athaliah	6 yrs		Jehu	28 th, *i. e.*, 27 yrs	
Jehoash, 40 th, *i. e.*	39 yrs		Jehoahaz	17 th, *i. e.*, 16 yrs	
Amaziah, 29 yrs	14 yrs		Jehoash	16 yrs	
		59			59
	15 yrs		Jeroboam, II	41 yrs	
Azariah	52 yrs		Interregnum	12÷5 mo	
			Zachariah, &c	0+7 mo	
			Menahem	10 yrs	
			Pekaiah	2 yrs	
			Pekah, 20 yrs	1 yr	
		67			67
Jotham	16 yrs			19 yrs	
Ahaz, 16 th, *i. e.*	15 yrs		Anarchy	9 yrs	
Hezekiah, 29 yrs 6 th *i. e.*	6 yrs		Hoshea	9 yrs	
		27			27
		254			254
(Added, 260.)			(Added, 241-7 mo.-7 ds.)		

§ 24. It is worthy of note how little variation has to be made from the Bible figures, thus to balance the reigns in the two kingdoms. The reigns in Judah, as here given from scripture, add up just 260 years: but three of these are an overlap of Jehoram upon his father, Jehoshaphat, as everybody concedes, and scripture itself teaches. (Comp. I Ki. xxii: 42; II Ki. iii: 1, and viii: 16), and 3 years are only apparent, being the *current* year given for the *complete* years, 1 less, in three cases, at Jehoram, Jehoash and Ahaz. Thus, the 254 years appear at once. (So also Josephus, see § 55.)

NOTE.—The 254 from Solomon's death to the capture of Samaria is about the same in the Modern Jewish chronology; for that has Sol. 40 +Israel, 256+Judah, 114, to beginning of captivity in the 4th year of Jehoiakim—"410" years. They evidently took the total of Judah's reigns, viz., 260 years, omitting only 3 or 4 of the 6 years' omission here shown to be required. The Talmud itself, compiled in B. C. 32, says (at the end of *Solomon the Wise*), "Four hundred and thirty-three years (433) elapsed between the date of Solomon's reign and that of the temple's destruction;" that is 40+260+133=433. And thus it has the interval 260 of exact Bible addition without any reduction.

All the early kings of Israel seem to have their reigns thus given *current, i. e.*, 1 more than *complete* years; and Schwartz thence infers (Bib. Sac., 1888, p. 71), that they must *always* be so reckoned. But the proper rule is that only as the synchronism of the reigns require it, must any number, whether in Israel or in Judah, be considered as current rather than complete. There are nine such cases in Israel, besides two evident interregnums or periods of anarchy not accounted for.

§ 25. All the numbers of the foregoing table are fully confirmed by the numerous synchronisms and cross-references between particular years of contemporaneous kings compared, as given in the books of Kings and of Chronicles. And only a few comments are needed to harmonize all the Bible data. This is seen by the following table:

TABLE OF SYNCHRONISMS.

JUDAH.		B.C.	ISRAEL.
1st Rehoboam, 17...		974	=1st Jerob., 22 (nd).
(18th) Rehoboam	=1st Abijah, 3	957	=18th Jeroboam
1st Asa, 41, 41st	=(4th Abijah)	954	=20th (20) [21st]
2d Asa		953	1st Nadab, 2 (nd).... =(22d) Jeroboam
3d Asa		952	(2d) Nadab... =1st Baasha, 24 (th)
26th Asa		929	1st Elah, 2 (nd)... =(24th) Baasha.
27th Asa		928	(2d) Elah Omri... =Zimri, 7d.
31st (31) Asa		923	(7th) Elah Om. 6... =1st Omri (6) 12 (11).
38th Asa		917	1st Ahab, 22 (nd) ... =(7th) Omri.
(42d) Asa	=1st Jehosh., 25 (22).	913	4th (4) [5th] Ahab.
(1st Jehoram)	=17th (17) [18th]	896	(22d) Ahab... =1st Ahaziah,2 (nd)
2d Jehoram	=18th (18) [19th]	895	1st Jehoram, 12... =(2d) Ahaziah.
1st Jehoram, 8 (th)	=(23d)	891	5th Jehoram
(4th) Jehoram	=(25th end.,he died.	888	(8th) Jehoram
(8th) Jehoram	=1st Ahaziah, 1	884	12th, 11th (11) Jeho..
1st Athaliah, 6	=(2d) Ahaziah	883	(13th) Jehoram... =1st Jehu., 28th (27)
(7th) Athaliah	=1st Jehoash, 40 (th)	877	=7th Jehu.
	23d (22d) [21st]	856	1st Jehoahaz, 17 (th). =(28th) Jehu.
	37th (37)	840	(17th) Jehoahaz... =1st Jehoash, 16.
1st Amaziah, 29	=(40th)	838	=2d (2) Jehoash.
(3d) Amaziah		836	(1st Jeroboam, 53)... =(5th) Jehoash.
15th Amaziah		824	1st Jeroboam, 41 [40]. =[17th] Jehoash.
(30th), 15 years after.	=1st Azariah, 52...	809	(16th) 27th Jeroboam.
	(27th) Azariah	783	(42d) Jeroboam... =Interregnum, 12.
	38th (38) Azariah	771	(54th) Jeroboam... =1st Zacharia, 6 mo.
	39th Azariah	771	1st Shallun, 1 mo... +5 mo.
	39th (39) Azariah	770	=1st Menahem, 10.
	50th Azariah	760	1st Pekaiah, 2... =(11th) Menahem.
	52d Azariah	758	(3d) Pekaiah... =1st Pekah, 20.
1st Jotham, 16	(53d) Azariah	757	=2d Pekah.
(17th) Jotham	=1st Ahaz, 15 (th)	741	=17th (17) [18th]
20th Jotham	=(4th Ahaz)	738	1st Hoshea... =(21st) Anarchy, 9.
	12th (12)	729	1st Hoshea, 9.
1st Hezekiah, 29	=(16th) [15th]	726	3d (3) Hoshea.
4th Hezekiah		723	7th Hoshea.
6th (6) [7th]	=After 3 years	720	9th (9) Hoshea... Capture of Samaria

THE KINGS

The one thing remarkable about this table is, that the dates B. C. here given are none of them assigned by ourselves, or by any human authority; but come where they are of themselves from the scripture numbers themselves (set opposite to them in order). None but the Bible numbers (and all the Bible numbers) are used in the table; yet these, simply interpreted and set in order, of themselves give the B. C. dates here exhibited, as their necessary and unmanufactured result. THIS SELF-INTERPRETATION *of the Bible datings, containing so many and so repeated numbers and cross-references, is a perfect demonstration of its accuracy. And no theory of how the events* OUGHT *to be dated, can avail to set aside this simple artless exhibit of how the events* ARE *here in the Bible plainly and certainly dated.*

§ 26. In the foregoing table, the parts in parentheses ( ) are simple necessary inferences, the parts in brackets [ ] are from Josephus; all the rest is taken from the scripture. What is remarkable is, there is no deviation here from scripture figures (besides the current and complete year often interchanged), except the 3 year overlap upon Jehoshaphat's reign, plainly indicated in scripture, and the "23d Jehoash" changed to the 22d Jehoash," in accordance with Josephus' copy, "21st year" or 21 years. (Ant. 7, viii: 5.)

THE SCRIPTURE NUMBERS, AS ABOVE.

There are in the table 92 scripture numbers, here all harmonized together, as follows: In the days of
   Rehoboam.   I Ki. xiv: 20, 21, "22 yrs., 17 yrs."; ver. 25, "the 5th yr. of Reho."   (969 B. C.)   So II Chron. xii: 13, "17 yrs."
   Abijam.   xv: 1, "18th yr."; ver. 2, "3 yrs."   So II Chron. xiii: 1, 2, "18th yr., 3 yrs."
   Asa.   xv: 9, "20th yr."; ver. 10, "41 yrs."; ver. 25, "2d. yr., 2 yrs."; ver. 28, 33, "3d yr., 24 yrs."; xvi: 8, "26th yr., 2 yrs."; ver. 10, 15, "27th yr., 7d."; ver. 23, "31st yr., 12 yrs., 6 yrs."; ver. 29, "38th yr., 22 yrs."   So II Chron. xvi: 1, "36th yr. [26th]"; ver. 12, "39th yr."; ver. 13, "41st yr."
   Jehoshaphat.   xxii: 1, 2, "3 yrs., 3d yr."; ver. 41, "4th yr."; ver. 42, "25 yrs."; ver. 51, "17th yr., 2 yrs."; II Ki. iii: 1, "18th yr." So II Chron. xx: 31, "25 yrs."
   Jehoram.   II Ki. i: 17, "2d yr."; viii: 16, "5th yr."; ver. 17, "8 yrs."   So II Chron. xxi: 5, "8 yrs."; ver. 19, "2 yrs."; ver. 20, "8 yrs."
   Ahaziah.   viii: 25, "12th yr."; ver. 26, "1 yr."; ix: 29, "11th yr."   So II Chron. xxii: 2, "1 yr."
   Athaliah.   x: 26, "28 yrs."; ver. 4, "6 yrs."; ver. 5, "7th yr."   So II Chron. xxii: 12, "6 yrs."; xxiii: 1, "7th yr."
   Joash.   xii: 1, "7th yr., 40 yrs."; xiii: 1, "23d yr., 17 yrs."; ver. 10, "37th yr., 16 yrs."   So II Chron. xxiv: 1, "40 yrs."
   Amaziah.   xiv: 1, "2d yr."; ver. 2, "29 yrs."; ver. 17, "15 yrs."; ver. 23, "15th yr., 41 yrs."   So II Chron. xxv: 1, "29 yrs."
   Azariah.   xv: 1, "27th yr."; ver. 2, "52 yrs."; ver. 8, "38 yrs."; ver. 13, "39th yr., 1 mo."; ver. 17, "39th yr., 10 days,"; ver. 23, "50th yr., 2 yrs."; ver. 27, "52d yr., 20 yrs."   So II Chron. xxvi: 3, "52 yrs."

Jotham. xv: 32, "2d yr."; ver. 33, "16 yrs." So II Chron. xxvii: 8, "16 yrs."

Ahaz. xvi: 1, "17th yr."; ver. 2, "16 yrs."; xv: 30, "20th yr. of Jotham"; xvii: 1, "12th yr." So II Chron. xxviii: 1, "16 yrs."

Hezekiah. xvii: 6, "9th yr. of Hoshea"; xviii: 1, "3d yr." ver. 2, "29 yrs."; ver. 9, "4th yr.—7th yr."; ver. 10, "3 yrs., 6th yr.—9th yr."; ver. 13, "14th yr." So II Chron. xxix: 1, "29 yrs."; ver. "3, 1st yr."

The table shows so close a conformity of our dating (and that of Usher) with the scripture data, that there are needed for difficult passages only a few.

EXPLANATIONS.

§ 27. JEHORAM. In the "5th year" of Joram of Israel, Jehoram of Judah began his "8 years" (II Ki. viii: 16, 17): and in the *beginning* of the "12th year of Joram," Ahaziah of Judah began his "1 year," (ver. 25, 26) *i. e.*, at the *end* of Joram's "11th year" (ix: 29). Thus, Ahaziah's 1 year covers Joram's 12th year, since they both died at the end of Joram's "12 years" (viii: 28, and ix: 24, 27). Therefore, Jehoram's "8 years" can reach only from Joram's "5th year" *begun* to his "12th year" *begun*, or 7 full years; and the "8 years" must mean the 8th year *current*. But as Jehoram thus began 4 years after Joram (in his "5th year" begun), whose reign began in Jehoshaphat's "18th year" ending (iii: 1)=2d year of Jehoram's *joint* reign (called a "mistake" in the Bib. Sacra., Oct., 1870, p. 641)—therefore, Jehoram begun those 8 (7) years after (18+4=)22 years of his father Jehoshaphat's reign of "25 years" (I Ki. xxii: 42). And consequently, Jehoshaphat was still alive when his son Jehoram began his 8 (7) years, just as is expressly stated (at II Ki. viii: 16, 17). And the remaining (25—22=)3 years of the father's reign lap over upon Jehoram's 8 (or full 7), giving but (7—3=)4 years of Jehoram alone, after his father's 25 and at death.

NOTE. Several writers (Hales, Cunningham, Jarvis, Bowen, Elliott, Browne in Coleman, Akers, Seiss, and "Time of the End," *Boston, Jewett, 1856*), entirely neglect the overlap of Jehoram's reign, calling the three reigns 41+25+8, and so enlarging the interval back to Solomon by 4 years. But this violates II Ki. viii: 16, 17, and all the dates back to the reign of Ahab.

§ 28. OMRI. According to I Kings xvi: 8, 29, there were twelve years from the accession of Elah to that of Ahab. So that, as Elah reigned one of those years (ver. 8, 15), therefore the "twelve years" of Omri (ver. 23) means the twelfth year current, or eleven full years only; as in the case of all these adjacent reigns in Israel. The "thirty-first year" of Asa here must mean full thirty-one years; so that there were for Omri after this, six full years to the "thirty-eighth year" (ver. 29), and "six years" back to the "twenty-sixth year" (ver. 8); *i. e.*, five full years of anarchy, besides one year left for Elah. At II Chron.

xv: 19 and xvi: 1, the "35th year" and "36th year" are evidently a corruption for 25th and 26th; and Josephus so has the numbers in his copy (So Scott.)

§ 29. JEHOAHAZ. According to II King xiii: 1, 10, Jehoahaz seems to have room for but fourteen of the seventeen years reign there assigned him. Therefore, his reign (like so many in Israel) is *current* 17th, or but sixteen full years; and the "37th year" (at ver. 10) must mean 37th *ending*, or full thirty-seven years (*i. e.*, 38th beginning; some 70 copies read "39th." See this explained in Clinton, and by Newman in Kitto.) Moreover, we must correct the "23d year" (ver. 1) to 22d year; for, Josephus' copy has it "21st" (*i. e., ending*)—and Jehu's 28 *current* or 27 full years (as in Josephus) reach only thus far (the 28 for Jehu, carrying us back to his conspiracy before Joram's death (II King ix: 14, 24.) This reckoning makes the "40 years of Jehoash of Judah (xii: 1), to be *current* 40th, or full 39 years.

§ 30. JEROBOAM II. According to II King xiv: 17, 23, with xv: 1, there was a (27th—16th =) 11 years *regency* of Jeroboam II with his father Joash; concerning which we read in the marginal references of Scott's Bible, "his father made him consort at his going to the Syrian wars." See also II King xiii: 13, 17, 22-25.

NOTE. But Newman in Kitto prefers to call the "27th year" a corruption for 17th or 16th: so Petavius, Usher, Marsham, Clinton, Winer, Bowen, Elliott. And some, without any warrant, put an interregnum of 11 or 12 years before Azariah at xv: 1, thus lengthening that much the interval back to Solomon; so Hales, Jarvis, Akers, Comprehen. Com., and "Time of the End." But (as Clinton remarks) this has no possible ground, and it doubles the difficulty about the interregnum in Israel, etc.

Moreover, from II Kings xv: 8, we learn that there were (15 + 38 =) 53 years from the beginning of Jeroboam II to the accession of his son, Zechariah; from which, deducting his 41 years' reign (xiv: 23), we find an interregnum of 12 years.

NOTE. Clinton and others say 11 years. But Newman in Kitto prefers to lengthen Jeroboam's reign, as 51 instead of 41 years.

§ 31. JOTHAM. We are told at II Ki. xvii: 1, that Hoshea began his 9 years at the end of the "12th year of Ahaz;" but in xv: 30, he is said to have commenced, or rather to have killed his predecessor (with intervening *anarchy*) 9 years earlier, namely, in the "20th year of Jotham." From this it would seem that Jotham lived 4 years after his "sixteen years" of reign ended (xv: 33), or rather find an explanation given here (at §109). See to the like effect the British Commentary of Jamieson.

NOTE. Newman in Kitto prefers to reject the "20th of Jotham" as corrupt, and to change the "20 years" of Pekah (ver. 27) to 30, so as to cover the anarchy.

§ 32 HEZEKIAH. As Hoshea began in the "12th year of Ahaz" (II Ki. xvii: 1), whose successor, Hezekiah, began in Hoshea's "3d year"

(18: 1), therefore, there can be but 3 years between the accession of Hezekiah and the *end* of Ahaz' 12th year; and Ahaz' "16 years" (xvi: 2) must be *current* 16th, or only 15 full years, and it must be Hoshea's "3d year" *ending*. Hence, "the 6th year of Hezekiah, that is the 9th year of Hoshea" (xviii: 10) is *6 full years of Hezekiah* and 9 full years of Hoshea (xvii:1), so as to make "the end of 3 years" from the "4th year of Hezekiah, which was the 7th year of Hoshea" (xviii: 9, 10). Some wrongly put this capture of Samaria after only 5 years of Hezekiah. His age at accession was "25 years" (ver. 2), and his father's age at accession was "20 years" (xvi: 2), and the father's intervening reign of 15 years brings his age at death up to 35; from which, taking Hezekiah's age then as "25 years," we have his father but 10 years old at his birth! So that, one or the other of those age numbers must be wrong.

§ 33. The above are about the only scripture points needing explanation. The self-adjusting table here given, though constructed without any regard to the common chronology of Usher, yet shows a remarkable agreement with it; the only obvious variation being a change in the starting point, B. C. 587 (not 588) for the destruction of Jerusalem, bringing B. C. 1014 (not 1015) for the beginning of Solomon's reign. This shows how nearly he must have used our own simple process of interpretation. Let us here note the common-sense simplicity of this.

CHAPTER II.

THE BIBLE METHOD.

§ 34. The reason why all our numbers in the tables (§ 23, 25) fall together so harmoniously, without effort on our part, and with scarcely any deviation from the scripture text, is because we have here adopted the only natural and rational method of ascertaining what is the Bible chronology of this period. We have merely *let the scripture speak for itself and harmonize its own reckoning* without interference from us. We adopt NO THEORY (as do the destructive critics) prejudging how the reigns and synchronisms *must* have been calculated; but we allow them each and all to tell their own story, and combine as they will. As we have the reigns and their multiplied synchronisms in the two contemporary kingdoms of Judah and Israel, there is no honest way but to put all these numbers together into *one harmonious whole*, speaking their own language with *the least possible change* of figures. This method reveals only *three slight self-evident adaptations*, as follows:

§ 35. (1.) Any single synchronism allows one year of variation in the reckoning; and a double synchronism allows a variation of two years, if the context so requires. Thus, if a reign in one kingdom begins in the "third year" of a reign in the other kingdom, it may be either near the beginning or near the end of that third year; that is, after two years or after three years of reign. (See example II Chron. xvi: 3, comp. 1 Ki. xv: 10.) Again, if a reign begins in the "third year" and another in the "eighth year," the interval may be simply five years; or the first date may be at the beginning of the third year and the second at the end of the eighth year, giving an interval of six years; or the first may be at the end of the third year and the second at the beginning of the eighth year, giving an interval of but four years. (See example I Ki. xv: 1, 9, comp. ver. 2; and II Ki. xv: 17, 23.) No greater variation than this is in harmony with the figures; but a variation within these bounds is no violation.

§ 36. (2.) A length of reign is ordinarily to be understood as so many full years, the fraction less of one reign being offset with the fraction more of another; but sometimes, the fractional year may have been (by a careless way of the first scribe) allowed to both reigns, requiring a year to be deducted from one or the other of the two reigns. But the synchronisms in the context show such an over-numbering, and no error results. For example "Jeroboam twenty-two years" is required by the contiguous synchronisms to denote a reign to his "twenty-second year," *i. e.*, twenty-one full years only. The fact that this usage is found with the first seven kings of Israel, only shows the habit of that earlier scribe; and it does not warrant Schwartz (Bib. Sac., Jan., '88) in imposing this as a *fixed rule* for all the kings of Israel and denying it to any king of Judah. The artless Bible historians were not tied down to mathematical canons such as modern critics are disposed to invent for them; much less would the same author have two sets of kings intermingled in his dating with a *different rule* for each set. Our only authority for letting any reign go as one year less than its nominal figure, is the requirement of the writer's own synchronisms in the context, proving necessarily how he, in that case, was reckoning. We have no right otherwise to modify the value named, and thus do violence to his figures.

§ 37. Doctor Orr of Scotland (in the *Pres. Review*, Jan., 1889), in order to make out a scheme of Bible chronology in accordance with alleged Assyrian dates, applies the arbitrary rule, that all Bible reigns both in Israel and in Judah must be reduced one year; claiming that every reign is given inclusive of the fractions reckoned at both ends, like the "three days" ascribed to our Savior in the tomb. But it is altogether unnatural to suppose that inclusive mode of reckoning applied rigidly to all numbers, to successive reigns and larger periods, which certainly were intended to express the actual length of time. For instance, the age of Moses is given as "full forty years" when he fled to Midian (Acts vii: 23); his stay there is given as full "forty years expired" (ver. 30); and his wilderness sojourn is given as "forty years" (ver. 26); while the whole is summed up as "120 years" of life (Deut. xxxiv: 7). And so of the reigns and ages generally. It is preposterous to foist upon the artless Jewish annals any such machine system of stereotyped and premeditated curtailment as the destructive critics are trying to devise for the accommodation of their Assyrian reckoning. The very diversity and contrariety of their theories prove them to be all fallacious.

§ 38. (3.) A synchronism may require either a *vacancy* (anarchy or interregnum) understood after the father, or a *regency* understood with the father named. But which is required in each case, depends upon the surroundings of the text. Such are the two difficult synchronisms of II Ki. xv: 1 and 8. The first presumption is in favor of an interregnum; because this is *letting the scripture speak* for itself without any explanation attempted. And therefore we let this interpret verse 8; there being nothing in the way of this purely biblical interpretation. We would do the same at verse 1, were there not three biblical facts against it. (*a*.) The fact that Azariah was taken "by the people" at or even before his father's death, and made king (xiv: 19-21), which forbids an interregnum between. (*b*.) The fact that an interregnum here would double the interregnum after Jeroboam, which is impracticable. (*c*.) The fact that such a doubling of interregnum cannot be avoided by supposing a mere regency of Azariah with his father to be referred to in verse 8, since verse 13. etc., forbid. Therefore, we have to conclude that verse 1 refers to a regency of Jeroboam with his father not reckoned in his "forty-one years" given; and this harmonizes the whole account without any mutilation.

§ 39. As for supposing more than a regency, a real *overlap* or joint reign *reducing the length of reign given*, this can not be allowed; for it would be a violation of the text, which, unless there is proof to the contrary, must be accepted as meaning to give by the successive reign lengths the whole space of time passed over in those reigns. Hence we can not let a *supposed* joint-reign reduce the *declared* lengths of reign; unless, indeed, there is an express statement to that effect, as there is in one case only, the case of Jehoshaphat and Jehoram, I Ki. viii: 16. It is sometimes said, as by Schwartz, that our Bible chronology is inconsistent, in having verse 8 make an interregnum and verse 1 a regency; but the above explanation shows, that, on the contrary, one consistent rule is followed, of letting scripture in each case speak for itself, with no theory interposed, the Bible numbers being allowed to fall into place of themselves, giving such result as they will.

§ 40. NOTE. That Zechariah's six months of reign, ver. 8, was only the culmination of a period of anarchy following Jeroboam's death, appears from the very wording of the narrative in scripture. At every other reign we are told that this king and that king "began" to reign in the year mentioned; but in this particular case there is a striking variation: "In the thirty and eighth year of Azariah, king of Judah, did Zechariah, the son of Jeroboam REIGN [not *begin* to reign] over Israel IN SAMARIA six months." That is, he only then, and for a few months, succeeded in getting to actual *reign* in the capital "Samaria," on account of a long preceding anarchy, which now resulted in his own speedy murder (after only six months) by a usurper, who in turn was immediately assassinated by another usurper Menahem—who only succeeded by regular war and conquest of the people (ver. 8-15). Scripture thus makes it plain, that Zechariah's real claim to the throne was during the thirteen years of anarchy, though his actual possession of the throne was only the last six months of it.

§ 41. Indeed, all the last years of Israel were so anarchical, that it is no wonder that, after the subsequent murder of Pekahiah by the usurper Pekah, and after his murder by the new usurper, Hoshea, (with aid from the Assyrian king), this last usurpation failed for nine years to get Hoshea really seated upon the throne, there being that much of new anarchy between the reign-lengths given in scripture. The cause of anarchy in this latter case is more fully shown by the Assyrian inscription, which (as Schwartz himself informs us) reads: "I [Tiglathpileser] slew Pekaha, and Hosea I made king." As it was this very Assyrian king whom Ahaz of Judah (in the first part of his reign) hired to come against Pekah of Israel (II Ki. xvi: 5, 7-10)—as it was he who really caused the death of Pekah (through Hoshea instigated by him), surely such new usurpation in Israel, through a foreign invasion, as well as domestic massacre, was calculated to intensify the anarchy of embroiled Israel, and prevent Hoshea, for a long time, from reaping the reward of his treachery, or being allowed to occupy in "Samaria" the throne which he had usurped and could only gain at length by Assyria's aid.

BUT ONE BIBLE METHOD.

§ 42. By the above three simple common-sense adaptations of the one common-sense method of interpretation, the Bible numbers (both reigns and synchronisms) are all happily reconciled with each other. And in such a harmony of many complex reckonings, there is a moral assurance that we have the mind and intent of the Bible writers, such as no other method of treating the matter can give. In contrast with it, look at the mutilating processes applied to scripture by speculative manipulators of Assyrian dates. These are *theories* for the *reconstruction* of Bible Chronology, in striking contrast with our plan of simply ascertaining it as it is. Mr. Schwartz claims that there are *three methods* of reckoning Bible dates, instead of the only correct way here claimed: (1) By adding up the lengths of reigns as given for Judah; (2) By adding up the lengths of reigns as given for Israel; (3) by selecting from among the synchronisms given such as will serve to make out the length of time desired!

This last is little better than the theory adopted by Dr. Orr (Pres. Quar., New York, Jan., '89) that all the synchronisms given in the scripture history are spurious, being interpolations made by a later editor, whom he calls *the synchronist;* so that he makes a Bible chronology to suit himself, using only such synchronisms as please him, and throwing the rest away! Such is the "higher" criticism of chronology with which we are being so largely entertained. Who does not see, that every one of these conflicting methods is partial, one sided, and unfair to the full scripture truth?

§ 43. It must be evident to all, that the only impartial, unprejudiced, and honest way is that which we here adopt, to *let the Bible numbers tell their own story*, without any theories or canons imposed. This fair and faithful method takes *every* regnal number in Judah or in Israel, and *every* synchronism given (without selection), and combines the whole, reigns and synchronisms, in one complete and consistent harmony, without any mutilation or collision of numbers. It is wonderful that such a harmony is found; and this is the best proof of the inerrancy of scripture, and of our having the right view of its numbers. How contrary to this are the diverse distorting schemes cited above!

The proposed adding up of reigns in one kingdom to the exclusion of the other, is entirely one-sided, and, therefore erroneous (as seen in the errors of Hales and others.)* As for a culling out of synchronisms to suit each theorizer's whim, that is intolerable. Instead of being "the synchronistic method," as Schwartz claims, that is the abdication of all real method. Instead of having *three diverse chronologies*

---

* Take, for example, what the book editor of the S. S. Times (June 9, 1894, p. 363) asserts: "There are just two systems of chronology for this period (from Solomon to the capture of Samaria), the biblical and the Assyrian, each computed at its *prima facie* value. The true chronology is either one or the other of these two, or else some combination of them that has not yet been demonstrated and adopted. The biblical numerals, computed at what appears to be their value, make the first year of Jeroboam I to be 982 B. C.—The chronology of Usher is a compromise," etc.

What is said here about the issue, as between the one chronology of the Bible and the alleged chronology of Assyriology, is just right. But there can be *no compromise* or "combination" between them, without a rejection of both. And the one obvious Bible Chronology is here very foolishly given as *the added reigns of Judah, with all the other scripture datings ignored*. Thus: 260 years of added reigns + 722 B. C. taken for the capture of Samaria = "982 B. C." here given for the death of Solomon. Of course, such an *un*-scriptural dating will have to be "compromised" and rejected. But the obviously scriptural date derived from *all the datings* harmonized, we show to be 254 years of reigns + 720 B. C. at the capture of Samaria = 974 B. C., as the true Bible date of Solomon's death; and the issue is between this alone and the claims of Assyriology. The 254 is demonstrably the correct scripture interval, and not a compromise even if Usher does have it.

We insist upon starting with scripture, "computed at its *prima facie* value," which is the true value; and the 260 years taken at its value for the interval before us, as made up from a part of its datings with the rest ignored, is certainly not the scripture's correct or "*prima facie* value."

of the Bible, we are offered *three unreasonable theories* beclouding its one simple reckoning, with neither of which have we anything to do. Our own procedure is as different from all these as light is from darkness. It can not be stigmatized as "another theory" in competition with those theories. We have no theory on the subject; we do not believe in studying scripture with preformed theories to be therefrom proved. All our business is to discover the one self-asserting, self-harmonizing chronology of the Bible. If it is found clashing with some outside dating, and is, therefore, to be rejected as untrue, that is an after question, which must be honestly decided by itself.

§ 44. It is plain that the sacred writers *meant* what they say; and they either told the truth (to the disproval of what contradicts them), or else they mistook the facts and wrote their history incorrectly. What they meant and said (whether true or false) is a matter of impartial exegesis simply, which we have resolved to know. And we think we have ascertained it very nearly in the tables we have drawn up. It is entirely disingenuous for scholars to twist and tear the Sacred Word, trying to distort its simple teachings into alleged agreement with something they have found outside of it. There is no honoring of scripture in such forced agreement. It were better to concede discrepancy between sacred and profane history, and let either record prevail according to the weight of its own authority. Let us own the truth, and treat the Book honestly "though the heavens fall."

CORROBORATIONS.

§ 45. The harmony of dates as herein set forth leaves so little difficulty with any passage, and is at the same time so undesignedly accordant with the accepted Usher chronology, as to commend itself at once as the true Bible dating. But there are certain important corroborations of our reckoning. First, we have the confirmatory evidence of *prophecy*. Ezekiel (in iv: 1-9) foretold "40 years" for filling up the iniquity of Judah, that is, from the 18th of Josiah (when he began his prophecy, Ch. i: 1, 2), to the final capturing four years after the destruction of Jerusalem (Jer. lii: 12, 30)—*i. e.*, from B. C. 623 to 583; and he foretold "390 years" for final finish of Israel, from the finished revolt of Jeroboam a year after Solomon's death, to this same final ravaging of the whole land—*i. e.*, from B. C. 973 to 583, just as in our table. Josephus (Ant. 10, iv: 4) thus reckons the prophecy of Ezekiel as covering "391 years" from the death of Solomon; minus 40 = 351 (corrupt 361) to the "18th of Josiah."

§ 46. The 490 years interval from temple to temple (§ 49), was regarded as the fulfillment of prophecy, as in II Chron. xxxvi: 20, 21. "They were servants to him [the king of Babylon] and his sons, until the reign of the kingdom of Persia. To fulfill the word of the Lord by the mouth of Jeremiah, until the land had enjoyed her Sabbaths; for as long as she lay desolate she kept Sabbath, TO FULFILL THREE-SCORE AND TEN YEARS," foretold. (See Lev. xxv: 4-26, and xxvi: 34, 35; Jer. xxv: 11, 12, and xxix: 10; Zech. i: 12.) These seventy Sabbatic years of captivity x 7 = 490 years, or 10 jubilee periods, reached from the completely finished temple at B. C. 513 (F, § 35) back to the finished temple of Solomon at B. C. 1003. This Divine arrangement of time (made to preserve the true Sabbatic reckoning, and to induce a Sabbatic revival after the captivity),* was an intimation; that, as soon as God's people got fully equipped for their worship, they began to decline therefrom. Sad truth of all ages! We have here a signal confirmation of the Bible Chronology of this Sabbatic interval from temple to temple, as taught also by Josephus and the Jews.

§ 47. Uncanonical Jewish authors confirm our reckoning, showing the Bible datings as well understood in their times. Josephus (Ant. 10, viii: 4) expressly states the duration of the Jewish kings, including "20 years" for Saul, as being "514 years, 6 months and 10 days;" which is our own addition of the reigns just as the Bible gives them (even to the months and days), from 20 years before David to the death of Jehoiachin the last surviving king, (38—11 =) 27 years after the destruction of Jerusalem (II Ki. xxiv: 8, 15, and xxv: 2, 4, 27; Jer. lii: 5, 31). Thus we have 20 years + David, 40 + Sol., 40 + Israel, 254 + Judah 133 + 27 of captivity = 514 years from B. C. 1074 to 560.

Josephus also (9, xiv: 1) gives the duration of Israel (reckoning simply by its given reign-lengths added), as 240 yrs., 7 mo., 7d.," while the Bible figures (changing his Jehu 27 to 28) add up 1 year more, as here at § 23. (For the months and days, see II Ki. xv: 8, 13, and I Ki. xvi: 15.) We see by this how accurately preserved we have the Bible numbers, just as Josephus and the Jews originally had them. Moreover, the Jewish Priest Record copied by Josephus (20, x) gives the old standard interval, from Solomon's temple to the Cyrus decree for rebuilding it, as "466 yrs., 6 mo. and 10 days," *i. e.*, from B. C. 1003 to 537-6—just as our table has it. (See further testimony of Josephus at § 55, of Eupolemus and Demetrius at § 54, and of the Talmud at § 24.)

§ 48. There has been discovered in our day a wonderful monumental confirmation of the Bible chronology as our table sets it forth. "In the stèle of Mesha, King of Moab, he states that Omri and his house reign exactly 40 years." (See Schwartz.) Now we are told of Omri (at I Ki. xvi: 23), "Six years reigned he in Tirzah;" *i. e.*, as only the ruler of a faction (ver. 21, 22)—the other 6 of his total " 12 years " being alone known abroad as *actual reign* without a rival, began in the "31st year of Asa," in the now permanently established capital "Samaria" (ver. 24). And from the beginning of Omri's 6 years of

---

* See Neh. x: 31; Jos. Ant. 11, viii: 5.

actual reign to the death of his last grandson, Joram (the end of the dynasty), is by our Bible Chronology just 40 years, B. C. 923-883.*

What is striking about the agreement is, that this chronology was formulated by us (as given in the table § 25) many years ago, from the Bible alone, before anything was known of the monumental inscription from Moab. The peculiar value of this 40-year verification is, that it covers the joint reign of Jehoram of Judah with his father, Jehoshaphat, the only case where our chronology has an overlap of the regnal years, and proves our reckoning (at that, its most difficult point) to be correct. Besides, it confirms the *full 13 years* between Ahab and Jehu, which proves that it can not be those kings referred to (as alleged) in the Assyrian canon.

NOTE. Schwartz tries to make the 40 years of the Moabite inscription cover the whole rule of Omri, before he got full possession of the throne in *Samaria* (contrary to "the 31st of Asa" in verse 23); and for that purpose he reduces the reigns as found in Scripture, from (Omri 6+Ahab 21+Ahaziah 1+Joram 12=) 40 — See § 25 — down to (6+19+1+9=) 35+5 more of Omri's previous rule=40 in all. But what a perversion is here of the Bible's figures for Ahab and Joram! This is a fair specimen of the steps taken, in the now popular *reconstruction* of Bible numbers in the interest of alleged Assyriology.

CHAPTER III.

JUBILEE RECKONING.

§ 49. This Bible dating is thoroughly fixed and assured by the jubilee reckoning of the Jews. They and their scribes noted from the first the striking fact, that the final founding of the second temple by royal decree, in the 2d of Darius (B. C. 520), was just 490 years after the first founding of Solomon's temple in the 4th of Solomon (put at B. C. 1010); these 490 years being just 10 jubilee periods of 49 years each, or in other words "70 weeks" of years like those described in Daniel's prophecy. And what was still more notable, the dedication of Solomon's temple 7 years after its founding (or in B. C. 1003), was thus the YEAR OF JUBILEE; giving 490 years or 70 weeks, or 10 jubilee periods, thence to the 9th of Darius (B. C. 513) as also a jubilee year.

§ 50. It was for this reason, although Ezra vi: 15, records the second temple as "finished" at the close of "the 6th year of the reign of Darius the king," yet "the dedication" which is thereupon described (ver. 16) as connected with a passover following (ver. 19-22), is said by Josephus to have been "in the 9th year of the reign of Darius," the

---

*In the Bib. Sacra (July, 1870, p. 642), our reckoning of the 40 years is verified, but there is much unnecessary confusion thrown over the computation.

temple being "built in 7 years' time," he says, as was the first temple. (Antiq. 11, iv: 7.) No doubt there was an adjustment of both these dedicatory occasions to the jubilee dates, to which providentially the building operations were brought so nigh. And the coincidence in each case was well fitted to stir the Jewish heart. (See § 46.)

§ 51. This ten-fold jubilee reckoning, or 70 weeks' dating (made more correctly 491 years by reckoning the 4th of Sol. as B. C. 1011) thus fixed in their temple history, and mixed with their most sacred associations, became the favorite measuring line of Jewish history, by which as a talismanic time-length of 490 years, they ever afterwards endeavored to map out all the ages. Step by step they theorized with this magic meter applied to Bible dates; even sometimes corrupting figures by conjectural emendations, when they did not quite agree with inexorable jubilee adjustment. Until, after a time, they had a full-fledged jubilee theory of Jewish history, which shows itself in the "Book of Jubilees," issued in about the New Testament time.

§ 52. The republic of scholars owe a debt of gratitude to Professor Schodde of Alleghany University, for his invaluable service in recently translating from the Ethiopic this memorable book of Jewish lore, showing the Hebrew method of dating scripture in the time of Christ. Thanks to the Bibliotheca Sacra for giving his translation to the public (see the Nos. during 1886-7); though it now can be had in book form. The same jubilee reckoning appears in the modern Jewish chronology, still followed by them; which was set forth soon after the Book of Jubilees, viz., in about A. D. 130, through the labors of the famous Rabbi Akiba. That chronology calls this year (A. D. 1888) their year A. M. 5649; putting the creation 3761 years B. C. And these 3761 years B. C. they make up as follows (as given by Hales): Before the flood 165(6)+to Abraham 29(0)+to the exodus 50(3)+to Solomon's temple 480th+to the captivity 410+70+40 to the Seleucic era+312 to A. D.—total 3760¼, or the 3761st year.

§ 53. The Jews in their ignorance of history during the dark ages following the close of the Old Testament, regarded the Persian Empire as having lasted but 52 years, to the 32d year of Darius Hystaspes, the last date of the Bible. (Neh. xiii: 6. *See Prideaux's Connection, I., p. 218, anno 486.*) And of these 52 years, the modern Jewish chronology gets but 40 after the 70 years of captivity, as if 20 years only were allowed from the temple dedication to the 20th Artaxerxes. For, as Jewish tradition put the finishing of the temple 20 years after the Cyrus-decree for restoring it, which decree ended the 70 years captivity as prophesied by Jeremiah, (Dan. ix: 1, 2; Jer. xxv: 1, 11, 12, comp. Ezra vi: 3, 15), we see that half the Persian 40 allowed in the modern Jewish chronology, really belonged before the temple dedication.

So that, we find therein the full jubilee reckoning, thus: From creation to the exodus (as there adjusted) 1656+290+503=2450th year, or 50 jubilees; then 480 (construed as reaching to the beginning of Solomon and of preparation for the temple, I Ki. v: 17, 18, as indicated in the arrangement of the LXX text)+10 of Solomon to the dedication=490 years, or 10 jubilees: or 480+410+70+20=980 years, i. e., 20 jubilees to the dedication of the 2nd temple (as if 490 from B. C. 1013 to 533 and 513 for "the second temple bulit"), viz., 70 jubilees back to the creation; and then 20+312+A. D. 159=490 years, or the "70 weeks" of Daniel, made to reach on beyond their own day (A. D. 130), with current jubilee reckoning ignored now that their land was lost * so as to controvert the Christian claim, that the 70 weeks of Daniel were more than out, and Messiah had already come.

§ 54. We thus know, from the modern Jewish chronology, as well as from the reckoning of Josephus, and of Eupolemus before him, and other ancient authorities (as we fully show elsewhere, that the ten-jubilee period of 490 years from temple to temple, was well established from the first, as the basis of all ancient chronology. Eupolemus,

---

*Schwartz tells us, that some of the rabbis give the taking of Jerusalem by Titus as 35 years after a jubilee. That is, having lost the jubilee reckoning in passing from the Old Testament, they started a new jubilee period from the famous Maccabean Era, B. C. 163, in place of the current jubilee B. C. 170); which, after (4 times 49=)196 years brought a jubilee at (196—163 B. C.=)34 A. D. (in place of the correct A. D. 27); so that 35 years from its ending (in A. D. 35) reached to September, A. D. 70. This made a jubilee come 63 years afterward, at A. D. 132, exciting the Jews remaining about Jerusalem then to revolt in hope of the city's restoration, as had occurred 63 years after its previous ruin (reckoned as from B. C. 583 to 520, as in Josephus. See *Rest. of Jos.*, § 28-30). This Rabbinical reckoning of jubilees was evidently gotten up at that era (A. D. 130) when their false modern chronology was invented; and it was what led to the Jewish outbreak which the Emperor Hadrian then quelled. (See Period A, B, § 15.)

But even this Rabbinical chronology retains traces of the correct Old Testament dating of the Jewish kings and captivity, with the true jubilees *then* existing. Thus: It has the accession of Solomon as if rightly at B. C. 1013, minus "410 years" to B. C. 603, minus "70 years" to B. C. 533 for Cyrus and "second temple built," minus 20 years to B. C. 513 (or 603 to 583 and 513), for Josephus' 9th Darius and the temple finished. But this 9th Darius being falsly treated as at the accession of Alexander the Great (as conquering *this* Darius) in B. C. 532 (a loss of 181 years), a minus 20 reached B. C. 312, the Seleucic Era. This made (20+20=)40 years only from the well known B. C. 312, the spurious "B. C. 352," as the time of 1st Cyrus decreeing "the second temple built." (As taken from Ganz by Hales, my notes iv: 11.) Those who give Darius 23 more years, or 32 years in all (as cited above from Prideaux), must thus have reduced the previous "70 years to 47 years, as if from 587 B. C. to 540," for the dates for "the temple burnt" and again "built."

mentioned by Clement Alex., as writing in B. C. 174, giving 5149 years from the creation down to B. C. 294. This he could not make out without the 490 years from temple to temple. The same is indicated by Demetrius, who wrote in B. C. 220 a history of the Jewish kings. (See citation of Alex Polyb., in Euseb. *Praep. Evang.*, ix: 21, Jackson's Chronol.)

§ 55. Josephus' testimony (War. 6, iv, 3, and x. 1) is, that from the completion of the second temple back to the completion of Solomon's temple, was ("1130−639"=)491 years, *i. e.*, 490 years to Solomon's dedication put as one year later. And this interval he makes up as follows: The 70 years captivity+the "639" years at its close =709 years (or "2177−1468"): and this 709+421="1130 years" back to Solomon's finished temple (after 70+421=491 years); which 1130+9 of Sol.+40 of David="1179 years" to the beginning of David's reign; *i. e.*, ("1179− 709"=)"470" [not '477'] before the 70 years of captivity, begun at the *completed capturing* (the 23d of Neb., Jer. lii: 30, Antiq. 10, ix: 7).

The 470−49=421 being thus from 9 years of Sol. to the 23d of Neb., it is 417 to the destruction of Jerusalem in the 19th of Neb., or (417+7 =)424 years *duration of the temple* from its founding at 2 years of Sol. (One year more being here in the war allowed for *joint reign* with his father—whereas, in the Antiq., 3 years put to Solomon alone reduce the 424 to 423.) The 423-4 years duration of the temple is just the scripture reckoning; and is plainly made up thus: The 133 years after Samaria captured+the 254 before (to B. C. 974)+36-37 of Sol=423 −4 years (to B. C. 1010-1011). Thus we see that Josephus used the *scriptural 254 years duration* of Israel, not the gross 260 of added reigns in Judah, as Schwartz contends. This harmonized reckoning of Josephus is fully expounded elsewhere; and all his values show that 490 years were universally understood as separating temple from temple.

GIVEN JUBILEE YEARS.

§ 56. We have sufficient indications of the very years in which the ancient jubilees occurred, to fix the place where the 490 year period from temple to temple belongs. The building and dedication of Solomon's temple plainly indicate the Sabbatic and jubilee year (I Ki. vi: 37, 38): "In the 4th year of Solomon was the foundation of the house of the Lord laid, and in the 11th year was the house finished. So was he seven years in building it." (Ch. viii: 2): "And all the men of Israel assembled themselves unto King Solomon, at the feast of the month Ethanim, which is the seventh month [the month for sounding the jubilee trumpet]. And they brought up the ark of the Lord. So the king and all the children of Israel dedicated the house of the Lord. And at that time Solomon held a feast, and all Israel with him, * * * seven days and seven days, even fourteen days;" *i. e.*, 7 for the ordinary celebration, and 7 for the jubilee dedication (Ver. 2, 63, 65.) "They kept the dedication of the altar seven days and the feast seven days; and on the three and twentieth day of the seventh month he sent the people away unto their tents, glad and merry in heart for the goodness of the Lord." So the tabernacle feast lasted (as usual) from the 15th to the 22d of that 7th month; and if the dedication feast *preceded* it from the 8th to the 15th, it would make 14 days (the 8th to the 22d). The festivities would begin from the 8th (at sunset), and on the morning of the tenth the jubilee trumpet had to sound, as commanded in Lev. xxv: 9: "Seven Sabbaths of years shall be unto to thee forty and nine years. Then shalt thou cause the trumpet of the jubilee to sound on the tenth day of the seventh month; in the day of atonement shall ye make the trumpet sound throughout all your land."

§ 57. Usher, and most chronological authorities, accept that year B. C. 1003, following Solomon's temple, as the Jewish jubilee.*

Reckoning by the vulgar text of I Ki. vi: 1, we shall have 8 years of building the temple+the "480th"=487 years from that jubilee back to the exodus. So that the common chronology has the first ten jubilees, or 70 weeks' period of 490 years, reaching from (490-487=) *3 years before leaving Egypt* to the dedication of Solomon's temple. That is, the first jubilee period of 49 years is reckoned from three years before the exodus to six years after the entering of Canaan, when, at the 7th year of Joshua, as the first Sabbatic of Canaan possession, is understood to have been the celebration of the first jubilee finished.

§ 58. Thus we read (at Josh. xi: 23): "So Joshua took the whole land * * * and the land rested from war." (Ch. xiv: 6–10): "And Caleb * * * said unto him * * * forty years old was I when Moses sent me to spy out the land * * * and now, behold the Lord hath kept me alive, as he said, these forty and five years * * * and now, lo, I am this day fourscore and five years old." That is, five years after the arrival in Canaan, in the 6th year, the land had pretty much been conquered. Thereupon, in the 6th year, the land was divided by lot (xviii: 1, 10, and xix: 51); and cities of refuge were established (ch. xx, xxi). And by this view the seventh year having

---

* "This dedication did not take place till eleven months after the completion of the edifice. The delay most probably originated in Solomon's wish to choose the most fitting opportunity, when there should be a general rendezvous of the people in Jerusalem; and that was not till the next year. THAT WAS A JUBILEE YEAR; and he resolved on commencing the solemn ceremonial a few days before the feast of tabernacles, which was the most appropriate of all seasons." (Dr. Jamieson in Brit. Com. on I Ki. viii: 1.)

come, "the Lord gave them rest round about" (xxi: 43, 45); and with Sabbatic rest closed with jubilee rejoicing, the two and a half tribes were dismissed from war to their home beyond Jordan (ch. 22). Not till "a long time after" this was it that "Joshua waxed old and stricken with age" (xxiii: 1; xiii: 1, out of place). Compare Period D, § 8, 9.

§ 59. From that 7th of Joshua (made the 8th by Usher), B. C. 1444 back through the first jubilee period of 49 years, we are carried to B. C. 1493, three years before the exodus in B. C. 1490 (Usher says 1491). And from that B. C. 1493 at the beginning of jubilees, the first ten jubilees or 490 years take us to Solomon's dedication, B. C. 1003. And the next 490 take us to B. C. 513, the dedication of the second temple (according to Josephus, above). Whether the former of these periods is right (as given by the vulgar text of I Ki. vi: 1), or whether that text ("480") and that reckoning, taken from the modern Jewish chronology, which is plainly founded on the peculiar jubilee theory of Jewish history, is a corruption suggested by and meant to complement the 490 period between the two dedications, which is undoubtedly correct; this question is fully discussed by us elsewhere, and we can not enter upon it here. (See Period D.)

§ 60. Though the appointed Sabbatics and jubilees were but little maintained by the apostate Jews, yet the *reckoning* of them was kept up down to the New Testament times and as long, at least, as Jerusalem remained. In their faithful observance was a divine promise of two years' food extraordinarily provided (Lev. xxv: 11, 19, 22): "I will command my blessing upon you in the sixth year, and it shall bring forth fruit for three years. And ye shall sow the eighth year, and eat of old fruit until the ninth year, until its fruits come in ye shall eat of the old store." But when they failed to carry out the jubilee enfranchisement required, the promise failed, and disaster came. The seventy years of captivity were brought in that the land might "enjoy her Sabbath" of which she had been deprived. (Lev. xxvi: 20, 33, 35; II Chron. xxxvi: 21.)

§ 61. From the jubilee of Solomon, B. C. 1003, six jubilee periods or 294 years carry us to B. C. 709, when there was evidently a jubilee, in about the 17th year of Hezekiah's reign according with the description given. (Isa. xxxvi: 1; xxxvii: 8, 30.) "And this shall be a sign unto thee; ye shall eat this year such as grows of itself; and the second year that which springeth of the same; and in the third year sow ye and reap, and plant vineyards and eat the fruit thereof." This makes Hezekiah's reign begin about B. C.726, as required by the accepted chronology given above (§ 25).

§ 62. Other jubilees must have come at B. C. 611, near the end of Josiah's reign; and at B. C. 562, "in the midst of the years" of captivity

(Hab. iii: 2). In that year, the (B. C. 598—562=)" 37th year of the captivity of Jehoiachin" (II Ki. xxv: 27; Jer. lii: 31-35), he was appropriately given his jubilee liberty, and raised to honor: so that, by this foretokening of captivity to end, God did "in wrath remember mercy." Another jubilee came at B. C. 513, when the second temple was dedicated (according to Josephus) and the captivity came fully to an end; and then again at B. C. 464, the close of Xerxes' reign. From that date, ten jubilees or 490 years carry us to A. D. 27 as the jubilee year. This it plainly was, leading Christ, then in the first year of his ministry, to read in the synagogue from Isaiah (very likely the appointed lesson for the occasion) that memorable jubilee passage: " The Spirit of the Lord is upon me, because he hath sent me to *set at liberty* them that are bruised, to preach THE ACCEPTABLE YEAR of the Lord. And he closed the book, * * * And he began to say unto them: This day is this Scripture fulfilled in your ears." (Luke iv: 17, 21). That is, " In this jubilee, this acceptable year, I come preaching jubilee freedom and deliverance to the captives of sin."

§ 63. At 49 years before this A. D. 27, *i. e.*, in B. C. 23, the 14th of Herod (from B. C. 37), occurred the last previous jubilee, and a sad time of famine it was. Josephus (Antiq. 15: xx: 1) says: "Then in this very year, which was the 13th year of the reign of Herod, very great calamities came upon the country * * * The ground was barren. When the fruits of the first year were spoiled, and whatever they had laid up beforehand was spent, the misery increased upon them; and that not only in this year, but what seed they had sown perished also, by reason of the ground not yielding its fruits in the second year," the 14th of Herod.

§ 64. Concerning this, Whiston, the editor of Josephus, observes: "This famine for two years that afflicted Judea and Syria in the 13th and 14th years of Herod, which are the 23d and 24th years before the Christian era, was remarkable. It is well worth our observation here, that these two years were a Sabbatic year and a year of jubilee, for which Providence, during the theocracy, used to provide a triple crop before hand; but they became now, when the Jews had forfeited that blessing, the greatest years of famine since the days of Ahab."

GIVEN SABBATIC YEARS.

§ 65. Thus evident are the true jubilee reckonings. There are similar plain indications of Sabbatic years. The ideal Sabbatic was a time, not only for rest and recuperation of the land lying fallow for a year, but for rest and recuperation to the agriculturist himself, usually so driven and confined (as we see in our day) by the exacting and unremitting duties of farm life. How else can *he* have any "vacation," such as men in other walks of life plan for themselves? When, among the Jews, the land lay at rest, and debts were released, and bondmen went free, then there was a season of leisure, convenient for religious, social, educational or political convocations; when the people generally could be stirred up to any great enterprise or reform that might be needed.

§ 66. Such a revival seems to have occurred in the Sabbatic that came 70 years after the founding of Solomon's temple, viz., in B. C. 940. For that appears to be the 15th year of Asa's reign in Judah, reckoning 36 more of Solomon+17 of Rehoboam+3 of Abijah+14 of Asa= 70 years from beginning to beginning of Sabbatic. Then, early in Asa's 15th year (according to II Chron. 15th ch.), there was a notable time of reformation, assembling and worship.

§ 67. And 28 years later, at the Sabbatic of 912 B. C., near the beginning of Jehoshaphat's reign, may have occurred the remarkable work of missionary preaching recorded in the 17th chapter, particularly at ver. 7-10, when the king sent many evangelists to "teach in the cities of Judah," and "they had the book of the law of the Lord with them, and went about throughout all the cities of Judah and taught the people and the fear of the Lord fell upon all the kingdoms of the land that were round about." This is said to have been in Jehoshaphat's "3d year," which, if reckoned in this particular case from Asa as reigning but 40 full years (xvi: 13), or rather, if reckoned from Asa's total disability the year before (ver. 12), agrees with the Sabbatic B. C. 912, after 42 years from Asa's accession.

§ 68. In like manner John Baptist came preaching in the Sabbatic of A. D. 26-7, which culminated in the jubilee of A. D. 27. A wonderfully convenient season that, for such a wide-spread reformation, when, with more than ordinary leisure the people flocked to him from every direction, and there "went out to him Jerusalem and all Judea, and all the region round about Jordan." (Mat. iii: 5.)*

The well-established calculation of Daniel's "seventy weeks" of "Messiah the Prince" (ix: 24-27), is from the Sabbatic ending in B. C. 457, the 7th year of Artaxerxes, when Ezra went to Jerusalem with the king's decree of restoration, onward 490 years to the Sabbatic ending in A. D. 34, when Saul was converted, and the gospel was fully opened to the Gentiles. The preaching of John Baptist, of Christ, and of the Apostles, "confirmed the covenant with many for one week" Sabbatic, from A. D. 26-7 to 34; and "in the midst of the week," A. D. 30, the death of Christ caused the "sacrifice and oblation to cease," the Messiah being then "cut off."

---

*That we have the right reckoning of the sabbatics is further evident from Josephus' description of a Sabbatic at the death of Simon, B. C. 135, and at Herod's conquest of Jerusalem, B. C. 37 (Antiq. 13, viii: 1, and 14, xvi: 2). Also at B. C. 163. (See Period F.)

§ 69. But the most distinctly notable Sabbatic in Jewish history, is that of B. C. 590, *i. e.*, 21 years after the previous jubilee of B. C. 611. This was at the end of the 8th year of Zedekiah's reign, at the close of whose 11 years' reign (3 years later) in B. C. 587, Jerusalem was destroyed by Nebuchadnezzar. (Usher says B. C. 588, Hales, 586; we elsewhere prove that it was 587.) For Zedekiah "after 8 years" (Josephus. Ant. 10, vii: 3) of subordination rebelled against Nebuchadnezzar (II Chron. xxxvi: 11-13, II Ki. xxiv: 17-21). So that Nebuchadnezzar came against Zedekiah "in the 9th year of his reign" (xxv: 1), besieging Jerusalem till its destruction at the end of Zedekiah's 11 years (ver. 2, 8).

§ 70. The siege was raised temporarily by the approach of Pharaoh from Egypt (Jer. xxxvii: 53); whereupon Jeremiah was cast into prison (ver. 6-21). "In the 10th year of Zedekiah" the siege was renewed (xxxii: 1-3). Jos. (Ant. 10, vii: 4) says it was on "the 10th day of the 10th month in the 10th year of Zedekiah," just a year after the siege began before (II Ki. xxv: 1), with "18 months" of further siege, till the city was taken "on the 9th day of the 4th month in the [end of the] 11th year of Zed." (Jos. viii: 1, 2). Now, *before* this return of Nebuchadnezzar to the siege (Jer. xxxiv: 21, 22), *i. e.*, some *two years before the taking of the city*, Jeremiah rebuked Zedekiah and the princes for having broken a covenant made at the Sabbatic year (then just past) giving liberty to the bondmen, according to the Sabbatic law of Moses (ver. 8-22). See Period F, § 29.

§ 71. This proves, that that Sabbatic was *three years* before the taking of the city, when Zedekiah had reigned 8 years, and revolted from Nebuchadnezzar. Taking advantage of the Sabbatic year of liberation (B. C. 590), Zedekiah declared *his own* independence, securing the popular enthusiasm in it by pledging also the required Sabbatic enfranchisement of those in servitude. (Chap. xxxiv: 8, 9.) "This is the word that came unto Jeremiah from the Lord, after that the king Zedekiah had made a covenant with all the people which were at Jerusalem, to proclaim liberty unto them; that every man should let his man-servant, and every man his maid-servant, being a Hebrew or a Hebrewess, go free; that none should serve himself of him, to wit, of a Jew, his brother."

§ 72. This was a concession to duty and to God, adhered to but a little while, under the alarm of Nebuchadnezzar's approach to the siege. But when the siege was temporarily raised, about the end of Zedekiah's 9th year (B. C. 589), he became haughty, and the pledge was disowned and broken (ver. 10, 11). "Now when all the princes and all the people which had entered into the covenant, heard that every one should let his man-servant and every one his maid-servant go free, that none should serve themselves of them any more, then they obeyed, and let them go free. But afterward they turned, and caused the servants and the hand-maids whom they had let go free, to return, and brought them under subjection for servants and for hand-maids."

§ 73. Thereupon, Jeremiah denounced God's anger.

Verse 12-17: "Thus saith the Lord, the God of Israel: I made a covenant with your fathers, in the day I brought them forth out of the the land of Egypt, out of the house of bondage, saying, At the end of seven years let ye go every man his brother, a Hebrew, which hath been sold unto thee; and when he hath served thee six years, thou shalt let him go free; but your fathers hearkened not unto me, neither inclined their ear. And ye were now turned, and had done right in my sight, in proclaiming liberty every man to his neighbor; and ye had made a covenant before me, in the house that is called by my name; but ye turned, and polluted my name, and caused every man his servant, and every man his hand-maid, whom he had set at liberty, at their pleasure, to return, and brought them into subjection, to be unto you for servants and for hand-maids. Therefore, thus saith the Lord, ye have not hearkened unto me, in proclaiming liberty every one to his brother and every man to his neighbor: Behold, I proclaim a liberty for you, saith the Lord, to the sword, to the pestilence, and to the famine; and I will make you to be removed unto all the kingdoms of the earth," etc.*

---

* Prideaux (Connec. Pref., page ix) discards all jubilee and Sabbatic reckoning, saying of this passage (Jer. xxxiv: 8-10): "Every Hebrew servant was to be released in the 7th year of his servitude, though it were neither a jubilee nor a Sabbatical year." But, though this general principle, that no Hebrew should serve over six years, was the first thing announced (at Ex. xxi: 1) before the Sabbatic year was arranged (at Ex. xxiii: 9, 10), yet upon the full establishment of that Sabbatic year as a *land-sabbath* (Lev. xxv: 1-7, 20), it was constituted a "*year of release*" (Deut. xv: 1, 9, 12, and xxxi: 10), for the canceling of all Hebrew debts, and consequently all claims for service. That the fixed Sabbatic year was thus introduced for the carrying out and insuring of the previously ordained principle of 7th year rest and release, is evident from the fact that Moses thus set it forth fully in his final address in Deuteronomy.

He there (in Deut.) says nothing about it as a *land-sabbath* (described in Leviticus), but he fully explains it as a *bankruptcy law*, or "release" of debtors, and a release from servitude. Notice particularly, that in the midst of his discourse on this "year of release" coming "at the end of every seven years" (Deut. xv: ver. 1, 9, and ending at ver. 18), he introduces at ver. 12 the release of *service* "in the 7th year," without any particle or note of transition as if to another subject, showing plainly that he reduces the whole to one Sabbatic institution. When the Sabbatic year came round, and they were releasing all their brother Hebrews from *debt*, they could not help being reminded of that *special debt* of service which they were required also to release. They *then* would see that this obligation, too, was carried out; and especially when (as in Jer. xxxiv: 8-17), the congregation generally took it up as a reform. This reformation made (as we show) in the very "year of release," or Sabbatic year (ending B. C. 590), as well as that other reformation, of Nehemiah (x: 31), made in the Sabbatic year (ending B. C. 443), just 21 Sabbatics afterward, both show that we rightly calculate the Sabbatic years of the Jews.

§ 74. Here we have an express exhibit of Sabbatic law, and its historical application, a thousand years after its establishment; showing us in striking language *the exact date of its reckoning down to that time* (B. C. 590), and proving that we have the Sabbatic and jubilee reckoning correct, with the destruction of the city in B. C. 587. The chronology of Jewish history back to Solomon's temple is thus placed on an impregnable basis.

CHAPTER IV.

UNFOUNDED THEORIZINGS.

§ 75. Thurman in his chronology, (The Bible Chronology established by Wm. C. Thurman, 3d Ed., Phila., 1864), laboring to make out a particular scheme of dates, undertakes to get the Sabbatic of Zedekiah *later in his reign*, or near the time of the city's capture, instead of three years before, as we have proved it above. He says the covenant of emancipation was not made until under the alarm of Zedekiah's sending to Jeremiah at the first siege in Zedekiah's ninth year (Jer. xxxvii: 3-5); and even then he claims that it was only a covenant in *anticipation* of the Sabbatic year, which did not begin (he alleges) till the next spring, the last of Zedekiah's tenth year. But this makes the Sabbatic itself to be spent in a re-enslavement of bondmen, who had been freed before it began! for they had certainly enjoyed a period of actual freedom (xxxiv: 10, 11, 16). And *after* the rebuke for their re-enslavement, the siege had not re-begun (ver. 21, 22), viz., in the tenth of Zedekiah (xxxii: 1, 2), *i. e.*, eighteen months before the capture of the city. How certain that *their temporary release was ended* at least two whole years before the city was destroyed. How impossible any such theory as that of Thurman!

§ 76. He thus claims that the Sabbatic began as late as the spring of B. C. 588 (instead of 590), and so twenty-one years before, in the spring of B. C. 609, when Josiah died. Otherwise, he claims, Josiah would commence offensive war in a Sabbatic year, which could not be. But, as the true jubilee reckoning here shown has the Sabbatic ended on the day of atonement in the autumn of B. C. 590, and so of B. C. 611, it was all over a year later in 610, the year before Josiah's death; that is, long before he entered the war in which he was slain. Moreover, Thurman makes the Sabbatic fourteen years before, to be in B. C. 623, the eighteenth of Josiah, instead of the correct 625. And still more strangely, he makes that eighteenth of Josiah (as B. C. 623) to be the jubilee Sabbatic! whereas the jubilee was B. C. 611, as we have thoroughly proved.

§ 77. Thus wildly does Thurman speculate; and all his chronology of the ages is founded on this misplacement of all the Sabbatics by two years and of all the jubilees by twelve years! This is only a specimen of the many reckless and uncritical theories of chronology that have been put forth in our day. We are sorry to say that the scholarly Bunsen himself indulges in such fanciful theorizings. And very recently, a writer in the Bibliotheca Sacra (January, 1888) sets forth with much ingenuity a scheme of the sort. He sets aside the whole established chronology of Jewish history, giving a new reckoning throughout; which he bases upon a jubilee theory of his own, with the established dating of the jubilees and Sabbatics (as shown above) *entirely ignored*. He starts his jubilees backward from A. D. 32 put as a jubilee! instead of the well known A. D. 27; thus having no jubilee and no Sabbatic in all his reckoning correct.

§ 78. He puts the "seventy weeks" as reaching from jubilee to jubilee, *i. e.*, from his A. D. 32 back 490 years to his 458 B. C. (he says) as a jubilee year; instead of the correct jubilee 464. He thus has not even learned how to carry any number of years from a date A. D. to a date B. C., or *vice versa*, viz., with 1 extra added to the date (because of two years, 1 B. C. and 1 A. D., with no year o between; so that, from A. D. 34 to B. C. 437 are 490, not 491 years). His jubilee A. D. 32 requires jubilee B. C. 459, not 458 as he puts it, entirely oblivious of even chronological arithmetic. Thus, all his jubilee and Sabbatic reckoning, back through the dates of the Jewish kings and the whole Bible history, is based on this erroneous and inconsistent calculation. And so, by his own peculiar jubilee theory, he gets (B. C. 458+490=) 948 B. C. as a jubilee year—and then he has (B. C. 948+490=) 1438 B. C. as the beginning of jubilee periods *at* his Exodus, instead of Usher's, two or three years *before* the Exodus.

§ 79. But as he has the death of Solomon in B. C. 929 (or forty-five years after its Bible date, B. C. 974); and as he has also devised a peculiar date for the Exodus as B. C. 1438; therefore, in order to use "the 480th year" of I Ki. vi: 1, he has to say (1438—480th=) 959 B. C. for "the fourth of Sol." or 962 for the beginning of his reign. Thus he has arbitrarily reduced the reign of Solomon from the scriptural forty (or 39 sole) to thirty-three years only (from B. C. 962 to 929)! And he has the dedication of the temple in the 11th of Solomon or B. C. 952, *four years before his jubilee* of 948 B. C. It is only by such mutilating of numbers, such unsabbatic reckoning of events, that the destructive critics are enabled to lessen by forty or fifty years the scriptural time back to Solomon, as they feel obliged to do in order to satisfy the supposed demands of Assyrian chronology. This process of mutilation is applied to all the multiplied regnal numbers and synchronisms so interlocked throughout the books of Kings and Chronicles—with utter disregard of jubilee and Sabbatic requirement. And this course is pursued as if on the presumption, that any sort of critical handling will answer for the Bible—no matter how authentic and well proved its data—to save a pagan record (supposed to be deciphered and explained without possibility of mistake) from appearing to have any misspelling of names or any defect of reckoning about it!

§ 80. Thus the current method of procedure is, *first* to fix out from inscriptions excavated of late in Assyria, a pagan chronology assumed to be perfect and infallible; and *then* to attempt a reconstruction of the sacred writers into harmony with it. The time has fully come for a reversal of this process. We have first ascertained what the Bible chronology is, and must be, in the harmony of its own consistent exegesis; and now only are we prepared to learn if the Assyrian inscriptions can be reconciled with it. Not God's word harmonized with a heathen record, but the heathen record harmonized (it may be) with God's well verified word. That second stage of the process must be reserved to another article. The subject may well be investigated from this Bible standpoint; with the presumption thus fixed, that, by multitudinous datings of diverse writers in different kingdoms, fortified by numerous verifications, there is no chance of mistaking the Bible chronology back to the reign of David; and that (unless otherwise disproved) there is no event of human history whose date is more certain or more simply demonstrable, than the dedication of Solomon's Temple in B. C. 1003.

PART III.

Assyriology and the Jewish Kings.

SHOWING THAT THE BIBLE CHRONOLOGY CAN NOT BE IMPEACHED.

§ 81. We have shown that Scripture has an exact and certain Chronology; especially fixing the interval of Israel's duration from the accession of Jeroboam I to the capture of Samaria as 254 years, from B. C. 974 to 720. But now Assyriology comes forward, and with its excavated and deciphered inscriptions, claims to prove that the Bible Chronology is wrong, having the times of Menahem and Azariah over twenty years, and the times of Ahab and Jehu (with all beyond) over forty years too far back. We are here to investigate whether the Assyrian inscriptions do give a different dating to the kings, or whether, on the other hand, they can be harmonized with the Bible Chronology. The larger part of the inquiry comes under two heads, (I) as to "Pul" of Assyria and "Ahaz" of Judah, (II) as to Ahab and Jehu of Israel.

FIRST DIVISION.

" Pul " of Assyria and " Ahaz " of Israel.

CHAPTER I.—Who Was " Pul, King of Assyria?"
II Ki. xv: 19, 29; I Chron. 5: 26.

§ 82. While many monuments and inscriptions of the earlier and the later Assyrian kings have been found and deciphered within the past generation, the period for 25 to 50 years preceding Tiglath-pileser is remarkably destitute of any discovered inscriptions. "The total absence of contemporary dated documents during these reigns (previous to Tiglath-pileser) is remarkable; and the Assyrian Canon is here the only proof of the reigns of these kings." (*Geo. Smith, Ep. Can., h. §3, 116.*)

For this reason, the statements of different Assyriologists concerning these kings and their reigns, are very mixed and confusing. The Assyrian " Eponym Canon " indicates the following reigns, as given by Smith:

Vul-nirari,	beginning about B. C.	812.
Shalmaneser,	"	"	783.
Assur-daan,	"	"	773.
Assur-nirari,	"	"	755.
Tiglath-pileser,	"	"	745.

§ 83. Concerning the first of these, "Vul-nirari," Rawlinson (in Smith's Bible Dic., Art. Pul) says: " The Assyrians have a king, the grandson of Samsi-vul, whose name is read very doubtfully as 'Vul-lush' or 'Iva-lush,' at about the period when ' Pul' must have lived (say B. C. 800-750). He states that he made an expedition into Syria," etc. Chamber's Cyc. (1880) calls him " Iva-lush, probably the Pul of the Scriptures." It also says: " With this king ends the first dynasty (at Tiglath-pileser), in which we have eighteen monarchs from Bel-lush to Iva-lush (1273-747 B. C.), where begins the later Assyrian Empire." The " eighteen monarchs" include the four upper names given above, and yet the writer says the uppermost (Vul-nirari) *ends* " the earlier empire." The Encyc. Brit. (1887) calls him not Vul-nirari but " Rimmon-nirari, 811-782 B. C." And it adds: " The first Assyrian Empire came to an end in B. C. 744, being overthrown by the usurper Tiglath-pileser after a struggle of three or four years. He, in 740, took tribute of Menahem (which a false reading in the Old Testament ascribes to a non-existent Pul."

§ 84. Rawlinson (in Smith's Bible Dic. Art. Assyria) says, that after " Salmanasur (B. C. 860-825), his grandson (Vul-nirari, the intermediate father being Samsi-vul) is thought to be Pul, Phul, or Phalech, the first Assyrian king named in Scripture. * * * By the synchronism of Menahem, the date of Pul may be determined to be about 770 B. C., *i. e.*, twenty-three years before Babylon became independent, according to Ptolemy's Canon, in B. C. 747." This is the view of George Smith, the distinguished Assyriologist, in his "Assyrian Eponym Canon." The British commentary of Dr. Jamieson (1872) says: "This name 'Pul' has been recently identified with that of Phalluka on the monuments of Nineveh, and that of 'Menahem' has been discovered also."

Prof. Oppert (1868) gave the names of the kings thus: Samsi-vul="Samas-bin;" Vul-nirari="Belochus" (with Semiramis); "Shalmaneser;" Assur-daan="Assur-edibel;" Assur-nirari="Assur-likhis." Rev. D. H. Haigh, another Assyrian scholar (1871) gave the names thus: Samsi-vul="Samsi-barku;" Vul-nirari="Barka-narar," "Salmanaris;" Assur-daan="Assur-idili;" Assur-nirari="Assur-narar;" Tiglath-pileser="Tukulti-palesar." (See in Geo. Smith's Ep. Can., p. 3-6.)

§ 85. In this diversity of the decipherings, it is somewhat difficult to determine the exact truth. We have here found the reign beginning B. C. 812 (and taken as that of "Pul" by George Smith, and Chambers' Cyc., and Smith's Bible Dic.), given with seven different spellings of the king's name, viz., as Vul-nirari (by the Canon of Geo. Smith), as Rimmon-nirari (by the Encyc. Brit.), as Barku-narar (by Haigh), as Bel-ochus (by Oppert), as Pul, Phul, or Phalech (by the Bible Dic.), as Phalluka (by the British Com.), and as Iva-lush or Vul-lush (by Chambers' Cyc. and Rawlinson). We can only say, that the "Vul" in the Canon forms a sufficiently near identification with the "Pul" or Phul of the Scriptures.

Now then, in consistency with the Scripture dating, we may adopt either of *three* theories concerning the identity of "Pul." (1.) We may, with the authors cited above, consider Pul as the Assyrian king "Vul-nirari" (or Phal-luka, or Bel-ochus, or Iva-lush), who ascended the throne in B. C. 812. Or (2), we may recognize Pul in the Assyrian king "Assur-daan" (or Assur-dana-pul) who ascended the throne in B. C. 773, as being the famous "Sar-dana-pulus" at the end of the earlier Assyrian Empire. Or (3), we may regard Pul as the subsequent Tiglath-pileser himself (or Takulti-pal-eser or Pulus), in the character of a *usurping* king of Assyria long before his regular accession to the throne at Nineveh in B. C. 745.

1. VUL-NIRARI.

§ 86. George Smith (in the Ep. Can., p. 183) thus gives his reasons for accepting this king as the "Pul" of Scripture:

"It has been one of the greatest problems of Assyriologists to discover which king of Assyria is called Pul in the Bible. This question forms the key of the whole chronological problem. My own theory for the solution of the problem is founded on the principle I have followed out in all these dates, the principle of taking the Assyrian records to be correct as to Assyrian dates, and the Hebrew records as to Hebrew dates. The date I fix for the accession of Zachariah, king of Israel, (and Menahem) is B. C. 773; according to our marginal dates, the submission of Menahem to Pul took place within two years of this, that is, in B. C. 771. Now it is a curious fact that in this period, at the commencement of the reign of Menahem, the Assyrian Canon registers two successive expeditions to Palestine, in B. C. 773 to Damascus, and in 772 to the neighboring city of Hadrach. These expeditions so closely correspond in time with the Biblical date of Pul's expedition, that I am strongly of opinion that one of these campaigns was the occasion on which Menahem invoked the aid of the Assyrian monarch.

"The expedition of B. C. 773 occurs, however, according to the Canon, in the reign of Shalmaneser III, whose name can not by any process be tortured into a resemblance to Pul. This objection I think can be explained by a curious notice in two inscriptions of Vul-nirari, the predecessor of Shalmaneser. From this notice I judge that Shalmaneser was the son of Vul-nirari, and did not reign independently, but was associated with his father during his lifetime; and I believe that Vul-nirari continued to reign at least as late as B. C. 773. The passage in question reads: 'Palace of Vul-nirari, the great king, king of nations, king of Assyria. The king, whom in his son, Assur, king of the spirits, has renowned, and a dominion unequaled has given to his hand.' This allusion to Vul-nirari being renowned through his son points to his being associated in the government.

"Again, in his principal inscription, Vul-nirari celebrates a special expedition to Damascus, and immediately before it states that he took tribute from Tyre, Sidon, the land of Omri (or Israel), Edom and Philistia. Now, the expedition to Damascus in B. C. 773, is the only one in the Eponym Canon to that place which comes anywhere near the time of Vul-nirari; and his statement that he took tribute from the land of Omri corresponds precisely with the Biblical statement that Menahem, king of Israel, paid tribute to Pul.

"It has been conjectured for many years that the name of Vul-nirari contains the elements of the Biblical Pul. Pur or Pul is one of the well-known values of the first element in the name, and it was quite in accordance with Assyrian custom to shorten similar names in common use; thus, the king Agukak-rimi is generally called Agu, and Ragmu-sevi-ina-namari, a long name in the Izdular legends, is often shortened to Ragmu. So the name Vul-nirari, which was probably Pul-nirari, was quite possibly shortened to Pul.

"On the strength of the inscription in which he states that he subdued and took tribute from the land of Omri, or Israel, Sir Henry

Rawlinson, some years back, identified Vul-nirari with the Biblical Pul; but he afterward abandoned this view when he discovered the Eponym Canon."

§ 87. We might object to this view, that it requires Menahem to begin in B. C. 773 or before; whereas we can not, without violation of the Scripture numbers, make him begin before B. C. 770 (or at most 771). For the 1st year of Pekah, beginning "in the 52d year" of Uzziah, can not be earlier than (the "16 years" of Jotham + the "16 years" of Ahaz =) 32 years added to Hezekiah's accession (B. C. 726), that is, corresponding with B. C. 758; and Menahem's accession "in the 39th year" of Uzziah, can not be more than (52d-39th =) 13 years earlier, viz., in (758 + 13=) 771 B. C., instead of the 773 that Smith claims (by stretching Menahem's "10 years" to 12 years from B. C. 761 to 773).

But this objection may be overcome thus: The years 770, 771 B. C. are (as Smith remarks) anomalous in the Canon. For they have as eponyms, 771 "the king," 770 "the tartan," or commander-in-chief, which are here entirely out of their order, with no other prime ministers following, but with rulers of cities proceeding before and after as if not interrupted by those two extraordinary eponyms. (See Ep. Can., p. 63, 25.) Smith tries to explain this by saying (p. 82): "It is conjectured that the reason for this omission (of so many officials who ought here to come in as eponyms) lies in the fact that these officers had so recently held the office of eponym during the last reign that their names were passed over." But this is unlikely, because just afterward, at the accession of Tiglath-pileser, where the succession is just as recent, no such omission of officials occurs.

§ 88. The two anomalous eponyms at B. C. 770, 771, have led Rev. D. H. Haigh to assume that there is here a *gap* in the Canon of 10 or 15 years, wherein the omitted eponyms belong. This Smith rejects, yet says: "But it must be allowed that in this place, if anywhere, a gap should take place, as there is a break here in the titles of eponyms." We suggest not a gap but a mere *excess* here of these two years not really belonging in the Canon.

It will be noticed as a curious coincidence that these two eponyms are not found on any except one of the seven copies of the Canon which we possess, namely, on copy I. (See Ep. Can., p. 35, 46, 47.) Suppose now that in making copy I (at p. 35) the scribe or artist at this point glanced wrongly at the years 752-3 of the copy which he was following, instead of the right place (after 772) which he had reached, then, *by mistake* he would write at 771, "Assur-nirari, the king," and at 770 "Samsi-il, the tartan." But directly, discovering his mistake, he would *erase these two lines*, as seen on copy V (p. 46), and would go on with the right names. (As at 769, 768, etc.) Then, afterward, some one seeing the two lines vacant, and *supposing* that two eponyms were there accidentally obliterated, might scrutinize the erasure to discover the lost names. He makes out the partial name, "Assur———king," and the next line, "Samsi-il tartan," but is at a loss to fill out the Assur———king; and remembering that he has heard of a king "Assur-dana-pal"—(see directly, § 89)—which name he finds nowhere on the list, he concludes that this must be the lost name, and inserts so much of it as the space between "Assur" and "king" allows, so that the two lines now read "Assur-daan king" and "Samsi-il tartan." And thus we have copy I, with these two erased lines (of real vacancy) wrongly filled up with names. The expeditions named in copy V might be further conjecture, made because all the years in this copy had expeditions put to them.

So then, if years 770, 771 are spurious in the Canon, then the eponyms and expeditions now set at years 772, 773 belong in their place, and there is *here no change of kings;* but Shalmaneser continues right along till B. C. 755, and the tribute of Menahem to Pul as the still living father Vul-nirari, might be during the "expedition to Damascus" 771, or that "to Hadrash" 770, or even later. With this small correction which we suggest in the Canon, this theory concerning Pul as Vul-nirari may be maintained, as is done by George Smith, and Chambers' Cyc., and Smith's Bible Dic.

2. ASSUR-DAAN.

§ 89. This king's name looks as if a contraction from "Assur-dana-pal," the name of a son of King Shalmaneser in the previous century. "It is related, in the monolith inscription of Samsi-vul III (beginning B. C. 825), that during the reign of his father, Shalmaneser II, another son of that king, named Assur-dain-pal, revolted against him, and was followed by twenty-seven districts of Assyria, principally in the east and south. These districts were subdued, and again brought under the rule of Shalmaneser by Samsi-vul, who afterward succeeded to the throne instead of the rebel prince." (*Ep. Can., p. 73.*) So, "Assur-daan," as a son of the next Shalmaneser, may have had the same name "Assur-dani-pal" as in the earlier case; which he perhaps tried to shorten by dropping the *pal*, to distinguish himself from that other Assur-dani-pal who had reigned *in rebellion*. Having a double name, he would naturally reject the second or *nick-name* Pal or Pulus, used by his enemies in sarcastic allusion to that case of rebellion. But that very name Pal or Pul would be the one which would reach the Jews, and would find a record in their scriptures, which up to this time had no mention of an Assyrian name. In this view, the tribute of Menahem, if not as early as the "expedition to Hadrach" in 772 B. C., might be as late as the "expedition to Hadrach" in 765 B. C., or else some time between.

§ 90. This theory concerning Pul will serve to clear up the account of Ctesias, the early Greek historian (B. C. 400); whose story of those times has always perplexed scholars, while giving color to all attempted histories of Assyria until the present generation of inscription decipherment. He depicts the effeminate "Sardanapalus" as the last king, precipitating by his folly the overthrow of Nineveh; which (he says) fell a prey to the united onset of Arbaces of Media and Belesis of Babylon. But he gets those events back at about B. C. 842, i. e., 282 years before the conquest of Media in B. C. 560. Very likely he heard of the rebel "Assur-dani-pal," son of Shalmaneser, who undertook to reign not far from that time, as seen above; and calling him "Sardanapalus," applied to him facts which really belonged to the later "Assur-dana-[pal]" whom we have here indicated, as beginning to reign in B. C. 773, being one of the very last kings of the earlier empire.

And what Assyrian king was really meant by "Sardanapalus?" And at what date did he reign? This has been a great puzzle to historians. The name (in that form) does not occur on the monuments, or in the Eponym Canon. But it would seem that it must have come from the royal name "Assur-dani-pal;" for the "Assur" readily becomes "Sar," the *consonants* being the same, both in this part and throughout the name. If, as we here suggest, the full name of king "Assur-daan was Assur-dana-pal," then, as being the real "Sardanapalus," that might be true of him which Ctesias relates. For, it would seem from the Canon that this king might be effeminate, not accomplishing much; since, instead of an "expedition" *every year*, as in previous and later reigns, the record gives no expedition in 9 of his 18 years, but mentions a stay "in the country" in 4 of the years, and a "revolt" in some great city in 5 other successive years. This state of the case on his part and of dissatisfaction on the people's part, well matches the account given of Sardanapalus. (See Schwartz' Review, p. 4.)

§ 91. The next king, "Assur-nirari," may have been the Median "Arbaces," who is described by Ctesias as conquering Sardanapalus, and reigning in his stead. And as to the Babylonian "Belesis," who (he says) aided Arbaces, receiving the rule of Babylon as his reward, it is indeed generally agreed that Belesis was that "Nabonassar," who in B. C. 747 got possession of Babylon, founding the Nabonassan Era of Ptolemy's Canon from that date (February 26, B. C. 747). Perhaps he was aided by Arbaces, in return for help in overcoming Sardanapalus 8 years before (in B. C. 755). Thus the much disputed history of Ctesias may be set to rights.

The above account agrees mostly with that long ago given by such historians as Prideaux, Rollin, Anthon, etc.—Anthon's Classical Dictionary (following Ctesias) says: "Arbaces, a Median officer, conspired with Belesis, the most distinguished member of the Chaldean sacerdotal college, against Sardanapalus, King of Assyria. After several reverses, he finally succeeded in his object, defeated Sardanapalus near Nineveh, took the city, and reigned in it 28 years [as if covering the two reigns B. C. 755-727]. With him commenced a dynasty of eight kings, of whom Astyages (about B. C. 600) was the last." "Arbaces promised Belesis, in case of success, the government of Babylon, which the latter, after the overthrow of Sardanapalus, accordingly obtained." Says Rollin (Anc. Hist., Vol. II, p. 60): "Belesis is the same as Nabonassar; in the Holy Scriptures he is called Baladin." Arbaces, governor of Media, formed a conspiracy against Sardanapalus. Belesis, governor of Babylon, entered into it. Nineveh was taken, Babylon was given to Belesis" (p. 58-60). "Several writers believe that Arbaces then immediately became sovereign. Heroditus is not of this opinion" (p. 58). "Pul is supposed to be the king of Nineveh who repented with all his people at the preaching of Jonah. He is also thought to be the father of Sardanapalus, the last king of the Assyrians, called, according to the custom of the eastern nations, Sardan-pul; that is to say, Sardan, the son of Pul" (p. 58). This last idea of Rollin agrees with view 1 above combined with 2, treating Pul as Vul-nirari, and Sardanapalus as his son (or grandson) Assur-daan-[pal].

§ 92. Prideaux (at year 747) says that on the fall of Sardanapalus, not only did Arbaces become the sovereign in his stead (suggested above as possibly the "Assur-nirari" of the Canon), but that Arbaces was actually Tiglath-pileser, who, as a result of that conspiracy and overthrow of Sardanapalus, left Babylon to the rule of his confederate Belesis or Nabonassar-baladin, and himself (as Tiglath-pileser) got possession of the throne at Nineveh. This is not accepted by Rollin and others who follow Heroditus, and make Tiglath-pileser a different usurper distinct from Arbaces.

Chambers' Cyc. says of the *final* overthrow of Nineveh (about B. C. 609): "It is uncertain whether Nineveh was destroyed under King Assher-emib-alli, or under a successor, the Saracus of Berosus, the effeminate Sardanapalus of the Greeks." And the Encyc. Brittan. treats "Assur-bani-pal" (beginning B. C. 668 in the Canon) as being Sardanapalus, the last king of Assyria. This late placing of the enigmatical "Sardanapalus" of Ctesias and the Greeks, or the supposition of a second monarch of the same name, is perhaps a doubtful theory. May not all conflicting schemes be harmonized upon the view of Sardanapalus we have here given, as being the "Assur-daan-[pal]" of the Canon?

3. TIGLATH-PILESER.

§ 93. Those who think the name "Pul" can be best identified with that of Tiglath-pileser, may adopt that view without impairment of the Scripture history, as we proceed to show. It is agreed that

Tiglath-pileser, the real beginner of the new empire, was a *usurper*. The Encyc. Brittan. says: "The first Assyrian Empire came to an end in B. C. 744, being overthrown by the usurper Tiglath-pileser, after a struggle of three or four years." Now, it may have been not alone four years of final fighting, but many years of struggle begun by open usurpation, that preceded Tiglath-pileser's final accession to the throne. For, the Eponym Canon indicates that there was commotion in Assyria during that period, for 18 years before Tiglath-pileser's accession in B. C. 745.

Back there at B. C. 763, the Canon reads, " revolt in the city of Assur;" next year, 762, "revolt in the city of Assur;" next year, 761, "revolt in the city of Arbaha;" next year, 760, "revolt in the city of Arbaha;" next year, 759, "revolt in the city Gozan." Five successive years of "revolt," in place of each year's recorded "expedition" usual to other reigns. And then at B. C. 746, the year before Tiglath-pileser's accession, there is a similar record, " revolt in the city of Calah," *i. e.*, in the old capital city, not far south of Nineveh. (Gen. x: 11.) This last outbreak, almost under the walls of Nineveh, was seemingly the crowning onset of the usurper, whose opening onset 17 years before had been by "revolt in the city of Assur," that other capital, 60 miles south of Nineveh (toward Babylon). If it was the war-like Tiglath-pileser thus fomenting trouble through the land, the starting-point of all on his part may have been an open usurpation of the throne about 772 or 3 B. C.; after which, being disowned by the government (in 769), his embittered passion would stir up the subsequent revolts, raising him finally to the fully-acknowledged kingship over the whole realm.

§ 94. This view of the matter will furnish a new explanation of the two anomalous eponyms found at years 770, 771 of the Canon, a different explanation, confirming the accuracy of the Eponym Canon. Suppose then, that the original Tiglath-pileser, then known only by his private name Pulus, usurped the Assyrian throne, overwhelming the officials, and compelling them (as the common custom for a new king) to put him as eponym of B. C. 771, under the title of king "Assur-daan" (the other part of his double name "Assur-dana-pal" or pul.) This compulsory honor would follow to "the tartan" in B. C. 770. But by that time the indignant officials may have wrought up the people to effectual resistance. And under the leadership of the preceding king, Shalmaneser newly acknowledged, either driving out the usurper from Nineveh, or themselves removing as the real government to another of the capital cities, Calah or Assur, they would refuse longer to follow his bidding; but, being in possession of the Eponym records, they would again go on with the old order of eponyms, as if those two had not been forcibly interjected.

There is in the Canon some indication of a removal of the government for a time from Nineveh. If in B. C. 769, when the usurper was disowned, the loyal government (under Shalmaneser still) set up its authority at the old capital Assur, leaving the intruder possessing Nineveh for awhile; then we see why that usurper stirred up so continued a "revolt" year after year in that very "city of Assur" (B. C. 763, 762), followed by revolts in other cities, Arbaha and Gozan (B. C. 761, 760, 759). And when in B. C. 759, at the accession of a new king, "Assur-nirari," we read in the Canon, "from the city of Assur the return," we seem to see the new king with young valor driving out the intruder from Nineveh and making "the return from Assur" of himself and his government. Of course, the expelled usurper would still try to keep up a local sway, inciting revolts; until by revolt fomented at Calah, in the very face of the authorities, he got full possession of the throne.

§ 95. And now, in order that there should be no ousting of him again, as not the real king, the conqueror introduced a new feature in the record—and had the fact of his real accession recorded on the Eponym Canon of that year (B. C. 745); which reads: Eponym "Nabu-bel-uzur [governor of] Arbaha, in the month of Iyyar, 13th day, Tugulti-pal-esar the throne ascended." Such a record of the fact and date of a king's accession had never before been known in any copy of the Eponym Canon; and George Smith (page 206) says of it: "It should be noted that no accession is ever marked in the Assyrian Eponym Canon before that of Tiglath-pileser II. B. C. 745. It would appear that great precision was then introduced into the Assyrian records; and it is curious that the date of this change, B. C. 745, nearly synchronizes with the date of the commencement of Ptolemy's Canon at Babylon, B. C. 747, so that it is probable that some change in this respect took place at both capitals, at nearly the same time."

Anthon's Classical Dic. tells us, from Polyhistor and Berosus, through Syncelhus: "Nabonassar having collected the acts of his predecessors, destroyed them, in order that the computations of the reigns of the Chaldean kings (in Babylon) might be made from himself." As thus the usurping king at Babylon wanted to fix definitely the fact and date of his accession, so his companion usurper at Nineveh wanted to establish his right to the throne (before set aside) by an exact official record.

§ 96. The newly instated monarch of Assyria had already the name Pil-esar or Pulassur (the Dic. of Relig. Knowl. gives it as Pal-esarra); which seems to be only the last and first of his original name *inverted*—a very common custom concerning names in those times. Thus Assur-[dana]-pal would readily become Pal-assur or Pileser. But upon his new enthronement, he naturally prefixed a new cognomen, "Tiglath" or "Tukulti," as successor of an early Assyrian king of that name. With this view of Tiglath-pileser as an old usurper "Assurdaan-[pal]," *i. e.*, Pal-assur or Pileser restored—we have the Eponym Canon left with Shalmaneser, whose reign began in B. C. 783, still reigning at 771, 770, until B. C. 755, when his successor Assur-nirari might be the "Sardanapalus" of Ctesias, overthrown by the usurpers Arbaces (as Baladin or Nabonassar) with Belesis (as Pal-assur or Pileser) at the re-enthronement called Tiglath-pileser.

(NOTE.—The greatest objection to regarding Pul and Tiglath-pileser as the same, is, that the Scriptures seem so plainly to regard them as two distinct persons; as in II Ki. xv: 19, 29, 1 Chron. v: 26. For, the "he" in the latter verse evidently means *he the last named* (Tiglath-pileser), since Pul produced no such *captivity* as described.)

§ 97. If Tiglath-pileser was originally the very "Pul" of Scripture, then his mention (on his inscriptions) of "Menahem of Samaria" and "Azariah of Judah" is a very natural matter. For these two inscriptions, like the rest in his reign, are not dated; so that, as George Smith observes (page 116): "The annals of Tiglath-pileser are very mutilated; and the fragments referring to Palestine are so detached, that it is difficult to determine their dates. The dates given here are only approximate calculations, and future discoveries may alter them considerably." In these inscriptions (conceded to be among his earliest) he no doubt gives a combined reminiscence of all he had accomplished hitherto, without being particular to distinguish dates. This appears particularly from the aspect of that inscription which contains mention of *Minnichimmi* or Menahem. A great many diverse localities are mentioned as conquered, and then follows a list of tributes received,—"The tribute of Kutaspi of Kummaha, Rezin of Syria, Menahem of Samaria, Hirom of Tyre," and fourteen more named.

§ 98. These four that head the list seem to be peculiar cases of continuous standing; for in another early inscription, a similar list starts with three of them, and the first one heads another like list on an inscription several years later. Indeed, all the names deciphered on the earliest inscription are contained in the list on the subsequent inscription; and most of these are contained in the list many years later (viz: 14 out of 18 names.) This evident stereotyped character of these lists suggests the remarks of Geo. Smith (p. 179): "I am able to bring some evidence to show that these tribute lists were sometimes carelessly compiled, and in error as to names." (He mentions several cases of error, and says): "There is another instance in the tribute-list in the first expedition of Assur-banipal, which so far as it is preserved, contains the same names as that of Esarhaddon, about 13 years before, being most probably a literal copy of the earlier document, without any attempt to ascertain if these kings were still reigning, and if they really paid tribute. * * * These evidences of error in the tribute lists are accompanied by similar false statements as to foreign proper names in the annals of some of their kings, and should serve as a caution against attaching too much importance to a difference in a proper name between the Bible and the inscriptions."

Tiglath-pileser would not like to direct attention to the date of his first usurpation, when he was soon repulsed; so he mentions his achievements of those days in a general way in summing up his past exploits.

"The submission of Menahem, etc., appear in the annals of Tiglath-pileser in a paragraph that immediately precedes an event in the 9th year. * * * The events preceding the 9th year of Tiglath-pileser might be merely a *summary* or recapitulation, and they might have happened in any of the years" of Tiglath preceding. (*Schwartz' Letter*, Oct. 29, 1888, p. 20.)

§ 99. According to this view, Tiglath-pileser had dealings with Menahem and Azariah in those days (B. C. 771-769) when he was actually on the throne for a while, and was known in approaching Palestine as "Pul, King of Assyria." (The expeditions set down at those years may not have been his, but those of the then overshadowed Shalmaneser.) Indeed, the Hebrew word "Pul" or "Phul" means *his highness*, or *royalty*. Says Gesenius: "The name signifies either *elephant*, or *lord, king*, like the Sanscrit, *pala*, lofty, highest." (Compare the *pul* in names of Assyrian kings.) The derivation is from Heb. *pulay*, wonderful, mighty. So that the Jews, as yet unfamiliar with Assyrian names, would readily call this first king with whom they had to do, simply "Pul," *his highness, the mighty one*.

Indeed, so many of the Assyrian kings had *pal* at the end of their name, or *vul* (*i. e., phul*) at the beginning or end, as seen in the Canon, (viz: Assur-nazir-pal, Assur-dani-pal, Samsi-vul, Vul-nirari, covering over half, perhaps five-sixths of the 115 years previous to Menahem), that the simple Hebrews might think that "Pul" or Phul was a general term for an Assyrian *king*, like "Pharaoh" in Egypt. So that, whoever that particular king may be, whether either or neither of the three we have here proposed, the Scripture name Pul is amply accounted for, without any mutilation of the Scripture history or chronology. The original tribute paid to Pul was about 770 B. C., where the Bible puts it; while a mention of it, and a repetition of it, as "the tribute of Menahem," is given many years afterward by Tiglath-pileser.

CHAPTER II.—"THIS IS THAT KING AHAZ."
II Chron. xxviii: 22.

§ 100. When we have settled the question, "Who was Pul?" without viewing him as Tiglath-pileser—(for George Smith and others prefer the first view above, making him Vul-nirari—and we ourselves incline to the second view, making him "Assur-dana-[pal],")—then the new question arises, How could Tiglath-pileser on his monuments speak of dealing with "Azariah of Judah," as well as "Menahem of Samaria," who both died many years before Tiglath-pileser's accession in B. C. 745; the former in B. C. 757, and the latter in B. C. 760, by the Scripture dating? A careful study of the history will make the matter plain.

§ 101. It seems that Jotham, the pious father of Ahaz, gave him the name "Jeho-ahaz," meaning *whom Jehovah possesses*. And Tiglath-pileser, king of Assyria, calls him by that full name, in an inscription belonging about 732 B. C. Giving a list of tributaries, he mentions "The tribute of Kustaspi of Kummaha, * * * Metinto of Askelon, Jeho-ahaz of Judah, Chemosh-melek of Eden," etc.—22 countries in all. But this king of Judah was so wicked and idolatrous, more so than any of his predecessors or successors, that the Jews themselves disliked to attach the epithet "Jeho" (or Jehovah) to his name, and so for short they called him simply by the other part of his name "Ahaz." And they derisively said, "This is that king Ahaz!"

It was common, then as now, to abbreviate proper names in this way; and the difference in designation of the Bible records and the foreign record occasions no difficulty among scholars. All are agreed that the Jeho-ahaz of the Assyrian inscription is the same as the Ahaz of Scripture, who did just about that time pay tribute to Tiglath-pileser, as described here in II Chron. xxviii: 20-25. This variation of a name at the outset should prepare us not to be surprised, if we find other variations as we proceed. Thus, also, these late-discovered inscriptions from the excavated Assyrian ruins, furnish a wonderful confirmation of Scripture, in this and many other respects.

§ 102. But the name Jeho-ahaz itself was among the Hebrews convertible into Ahaz-iah (or Ahaz-jah), meaning *him who possesses Jehovah;* for this is in fact the same name as the other, only with *the two parts inverted*. Therefore, we find the same king called in close connection both Jehoahaz and Ahaziah, as in II Chron. xxi: 17 and xxii: 1. This inversion of names was common in those days. Moreover, this latter form of the name, Ahaziah, was so similar in sound and aspect to Azariah, which was more easily pronounced, that the two names were sometimes used interchangeably: as we find in the very case just referred to: II Chron. xxi: 17, and xxii: 1, with ver. 6. Here is the remarkable circumstance, that within 10 verses the same man is called, first "Jeho-ahaz," secondly "Ahaziah," and thirdly "Azariah." It is perfectly plain, then, that these three forms of the name were interchangeable; and "Ahaz," who was primarily "Jeho-ahaz," might also be called "Ahaz-iah," and likewise "Azariah." Accordingly, we find Tiglath-pileser, on two inscriptions some years earlier than the one above mentioned, calling Ahaz by this name "Azariah."

It would seem that *at first* Tiglath-pileser became most familiar with this form of the name as "Azariah." And why? We may learn why, by reading the story as given in II Ki. xvi: 2-9. "Twenty years old was Ahaz when he began to reign, and he reigned sixteen years in Jerusalem, and did not that which was right in the sight of the Lord his God, like David his father. But he walked in the way of the kings of Israel, yea, and made his son to pass through the fire, according to the abominations of the heathen, whom the Lord cast out from before the children of Israel. And he sacrificed and burnt incense in the high places, and on the hills, and under every green tree. Then Rezin, king of Syria, and Pekah, son of Remaliah, king of Israel, came up to Jerusalem to war; and they besieged Ahaz, but could not overcome him.

"So Ahaz sent messengers to Tiglath-pileser, king of Assyria, saying, I am thy servant and thy son: come up, and save me out of the hand of the king of Syria, and out of the hand of the king of Israel, which rise up against me. And Ahaz took the silver and gold that was found in the house of the Lord, and in the treasures of the king's house, and sent it for a present to the king of Assyria. And the king of Assyria harkened unto him; for the king of Assyria went up against Damascus, and took it, and carried the people of it captive to Kir, and slew Rezin."

§ 103. Notice now the perfectly abject posture of Ahaz, when thus early in his reign (lasting from B. C. 741-726), viz., in 740-738 B. C. (before his 4th year= Jotham's "20th year," II Ki. xv: 30), he bowed and truckled before the king of Assyria, begging him in piteous tones to come to his help against his enemies. "I am *thy servant*, and *thy son*," he said, "come up, and *save me* out of the hand" of Rezin and Pekah. Such was the letter which the "messengers" bore to Tiglath-pileser. No doubt, this fawning sycophant filled in that letter with adulation and self-flatteries, about his own pious ancestors and Assyria's great exploits in their day; telling how long his good grandfather "Azariah" had reigned in peaceable relations with the kings of Assyria, while Menahem of Samaria "had felt compelled to become voluntarily their tributary. "Come up," he cried, "and help me too, the son of such friendly ancestors, in my war with Samaria, and you too may gather in and perpetuate 'the tribute of Menahem of Samaria.'" He no doubt signed his name in full, "Jeho-ahaz," or "Ahaz-iah," laying full claim to the ancestral piety, and scorning the mere nickname "Ahaz," which the Jews in his impiety had learned to give him. "This was that king Ahaz!"

§ 104. Tiglath-pileser thus cajoled came with his armies, and conquered Pekah and Rezin for Ahaz, as he describes in his inscriptions of those very years (B. C. 740–738). But of course, he does not speak of his confederate as "Ahaz," but in full as he had signed himself

"Ahaziah." Or rather, he mixes up the names of the grandson and grandfather, whose fame had been portrayed to him, and (like the Jews themselves) he uses the more pronounceable form "Azariah," as the designation, on the monuments, of his Judean confederate. The pronunciation Azar-iah came more natural to an Assyrian, because they had so many names beginning with similar sound, "Assur—."

In the discovered fragments of his monument he writes: "* * * course of my expedition the tribute of the kings * * * Azariah of Judah like a * * * Azariah of Judah in * * * without number to high heaven were raised * * * their cities without number I pulled down, destroyed * * * to Azariah turned and strengthened him, and * * *." Again he says: "* * * Judah * * * of Azariah my hand greatly captured * * * right * * * tribute like that of * * * to his assistance the city of Ma * * * cities helping them * * * 19 districts of Hamath, and the cities which are round them, which are beside the sea of the setting sun in sin and defiance to Azariah had turned, to the boundaries of Assyria I added, and my generals governors over them I appointed * * * The tribute of Kustaspi of Kummaha, Rezin of Syria, Menahem of Samaria, Hirom of Tyre [and 14 others], gold, silver, lead, iron, skins," etc.

§ 105. We, in common with the great Assyriologist, Geo. Smith, and others, regard the Azariah here as meaning Ahaz-iah or Ahaz of Judah. Observe how well the coloring and aspect of the inscription fit the relation of Tiglath-pileser to Ahaz, as seen in the Bible story. He does not number him among his enemies or those made tributary; but he speaks of him more as if a confederate. As Geo. Smith remarks (p. 180), the meaning "is not quite certain, owing to the mutilation of the fragments." But the language seems as if meaning to say: "* * * their cities I pulled down [and then] to Azariah turned and strengthened him * * * 19 districts of Hamath * * * in sin and defiance to [against] Azariah turned, to the boundaries of Assyria I added [them]." Certainly, the distant northern regions of "Hamath" were not fighting for Judah, but more likely were confederate with their nearer intervening neighbors Samaria and Damascus *against* Judah. And so, Ahaz as at first in the distance an obsequious confederate of Tiglath-pileser, was loosely termed "Azariah:" but several years afterward, when Tiglath-pileser had proved false, and had come and exacted tribute (instead of being content with gifts), and "king Ahaz *went* to Damascus *to meet* Tiglath-pileser king of Assyria," and to confer with him in person (see II Ki. xvi: 10, 17, 18, with II Chron. xxviii: 19-21), then *better acquaintance* led to the record on the tribute list *more exactly*, as the tribute of "Jeho-ahaz of Judah."

§ 106. As to the mention made of the tribute of "Menahem of Samaria," we have already shown (§ 98) how little these tribute lists can be depended upon as recording only *what took place at the time* of writing, since they evidently sum up loosely the tributes of the past, including some of an established and permanent sort, kept in mention to swell the boastful claims. We have also suggested how Ahaz at this time had probably *reminded* Tiglath-pileser of Menahem of Samaria, and of his celebrated tribute offering, which might be now reenforced. So that it was not wonderful that when Tiglath-pileser had taken the hint, and had now in truth subdued Samaria and exacted tribute, he should set it down in the list as "the tribute of Menahem of Samaria" renewed. Perhaps his expression in the inscription, "* * * right * * * like the tribute of * * *" means "Azariah (or Ahaz) first acknowledged my right by a free-will offering like the tribute of Menahem." For certainly we know that that particular offering of money by Menahem became a famous incident to the Assyrians, long cited as a *current phrase* to express the *panicky purchase of peace*.

Notice how apt was that instance as an illustration of extravagant surrender. Menahem had just seized the throne of Israel with cruel butchery and savagery that made him very unpopular. (II Ki. xv: 16, 19, 20.) "And Pul, the king of Assyria, came against the land: And Menahem gave Pul a thousand talents of silver that his hand might be with him to confirm the kingdom in his hand. And Menahem exacted the money of Israel, even of all the mighty men of wealth, of each man fifty shekels of silver, to give to the king of Assyria. So the king of Assyria turned back, and stayed not there in the land." How eager Menahem was to give away other people's money, extorting it from them to purchase an undeserved peace for himself! His very name, "Menahem," signifies *their gift* (from Heb. *Minchah* gift; so *hadorah*, ornament, hence the proper name *Hadoram*, their ornament). And perhaps he got the name fastened on him by the people as a reminder of the "1,000 talents," *their gift*, extorted to purchase *his* peace!

§ 107. That we have rightly represented this as a current phrase long afterward used in Assyria, appears from the fact that not only does Tiglath-pileser mention "Menahem of Samaria" in his tribute list thirty years after the original event, but also Sennacherib, over thirty years later still, has the same "Menahem of Samaria" at the head of his list of tributes taken (Ep. Can., p. 132); as if to characterize all those tributes as (like his) *free gifts to purchase peace*. We are astonished that among all those whom we have found discussing this subject no one has ever mentioned this fact, that Sennacherib uses the phrase as well as Tiglath-pileser. If we must conclude (as many argue) from the mention of "Menahem," that he was living in the time of Tiglath-pileser, by the same logic we must conclude that he was living still later in the time of Sennacherib. Or, if some new and unheard-of ruler of the same name "Menahem," had arisen in

Samaria in the time of Sennacherib, then, perhaps (as Prof. Oppert sets forth, Ep. Can., p. 182), some unheard-of pretender of the same name had obtained power and paid tribute in Samaria in the time of Tiglath-pileser during that 9 years interregnum after the death of Pekah, while Hoshea was struggling for the throne (B. C. 738-729. See II Ki. xv: 30, and xvii. 1.)

§ 108. Rather, we say, whenever tribute was taken from Samaria, it was called "the tribute of Menahem of Samaria," as being a repetition of that. This George Smith shows by other examples taken from the inscriptions (page 195): "We can see how a name like Menahem might be continued in the list of Assyrian tributaries, and his country be accounted as subject to Assyria, long after Menahem and Pul were dead; the new king of Assyria ignoring the march of events, and not admitting that the tributary was dead, and the subject country in revolt." He adds the caution which we have cited in § 98. So then, we come to the conclusion, that the phrase "tribute of Menahem," occurring in Tiglath-pileser's inscription, is only a stereotyped expression, especially as connected with Samaria; and that "Azariah" is simply the diplomatic form for "Ahaziah," equivalent to "Jehoahaz." "This was that king Ahaz."

The concurrence of these names on the monument, seemingly out of place, is a singular incident; but it need not destroy our faith in the accuracy of Scripture; especially when we find the Bible Chronology, so indubitably demonstrated as it is by its own inherent combinations and corroborations, as well as by the chronology of Josephus. We can still honestly believe that the original tribute paid to Pul was about B. C. 770, where the Bible puts it; while a mention of it and a repetition of it, as "the tribute of Menahem," is given thirty years later in B. C. 738-740 by Tiglath-pileser, and again sixty years later by Sennecherib.

§ 109. There is another point that requires notice here. The gap or interregnum of nine years in Israel (from B. C. 738 to 729, which Scripture leaves unfilled after Pekah, George Smith proposes to fill up, by calling Pekah's "20 years" (II Ki. xv: 27), a corruption for "30 years." But the objection to this is, that this makes out not one but *two* impossible corruptions. For, the "20th year of Jotham" (in ver. 30) must also, in that case, be a corruption for "30th year of Jotham." But this last is unsupposable: for, the "20th year of Jotham," means simply the "20th year after Azariah;" * and if it intended to say

---

* The writer had (at ver. 5) named "Jotham," the successor of Azariah; but he had not yet come to any mention of such a king as "Ahaz" to follow. Therefore, he expresses his date here as the "20th year of Jotham," which was equivalent to *the 4th year of Ahaz*, after Jotham's death.

"30th year," this event would not be recorded here (so long before its occurrence), but at Ch. xvii: 1, where that point of time is taken up. The very language at this last-named place shows, that Hoshea's attempt to reign had up to this point been a failure. "In the 12th year of Ahaz, king of Judah, began Hoshea, the son of Elah, to reign in Samaria over Israel nine years." It is not said that then he began reigning, but then he began to REIGN IN SAMARIA NINE YEARS; showing that his previous rule was only as an unacknowledged usurper outside the capital. Notice, that all previous reigns are expressed differently, as actually begun in Samaria.

§ 110. Tiglath-pileser in one of his inscriptions speaks of going to "the boundary of the land of Beth Omri" [Samaria], and says: " Pekah, their king * * * and Hoshea to the kingdom over them I appointed * * * their tribute I received and * * * to Assyria I sent." Some Assyriologists date this inscription as in B. C. 732-730, and claim that *then* Tiglath-pileser must have himself *slain* Pekah, (though that word *slain* is wanting in the fragment); so that (they argue) the Scripture account of Pekah as slain by Hoshea in B. C. 738 must be wrong. But a good Assyriologist (Geo. Smith) calls this inscription a "General Summary" of events "from 740 to 730," telling us that all these inscriptions of Tiglath-pileser are very doubtful as to their date. This one is as likely to belong to B. C. 738 as anywhere else. It contains mention of *four places* as captured (Hadrach, Saua, Uznu Sihanu), whose capture is described in the inscription conceded as belonging in B. C. 738.

Indeed this inscription concerning Pekah and Hoshea, relates the capture of the very city "Abel [beth Maacha] which is the boundary of the land of Beth Omri" [Samaria]—the account of which is given in II Ki. xv: 29, showing that this expedition, wherein Pekah and Hoshea are named, is the very occasion here described by Scripture as connected with the change from Pekah to Hoshea (in B. C. 738). This is very confirmatory of the Bible truthfulness. Whenever the inscription was made, it was a mere recounting of what took place with Pekah in B. C. 738, (Tiglath-pileser's instigation to his death by the hand of Hoshea). And when he says, "Hoshea I *appointed* over them," he does not tell us how long it took the "appointed" Hoshea to get possession of the capital Samaria, as the *de facto* king.

SECOND DIVISION.

Are "Ahab" and "Jehu" on the Monuments?

CHAPTER III.—The Inscriptions.

§ 111. When the mystery as to Pul, Menahem, and Azariah, is settled, there remains the question: Are the names of "Ahab" and "Jehu" found on the Assyrian monuments, as alleged by many Assyriologists, with dates still further removed from those of Scripture, requiring the whole Bible chronology of those and previous times to be reduced forty or fifty years? The facts are these:

An inscription of king Shalmaneser, dated with the eponym of B. C. 854 according to the Canon, contains as follows: "In the eponymy of Dayan-assur, the month Iyyar, 14th day, from Nineveh I departed, the river Tigris I crossed," etc. "From Argana I departed, to Aroer [Quqa] I approached, Aroer my royal city I pulled down, destroyed, and in the fire I burned; 12,000 chariots, 12,000 carriages, and 20,000 men of Dadidri [Benhadar] of Syria, 700 chariots, 700 carriages, and 10,000 men of Irchulin [Irhuleni] of Hamath, 2,000 chariots and 10,000 men of Achu-abbu mat Sir'lai [Ahab of Sirhala], 500 men of the Goim, * * * "These 12 kings to his aid he brought, to make war and battle to my presence they came," etc., * * * with them I fought. From Aroer to Kirzan their overthrow I accomplished," etc.

§ 112. In two other inscriptions (undated) he gives the same account more briefly, saying it was "in my sixth year," and describing the confederacy as "Benhadar of Syria, Irhulini of Hamath, and the 12 kings beside the sea, * * * with them I fought." He repeats about the same in two other inscriptions, as to what occurred "in my tenth year" and "in my eleventh year;" and in two other inscriptions besides, one of them as "in my fourteenth year." In still another inscription (also undated) he says: "In my eighteenth year * * * Chaza-ilu [Hazael] of Syria * * * with him I fought * * * To save his life he fled. After him I pursued, in Damascus his royal city I besieged him * * * In those days the tribute of Tyre and Sidon, of Iaua [Jehu] son of Omri I received." In yet another inscription he says: "Tribute of Iaua son of Omri, silver, gold, bowls of gold, cups of gold, bottles of gold, vessels of gold * * * royal utensils, rods of wood I received of him." And in another he tells of "my twenty-first year," and says he conquered Chaza-ilu of Syria."

☞ In the above, the names in brackets [ ] are as George Smith gives them; before the brackets they are as given in the Dic. of Relig. Knowledge (1889).

§ 113. The larger part of professional Assyriologists contend that the "Acha-abbu mat Sir'lai" given as conquered by the king in his "6th year," means "Ahab of Israel" put as at B. C. 754; and that the "Iaua, son of Omri" given as put under tribute in the king's "18th year," means "Jehu, successor of Omri," in Israel put as at B. C. 742; which are 42 and 41 years after the Scripture dates for the death of Ahab (896) and the accession of Jehu (883). On the contrary, we (with George Smith and others) claim that it can not be so, for *three reasons*, which concern, (1) the *contingencies*, (2) the *names*, (3) the *surroundings*.

1. There is no certainty in the Assyrian deciphering and dating; while on the other hand the biblical reckoning is settled by indubitable demonstrations and corroborations, as shown in our "Chronology of the Kings." The continuity of the later part of the Eponym Canon is pretty well assured back as far as B. C. 763, by an *eclipse of the sun* recorded in the Canon as occurring "in the month Sivan of that year; which eclipse has been calculated by Mr. Hind, and the results tabulated by Mr. Airy, the Astronomer Royal, showing that eclipse to have been June 15th, B. C. 763. (*Ep. Can., p. 83.*) And the very facts as recorded in Scripture being explainable in accordance therewith, as we have shown, form a decisive confirmation of that part of the Canon. But we have no assurance that there are not one or more *gaps* in the Canon before that date, as maintained by the Assyriologist Rev. D. H. Haigh and others. (Prof. Oppert also argued for a long gap.) In this state of things, no chronology can be made out from the Canon which will *positively* confute the accuracy of the assured Scripture datings.

2. The names on the inscriptions of Shalmaneser, which are deciphered and construed as meaning "Jehu" and "Ahab," can not be *proved* to stand for those kings of Israel.

(*a*) As to Jehu.

§ 114. The inscription reads "Iaua, son of Omri" as given in the Dic. of Religious Knowledge (1889), and "Yahua, son of Khumri" as given in Chambers' Cyc. (1880). Now the "son of Omri" means merely that the king named was *king of Samaria*, that city being well known as founded by "Omri," king of Israel. (I Ki. xvi: 22-24.) So that, among the Assyrians, Samaria was ever after known as *the city and kingdom of Omri*. It is so called not only in the inscription of Shalmaneser before us, but also in the inscription of Vul-nirari (beginning 812 B. C.), who names the countries from which he exacted tribute thus: "Tyre, Sidon, Omri [*i. e.*, Samaria], Eden, and Philistia." And in an inscription of Sargon (B. C. 715) he describes the people substituted for the Israelites, when Hoshea and his forces were conquered and carried into captivity, as being "enslaved and caused to be placed in the land of Beth Omri," *i. e.*, 'the land of Samaria, the house or home of Omri.' Tiglath-pileser also uses the same expression for Samaria, "Beth Omri," as we have seen before. Thus Omri=Samaria, as all are agreed; and the king *Iaua* or *Yahua* named by Shalmaneser must have been a Samaritan or Israelitish king.

But not Jehu. For, the son of Jehu, viz: "Jehoahaz" is just as readily identified with the *Iaua or Yahua* of the inscription, as the father Jehu is. Indeed, the Dic. of Relig. Knowl. gives *Iau-chazi* as the way "Jeho-ahaz" is spelled by Tiglath-pileser. As *Iau* means "Jeho-[ahaz]" in the later day, so *Iaua* merely means Jeho-[ahaz] in the earlier day. It was very common to omit one half of a double name, as we have seen before. Now the reign of Jeho-ahaz was, according to Scripture, 17 years long, from B. C. 857 to 840; and in the last part of his reign, at B. C. 842, was the very time when, according to the Canon, Shalmaneser, of Assyria, received tribute from him. This is a most beautiful confirmation of the accuracy of Bible History and Chronology, as well as of our interpretation put upon the monumental inscription. Each satisfactorily corroborates the other.

(*b*) As to Ahab.

§ 115. The inscription reads, "Acha-abbu mat Sir'lai" as given in the Dic. of Relig. Knowl., which is "Ahab of Zirhala" as George Smith gives it (in Ep. Can., p. 189). And he there says of it: "The Rev. D. H. Haigh has pointed out, that Zir is not the usual reading of the first character, and that the name should be Suhala; and he suggests that the geographical name Samhala or Savhala, a kingdom near Damascus, is intended in this place, and not the kingdom of Israel. The hypothesis of Rev. D. H. Haigh may be correct; certainly he is right as to the usual phonetic value of the first character of this geographical name; but on the other hand, we find it certainly used sometimes for the syllable *zir*. Even if the view of Rev. D. H. Haigh has to be given up, and if the reading 'Ahab the Israelite' has to be accepted, it would be possible that this was not the Ahab of Scripture. The time when this battle took place, B. C. 854, was, according to the chronology here suggested, during the reign of Jehoahaz, king of Israel, B. C. 857, to 840; and at this time part of the territory of Israel had been conquered, and was held by the kingdom of Damascus; it is quite possible that in the part of the country under the dominion of Damascus a ruler named Ahab may have reigned, and that he may have assisted Benhadad with his forces against the Assyrians." (*Geo. Smith.*)

§ 116. It is doubtful if *Zirhala* or *Sir'lai* means Israel. For, that was not the Assyrian way of mentioning the domain of a king; but they distinguished him by the name of his capital city or district, as seen in the list of Shalmaneser before us. The proper word here would have been Samaria or Beth Omri, as in other places. But if any one feels constrained to accept the meaning there as "Israel," it must be on some such ground as that given in the Dic. of Relig. Knowl., namely, that though "the first syllable of Yisrael (Israel) is lacking in *Sir'lai*— the terminal *ai* being simply the adjective ending in Assyrian, the whole has been reasonably identified as "Ahab of the Israelitish land." If then the *mat Sir'lai* be identified as "the Israelitish land," still the first half of the king's name given Acha, is no more like the name *Ahab*, than it is like the name *Ahaz*, which is half the name Jeho-ahaz (or its equivalent Ahaz-iah, as we have seen, § 102).

§ 117. But what of the "abbu"? Our supposition is, that this is not meant as a second half of the *name*, but as the *title* given to the individual named, like the title *tartan* in Assyria. Gesenius in the Hebrew Lexicon defines thus: "Ab, *father*. It is a primitive word (like am, *mother*, imitating the simplest labial sounds of the infant child); and it is common to all the Semitic dialects, Arabian, Chaldean, and Syriac. (Abbu, *his father*.) But the word *father* often has a wider sense, forefather, ancestor, founder, author, benefactor, master, teacher (or protector)." The word is often appended to personal names, as *Eli-ab*, God my father, *A-binad-ab*, *Aholi-ab*, etc. The British Com. of David Brown on Rom. viii: 15, says: "Abba is the Syro-Chaldaic word for *father;*" and an Assyrian king would understand and use this word in that sense.

Our supposition is, that the king of Israel obtained an audience with Shalmaneser, either before or after the battle, and told him all the truth; that he was not an enemy to Assyria, but was forced into this alliance by Benhadad of Damascus, who was all the while distressing Israel (See II Ki. xiii: 3, 4), that he would willingly be subject or tributary to Assyria if she would protect him from the tyranny of Syria; that he was only acting in defense of his country, as the "father" or *patriarch* or protector of Israel, which was signified by his very name, part of which (Jeho-) meant Jehovah, the God and Father of Israel; that he was willing to act under the protectorate of Shalmaneser, as thus simply the father of his country, a subordinate under a greater king. It was common thus to speak of a ruler as a Father to his people. (See Isa. xxii: 21; Jer. xxxi: 9, etc.) So Shalmaneser, recognizing that title *abba* "father" by which Jeho-ahaz called himself in asking of him favor and alliance, wrote him down on his inscription as "Acha (for Ahaz or Jeho-ahaz) Abbu mat Sir'lai" (father or protector of the Israelite land). This was by the Canon in B. C. 854, the 6th year of Shalmaneser, and it was about the 3d year of Jeho-ahaz' reign of 17 years (from B. C. 857 to 840), just as indicated in the story in II Ki. xiii; 3-6.

§ 118. In this unusual designation of a tributary we seem to see a touch of sympathy rather than of sarcasm on the part of Shalmaneser. At any rate pity was shown in response to the earnest entreaty.

Wicked as Jehoahaz was in some respects, he did act the part of a suppliant in behalf of his land, and there was a favorable response (II Ki. xiii: 4-6). Hear it: "And Jehoahaz besought the LORD, and the Lord hearkened unto him: for he saw the oppression of Israel, because the king of Syria oppressed them. AND THE LORD GAVE ISRAEL A SAVIOR [who else but Assyria?]; so that they went out from under the hand of the Syrians; and the children of Israel dwelt in their tents as aforetime." Here we have a vivid picture of just the way in which Shalmaneser seems to have responded to an appeal of Jehoahaz. He befriended Israel, and subordination to the *far-off* Assyrian empire, by the protection and intimidation that it afforded, proved a salvation of the land from the *near* Syrian oppression.

This explains why in all Shalmaneser's accounts of this conquest, upon six different inscriptions in different years, while mentioning the two previous names, Damascus and Hamath, he never again mentions Israel among his conquests after that first allusion to "*Abbu mat Sir-lai.*" He had accepted that land in a different attitude from the rest. Shalmaneser kept off their enemies, and Jehoahaz was very willing to pay him tribute for his protection, as we have already seen he did near the close of his reign (in B. C. 842). This surrender to Shalmaneser also explains why Jehoahaz was left with such a mere handful of forces. (II Ki. xiii: 7.) "Neither did he leave to Jehoahaz but fifty horsemen and 10 chariots and 10,000 footmen." Why? Because Shalmaneser took from him "2,000 chariots and 10,000 men," as he says in his inscription. This havoc made of Israel's resources was all brought about by Syria's outrages, compelling the confederacy against Shalmaneser.

§ 119. It may be a surprise to some that Shalmaneser should call the same king of Israel by two different names—in his 18th year naming him *Iaua* or *Yahua*, *i. e.*, Jeho-, and in his 6th year naming him *Acha* or Ahaz. But we have seen how common it was thus to divide a name into its two parts (Jeho-ahaz=Ahaz-iah), and to use either half alone, as occasion or impulse suggested. And we have fully exhibited a case, the very parallel to this, and with *the same compound* name, "Jeho-ahaz" thus separated years apart. If any one is troubled with two different names given to one person by the same speaker or writer, we simply leave him to the solution of the question why the same writer of II Chron. ch. xxi and xxii has within 10 years (at ver. 17, 1, 6) called the same king by *three* different names!

§ 120. Our view above given concerning II Ki. ch. xiii, and the striking expression there, "THE LORD GAVE ISRAEL A SAVIOR," was all written out and published abroad a number of years ago, before we had seen or heard anything of the view of George Smith, the famed Assyriologist in his "Eponym Canon," wherein he maintains the same as we do concerning that expression and that chapter, as the true exhibition of the events mentioned by Shalmaneser. We refer to this fact because it shows how independent thinkers without communication arrive at the same conclusion as reasonable and satisfactory, and gives additional proof of the correctness of our results. (Our suggestion in regard to "abbu" we have found nowhere.) The full study of this great Salvation to Israel forms a very interesting section in the comparison of Assyrian and Jewish history, and it exhibits one of the very best evidences of the correctness of the Bible Chronology, and its harmony with archæological research when fully and fairly investigated.

CHAPTER IV.

THE SURROUNDINGS.

3. The historical surroundings of the life of Jehoahaz agree with facts given in the Shalmaneser inscriptions, better than do the surroundings in the times of Ahab and Jehu.

BENHADAD AND HAZAEL.

§ 121. It will be at once objected, that Shalmaneser in his sixth year and afterward tells of conquering "Benhadad of Syria, and in his eighteenth year and afterward tells of fighting "Hazael of Syria;" whereas, there was (as alleged) no king of Syria but Hazael, through all the reign of Jehoahaz. To that we reply: This is making Hazael reign from about six years after Ahab's death (II Ki. viii: 15, 16), through the reign of Joram (7 years), and Jehu (28th year) and Jehoahaz (17 years, II Ki. xiii: 1, 22, 24) and through three years at least of Jehoash, a very long reign of 54 years, from B. C. 891 to 837 according to Scripture—and with fierce warfare at the very close. (II Ki. 12: 17-21.) Such a protracted warlike reign was not likely to occur in those troublous times. On the other hand, the obvious impression of II Ki. xiii: 3, with ver. 22, is, that the reign of Jehoahaz, while preceded by the reign of a Hazael, contained the reign of a Benhadad, his son, and that Jehoahaz' reign ended in the time of *another Hazael*. For, ver. 22 does not teach (as some assume) that this last Hazael was reigning "all the days of Jehoahaz," in contradiction of ver. 3, but only that this last Hazael "oppressed Israel all the (remaining) days of Jehoahaz, *i. e., as long as Jehoahaz lived*. The ver. 3 can not be speaking of the Benhadad of ver. 24; for the latter was not like the former a successful oppressor of Israel "all his days," but was a weak king who was beaten by Jehoash three times, and lost all "the cities which his father (Hazael) had taken out of the hand of Jehoahaz by war."

§ 122. We are right, therefore, in claiming that the first Hazael died not far from the time when Jehoahaz began his reign, say in his second year, B. C. 755-6; that in B. C. 754 Shalmaneser found his son Benhadad on the throne; and that twelve years later, in Jehoahaz' 15th or 16th year, B. C. 742, when he paid tribute to Shalmaneser, a second Hazael was on the throne of Syria, having reigned (say) four years, from B. C. 746. This second Hazael must have reigned at least ten years; for at the death of king Joash of Judah (B. C. 736) Hazael was alive (II Ki. xii: 17-21; II Chron. xxiv: 23-25). J. Schwartz, Assyriologist, of New York, objects, that this will allow more Syrian kings than Josephus makes out. Josephus (Antiq. 7, v: 2) says: "Nicolas of Damascus makes mention of the first Syrian king, Hadad, in the fourth book of his history, where he speaks thus. '* * * Hadad reigned over Damascus and the other parts of Syria, excepting Phœnicia. He made war against David, the king of Judea. * * *' He says of his posterity, 'When Hadad was dead, his posterity reigned for ten generations, each of his successors receiving from his father that his dominion and this his name, as did the Ptolemies in Egypt. But the third was the most powerful of them all; he made an expedition against the Jews, and laid waste the city which is now called Samaria, in the reign of Ahab.'"

§ 123. Schwartz tells us that this means "ten kings from Hadad to Rezin," and that the Assyrian records name *three* Syrian kings between Rezin and the last Benhadad. George Smith (Ep. Can., p. 191) gives but two from the inscriptions, viz.: "Hadara," in the inscription of Tiglath-pileser, given on p. 121, and Mariha in the inscription of Vul-nirari, given on p. 115. We find, therefore, the following, as the list of Syrian kings:

1. Hadad, in the reign of David and Solomon; II Sam. viii: 5, 6, 14; I Ki. xi: 14-25.
2. Benhadad I, son of Hadad, in Asa's time; I Ki. xv: 18.................B. C. 936 917
3. Benhadad II, in Ahab's time; I Ki. xx: 1, 34.........................B. C. 917-891
4. Hazael I, in Jehu's time; II Ki. viii: 7, 15...........................B. C. 891 856
5. Benhadad III, in Jehoahaz' reign; II Ki. 13: 3 ....B. C. 856 846
6. Hazael II, in reign of Jehoahaz and Jehoash; II Ki. xiii: 22-24......B. C. 846 835
7. Benhadad IV, in reign of Jehoash and Jeroboam, II Ki. xiii: 25......B. C. 835-810
8. Mariha, in reign of Jeroboam, inscrip. Vul-nirari....................B. C. 810 780
9. Hadara, in reign of Menahem, inscrip. Tiglath-pil..................B. C. 780-750
10. Rezin, in the reign of Pekah; II Ki. xv: 37..........................B. C. 750 738

If a third king be inserted between 7 and 10, then Hadad is not numbered, but only his successors, as intimated in the language used, "when Hadad was dead, his *posterity for ten generations* reigned."

§ 124. Schwartz rejects our 5 and 6, and makes up the total 10, by substituting two unauthorized names at the start; that is, he has "1, Hadarezer; 2, Rezon; 3, Hezion; 4, Benhadad I," etc. Here "Hadarezer" is a mistake for Hadad; and "Rezon" (from I Kings xi: 23, 24) is a temporary partner during Hadad's time, and not one of his ten "posterity" referred to by Nicolas. (Hazael was probably of the family.) "Hezion" (from I Ki. xv: 18) is no king at all, but only an ancestor of kings ! The Hebrew reads: "Asa sent them to the son of Hadad, (the son of Tabrimon, the son of Hezion) king of Syria." The parenthesis merely gives the *ancestors of Hadad* (the founder of the family) as Rezon's descent is given at I Ki. xi: 23. George Smith puts in both the "Tabrimon" and the "Hezion" as two additional kings of Syria, calling the latter the same as "Rezon" and he strangely makes out *two kings* of Syria at I Ki. xx: 34! There is some confusion as to the original Hadad. Josephus thinks he was actually reigning in Damascus when David conquered Hadarezer, king of Tobah (II Sam. viii: 3, 4). Schwartz confounds him with Hadarezer himself.

§ 125. But the fact seems to be, Hadad was an Edomite, and "yet a little child" at that time (comp. II Sam. viii: 3, 14, with I Ki. xi: 15-17). He fled from David as Rezon fled from Hadadezer, when David conquered Edom and Zobah, I Ki. xi: 17-23, comp. II Sam. viii: 3, 14. Long afterward they both met at Damascus, got possession of the kingdom, and there reigned together for a while (I Ki. xi: 24, "and *they* [Hadad and Rezon] went to Damascus, and dwelt therein and reigned in Damascus"). Rezon died, and Hadad (or his son) became sole king of Syria after Solomon's time, as the British Com., Jamison, says. The very writer Nicolas, who is our only authority for there being just ten "posterity," particularly affirms that "*the third* king was the Benhadad II who in Ahab's day besieged Samaria (I Ki. xx: 1), just as we put it. Whereas, Schwartz makes him the *fifth* king in order.

If Josephus is right in saying, that any Syrian king was on occasion called by the one name Benhadad, or "Son of Hadad" the father of the line, just as kings of Egypt were all called "Ptolemy,"—then, even a Hazael in the time of Jehoahaz might, on an Assyrian monument, be written as "Ben-hadad," and it would answer the purpose of the canon. But we have made it plain that we have the Syrian kings right with a *second Hazael* in the list. So certainly is there a "Benhadad" in the reign of Jehoahaz (B. C. 854) to answer all the purposes of the Assyrian Canon and inscription! In this respect the *surroundings* are all that can be required.

The Ahab-Jehu Interval.

§ 126. In respect to reign adjustment, the surrounding facts of Ahab and Jehu can not possibly be made to fitt he inscription, while at Jehoahaz' reign the dates and the inscribed facts exactly match. Between the death of Ahab and the accession of Jehu were 13 years, viz., Ahaziah "2 years" (or 2d year) from "the 17th year" to "the 18th year" of Jehoshaphat, and Jehoram "12 years" from "the 18th year of

Jehoshaphat" to the death of Ahaziah of Judah (I Ki. xxii: 51; II Ki. iii: 1, and ix: 16, 24, 27). The 13 years is thus determined, not only by lengths of reigns in Israel, but also by three synchronisms with Judah, viz., the "17th year" and the "18th year" of Jehoshaphat, and the death of Ahaziah.

And it is further established by the given reigns in Judah, viz., Jehoshaphat's "25 years" (I Ki. xxii:42, II Chron. xx: 31) after 22 of which, viz., in the 5th year of Joram, king of Israel," Jehoram of Judah began his "8 years" (II Ki. viii:16, 17, II Chron. xxi:5). But the "8 years" means only that he ended in *his 8th year* after 7 full years. For, beginning "in the 5th year," he ended "in the 12th year" of Joram of Israel "the 11th year" then ending—when Ahaziah succeeded him "1 year" (II Ki. viii: 25, 26, and ix: 29, II Chron. xxii: 2). Thus Jehoshaphat lived 3 of his 25 years after his son Jehoram's 8 (or 7) began, it being then 5 years after Ahab's death. And these 5 years added to the 8 years of Jehoram and Ahaziah = 13 years as the interval between Ahab's death and the death of both Judah's and Israel's kings, at the accession of Jehu. The same is proved by the synchronisms, Jehoshaphat's first year, we are told, began in "the 4th year of Ahab" (I Ki. xxii: 41); so that, the 23d of Jehoshaphat began in the 26th of Ahab (had he lived) *i. e.*, 5 years after Ahab's death, given as "the 5th year" (beginning) of his second son, Joram's reign. And hence, after 8 more years through the 12th and last year of Joram, must be (5+8=)13 full years from Ahab to Jehu, and must reach through (22+8=)30 years of Jehoshaphat (had he lived), leaving (30—22=) the 8 years for the reigns of Jehoram and Ahaziah in Judah.

§ 127. Thus we know for a certainty, that if the Bible story is any true history at all, its interval between Ahab and Jehu is full 13 years, fixed and assured by so many eras and datings of reigns in two kingdoms recorded in two different books, that it can not possibly be made less. (If urgency should try to assume some further fractional excess needing deduction, the interval certainly could not be got below 12 years.) So that a summer campaign *in the first year of Jehu*, must be 14 years after a summer campaign *in the last year of Ahab*. And, since, Assyriologists generally concede that the campaign in which Shalmaneser fought Benhadad could not be in Ahab's last year (when Ahab was slain fighting *against* Benhadad), but must be in the next before his last year, therefore, this could not be less than 15 years before a campaign in the first year of Jehu. By closest pinching, the interval between the two events could not be made less than 14 years. Whereas, the Assyrian inscription demands only 12 years, from the 6th to the 18th year of Shalmaneser (by the Eponym Canon, B. C. 854-842). This proves unmistakably, that the application of this inscription to such events ascribed to Ahab and Jehu is erroneous, and that our application of it to the reign of Jehoahaz is reasonable and true.

Any attempt to reconstruct the multiplied scripture numbers given above, which go to fix the 14 or 15 years' interval, so as to crowd it down to the 12 years wanted, must be abortive; even as the attempts of Schwartz and of others have been shown to be abortive. For the reduction can not be forced, without such a mutilation of the Scripture numbers given, as would leave it a repudiated record, not by any possibility corrupted to what it is, but necessarily and originally a *false history*, gotten up by writers who did not know what they were talking about. The same may be said of all the circumstances and surroundings of the history; they can not be made to agree with the theory of Ahab and Jehu as brought under subjection and tribute to Assyria. (See a remarkable monumental confirmation at § 48.)

The Course of Events.

§ 128. "It does not seem likely that the biblical Ahab, who was the foe of the king of Damascus, sent any troops to his aid; at least, such a circumstance is never hinted at in the Bible, and is contrary to the description of his character and reign. Under these circumstances, I have given up the identification of the Ahab who assisted Ben-hadad at the battle of Quarqar, B. C. 854, with the Ahab, king of Israel, who died, I believe, 45 years earlier." (*George Smith, Ep. Can., p. 190.*)

It is irrational to think of Ahab as ever a confederate helping Benhadad. For, the Scripture history of Ahab, which seems on its face reliable and in harmony with all that precedes and follows, presents Ahab as repeatedly at war with that arrogant Benhadad, and successful against him and his *confederates*, "thirty and two kings" (I Ki. xx: 1-6, 11, 20, 21, and ver. 26, 29, 30),—and at last as meeting his death in fighting him. (Chap. 22.) After his victories Ahab had been too lenient in letting Benhadad live, and a prophet had warned him that he would suffer for it (xx: 34, 42). Benhadad broke his promise to restore the cities of Ramoth Gilead; and after the novelty of three years without war between Syria and Israel (xxii: 1), Ahab again, in company with Jehoshaphat, went forth against Benhadad, for the recovery of Gilead (ver. 3), and Ahab was slain (ver. 17). Now it is in that intervening truce of three years (which probably contained only two whole years, after the Jewish fashion of speech), that Assyriologists try to work in the inscription account of Benhadad conquered at Aroer (or Quarqar) with his confederate Ahab and others.

That is, they would represent Ahab as fighting in helpful confederacy with Benhadad, only one year before Ahab died fighting against Benhadad, for a grievance existing all these years—and less than two years after Ahab had awfully whipped—almost annihilated Ben-hadad, mercifully letting him off with his life, upon a promise which being forthwith broken compelled this last fatal fight. Does the theory of an intermediate alliance of *Ahab under Benhadad* look at all likely or reasonable on its face? Here was Benhadad completely broken up and crushed two years in succession by Ahab, 100,000 of his men slain in one day, and 27,000 the next day (Ch. xx: 29, 30, 21), yet represented as within two years heading a confederacy with large forces against Assyria,—and stranger still, as having under him as subaltern that very King Ahab to whose mercy he owed his life, and whose new rage he was already exciting by breach of the life-pledge he had given!

§ 129. So absurd is the theory that the Assyrian inscription refers to the Scripture Ahab, that Chambers' Cyc., while accepting the inscription of the 18th year of Shalmaneser as meaning Jehu, yet omits all mention of the inscription of his 6th year, as being altogether too doubtful to be claimed as meaning Ahab. And Dr. Orr, in the Presbyterian Review (New York, January, 1889), while in general sustaining the Assyrian dates as against those of the Bible, yet after all his endeavor to work in Ahab, decides as most probable, that the name interpreted as Ahab is an *Assyrian mistake*. He says (p. 57): "The date for the death of Ahab is about a year too high to admit of his presence at the (Assyrian) battle of Karkar in B. C. 854, which yet, it is allowed, can not be put earlier than Ahab's last or second-last year, This raises an interesting question. Wellhausen strongly contends, and Kemphansa agrees with him, that the king who sent a contingent to the battle of Karkar *could not have been Ahab*. There is the chronological difficulty; but apart from this, it is agreed that *it is in the highest degree improbable* * * * *that Ahab should fight as a voluntary ally of Benhadad*. * * * Wellhausen therefore thinks that the battle of Karkar took place *after* the battle of Ramoth Gilead; that the king who sent a contingent to it was not Ahab but Joram; and that the mistake in the name arose from the ignorance or carelessness of the scribe, who knew nothing of the changes on the throne of Israel. There is much to be said for this view." Thus distinctly is it confessed by Assyriologists, that no dependence can be put upon the Assyrian naming of a Jewish king.

§ 130. There was no place for either voluntary or forced alliance with Syria, till long after the days of Ahab. In the reign of Ahab's successor Jehoram, still "the king of Syria warred against Israel" (II Ki. vi: 8), but was not successful (ver. 23); and yet afterward (ver. 24) "Benhadad, king of Syria, gathered all his host, and went up, and besieged Samaria;" but was beaten (vii: 6, 7). Still again, after some years, Jehoram was in "war against Hazael king of Syria" (viii: 28); in which war Jehoram was wounded, and soon was slain by Jehu (ix 24). When Jehu, thereupon, under appointment of God, was so valiently sweeping down all enemies—was such a dashing, daring, successful king as he the man to succumb without a fight and pay the first tribute to a distant power, as alleged? For, be it noticed, the

Assyrian inscription says nothing of any fighting with "the son of Omri" only of tribute received from him, as if a natural expected continuation of past affairs. This fits the case of Jehoahaz, as we saw, but is quite out of place as a first payment of tribute from such a man as Jehu.

The warfare against Syria went on. In Jehu's time, about B. C. 860, we read (II Ki. x: 23): "In those days the Lord began to cut Israel short. And Hazael (king of Syria) smote them in all the coasts or Israel," Jordan, Gilead, Galilee, etc. It was war, war, continually repeated war between Israel and Syria; and now at last it was getting to be more fatal to Israel. But it was not till Jehu's son, the weak Jehoahaz, ascended the throne and reigned from B. C. 856-7 to 840 (II Ki. xiii: 1), that there seems any place for the king of Israel to be found in a *strained* confederacy with any Benhadad or Syrian king. Then at length the king of Syria had got the upper hand, and could dictate terms; and he soon after turned his arms against Judah also (xii: 17).

§ 131. Israel was left, under its feeble Jehoahaz, to submit to the Syrian oppressions (xiii: 1-3): "The anger of the Lord was kindled against Israel, and he delivered them into the hand of Hazael, king of Syria, and into the hand of Benhadad, the son of Hazael, all their days." So that, as now, reduced to be an unwilling confederate with the king of Syria, Jehoahaz may well have got beaten with him in a conflict with the king of Assyria, in B. C. 854, two or three years after he (Jehoahaz) began to reign, just as the inscription of Shalmaneser describes.

Or rather, he may have taken the opportunity to become a betrayer instead of a helper of Benhadad, by getting the Assyrian monarch to be to him "a savior" from the rapacity of Syria (xiii: 4, 5). The struggle would still go on between the *neighboring* nations (ver. xxii); but the overshadowing favor of the *far-off* monarch toward Jehoahaz would keep Syria somewhat in check and Jehoahaz would gladly of his own accord pay tribute to Assyria for this protection, as the inscription describes concerning this "son of Omri," in B. C. 842.

CONCLUSION.

§ 132. We see not how it could be possible for Israel to receive so great an onset from Assyria as the inscriptions suppose—Israel's first connection with that great world-power—without any allusion to it in the Jewish history, so full and complete; which is the predicament in which the critics who claim Ahab and Jehu as the kings referred to, find themselves placed. But if the reference was to Jehoahaz, then we have in the Jewish history a striking allusion to this great turn in Jewish affairs—an allusion obscure indeed, as we might expect it to be because calling that great world-power "a savior," which was yet to be the waster and destroyer of Samaria—but an allusion whose mystery hitherto is now happily cleared up by these Assyrian inscriptions excavated, so well bringing forth the meaning and corroborating the truthfulness of God's Holy Word.

Nebuchadnezzar too, of Babylon, was spoken of as in some sense a savior of Judah from utter extinction, by the very means of his capturing Jerusalem; and the captives were exhorted to go cheerfully, under the saving mercy, to the exile in Babylon. (See Jer. xxvii: 6-17, and xxxviii: 2, and xlii: 11, and xliii: 10.) So light comes out of darkness; and the truth of Scripture emerges from the smoke and error of criticism!

PART IV.

Comparative Reliability of The Jewish and The Pagan Chronology.

CHAPTER I.

Assyriology and the Bible.

§ 133. The chronology of the Jewish Scriptures for their 491 years from the second year of Darius, B. C. 520, to the fourth of Solomon, B. C. 1011, is what we here compare with the chronology of the same time as given by the surrounding nations, Assyria, Egypt, Tyre, etc.

In all past ages, the Bible Chronology, back through the Jewish kings (to the beginning of David's reign as in B. C. 1053 or 5), has been accepted universally as the only reliable reckoning we have; Assyrian, Egyptian, and Tyrian data being seen to be very uncertain, and unworthy of comparison with the Scripture authority.

But there has now (in 1892) arisen a belief, particularly among Assyriologists, that the "Eponym Canon," so-called—a record deciphered from the inscriptions unearthed at Nineveh by Layard, and described by Sir Henry Rawlinson in the London Athenæum for May and July, 1862—give us a sure chronology of those times, differing greatly from the Scripture reckoning: which (they say) must be corrected accordingly.

Our purpose is to show that there is no certainty about the alleged new chronology; that the Bible history and chronology still remains more reliable than any other; and that it is altogether premature to alter our ancient dating, as some are beginning to do, * or to lose faith in Scripture as a true and reliable history of the ancient ages.

§ 134. The first and foremost claim of an Assyriologist will be that Scripture is *only a book*, copied from age to age, and so liable to all kinds of corruption and alteration; while the inscribed rock or plaster is, we are sure, the original, just as prepared two or three thousand years ago. So the monumental statement is thought to have vastly more authority than any book utterance can have. But this depends, as we shall see. There may be much less difference than at first supposed, in the authority of stone or mortar over parchment or paper.

The weight which any document has in determining truth, depends (1) upon its source, (2) upon its contents; and both must combine to give authority to the writing. Though the source of an excavated monumental inscription should give it at first glance a greater authority than if transmitted on more perishable material, yet its contents when studied may be found so much less clear, and decisive, and self-convincing, as to be entirely overcome in weight by the paper statement.

If in some old cemetery a grave-stone should be found, stating that the deceased died in A. D. 1767 on the very day when American Independence was declared, that would not revolutionize the accepted date of the American Revolution as contained in books. And if an Assyrian inscription has been found, with obscure or uncertain indications of some Bible event out of its place, that is not sufficient to overturn the unmistakable dating of Scripture history.

§ 135. What are the facts? On the one hand we have the Jewish Scriptures, of whose correct transmission to us from the very times of the kings, without serious alterations or mistakes there can be no doubt, and no one has a doubt; † while the time covered by those kings is therein clearly and repeatedly explained in multiplied dates and cross-dates so fixed and determined as to make certain that we have the very

---

* Some of the Lesson Helps to our International Sunday School studies are already giving changed Bible dates, drawn from the uncertain theories of Assyriology.

† To show how surely the Bible numbers are transmitted to us unchanged, as certainly as if found inscribed on contemporary monuments, notice the following facts: The great historian, Josephus, in the first century, avowedly quoting from the Hebrew Scripture, gives the same total of added reigns in Judah and Israel as we have now in our Hebrew Bible. This we have elsewhere shown. And now I find in the Talmud ("Solomon the wise," p. 204 of London Ed., 5636, A. M.), that from Solomon's reign to the destruction of the temple was "433 years;" which is precisely what the reigns as given in our Hebrew Bible still add up, thus: Solomon 40 + to capture of Samaria 260 + to end of Zedekiah 133 = total 433. It is evident that there has been no mutilation of the original.

reckoning intended by the writers, and to leave no possibility of our misunderstanding the length of time they meant to describe. The writers are reliable, their own statements are plainly before us, and the meaning can not be mistaken. If ever there was an indisputable record of assured dates, it is here in the Jewish history of "the kings."

§ 136. On the other hand, Assyrian research has unearthed for us certain fragmentary tablets of those olden times, inscribed with a long list of Assyrian names, which are interpreted as designating the successive years; some of which names are found given on other monuments, which in a few cases are thought to allude to Jewish incidents; and those names counted up, as meaning one year to each name, do not make out so many years as the Jewish history claims between those incidents thought to be alluded to. So that, if this Assyrian theorizing be considered true and infallible, the Bible account must be false in all its dating, and over 40 years must be dropped out of its details, item by item, greatly mutilating its various statements, to bring it into agreement with this (so called) "Eponym Canon" of Assyria thus treated as infallible.

§ 137. It will be seen at once, how precarious and uncertain is this Canon reckoning, compared with the sure word of Scripture; and how evidently the seeming superiority of the monumental *source* of information is outweighed by the obscurity and uncertainty of its *contents*. So that the sure and plain-speaking Bible has more historical authority than the enigmatical Canon, and can never be overturned by it without further light. The Assyrian inscriptions do indeed give wonderful confirmation to the scriptural events as occurring about as the Bible records them. But those Assyrian items are not dated with sufficient definiteness and certainty, to put the precise and assured dates of Scripture in fault.

Let us examine the Canon reckoning more closely, and see how much of authority it has as an alleged infallible chronology. There are three respects, in which we shall find its certainty impaired; (1) as to the perfect and sure *consecutiveness* of years; (2) as to the certain accuracy and infallibility of those *reporting* the list of names; (3) as to the correctness and certainty of Assyriologists in their *interpreting* of events referred to and their identifying of names alleged.

§ 138. (I.) As to the perfect and sure *consecutiveness* of years indicated by the list of names, Geo. Smith in his valuable work on "The Eponym Canon," London, 1875 (p. 22), thus explains the case:

"In Assyria, the practice of dating documents according to the regnal years of the reigning monarchs was seldom used; by far the greater number of inscriptions being dated by the names of certain officers called by the Assyrians *limu;* a word which, by general consent, is translated 'eponym.' The Assyrian *limu* or eponyms were appointed according to a general rotation; and each one in succession held office for a year, and gave name to that year; the usage of the Assyrians in this respect being similar to that of the Archons at Athens, and the Consuls at Rome. The Lord Mayors of London are also appointed for a year, and a parallel case would be presented if we dated our documents according to the years when successive Lord Mayors held office, calling the years after their names."

Now we see at once how uncertain is such a mode of dating applied to long periods of time. The same official may at times serve two or more years in succession, or years of peculiar emergency may occur when no assignment takes place. Periods of tumult or revolution may come interrupting the order. And when after a time the old list is written down to date, the new names may not be rightly joined to the old. Thus in various ways the consecutiveness of the years may be broken up.

§ 139. Mr. Smith gives the naming of years by the Roman consuls as an illustration. This plan was accurate for a few years *at the time* of occurrence; but it was found often misleading, in dating back after a long period had elapsed. We all know how mixed up became the consular reckoning, as used by the early Christian chroniclers for measuring the times of the New Testament history. Thus Epiphanius (A. D. 403) omitted the consuls of A. D. 4 in explaining the years of Christ's life, as shown by Clinton (Fas. Hel., at A. D. 14). From him this error in the consular list was propagated down the ages in the "Paschal Chronicle." And Eusebius got an extra consulate interpolated at A. D. 69. Afterward Prosper and Victorius had the early consuls much disarranged. (See my "History of the Early Christian Chronicles," p. 41-49.)

How uncertain must be such a method of dating long intervals, with no lengths of reign given, and no periods of time designated (such is the Assyrian reckoning)—compared with the Jewish method, giving the length, the beginning, and the end of each reign, with the interlocking synchronisms, and dates of two contemporaneous series of kings, in Judah and Israel, and with long prophetic and typical periods comfirming the whole. Some writers speak of the wonderful excellence of the Assyrian chronology, and even present it in disparagement of Bible chronology as far less reliable. But looked at carefully and honestly, that Pagan method can no more stand before the Scripture dating than a candle can illuminate the sun.

§ 140. It does not matter whether we can point out any break in the order of Eponym years; the system is liable to such breaks, and this destroys the certainty of its chronology as a whole, whatever assurance we have about particular parts of it. Some of the shrewdest Assyriologists, Oppert, Haigh, etc. (see Eponym Canon, p. 73), have thought they saw evidence of gaps; and whether they were right or wrong, we ourselves perceive great possibility of more or less interruption of the order especially in the early part of the canon, from B. C. 820 backward, where the canon is most meager (giving only the list of *names* without any explanation of their office or mention of anything occurring in each year). It is in this meager part of the canon, that the greatest conflict with Scripture is imagined; and just here is the most uncertainty in the canon itself.

§ 141. When the canon's list of names has been applied to reach backward to B. C. 820, soon after Sam-si-vul III began to reign, we find that there, at B. C. 820 and 821, there is extant *only a single copy* of the canon (called copy I), with nothing to confirm its names, or the number of the names there belonging. There it seems as if the original list ended; and in adding what follows, which was not done until 120 years afterward (as shown by George Smith, Ep. Can., p. 151), there may very easily have been an interruption of the regular order.

Rev. D. H. Haigh, Assyriologist (Ep. Can., p. 73), believed there was a gap hereabouts, at B. C. 829; and thought he could show the length of it as 19 years. But without accepting his view, we see how greatly possible it is, that hereabouts, at the close of Shalmaneser's reign, in the tumult of those times, there may be a gap of some years in the record of names.

Says George Smith (Ep. Can., p. 73): "It is related, in the monolith inscription of Samsivul III [beginning B. C. 825], that during the reign of his father, Shalmaneser II, another son of that king, named Assurdainpal, revolted against him, and was followed by twenty-seven districts of Assyria, principally in the east and south. These districts were subdued, and again brought under the rule of Shalmaneser by Samsivul, who afterward succeeded to the throne, instead of the rebel prince."

§ 142. Who does not see the likelihood of interruption in the record of Eponyms during such a rebellion, and of a gap occurring in the joining on of the subsequent list, not made up till 120 years afterward? There is an unprecedented incident of B. C. 828, given by the canon for that year, which corroborates this suggestion. The canon gives "Shalmaneser, the king," as Eponym of that year again, after he had been Eponym 30 years before. This return to a position occupied by no other king but once, may either have instigated the rebellion that occurred, or may have resulted from it as a re-instatement of the king. In either case, the Eponym list had hereabouts an interruption of order, very possibly resulting in a loss of some years' reckoning.

We do not present this as proof of a gap. We only show that a gap is possible. It can not be proved, and probably never can be, that there was no gap in the canon; and that being so, there can be no such certainty as some claim in the Assyrian dating, wherewith to set aside the sure record of Bible history. We may have pretty good confidence in the later part of the Eponym canon, where an eclipse of the sun in the month Sivan of B. C. 763 gives confirmation* (though not full assurance; because the day of the month is not given, nor the degree of eclipse, so that in a choice of many years, there might be a duplicate eclipse within that month). But as to the earlier and more meager part of the Canon, where the chief conflict with Scripture is alleged, we can have no assurance at all.

§ 143. (II.) As to the certain accuracy and infallibility of those *reporting* the Eponym list of names to the sculptor, George Smith, the esteemed Assyriologist, informs us (p. 151): "The earliest known copies of the Assyrian Canon mere made in the reign of Sennacherib (about B. C. 700), that is, about 150 years after" the alleged reference to Ahab and Jehu. What proof have we that these first copies give an accurate account of those earliest years occurring so long before their time? Why was not the engraver or sculptor of B. C. 700 liable to have the period from B. C. 890 to 820 somewhat disarranged? If New Testament scholars could bring no evidence for the events narrated in the four gospels, except a first reference to them 150 years after their alleged occurrence, with no known existence of those gospels till that late date—certainly there would be a great outcry of scepticism against the claim of certainty as to the New Testament history. What better claim has the alleged Assyrian dating of Ahab and Jehu to be considered a certainty?

§ 144. Man is fallible. And even an Assyrian fashioner of inscriptions was liable to get in a mistake, either of a name, or of its spelling, or of the location of an incident occurring 150 years before his time. Even an Assyrian inscription is not necessarily infallible. A Pagan writer or engraver was just as likely, to say the least, to commit a blunder concerning Jewish affairs, as was a native Jew in writing by

---

* Yet, that very fixing of the Eponym Canon at B. C. 763 may prove that there is an *omission of one year* somewhere after that in the Canon. For, as Schwartz tells us (*Letter*, *April*, *1893*), "Ptolemy's Canon has the accession of Esar-haddon, Assur-banipal, Nabonassar, Nebuchadnezzar, and Evil-merodach, at B. C. 680, 667, 625, 604, and 561, all one year too late by the Eponym Canon." Instead of proving by this (as Schwartz attempts, and even Geo. Smith thoughtlessly allows, Ep. Can., p. 102) that Ptolemy's Canon *post*-dates the reigns—a theory entirely untenable (see Period F, § 2)—this discrepancy more likely shows that the Eponym *Canon has lost one year* (say) right before "Eponym Shalmaneser, king of Assyria," B. C. 723. For, there would regularly come as Eponym the governor of Arbela, and there is there *but a single copy* of the Canon; so that, the omission might readily occur in the confusion at the death of the king, so peculiarly then *just serving as Eponym*. With a year there inserted, the Eponym Canon would agree with Ptolemy's Canon in all the dates referred to, and so (by that indisputable authority) would be greatly confirmed as far back as B. C. 763.

authority the history of his own land in his own time. The Pagan was only stringing together lists of names handed down to him from 150 years before, with no certifying or rectifying number accompanying them. Whereas, the Jew was an official recorder of the current history, giving numbers of years and coincidences of reigns in two kingdoms, and passing his work along from one generation to another of official history.

We say nothing here of any divine inspiration or special providence, guarding the Jewish history against error. We only claim, that the *method* of record and transmission gives far greater credibility to the Scriptural than to the alleged Assyrian chronology, and more than counterbalances any advantage thought to arise from an unearthed inscription over a written book. Look, for illustration, at the carefulness, fullness, and assured contemporary accuracy of the Jewish period from Solomon's death to the reign of Elah, the fourth king of Israel—as given in the book of Kings.

§ 145. " Rehoboam reigned 17 years, and Jeroboam 22 years (I Ki. xiv: 20, 21); in Jeroboam's 18th year Abijam of Judah began his 3 years (xv: 1, 2); in Jeroboam's 20th year Asa of Judah began his 41 years (ver. 9, 10); in Asa's 2nd year Nadab of Israel began his two years (ver. 25); in Asa's 3d year Baasha of Israel began his 24 years (ver. 33); in Asa's 26th year Elah of Israel began his 2 years " (x: 8).

This Bible reckoning, put into tabular form, *has* to read as follows:

JUDAH.	B. C.	ISRAEL.
1st Rehoboam 17 .... =974= .... 1st Jeroboam 22 (nd)
(18th) " = 1st Abijam 3 .... =957= ....18th "
1st Asa 41 = (4th) " .... =954= ....20th " (ended)
2nd " .... =953= 1st Nadab 2(nd) = .. (22nd) "
3d " .... =952= (2nd) " = ... 1st Baasha 24 (th)
26th " .... =929= 1st Elah 2(nd) = ... (24th ")
Total.............................. = 45 years. (See § 25.)

§ 146. Here the reigns in Judah (17+3+25) just equal the total 45 years elapsed, and explain and establish the reigns in Israel, as each reckoning in the terminal fractions of a reign as if 1 whole year, (which shows the custom then of the Israelite scribe). The Bible numbers can not possibly be put together (without the violation of any one of them), except thus to make out 45 years; so that there can be no chance for dispute about the chronology. The numbers given are so numerous, and the datings and cross-synchronisms are so carefully interwoven, as to show that it must have been *contemporary* history given by those on the spot; while the complication of the dating explains its own method, and rectifies what otherwise might lead to error.

This is only a fair specimen of the whole history and chronology of the kings as given in Scripture; where it is reiterated and confirmed with the same figures in the books of Chronicles, and in Isaiah, etc.,—

giving us one whole consistent and unassailable chronology. No author, ancient or modern, has taken such pains to explain carefully and fully the datings of his history, as have these sacred writers. And their figures simply put together and allowed to speak for themselves (without change), give us the most determinate, exact, and certain chronology that has ever been found, or is likely to be found, in the world.

§ 147. That we have before us the very facts and figures given by the writers of the books of "Kings" without any serious corruption, and that they are as genuinely the original text as if transmitted on an excavated monument, is certain from the same numbers given in the books of "Chronicles," and in the prophetic books, as also in the Septuagint translation into Greek (B. C. 200). It is also known from Josephus, using the same unchanged text and figures; as well as other Jewish authors, and the New Testament writers, and the Chronicles prepared in the later centuries. Moreover, the scripture datings are so blended and interwoven into one whole, by synchronisms and cross-reckonings, that there can be no corruption of a few figures, whose correction might satisfy the Assyrian theorizings.*

§ 148. The Bible Chronology of the Kings must stand or fall as one whole; for as we have the text, it is certainly not to any extent corrupt, but is just what its authors meant it to be. If Assyriology overturns it, that whole scripture history is made to be misleading and false; and those who wrote it are convicted of relating as history what they knew little about. On the contrary, the Bible dating carries on its face the evidence of its truthfulness.

Compare the careful method of contemporary dating in scripture with the mere stringing out of names to represent years, reported to us 150 years after they were passed, as seen in the Eponym Canon; and say which is the most reliable and sure. Nothing in history can be more certain than that the bible numbers put together without mutilation give just 254 years to the kingdom of Israel, from the death of Solomon to the capture of Samaria (B. C. 974 to 720). The mere string of Eponym names from Nineveh, in their meagerness and fallibility of information, can never reduce this to about 210 years, as Assyriologists claim.

§ 149. (III.)—As to the correctness and certainty of Assyriologists in their *interpretation* of events and their identification of names, alleged to be found in the inscriptions. It must be conceded that there

---

*This is shown by the sweeping and destructive mutilation of scripture made by every recent scheme put forth attempting such a forced agreement of the Bible with the alleged requirements of Assyriology. See the treatise of J. Schwartz of New York, in the Bib. Sacra. for Jan. and July, 1888; and that of Dr. Orr of Scotland, in the Pres. Review for Jan., 1889. (See also my criticism of these schemes.)

are great difficulties in the decipherment and exposition of excavated monuments; and that there have been considerable differences of opinion among the ablest scholars concerning the contents of inscriptions found. How could we expect certainty in understanding records consisting mostly of proper names, especially those names which were foreign to the language of the recorder? Every one knows the diversity of naming and of spelling names even within a single language; how much greater the confusion when names and terms are roughly translated into a strange tongue by invading armies and carried off for mention in an alien clime.

We are continually laughing at the mistakes of foreign writers concerning names, times, and places in our own land. Yet many archæologists speak with the greatest confidence of identifications which they think they see, in the mention of places and persons, three or four thousand years ago, by rude foreign inscribers who knew little or nothing about the localities or the personages referred to. Valuable hints may often be got from similarity of names on ancient monuments to other names we know of; and sometimes plausible theories may be thence deduced. But there can be little *certainty* in many such speculations, where few details and mostly mere names are given. Scholars, elated with antique discoveries, are apt to speak with too much assurance as to their inferences therefrom. We commend the greater modesty and caution of George Smith, one of the most esteemed and trustworthy Assyriologists, who candidly owns the difficulties of identification, and sees no necessity of setting the Eponym Canon in collision with Scripture. *

§ 150. Those whom we find speaking so confidently of the Scripture chronology as quite set aside by three or four supposed identifications of Jewish names in the Assyrian inscriptions far out of their scripture place, are by no means so certain about this as they claim to be. They are but fallible men like the rest of us; and their interpretation of the facts may be wrong. In the other chapters of this treatise, we have fully examined those facts of Assyriology; and we think we have shown, that they give us no assured evidence of untruthfulness or error in the Bible Chronology.

Assyriology, in its *source* and its *contents*, carries far less authority as to assured accurate dating, than does the Jewish history. And the same is still more emphatically true of the Tyrian and Egyptian annals; which are only random items and uncertain lists picked out here and there from written manuscripts, like the Bible, only far less reli-

---

* " Professor Hechler, in his address before the Oriental Congress in London, on ' Assyriology and the Bible,' asserted that the harmony of the books of Kings and Chronicles could be established by archæology." (*Boston Watchman, Oct., '92.*)

able than that. We may rest assured, that the Jewish history will yet long stand, as the correct and trustworthy history of ancient times. It must stand, at least until far greater evidence is found in disproof of it, then has yet been brought forward.

CHAPTER II.

TYRIAN HISTORY AND THE BIBLE.

§ 151. *Does the Tyrian History contradict the Bible Chronology of Solomon's Temple as begun in B. C. 1011?*

"The date of the revival of Olympic games by Iphitus is, according to Eratosthines (B. C. 200) at 884 B. C.; according to Callimachus (B. C. 250) at 828 B. C.; Mr. Clinton prefers the latter date." "The Olympiads began to be reckoned from the year 776 B. C., in which year Corœbus was victor in the foot-race. We have lists of the victors from that year." (*Anthon's Class. Dict.*)

So then, the first of the revived Olympic games was (828-776=) 52 years before the first numbered Olympiad.

Now, Josephus, using the historian Menander (B. C. 300), speaks of the building of Carthage as 143 years and 8 months after the building of Solomon's temple (vs. Ap. I. 17, 18.) He thus puts it, according to his Bible Chronology (1011, Antiq. 1010), at (1010—144=) 866 B. C.; *which is 38 years before the first Olympic games* in 828 B. C.

Thus it seems, that the historian Menander, B. C. 300, (if cited rightly by Josephus) had the 7th year of Pygmalion, king of Tyre, and the flight of his sister Dido for the building of Carthage, at the year 866 B. C., 38 years before the first Olympic games of Iphitus in B. C. 828.

§ 152. But soon after, Timæus (B. C. 260) expressed this as "*the 38th year before the first Olympiad,*" thus (perhaps by mistaking his predecessor Menander) speaking of the building of Carthage as if 52 years later, viz., at (866—52=) 814 B. C., (i. e. 776+38.) Dionysius of Hulicarnassus (B. C. 30) in citing Timæus says, he knows not "by what canon" he thus dates, as if there was a doubt about its correctness, in view of Menander's different "canon."*

---

*That Timæus might be mistaking Menander, will appear from what is said by Anthon: "The historical work of Timæus did not contain a synchronistic relation of events, but consisted rather of detached portions of history, in each of which the author treated separately of some important event. Cicero cites Timæus. * * * Polybius, and after him Diodorus Siculus, have charged Timæus with credulity and unfairness. * * * The ancients praised his geographical knowledge, and his care in indicating the chronology of the events which he describes. He appears also to have composed another work on the Olympiads, and it is said *he was the first* historical writer that employed this era." Hence any error of his would be largely copied.

Cicero, B. C. 50 (who cites from Timæus), puts the building of Carthage thus like him as being the 39th year (or 38 years) before the first Olympiad, and 64 or 65 years before the founding of Rome. That is, B. C. 776+38=814—65=749 B. C. for Rome. (Or rather, B. C. 753 for Rome according to Varro, who lived in "closest intimacy with Cicero," says Anthon, +65=818—28=780 B. C. for beginning of the 1st Olympic period—as said to be reckoned by Africanus and others.)

Velleius (A. D. 20) has this same "65 years" before Rome, as if drawn directly from Cicero; *i. e.*, 748 B. C. +65=813, for the rise of Carthage, which he says was "668 years before its fall in B. C. 145-6. (Rollin says 145, Anthon 146.)

Long afterward, Eusebius (A D. 300) at his year B. C. 145-6 says: "Carthage surrenders to Scipio, having stood 669 [other reading 668] years"; which carries us to the same 813-14 B. C. for its founding.

§ 153. These five writers, Timæus, cited by Dionysius, Cicero, Velleius, and Eusebius, are the only ones found giving B. C. 814 for the building of Carthage. And their statements all seem to be derived from the first writer (Timæus), whom Dionysius directly cites, and who seems to have wrongly construed the previous reckoning of Menander (found in Josephus), the only really Tyrian annalist, as meaning "38 years before the 1st Olympiad," whereas he had it *38 years before the 1st Olympic of Iphetus*, viz., at B. C. 866 instead of 814.

This 52 years' difference between the two datings of Carthage has come down to us from the ancients. And the earlier date of Menander is, to say the least, as likely to be true as the later date; because given by the earliest author (B. C. 300), and he the only special annalist of Phœnician affairs, giving specifically the lengths of reigns making up the time, as none of the other writers do.

§ 154. Indeed, no other writer but Menander explains his date, as that of the flight of Dido from her brother Pygmalion, king of Tyre. Menander (in Josephus) makes this B. C. 866 to be "the 7th year" of Pygmalion's 47 years of reign. And who can show that this is not the date of his reign? If those later writers mistook Menander's 38 years before the first Olympic year of Iphitus (B. C. 828) as meaning "38 years before the first Olympiad" (B. C. 776), this error of 52 years later was merely disconnecting the building of Carthage from the flight of Dido; or else it was assigning her flight and the reign of Pygmalion to a later date than than that given by Menander's reigns. In either case, the earlier writer Menander was most likely to be correct. And at any rate, his *reckoning* as 52 years earlier than the other reckoning indicates plainly that the difference arose from the different numberings of Olympic years (52 years apart, from 828 and from 776 B. C.) So that, whichever is right (866 or 814), there is no necessary discrepancy with the Bible Chronology; which (by Josephus) has Solomon commencing the temple at (866+Menander's 144=) 1010 B. C., or (814 +Timæus' 196=) 1010 B. C. (See Restor. of Jos., § 51.)

§ 155. Some attempts have been made, by *comparison of different* dates and writers, to make out the B. C. 866 to be impossible as Menander's reckoning. Thus, Aristotle's statement that Utica was built 287 years before Carthage, is put with Pliny's statement, that Utica originated 1178 years ago (*i. e.*, from A. D. 77 back to B. C. 1101); from which taking the 287, we have 814 not 866 B. C. Again: The statement of Castor of Rhodes, that there were 382 years from the Lydians down to the end of the Phoenician dominion over the sea, is put with a roundabout calculation from other writers, of the Lydian kingdom as beginning B. C. 1197; so that 1197 (changed to 1196!)—382=814 B. C. Once more: Justin's statement, that Tyre was built in the year before the destruction of Troy, is put with Josephus' statement, that Tyre had been built 240 years when Solomon began his temple (Ant., 8, iii: 1); so that, calling the destruction of Troy 1197 B. C., we have 1198—240=958 B. C. for the beginning of Solomon's temple; whence Menander's 144 years carry us to B. C. 814, not 866.

§ 156. But no such mingling of one writer's date of one event with another writer's date of another event, proves anything concerning either's estimate of the interval between. For instance: Who knows that Pliny believed in Aristotle's 287 years from Utica to Carthage? —without which he could not believe in Carthage as built in B. C. 814. And who knows that Josephus thought Tyre was built the year before Troy fell, or in the year 1198 B. C.?—without which he could not think Solomon's temple began in B. C. 858. And who knows that Justin thought there were 384 years between the beginning of Tyre and of Carthage?—without which he could not think the latter to be B. C. 814. And so of every similar case. One or the other writer may be mistaken;* and the self-confirming Bible Chronology can not thus be overturned.

§ 157. It is by such coupling of diverse authors, that J. Schwartz tries to boast of *twelve* ancient writers as testifying to B. C. 814, instead of the *five* shown above, all derived from one (probably mistaking) source, viz., Timæus, as we have seen. (*Letter, Nov. 29, 1888.*)

Look at the matter again. We can not with any assurance combine the date given by Cicero and others for the building of Carthage, with

---

(*Note.—That Josephus himself may perhaps be mistaken as to Menander's amount of years, appears from the fact, that he (Josephus) puts the founding of Solomon's temple in "the 12th year" of King Hiram of Tyre; while we know that it was much later than that in Hiram's reign. (See II Sam., v: 11, and I Ki. v: 1.) Moreover, Hiram's reign as he cites it from Menander is but "34 years," while it requires his whole life of Hiram, "53 years," to make out his total down to Dido. This whole matter of Hiram's reign seems to be given wrongly.)

the interval given from Menander for the flight of Dido. How long was the building of Carthage after Dido quit Tyre? Who knows? Menander makes her brother Pygmalion still reign at Tyre 41 years after "his sister fled away from him;" and she, after a while getting up an expedition, and subsequently stopping with her fleet in Cyprus, may have lived as long as her brother, before in Africa she saw Carthage rebuilt.

§ 158. We now give a sure proof, that the Bible Chronology cannot, by any device, be reconciled with the date 814 B. C. of Timæus for the building of Carthage, and at the same time with the 144-year interval of Menander back to the temple. This makes Solomon's temple to begin at (814+144=) 958 B. C.; and Schwartz so assigns it. But when he and others interpret the Assyrian Chronology in the Eponym Canon as referring to Jehu, king of Israel, the first year of Jehu is thus compelled to be no later than B. C. 841; leaving but (958-841=) 117 years from the founding of the temple to Jehu. Now, scripture makes the time from Jehu back to the death of Solomon to be 91 years, and the multiplied interlocking cross-dates or synchronisms utterly forbid any shorter reckoning. To which adding only 36 of Solomon's "40 years" back to his "4th year," makes (91+36=) 127 years, as the shortest possible interval from Jehu back to the founding of the temple, or from 841 to 968 B. C.

This latest possible date is 10 years (or at least 9) earlier than the 958-9 B. C. which Timæus' 814 + Menander's 144 requires. So that, to overcome the discrepancy, Schwartz* has to reduce Solomon's "40 years" reign arbitrarily by six years! and then to reduce the subsequent interval to Jehu by 3 years more, so as to reach B. C. 959 (substituted for 958),—in violation of numerous concurring synchronisms and reign-lengths of Scripture! Such mutilation of the Bible is not *harmonizing* it with profane chronology, as professed; but it is treating the inspired book as *utterly inaccurate* in its historical accounts.

CHAPTER III.

Egyptian History and the Jewish Kings.

§ 159. It is claimed that Egyptian chronology puts the beginning of Shishak's reign (I Ki. ii: 40 and xiv: 25) as much as 40 years too late to agree with the scripture date of Solomon's death as B. C. 974. We proceed to show, that the Egyptian reckoning is altogether uncertain, and cannot set aside the Bible Chronology, which is so well assured and indisputable in its data.

---

*Theolog. Monthly, London, 1889, March, p. 163.

There are three sources of argument used for the Egyptian dating claimed. (1) The added Egyptian dynasties of Manetho. (2) Manetho's mention of the Olympic era. (3) Astronomical allusions.

MANETHO'S DYNASTIES.

§ 160. (I.) The added Egyptian Dynasties of Manetho. George Rawlinson, in his History of Ancient Egypt (Vol. II, p. 7) says: "Thus far back (to 'Tirhakah', II Ki., xix: 9) the dates are as nearly as possible certain, and accord with Scripture. From the date of Tirhakah's accession, we are thrown almost entirely upon Manetho,"— who wrote his history of Egypt nearly 500 years after Tirhakah. Here let us remark, how uncertain is any reckoning that depends upon Manetho. His work is lost; and we have to rely altogether upon the conflicting accounts of it contained in various authors.

Says Anthon (*Class. Dic.*), "Considerable fragments are preserved in the treatise of Josephus against Apion; but still greater portions in chronicles of George Syncellus, a monk of the 9th century, which were principally compiled from the chronicles of Julius Africanus and from Eusebius, both of whom made great use of Manetho's history. The work of Africanus is lost; and we only possess a Latin version of that of Eusebius, which was translated out of the Armenian version at Constantinople." It will be seen at once how undecisive must be differing data derived thus second and third handed from the original historian, even supposing him to be fully reliable, which is a matter in question.

§ 161. The Encyc. Brittanica (newest edition, art. Egypt) tells us: "Manetho gave a list of 30 dynasties and the length of each, with in some cases the duration of the indivual reigns. Manetho's list is unhappily in a very corrupt condition." Schwartz says: "Manetho's dynasties have not come down to us in their original form, but through successive corruptions, in which each successive author tried to accommodate them to his special 'system' of Biblical chronology. It is therefore necessary, by comparing the various versions, to restore the original form of the lists." Yet Schwartz thinks to make out an *assured* date for Shishak (contrary to that of the Bible) from data so confused and corrupted as these! And to make out such an anti-biblical reckoning, he entirely throws out one dynasty, and makes the dynasties overlap each other; while Schwartz and Bunsen, and other kindred critics, greatly disagree as to the manner and extent of the overlap. (See period D, § 102).

§ 162. Prof. Lepsius and M. Mariette are the two Egyptologists who give a definite arrangement of the dynasties throughout. (See in *Encyc. Brittan.*) Their tables of dynasty lengths agree, from the beginning of the 19th dynasty to the beginning of the 22d, total 482 years

(Eusebius makes 502 or 510.) M. Mariette has Shishak beginning the 22d dynasty B. C. 980, Lepsius 961. This 22nd dynasty Lepsius makes 174 years, and M. Mariette makes it 170 years, *or 54 years more* than the "116 or 120 years" given by Africanus. Bunsen well says: "It is generally admitted that, according to the monuments, [we add according to the Scriptures also], *more time must be allowed* for the entire reigns of the 22nd dynasty" than this "120 years" of Africanus *seems* to give. So he arbitrarily makes it 148 years (from B. C. 948), while Schwartz arbitrarily calls it 143 years (from B. C. 937). Here, then we are all afloat, and any *assured* dating is out of the question. Here are *four different lengths* given for the 22nd dynasty (from the accession of Shishak downwards) by as many different writers of Egyptology; viz., 143, 148, 170, 174 years! How evidently uncertain is the whole reckoning. Hence, our calculations of the dynasty as 154 or 159 years is as likely to be true as any of the others.

§ 163. George Rawlinson (Vol. II., p. 7) tells us: "To the two dynasties preceding the 24th, (viz. to the 22d and 23d dynasties), Manetho assigned 209 years, according to Africanus in Syncellus;" which makes the 22d dynasty 120 + 89 years for the 23d, (or 160 + 49 see § 166). He says: "The Saite dynasty (the 24th) consisted of but one king, Bocchoris, who reigned 44 years according to the Manetho of Eusebius in Syncellus;" which, with the death of Bocchoris (at the accession of Seveh or "So," II Ki. xvii: 4) put as B. C. 722, makes "Shishak begin (B. C. 722 + 44 + 209 =) 975 B. C.," says Rawlinson,— (adding, that the 6 years only of Bocchoris in Afric.'s Manetho would reduce it 38 years).

Thus Rawlinson finds Manetho's dynasties giving B. C. 975 for the beginning of Shishak; while M. Mariette finds it B. C. 980, *i. e.* 5 years earlier. And the accession of "So" was probably as much as 5 years earlier, in B. C. 727, instead of 722. (It must be before Hoshea's 9 years from B. C. 729 to 720 had far advanced. See II Ki. xvii: 1-4.) Both these distinguished Egyptologists thus found the dynasties of Manetho yielding a date for Shishak in harmony with Scripture.

The Olympic Era.

§ 164. (II.) Bunsen remarks, that "Manetho states positively that the first Olympiad was celebrated in Egypt during the 40 years' reign of Petubastes, the first king of the 23d dynasty." It must be remembered that Manetho was writing more than 500 years after the time spoken of, and might easily mistake as to a date so far away; so that this remark, if correctly reported, and if meaning just what is ascribed to him, (which may be doubted), can have no such sure authority as to overturn the assured dating of the contemporary Scripture history.

Besides, there is something peculiar in the expression as to *celebrating* an "Olympiad," instead of holding Olympic games, and as to this being "in Egypt," rather than at Olympia in Greece. This suggests that the reference is not to the current Olympic Era, 776 B. C., but to the beginning of the first Olmpic *period* of 4 years, as *ended* not begun (by Egyptian estimate) at 776 B. C., *i. e.*, as beginning B. C. 780; or even as beginning back at B. C. 828, when Iphitus first revived these Olympic games, according to Callimachus, (endorsed by Clinton, *Fas. Hel., vol. 2, p. 408, note h.* So in *Anthon's Class. Dic., Art. Olympia.* (See here, § 151.)

If the Olympic era referred to means B. C. 828, then the 22d dynasty may end anywhere from B. C. 868 to 828, and even the 120 years given by Africanus for the 22d dynasty will carry us to any point from B. C. 988 to 948 for the beginning of Shishak; which agrees with the scripture dating of him, as reigning at B. C. 975.

§ 165. But if the Olympic era referred to means B. C. 780, as the beginning of a first Olympic period supposed then to begin, (with the first Olympiad *ending* in B. C. 776,)—this will accord with Schwartz' own reckoning of Olympiads, by which alone (as ante-dating B. C. 776) he makes out his chronology of the period, (he making Africanus have the Olympiads beginning as early as B. C. 779). And this will also give a scriptural dating for Shishak.

For, Manetho's naming of the celebration of a first Olympiad in connection with the reign of Petubastes' 40 years, would be a very vague way of speaking, unless he meant that that reign *did not close* till that date, or had some such special reference. Therefore, the 40 years are as likely as any way to begin at (B. C. 780+40=) 820 B. C. as the beginning of the 23d dynasty (instead of M. Mariette's 810, Bunsen's 800, Schwartz' 794, or Lepsius' 787.) Then, the 120 years given by Africanus from Petubastes to Shishak, which all the critics enlarge one way or another, is best considered as having originally referred not to the beginning of Shishak, but to his end in (B. C. 820+120=) 940 B. C. So that, the reign of Shishak (34 years in Syncellus) is to be added to the 120 years of Africanus, making 154 years as the real length of the 22d dynasty (rather than the 143, 148, 170, 174 of the various authors.) This carries us to (B. C. 940+34=) 974 B. C. for the beginning of Shishak, the very year of Solomon's death according to the Scripture chronology. It might be the news of a new dynasty in Egypt (inimical to Solomon's father-in-law), that led Jeroboam to flee to that particular retreat just before Solomon died. (See I Ki. iii: 1, comp. xi: 40.) *

---

* For our reckoning of Manetho's Olympic reference as putting it earlier than B. C. 776, we have the sanction of Schwartz, as seen above. For our inclusion of all the 40 years of Petubustes in the pre-

§ 166. Suppose we understand Manetho as putting the end of Petubastes' 40 years at the Olympic B. C. 776. This carries the beginning of that king (and dynasty) to B. C. 816, and requires dynasty 22 to be only 159 years long (similar to Rawlinson's value—see above—), in order to reach B. C. 975, as a scriptural dating point for the reign of Shishak. (M. Mariette increases the 159 to 170, and Lepsius to 174 years.)

Rawlinson notes, that Manetho in Eusebius has the 23d dynasty but 44 years, (like the 24th); so that, Manetho has here left out (89—45=) 44 years, and may have offset (in Euseb.) by adding 40 or 45 to the previous 22d dynasty, making it thus (120+40=)160 years (as seen in §163), or even 165, (not Mariette's 170 or Lepsius' 174.) Then, by *Manetho in Eusebius*, we have the 22nd dynasty 160 years from B. C. 975 to 815 (or even 165 years from the B. C. 980 of Mariette), and the 23d dynasty 44 years from B. C. 815 to 771, and the 24th dynasty also 44 years from B. C. 771 to 727, as the death of Bochoris and the beginning of "So" (or Shabak) in the 3d year of Hoshea, (II Ki. xvii: 1-4), which last (727) is a more reasonable date than the 722 of Rawlinson, (see §163.) And these dates, B. C. 975 for the accession of Shishak, and B. C. 815 for the accession of Petubastes are in accordance with the requirements of the case. (See §164. Also, Period D, §115.)

Thus to put the beginning of Petubastes (and the 23d dynasty) in the neighborhood of B. C. 820, is certainly a more reasonable assignment than the later dates given, (M. Mariette 810, Bunsen 800, Schwartz 794, Lepsius 787). For, the next two dynasties (23d and 24th)

Olympic period, we have the sanction of Bunsen, when he says, that with that 40 and the 120 of Africanus preceding it (total 160 years) reckoned from his (Bunsen's) beginning of Shishak's *sole* reign (as in B. C. 935), we should have B. C. 775; so that, the year of the 1st Olympiad in B. C. 776 would have fallen in the reign of Petubastes. Then again, for our reckoning of the "120 years" of Africanus as reaching back only to the *end* of Shishak, we have also the sanction of Bunsen, when he takes the smaller "116 years" of Africanus, and reducing it to 114, makes this reach back from Petubastes (B. C. 800) to his end of Shishak (as 914)+34=948 B. C. for his beginning of Shishak.

Thus we have every step of our reckoning (B. C. 780+40+120+34= 974 B. C.), endorsed by these critics themselves; which shows that this our combination of those values is as likely as any reckoning to be right. Our treatment of the "120 years" *without alteration* is certainly more simple and rational than that of Bunsen in arbitrarily reducing it to 114, or that of Schwartz in arbitrarily increasing it to 130 back to Shishak's invasion, or 143 to his accession.

(This notion of Schwartz, that Africanus (in giving but 21 years to Shishak), purposely left out 13 years as being before the invasion, and that Eusebius also (in giving Petubastes but 25 years), purposely left out 15 years as being before the Greek Olympic era reckoned as 779 B. C., is certainly more fanciful than convincing.)

will rightly give us 92 years, from B. C. 820 or 816, to B. C. 728 or 724,. as the proper date of the scriptural "So" beginning the 25th dynasty.

Both Bunsen and Schwartz give dynasty 23 as 58 years (the same as Lepsius); and Bunsen puts dynasty 24 as 34 years; making 92 years as just given. Rawlinson says that Eusebius has Manetho's dynasty 24 as 44 years, and the 23d also as 44, making the two 88. But he tells us that Africanus gives Manetho's 22d and 23d together as 209 years, which +Eusebius' 44 for dynasty 24=253 years, from B. C. 722 (for "So") back to B. C. 975 (for Shishak.) So says Rawlinson. And thus, Manetho's dynasties, when taken *continuously*,—without one whole dynasty dropped out completely (as done by the critics) under the unproved assumption of contemporary reigns, are found to be in complete agreement with Scripture.

§ 167. For there (in II Ki. xvii: 1-4) we read of Hoshea, who reigned B. C. 729-720, as seeking alliance with "So (Sabaco), king of Egypt;" which therefore must have been somewhere from B. C. 728 to 722, as just now reckoned. And (at xix: 9) we read of "Tirhakah, king of Ethiopia," kinsman of Sabaco, (*see Prideaux, year 710*), as coming to attack the Assyrian king (in B. C. 712-708). Thus that 25th dynasty began with "So" or Sabaco somewhere before B. C. 728 or 722. (Usher has it 727, Rawlinson has it 722). "It was then that Sabaco, king of Ethiopia, having taken Bocchoris (who constituted the 24th dynasty), and burned him alive, set up the new or Ethiopic dynasty, the 25th of Manetho." (*Chambers' Cyc. Art. Egypt.*) *

---

* "After reigning 8 years, Sabaco (or So) was succeeded by his son Sevechus, whom Heroditus calls Sethon." (*Prideaux yr. 720*). Rawlinson says of "the synchronism of Shabak (Seveh or So) with Hoshea,"—"It is generally allowed, that the 'So' or Sevek of II Ki. xvii: 4 represents Shabak, in whose name the k is unimportant, being merely the suffixed article. (See Brusch)." Anthon (*Art. Egypt*) tells us: "The (four) names inscribed on the monuments are Schabak, Sevek-otheph, etc., all of whom are mentioned either by Greek or sacred historians, under the names of Sabacon, Sevechus, etc. No more than three of these kings are mentioned in the list of Manetho as belonging to this dynasty, the last being included in that which follows."

But Bunsen names the father Zeth or Sethos, making his reign (as 31 yrs.) an addition to the 23d dynasty, with 23 yrs. of it spent alongside of Bocchoris of the 24th dynasty (as contemporary), and making the last 8 yrs. of it spent (seemingly in joint reign) with the son Sevek (as ending B. C. 711). He says: "The last king of the 23d dynasty was Zeth, long recognized as the Sethos whom Heroditus helps us to identify with the advance of Tirhakah, B. C. 711." M. Mariette has the 24th dynasty only 6 yrs. (B. C. 721-715), and Lepsius has it but 13 yrs. (B. C. 729-716). Schwartz begins the 26th dynasty at B. C. 692, and throws out entirely the 25th dynasty, as contemporary with the 24th and 26th. It is only by such gratuitous violations of Manetho's dynasties, that the critics try to make out their later dating of Shishak. How unreliable such chronology!

Astronomical Allusions.

§ 168. (III.) Schwartz (Letter, Oct. 29, 1888) says: "Shishak 34 years from B. C. 937 to 903, then Osorkon I for 19 years to B. C. 884, then Tukelut I; his 15th year=870 B. C., in which an eclipse of the moon is recorded, as occurring on the 25th of the month Mesori; and the only eclipse visible in Egypt during that 9th century B. C. that fell on the 25th Mesori was in B. C. 870." But what if the eclipse occurred (say) forty years earlier, in the previous century? In 40 years, 25 Mesori would range through 10 days of the Julian year during which it would be very remarkable for *no eclipse of the moon to occur*,—since *every lunar* eclipse is visible in all places. Besides, we have no assurance, that the reigns were only 67 years from this eclipse back to I Shishak, as Schwartz here makes them. So that, there is *no certainty* about this astronomical argument.

§ 169. Again Schwartz says: "My researches place the 1st yr. of Tukelut II in B. C. 852 (or 32 years after Tukelut I began); so that his 11th year would be B. C. 842;—in which year we are told that the rising of Sothis heliacally was on the 1st of the month Tybi; and that 1st Tybi fell on July 20 (the Sothiacal date) only in B. C. 845-2." But, though July 20 was the Sothiacal date in the time of Censorinus, (A. D. 238), it was not so in B. C. 842. Besides, Mr. Schwartz' "researches" may be misleading; and we have no assurance that the reigns were only 85 years from the 1st Tukelut II back to the 1st Shishak, as Schwartz here makes them. There may have been 123 years or more back to B. C. 975 or earlier, as the researches of others indicate. So that, there is *no certainty* about this astronomical argument.

§ 170. On the whole, our calculation of Shishak (from Manetho) as beginning the 22nd dynasty in B. C. 975 or 4, the year before Solomon's death, in conformity with Scripture reckoning, is as reasonable as any of the theories devised by the critics. At the same time, the entire discussion shows, how very *uncertain* are all those outside historical reckonings, compared with the full, duplicated, harmonious Bible chronology.

The result of all is, that the Egyptian chronology plainly can give us no assured dating to compete with Bible chronology, or to set it aside as incorrect. And it is just so with the Tyrian and the Assyrian data. All these pagan reckonings are vague and uncertain, as compared with the Hebrew records, which we have shown to be very exact and evidently prepared upon the spot with careful effort to measure the time.

The best that these outside figurings can do, is to show, that *if* Scripture itself should be found to require a later dating of Shishak and Solomon, the pagan reckonings could be made to conform thereto. But with the Bible chronology as it stands, there is nothing outside that can prove it untrue.

[The reply to Schwartz Review is left in MSS.]

PERIOD D.—THE JUDGES.

PART I.

FROM THE EXODUS TO SOLOMON'S TEMPLE.

CHAPTER I.

THE INTERVAL OF THE 580 YEARS.

§ 1. The dates and the length of time from the exodus to David, are very distinctly and unmistakably given us by Paul, in his speech at Antioch, Acts xiii: 17-22; making, to Solomon's Temple, as follows:

```
Moses, in the wilderness,        40 years, Acts xiii: 18.
Joshua, until the allotment,      7    "      "    "    19*
Judges, to and with Samuel,     450    "      "    "    20†
Saul, the first king,            40    "      "    "    21
David, the man of God,           40    "    II Sam. v: 4
Solomon, until the Temple,        3    "    II Chron. iii: 2
```

Total, 580 years.

This period of 580 years, therefore, is most clearly and decisively the true Scripture interval from the Exodus out of Egypt to the founding of Solomon's Temple. In I Ki. vi: 1, the date of the temple is given as "in the 480th year"; where the 4 (instead of 5) is evidently a mistake of copyists, which was not misleading Paul, as it is misleading many in our day.

There are known to be two or three instances (at the least) in the Old Testament of the miscopying of a single figure; and it is wonderful that there are no more. One of the cases is at II Chron., xxxvi: 9, "Jehoiachin was eight years old when he began to reign;" which is corrected by II Ki., xxiv: 8, "Jehoiachin was eighteen years old when

---

* "Destroyed seven nations" is equivalent to "gained possession in seven years." The allotment began in the 47th year, *i. e.*, 46½ years from the Exodus; as we learn from Josh., xiv: 1, 2, 7, 10, comp. with Num., x: 11, and xiii: 25.

†As to the revised reading of this text see § 27.

he began to reign." So, the "480th year" of I Ki., vi: 1 is corrected by the enumeration of Paul in Acts 13th. We may perhaps fairly assume, that God has not suffered any copyist's error of this sort to creep into His Word without some means of correcting it, as in these cases.

The "450 Years."

§ 2. The precise agreement of Paul's enumeration with the number given in I Ki., vi: 1, as thus set right, is proof that his value "about 450 years" is the true interval from the allotment of Canaan to the beginning of the kingdom under Saul. And this is the exact amount found by adding up the several lengths of time given in the book of Judges, with 40 years added from the first-named oppression of "Chushan-rishathaim 8 years" (Ju., iii: 8), back to Joshua's allotment of the land.

The book of Judges plainly intends to give a continuous history, with its successive numbers showing the whole length of time occupied. The honest way, therefore, is to add up all its numbers as giving the period that it covers, leaving the subsequent books (of Ruth and Samuel) to begin back upon the same period, if they so appear. Treated in this fair manner, the book of Judges adds up just 410 years; and the "about 450 years" of Paul for possession of the land and for "judges," evidently means to *cover the book of Judges*, with a terminal 40 years for the events at its beginning and close.

This mode of adding up the 450 years made the judges to end with the book of Judges, viz., with Samson's 20 years at chap. xvi: 31, *where the book properly ends*. For, the last five chapters of Judges are an Appendix, belonging chronologically to the anarchy that prevailed in the time of the first two chapters, until Othniel, the first of the Judges (iii: 9). "In those days there was no king (or judge) in Israel; every man did that which was right in his own eyes." (Ju., xvii: 6, and xviii: 1, and xix: 1, and xxi: 25.) It is in this order that Josephus gives the history (Antiq., 5, ii) and all expositors are agreed in this arrangement.*

§ 3. Moreover, the following book of Ruth, and the first chapters of I Sam. are cotemporary history, dating back into the time of the book of Judges, as is now generally agreed. Samson's dying slaughter of the Philistines, with which the order of history in Judges ends (with chap. xvi), so emboldened God's people, that "Israel went out

---

*We must add, by way of postscript, that in the Bib. Sacra (Oct., 1891, p. 660, 661), appears a treatment of this Appendix to Judges as if belonging there chronologically. It is one of the most astounding oversights by professed bible scholarship that we have ever seen committed in so high a quarter.

against the Philistines to battle "; which battle resulted in Eli's death, as narrated in I Sam., iv: 1-18. So that Eli's 40 years of judging (ver. 18) had counted backwards over Samson's 20, and beyond, covering the last 20 of the Philistine invasion (Ju., xiii: 1). Eli ruled at Shiloh where the ark abode; and Samson ruled at the same time in the more southern or Philistine country. This is the reckoning as still given in our common chronologies (from Usher); that of Scott's bible, for instance, which describes it as the reckoning of "some learned men. (NOTE.—The Septuagint has Eli ruling but 20 years, *i. e.*, the same 20 as Samson, following the Philistine 40 years.)

But to reckon the well-understood "450 years" *of the judges* as thus beginning at Joshua's apportionment of the land, would not agree with the fact that the *first judge*, Othniel, did not begin till long after that (Ju. iii: 9); so that, some were led to substitute (for this 40-year interval at the beginning) the 40 years of Eli as if additional at the end. So Eusebius gives it. Still, this left no time for Samuel as one of the judges; concerning whom Josephus tells us (Antiq. 6, xiii: 5): "He governed and presided over the people alone, after the death of Eli the high-priest, twelve years, and eighteen years together with Saul the king." These 12 years given to Samuel as judge, allowed but 28 of the 40 to go back *before the judges*, to reach Joshua's allotment of the land.

§ 4. And Josephus, accordingly, reckons it just this way. For he says (Ant. 5, i: 29), "Joshua became Israel's commander after Moses' death twenty-five years;" that is, 18 more after the 7 years at the allotment of the land.* (So Julius Africanus, A. D. 221, also puts it.) And then Josephus adds (6, v: 4), "In the days of Moses and his disciple, Joshua, who was their general, they continued an aristocracy; but after the death of Joshua, for 18 years in all, the multitude had no settled form of government, but were in an anarchy [as also says Ju. xvii: 6, etc.]; after which they returned to their former government, they then permitting themselves to be judged by him who appeared to be the best warrior, and most courageous; whence it was, that they called this interval of their government 'the judges.'"

These "18 years" of "anarchy," therefore, reach to the first judge Othneil (iii: 9), including the 8 years subjection to Chushan (ver. 8), with 10 years before; which 10, with the 18 years of Joshua after the allotment, amount to 28 years here at the beginning, with the 12 of Samuel at the close, making up 40 of the 450-year period. Thus this period, according to the Bible and Josephus, is constituted as follows:

---

* Eusebius gives Joshua 27; and he wrongly treats this whole reign of Joshua (instead of his first 7 years), as excluded from the "450 years of Acts xiii: 20; and he thus increases Paul's total, 580 from the Exodus, up to the 600 years which *he* attributes to Paul.

§ 5. Period of the Judges.

```
   Joshua ......  18 more    ⎫         Josephus, 5, i: 29.
   Anarchy ....  10          ⎬ 28         "      6, v: 4.
   Chushan.....   8          ⎭         Judges,  3: 8.
1. Othniel .....  40                      "      11.
   Eglon .......  18                      "      14.
2. Ehud........  80                       "      30.
   Jabin........  20                      "      4: 3.
3. Barak.......  40 (& Deb.)              "      5: 31.
   Midian ......   7 [ ]                  "      6: 1.
4. Gideon......  40                       "      7: 28.
5. Abimelech...   3                       "      9: 22.
6. Tola........  23 (22) [ ]              "     10: 2.
7. Jaïr ........  22                      "      3.
                ─────                              
   ("300 years") 329 [" over 300."]       "     11: 26.
   Ammonites ..  18                       "     10: 8.
8. Jephthah ....   6                      "     12: 7.
9. Ibsan........   7                      "      9.
10. Elon ........  10                     "     11.
11. Abdon ......   8 [ ]                  "     14.
    Philistines...  40 Eli 20             "     13: 1.
13. Samson......  20 Eli 20               "     15: 20.
14. Samuel......  12                    Josephus, 6, xiii: 5.
                ─────
    Total........450*                   Acts,    13: 20.
```

(Bracket groups: 410 years total; I Sam. iv: 18; 12)

These Scripture numbers are all given just the same by Josephus, except the three marked [ ], which are not clearly stated by him, (Tola not being mentioned at all), though his aggregate requires all but Abdon. This shows that our Hebrew bible is uncorrupted and just as he had it (in the main), and that his view of the whole interval was about the same as that of Paul, living at about the same period. The reckoning agrees with the round number "300 years" mentioned in the book of Judges (xi: 26) and in Josephus (5, vii: 9), as seen above.

§ 6. Thus evident is it, that we have here the true Bible reckoning. Every number is given in the Scripture itself, except the length of Samuel's *separate* rule (12 as part of the "20" at I Sam. vii: 2), and the gap after Joshua's allotment. And these two points (at beginning

---

*Josephus' reckoning, with 1 year given to Shamgar (Ant. 5, iv: 3; Ju. iii: 31), will give the total as 451, (i. e., "*about* 450 years," as Paul says); and this Josephus offsets by only 2 (not 3) years given to Solomon,— the 40th year of David being dropped as a year of joint reign with Solomon. This makes Josephus have David begin B. C. 1053, instead of the B. C. 1054 of our reckoning here. The reader may decide which is right. Clement Alex. interprets Paul's "about 450" (like Josephus) as 451, but with Josephus' extra 12 put into it, making it "463." (See Restor. of Jos. § 92.) See Appendix A, here, § 41.

and end of the 450 years period) are very clearly established by Josephus; while their amount and the total interval are decisively fixed by the figures of Paul.

But it is around these two points that the chief divergences of opinion and variations of reckoning have arisen. By adding Eli's 40 years (with or without Saul reduced 20 years), one and another of the Jewish teachers and early Christian fathers, got the interval from the Exodus to the Temple as 600 or 620 years (instead of Paul's 580). Josephus, reckoning the full (Philistine 40 + Samson 20 + Eli 40 =) 100 before Samuel, instead of the right 60,—and then reducing Saul's 40 to 20,—made out 20 too many, or a total of 600 (as given in Eusebius).

But for a reason which we elsewhere explain (see here, § 69), Josephus reduced the 600 to 592, by letting the 8 of Abdon overlap (not naming it in his account). Subsequently, Theophilus (A. D. 171) got the interval to 612, so using the 612 of Jos.' Priest-Record as if ending at the 4th of Solomon. (The Paschal Chronicle gets in 20 more, making 632.) Clement Alex. increased the "450 years" of Paul by 13 years up to "463"; and he had the 592 to the temple, though sometimes calling it 573 and 566 (which last number Eusebius cites as "from the Syrian Records"). *See Jackson.* All these values are derived from a 580 years' reckoning originally *understood*, but not expressed in I Ki. vi: 1.

THE EXODUS DATE.

§ 7. In Period E, § 5, we have shown, that Solomon began the temple in the 4th year of his 40 years' reign, B. C. 1011, *i. e.*, 3 years from his coronation or from his father's death. (See here, § 41.) With our interval of 580 years back from this point, we reach (1011 + 580 =) 1591 B. C. as the date of the Exodus. But with "the 480th year" of I Ki. vi: 1, we reach only (1011 + 479 =) 1490 B. C., not Usher's 1491, as the Exodus date.

No early writer gives any such smaller reckoning as "the 480th year," until it is set forth by Eusebius (A. D. 325). In agreement with many able scholars, we judge that this 480 must be a corruption of the text, that crept in not very long before Eusebius' day. (This is fully discussed here, in Part II, § 58.) We here proceed with the proof, that 580 (not 480) is the correct Scriptural number.

SABBATIC CONFIRMATION.

§ 8. The 580 years reckoning gathered from Paul and the Judges, is shown to be right by the Sabbatic and Jubilee reckoning of the Jews. Josephus instructs us (Antiq. 14, xvi: 2), that a Sabbatic year ended at Herod's conquest of Jerusalem, in the autumn of B. C. 37 (as well as B. C. 163, etc.),—with Jubilee Sabbatic ending in B. C. 23. So that it was a Jubilee at A. D. 27, when Christ spake as in Luke, iv: 19; and just 21 Jubilee periods before, in B. C. 1003, Solomon's temple was dedicated (1 Ki. viii: 63, 65), at a Jubilee as is generally agreed. And 12 Jubilee periods, or 588 years before, carry us to B. C. 1591 as the Exodus date, 580 years before the founding of the temple in B. C. 1011. So that, by this reckoning, the starting point of Jubilees was at the Exodus, where it should be, at the grand epoch of Jubilee deliverance. (See Period E, § 49, etc.)

Hence the first Jubilee period of 49 years ended at 9 years of Joshua (viz., at Josh. xxii: 1-34), when, the land being conquered and divided by lot, the 2½ tribes were sent away, and all settled down to their home cultivation of the country. Not until then could they begin to count their six years of established land-culture, followed by a 7th "Sabbatic year," as required. (Lev. xxv: 3.) They could have no Sabbatic till six years of orderly tillage; and no such orderly tillage was there in the turmoil of war.

§ 9. In the first seven years Joshua "destroyed seven nations" (Acts xiii: 19), finishing the chief conquest of the land, and beginning its allotment, as at Josh. xii-xv. But after a few tribes had received a temporary apportionment, there was a suspension of the work, and considerable delay in thoroughly surveying and more equitably allotting the land, (Josh. xviii: 2, 7, etc.); until cities of refuge were assigned, and cities for the Levites (ch. xx, xxi). And after that, when (in ch. xxii) the 2½ tribes had been sent away over Jordan, and, the army being disbanded, all were settled in their homes,—then at length, after 9 years in Canaan, the nation felt that their Jubilee of finished exodus and inheritance had come; and that, in beginning now their peaceful home tillage, and no longer living as they had on the spoils of war, they must count first six years of husbandry and then a Sabbatic year of rest, according to command.

Is not this a more reasonable view of the begun Sabbatics (at 9 years of Joshua or 49 from the Exodus), than the view maintained by some (the Usher Chronology, for instance),—that the Israelites held their first Sabbatic year, and let the land rest, as soon as they had been there 6 or 7 years only, fighting all the while and gathered in battle array, away from any settled homes? Would they, or could they, observe a Sabbatic year with no non-Sabbatic or cultivation years before it, and with no reference to a 49 year Jubilee interval preceding it? This Usher reckoning makes the Jubilees all date as from 2 or 3 years before the Exodus, instead of all pointing back (as they should) to that great honored epoch of Jubilee freedom to the Jews. We feel assured, that we rightly reckon the Jubilees from the Exodus date, as the Modern Jewish Chronology does. (See Period E, § 57-59.)

THE "14 GENERATIONS."

§ 10. The same appears more certain from the Jewish reckoning of *generations*, as given in Mat. i: 17. For convenience and symmetry they made summaries of generations conformable to the Jubilee periods. From Abraham to David they reckoned 70 years to a generation, in accordance with the teaching (of Moses?) in Psm. xc: 10.* So that, the deliverance from Egypt in 215 years from the arrival of Jacob there was said to be "in the fourth generation" (Gen. xv: 16), i. e., *after 3 times 70 or 210 years.*

And *names* were taken (of distinguished successors) to conform to this number of generations: as at Ex. vi: 16-20, Levi, Kohath, Amram, Moses. So at Mat. i: 3, Judah, Phares, Esrom, Aram, four names (after Abraham, Isaac, and Jacob) finishing the first seven generations of 70 times 7=490 years in all. As many more added, or 980 years in all, make 20 Jubilee periods, or twice "seventy weeks" of years, or the "fourteen generations," reaching from B. C. 1983, the Jubilee year, or year following the offering of Isaac (at 12 years of age in 1984) down to B. C. 1003, the Jubilee year of temple dedication, following the year of finished temple sacrifice (on the same Mt. Moriah, in 1004.) This was about 980 years from Isaac's birth to Solomon's accession; that is, *14 generations (of 70 years) from the call of Abraham to the reign of David.*

§ 11. Thus was the generation reckoning of the Jews conformed to their favorite Jubilee periods, especially to those two celebrated Jubilees of sacrifice on the mount, B. C. 1003 and 1983, just 20 Jubilee periods apart. And this generation reckoning gives

```
    7 years for building the temple.
  580 years back to the Exodus.
  430 years back to Abraham's arrival, (see period C.)
  —37 years to the offering of Isaac.
  ―――
  980 years=14 generations.
```

---

*From David downward, the Jews halved the reckoning to an *average* duration of 35 years for a generation of people, instead of 70 years for individual life; having now 10 (instead of 20) Jubilee periods, viz, 490 years to 14 generations. So that, the second "14 generations" in Matthew reach from the temple Jubilee B. C. 1003 to the second temple Jubilee B. C. 513 (or about 490 years from the accession of David, to the death of the last king, in "the carrying away into Babylon," Jer. lii: 31). And the third "14 generations" reach 490 years from the second temple Jubilee B. C. 513 to the Jubilee of Herod, B. C. 23; or (roughly) from the generation containing the former date to the generation (of 35 years) containing the later date and the birth of Christ. (In the Bib. Sacra, 1888, p. 452-463, is a most complex, artificial, and unsatisfactory theory of these "generations.")

The Passover Sabbath.

§ 12. We have found confirmation of our 580 years reckoning in the Jubilee and Sabbatic years of the Jews. We shall now find similar confirmation in the Passover Sabbath. In connection with the passover, "the morrow after the Sabbath" was a notable day, the day of "first fruits." (Lev. xxiii: 11, 15, 16.) Some think "the sabbath" here means the 15th Nisan, the first of the seven days feast of unleavened bread; so that the first-fruit offering would always be on the 16th Nisan. But we have shown conclusively, (N. T. Appendix A, § 58), that "the sabbath" here means *the weekly sabbath* coming on any day of the paschal feast, from the 14th to the 20th Nisan inclusive; so that, the first-fruit offering came on any day of the seven days feast, from the 15th to the 21st Nisan inclusive.

The first occurrence of the first-fruit offering, on entering Canaan, is recorded in Josh. v: 10, 11; where we learn, that the eating, and nesessarily the offering, of first-fruits was "*on the morrow after the passover*"; which we are expressly told (in Num. xxxiii: 3) means "on the 15th day of the first month" Nisan. We thus learn unmistakably, that "the morrow after the sabbath" being then on the 15th Nisan, that *weekly sabbath* was on "the 14th of Nisan at even" when the passover was observed. And we thus have the concurrence of a fixed date (the Saturday sabbath) with an astronomically assignable date (the 14th day of a lunar month.) See period G, § 58.

§ 13. This is the same concurrence, by means of which we have astronomically demonstrated the Date of Christ's Death; and by this same means we may now determine the correctness of our date assigned for the Exodus, viz., B. C. 1591. For, we here demonstrate, that just 40 years after our Exodus date, viz., in 1551 B. C., the 14th of Nisan ended (as it should) at sunset on SATURDAY, April 16 (O. S.),—just as required by Josh. v: 10, 11, and Num. xxxiii: 3.*

Then, just 40 years before this, the original passover of the Exodus occurred, at sunset of THURSDAY, April 8, B. C. 1591; and Friday was the 15th Nisan (or Abib), when the Israelites left Egypt (Num. xxxiii: 3). So that, adding 29 days, "the 15th day of the second month" was on SATURDAY, when they came unto the wilderness of Sin (Ex. xvi: 1). Then, after 6 days of gathering manna, there followed the SATURDAY

---

*By the same process we learn, that in B. C. 1451, the 14th of Nisan ended on *Tuesday*, April 20; but in B. C. 1450, it ended on *Saturday*, April 9. So that, the (1451+40=) 1493 B. C. (of Usher) will not answer; though the 1450+40=) 1490 B. C. would do, so far as Joshua's passover is concerned, but the week-day of the Exodus and of the arrival at Sin would not harmonize as above. (For the whole astronomical process, see Appendix B, § 44.)

"Sabbath" (ver. 5, 22-26). Here we have a most wonderful concurrence of dates, astronomically fixed, such as could hardly thus combine harmoniously with Scripture in any other Exodus assignment. B. C. 1591 seems to be proved as the year.

The view we here present, that the original reckoning at I Ki. vi: 1 was 580 years, and that there was no "480th" in the original text, was ably argued by the learned John Jackson, in his *Chron. Antiq.* (London, 1752, 3 vol. folio). And it was also defended in Elliott's Chronology, and elewhere; (though none of these writers have found the true year of Exodus, B. C. 1591, because of error in period E.) We besides appeal to the following

Ancient Authorities.

§ 14. In demonstration that we have rightly the reckoning of Paul for the period of the Judges as about "450 years," and the whole time intended at I Ki. vi: 1 as 580 years from the Exodus to the temple,—we have the testimony of several ancient authors at and before the time of Paul, giving us about the same values, as what they learned from the Scriptures of their day.

First, we name Josephus (in Paul's own day), whose general reliability none can question. (See Rest. of Jos., Appendix A.) In his full and careful history drawn from the Old Testament, and in his other works, he repeatedly and constantly gives the interval from the Exodus to the temple as "592 years." (See Rest. of Jos., Appendix G.) And upon examining his method of reckoning, we find that he derived this number from a 580 years value previously understood (but not expressed) at I Ki. vi: 1. We have not room here to explain this in full; but we give the complete exhibit in our succeeding treatise, ("Origin of the 480th year," § 69 here). It is plain, that there was no such reading as "480th year" in the Scripture text in the time of Josephus (and Paul); for, if there had been, he would not, in entire neglect and evident ignorance of it, have given and insisted on the larger value, as he does.

§ 15. We next cite two noted Jewish historians, who wrote about 200 years B. C.; namely Eupolemus (B. C. 174) and Demetrius (B. C. 210). These authors give the LXX chronology as 2262 years from creation to the flood+1362 to Jacob's going to Egypt+215 to the Exodus —3839 A. M. for the date of the Exodus+"1310" years to the 5th year of king Demetrius in Asia, B. C. 294; saying that this latter date was "5149 A. M.," which (says Jackson) was 1012—294 B. C.—718 years after the 4th year of Solomon. So that, they have ("1310"—718=) 592 years from the Exodus to the 4th of Solomon, *the same as Josephus has*. They know nothing of a "480th year" in Scripture, but only the longer reckoning derived from 580, perhaps in the same way as Josephus derived it. (See Rest. of Jos., Appendix G.)

The Old Priest Record.

§ 16. We now come to the original document, most plainly corroborating our view. The Priest Record of the Jews already referred to as used by Josephus, gives the lengths of the high-priesthoods from the Exodus to the end of the captivity, as "612 years" to the death of Zadok (in Solomon's reign), and then "466½ years" to (and including) the captivity. This makes (612+466=) 1078 years, or just (1078÷49=) 32 jubilee periods complete, between the start of jubilees at the Exodus date and the jubilee at the close of the captivity.* This was probably the official record of the Jews, and it agrees exactly with the Scripture Chronology which we have shown in Period E, and with the 580 years which we claim as Scripture in Period D.

§ 17. For we proved the Scripture interval, from the founding of the temple in the 4th of Solomon, to the beginning of the second temple in the 2nd of Darius, to be 491 years (from B. C. 1011 to 520), just as given by Josephus himself in the War; or, 490 years (10 Jubilees) from Solomon's dedication in B. C. 1003 to the traditional dedication given by Josephus at B. C. 513.† Now, the (612+466=) total 1078 years of the Priest Record reaches back from its traditional B. C. 513 as the end of captivity to B. C. 1591 as the Exodus date, just where our 580 years reckoning puts it. That is, the total 1078 of the Priest Record, minus the 490, leaves 588 years before Solomon's dedication, or 580 be-

---

*That the "466 years" is meant to include the captivity, is apparent from three facts: (1) This Priest Record says, that in this interval "eighteen priests took the high-priesthood at Jerusalem; and, though it names Jozedek as the last one at the capturing, yet Josephus' own list (given at Ant. 10, viii: 6) has but 17 after Zadok, even including his omitted Azarias, and requires the addition of Jozedek's son Jeshua who served at the restored temple. (2) This Priest Record itself goes on to give the next interval down to the Maccabees, beginning it from the restoration after captivity, as all scholars are agreed. The only question raised is, at what particular point of the restoration it begins; which shows that the previous captivity is certainly included in the previous interval. (3) The Priest Record designates its latest interval as the period of "democratical government," which shows that its calling the previous interval a period of "regal government" meant, that the Jews were under royalty (domestic or foreign) until the "democratical government" was fully established by them at the end of 70 years captivity. (See Rest. of Jos., § 37.)

† Ezra vi: 15, 16, appears as if putting no time between the finishing and the dedicating of the second temple. But as at Solomon's temple there was a year's delay after the finishing, purposely to bring the dedication at the Jubilee festivity (from B. C. 1004 to 1003),—so Josephus in the Priest Record follows the traditional view, that there was similar delay at the second temple, purposely to bring this dedication also at the Jubilee date (*i. e.*, from B. C. 516 in Ezra vi: 15, to B. C, 513 in verse 16, the 6th to 9th Darius.) See Restor. of Jos., § 24.

fore the beginning of the temple, just as we claim. This shows that (612—580=) 32 years of the Priest Record's "612," extend beyond the beginning of the temple to the death of Zadok.

§ 18. Thus the 612+466=1078 of the Priest Record is the very 580 +8+490=1078 of our reckoning drawn from Scripture, in agreement with Josephus and Paul. Does not this prove that we are right, and that this Priest Record is the original and official dating of the Jewish history found in the Bible?

The 1078 years of the Priest Record + the 400 years preceding the Exodus (Gen., xv: 13; Acts, vii: 6), give 1478 years back from B. C. 513 to B. C. 1991, as the date of Ishmael's Egyptian "mocking" of Isaac (at 5 years of age). So that, 8 years later (reducing the 1478 to 1470 years back) at B. C. 1983, the Priest Record had 1470 years of *priestly sacrifice*, or (1470+49=) just 30 Jubilee periods,—from the Jubilee following the second temple sacrifice, back to the Jubilee following the Isaac sacrifice (a year after he was 12 years old). A notable concurrence of the Priestly with the Jubilee period!

The Church Fathers.

§ 19. We further summon as witnesses all the early Christian fathers and chroniclers, Theophilus of Antioch (A. D. 171), Clement Alex. (189), Julius Africanus (221), the Paschal Chronicle, etc.; who all give the longer interval from the Exodus to the temple, and know nothing of the "480th year." Clement Alex. gives Josephus' reckoning 592 years, but he really makes out the true 580.* Theophilus increases it to 612, the Pas. Chron. to 632. Eusebius had 600, Syncellus made it 659, and attributed to Africanus 741. Eusebius (A. D. 320) is the first writer proclaiming "the 480th year"; but he also gives Paul's reckoning as 600 (he should say 580), calling it the "apostolical tradition." †

---

* Clement Alex. gives the 592 years of Josephus, Demetrius, etc. (as seen in the Rest. of Jos., Appendix G), attributing the reckoning to the "barbarians" or non-Christians. But he really by his numbers makes the true 580 (though he wrongly adds). For, he puts the "about 450" of Paul as being "463," and follows it by 27 years to David, increasing the one and decreasing the other by 13, and so reaching no change of total, thus:—Moses 40+Josh. 7+Judges 463+27 to David+David 40+Solomon 3=580 years. But by leaving out the 7 of Joshua, he adds it up as only "573." And again he adds it thus: 40+7+Paul's 450th+27+40+3="566" years only,—all evidently false addings, founded on the true 580.

† Eusebius gives all the items from the book of Judges, the same as in Josephus; except that Samuel is increased 8 (from 12 to 20), making Samuel and Saul amount to 40 years, and increasing the 592 to 600; with Josephus' loss of 8 years at Abdon changed to a loss of 8 years from the 10 of anarchy after Joshua, leaving but 27 years from Moses to Chushan (as if all belonging to Joshua.) This 600 years reckoning of

§ 20. A still more striking witness is Origen (A. D. 220). "Origen (*Com. in Joh. p. 187*) cites the text I Ki., vi: 1, *leaving out all that part*" about the 480th year interval. (*Jackson, Chron. Antiq.*) Here is as good a proof of what Ovigen found or did not find in his copy of the Old Testament, as if we had before us his own Ms. of the book of Kings. And this is much earlier than any Ms. of Scripture that we have. What further proof is needed, that the "480th year" is an interpolation, not introduced into the Hebrew text until as late as the 3d century, a short time before Eusebius?

CHAPTER II.

ATTEMPTED DEFENCES OF "THE 480TH YEAR."

§ 21. There are many who (with the Usher Chronology) attempt to maintain "the 480th year" as the genuine originally given length of time in I Kings, 6: 1. This 100 years of decrease from the 580 of the items given in Scripture, is sought to be made out in different ways.

1.—The old method, reported by Eusebius as "Jewish tradition," was, to drop out the periods of foreign oppression named in the Scripture narrative, they being treated as contemporaneous with the periods of rule given to the judges. But there are insuperable objections to this view.

§ 22. This is to treat the book of Judges in a manner entirely anomalous, and unheard of in the interpretation of any other history. The book (until the appendix is reached at chapter 17) is on its face a plain and orderly account of *successive* events, carefully giving the time-length of the peaceful periods and of the *intervals between* them. Notice how explicitly the author introduces his history (at ii: 13-21), as containing successive and *alternating periods* of servitude and independence (particularly ver. 18, 19). And notice also how similarly Samuel (at I Sam., xii: 9-11) and all the sacred writers ever afterward described those alternating periods of peace and distress. A fondness for round numbers may have led the writer, in some instances, to put a successive 19+ and 41— as 20 and 40, or the like; but we have no good reason to distrust the numbers, as meant for an accurate account of the lapse of time.

Eusebius is adopted by Jackson as his own chronology; except that he lets Samson's 20 years cover 20 years of the previous Philistine invasion, thus reducing the total to the right 580 years, which is Jackson's reckoning. WE prefer to use the same 580 years, with the items of Josephus (and Paul), instead of Eusebius (and Jackson)—namely: 10 not 2 of anarchy after Joshua's 25 years, offset by 12 not 20 for Samuel, with 40 for Saul not an extra 40 for Eli.

§ 23. For instance, at the first transition (Chap. iii) we read (verse 11): "And the land had rest forty years. * * * And the children of Israel did evil again—and because they had done evil (ver. 14), the children of Israel served Eglon, the king of Moab, eighteen years; but when they cried unto the Lord (ver. 30), Moab was subdued that day under the hand of Israel, and the land had rest fourscore years." No ingenuity can make it believeable, that those 18 years of *intervening foreign servitude* are meant to be included as a part of either period when "the land had rest."

So, also, when "the Lord delivered Israel into the hand of Midian seven years," (vi: 1)—to include this either within the previous rule of Deborah when "the land had rest forty years" (v: 31), or within the subsequent rule of Gideon when "the country was in quietness *forty years in the days of Gideon* (viii: 28), *i. e.*, *after* his conquest of Midian —this seems really absurd. Moreover, in Deborah's time when "the land had rest forty years," to include in this Jabin's period when "for twenty years he MIGHTILY OPPRESSED the children of Israel" after "Ehud was dead" (iv: 1-3)—this seems equally absurd.* And so of the whole book.

II.—In fact, so plain are the incongruities of this theory, of the foreign oppressions as included in the reigns, that for a long time it has been practically abandoned. And instead of it, various plans of *overlapping* the reigns have been devised. A period of anarchy after Joshua, without any reign, has to be allowed; and hardly any two writers can agree as to the amount of this, or as to the right places for making the overlap of reigns.

§ 24. A common way of trying to make out the 480th year is seen in Scott's Bible, and is elaborated by J. Schwartz in the Bib. Sacra, (July, 1888, p. 449). The 40 years of Philistine oppression (xiii: 1) are *dated back* over the previous reigns, beginning (it is said in the west) when the oppression of the Ammonites began (in the east, x: 8). And this is alleged, merely because "the Philistines" are named there (at x: 6, 7)!—though the very next verse (8) carefully distinguishes, that the oppression begun "that year" was that of the Ammonites, "on the other side Jordan"—in Gilead. And by this theory, the 20 years of Samson, as well as the 40 years of Eli, are also dated back, as all going on *during those 40 years of Philistine oppression!* So that, the 109 years (of chap. x to xvi inclusive) after Jair to the death of Samson, as given in Scripture (see our table before), are thus reduced into the one item of Philistine oppression "40 years," with 69 years entirely cast away!

---

* Deborah was perhaps *mitigating* the oppression during those 20 years of Jabin (see iv: 4); but those 20 years certainly were not included in the following 40 years of "rest."

§ 25. But even with this plan decided upon, hardly any two writers can agree upon other required overlaps. The incongruities and contradictions of different attempts made, we fully show in Appendix C, § 47 (which see). In such ways is the whole chronology of the judgeship period thrown into confusion; though it is so simple and definite when the full Scripture numbers are followed, as shown above.

Indeed, it is from this cause chiefly, that it has become fashionable, even among scholars, to say, that the Bible Chronology generally, and particularly in this period, is very confused and unreliable. It is so, when you depart from the simple Bible record (compared in all its parts, and so found consistent and plain), and undertake to fashion it over to fit some fictitious number or plan. The Scripture *numbers* are as authentic as any other Scripture statements; and in the whole Bible datings we find as yet but three or four miscopyings of a figure, (as few and as easily correctible as other slips of the pen). Thus the Scripture dates and periods of time are wonderfully lucid and definite, more so than any history we know of, whether ancient or modern.

§ 26. Rightly studied and accepted as a whole, Bible Chronology is one of the exact sciences. It forms a most convincing evidence of divine inspiration; as we have shown in our treatment of its various periods. For instance, in the period before us, take the simple inspired statements of Paul, compared with the book of Judges (unmutilated), and all the numbers harmonize most beautifully together, as seen above (in our tables, § 1, 5); with all the complaints about confusion and uncertainty brushed out of the way.

Revised Reading of Acts, xiii: 20.

III.—Some of late have tried to bring confusion into the clear statements of Paul in Acts, 13th, by pleading the new reading of verse 20 (given in the Revised Version); as if it could be twisted into a *dating backward*, or as saying "450 years *after* Abraham's (or Jacob's) day," or the like. But,

§ 27. (1) What has Abraham's (or Jacob's) day to do with the story Paul is telling, concerning God's guidance of " this *people* Israel" from Moses to David, beginning (as he does) most explicitly from the Exodus? He is plainly meaning to give an exact outline of that definite period, with the correct intervals of time that elapsed from Moses to David, showing how long it took to prepare the Israel redeemed from Egypt for the kingdom of David and his son Messiah. And to pervert his plain teaching, of *the time the land was given* to this people Israel as democratically *their own*, until they voluntarily gave it away to a king, (see I Sam., viii: 14),—to pervert this as if an irrelevant reference back to some unknown date, which nobody can fix,—this is only to throw ourselves gratuitously into that very confusion of chronology, of which we forthwith proceed to complain.

§ 28. (2) As the common reading of our King James Bible certainly does not admit of such a perversion, no more does the new reading admit of it. The revisers did not think that view possible, as is shown by the "for" they insert. Neither their construction nor the Greek idiom allows us to understand it "450 years *after*" some vague unnamed date; but the land is given as theirs "*for* 450 years," till they give it away. If the changed order of the words must be accepted, (which is by no means certain), that somewhat peculiar order is accounted for, thus:

Paul first names the 450 years of possessing the land democratically until King Saul: but after giving the number, he bethinks himself to add (parenthetically), that *after a part* of this period had elapsed, there were judges ending with Samuel. So the sentence is to be understood in this way: "He apportioned the land as theirs about four hundred and fifty years (and afterward gave Judges) till Samuel the prophet," who was superseded by King Saul. The parenthetic clause was meant to express, that the period of the Judges was *not the whole* 450 years of inheritance, but began somewhat later, as we have seen (above) that it did.

§ 29. And that the *beginning of the kingdom* under Saul was a notable epoch, fit to be used by the Scriptures, as making the *end of 450 years* of democratic possession of the land, will appear very obvious to any one reading the 8th chapter of I Samuel; where this man of God so strenuously warns the people, that in obtaining a king, they are surrendering to him their land and its very soil, which had been graciously given them to be enjoyed as their own in severalty. "And he said: This will be the manner of the king that shall reign over you: He will take your fields, and your vineyards, and your olive-yards, even the best of them, and give them to his servants. And he will take the tenth of your seed,—and the tenth of your sheep, and ye shall be his servants" (ver. 11, 14, 17). The people's decision to have a king is called a *rejection of God* and of the democratic homestead God had given them in bringing them "out of Egypt" (x: 18, 19). And so, that "450 years" interval became a marked period in the history of Israel's discipline, which Paul did not fail to emphasize.

§ 30. (3) It is by no means certain that the revisers' new reading of the text is right. The early Christian fathers read Acts, xiii: 20 just as we do, with the 450 dating forward over the Judges. Earlier than any of our Greek manuscripts of the New Testament, Eusebius (A. D. 320) wrote, affirming that "Paul says there were 450 years of Judges.", (Hist. ch. 16, Migné 150.) This testimony is better than even another *uncial Ms.*, in confirmation of the King James text of the passage; or at least, it confirms the sense we draw from the passage. For if, as changed in the Revision, it compels a different meaning, then certainly the copies used by the learned Eusebius (who would seek out the best copies) did not contain the Revised text. This is a very strong argument for the King James text; or at least, it demonstrates that the "450 years" covers the period of the Judges, as we claim.

§ 31. Thus Paul's dates are simple and plain, and there is no need of any confusion or mistake about the chronology, if we only take the numbers as they are given. The attempt to get rid of the 450 years of democratic land possession, is only a part of the attempt to maintain the wrongly copied "480th year" of 1st Kings; and the whole procedure is a most destructive one, violating numerous Scripture numbers (as well as statements), just to save that one number "480." We in our next chapter discuss fully the reasons that probably led to the miscopying of it (as 480 instead of the original 580); and when Paul's rectification of it is accepted, everything is left plain.

§ 32. THE I SAM. vii: 2.

IV.—There are many who make a needless complication of the "20 years" statement in I Sam. vii: 2, and some other datings in the same book. That is an *incidental* remark of the writer, introduced by natural suggestion. When speaking of the ark taken to a certain place, it was natural to mention *by the way* how long it was there; and to confound things, as is done, by understanding this as *a gap* of 20 years in the history (a Philistine servitude, say some, the first half of 40 years in Jud. xiii: 1, says Schwartz), intervening before the next event given, Samuel's victory over the Philistines—is an altogether needless derangement of the chronology. The writer simply remarks in passing, that after the ark was recovered from the Philistines, remaining a long while (about 60 years) at its new resting-place, Israel attended faithfully to the worship of God in connection with it *for the first twenty years;* that is, during the twenty years of Samuel's full care over them, from Eli's death and the return of the ark, until the rejection of Saul as king, which led Samuel to retire from *public* affairs to a more private administration. (Comp. xv: 35, and vii: 15.)

§ 33. In this verse (vii: 2), instead of "Israel lamented," the Revision *marg.* has "Israel was drawn together;" and Gesenius' Hebrew Lex. (at נהה *Nahah*) translates it, "'all the house of Israel assembled themselves after Jehovah,' *constr. pregnans* for 'they all with one mind followed after Jehovah.'" And (at ויהי hahyah) it tells us that after "it was" the seeming *and* often means *that*, "it was that, and it came to pass that." So that, we should read here, "the time was long; and it was twenty years that the house of Israel was drawn together after Jehovah." It was not twenty years of Philistine servitude, but twenty years of happy ark-service and worship under Samuel, until the rejection of Saul.

These "20 years" covered the 12 years of Samuel's separate judgeship from Eli's death to Samuel's address at the beginning of Saul's reign, and 8 more years till Saul was cast off, and the people again strayed from God. And it was near the beginning of these twenty years (and not at their close) that Samuel's reformation of the people and triumph over the Philistines occurred (as vii: 13 asserts). This is just the way in which Josephus clearly arranges the years of Samuel; and his account is reliable and in accordance with the Bible. There need be no confusion of reckoning here; for Paul's account in Acts is exactly conformed to these same years of Samuel and of Saul. (See the tables at our beginning.)

§ 34. It seems that Samuel was born at about the beginning of Eli's 40 years judgeship, being 12 years old when called of God, Eli then being 70 or "very old" (as said at ii: 22, comp. iv: 15). So that, at Eli's death (aged 98) Samuel was about 40 years old, and then judged 12 years till he was 52; at which time he is called "old" (at viii: :1) and "grey-headed" (at xii: 2). This does not mean "very old," as in the case of Eli at 70. The Levites generally were regarded by the Mosaic law as too old for full service at the age of fifty (Num. iv: 3, 23, 30, and viii: 25). As Samuel lived on through the greater part of Saul's 40 years of reign, he must have been 80 or 90 years old at his death.

Other Points.

§ 35. Professor Harper (in the *S. S. Times*, July 20) thinks that there must be a gap of some years at chapter xi, because Saul is a young man up to that time, and forthwith (at xiii: 1, 2) he has a grown son Jonathan going to war. But the real account is rather this: Chapter ix and x to ver. 17 is an *episode*, or going back to narrate *previous* private affairs, suggested to the writer by his account of the public complaints in chap. viii. When the people beg for a king, the writer is reminded to go back and tell how, years before, Samuel had *privately* anointed a youth to become *ruler* sometime (not then expressed as a *king*); after which episode he resumes (at x: 17) the account from chap. viii about the *public* demand and selection of a KING.

That the demand for a king (chap. viii) connects close with the account of Nahash (at chap. xi) is shown by what Samuel says at xii: 12. And that the private anointing was years before is evident from the whole story of it, which represents Samuel as at that time in his prime, going about all his official circuit from place to place, long before he had on account of years devolved much upon his sons, which led to the open demand for a king. Thus Saul, like David, was privately set apart years before his public recognition.

§ 36. Here we see an important principle followed in the writing of scripture as of other history. It is the principle of *retrospection* and *anticipation*. Some open event often suggests to a writer some previous preparatory incident, which he proceeds to interject into the account.

Nowadays, the use of the pluperfect (*had* been) carries us thus backward, and saves all mistake as to the order of time. But in the lack of a pluperfect tense among the Hebrews, we have to watch the narrative more carefully to see when there is really a pluperfect sense. This idiom will explain many points of chronology in the bible, which some have thought obscure. For instance, the case before us; and also Gen. i: 16, which means, "And God *had* made two great lights" (the sun and the moon; that is, had made them before the six days began, and now only *set* or exhibited them for regulators of day and night on the earth's surface, by clearing away the clouds.

§ 37. In like manner, when a writer has struck upon a subject, he incidentally *anticipates* the result of it, in order to finish that point before going on with his current narrative.* Thus, as we have seen here at I Sam. vii: 1, having told how the ark got to Kirjath-jearim, the writer incidentally pauses to mention how long it there was treated with respect; and then, at ver. 3, he returns to the events that followed its being brought there.

Thus, also, at xvi: 14, the writer having just told how the Spirit of the Lord first came upon David, is reminded to tell how, years afterward, that Spirit of the Lord left Saul, and David was called in to drive away the evil spirit that disturbed him. When this episode of *anticipation* is finished with the chapter, the writer (at chap. xvii) goes on with his regular history. And it will be found that the affair of the episode belongs near the beginning of chap. xviii.† It was very likely Jonathan here awakened to love, who *afterwards* was the "young man" (xvi: 18, Revision) that came forward and had David sent for. This arrangement relieves the otherwise inexplicable mystery of Saul's not knowing David, at xvii: 55-58. (Note that David had become a "valiant *man of war*," xvi: 18.) It also gives time for the change in Saul at xviii: 8, otherwise unaccountable. In ver. 6 it seems to be David's later slaughter of Philistines (see Revision *marg.*) not Goliah alone referred to. And xvii: 15 refers to David's going "to and fro" (Revision) from his home to Saul's *army* (ver. 19).

§ 38. A similar case occurs at Gen. xxxv, where the writer finishes up Jacob's affairs in Canaan, and is led by the mention of Esau (in ver. 29) to go on and give the whole subsequent genealogy of Esau's race. Whereupon, he *returns* (at chap. 37) to begin the story of Joseph, which probably *dates back* before the events of the 34th chapter, ‡ when Jacob, returning from Padan-aram, first came and tarried awhile with his

---

* Thus are readily explained the interjected events of Gen. xxxviii, etc., on which the critic Astruc (A. D. 1750) based his *documentary* theory. (See Bib. Sacra, 1884, Oct., p. 673: and here, Period C, § 29.)

† Note that xvii: 55 to xviii: 5 is wanting in the lxx. See Revision.

‡ See Appendix D, § 54.

father Isaac at Hebron. (Comp. xxxi: 3, 30, and xxxiii: 18, and xxxv: 9, 15, and xxxvii: 14.) This we have fully shown in the Bibliotheca Sacra, July, 1887, p. 553.

A few such common-sense principles of interpretation, applied to the Bible history as to other books, give us an harmonious Scripture Chronology: which is wonderfully complete and satisfactory, greatly confirming our faith in the Word of God. The loose remarks we so often hear, about the uncertainty of Bible dating, and the little importance of correct dates, are made by those who have not *thoroughly* studied this subject.

§ 39. As to the Egyptian monuments and inscriptions, the light which they give toward fixing the date of the Exodus, is as yet very vague and uncertain: and the most learned Egyptologists are very widely divided in opinion as to the year, and as to which of the Pharaohs was then in power. Their results will agree with the date we give as well as with any others. This we will proceed to show in a future number,—Part III, § 101.

§ 40. A life study of the subject has convinced us, that the safest way is to search out and stand by the Bible datings in their simple and harmonious consistency, as *presumably correct;* and wait for any fuller scientific researches, to see if they can *thoroughly prove* at last that such a palpable interpretation of the Bible is incorrect. It will be time enough to begin tampering with the record, and readjusting the obvious scripture dates, when excavation of inscriptions has fixed some date *for certainty*, with the concurrence of investigators generally,— a point far from being reached at present. Till then, we candidly own our faith, that the simple BIBLE will come out uppermost in all respects.

APPENDIX A.

For § 5 note.

THE "4TH YEAR OF SOLOMON."

§ 41. In the Bib. Sacra (July, 1888, p. 447), J. Schwartz, Egyptologist, of New York, says: "For some peculiar reason, not yet satisfactorily explained, the early Christian chronologists placed the building of the temple in the 2nd, in place of the biblical 4th year of Solomon." Some light may come from the following:

The early chronologists largely followed Josephus: and Josephus reckoned a joint reign of Solomon with his father. (See I Kings, 1st chapter.) So that Solomon's 4th year in all was reckoned as *but 2 years after his father's death*. The founding and finishing of the temple in the "4th" and "11th" years of Solomon (I Ki., vi: 1, 38) were in B. C. 1011 and 1004, the death of David being in B. C. 1013, but with the reign of Solomon beginning in B. C. 1014, and with that intermediate year B. C. 1014-1013 as a joint reign. This made David begin in (1013+40=) 1053 B. C., and Solomon end in (1014—40=) 974 B. C., with only 79 (not 80) years to both reigns. And this made only 42 years and 49 years from the beginning of David to the beginning and finishing of the temple, with one year more (an 8th of the temple, a 50th in all) to the dedication in B. C. 1003.

§ 42. This is just the chronology which Josephus gives in his earlier work, the War; and this correct dating of Solomon's temple as begun in B. C. 1011, when put with the "480th year" (in I Ki., vi: 1), gives the Exodus as B. C. 1490 (not Usher's 1491), or, put with the corrected 580 years, it gives the Exodus as B. C. 1591, the Bible date we claim. (See § 13, note.) But now, on the other hand, if we treat the temple founding in B. C. 1011 as "the 4th year of Solomon" *alone*, (not 2 years but 3 years after the death of David), then the year of joint reign is B. C. 1015-1014 (being an extra year in addition to Solomon's 40); and David's accession is then B. C. 1054 (not 1053), and the total of both reigns is 80 (not 79) years. But, as in this case Josephus' 1 year of Shamgar is dropped instead of his 1 of Solomon dropped, the Exodus and all previous dates remain unchanged. It is by this latter method, with David's accession at B. C. 1054, that we reckon here, (at § 1, etc.); while Josephus always has it at B. C. 1053. Which is the more correct, everyone may judge for himself.

§ 43. We have given above the chronology of Josephus in the War. But in the Antiquities, he seems to change the temple one year, while still retaining David's accession as B. C. 1053. He there reckons "the 4th year of Solomon" as *not including* the year of joint reign B. C. 1014-1013, but as 3 years (instead of 2) after the death of David in B. C. 1013, viz., in 1010 (not 1011), for the founding of the temple. This was to understand the "4th year" and the "11th year" of Solomon as 43 and 50 (not 42 and 49) years after David's accession, from B. C. 1010 to 1003 (instead of 1011 to 1004 as previously)—with *the 8th year omitted*, i. e., with the dedication in B. C. 1003 taken as the same 7th year as the finishing of the temple.* But this change of 1 year in the founding of the temple (from 1011 to 1010) made Josephus' "592 years" reach 1 year later for the Exodus, and for all the previous chronology.

---

*To reach this result, Josephus had only to regard *the finishing in the 8th month* (I Ki., vi: 38), to mean simply, that the 7 days feast of tabernacles in the 7th month followed by the 7 days feast of dedication (II Chron. vii: 9) finished up the 7th month; so that, the 8th month had arrived when "the house was finished, with all the appurtenances thereof, and *with all the ordinances thereof*" (I Ki., vi: 38, Revision, *marg*.). Some Scripture reasons may be pleaded for this view, which we have exhibited in a supplement.

APPENDIX B.

For § 13.

THE ASTRONOMICAL DATE.

We know from Josh. v: 10, 11, (with Num. xxxiii: 3), that the *day of first-fruits* on entering Canaan came on "the 15th day of the 1st month" Nisan. So that, it being necessarily "on the morrow after the sabbath," (Lev. xxiii: 11, 14), the sabbath that year must have come on SATURDAY THE 14TH OF NISAN. Our purpose is, to find whether, in our year for Joshua's entering Canaan, viz., B. C. (1591—40=) 1551 B. C., the paschal 14th Nisan did come on SATURDAY. (See Period G, Appendix A.)

§ 44. The astronomical process for the Exodus dating, is just as in our New Testament reckoning (Period G. § 34, etc.). It goes as follows: From A. D. 1855 to B. C. 1550=3404 years (just divisible by 4); which ×365¼=1243311 days from Julian (or O. S.) Jan. 6, A. D. 1855, to Julian Jan. 6, B. C. 1550; or (—90 days=) 1243221 days back to Apl. 6, B. C. 1550, at 8¼ A. M.

On the other hand, an exact lunation, 29d. 5305885 being × 42100 lunations = 1243237d. 77585, which is 16d. 776 excess over the 1243221 days to April 6. Or, adding acceleration of the moon's motion for 3400 years (viz., the .154 of a day), we have 16d. 93 excess back to the new moon in that April.

This excess carries the new moon from the April 6 at 8¼ A. M. back that much earlier, to March 20 at 10 A. M. in B. C. 1550. Then, if 1 Nisan began at sunset of March 22, the 14 Nisan ended at the passover sunset of April 5,—which was *Wednesday*, and will not answer our purpose. This passover was very nearly on the equinox: which was then April 4-5, as seen thus: A. D. 325+B. C. 1550=1874 years+ 130 yrs. (for each day-change)=14d. 4+Mar. 21=April 4-5.

The next year after, viz., B. C. 1549, had the new moon (29d. 5306 ×12=) 354d. 367 from 366 days=11d. 15 hours earlier than the Mar. 20 at 10 A. M., and also 29d.—12¾h. (or 1 lunation) afterwards, *i. e.*, on April 7 at 7¾ A. M. Then, if 1 Nisan began at sunset of April 9, the 14 Nisan ended at the sunset passover of April 23,—which was *Tuesday*, and will not answer our purpose.

§ 45. In the next year *before* B. C. 1550, *i. e.*, in 1551, the new moon was 10d. 15h. *later* than the Mar. 20 at 10 A. M., viz., on March 31 at 1 A. M.* Then, if 1 Nisan began at sunset of April 2, the 14 Nisan ended at the passover sunset of April 16,—which was SATURDAY, as the Scripture requires.

This fact, that April 16, B. C. 1551, was SATURDAY, we learn by the Rule given at Period G, § 40, thus: One less than the year is 1550, which+28 leaves 10, and this+7 leaves 3, to which we add 2 (for the two 4's in the 10), and add 1 more (for the rest of the 10), making 6 days

---

*This is the mean reckoning, which corrected will be about 3 hours later, both for new and for full moon.

before Sunday, *i. e.*, Monday, March 0 and 28, and April 4; whence, SATURDAY was April 2, and 9, and 16, in B. C. 1551.

At this sunset of Saturday, April 16, B. C. 1551, the Israelites must have kept their passover, at the close of their Sabbath day—just as described in Josh. v: 10, 11—with the First-fruit offering coming the next day, *i. e.*, "on the 15 Nisan, the morrow after the passover" (see Num. xxxiii: 3). As that was their first passover upon entering Canaan, it was just 40 years after their original passover at the Exodus; so that the Exodus was in (1551+40=) 1591 B. C.

Now in those 40 years, there were 495 lunations, which × 29d 5305885 =14617d. 64, *i. e.*, 7d 15½h more than the (40 × 365¼)=14610 days in 40 years. This carries the new moon of Mar. 31 at 1 A. M. in B. C. 1551, to be in B. C. 1591, on March 23, at 9½ A. M. And if 1 Nisan began at sunset of March 25, then 14 Nisan ended at the passover sunset of April 8—which was *Thursday*. For, 1591—1=1590+28 leaves 22+7 leaves 1+5 (for the 4's in 22)+1 (for the rest of the 22)=7 or 0 days before Sunday, March 0 and 28 and April 4. So that April 8 was Thursday. Therefore the Exodus on the next day, the 15 Nisan, was FRIDAY, April 9, B. C. 1591.

---

§ 46. So much for the Exodus date B. C. 1591, as derived from the 580 years interval. Now look at the Usher date of the Exodus B. C. 1491, as derived from "the 480th year" (given in the present text of I Ki. vi: 1). Usher takes his B. C. 1012 for the founding of the temple in "the 4th year of Solomon," and says, B. C. 1012 + the "480th"= 1491 B. C. for the Exodus; which brings the passover of Josh. v: 10, 11 at (1491—40=) 1451 B. C.

But in that year the passover was *Tuesday*, April 20, B. C. 1451; so that the *Saturday* passover of Josh. v: 10, 11, could not be that year. Whereas, the year after, the passover was 11 days earlier, on SATURDAY, April 9, B. C. 1450. (This we learn by the same process as above, reckoning either with the 100 years difference, or with the whole interval from A. D. 325.) Therefore, the passover of Josh. v: 10, 11 might be in that year 1450, and the Exodus might be in 1490 B. C.; but it was not possible in B. C. 1491.

This proves the correctness of our date B. C. 1011 (not 1012) for the 4th of Solomon at the founding of the temple; for, 1490—the 480th= 1011 B. C. Moreover, we thus find Usher's 1 year too early at the destruction of Jerusalem (B. C. 588 for 587 propagated all the way back to the Exodus (B. C. 1491 for 1490.)

In the above reckoning, we have put 1 Nisan as beginning when the moon was about 2 days old. For, the new month and the new year was not commenced till the new moon festival was observed, after report of the new moon seen, and then proclamation and congregating for the purpose. All which, in that early day of rude observation, must usually cover two days at least after change of the moon—and especially as clouds often prevented the observation. (See Period G, § 31.)

APPENDIX C.

For § 25.

Attempts to Make "480."

§ 47. To show the incongruities and contradictions of all attempts to reduce the Scripture numbers to the 480th year, we will here compare the current Usher method in Scott's Bible with the later method of J. Schwartz in the Bib. Sacra, (July, 1888, p. 451). The interval from the Exodus to the Temple being for convenience divided at the Ammonite invasion (Jud. x: 7), the periods before and after that point we call the Pre-Ammon and the Post-Ammon periods. And the figures are these:

	Scripture.	Scott.	Schwartz.	Error. Scott Sch.	Dif. Sch.
Moses	40	40	40	—46 —21	+25
Pre-Ammon	336	290	315		
Whole	376	330	355		
(Total=)	580	479	479)		
Whole	204	149	124		
Post-Ammon	161	106	81	—55 —80	—25
David 40, Sol. 3	43	43	43		
				—101 —101	0

The *difference* of the two periods in the two writers is 25 years, which Scott adds in as extra 25 years of Samuel, but which Schwartz takes off from Samuel and adds in after Chusan. For Scott has the peculiar scheme, of letting Ehud's 80 cover both Eglon's 18 and Othniel's 40, thus losing 58 years,—25 of which Schwartz thus restores. This leaves 33 still to be restored after Chushan; which Schwartz (making up correctly all the 301 total of the numbers given in Judges down to the Ammonite invasion), accomplishes by substituting 33 taken from *before* Chushan, thus:

§ 48. The Scripture amount before Chushan is (anarchy 10 + Joshua 25=) 35, which taken from the true Pre-Ammon amount 336, leaves 301 as the amount of the numbers given in the book of Judges from Chushan to the Ammonite invasion. But Scott's loss of 58 after Chushan reduces this 301 to 243, which taken from his required Pre-Ammon amount 290, leaves 47 as his amount before Chushan. (By an oversight, Scott's Bible has 2 years more (making 49), caused by a loss of 2 from Jabin's 20.) Schwartz reducing this 47 by 34 (as just seen) has left but 14 years from Moses to Chushan,—including the whole reign of Joshua and the anarchy that followed!—or only 301+14= 315, instead of the correct 336, down to the Ammonite invasion. This necessitated feature of deficiency after Moses in the Schwartz method is alone sufficient to condemn the whole scheme; while in avoiding this, Scott's necessitated method of dating back Ehud's 80 years of "rest" over not only Othniel's 40 but also Eglon's 18 years of Moabite tyranny over Isrsel, is alone enough to condemn that scheme also.

And further, Scott's scheme of losing so much after Chushan reduces his total from Moses to the Ammonite invasion,—by a net 58— (his 47-35)=46,—from the 336 down to 290 years; in violation of the "300 years" given at Ju. xi: 26. But notice now the incongruities and errors caused by this whole plan of overlapping the reigns *after* the Ammonite invasion.

§ 49. (1) In xiii: 1, the people "did evil *again*" (*marg*. "Heb. added to commit evil"), *after* the events and dates given before. So that the 40 years of Philistine oppression now to be brought upon them can not be thrown back, as if it stated that they *had* transpired already.

(2) This back reckoning makes Abdon (xii: 13) reach 9 years after the death of Samson and Eli! and so his 8 years are dropped out entirely by many. Schwartz has these 8 years of Abdon ruled along with Samuel, as the first part of the latter's supposed 20 (at I Sam. vii: 2) spent *during Philistine oppression*, in direct contradiction of verse 13. And he says that Josephus had Abdon's 8 years thus reckoned; though it is notorious, on the contrary, that Josephus has Samson and Eli *between* Abdon and Samuel, as necessitated by his aggregate number 592 years.

(3) The 20 years judgeship of Samson (xv: 20 to xvi: 31) *begins* "in the days of the Philistines," reaching 20 years after their 40. What sort of a judgeship would his be (and that of Jephthah, etc., put at the same time), with the people "delivered into the hands of the Philistines" all the while?

§ 50. (4) The last 20 years judgeship of Eli, (which is all the lxx gives him, under the administration of Samuel, as described in I Sam. iii: 20 to iv: 1,—synchronizing with Samson's 20,—could not be during the subjection to the Philistines. For though there was subjection before (Jud. xv: 11), yet when Samson's 20 years began "in the days of the Philistines" (ver. 20), he kept the Philistines subdued while he lived, as seen by chap. xvi.

(5) A leading absurdity is, that, after the 40 years of Philistine oppression, thus made to cover all Samson's and Eli's judgeship, this

view makes *another Philistine oppression of 20 years immediately to follow* after Eli's death,—interpreting in this way I Sam. vii: 2-12. Think of *sixty years* of continuous Philistine domination! yet at Jud. xiii: 1 limited to forty years! But the Philistine battle at I Sam. iv: 1, and after 7 mo. at vii: 7, was not a new oppression of 20 years, but only a new attempt after the death of Sampson, and ended all their attempts (ver. 13). See § 32.

§ 51. (6) To be rid of this extravagant 60 years of continuous Philistine domination, the resort of Schwartz is, to let the "40 years" oppression of Jud. xiii: 1 cover the "20 years" mentioned at I Sam. vii: 2, as the last half of the Philistine domination; during all which last 20 years of foreign servitude Samuel's administration was going on! This is in direct contradiction of I Sam. vii: 13, which says: "So the Philistines were subdued [by Samuel], and they came no more into the coast of Israel; and the hand of the Lord was against the Philistines *all the days of Samuel.*"

(7) To escape this difficulty, the Usher chronology in Scott's Bible has Samuel's rule delayed till after the alleged Philistine domination at I Sam. vii: 2 is over; and so puts in an extra 25 years for Samuel after that,—reducing Saul from 40 to 20 for the purpose. By this plan, the first 20 years of the Philistine dominion is covered by the judgeship of Eli taken as only 20 years. So that the Scriptural "40 years" of Eli reach back 20 years before the Ammonite invasion (as seen in Schwartz)! and Samson's beginning to "judge Israel" is only the beginning of a 40 years domination of Philistia over them!

§ 52. (8) Trying to relieve this last absurdity, Schwartz introduces a worse one. He puts Samson's 20 years along later, to begin from the death of Eli, and cover *the last 20 years* of Philistine domination (as the "20 years" of I Sam. vii: 2). This is saying that "Samuel judged the children of Israel in Mizpeh" (I Sam. vii: 7) during *all the time when* "Samson judged Israel twenty years," *while also* Jephthah, Ibsan, and Eglon "judged Israel," (Jud. xii: 7-11, and xvi: 31)—and *while at the same time* the people were under two foreign dominions, being "delivered into the hands of the Philistines 40 years" (Jud. xiii: 1), and being "sold into the hands of the children of Ammon," 18 years of *the same time* (x: 7, 8)! Surely, a wonderful combination of mixed up simultaneousness! Thus Samuel's victory over the Philistines is made one with Samson's death-triumph over them; while all Samuel's previous twenty years of "judging Israel" (I Sam. vii: 2, 6, 13) is represented as a domination of Philistia!

(9) Josephus takes 20 from Saul's 40 years, but adding them to 20 more as a 40 of Eli put in (with Abdon's 8 not added), he gets (40—28 =) 12 extra, instead of a loss from this lessening of Saul. Scott has the 20 from Saul put upon Samuel, thus not reducing the time after Eli. But Schwartz drops entirely the 20 years taken from Saul, and so has

but 40 years left from Samson to the reign of David!—while Saul is given only 20 years, and Samuel full 40 between Eli and Saul!

§ 53. (10) All these methods are in violation of the history contained in the book of Ruth. It is generally taken for granted, that Ruth lived in the *early days* of the Judges. But Josephus positively asserts (Ant. 5, ix: 1), that it was "under Eli, the high priest and governor of the Israelites." And the contents of that book, its pleasant and peaceful story of domestic life, requires such an assignment, rather than in previous warlike and disorderly times.* Now Ruth's son Obed was grandfather of David (Ruth iv: 17); and this requires his birth to be 70 or 80 years before David's reign. Accordingly, our Scripture reckoning gives (Saul 40 + Samuel 12 + Eli 40 =) 92 years to the beginning of Eli; or 72 years to the end of Philistine oppression, at the beginning of Samson's 20 years.

Whereas, the Usher reckoning (in Scott) has but (20 + 25 =) 45 years, and Schwartz has but (20 + 20 =) 40 years back to the end of Philistine domination; while the latter has but 60 years to the full sweep of their warfare, in the very region of Bethlehem, the home of Boaz and Ruth,—before Samson began to restrain the enemy! This deficiency of time, as well as the diverse and contrary methods attempted, all shows how impracticable the shortened system is, which tries to get only the "480th year."

APPENDIX D.

For § 37.

That "Canonical Formula."

§ 54. Some have thought, that the events narrated in the first chapter of Judges did not occur "after the death of Joshua," as said in verse 1; simply because in verse 10, 11 two cities, Hebron and Debir, are named among those assailed by the army of Judah; which two cities are given at Josh. x: 36-38, as fully conquered and utterly destroyed by Joshua (ver. 40).

Certainly, Jud. i: 10-15 is a parenthetic digression, taken from Josh. xv: 14 19, by way of *retrospection;* being suggested by what is said in Jud. i: 9. So that verse 10 properly reads thus: "And Judah went against the Canaanites that dwelt in Hebron. (Now the name of Hebron *beforetime* was Kirjath Arba; and *beforetime* they slew Sheshai," etc., to ver. 17, all properly in the parenthesis.) But the previous topic, *Judah's warfare in concert with Simeon*, which occupies verses 1-9 and is resumed at ver. 17 onward, belongs after the death of Joshua just as certainly, as verse 1 asserts.

---

*A writer in the Bib. Sacra (Oct. 1891, p. 659) urges this view. Perhaps there is a gap before Boaz, in the genealogy. (Ruth iv: 21.)

§ 55. It was Joshua, not a league of Judah with Simeon, that conquered "all the country of the hills, and of the south, and of the vale, and of the springs," and "all the mountains of Judah," as recorded in Josh. x: 40, and xi: 21. Such a sectional league of two tribes, to fight in their "lot" at the people's demand (Jud. i: 1-3), would have been entirely unnatural and out of the question under Joshua's generalship, and especially then, when the land had not been *allotted*. And, though of those found in the conquered places Joshua "left none remaining, but utterly destroyed all that breathed," yet of course some had escaped before their cities were fully invested, and returned afterwards (in Israel's lukewarmness) to recover their possessions. So that, there was real occasion for Judah (with Simeon) to go "down against the Canaanites that dwelt in the mountain, and in the south, and in the valley"—"after the death of Joshua," as told in Jud. i: 1, 9.

§ 56. Yet, strange to say, the writer in the Bib. Sacra. (Oct. 1891, p. 652), argues at length, that *all* this opening portion of Judges belongs back in the time of Joshua; and that the first dating clause, "after the death of Joshua," must be *an interpolation*, which should be struck out! And, stranger still, he argues,—that because the story of Ruth does not belong till the judgeship of Eli, which is recorded (not in the *book* of Judges, but) in I Samuel,—therefore its dating (put at Ruth i: 1, "Now it came to pass in the days when the Judges ruled," etc.), is also spurious, and should be erased! Just as if Eli and Samuel did not belong among "the judges;" and just as if Eli's judgeship (because forsooth not recorded in the *book* of Judges) was not "in the days when the judges ruled"! Was ever greater folly than this set forth as bible criticism?

The writer even quotes approvingly (p. 660) the random talk of an author, about the foul stories in the last chapters of Judges (concerning Micah, Gibeah, etc.), as being entirely incongruous for the times of Naomi and the "pastoral idyl" of Ruth. He seems to be entirely ignorant that those last chapters of the book (xvii–xxi) are universally recognized as an appendix, belonging chronologically at the beginning of Judges (see xxi: 25), and have nothing to do with "the days when judges ruled,"—and when Ruth and Naomi are declared to have lived!

§ 57. Now comes the climax. Upon this ground alone,—of the two books of Judges and Ruth alleged to be wrongly dated at their opening, the writer before us would *blot out every date* given at the beginning of the books between Deuteronomy and Chronicles, as a conjectured spurious "canonical formula" put in by an editor in uniting the books together, and needing to be expunged! Was ever a wholesale scheme of Bible mutilation reared upon so flimsy a basis? The critics seem to be finding enough fault with Scripture, without the need of gratuitous errors thus foisted upon it.

We recite this case, as a sample of the treatment which the Bible is receiving, and especially its chronology, from alleged scholars, who merely skim its surface, seemingly bent on nothing but to pick all the flaws they can.

PART II.

Origin of the "480th Year" Reading.

In I Kings vi: 1.

§ 58. What we are here to undertake is, first, to prove that no such number as 480 was originally in the Scripture text; and secondly, to show (as far as we can) how it comes to be now there.

CHAPTER I.

No 480th Originally.

We have learned by our study of the chronology of the Judges, that the founding of Solomon's temple in his 4th year was 580 years from the exodus, not "the 480th year" as given in I Kings vi: 1. It follows that the 480 must be a corruption of the Hebrew text; and there is such corruption of the original text in several Old Testament passages, especially in the case of *numbers* (as at II Chron. xxxvi: 9, comp. II Kings xxiv: 8). The cause or reason of such a corruption may sometimes be traced; and in the case before us, it becomes an interesting and useful study to search out (if we may) the origin of this 480 error.

§ 59. In our modern times a new theory of the exodus has come into vogue, making it but about 300 years, instead of the "480th year" before the temple, *i. e.*, about B. C. 1300. This view has been set forth by Brugsch and other Egyptologists, as a supposed necessity arising from their study of the monuments. The large number of Bible scholars who follow chronologically these speculations of the archæologists, of course reject "the 480th year" of I Kings as altogether too large. On the contrary, we show by Egyptology itself, that this "480th year" is a corruption 100 years too small. The number of those who still adhere to "the 480th year" as correct, is very small.

§ 60. We know for a certainty, that the 480 could not have been in the Hebrew text in the New Testament times. For, not only does the testimony of Paul (in Acts xiii: 17–22) prove this, as we have shown, but also the testimony of Josephus (written about the same time), together with earlier Jewish historians, is decisive on the point. Josephus and Paul in the first century, as well as Theophilus, Clemens Alex., Hippolytus, Julius Africanus (A. D. 200), and other early chroniclers of the church, all found no such number there in Kings; but all their reckonings of the Bible times are based upon the larger number, 580 years, between the exodus and the temple. Let us examine this matter particularly in regard to Josephus, the most careful and reliable of all ancient writers, in his work of rehearsing fully the substance of the Old Testament records. (See here, § 100.)

In his "Antiquities of the Jews," he recounts to us in full detail the history found in the Old Testament; and his work contains (he says in his preface) "all our antiquities and the constitution of our government, as interpreted out of the HEBREW Scriptures." Using thus the original Hebrew text, as he does, we can see from his statements what his copy of the Hebrew Scriptures did, and what it did not contain.

§ 61. When he comes to the founding of the temple at I Kings, 6th chapter, he gives very explicit datings of that event, based on the number 580 (as we will presently show); and he manifests no knowledge whatever of any such contrary number or reckoning as the "480" now found in that passage. In several other parts of his work, and especially in his other work, "The Jewish War," he reiterates that same larger reckoning of the interval between the Exodus and the temple; and everywhere he is in utter ignorance of any such lesser reckoning 480, as ever seen or heard of in his time. Therefore, it is simply impossible that this number could have been in the Hebrew text as used by Josephus, as well as by Paul, by Africanus, and by other ancient Bible scholars.

We must here remark, that the chronology of Josephus, when carefully studied, is a simple and harmonious system, drawn from the numbers given in the Hebrew Bible as he understood them; and it is not any such jumble of conflicting dates as has been imposed upon him by diverse editors, trying to amend, but sadly corrupting his text. A thorough sifting of his work has led to a "Restoration of Josephus" in respect to datings (which see); showing a methodical and beautiful harmony of the whole, accordant with the Hebrew text as interpreted by him. We shall see parts of this restored chronology as we proceed.

§ 62. Josephus uniformly makes the interval "592 years" from the exodus to the temple begun "in the 4th year of Solomon's reign."* But how does this comport with the "612 years" found in his writings? Josephus is thought by many to be vacillating in his chronology, and to have other numbers besides the 592 years for the interval between the exodus and the temple. For instance, the 612 is a value named. But this number is given by Josephus (at Ant. 20, x, 1), not as a length of reigns, but as the length of priesthoods from Aaron through Zadok to the end of building (I Kings ix: 10); though he loosely speaks of it as if reaching only to the building of the temple. Zadok's priesthood, re-established by Solomon (I Kings ii: 35) is included in the 612 years (as required by the number of priests given, 13; see Antiq. 5, xi, 5, and 8, i, 3); and it covers probably a large part of Solomon's reign.

---

*See Appendix G, in "Restor. of Jos.," § 90.

Josephus no doubt understood it as thus covering the "20 years time" that Solomon spent in building. (Antiq. 8, v, 1, 3, I Kings vii, 1), from the 4th year to the 24th of Solomon. This is shown by the reduced period "466 years" (given in the same passage as the 612) for the length of priesthoods to the return from captivity—in place of Josephus' whole 491 years (War. 6, iv, 8). Thus he understood his 592 as in agreement with the 612—20.

It is plain that this closing episode of Josephus' Antiquities (20, x,) is a sort of Appendix, giving the Priest Record, as drawn from the Jewish archives. It was not a part of Josephus' own chronology. And he in fact misunderstood it, as we show in our "Restoration of Josephus." The 612 thus somewhat obscured in meaning, Josephus mentions in one other place (Apion ii, 2), as if ending at Solomon's temple; but whenever speaking exactly he has his own 592 years' interval. (See Appendix A, § 85.)

The 612 Years in Josephus.

§ 63. The 612 years is, in fact, a wonderful confirmation of the original reckoning to the temple as built after 580 years; it being in exact accordance with that Scripture dating. For, the Bible reckoning of Josephus in the war makes ("1030"—"639"=) 491 years from the end of captivity back to Solomon's finished temple, or (491+7=498) to the temple founded; while the Scripture makes 580 years before that to the exodus. And the total of these is (498+580=) 1078 years from the end of captivity back to the exodus, *i. e.*, from B. C. 513 to 1591. On the other hand, the Priest Record, with its 612, gives ("612"+"466"=) 1078 also, the same number of years for the same interval of events. How striking the coincidence! How marked the proof, that the Priest Record, and Josephus, and Scripture, all rest on the same basis of chronology!

Thus the Priest Record reckoning seems to have been developed historically as follows:

	1603	Exodus	1591	1011 begins Temple 1003 ded.	Zadok	1 Cy. 537	2 Da. 520	9 Da. 513	Total from Exodus
Scripture Reckoning.			580	+8+	466	+17+7=			1078
Jubilee Reckoning…			588	+	490				
Priest Reckoning…			{ 588	+	24+466				} 1078
			{	612	+466				
Josephus' War……	{ 12+		580	+8+	12+466	+ 5+7=			⎫
			592		+20+471	+7=			⎬ 1090
			592	+	491	+7=			⎭
			592	+ 8+	490	=			

§ 64. We thus see how a misunderstanding of the Priest Record has misconstrued its "612 years" of priests ending during Solomon's reign, as if they reached only to the founding of the temple, whereas they include 580 years only down to that event. Here then we have this earliest form of the Jewish chronology (evidently arranged before Josephus), giving us the 580 years as the correct reckoning at I Kings vi: 1. This Priest Record thus confirms and vindicates our revision of the text, in accordance with Paul's account in the 13th chapter of Acts. It was only by mistaking the distance by which the "612" overlapped Solomon, that Josephus got his "592 years" at the founding of the temple, in place of the correct 580 years which the Priest Record had intended.

The great question now is this: How was it possible for Josephus to give the "592" as his only reckoning, if his Hebrew Bible, which was his only authority, gave the "480th year" as we now have it (at I Kings vi: 1)? Or how any better, if the Lxx version, which he must have known, gave the "440th year" as we now have it? Or how any better, if the I Kings vi: 1, then read or meant 580 years as we allege?

The Original 980.

§ 65. Our answer is: The I Kings vi: 1, did not originally read as it now does, namely:

"And it came to pass, in the four hundred and eightieth year of the exodus [*Heb. and Gr.*] of the children of Israel from the land of Egypt, in the fourth year of Solomon's reign over Israel, * * * that he built [*Rev. Marg.*] the house of the Lord."

But it probably read or was understood thus—with the part in brackets [ ] at first as a mere gloss in the margin:

"And it came to pass [in the nine hundred and eightieth year from foreign affliction from the land of Egypt], in the fourth year of Solomon's reign, * * * that he built the house of the Lord."

Whether the clause in brackets [ ] was in Josephus' day actually in the text, or was only a note put by some one in the margin, or was simply a traditional understanding of the date at that point, we do not here say. We only claim that in Josephus' time the dating of the temple was *so understood*.

§ 66. That well known "980 years" from foreign affliction, as handed down, had been understood to date from the same point as the "400 years" of foreign "affliction" foretold in Gen. xv: 13; viz., from the mocking by the Egyptian Ishmael (Gen. xxi: 9-11), just after the weaning of Isaac; which was when Isaac was five years old, *i. e.*, 30 years after Abraham's arrival in Canaan (980 years before B. C. 1011, viz., in B. C. 1991).

Therefore, as the "400 years" of affliction from the mocking of

Isaac reached to the exodus out of Egypt (see in Period C), so the "980 years" contained (980 — 400 =) 580 years after the exodus to the founding of the temple in B. C. 1011. And the offering up of Isaac on Mount Moriah being understood as 7 years later than the mocking (viz., at 12 years of age), the same 980 years reached thence to the finishing of the temple on Mount Moriah 7 years after the founding (viz., in B. C. 1004). The double dating (to the temple as begun and as finished) seems accordant with the exact language used—after so long "he *built* the temple." Moreover, the 980 years were just 20 Jubilee periods (of 49 years each), from the year after the offering of Isaac to the year of dedication following the finished temple, *i. e.*, from B. C. 1983 to 1003.

§ 67. That the age of Isaac at being brought to the altar was 12 years (not 25 as some put it), is evident from the fact that Jewish tradition thenceforward made this the age at which youth were brought to the temple service, as seen in the case of our Lord (Luke ii: 42). It is moreover obvious, from the childish submission of Isaac, and from his being called "the lad," and being so easily "bound and laid on the altar" by his aged father. (Gen. xxii: 5-9.) Such then seems to have been clearly the original understanding of the temple's date, as "980 years" after Isaac, or "580 years" after the exodus, as seen in the reckoning of Paul. (Gal. iii: 7; Acts xiii: 17-22.)

There were reasons why this particular dating, "980 years," was impressed upon the Jewish mind, and minuted (as text or as gloss) at I Kings vi: 1, while there are in the Bible so few long comprehensive reckonings like this. The sacrifice of Isaac was a marked event, typical of the Messiah; and the after selection of that very spot, on Mount Moriah, as the site of the temple, where sacrifice was continually to be offered, and where Messiah was to manifest himself, was an intended and notable concurrence,*—timed seemingly on purpose at 980 years, as a peculiar and significant number in Jewish Chronology.

---

*That the coincidence of place was specially noted and marked, appears not only from the scripture account, giving name to the spot as "the mount of the Lord" (Gen. xxii: 2, 14; II Chron. iii: 1), and from Josephus, who repeatedly declares that the temple was built on the spot where Isaac was offered (Antiq. 1, xiii: 2, etc.), but also from the identification which the Samaritans afterward attempted of Mt. Moriah with Mt. Gerizim. (See Bib. Sacra, Oct. 1868, p. 765.) The great wonder expressed in that article, that no mention was made in Jewish literature of the striking coincidence of place, is somewhat met by our exhibit here of the *dated interval* (980 years) as the early Jewish expression of interest in the coincidence. The writer of that article (at p. 375) is staggered at the improbability of God's countenancing such a chance for local superstition. But certainly it was not beneath the dignity of Divine Providence to encourage such a typical coincidence of time and place prospective of the Messiah, for the strengthening of Jewish faith in those crude times,—as witness the "seventy weeks" of Daniel given for the same purpose.

§ 68. For, this 980 is just twice 490 years, or twice the "seventy weeks" of Daniel; that is, twice 10 *Jubilee periods* of 49 years each; and twice 7 generations of 70 years each (as generations were then reckoned, Psa. xc: 10), making the "14 generations" of Mat. i: 17 (*i. e.*, 14×70 = 980). This 14 generation arrangement at the opening of Matthew, is a striking proof of our view, that the time from Abraham (and Isaac) to David (and Solomon's temple) was 400 + 580 = 980 years, not 400 + 480 = 880 as the shortened reckoning makes it. (See our exposition of Mat. i: 17, in "Chronology of the Judges, here § 10.)

Jewish scholars always made much of this Jubilee reckoning, by 49 and 490 years, as before shown. (See Period E, § 69.) In their various writings they reckoned Jubilee periods from the creation downward. And such a marked interval as the twice 490 years seen to exist between Isaac on Mount Moriah and the temple built on Mount Moriah, would naturally awaken their enthusiasm, and cause a noting of that particular epoch at I Kings vi: 1—in continuance of the "400 years" of it ending at the exodus. This will well account for a "980 years" put as text or marginal note in the early Hebrew of that passage in Kings.

And thus we have the original of I Kings vi: 1, without any "480th" in the text, as now, but probably with a note in its margin, saying, "980 years from foreign affliction"; which was understood as meaning (980—400=) "580 years from the exodus out of Egypt."

§ 69. But this original understanding of the matter had been lost sight of in Josephus' time (except as Paul was inspired to accuracy). For, we find Josephus, contrary to previous tradition, saying of Isaac at the time he was offered on Mount Moriah, " Now, Isaac was twenty-five years old." (Antiq. 1, xiii: 2.) That is, he makes that sacrificial event to be, no longer *seven*, but *twenty* years after Isaac's 5 years, when the "400 years" of affliction began. So that, he has there but (400—20=) 380 of the 400 years left, instead of the (400—7=) 393 before understood.

This change of 13 years made him say: The still known "980 years" from the Isaac sacrifice to the temple built on the same Mount Moriah—minus the 380 (left of the 400)=600 years from the exodus to the dedication of the temple; which is "592 years" to the founding of the temple 8 years before. Here at length we find the origin of Josephus' error, in putting 592 years instead of the right 580.

§ 70. When for some reason Josephus had changed the traditional and correct age of Isaac at being offered, from 12 to 25 years, his error of chronology would have been 13 years; *i. e.*, 593 after the exodus instead of 580. But he at the same time made another mistake of 1 year, in treating the terminus of the 980 (and so of his 600) as at the *dedication* instead of the *completion* of the temple, 8 years instead of 7 years after the founding, so getting (600—8) instead of (600—7). He was thus confounding the 980 of *sacrifice*, from B. C. 1984 to 1004, with the 980 of *Jubilee* reckoning, from B. C. 1983 to 1003. And by this means, he made his *excess* of chronology 12 years (not 13), from 12 years to the 25th year of Isaac, *i. e.*, from B. C. 1591 to 1603 for the exodus; and thus he exactly offset (or caused) his 12 years *deficiency* of reduction from the 612 (reduced 20 years instead of 32)—so leaving also a void of 12 years at the end of the "466 years." (See Rest. of Jos., § 27.)

He took his 592 as the 612—20, in the way we have seen, and we can account for his doing so; for he certainly had no Scripture number to contradict it. And it is evident that in Josephus' day there could not be in I Kings vi: 1, any such number as "480," or even "580"; but there might be simply the "980 years" from Isaac, either in the text, or more likely as a mere note in the margin. And from this "980 years" he must have worked out his 592 years, as we have here seen. Which number of his differs from the true original 580 years from the exodus only because he put the Mt. Moriah sacrifice at 25 instead of the correct 12 years of Isaac's age (with also 1 year of error at the dedication).

And thus Josephus has, from Abraham's arrival in Canaan 25 years to Isaac's birth + 25 to Mt. Moriah + 380 to the Exodus + 592 to the temple=1022 years (*i. e.*, 430+592) back to Abraham's arrival, as he himself gives it. (Antiq. 8, iii: 1, corrupted 1020.)

See Josephus' whole chronology, at "Rest. of Jos." § 18.

The 592 reckoning found previous to Josephus, in the Jewish historians, Eupolemus and Demetrius, may have originated the error, which Josephus only followed.* But the 612 of the Priest Record in Josephus (Antiq. 20, x: 1) was no error, but only an adaptation of the true "580 years" itself, as we have shown.

CHAPTER II.

THE SEPTUAGINT "440."

§ 71. The error of Josephus in his "592 years" arose from his forgetting that the original "980 years" began with the "400 years" of foreign affliction, not with the offering of Isaac. But others, while not thus shoving down the 980 as beginning later than the 400, yet had long before Josephus adopted a *double reckoning* of the "430 years" of sojourning; which led on to the present corruption of the text. Thus:

Since, in Ex. xii: 40, the "430 years" is called "the SOJOURNING of the children of ISRAEL," an opinion arose that this number began strictly with the sojourning of Israel himself (or Jacob) rather than of

---

* See Appendix G, in "Restor. of Jos.," § 93.

Abraham; that is, when he left home for Haran (Gen. xxvii: 43), taken as at 56 years of his age, or (130—56=) 74 years before he stood before Pharaoh (Gen. xlvii: 9). This made that period of "sojourn" begin (215—74=) 141 years later; or 25 from Abraham's coming + 60 from Isaac's birth (Gen. xxv: 26) + 56 years from Jacob's birth=141 years later than Abraham's coming to Canaan, the original date of sojourn. (Appendix C, § 96.)

This delay of 141 years in beginning the "430 years" of sojourn carried down its ending to 141 years after the exodus, viz., to the judgeship of Ehud, at the *end of foreign servitude*, after the children of Israel *served* Eglon, king of Moab, 18 years" (Jud. iii: 14). For the years from the exodus are as follows: Moses 40+Joshua 25+anarchy 10+Chushan 8+Othniel 40+Eglon 18=total, 141 years. (See Chron. of the Judges, here § 1, 5.) And that this ended foreign servitude, see Appendix B, § 88.

§ 72. The 141 years thus taken from the beginning of the "430 years" of sojourning and added to their end, constituted a second reckoning of the 430 years, viz., from "Israel" to Ehud; with the first reckoning still retained (Ex. xii: 40, comp. ver. 41), in accordance with the Jewish fondness for *double reckoning* of dates, of which we are having constant examples as we proceed. (See here § 66, etc.) And this second "430 years," from Israel to Ehud was looked upon as a period of "sojourning" and of servitude to foreigners, mostly in Egypt, and also in Canaan. So that the Lxx translators put in the gloss at Ex. xii: 40: "they sojourned in Egypt *and in Canaan*," placing the Canaan sojourn *after* rather than before that of Egypt. By thus making *an after sojourn* in *Canaan* cover a part of the "430 years," they plainly show their method of carrying down that period below the Exodus. (See Appendix, § 88.) Moreover, those translators finish out the book of Joshua (or the "hexateuch") to reach down to this era of Ehud, as we see in the Lxx, at Josh. xxiv: 33, onwards. (See Appendix B, § 90.)

Knowing still the (980—400=) 580 years, dating from the exodus to the temple, but using the new era of Ehud, 141 years after the exodus, as an era of ended foreign servitude or of INDEPENDENCE, the Jews now came to speak of the (580—141=) "440th year" of this *independence era* (after the lengthened hexateuch) as the date when Solomon commenced the temple.

§ 73. The use of this "440th year" of independence was encouraged, not only by the fact that this number 440 expressed the years of comparative freedom downward from Ehud with 141 years of unsettled condition left out, but also by the further fact, noticed by the Rabbis, that this 441 would likewise express the reigns and judgeships from the exodus to the temple with the interregnums of foreign invasion omitted as of no account in Israel's nationality. Thus, the anarchy after Joshua was 10 years+Chushan 8+Eglon 18+Jabin 20+ Midian 7+Ammon 18+Philistines 40 (at Jud. xiii: 1)+20 years at I Sam. vii: 2=141 years of total invasion to be dropped out from 580, leaving the "440th year." (See Chron. of the Judges here, § 5.)

The originators of this "440th year" reckoning may therefore have intended to include the 141 years of separate foreign invasion (all the way down to king Saul) in with the Egyptian oppression, leaving the "440th year" to express only *the 440th year of reigns* or of Jewish supremacy. They thus *meant no shortening* of the chronology.

§ 74. This "440th year" of freedom from servitude or foreign "affliction" (Gen. xv: 13), was a gloss in the margin of I Kings vi: 1, put as a current and correct application of "980 years" found in the margin of other Hebrew copies. The Lxx editors, choosing to insert this (as a supposed correct date) in their translation—it seemed to them more popular and patriotic to mention merely the length of their independence, than to include the long period of their affliction under foreign oppression. And these Greek translators being in Egypt, and translating for Egyptian use, would naturally make the national life of Israel *as short as they could* at the building of their one great temple; because this would best comport with Egyptian ideas of piety, the earliest work of all their kings being the erection and adornment of magnificent temples to the gods. The "440th year" of independence put at the founding of Solomon's temple, answered this purpose better than would the retention of the "980 years" from foreign affliction.

§ 75. But in choosing this "440th year" reading of the margin for insertion in their Greek translation, they mistook its meaning, and instead of its exact Hebrew sense "440th year from *servitude*," or foreign affliction, they rendered it into Greek as it now stands, "440th year of *Exodus from Egypt*"—supposing that to be the thought intended. They thus innocently but carelessly dropped out 141 years from the chronology. For, while the inditer of the gloss correctly meant "440th year of *final* freedom from foreign servitude in general at Ehud, the translators, by giving it as the *special exodus from Egypt*, have thrown out all the 141 years between. Such was the Septuagint when it was issued, over 200 years B. C. But still, there was no such number in the Hebrew, and Paul and Josephus, and writers generally, were guided by reference to the "980 years" gloss handed down from the first.

We here see that the Septuagint error of shortening the chronology arose from a forgetting of the double reckoning of the "430 years," as ending at Ehud as well as at the Exodus. The Ehud era being lost sight of, the "440th year" got put back from that place as if beginning at the Exodus. And so the changed expression, "exodus from Egypt," crept into the Septuagint text.

§ 76. A PRESUMPTION. It may well be presumed that it was not the Lxx translators themselves who got in the changed expression "exodus from Egypt" (though they did insert the "440th year" gloss); but that the change of expression was a *corruption* that crept in long afterward. Otherwise, there could not be (as there is both in Josephus and in the New Testament) an absence of all knowledge of the shorter reckoning between the exodus and the temple, while the longer reckoning is so constantly reiterated as drawn from the Old Testament itself. How and why this reduced reckoning came in is the question. There is no trace of it till it is cited by Clemens Alex. about A. D. 200. We quote from J. Schwartz in the Bibliotheca Sacra (July, 1888, p. 447):

"Clement of Alexandria, who flourished about A. D. 192, or over 100 years before Eusebius, among a mass of undigested extracts from chronologists before his time (contained in Book I, chap. xxi of his 'Stromata'), gives the following fragment: ' From the birth of Moses till the captivity, 972 years * * * From the reign of David till the captivity, 452 years 6 months.' (*Ante-Nicene Lib., Vol. iv, p. 432.*)"

These "452½ years" are plainly the length of the Jewish kings from the *end* of David to the end of Jehoiachin in captivity. (See Rest. of Jos. § 52, 53.) And this is the correct Scripture value, viz., from B. C. 1013 to 561—452 years+½ year from spring to autumn; just as Josephus (War., 6, x: 1) gives it, "470½"—David 40+22 last years of Jehoiachin—the "452½" here. Josephus also has it as (452½+David 40+22 of Saul=) "514½ years" for the whole duration of the kings after Samuel, (so he says in Antiq. 10, viii: 4, with 6, xiv: 9).

§ 77. Thus this fragment in Clemens Alex. gives (972—452½=)519½ years from the end of David back to the birth of Moses, which is (519—80=) 439 years back to the exodus from the death of David, and this gives 440 years to the 2d of Solomon *alone*, regarded as the 4th of Solomon's whole reigning at the founding of the temple. Here, then, we have the first intimation anywhere in history of such a shortened reckoning as the "440th year" from the exodus to the temple.

This shows that at some time (the reader may judge when) before Clement in the 2d century, the Lxx had received this exodus interpretation. Its previous reading, the "440th year of the exit of the children of Israel from *foreign affliction*" (meaning from Ehud downward), had very naturally been misunderstood as meaning "from the exodus out of Egypt," and no doubt, by a gloss in the margin, the text itself became corrupted to its present form. There may have been no intentional corruption, but only a natural misunderstanding of the meaning. And the new reading, as apparently plainer and better, would soon find its way into all new copies. So that, as we have no very early manuscripts of the Lxx, we find no copies with the earlier reading.

CHAPTER III.

The Hebrew "480."

§ 78. When the Lxx had thus become unintentionally corrupted to its present form, the original Hebrew was easily misunderstood, for it probably had in its text no back date at I Kings vi: 1, except (perhaps) a marginal gloss, saying "980 years from foreign affliction," abreviated, it may be, to read simply "980 years." Its anciently known reference to Isaac being forgotten, it was thought that the Lxx's number must be more nearly correct. So that, a conjectural emendation was inserted [480] for the 980, bringing it into nearer agreement with the Lxx. This may have been at first a mere gloss in the margin, but as appearing to be a very reasonable correction, it would soon find its way into the text.

§ 79. There were reasons why, instead of the Lxx's "440" being adopted into the Hebrew, there was simply the change made of a figure (980 to 480.) The Lxx now having come to read "in the 440th year of exit (or exodus) of the children of Israel from Egypt," was understood as really denoting the 440th year of *full exit and entrance to Canaan*, requiring the addition of the 40 years in the wilderness to give the whole interval. And when the reigns and judgeships were now added up, as being the items supposed by some to be alone included, they were found to be more accurately a total of the "480th year."—the previously supposed 141 years of interregnums being more correctly but 101 years. For, the "40 years" at Jud. xiii: 1, were seen to cover only 20 years before the 40 years of Eli. So that there was in the book of Judges (anarchy 10+Chushan 8+Eglon 18+Jabin 20+Midian 7+Ammon 18+Philistines 20=) 101 years of invasion, taken from the full amount 580, and leaving the "480th year" which has been put into the present Hebrew text.

§ 80. The total of the numbers given us in Scripture from the exodus to the temple is certainly 580 years, as shown in our "Chronology of the Judges." (§ 1, 4.) If that total number was ever inserted in the Hebrew text, as a gloss rightly derived from "980" (minus 400 years of affliction)—then the present "480th" of the Hebrew text is simply a corruption from that "580th" by the mere accidental change (in some copy giving the numbers by *letters*) of 5 into 4, or (in Hebrew) ה into ד; *i. e.*, the mere failure to insert one slight little dash (1). But one way or another, there was now made an actual corruption or reduction of one hundred years from the chronology—a result never known or heard of before that time. When and by whom was the present corruption made?

Eusebius (A. D. 320) is the earliest writer found to have any knowledge of the "480th year" reckoning.* He says (Hist. ch. 16, Migne, p. 150): "From the Exodus to the Temple are 600 [580] years according to the Apostle, but by the Hebrew Scriptures is put as 480 years." He goes on to give the Christian fathers before him, Africanus, Clement, and Theophilus, as also all having the longer reckoning. But he himself abandons this "Apostolic tradition," as he calls it, and adopts the "480th year," which he calls "Jewish tradition;" saying, "the Jewish doctors affirm the 480 to be made out by not reckoning the foreign rulers separate."

This last statement of Eusebius reveals the secret as to how the interval got reduced. It was a leaving out of the periods of invasion; at first, no doubt, as a mere slighting of those years in the record, without denying their reality as lengthening the time; but afterward, an ignoring of them entirely, as is done by many now.

§ 81. Eusebius gives, as the principal reason for rejecting the longer reckoning, the fact that, of the "14 generations" in Mat. i: 17, "only *five* names are given after the Exodus (he should say *six*), viz., Naason (Num. i: 7), Salmon, Boaz, Obed, Jesse, David; making each generation too long (600+5=120) as he says. He should say, 580+6 =96. Thus is he led astray by not perceiving (what we have shown in "Chron. of the Judges," here § 10) that the "14 generations" denote merely "*14 seventies*"=980; and that the *names* are not to be taken as an exact list of all the links of descent, but are only meant to give life to the several steps.†

It is thus probable that some time in the 3d century, between Eusebius and Clement, or even earlier, the "480th year" reading crept into the Hebrew text. And it looks as though it came from the Jews, who in those days were the chief handlers of the Hebrew Scriptures. "On account of the prevalent ignorance of the Hebrew and Chaldee languages among the early Christians, the Alexandrian Greek version (or Lxx) was the authority employed." (*Chambers Cyc. Art. Bible.*) While the church thus trusted to their Greek copies, the Jews clung to their Hebrew text, and had it pretty much in their control. They were very faithful custodians of Scripture until they were cast off for their rejection of Christ; but after that their malignant opposition to Christianity tempted them to any measure which would oppose it.

§ 82. About A. D. 130, their leader, Rabbi Akiba, originated their modern Jewish Chronology, to which they still adhere; and in this

---

* J. Schwartz, in the Bib. Sacra (July, 1888, p. 447), has tried to make out a knowledge of the 480th year reckoning in Castor of Rhodes, just before Clement; but the figuring is very complicated and far-fetched, and reaches no reliable result.

† See a similar case explained in Period C, § 12.

they made the age of the world as short as they could, in order to deny the Messiahship of Jesus by alleging, that "the last times" required by prophesy had not yet arrived when he appeared. This chronology (found in the present Jewish calendar) as fully established in the 3d century, has from Creation the 2451st year to the Exodus+480 to the Temple+410 to the Captivity+490 to Jerusalem's overthrow by Titus =total 3831st year (minus A. D. 70)=3761st year B. C., instead of Usher's 4004. This seems to be, then, the origin of the "480th year" assigned at the founding of the temple,*—along with the greater error of only (490—A. D. 70=) 419 years put from the beginning of the captivity to the Christian Era! Such is the blundering Jewish reckoning of their Hebrew chronology.

Aquila was a pagan who became a Christian, and then apostatized to Judaism; and in A. D. 138 he put forth his Greek translation of the Old Testament, to take the place of the Septuagint, which the Jews had by that time pretty generally discarded as too favorable to the Christians. If Aquila, under the teaching of Rabbi Akiba (who was his preceptor) adjusted his Greek version with the "440th year of the *exodus from Egypt*" at I Kings vi: 1, in the way we have indicated above—it would soon find its way as a seeming improvement into all copies of the Greek Lxx, because his version was at once accepted as more correct than that. And it would not be long before the Hebrew text itself would show its gloss (and then its corruption) "480th year," as we have shown. "Origin cites the text I Kings vi: 1, leaving out all that part (concerning the exodus); nor is it in that parallel place of Chronicles." (*Jackson*.)

§ 83. There is one fact very noticeable here: "All the eastern copies of the Hebrew have 1656 years before the flood; but all the western copies have 1556, leaving 100 from Jared; so we are told by an author of good credit." (*Jackson*.) It would thus seem, that older copies (scattered in the west) had no 480 reducing the period from the Exodus to the Temple by 100 years, but had instead a 100 reduction before the flood. Whereas, when eastern copies, by insertion of the 480 would lower the whole chronology 100 years, an offsetting 100 years was added to Jared, to keep the total A. M. unchanged, viz., 3761 B. C., as in the modern Jewish Chronology. This looks like a purposed adjustment of the reckoning about the 2d century. (See Period A, B, § 27.)

But we need not here allege any intentional corruption of I Kings vi: 1; though such complaints have been freely made by many writers.†
We have shown sufficient grounds for explanatory words, inserted in

---

*Eusebius says he took it from "the Jewish doctors."
†See Appendix D, § 99.

the margin, and finding their way into the text, as a supposed correction or improvement. And this is all that we feel called to insist upon. But, one way or another, the "480th year" reckoning must have crept into the Scripture account at some period, seemingly later than when Paul, and Josephus, and the other early writers lived. (See Appendix E, § 100.)

Conclusion.

§ 84. So then, we seem to have shown, that the present "480th year" in our I Kings vi: 1, is a corruption, from an original reckoning 580 years, probably written as "980 years" from Isaac, and changed to 480th year by mistake, as a supposed correction of the number. There appears but one question unanswered, viz: Was the number "980" in the original Hebrew as Josephus and Paul had it—or was the text without a date at that point, until the "480th year" was subsequently put in? The deranged order of the Lxx text favors the latter view; but the change to "480th" favors the former view.

If the Hebrew text originally had "980," the form of statement then must have been different from what it now is; not "480th year of exit from Egypt," but "980 years from foreign affliction," or the like. And so also, when the "440th year" was a mere gloss to the Lxx, it must have read "440th year of exit from foreign affliction," not as now "440th year of exit from Egypt." But most likely, there was originally *no number given* in the text of I Kings vi: 1. If it were there in Kings, why is so marked a date omitted in the later chronicles going over the same events?

We have thus given a plausible account of the way in which the corruption of our present I Kings vi: 1, may have come about; while yet the New Testament writers, with Josephus and others, had for a certainty no such number there as we now have. The real value, the 580 years, carries us from the founding of the temple "in the 4th year of Solomon," B. C. 1011, to B. C. 1591 as the true date of the exodus, not B. C. 1491 as Usher has it.

APPENDIX A.

For § 62.

Josephus and the Priest Record.

§ 85. We have shown before (in the previous Period E) that Josephus reckoned the 70 years captivity as ending at the Jubilee B. C. 513, regarded by tradition as the time of the second temple's dedication (delayed like Solomon's dedication to concur with the Jubilee). And we now see that in this Josephus was only following the Priest

Record given by him (which perpetuates that tradition), though he mistakingly thought that record lacked 12 years of reaching down to B. C. 513, and therefore added 12 years to it to make his own chronology, as we shall presently see. (§ 86.)

The true Bible chronology, as we showed in Period E, has a marked interval, 466 years, as *the duration of reign to David's line*, from the accession of David in B. C. 1053 to the destruction of Jerusalem in B. C. 587. This same interval was applied by the Jews to reach from Solomon's dedication 50 years later in B. C. 1003, down to the Cyrus decree for restoration as also 50 years later in B. C. 537. And this same interval was applied in the Jews' Priest Record as reaching from the death of Zakok (taken as 24 years after Solomon's dedication (as also 24 years after the Cyrus decree), viz., in B. C. 513. These were all correct applications of the "466 years" interval. (See Restor. of Jos., §§ 42, 43.)

§ 86. But in after times Josephus mistook the Priest Record's 612, as reaching down only 20 years after the 4th of Solomon (the definite *period of building*, 1 Ki. ix: 10), instead of 24 years after the 12th of Solomon, the time of dedication. This made a difference of 8+4=) 12 years, causing the Priest Record's, 466 years to fall 12 years short of its true terminus in B. C. 513. He therefore had to add these 12 years as 5+7) to reach first the 2d and then the 9th of Darius), and in this way he, in his own reckoning, reached 12 years earlier than the Record, viz. (1591+12=) 1603 B. C. for the exodus, with (580+12=) 592 from thence to the temple.

(NOTE. Since the continuator of the Priest Record, who, before Josephus had appended the "414 years" down to the Maccabees, began it, by a similar mistake, at the 2d instead of the 9th Darius, there is thus now in the Priest Record *an apparent excess of only 7 years* instead of the 12 put in by Josephus.)

§ 87. As Josephus thus increased by 12 both the Priest Record total 1078 (up to 1090) and its earlier portion 580 (up to 592), his remaining portion (1090—592=) 498 was thus left the same as that in the Priest Record, viz., 1078—580=) 498 years from the 4th Solomon to the 9th Darius. or (498—8=) 490 years from dedication to dedication (B. C. 1003 to 513). This makes 491 years from the founding of one temple to that of the other (put as B. C. 1011 to 520)—just as Josephus gives it in the War, in precise accord with the Priest Record, as here seen. (See further in Period E.)

Thus the Bible chronology seems to have been developed historically, first into the correct reckoning of the Priest Record, and then into the modified reckoning of Josephus (correct from temple to temple), as seen in the table at § 5.

APPENDIX B.

For § 71.

THE INDEPENDENCE ERA OF EHUD.

§ 88. We find in the Greek Septuagint *three* striking and related peculiarities, which combine to show the theory upon which its chronology at I Ki. vi: 1, is based.

(1) The passage at Ex. xx: 40, has in the Lxx an inserted clause, as follows: "Now the sojourning of the children of Israel, which they sojourned in the land of Egypt AND IN THE LAND OF CANAAN was 430 years." (The Samaritan pentateuch has a similar clause, but inserted *before* instead of after the mention of Egypt.)

§ 89. (2) The Lxx has I Ki. vi: 1, reading "in the 440th year," instead of the 480th year of the Hebrew text. Moreover the whole passage (from v: 16, to vi: 2) is transposed and confused, showing that it has been tampered with. It reads thus:

I Ki. v: 16, "—the people that wrought in the work. 17. And they prepared the stones and the timbers [three years. And it came to pass, in the four hundred and fortieth year of exodus of (the) children of Israel from Egypt, in the year the fourth, in month the second of the King Solomon reigning over Israel,]

17. And [that] the king commanded that they should take great costly stones for the foundation of the house, and hewn stones.

18. And the men of Solomon and the men of Huram hewed and placed them.

vi: 1. In the year the fourth he founded the house of the Lord, in month of Zif, even in the second month.

(38.) In the eleventh year, in month Baal (that is the eighth month) the house was completed, etc. [No "seven years."]

2. And the house which the king built for the Lord," etc.

REMARKS.

The original lxx evidently was without the sentence in brackets []; without which, that version reads much like the Hebrew—except that ver. 38 is brought back to fill out ver. 1 with the finished temple dating (instead of the exodus date).

After the inserted "three years," on the margin was the gloss contained in brackets [], which afterward wrongly got into the text. This is evident from the awkward manner of its insertion, in the wrong place (at v: 17, instead of vi: 1—introduced by "And" without any following verb—and repeating the year and month of ver. 1).

Subsequently, by way of supposed correction of the lxx, the gloss was inserted in the Hebrew also, at the more fitting place (ver. 1) as "480th" not 440th—thus avoiding the repetition of the year and month.

§ 90. (3) The Lxx has the book of Joshua not ending as does our Bible with the Hebrew verse 33 of the last chapter, but has an additional paragraph, as follows:

"In that day the children of Israel took the ark of God and carried it about among them; and Phinehas exercised the priest's office in the room of Eleazar, his father, till he died; and he was buried in his own place Gebaar [the hill]. But the children of Israel departed every one to their place and to their own city. And the children of Israel worshiped Astarte and Ashtaroth, and the gods of the nations round about them; and the Lord delivered them into the hands of Eglon, King of Moab, and he lorded it over them eighteen years."

This is an abridgement of the history given in Judges (i: 1, to iii: 30), taking its statements particularly from ii: 6, 12, 13, and iii: 12, 14; but the first statement about Phinehas and the ark has no parallel. The early Jews, in framing the Lxx version, evidently followed in this matter a tradition, which linked the book of Joshua with the five books of Moses as a "hexateuch," carrying the history to the end of Jewish *servitude*. And they understood that the nation did not really gain its independence till Ehud's 80 years of peace, after the 18 years of servitude to Eglon, King of Moab; with which latter events, therefore, the book of Joshua (or of subjugation) was considered as properly closing.

§ 91. Caleb's nephew Othniel, really the first "judge," seems to have been looked at as simply a survival of " the days of Joshua and of the elders that outlived Joshua" (ii: 7); and so long as the ark was "carried about among them," without a settled headquarters for the people,* their actual exodus out of Egyptian bondage was not looked back upon as complete. They thus came to regard the accession of Ehud,—when he "blew a trumpet" and cried "Follow after me!" completely routing Moab,—as a grand epoch in their history: from which they dated forward and backward, as the dividing line of colonization (or pilgrimage) and of nationality. And it is this era of *finished independence* that seems to have been originally meant by "the 440th year" at I Ki. vi: 1, of the Septuagint.

§ 92. Can any one in any better way than this account for the fact, that the Lxx has this *different number* of years, put with the singular

---

* It would seem, from the above extract from the Lxx, that after the "tabernacle" was located at Shiloh (Josh. xviii: 1, 10) the "ark" itself was from time to time "carried about" for safety or for prestige, in those troublous times, until it was fixed in its place at Shiloh upon Ehud's triumph. (Jud. iii: 30, and xviii: 31. See I Sam. iv: 4.)

fact, that it has also this parallel addition at the close of Joshua, which just meets the requirements of the changed number (440),—together with the other fact, that at Ex. xii: 40, a sojourn "in Canaan" is *added as following* the sojourn in Egypt? The *seventy* translators who so publicly by official authority sent forth the Septuagint from Alexandria, certainly would not boldly *change* the number contained in the well-known Hebrew Scripture, except as they supposed themselves to be giving an *equivalent date* more understandable or acceptable in their times.

It was natural for the Jews, and especially there in Alexandria, surrounded by an Egyptian atmosphere, to lump all their original servitude in with the Egyptian bondage, and not concede that they had been actual slaves to other nations after their boasted exodus was complete. And they did not like to magnify the time after their full freedom before their most illustrious monarch had built their world-famed temple; when everybody knew that the *first business* of Egyptian monarchs was to erect their stately temples of worship. They therefore preferred to date Solomon's Temple back only from the era of their full independence, with distinct recognition that it was *before that era* in the times of Moses and Joshua and their immediate colonial successors, that "the ark" of their worship was allowed to wander about without a home.

§ 93. And that there was some excuse for this traditional era of Ehud as *the end of national servitude*, will appear from the fact, that up to that point the Scripture expression used is, "The children of Israel *served* Chushan-rishathaim," "The children of Israel *served* Eglon" (Ju. iii: 8, 14); *i. e.*, they were in *actual servitude* or subjection, whereas no such expression occurs afterward. It is only said that the enemy "oppressed" (iv: 3) "prevailed against" and "impoverished" (vi: 2, 6), "vexed" and "distressed" (x: 8, 9), and "came into the coasts of Israel (I Sam. ix: 13), in order to prove Israel" (Ju. iii: 1-5). It was only in banter that the Philistines considered themselves "rulers" and the Hebrews their "servants" (I Sam. iv: 9; Ju. xv: 11); they were simply annoying invaders, not subjugators like Chusham and Eglon, in the former days of real servitude. At least, so the Jews liked to look back upon it in after times, putting an era of comparative independence from Ehud onward.

Moab (like Edom), though unmolested, yet refused a passage to the Israelites when they entered the land. (Num. xxii.) Moab, under Balak, opposed their progress, and caused a great plague to Israel. Hence Balaam's famous Messianic prophecy (Num. xxiv: 17), "I shall see him, but not now: I shall behold him, but not nigh: there shall come a star out of Jacob, and a scepter shall rise out of Israel and shall SMITE the corners of MOAB, and destroy all the children of Sheth."

It was just 100 years afterward, when Eglon (king of Moab in Balak's place) had subjugated Israel for 18 years (their last real bondage); and Ehud, as a typical "star out of Jacob and scepter out of Israel," came and *smote* most terribly Eglon and *Moab*, with slaughter of 10,000 (Jud. iii: 12-30). "And there escaped not a man. So Moab was subdued that day under the hand of Israel; and the land had rest four score years."

§ 94. No wonder that the Jews seem to have regarded this accession of Ehud as a great era in their history, the end of their bondage, and their full attainment of Canaan. No wonder that they looked upon Ehud as the Star and the Scepter smiting Moab, the type of their very Messiah. Those 100 years (plus the 40 in the wilderness) they were disposed to class with their earlier bondage, rather than with their later freedom; and this was what seems to have led to the corruption of I Ki. vi: 1, from its original intent (580) to be as we now have it, "the 440th year" of the Septuagint.

Josephus (Antiq. 5, v: 1) calls the 80 years of Ehud "a short breathing-time after the *slavery* under the Moabites"; and his editor, Dr. Whiston, takes advantage from this remark to suggest, that Josephus may have intended only 8 years instead of 80 for Ehud, thus seeking to reach the shortened "480th year" of I Ki. vi: 1. But such a surmise is entirely foreign to all Josephus' reckoning. He only means, that 80 years of freedom seemed but "short" *compared* with Israel's preceding 400 years of trouble. In reality, the 80 years of Ehud were lengthened into (80+20+40=) 140 years of comparative quiet. For the intervening "20 years" of Jabin's *oppression* (not of servitude) were relieved seemingly by the simultaneous administration of Shamgar and Deborah before the victory of Barak. (See Ju. iii: 31, and iv: 4, "at that time.") Some expositors have omitted those 20 years from their list of omitted foreign servitudes. (See Scott's Bible.)

§ 95. There was also, in the Jewish *double method* of reckoning epochs, a special reason for this epoch of Ehud. As the Lxx puts the period "430 years" distinctly as that of the sojourning "in the land of Egypt *and in the land of Canaan*" (not Egypt alone as in our Hebrew); and as the Samaritan copy has the same in different order, viz, "in Canaan and in Egypt"; it is obvious that the Jews understood this period as covering *the whole time of pilgrimage*, however reckoned —whether from Abraham's first coming to Canaan and Egypt down to the first exodus (where the number is put), or, as applied particularly to ISRAEL, from the time of Israel's going off to sojourn in Haran to the time of Israel's perfected exit out of servitude (with a wandering ark) at the triumph of Ehud. For this latter interval they made "430 years" as truly as the other. (This we show in our next Appendix.)

(NOTE. The translators of the Lxx were led to the insertion of their extra clause ("and in the land of Canaan") in the text of Ex. xii: 40, as a necessity of their wrong rendering — "the sojourning—WHICH THEY sojourned." For they saw that it was not true, that the 430 years' sojourning was *all in* Egypt. That notion, which some now adopt, did not enter *their* minds. The revisers, unfortunately, adopt their rendering without their added clause to preserve the truth. But, doubtless, our received English version has it right. "Now the sojourning of the children of Israel WHO SOJOURNED in Egypt, was 430 years." This is strictly true, and does not assert that the 430 years was all spent in Egypt.)

APPENDIX C.

For § 71.

ISRAEL'S STAY IN HARAN.

§ 96. The "430-year" interval was reckoned from "Israel" himself, as well as from Abraham. That is, as Ehud began at the (40+25 +10+8+40+18=)141st year after the Exodus, for a second ending of the 430-year period—so Israel's removal to Haran was regarded as (Ab. 25+Isaac 60+Israel 56 =) the 141st year after Abraham's arrival in Canaan, for a second beginning of the 430-year period. This shows an early Jewish opinion, that Israel went to Haran when 56 years old (not 77 as usually reckoned);* and that his stay there was 40 years (instead of 20). Perhaps they understood Gen. xxxi: 41 as meaning, "I have been twenty years in thy house; *also* I served thee 14 years and 6 years;" instead of viewing the two clauses as covering one and the same 20 years, as is commonly done.

In Gen. xxxi: 38, 41, the Hebrew has no verb "have been," and no word "thus;" but the (*zeh-zeh*) at beginning of the two sentences may be *adversative*, "this—that," or "one—another;" just as at I Ki. xxii: 20. Thus these old Jews seem to have read the passage, verse 38, "*This* twenty years I (have been) with thee" working *on shares*, with no damage to thy flocks; verse 41, "*That* (first) twenty years (was) in thy house," serving, first for wives and then for flocks, (as at xxx: 32, "and they shall be my hire" for the six years over-work already performed; and so henceforth).

§ 97. It thus appears, that the compiler of Genesis, after entering upon the family register at xxix: 31, went on to finish it, without mixing in business arrangments (a common method of writing history); and then, at xxx: 25, went on to give the *revision* of business arrangments then made, after some 34 years spent with Laban. This leads him now, at xxx: 29, to *go back* and relate the previous origin of these business arrangements, when "20 years in Laban's house" had elapsed, xxxi: 41, "for he (Jacob) *had* said unto him," etc. (ver. 29.)

---

*They called Joseph 40 (not 39) when Jacob was 130, making Jacob 96 (not 97) on leaving Haran.

Thus Laban's offer at xxx: 28, is a *repetition* of his previous proposal in ver. 31, made some fourteen years before; and the repetition of statement here (in ver. 29 and 31) plainly shows a lapse of time between two bargains. At the second bargaining in ver. 28, after complaint of "wages changed 10 times" (xxxi: 7, 41), Laban has to promise clearly to *stick to his bargain*, and say, "appoint me thy wages, and I WILL GIVE IT," *i. e.*, without further variation. And thereupon (after the episode of ver. 29-36, belonging back after xxix: 30), the account goes on, at ver. 37-43; to relate what occurred for the remaining six years, which make up the 40 years of Jacob's abode in Haran. The first 20 years were in "Laban's house" (xxxi: 41), buying wives and cattle (down to xxx: 32, "they shall be my hire," *i. e.*, for the past six years overworked);—and the last twenty years were *on shares* "with Laban" (xxxi: 38), with no ground of complaint.

The Westminster S. S. Quarterly, for April, 1894, says, Jacob's return from Haran was "20 years, or, according to other authorities, 40 years, after the vision at Bethel." In the S. S. Times, Feb. 24, 1894, Prof. Beecher, of Auburn, says: "An obscure tradition affirms that there was an interval of 20 years between the 14 years and the 6 years, regarding the 20 years of verse 38 as different from the 20 of verse 42. That there was such a long interval the facts conclusively show." (He recites them.)

The learned Dr. Kennicott accepts as correct this old traditional view of the Jews, putting Jacob's sojourn 40 years. (See *marg.* of *Polyglott Bible*, Gen. xxvii: 1.) And there is certainly some ground for this view, that there was a 20 years of *serving* and an additional 20 years of *sojourning*. Jacob was certainly 96 or 97 years old at his return to Canaan, (Joseph being about 6, see Gen. xxx: 25, and xxxi: 41); and there were 90 or 91 years difference in the age of Joseph and Jacob (see xli: 46, 47, and xlv: 6, and xlvii: 9); and so Jacob was 56 or 57 not 77 at his leaving home. For,

§ 98. (1) That is the more likely age for Jacob to go seeking a wife, (xxviii: 1, 2, comp. xxvii: 41). Esau was married at 40 (see xxvi: 34).

(2) The longer sojourn seems necessary to account for all the births and acquisitions in Haran. (Ch. xxix to xxxi.)

(3) Also, to account for the advanced boyhood of Reuben before the birth of several of his brothers. (xxx: 14.)

(4) To account for the difference of age seemingly required between Joseph and his brethren. (Ch. xxvii, etc.)

(5) To account for the mature age of the daughter Dinah, as given before the birth of Benjamin on the way to Isaac. (Ch. xxxiv: 25, and xlviii: 7.)

(6) To account for the successive births and marriages of Judah's

children, and the birth of children's children, the great grandchildren of Jacob, all within 33 years after leaving Haran, and within 42 years after Judah's own birth, if there were but 20 years' stay in Haran. (Ch. xxxviii and xlvi.)

All these facts of the Scripture narrative seem to require the births (of xxix: 32, to xxx: 21) to be not shut up within 7 years; as a 20-years' stay in Haran puts them, but to be strung along through 27 years, as a 40-years' stay makes them.

However, those afterward who took Gen. xxxi: 40 in the common view as covering but 20 years of sojourn, had the 161st year (instead of 141st) from Jacob's 75 yrs. back to Abraham's coming; and they tried to parallel this by making out the 161st year (instead of 141st) from the exodus to Ehud. This they did by lengthening Joshua 2 years (from 25 to 27) and lengthening the subsequent anarchy 18 years (from 10 to 28), as we find the numbers given by Eusebius. Thus having the 161st year down to Ehud, the adding of "the 440th year" of the lxx, made just 600 years to the temple, instead of the correct 580th year. Here, then, is seen one source of the *enlarged reckoning* (600, etc.) of this interval, which so prevailed in later times, and which we more fully discuss elsewhere.

APPENDIX D.

For § 83.

CORRUPTION OF THE SCRIPTURE TEXT.

§ 99. From the *Chronol. Antiq.*, by John Jackson, London, *1752, 3 vol. folio.* "The Hebrew was corrupted by the later Jews themselves, and so the Christians were imposed upon. The true chronology was divinely preserved in Josephus, who says he followed the Hebrew copies. The corruption is no older than the 2d century. Augustine (*De. Civ. Dei. xv: 1*) relates, that the Jews were suspected of having corrupted their copies (as to the antediluvians) out of envy to the Christians, and to diminish the authority of the Greek Scriptures used by the Christian Church,—and to confound the time of Christ's coming. This was easy to be done through their Sanhedrim, who controlled all Jews. * * * In the 2d century great changes were made in the Hebrew. For, the new Greek translations of Aquila (A. D. 128), Theodotian (185), and Symmachus (200) vary much from the Septuagint. In this corrected Hebrew the whole chronology was shortened.

"Few Christians understood the Hebrew, so that it was easy to corrupt it; and most Hebrew copies were lost at the destruction of Jerusalem, and the destruction in the reign of Hadrian. Then Aquila was employed to get up a new translation (in A. D. 128), and this was the only reason for it. Epiphanius (*De Mensa, p. 171*) says that

Aquila perverted the Hebrew text to invalidate the prophesies concerning Christ, etc. It was promoted by the false Christ that the Jews then got up. Justin Martyr (A. D. 142) mentions several instances of the altering and erasing of prophesies concerning Christ in the lxx.

* * * Abul-Pharagius is very express in charging the Jews with this mutilation for this purpose.

"Eusebius followed a groundless Jewish tradition, including the foreigners in the reigns; which led to error of opinion concerning this period. The I Ki. vi: 1, has been corrupted by the Jews, and the ' 480 ' was not known to the ancient Jewish and Christian writers. Eusebius is the first that mentions the 480. * * * Very likely the 480 was inserted in I Ki. vi: 1, to support the 'Jewish tradition' mentioned by Eusebius, of foreigners included in the reigns, and as a contrivance to shorten the chronology, getting it nearly as in the Lxx before Eusebius (viz., 440). But there was no number there known by Paul or Josephus, either in Greek or Hebrew. It was introduced no later than the 3d century. For Origen cites the text I Ki. vi: 1, leaving out all that part. Nor is it in the parallel place of Chronicles. And Panadorus (A. D. 400) found fault with Eusebius for this. Also Syncellus." (See Periods A, B, § 20.)

See also Russel's Connection of Sacred and Profane Chronology (Wheeler's edition) Vol. 1, p. 79-81, which is cited by J. Schwartz in Bib. Sac., 1888, p. 447.

APPENDIX E.

For § 83.

The Reliability of Josephus.

§ 100. The learned Wm. Whiston (A. D. 1750), in highly eulogizing Josephus, says: "Let me set down the sentiments of, perhaps, the most learned person and the most competent judge that ever was, as to the authority of Josephus,—I mean of Joseph Scaliger (A. D. 1600) in his *Emend. Temp.*, p. 17: 'Josephus is the most diligent, and the greatest lover of truth of all writers; nor are we afraid to affirm of him, that it is more safe to believe him, not only as to the affairs of the Jews, but also as to those that are foreign to them, than all the Greek and Latin writers; and this because his fidelity and his compass of learning are everywhere conspicuous.'"

Eusebius (A. D. 320) often quotes from Josephus as reliable authority, and says (Hist. i: 11): "Since this writer, sprung from the Hebrews themselves, hath delivered these things in his own work, what room is there for any further evasion?"

Ambrose (A. D. 360) says of Josephus: "He is an author not to be rejected." "If the Jews do not believe us, let them at least believe their own writers. Josephus, whom they esteem a very great man, hath spoken truth. It was no prejudice to the truth that he was not a (Christian) believer, but this adds more weight to his testimony."

Isidore (A. D. 410) calls Josephus "a Jew of the greatest reputation, and one that was zealous of the law; one also that paraphrased the Old Testament with truth, and acted valiently for the Jews. He made interest give place to truth, for he would not support the opinion of impious men."

Sozomon (A. D. 440) says: "Now Josephus, the son of Mattathias, a priest, a man of very great note both among the Jews and the Romans, may well be a witness of credit as to the truth of Christ's history."

Cassiodorus (A. D. 510) calls Josephus "a man of great nobility among the Jews, and of great dignity among the Romans," a reliable source of "truth."

The Chron. Alex. (A. D. 640) cites Josephus as "a wise man among the Hebrews." And Malela (A. D. 850) calls Josephus "the philosopher of the Hebrews."

PART III.

The Pharaoh of The Exodus.

§ 101. We have shown the date of the exodus according to Scripture.* But does not modern research into Egyptian antiquities require a different dating? No. Egyptology is unable to determine the date of the exodus; and the Bible reckoning must stand upon its own merits. For, look at

CHAPTER I.

Egyptian Chronology.

(1) There is no Egyptian account of the exodus. This is conceded by all. Their monuments and inscriptions recorded achievements, not disasters. It is only incidental circumstances that can be picked out here and there, to indicate where the exodus *might have been;* and there are in Egyptian history several such possible epochs, hundreds of years apart, where such an event might well have come in. It is not

---

*Usher gives it as (B. C. 588+424=B. C. 1012+480th=B. C. 1491. We show it to be more probably (B. C. 587+424=1011+580=)B. C. 1591.

likely that exploration will ever bring any determination of the case. For,

§ 102. (2) The Egyptians had no chronology, as the Hebrews so exactly had. Hear what George Rawlinson, the learned professor, of Oxford, says upon the subject:

"The great defect of the monuments is their incompleteness. The Egyptians had no era. They drew out no chronological schemes. They cared for nothing but to know how long each incarnate god, human or bovine, had condescended to tarry upon the earth. * * * They omitted to distinguish the sole reign of a monarch from his joint reign with others. A monarch might occupy the throne ten years in conjunction with his father, thirty-two years alone, and three years in conjunction with his son; in an Egyptian regnal list he will be credited with forty-five years, although his first ten years will be assigned also to his father, and his last three to his son. * * * Only one calculation of the time which had elapsed between a monarch belonging to one dynasty and one belonging to another, has been found in the whole range of Egyptian monumental literature; and in that, which is the (apparently) rough estimate of 400 years, neither the *terminus a quo* nor the *terminus ad quem* is determined.

"The only monumental list which is chronological at all, the Turin papyrus (as to the 18th dynasty), exists in tattered fragments, the original order of which is uncertain, while the notices of time which it once contained are in many cases lost or obliterated. * * * These many and great defects of the Turin papyrus it is quite impossible to supply from any other monumental source. A casual correction of the numbers given in the papyrus may be made from the annals of the kings; but there is no possibility of filling up its gaps from the monuments, nor of constructing from them alone anything like a consecutive chronological scheme, either for the early, or the middle (Hycsos), or even the later empire. This is confessed by most Egyptologists, though not as yet very clearly apprehended by the general public.

"Brugsch says: 'It is only from the beginning of the 26th dynasty (B. C. 692) that the Egyptian chronology is founded on data which leaves little to be desired as to their exactitude.' Bunsen says: 'History is not to be elicited from the monuments; not even its frame-work, chronology.' Stuart Poole says: 'The condition of the monuments with regard to the chronology is neither full nor explicit.' Lenormant says: 'The greatest obstacle to the establishment of a regular Egyptian chronology is, that the Egyptians themselves never had any chronology.' Even for the last empire a monumental chronology is absolutely unattainable." (*Rawlinson's Hist. of Anc. Egypt, Vol. II, Ch. 12, p. 2.*) See here, Period E, § 160, etc.

§ 103. (3) Egyptology can not even assign for certainty the time of any Egyptian king before Solomon, or tell within 100 years when any pharaoh reigned. The only means of putting in order at all the reigns of those ancient pharaohs, is the list of dynasties given by Manetho (B. C. 304); and his figures in some cases are proved by the monuments unreliable; while it is not even agreed in what cases the dynasties overlap each other, or when the reigns are successive. Compare such a jumble of reckoning with the careful and orderly specification of reigns and synchronisms and eras given in Scripture, and judge whether it is possible for any theory of Egyptian dating ever to compete with or disparage a plain Hebrew date. Egyptian darkness will not eclipse Bible light.

§ 104. (4) The excavated monuments of Egypt do not determine definitely the time in which those ancient pharaohs lived. They merely tell, in a few cases, how long one particular king reigned, not at what period of time his reign was located. There are four inscriptions sometimes cited, in which the rising of Sirius, the dog-star, is mentioned in connection with the dating of the seasons; and attempts have been made to deduce therefrom, astronomically, the years wherein those mentions are made. But it has been shown that no date of any reign can thus be definitely ascertained. (See this fully discussed in my essay on "Monumental Inscriptions and the Egyptian years.) Egyptologists assign their chronology of the ancient Pharaohs in entire contradiction and defiance of such calculations.

§ 105. (5) There is but one other means of information, by which alone a probable starting point has been reached for the locating of the ancient pharaohs. It is the remark of Theon (A. D. 365), that the Sothic era, running 1460 years, was called "the era of Menophres." This tradition is positively all we know of the time when any ancient pharaoh lived. And Egyptologists are all agreed in accepting this as the one reliable dictum upon which the ancient Egyptian chronology must be based.

As A. D. 136-9 is known to be the ending of the Sothis period, when Sirius rose heliacally on July 20, Julian, the I Thoth of the Egyptian rotary year, its beginning must be at (1460 yrs.—A. D. 136-9—) B. C. 1325-2. And this is the date which Theon says the Egyptians call "the era of Menophres," one of the pharaohs. Who was he? Egyptologists almost universally are agreed that it is "Meneptah," the son and successor of "Rameses II the Great," and fourth king of the 19th dynasty of Manetho. So that, as the Sothic era B. C. 1325-21 is taken as coming in the reign of Meneptah, the 19th dynasty is assigned as beginning about B. C. 1477, by putting in the three previous reigns as given by Manetho, whose lengths of dynasties also confirm the same.

§ 106. For, as given by Geo. Rawlinson (Hist. Anc. Egypt, 1889, p. 7), "Tirhakah [II Ki. xix: 9] reigned 26 years, and we may therefore place his accession in B. C. 698. Thus far back the dates are as nearly as possible certain, and from here we are thrown almost entirely upon Manetho, who makes the rest of the 25th dynasty 22 or 24 years, *i. e.*, to B. C. 722 for the accession of 'So' [agreeing with II Ki. xvii: 4]. Then the 24th dynasty is 44 years (from Euseb. in Syn.), and the 23d and 22d dynasties are 209 years (from Afric. in Syn.), carrying us to B. C. 975 for the accession of Shishak [the year before Solomon's death, in agreement with I Ki. xi; 40], or B. C. 935 if, at dynasties 25 and 24, the 22 yrs. and 6 yrs. (from Afric. in Syn.) be substituted for the 24 yrs. and 44 yrs. (from Euseb. in Syn.) [Mariette makes it B. C. 980.] Then the 21st, 20th, and 19th dynasties are (from Afric.) 474 years, or (from Euseb.) 502 years; making, when added to 975, the 19th dynasty begin B. C. 1449 to 1477 (the latter being the Eusebian reckoning throughout)." So says Rawlinson (abridged). Prof. Lepsius and M. Mariette (in *Encyc. Brittan.*) reduce the 19th dynasty from 194 to 174, which will make its Eusebian 19th dynasty begin B. C. 1457. Wilkinson, Birch, and Lenormant reduce the 19th dynasty to 160 years, which will make it begin B. C. 1443.*

§ 108. We may, therefore, set B. C. 1477 to 1443 as the limits for the beginning of the 19th dynasty, as assigned by Egyptologists from the Eusebian reckoning of Manetho's dynasties—in close agreement with the date obtained from the Sothis period as beginning in the reign of Meneptah. For, that B. C. 1325–2, with only Manetho's two preceding reigns given as 125 years, will make B. C. 1450, before putting

---

* THE 19TH DYNASTY.

§ 107. The Eusebian reckoning of Manetho's dynasties, both in the Latin of Jerome and the Greek of Syncellus, puts the—

	B. C. 21st. 20th.	B. C. 19th.	B. C. Begin.
Begin. of 22d dy............	=975+130+178=1283+	194=1477	=19 dy.
Another copy...........		(202=1485)	
The Armen. of Euseb...............	172=1277+	194=1471	(1479)
Lepsius & Mariette reduce to.........		174=1457	
Mariette has 980, & thus	1288+	174=1462	
But with Euseb.................		194=1482	(1476)
Wilkinson, Birch, and Lenormant reduce to........................		160=1443	
Afric. in Syn. (in Anthon) has........	135=1240+	210=1450	
(in Rawlinson)..........		209=1449	
(another copy)............		204=1444	
An. Old Chronicle has..........+121+	228=1324+	194=1518	
Lepsius has the 961 (14 less than Euseb.)	1269+	174=1443	
Others reduce to 935 (from Afric., making....		+174=1417	(or less.)

in any reign of Meneptah himself or of Ramses I, which may carry us to B. C. 1477. Here, then, at B. C. 1477 to 1450, is the highest probability that Egyptology can reach, for a date of beginning the 19th dynasty, as a basis of the *doubtful* chronology within two hundred years each way from that time.*

CHAPTER II.

Theories of the Exodus.

§ 109. With the 19th dynasty thus located within certain limits, there have followed three sorts of assignment for the exodus; (1) as being just before, (2) as being over a century before, (3) as being over a century after the 19th dynasty began.

1. The Midway Assignment.

§ 110. The standard reckoning of all who follow the Bible, and accept "the 480th year" date (of I Ki. vi: 1) has for centuries put the exodus just before the 19th dynasty, viz., in B. C. 1491 (as given by Usher), as the "480th" year added to "the 4th year of Solomon." This throws the event into the last reign of the 18th dynasty, assumed to be the reign of the last "Amenophis" of Manetho (as given by Josephus, *Vs. Apion*, i: 15). He is understood as the one who *expelled the lepers* from Egypt, according to Manetho's account there given.

This Amenophis reckoning of the exodus is given by the great Egyptologist Champolion (A. D. 1830), and will be found fully explained in Anthon's Classical Dictionary (A. D. 1856), Art. *Egypt* and *Sesostris*. Champolion puts the exodus in the 3d year of that Pharaoh (Amenophis), leaving 17½ of his 19½ years reign to go before the 19th dynasty taken as begun in B. C. 1473, thus making up the B. C. 1491 to the exodus. Pharaoh himself was not regarded as drowned in the

---

* The only exception to this as the universally accepted foundation of dating for those times, is the recent scheme of Jacob Schwartz, of New York, put forth in the Bib. Sacra. for July, 1888, and in the London Theolog. Monthly for March, July and August, 1889. He throws out the 21st dynasty entirely (as overlapping the 20th and 22d)! and so brings down the 19th dynasty to begin at the Sothic era B. C. 1325-2; with Ramses I there put as the "Menophres" of Theon; because (he says) Ramses I had "a throne name" *Menpehora*, which serves for identification. But this novel scheme so violates the dynasties upon a bare assumption (to make out a theory), and is so contrary to all views of Egyptologists, that we hardly need to consider it here.

Red Sea; but Roselini, thinking he was drowned, assigned the exodus to the very close of his reign, putting the 19th dynasty that much earlier.

There is little in the surrounding circumstances or incidents of that period to encourage the assignment of the exodus there. The story told by Manetho of Egyptian lepers expelled by Amenophis has little to fasten it upon the Hebrews; and the imputation was justly repelled by Josephus. Besides, this whole understanding of Manetho's "Amenophis," the expeller of lepers, as being the king ending the 18th dynasty, has been long ago universally discarded. So that there is nothing left to sustain this dating of the exodus, save the bare Scripture number "480th year," which would put it there. This itself is an argument against the genuineness of that number. Therefore, we turn to

2. THE EARLIER ASSIGNMENT.

§ 111. When the Scripture number (in II Ki. vi: 1) is taken as more properly "580 years," it carries back the exodus 100 years further to B. C. 1591, *i. e.*, into the middle of the 18th dynasty, in the reign of Thotmes III or IV, or thereabouts. And the circumstances and surroundings there are much more consonant with the event than in the other place. The particulars in this respect we will give at a later stage of the inquiry. This fact itself is evidence that the longer reckoning of the Judges and the earlier dating of the exodus must have precedence, as the more probable of the two Scripture views, and more accordant with the teachings of Egyptology.

Among Egyptologists Wilkinson long ago assigned the exodus to the reign of Thotmes III. (See *Anthon*.) And others put it at the end of Thotmes IV, giving special reasons therefor. Recently, Jacob Schwartz, of New York, has fully and with much force argued out the certainty (as he thinks) that Thotmes III was the Pharaoh of the Exodus. (*London Theolog. Monthly, March and July, 1889.*) There is much to be said in favor of Thotmes III and IV, or their epoch, as the times of Hebrew oppression and release. But we will not expatiate here. For, we must mention

3. THE LATER ASSIGNMENT.

§ 112. Egyptologists, almost universally, in rejecting (as they think they must) the old standard or midway view of the exodus as just before the 19th dynasty, have fallen upon a much later and entirely unscriptural date, having no warrant in the Bible, but utterly opposed to its teachings. They have assigned it to about the Sothic era itself,

B. C. 1325-2, saying, dogmatically and often sceptically, that the exodus *must* have taken place (*if at all*) in the reign of Menepteh, near the last of the 19th dynasty.

This theory has taken root only within this last generation, but is now entirely in the ascendant, especially among German and sceptical explorers of monuments and inscriptions. It is too much patronized and deferred to, even by Christian scholars, as if it might assist in Bible investigations; whereas, like the most objectionable form of the "higher criticism," of which it is in fact a part, it repudiates not only "the 480th year" of the Scripture text, but all its other datings,—reducing the interval from the exodus to the founding of Solomon's temple ("if there were any exodus") down to about (1310—1010 = 300 years! or at most 350 years by shoving down Solomon 40 or 50 years. Modern Egyptology thus sets aside the whole Bible Chronology, as of no account; though some attempt *to make it over* arbitrarily to suit the alleged requirements of monumental research.

The 18th Dynasty.

§ 113. It remains for us to find to what point in the 18th dynasty the earlier or "580 years" reckoning (deduced from 1 Ki. vi: 1) will take us back. This is no easy task, because not only is the length of the 19th dynasty greatly disputed (as we saw), but the whole reckoning of the 18th dynasty, and especially the last part of it, is in the greatest confusion, as conceded by all. Manetho in Josephus (Vs. Ap. I, 15, 16) gives the 18th dynasty as having 18 reigns with 327 years (as added, or 393 as stated by Josephus). But modern Egyptologists cut off the last 6 or 7 reigns, or all but 200 years.

Says the *Encyc. Brittan.*: "Manetho's list is here in a very corrupt state. If the line ends with the accession of Ramses 1 [right after Orus as the 11th king], we *can make* a sum of not much over 200 years for the line." If we end thus with Orus and his alleged daughter, Manetho's list has 12 rulers, with 208 yrs. and 3 mo. Mariette has it 241 years (from B. C. 1462 to 1703), seeming to add in the next three reigns, which make up 241 yrs. and 11 months.*

§ 114. But all that can be said with safety is what Schwartz asserts: "The *three last* kings are simply duplicates or repetitions of dynasty 19, as nearly all Egyptologists are agreed." Or, he should

---

*Schwartz (in the *Lon. Theolog. Monthly*, p. 154) takes out the last three reigns, 81 years (he says 87), and the next five reigns, 49 yrs. 10 mo. (he says 49); but he adds in an extra "13 years" at Horus; so that he has (89+49 10-12—13—) 117 yrs. 10 mo. less than Manetho's total 327, leaving 209 yrs. 2 mo. for his 18th dynasty,—very nearly as given above.

rather say, *the three kings before the last* are duplicates.* The very last king given in Manetho's list, as if ending the 18th dynasty, viz., "Amenophis, 19 yrs. and 6 mo.," is the most inexplicable of all, and has given rise to great diversity of opinion. But we show elsewhere † that this last king (wrongly located by Josephus) was probably *mentioned incidentally out of place by Manetho*, who was here simply referring back to "Amenophis IV," whom he had not named before, because it was a rejected reign (as the monuments show) and contemporary with "Orus" or his successors.

There is a circumstance which shows that we are right in this explanation. "Manetho says that the chief adviser of his Amenophis (the expeller of lepers) was his namesake Amenophis, *the son of Papis*." (Josephus, Vs. Ap. I, 26.) Now "the monuments show that the principal personage in the reign of Amenotep III was, in fact, Amenotep surnamed Si Hapi, that is, son of Hapi or Apis." (*Schwartz, § 4.*) Schwartz infers from this that the final "Amenophis" named by Manetho is this Amenotep or Amenophis III. But we learn rather, that it was the hitherto unnamed "Amenophis IV" who had as adviser the aged namesake who had been his father's prime minister,—that it was he, the son, to whom Manetho refers back. The driving out of lepers will more appropriately fit this reign of Amenophis IV.

§ 115. So then, this final "Amenophis" of Manetho's list being taken as Amenophis IV, and not to be counted (because he was a duplicate in the times of Orus and his successors), ‡ we have the *three* preceding reigns, "Armais, Rameses, and Armesses Maiammon," as being duplicates of the brothers "Armais" and "Rameses" with their successor "Sethosis," who are here given (in Jos., Ap. I, 15) as beginning the 19th dynasty. And thus we have Manetho's 18th dynasty as ending after Orus, with four successors occupying 45 years, 9 mo. ‖ Add to these the preceding "Orus 36 yrs. 5 mo. + Amenophis (III) 30 yrs. 10 mo. and we have (by this list of Manetho in Josephus) a total of 113 years of this 18th dynasty, reach-

---

* The last four reigns are these: "Armais, 4 yrs. 1 mo.; Rameses, 1 yr. 4 mo.; Armesses Maiammon, 60 yrs. 2 mo.; Amenophis, 19 yrs. 6 mo.:" total 85 yrs. 1 mo.

† See my essay "In the Days of Horus," etc.

‡ The details concerning these boundary reigns of the 18th and 19th dynasties, are discussed more fully in my essay, "In the Days of Horus."

‖ § 116. This takes off (4 1·12 + 1 4·12 + 60 2·12 + 19 6·12—) 85 yrs. and 1 mo. from the 327 years of Manetho's list in Josephus; leaving his 18th dynasty there as 241 years, 11 mo. long (Mariette says 241 for 18th dy.), as follows:

ing back to the death of Manetho's "Thmosis" or Thotmes IV; so that the last year of Thotmes IV, was *the 114th year* before the 19th dynasty.

This will leave 241 years in the 18th dynasty, *just the amount which Mariette gives.* And the total of Manetho's dynasties (as given by Eusebius) from this point will go thus:

18th dynasty		241 yrs.	1718 B. C.
19th "	(from Euseb.)	194 yrs.	1477 "
20th "	"	178 yrs.	1283 "
21st "	"	130 yrs.	1105 "
22d "	"	about 160 yrs.	975 "
23d "	"	44 yrs.	815 "
24th "	"	44 yrs.	771 "
			727 " (E, § 166.)
		991st year.	

Put this with what Schwartz informs us (Letter, Apl. 16, 1893): "Manetho made a summary of all the years he had enumerated, from the expulsion of the Hyesos in the 5th year of Amasis, first king of the 18th dynasty [then beginning], to the invasion and conquest of the Ethiopians in the 6th year [or at the end] of Bocchoris, and gave the total as 990 years." What a wonderful confirmation is this "990," that our reckoning of Manetho (from Eusebius) is right! (See Period E, § 166.)

Probable Exodus Date.

§ 117. Now the B. C. 1477 of the Eusebian Manetho (above shown at § 106), as the beginning of the 19th dynasty + this 113 years (Eusebius) of the 18th dynasty = B. C. 1590 (-91), just the date of the exodus required by the Scriptures, with the I Ki. vi: 1, read as the "580

The 18th Dynasty.

In Jos. Manetho.		*Monuments.*	*(Rawlinson.)*
1. Alisphragmuthosis.		1. Aahmes.	
2. Thetmosis,	25 y. 4 m.	2. Amenophis I.	
3. Cheron,	3 y.	3. Thotmes I.	
4. Amenophis,	20 y. 7 m.	4. Thotmes II.	} 54 yrs. Schwartz 53 y. 11 m.
5. Amesses (sis.)	21 y. 9 m.	5. Hatesu (sis.)	
6. Mephres,	12 y. 9 m.	6. Thotmes III.	
7. Mephramuthosis, 25 y. 10 m.		7. Amenophis II. (over 30)*	
8. Thmosis,	9 y. 8 m.	8. Thotmes IV. (over 6 y.)	
9. Amenophis,	30 y. 10 m.	9. Amenophis III. (over 35)	
10. Orus,	36 y. 5 m. 10. Amen IV.	10. Amenophis IV.	
11. Acencheres,	12 y. 1 m. 11. Horus.	11. } Three	} "33 years" Chambers.
12. Ruthotes (bro.)	9 y. 12. Three } "About	12. } sons	
13. Acencheres,	12 y. 5 m. 13. other } a genera-	13. } in-law	
14. Acencheres,	12 y. 3 m. 14. reigns } ation."	14. Horus.	

241 y. 11 m. (Mariette 241.)

* But Rawlinson says, "a short reign of 7 or 8 years."

No. 4 of Manetho appears put back to 2. The yrs. of Nos. 9, 10 may be exchanged.

years," which we have shown to accord with Scripture requirement. This is a somewhat remarkable coincidence; for here we have the exodus brought exactly to the last year of Thotmes IV, where former writers had assigned the event; and this date we reached unexpectedly, without any theory, by simply adding up the numbers of Monetho as given in Eusebius and Josephus.*

§ 118. The four reigns following Orus (in Josephus Manetho), and occupying 45 yrs., 9 mo., are, in the *Encyc. Brit.*, called three reigns occupying "about a generation"; and in Chamber's Cyc. and Rawlinson they are put as three reigns *before Orus*, said (in Chamber's) to occupy "about 33 years," *i. e.*, 12 yrs., 9 mo. less than Manetho's amount. This would reduce the distance back to the death of Thotmes IV to (113—12¾=) 100 years, or to his accession 109 years; which latter from the exodus as B. C. 1591 leaves B. C. 1482 for the beginning of the 19th dynasty, the same as given by Mariette with Euseb.'s 194 substituted for his 174.† (See § 107.)

§ 119. On the whole, the most probable beginning of "the 580 years" taken as the date for the exodus (meant in I Ki. vi: 1) is *at the death of Thotmes IV*, reckoned as in B. C. 1590 or 91, where we have found it here (§ 117). Nothing can be brought against this date for the death of Thotmes IV, and it is *about* the date set by Egyptologists generally. There are, indeed, two or three monumental inscriptions, which, *in the way they have* been interpreted, seem to date even Thotmes III as late as B. C. 1470 or 50; and Schwartz has taken advantage of this circumstance to attempt the lowering of all the ancient Egyp-

---

* Of course, a number of variations can be made upon this reckoning, by taking, on the one hand, the different assignments for beginning the 19th dynasty, and, on the other hand, different lengths of reigns in the 18th dynasty. For instance, to make the exodus reach (9 8-12+25 10-12=) 36 yrs. 6 mo. farther into the 18th dynasty, *i. e.*, to the death of Thotmes III, would require the reduction of the 19th dynasty to (194—35½=) 158 or 9 years; and Wilkinson, Birch, and Lenormant do reduce it to 160 years. Then the 19th dynasty will begin (1477—35½=)1442 B. C.; and Lepsius has it 1443 B. C. Again, we might say (113th+9 8-12 =) 122 yrs. back to the *accession* of Thotmes IV for the exodus; and then (B. C. 1590—122=) 1468 B. C. at beginning of 19th dynasty; which is about what Mariette and the Armenian of Euseb.'s Manetho make it.

† Schwartz reduces the four last reigns of 45¾ yrs. to a mere 13 (of "Osasiph" taken as Orus); and besides these 32¾ yrs. of reduction, he drops 6 mo. (from the 25 yrs., 10 months in Manetho); so that he has 33¼ yrs. less than the (113+35½=) 148½, or only 115¼ yrs. back to his end of " Mephres" (or Thotmes III). And then his 115¼ yrs. back to *his* place for the exodus, really reach (by Manetho's numbers) back only to 2¼ yrs. before the 113 to the death of Thotmes IV, where *we* reach the exodus. Thus he and we have the exodus about the same distance back into the 18th dynasty.

tian chronology by some 150 years! and so to bring Thotmes III as the Pharaoh of the exodus in harmony with "the 480th year of I Ki. vi: 1. (See in the *Lon. Theolog. Monthly, March, 1889.*)

But we have shown (in our dissertation on *Monumental Inscriptions and the Egyptian Year*), that, by a more rational interpretation of those Sothiacal manifestations referred to in the inscriptions, there is no such late dating of those ancient Pharaoh's; and that the Egyptologists are right, when (almost without exception) they assign Thotmes IV to about the date we put him, as ending in B. C. 1590 or '91. Here then, in accordance with I Ki. vi: 1 (taken as "580"), is the most probable assignment of the exodus.

CHAPTER III.

Reasons Given for Making Meneptah the Pharaoh of the Exodus.

§ 120. We have now gone as far as Egyptian chronology, in its uncertainty, can carry us, toward the reaching of a *probable* date for the exodus. It must be remembered, as we showed at the start, that only a probable date can be expected from this source. And we have shown that the *midway assignment* of the exodus as near the beginning of the 19th dynasty, or at B. C. 1491 as in Usher (in accordance with "the 480th year") is now almost entirely abandoned. This leaves only two theories: (1) The *Later Assignment* of the Egyptian Meneptah as the pharaoh of the exodus, about B. C. 1320; and (2) Our *Earlier Assignment*, which we here have indicated as the most probable Scripture dating, in accordance with I Ki. vi: 1, as meaning 580 years, and which makes Thotmes IV the pharaoh of the exodus, B. C. 1591. The decision lies between these two theories.

What, then, we have now to do, is first to notice the arguments used by Egyptologists, in favor of their unscriptural assignment of Meneptah as the probable pharaoh of the exodus. These we find set forth most fully by Prof. Ebers (in the *S. S. Times, Apl. 30, 1887*).

§ 121. (1) Various Egyptian papyri ascribed to the times of Ramses II and his son Meneptah, refer frequently to "the city of Rameses" (supposed to be Tanis). Ebers says: "The men who were compelled to carry bricks as serfs are called 'Aperu' and 'Apuiriu' by the papyri. * * * These papyri would give conclusive evidence of the exodus, if it could be proved that the 'Aperu' were Hebrews. Chabas was the first to pronounce them to be Hebrews, and all his colleagues agreed with him, until H. Brugsch objected to the view [also Essenbehr and M. Maspero, says Rawlinson]. * * * Stude, on account of difficulties connected with the sounds of the words, maintained that the Egyptian name 'Aperu' and

'Apuiriu' was not that for the Hebrews." Ebers himself thinks it was. The Encyc. Brittan. says doubtfully: "If the identification were certain, we should have much reason for dating the oppression under Ramses II, bringing the exodus under Menepteh. The difficulties of this theory are not slight."

§ 122. The main objection against understanding the word 'Aperu' to mean Hebrews, which Ebers himself says "appears to be of great weight," is that "among the monuments discovered by Mariette at Abydos, there is one, which, although it very probably belongs to the time of the 13th dynasty, that is, a long time before the Hebrews could have emigrated to Goshen,—yet represents builders who are called 'Aperu.' So then, it is certain, that the 'Aperu' was a general name for such laborers, without any special reference to the nationality as being Hebrews. Moreover, the same class of 'Aperu' are named *long after* the exodus of the Hebrews "at the beginning of the 20th dynasty, when it is said that 2,083 of them lived under Ramses III, in Heliopolis, the biblical On."

There is, therefore, no particular identification of Hebrews in Egypt in the time of Ramses II and Meneptah, more than at other times. Such representations of enslaved laborers at work are found 200 hundred years earlier than that; and indicate Thotmes III as the Pharaoh of the Hebrew oppression, full more strongly than in the case of Ramses II. (See afterward, § 131.)

§ 123. (2) The recent excavation of the ruins of Tell-el-Maskootah by the famous Geneva Egyptologist, M. Naville. have convinced scholars that this is the treasure city "Pithom" spoken of in Ex. i: 11; and as this was built along with another city "Rameses" (supposed to be Tanis), it is argued, that they must both have been built by the Hebrews for Ramses II as the oppressor of the Hebrews. But, what if we do thus have the interesting evidence of inspection, that the Hebrew account of those building operations is true? That by no means shows *when* they built those cities; it may have been generations before Ramses II reigned. It is said that statues of Ramesses II were found at the uncovered ruins. But that may only indicate that he *rebuilt or enlarged* works first built generations before by the Thotmes-es; which we know to have been the case in many instances. "The fixing of their sites (the treasure cities built) has no bearing at all on the question of date." (*Major Conder, translating the tablets.*) There is here no evidence that the exodus took place in those late times. The only real arguments for that date are the following:

§ 124. (3) One of the cities they built is called "Raamses" (Ex. i: 11). Therefore it may be argued, this building must have been done by the Hebrews *after* the Rameses began to reign. So it appears at first thought. But notice, that the land of Goshen itself was called "Rameses." (Gen. xlvii: 6, 11.) Therefore, the city built (or improved) was called "Raamses," perhaps as meaning chief city of the *land* of Rameses; and the Ramses kings may have got that name from the region where they originated, not the reverse. Many think the use of this name in Genesis, and perhaps also in Exodus is by prolepsis. "Pithom and the city afterwards called Raamses." We have no assurance, that any one of the Ramesides had yet reigned when the "treasure city" was built.

§ 125. (4) Ramses II made several invasions into Syria, passing with his armies through Palestine, and making conquests there; all which (it may be argued) must have occurred before the Israelites took possession of Canaan, since their Bible history gives no hint of any such Egyptian invasion after the conquest of Joshua. This argument, not named by Ebers and not generally put forward, is really the only point of any weight seeming to favor the late assignment of the exodus after Ramses II, contrary to the Bible chronology. But there is in this circumstance no real collision between Egyptian and Scripture history.

For, the book of Judges is by no means a full history of those times, but only an outline of the eras that marked the Jewish progress, with a few only of the most striking events mentioned which particularly affected the Israelitish estate. Foreign affairs not definitely related to them, are entirely ignored. And the Egyptian invasion of Syria was such. The scene of conflict was on the Orontes, north of Lebanon. "Kadesh on the Orontes" was captured, which was headquarters of the Amorites, classed under the general term "Hittites." But this was a region not pertaining to Israel, and the war there did not trouble them.

§ 126. True, the Egyptian army "went home in triumph through Palestine," as Rawlinson says, and Salem (or Jerusalem) and one or two other towns then unpossessed by the Israelites, but held still by Canaanites, were captured on the way. But no harm was done to Hebrews, who are not even mentioned in the Egyptian accounts, perhaps because they only formed the rural population of the country, not as yet much congregated in cities. The route from Lebanon down past Jerusalem was the public highway for all nations from Mesopotamia to Egypt, and the march even of an enemy that way, in those early times, did not molest the Jews sufficiently to be described in their brief history, so long as they as a people were let alone.

The Jews seem to have had a prejudice against even noticing their old oppressors; and the Egyptians in turn seem to have been shy of searching out or troubling a people whose strange Deity had wrought them such havoc. Providence appears thus to have reared a barrier of moral influence, or superstition, between the two races, to preserve (as at first to separate) the chosen people, left so near to their former foes. It is only in such manner, that we can account for the striking fact that nothing is said about Egyptian affairs through all the Scripture history of over 500 years, from Joshua to Solomon,— filling the book of Judges and the two books of Samuel. Besides about nine references to the exodus (Jud. ii: 1, 12, and x: 11, and xix: 30, I Sam. iv: 8, and vi: 6, and x: 18, and xii: 6, and xv: 6), there are only two mentions of an individual as an "Egyptian" in the days of David (I Sam. xxx: 11-13; II Sam. xxiii: 21). Not another word about Egypt during the 500 years.

§ 127. The whole lower region from Migdol of Egypt up to the Dead Sea was conquered by the Egyptians, as well as the regions beyond Lebanon. But Israel remained unmolested, as under the sheltering wing of Jehovah; until at length, after the mutual prejudice and shyness of the early times of first separation had died away, Egypt at length became the frequent helper of Israel against other foreign foes; insomuch that the prophets had to warn them against too much "looking to Egypt" for help.

Canaan was for a long time full of unsubdued cities and fortifications of the aborigines, which Israel could not conquer, as the book of Judges shows (Comp. Deut. vii: 22)— and it was even a help to Israel for Egypt to pass through and subdue such places, though not a matter to record as part of their own history. To see how readily an Egyptian army might pass through Palestine, and even capture such a fortress hostile to the Jews, without causing them any disturbance, look at the case of the Pharaoh whose daughter in later times Solomon married. (I Ki. iii: 1, and ix: 16, 17.) We are told, that thereupon "Pharaoh, king of Egypt, had gone up, and taken Gezer, and burnt it with fire, and slain the Canaanites that dwelt in the city, and given it for a present (or dowry) unto his daughter, Solomon's wife. And Solomon built Gezer." This inroad of Pharaoh was certainly not despoiling but helping Solomon, though an entirely foreign affair within Solomon's borders, not a part of Solomon's own administration or history. In like manner, the earlier doings of Ramses II and his associates were a real (though unmeant) help to Israel, not needing any special mention.

§ 128. In the Chicago "Advance (April 28, 1892, p. 346). Prof. Sayce announces the important discovery from the monuments, that Ramses III (B. C. 1200) conquered the "country of Salem" and the "Springs of Hebron," etc., which were *afterward* the territory of Judah. Here we have another Egyptian inroad made into Palestine still later by 100 years than that of Ramses II; which proves conclusively, that the late putting of the exodus as in Meneptah's reign is open to the same objection as the earlier assignment,—so that these later intrusions into the land can not be offered against either view of the exodus.

Here is a leading authority: "The chief strongholds were occupied by the Canaanites, Hittites, Jebusites, etc., during Egypt's 19th dynasty; and are so represented on the monuments describing the attacks on them by Seti I and Ramesses I. The open country was held by the Amorites, against whose iron chariots Israel could not stand (Jud. i: 19); so the district from the south border northward is called in the monuments 'the land of the Amorites.' (Comp. Jud. v: 6,) 'the highways were not occupied. * * * the villages ceased * * * war was in the gates (of the strongholds). Was there a shield or spear seen among 40,000 in Israel?' Thus the Egyptian armies in traversing Syria would encounter no Israelites in the field, and would only encounter Israel's foes." (*Fausset's Bib. Cyc.*, 1880, art. "Egypt.")

J. Schwartz, Egyptologist, of New York, also strenuously urges the same view.

§ 129. There is, therefore, nothing in the contemporaneous history requiring the later date for the exodus which Egyptologists claim. And we have absolutely nothing in connection with Meneptah, to indicate him especially as the Pharaoh of the exodus. Indeed, that claim is founded almost entirely upon the fitness of his predecessor Ramses II to be the previous pharaoh of the *oppression*,—as is indicated in Miss Edwards' opinion (here § 156.) But we have seen that the monuments and inscriptions no more point out Ramses II than they do Thotmes III (over 150 years before), as the oppressor of the Hebrews. We therefore turn now to notice the indications which favor this last named view of Thotmes III as engaged in the Hebrew oppression, with Thotmes IV as the Pharaoh of the exodus.

CHAPTER IV.

Reasons Pointing to Thotmes IV as Pharaoh of the Exodus.

§ 130. (1) We have already seen that the Bible Chronology which clearly brings the exodus "580 years" from the founding of Solomon's temple, viz., in B. C. 1591, thus carries it just about to the death of Thotmes IV, as assigned by Egyptologists generally, in accordance with the true reckoning of Sothiacal inscriptions. This date, therefore, has the primary advantage of being *in accord with Scripture*, whereas the Maneptah date (about B. C. 1320) is directly opposed to all Scripture reckoning,—as strongly opposed to the "480" number of 1 Ki. vi: 1, as to any other number over 300 years.

§ 131. (2) The inscriptions give the most vivid exhibit of foreign slaves (or the "Aperu") in the time of Thotmes, driven to their brickmaking work. "In a chamber of a tomb in the hills of Abd-el-Quviah, there is a graphic representation of the making of bricks by captives of Thotmes III, many of whom show strong Jewish features." (*Brugsch*,

Hist. Egypt, I, 375.) The overseers are represented with sticks, and 'insist with vehemence on obeying the orders of the great skilled lord,' * * * and the overseer speaks thus to the laborers: ' *The stick is in my hand, be not idle.*' "Compare this with the Biblical account (Ex. v: 17), where we have almost the identical words of the overseeer; and there can scarcely be any reasonable doubt that this pictorial representation and Biblical account of the oppression refer to the same thing." (*J. Schwartz*, in *Theolog. Monthly, London*, March, 1889, § 14 a.) See the description of this in Geike's *Hours with the Bible*.

And yet, so learned a man as H. B. Tristam, D. D., L. L. D., F. R. S., in the S. S. Times, April 14, 1894, falls into the mistake of saying: "When *Rameses*, the great builder, appears, he compels the foreign (Hebrew) shepherds to toil in the *unaccustomed* work of brickmaking and bricklaying." (!)

§ 132. (3) Says Schwartz. (Theolog. Monthly, § 14 b): "To make the identification doubly sure, there is a curious fact brought out by Palmer (Egypt. Chron. I, 194, 195), as follows: 'The monuments supply another indication, approaching still nearer to a proof that he [Thotmes III] and no other is the Pharaoh of the exodus [rather of the oppression, say 50 years before]. For, in the mounds of Heliopolis, one of the cities, according to the Lxx, which were fortified by the labor of the Hebrews, many sun-burned bricks *bearing the stamp of Thotmes III* have been used,—which on being broken show that they were made without straw; whereas ordinarily the earth of which these bricks are made is held together by a mixture of chopped straw. It is impossible not to see how this singularity is accounted for by the Scripture.'"

§ 133. (4) It is quite evident, and is generally accepted by scholars, that Jacob removed to Egypt under the reign of the Hycsos, or "Shepherd Kings," and not long before the close of their reign: so that the rising of "a new king that knew not Joseph" was the coming in of the new 18th dynasty, in which the several Thotmes-es ruled. (Comp. Gen. xlvi: 34, and Ex. i: 8.) Now the stay of the Israelites in Egypt was but 215 years, as all the Jewish and ancient chronology is agreed, and as is absolutely required by the apostle's language in Gal. iii: 16, 17. This distance after the Hycsos entirely forbids so late a date for the exodus as the reign of Meneptah in the last part of the 19th dynasty, and it readily agrees with the end of Thotmes IV in the 18th dynasty as the exodus date; 80 years from which carry us back (by Manetho's numbers in Josephus) to 10 years after the death of Thotmes I for the birth of Moses in the times of oppression; and 40 years more carry us to the beginning of the 18th dynasty, 16 years after the death of Joseph, as the dynasty of the "new king that knew not Joseph."

Says the Encyc. Brittan. (Art. *Egypt*): "There is the remarkable occurrence of a name similar to that of Jacob, or identical with it, in the record of the conquests of Thotmes III. This may only be a reminiscence of Jacob, as M. de Rongè suggests. But it would be more natural to take it to indicate that the exodus was anterior to [or in times not far from] the time of Thotmes.

§ 134. (5) Geikè (in *Hours with the Bible*, Moses, ch. III) says: "The Bible history demands the continuance of *a long reign*" in those days of oppression; and this he uses as an argument for Rameses II as the oppressor. (But what does he mean by saying, "Moses on his return to Egypt after his 40 years in Midian found *the same king* still on the throne"! On the contrary, see Ex. ii: 23, and iv: 19.) Rather is this an argument for Thotmes III as the great and long-reigning oppressor. His reign was 54 years, as all assert from the monuments, in which he included the previous reign of his *sister*, and most likely the reign of his *brother* before her. It is a striking story, the history of this family, from Thotmes I to Thotmes IV, during a period of 90 years, the period of Egypt's highest dominion and supremacy, as all writers concede. Read Rawlinson's glowing picture of those kings, especially of Thotmes III, and see how fitted was this king with his family to be the great oppressor of Israel.

§ 135. The great Thotmes I, dying, left his throne to his three children, two sons and a daughter. The elder son first reigned as Thotmes II (for 20 years and 7 months by Josephus); then the daughter Hatasu reigned (for 21 years and 9 months, according to Manetho in Josephus), a large part of it with her younger brother as partner. Then that brother reigned alone as Thotmes III (for 12 years and 9 months more). The whole reign of the three children (54 years by the monuments) was a period of unparalleled supremacy and autocratic power, as well as of building operations on the grandest scale, with enforced slave labor. Especially was Thotmes III the most brilliant as well as the most daring of all the Pharaohs, his spirit being dominant from his very boyhood when his father died, and leading him to swallow up to himself all the achievments of his brother and sister before him.

Such a family, and such a dominating spirit in it, might well be the operator of the Hebrew oppression. The birth of Moses will come after the first 9½ of the 54 years reckoned to Thotmes III (when Hatasu, "Pharaoh's daughter," was beginning to assume authority with her first brother), and the remaining 44½ years reckoned to Thotmes III will extend beyond Moses' flight to Midian,—while the reign of his son Amenophis II for 25 years 10 months, and of his grandson Thotmes IV for 9 years 8 months, will carry us just 80 years to the Exodus as ending the reign of Thotmes IV in B. C. 1590 [91].

§ 136. (6) Queen Hatesu was well fitted to be the "Pharaoh's daughter" who brought up Moses. For already then, in her comparative girlhood, she began to be prominent as ruling with her brother; and before long, on his death, she took the reins of government, striving for a long time to keep down her younger brother, Thotmes III. She seems to have been without family of her own; but ambitious and somewhat unscrupulous, especially as she grew older in power. And she might well wish to adopt an heir (like the beautiful Hebrew boy), in the hope to leave the throne to him, instead of the brother she was striving to displace. This trio of rulers, the children of one great Pharaoh, would well be called among the people "the daughter of Pharaoh" and "the sons of Pharaoh," without need of further designation. And yet, the pious Moses, growing up, might well fly from such a despotic schemer's house, and refuse longer "to be called the son of Pharaoh's daughter."*

§ 137. Josephus gives the name of Pharaoh's daughter as "Thermuthis," and he gives the Manetho name for Queen Hatesu as "Amesses." But in Eusebius the name of Pharaoh's daughter is "Merris"; and Rawlinson (Hist. Anc. Egypt, p. 133) says, "Thotmes III married Hatesu-Merira." As this is, in its first part, the name of his sister, Queen Hatesu, so it may in full be her name, and may thus show that "Merira," or "Merris," as in Eusebius, was indeed "Hatesu-Merira" the queen, daughter of Pharaoh. It would seem that this family name was taken on by the brother's wife, or else that he is represented as marrying his own sister with whom he reigned, (a custom common in that family).†

§ 138. (7) Though the Egyptians seem to have carefully avoided giving any account of the Exodus, so disastrous to them, yet Manetho betrays hints of the truth, mixed fabulously in his somewhat confused

---

* "Professor Hechler, in his address before the Oriental Congress in London, on 'Egyptology and the Bible,' expressed his firm conviction that the Pharaoh of the Exodus (oppression) was Thotmes III and not Rameses II, and—that the princess who saved Moses from drowning was just such a person as Queen Makara Hatesu."—(*Boston Watchman, Oct., 1892.*)

† Schwartz (in Essay, Jan., 1890, P. II, p. IV) says, that Jewish tradition "preserved by Artapanas and Abulfaragius," makes "Pharaoh's daughter" to be *wife* instead of *daughter* of Thotmes I, and that her name in Artapanas is "Merrhis," but on the monuments "Amon-Merit" (Rawlinson says "Arhmes"), his own sister, daughter of Amenophis I; who (those authors say) married Chenophres, called Cheop by Manetho in Josephus, that is Chanera Tutmes I. "Her name Merit explains the 'Thermuthis' of Josephus and the Tremotisa of Abulfaragius; for MERT reversed = TREM-otisa." (*Schwartz.*) The daughter "Hatesu" may have derived the name "Hatesu-Merira" or Merris from her mother. Egyptian notables generally had several names.

narrative. He describes the Hycsos or "Shepherd Kings" as finally bargained with, and allowed to leave the country peaceably; while the monuments show them to have been forcibly expelled. He has thus mixed in with that affair a tradition of another departure actually by permission, viz., the Hebrew Exodus, not very long after the Hycsos removal. Moreover, he says that the very king who bargained with them to go in peace was named Thermosis or Thetmosis, (*Jos. vs. Ap. I, 14. 15*), the son or descendant of another king, Alisphragmuthosis; whereas, the monuments show that the expeller of the Hycsos was Aahmes, first king of the 18th dynasty, a predecessor of the Thotmes kings.

We here see that Manetho mixes with the Hycsos account the name of the subsequent Exodus Pharaoh," Thetmosis," whom Schwartz therefore supposes to be Thotmes III, but whom we are showing to be more probably his grandson, Thotmes IV.

Still further, Manetho, in his later attempt (here § 26) to identify the Hebrews with the "lepers" banished by Amenophis IV, does thus imply, that there was a vague tradition of the Jews having gone from Egypt some time during the Amenophis and Thetmos kings, which he was here mixing with a subsequent banishment of lepers, perhaps some leprous remnant of the Hebrews, left behind in their flight. All these vague and misleading hints from Manetho point to a real Hebrew Exodus, known to tradition but concealed in Egyptian history, and lying somewhere between the story of the "Shepherd Kings" and the story of the "lepers." All the above arguments indicate Thotmes III as Pharaoh of the oppression, while other indications point out Thotmes IV as Pharaoh of the Exodus.

§ 139. (8) The monumental history indicates that after Thotmes IV, there had been a loss of troops as well as of laborers and builders in Egypt, leading to great efforts to replace them. We find that the immediate successor of Thotmes IV (viz., Amenophis III), though engaged in the erection of several structures, yet refrained from the grand military movements which had characterized his predecessors. " His reign was not very military. He did not extend the power of Egypt, either in the North or the South. He was content to make raids against negro tribes, and to carry off into captivity hundreds of their numbers. But it is absurd to speak of him as a conquering monarch. I can not agree with Brusegh in this. His negro-hunts were certainly not great wars." (*Rawlinson, Anc. Egypt, p. 142.*)

To such straits of negro-hunting were the Egyptians reduced, to get slaves for their brick-making and building operations, when they had lost their Hebrew subjects; and to such ignoble exploits were the weakened forces of Egypt applied, when they had been decimated by the disaster at the Red Sea. In the subsequent reign of Amenophis IV, "there were only a few military expeditions" (*Rawlinson*), and many discords followed. "Egypt was still recognized as Mistress of Syria; but we have no evidence of tribute from Mesopotamia subsequent to Amenophis III." (*Id.*) Long afterward, in the reign of Rameses II, we are told: "In reality, he himself does not appear to have shown any remarkable military genius, or to have effected any important conquests. * * * His object rather was to obtain captives, vast bodies of foreign laborers being necessary for his numerous and gigantic building projects." (*Rawlinson*.)

§ 140. Still at it, we see, trying to make good the loss of the Hebrews. We see that Rameses II, instead of building his structures by *their* service, was scouring the world for prisoners of war to take their place, long since vacated by the Exodus. His weak successor, Meneptah, was engaged in disastrous wars, "and built no great edifice. He was vacillating, and had the name of appropriating to himself the work of former kings, by erasing their names and substituting his own. He received into Egypt as new settlers several tribes of Bedouins, who were desirous of exchanging their nomadic habits for a more settled life; and he established them in the rich lands about the city of Pithom." (So says Rawlinson.) Instead of being at all like the oppressing Pharaoh of the Exodus, he was a weak monarch, evidently trying to re-settle the land of Goshen, long since depopulated by the departure of the Hebrews.

Rawlinson thus describes the doings of those times: "One, and perhaps the main, result of Rameses' expeditions was, the acquisition of many thousands of captives, some Asiatic, some African, carried off from their homes by the grasping conqueror, whose main object this seems to have been." Says Lenormant: "Man-hunts upon a monstrous scale were organized throughout the whole country of the Soudan. The aim was no longer, as under the Thotmes-es, to extend the frontiers of Egypt. The principal or sole object was to obtain slaves. Nearly every year there were great razzias which started for Ethiopia and returned dragging after them thousands of captive blacks of all ages and both sexes, laden with chains. And the principal episodes of these negro-hunts were sculptured upon the walls of temples as glorious exploits." It was of course in connection with his passion for 'great works' that Rameses desired and obtained this vast addition to his store of 'naked human strength.'" (*Rawlinson, p. 163*. See the like given in *Geike, ch. III.*)

Thus were the Rameses kings occupied in filling Egypt with slaves, made necessary by the Exodus of the Hebrews *before this* in the time of the Thotmes kings.

§ 141. (9) The *new religion* introduced into Egypt at the expiration of the reign of Thotmes IV, indicates the awakening of a moral influence, such as would be likely to follow the marvelous plagues and Red Sea disaster, when Jehovah did "marvelous things in the sight of their fathers, in the land of Egypt, in the field of Zoan." (Psa. lxxviii: 12.) Amenophis III, the immediate successor of Thotmes IV, whose sudden overthrow at the Red Sea may have brought him unexpectedly to the throne, was the son of an Ethiopian mother (for the father was the first monarch except Aahmes who had married a foreigner); and he himself married a strange foreign wife, Tai, whose nationality can not be made out. Under her influence new and foreign ideas of religion were introduced in this reign, having more reference to one supreme Deity than had been usual to the Egyptians. It was a sort of sun-worship in a higher form, the "sun's disk" being adored as representing the great God; and hence the wife encouraging it is thought by some to have been from Arabia. Possibly, she was married as some pious waif pitched upon in the superstitious horror awakened at the flight and miraculous escape of the Hebrews.

§ 142. At any rate, this king proceeded to "favor changes in the state religion, which were looked upon as revolutionary," says Rawlinson. He must be viewed as having paved the way "for the fuller establishment of the new religion" in the reign of his son. For, "he instituted a new festival in honor of the Solar Disc, exalting one God only." The son Amenophis IV next ruled under direction of his foreign mother, and fully carried out the new religion. He was a singular character, with strange foreign physiognomy; and the new worship created two great parties, and convulsed Egypt for a long time. Horus was set up as a rival king, and after a generation or two, under the Rameses kings of the 19th dynasty, the old religion was at length fully restored.

It is not hard to see in all this religious awakening under Amenophis III and IV, following right after the father Thotmes IV disappears, the moral effect for a season of Jehovah's miraculous manifestations attending the Exodus. Must not such displays of divine power have produced just such a revival of the idea of one Supreme Deity to be adored?

§ 143. (10) There are individual incidents known in regard to Thotmes IV and his successor, which point to him as the probable Pharaoh of the Exodus. He himself patronized particularly the deity of the great sphinx; and he "set up between the paws of the sphinx a massive memorial tablet on which he recorded his dream, and no doubt the happy accomplishment of his enterprises; (*see Birch Hist. Egypt, Vol. I, p. 415*); it was recently uncovered by Dr. Lepsius. (Birch, p. 418.)" So says Rawlinson, p. 140. It is reported that the inscription on this memorial tablet breaks off abruptly, as if left for further record of exploits (presumably not obtained by reason of some disaster to him); and that no naming of this Pharaoh has yet been found, though the names of the kings before and after him are recovered. (See the account in Dr. Cummings' work, London. Also, in the published discourse of Dr. Bailey, Ottumwa, Iowa.)

At any rate, his career was short. "He reigned only 8 or 9 years," says Rawlinson; who remarks (p. 140): "It would seem that Thotmes IV was *not the eldest son*, or expectant heir of his predecessor, since he ascribes his accession to the special favor of the deity" of his favorite sphinx, "who appeared to him as he slept, and raised his thoughts to the hope of sovereignty." (*See Brusegh.*) Thus Thotmes IV being not a "first-born," was himself spared in that great slaughter (Ex. xii: 29), when "at midnight the Lord smote all the first-born in the land of Egypt, *from the first-born of Pharaoh* that sat on his throne, unto the first-born of the captive that was in the dungeon." And the authors above referred to think there is evidence that the successor, Amenophis III also was not a first-born son. That he was young, and called unexpectedly to the throne, would appear from his taking for his prime minister an older namesake, "Amenophis Hapu," his second cousin, the grandson of his own grandfather, Amenophis II, as Rawlinson shows, (p. 140), and as Manetho testifies. (*Jos. vs. Ap.* 1, 26.)

§ 144. (11) From the Exodus to the beginning of Ehud (Jud. iii: 15, 30) were 141 years, (see § 72); and these reach from the end of Thotmes IV regarded as the Pharaoh of the Exodus, through the remaining 113 years of the 18th dynasty (see § 115), and 28 years into the 19th dynasty, or to about 11 years of the joint reign of Rameses II with his father, according to the current reckoning of those kings. This allows 5 years for Rameses I (according to Manetho in Josephus) +12 for Seti I, to the beginning of joint reign for Rameses II, and then the 21st year of Rameses II, in which he concluded his expeditions through Palestine by his final treaty with the Hittites near Kadesh, of Lebanon, will carry us to the 10th year of Ehud's peace in Israel. But if the 21st year were that of Rameses' *sole* reign after 59 of his father (as given by Manetho), then that treaty of his does not come till the 57th year of Ehud's 80 years of peace.

Hence we may say, that our view of the Exodus brings the exploits of Rameses II in the region of Lebanon, somewhere between the 10th and 60th of Ehud's 80 years. And this location for them in the midst of that long period of profound tranquility to Israel, is the most fitting place that could be found. The "480th year" of 1 Ki. vi: 1, will bring these operations of Pharaoh through Canaan to come about the time of Joshua's conquest of the land; when it would be simply impossible to occur (with Israel so up in arms) without a renewal of the Exodus conflict, and some mention made in the history. But when, in disarmed repose, the Israelites were long settled to their quiet husbandry, in accordance with our "580th year" reckoning, Egypt's monarch might, with his army, pass through, and even capture heathen towns on the way, without a ripple of disturbance to the Hebrew nation, as we have shown before. (§ 125-129.)

§ 145. Such encroachments on their enemies would even be a benefit to the Jews; though they would scarcely give their old oppressor, Egypt, the credit of it in their history. So long as the Hittite confederacy about Kadesh was thus kept under by Egypt, so long they were kept from invading Israel. But when, by the final league secured, they were made somewhat independent of Egypt, then it was not long before, at the death of Ehud, their leader, "Jabin, king of Canaan, who reigned in Hazor," near Kadesh, (Jud. iv: 1-4, 10) began a 20 years' oppression of the Jews. And the captain or prime leader of Jabin's confederacy (v: 2, 13) was that very Si-Sar-a (Sisera) whose name is indicated in the exploits of Pharaoh a little before against this Hittite confederacy! (*Schwartz*.)

(NOTE. Schwartz (*in Essay, Jan., 1889, P. II., p. v.*), makes the invasion of Pharaoh to come still later, and to be a conflict with Jabin himself, in connection with Deborah and Barak. He cites a general of the Hittite monarch antagonized by Pharaoh as being called "Si-Sar-a." But Schwartz' further attempt to reconcile these events with the "480th yr.," by dropping out 150 years from Egyptian history, is opposed to all the teachings of Egyptologists.)

§ 146. (12) For the foregoing and other reasons, we think we are safe in saying, that Thotmes IV is a *probable* Pharaoh of the Exodus, with Thotmes III as a probable Pharaoh of the oppression. The Egyptologist Wilkinson put Thotmes III at the Exodus; so also Schwartz; but we (with others) look with more favor upon Thotmes IV as consummating the oppression and perishing at the Exodus, in B. C. 1590 [91]. Nothing is claimed but a *probability* in this or any other date; and we deprecate the fashion of talking dogmatically concerning any pagan reckoning in those days of such chronological obscurity. Professor Ebers himself says: "We begin by admitting that, among the narrative works of Egyptian literature, nothing has been found as yet, which refers indubitably to the historical event of the Hebrew Exodus." (*S. S. Times, Apl. 30, 1887.*) We add, that no such discovery is likely to be made. Why, then, should he speak so positively of being sure that the time of Meneptah is the true and only possible date?

Miss Edwards, the noted Egyptologist, is much more modest in her utterance, and there speaks doubtingly concerning that assignment. The era of Menemptah for the Exodus is in violation of all Scripture numbers. But the era of Thotmes IV, as argued above, is in exact accordance with Bible Chronology as we have unfolded it in our previous essay. We are therefore disposed to rest in this Bible Chronology, till something more tangible appears to call it in question.

POSTSCRIPT. April 15, 1893. All the foregoing was written years ago, without knowledge that the Tel-el-Amarna tablets threw any special light upon the subject. But now come testimonies as follows:

§ 147. Listen to a good authority: "Major C. R. Conder, the famous Palestinian explorer and scholar, has made a translation of the *Tel-el-Amarna Tablets* discovered in 1887, at the site of the ancient Arsinoë in Egypt. They date from about 1480 B. C., and are written to the king of Egypt and some of his officials by Amorites, Philistines, Phœnicians and others, and include accounts of the conquest of Damascus by the Hittites, of Phœnicia by the Amorites, and of Judea by the Hebrews. Major Conder has endeavored to make an accurate translation, with no thought of supporting any particular theory of interpretation. He dissents sharply from Dr. Brugsch and the now fashionable theory which places the conquest of the south of Palestine by the Hebrews in the time of Seti II [or Meneptah], but claims that the tablets represent the conquest as much earlier, and as contemporaneous with the dates named in the Bible." (*Boston Cong'ist, Apl. 13, 1893.*)

"Major Conder contends that the Exodus had already occurred (at the time of the Tel-el-Amarna tablets), and that the Israelites were established in the mountains of Palestine when the correspondence occurred, in 1480 B. C." (*The Thinker," June, 1893, Christian Lit. Co.*)

"The Tel-el-Amarna tablets are composed of letters written from Palestine at the time of the Exodus by some of the very men named in the book of Joshua. The political condition of the land (and it is a most peculiar one) is the very condition pictured in Joshua. The name of the country and the names of the adjacent territories in these letters are identical with those in the Pentateuch." ("*Truth,*" *May, 1894, p. 241, Revell Co.*)

§ 148. "In 1888 at Tel-el-Amarna, half way between Thebes and Memphis, 100 miles south of Cairo, a large number of clay tablets were discovered, first by a peasant woman, at the site of the palace of Amenophis IV, on the east bank of the Nile. (See Prof. Jastrow's article in Journal of Bib. Lit., Vol. xi, 1892.) Some of these tablets are letters from Palestine, dated about B. C. 1400 to 1500, and five or seven are from Jerusalem, which mention menacing danger from the gradual encroachment from the Habiri, which Dr. Zimmern and others regard as none other than the Ibrim or Hebrews; either the descendants of Abraham remaining in Palestine, or (if the Exodus was in 1491) the Hebrews under Joshua taking possession of the promised land, as is far more probable. These letters tend to confirm the ordinary (Bible) date." (*Dr. Peloubet, in the Advance, May 3, 1894.*)

No! we remark, not to confirm the "ordinary" dating, 1491, but certainly to confirm our revised date, 1591. We have shown (at § 115) that the last year of Thotmes IV was 113 years before the 19th dynasty of Egypt, or B. C. 1591, and that Amenophis began 31 years later, in B. C. 1560, not reigning in "B. C. 1480," as the "Thinker" gives it above. The B. C. 1440 to 1450, where Peloubet would put Amenophis IV is down in the 19th dynasty; and it is not possible for that Pharaoh to be got down to so low a date as this, by any means, except the revolutionary and violent means of Schwartz. (See § 108, note.) The 40 or more years by which the Assyriologists reduce Shishak will not do it.

§ 149. Therefore, since Amenopolis IV reigned from B. C. 1560 to 1540, his reign was just in the days of Joshua, who (by our "580 years'" reckoning) began in (B. C. 1591—40=) 1551 B. C. So that the Tel-el-Amarna tablets were written in these very first seven years of Joshua, wherein he was taking possession of the promised land," *i. e.*, when the "580 years" are taken as the true Bible reckoning. But, taking the "480th year" of 1 Ki. vi: 1, the tablets were written one hundred years before Joshua, who in that case began (B. C. 1491—40=) 1451 B. C. Hence the certainty that these tablets do *confirm the Bible date*, not by the "ordinary" method of Usher with the 480th year, but with our 580 years' reckoning above.

Now mark! Here is a *demonstration from the inscriptions* of B. C. 1591 as the Exodus date, *just as we proved it from the Scriptures before knowing anything about this monumental proof?* Is not our unbiased result thus completely corroborated?

PERIOD C.—THE PATRIARCHS.

PART I.

From the Birth of Abraham to the Exodus.

§ 1. We next examine the period from the birth of Abraham to the Exodus of Israel from Egypt. In Ex. xii: 40, 41, we read as follows: "Now the sojourning of the children of Israel, who dwelt (or sojourned) in Egypt, was 430 years." This is the correct rendering as given in our King James Bible: and its statement is, not that Israel *dwelt in Egypt* 430 years, but that the whole "sojourning of" God's people (the Israelitish dwellers of Egypt) lasted 430 years. The Jews always understood this "sojourning" as covering all their unsettled state without a land of their own; particularly the time from the promise of Canaan to their going to take possession of it—that is, from Abraham's arrival in Canaan to the Exodus. All this time they "confessed that they were strangers and pilgrims on the earth." (Heb. xi: 13; Gen. xv: 13, and xvii: 8, and xxiii: 4, and xxviii: 4, and xxxvii: 1, and xlvii: 9.)

§ 2. Josephus very distinctly explains the matter. (Ant. 2, xv: 2), "They left Egypt in the month Xanthicus [Nisan], on the 15th day of the lunar month; four hundred and thirty years after our forefather Abraham came into Canaan, but two hundred and fifteen years only after Jacob removed into Egypt." The 215 years thus allowed to the patriarchs before Jacob's going to Egypt, is found to be the exact time given by Scripture. Thus: from Abraham's arrival at 75 years of age to Isaac's birth, 25 years + Isaac 60 at birth of Jacob + Jacob 130 when reaching Pharaoh = 215 in all. (Gen. xii: 4, and xxi: 3, and xxv: 26, and xlvii: 9.)

§ 3. After the 430 years had advanced about 10 years from Abraham's arrival in Canaan, God appeared to him and foretold how his numerous seed should become bondmen in Egypt; with the definite statement (Gen. xv: 13), "They—that is, Egyptians—shall AFFLICT them four hundred years." This 400 years affliction, of course, ended at the Exodus, along with the 430 years of sojourning. So that, it commenced 30 years later than the sojourning, that is, when Abraham had been 30 years in Canaan. Then Isaac was 5 years old, and (soon after being weaned) was mocked at by Ishmael, whose mother was Egyptian, (Gen. xvi: 1, and xxi: 8-14); and this was looked upon as the beginning of Egyptian affliction,—first from Ishmaelites (who sold Joseph into Egypt), and then from full-blooded Egyptians themselves. Josephus says (Ant. 2, ix: 1), "four hundred years did they spend under these afflictions;" and this language, though obscured by its position in the midst of the bondage, is meant to cover the whole period of affliction to Abraham's seed, beginning with Isaac at the mocking by Ishmael.

§ 4. Such was the understanding of Josephus and of all Jewish writers, both in ancient and in modern times, as seen in the Jewish Calendar and Chronology of the present day. And such is the reckoning given by the New Testament authorities, Paul and Stephen, and by all the church fathers down the ages. No other view was ever taken of the matter, and no longer estimate of the time spent in Egypt was ever dreamed of, so far as we can learn; until, in the present generation a few persons have decided, that the "430 years" were *all spent in the Egyptian bondage*,* and have thus increased the time from Abraham to the Exodus by 215 years.

§ 5. This new theory has arisen mostly from archaeological students and others, who, having first reduced the true 580 years period between the Exodus and the Temple to "the 480th year" of I Ki. vi: 1, wrongfully taken as genuine, have ended with rejecting that 480th year altogether, claiming (as almost all Egyptologists now do) that the interval was only about 350 years. This *loss* of over 200 years from Solomon's Temple back to the Exodus, leads them to seek in offset an *addition* of over 200 years before the Exodus, in order to restore Abraham to about his right place (near 2000 B. C.), where Egyptology itself requires him to be.

§ 6. But this pushing down of the Exodus to a 215-year later date, by putting the Scripture "430 years" as all spent in the Egyptian bondage, can not be sustained as true Scripture chronology. It is true, the Bible revisers have unfortunately encouraged this new theory, by adopting the Septuagint method of translating this Ex. xii: 40, thus: "Now the sojourning of the children of Israel WHICH THEY sojourned in Egypt, was 430 years," in place of our King James' rendering, "Now the sojourning of the children of Israel, WHO sojourned in Egypt, was 430 years." But, when the Lxx mistakingly so translated, knowing that this rendering gave a false impression of the whole time as if spent in Egypt, they felt necessitated to append "in Egypt *and Canaan*," to save the truth of the passage. And the Samaritan text

---

* So the Bib. Sacra., April, 1890, p. 291.

has the same, only with inverted order, "*in Canaan* and Egypt." Scott says of this gloss, "this is merely a *comment*, though a just one." And this comment of both those earliest versions proves conclusively that such a gloss is necessary, whenever the text is *so rendered*. But unfortunately the revisers have so rendered without putting in the required comment of the Lxx and Sam. to prevent mistake. It is plain, that our King James' rendering is the true reading when without comment inserted; and that there is really no encouragement in the passage for the modern notion, that all the 430 years were spent in Egypt. This is forbidden not only by all Jewish and Christian authorities, as before said, but especially by the inspired authorities of the New Testament.

§ 7. Paul's language (in Gal. iii: 16, 17) is this: "Now to ABRAHAM and his seed were the promises made. * * * And this I say, a covenant [of promise] confirmed beforehand by God, the law, which came four hundred and thirty years after, doth not disannul, so as to make the promise of none effect." This is perfectly decisive testimony, that the 430 years extend from "Abraham" to the giving of the law immediately after the Exodus. But the new theorists try to make the here-given "430 years *after*" to mean "after Jacob," not *after the covenant* of promise to Abraham, as it reads. This is preposterous. The apostle argues that a covenant-promise *so long standing* fully ratified, could not be nullified by a law coming *so long afterward*. Of course, he takes the *earliest* establishing of the covenant-promise, in order to express *as long a time as he can*; not the "400 years," but the full "430 years" back to Abraham's coming to Canaan, when the covenant-promise was first established.

§ 8. How unreasonable to suppose him pushing down his reckoning over 200 years less, at Jacob's coming to Egypt, when no such covenant-promise was inaugurated! If he could have said "over 600 years after" (as this new theory makes it), would he have limited it to just "430 years"? The apostle speaks distinctly of the Abrahamic promise as the *gospel* promise, "in Thee and Thy seed *shall all the families of the earth be blessed*;" which was given to Abraham at his first coming to Canaan (Gen. xii: 3), and we have no account even of the repetition of that *gospel* form of promise at Jacob's coming to Egypt. (xlvi: 3.) How unfit a dating place for it was this latter event, especially in the use which Paul was making of the date. It is plain as anything can be, that *Paul thought* the "430 years" was the age-length of the promise, dating from Abraham's coming to the giving of the law; whether he was correct in that thought or not. And it is not for us to deny the inspired accuracy of the apostle's statement.

§ 9. So, also, Stephen (in Ac. vii: 6) rehearses Gen. xv: 13, giving the "400 years," not as all years of the "bondage," but as the time of *affliction* wherein the alien nationality should "entreat them evil." Put the New Testament statements with those of Josephus and all other authorities, as well as the tenor of the Hebrew Scripture itself, and we find no warrant for the new theory of 430 years in Egypt. For, one token of Scripture is, the divine statement at Gen. xiii: 16, that "in the *fourth generation* they shall come hither again,"—that is, the bondage shall continue only into the 4th generation. Now, in our essay on "The Generations of Matthew i," (see our treatise on "The Chronology of the Judges, Period D, § 6), we have shown that a "generation" then meant simply 70 years, the appointed age of man (Psa. xc: 10). So that, "in the 4th generation" meant "in the 4th 70," *i. e.*, after (3×70)=210, or in 215 years.

§ 10. With this agrees the fact, that the four generations are expressly assigned by the sacred writers, with *four names* of father, son, grandson, and great-grandson, as in certain cases covering the time of the bondage, 215 years. (See Matt. i: 3.) This could not be if the bondage were 430 years; as is well shown in the Bib. Sacra (April, 1890, page 291). "The names, which are found without deviation in all the genealogies are—from Jacob--Levi, Kohath, Amram, Moses. (Ex. vi: 16-20; Num. iii: 17-19, and xxvi: 57-59; 1 Chron. vi: 1-3, 16, 18, and xxiii: 6, 12, 13.) Now unquestionably Levi was Jacob's own son. So, likewise, Kohath was the son of Levi, and born before the descent into Egypt (Gen. xlvi: 11). Amram also was the immediate descendant of Kohath. It does not seem possible, as Kurtz proposes, to insert missing links between them." All this is well said by Prof. Green in the Bib. Sacra.

§ 11. And we add, it is scarcely believable that any "missing link" can be inserted between Amram and Moses, as Prof. Green there tries to do. The record is this: Ex. vi: 20, "And Amram took him Jochebed his father's sister to wife, and she bare him Aaron and Moses." Num. xxvi: 59, "And the name of Amram's wife was Jochebed, the daughter of Levi, whom her mother bare to Levi in Egypt: and she bare unto Amram, Aaron and Moses, and Miriam, their sister." 1 Chron. vi: 3, "The children of Amram, Aaron and Moses and Miriam." Ch. xxiii: 13, "The sons of Amram, Aaron and Moses." Lev. x: 4, calls Amram's brother "Uzziel the uncle of Aaron," which also makes Amram the father of Aaron. Language could not express more explicitly than do all these passages, that the father of Aaron and Moses was Amram.

§ 12. And the ages of the successive parents show the same. At Ex. vi: 16-20, we are told the ages, thus: Levi lived 137 years, his son Kohath, 133, his son Amram, 137, his son Moses at the Exodus was 80 years old. We will say, that 65 years after the descent into Egypt Kohath begat Amram, and 70 years afterward Amram begat Moses;

then we have in Egypt, Kohath 65 years + Amram 70 years + Moses 80 years = 215 years in all to the Exodus.* Here we have very simply "the 4th generation" of God's promise (from Levi, the first to enter Egypt), with three generations or average 70's of lifetime between them. And does it not look plain and rational, that in the 215 years of stay, with successive parents living so long as these, this actual case occurred, of only four generations in succession?

The four successive lives in this case covering the whole time, would not prevent a greater number of lives in most cases occupying the time; even *ten* successive lives, of 21 years each at the birth of a son, might occur in the 215 years of bondage, as in the genealogy of Joshua. (I Chron. vii: 23-27. Prof. Green here wrongly reads *eleven* generations.)

§ 13. There are four difficulties in explaining Amram as *not* the father of Aaron and Moses: (1) We are told in two different books, that "Jochebed bare unto Amram, Aaron and Moses." (2) In two places we read, "the children of Amram, Aaron and Moses." (3) We are expressly told that Amram's brother was "the uncle of Aaron." (4) If at Ex. vi: 20, we make Aaron and Moses only remote *descendants* of Amram, we shall have to change ver. 21 and 22 in the same way, making "the sons of Izhar" and "the sons of Uzziel" to be only their remote *descendants*; which is supposing a very complex and unlikely combination of unusual terms here heaped up. Now any one of these variations of meaning may sometimes be found in Scripture, as Prof. Green has well shown. But the combination of all of them in such profuse unnaturalness upon all the varied mentions of this one case, is altogether beyond belief. It would never have been dreamed of, but for the desperate effort to make out 430 years of Egyptian bondage, by enough "missing links" imagined in the genealogy to make that possible.

§ 14. Prof. Green mentions one objection against the shorter bondage of only 215 years; namely, that in Num. iv: 36, the census of the adult male Kohathites gave "2750" of them at the Exodus,—and one man (Kohath) could not have originated this number, if he were only the grand-father of Moses,—and Amram, one of the four sons of Kohath (iii: 27), "could not have originated one-fourth of this number (or 687) in Moses' own days," if Moses were his son. So says Prof. Green. But look at the figures already given. With Amram 70 years old when his son Moses was born, we have (70+80=) 150 years from

---

* The Jewish historian Demetrius (B. C. 220) puts the birth of Amram 57 years after the descent into Egypt, and the birth of Moses 78 years afterward; so that he has 57+78+80=215 years. (*See Chron. Antiq. of Jackson, page 119.*)

Amram's birth to the Exodus. At the age of 30 each father might have 5 *sons* (and as many daughters); so that in (4 times 30 or) 120 years there might easily be $5 \times 5 \times 5 \times 5 = 625$ males; and in 30 years more (making up the 150 years to the Exodus), there might be 625 male adults, the youngest of them 30 years old. An average of 5 2-10 sons each will give 731 at the end; which is more than the 687 required.

§ 15. Again: If each father at the age of 37 years had 5 sons, then in (5 times 37 or) 185 years there might easily be $5 \times 5 \times 5 \times 5 \times 5 = 3125$ males) and in 30 years more (making up the 215 years of bondage), there might be 3125 male adults, the youngest of them 30 years old; and all coming from one man (Kohath) beginning at the descent into Egypt,—whereas only "2750" are required by Scripture.

Once more: If each father at the age of $32\frac{1}{2}$ had 5 sons, then in (6 times $32\frac{1}{2}$ or) 195 years there might easily be $5 \times 5 \times 5 \times 5 \times 5 \times 5 = 15{,}625$ males; and in 20 years more (making up the 215 years of bondage), there might be 15,625 male adults, the youngest of them 20 years old; and all coming from one man at the descent into Egypt. So that, if there were only 40 males to begin with, (and there were more than that, see Gen. xlvi: 8-27), there might easily be at the Exodus ($15{,}625 \times 40 =$) 625,000 male adults over 20 years of age. Whereas, only "603,500" are required by Scripture. (Num. i: 46.)

§ 16. Such is the rational census of that prolific people under the helping hand of God. (See Ex. i: 19, 20.) This completely removes, not only Prof. Green's objection in the case of the Kohathites, but also the popular objection often urged against the bondage of only 215 years,—that this was too short a time to produce such a population. Thus have we fairly set aside the only objections ever suggested against the 215 years reckoning of the Egyptian bondage; and the "430 years" of "sojourning" are thus left covering the whole interval from Abraham's arrival in Canaan to the Exodus out of Egypt,—just as St. Paul, and Josephus, and all other authorities taught it from the first. This makes the whole period ($75+430=$) 505 years from the *birth* of Abraham to the Exodus; as given by all ancient authorities.

§ 17. We found the Bible date of the Exodus to be B. C. 1591; which Josephus has 12 years too large, or B. C. 1603, on account of his 592 years after the Exodus instead of the right 580 years. Thus we have the scriptural date for the birth of Abraham as B. C. ($1591+505=$) 2096 B. C.; which Josephus increases 12 years to B. C. 2108 [7 in the Antiq.]) +his post-exilian error of 57 years.

Thus far back the chronology of human history is pretty well assured: Abraham born B. C. 2096 (by Usher, 1996).

§ 18. For a study of Jacob's stay in Haran (as 40 not 20 years), see Period D, Appendix C, § 96-99.

PART II.

WHEN WAS JOSEPH SOLD?

A CRITICAL STUDY OF GENESIS XXXVII.

[Reprint from the Bibliotheca Sacra, July, 1887.]

§ 19. Without troubling ourselves concerning the "higher criticism" of Genesis, we all have long acknowledged that its events are not in all cases recorded in exact chronological order. Gen. xxxvii: 2, 14. "Joseph being 17 years old," Jacob "sent him out of the vale of Hebron, and he came to Shechem." I judge that this account of Joseph belongs directly after xxxiii: 18, with only xxxv: 1-5, (9-15), 27 between. The writer at xxxiii: 18, having mentioned "Shechem," thinks best to go on and tell *all* about the residence there at a later date, leaving the account of Joseph's departure to come near to the whole story of his life, as a closing up of the book.

ORDER OF EVENTS.

§ 20. The real order of events seems to be this: Jacob found the vicinity of Shechem to be a good country for his flocks; and, therefore, either at first or afterward, "bought a parcel of a field where he had spread his tent" (xxxiii: 19) for a residence there. But he now tarried not long, for he must reach his father Isaac, whom he had not seen for so long. So he passed on to Bethel (xxxv: 1-5), where God appeared to him again (9-15), and he soon reached his father at Hebron (27). Isaac seems to have moved thither from Beer-sheba, further south, where Jacob left him in going to Haran (xxviii: 10).

Here Jacob resided near his father for some years, but sent his flocks back (more or less) to the better pasturage about Shechem; where, in charge of his sons, a part of the flocks may have lingered even from the first. When Jacob had been from Haran 10 or 12 years, the departure of Joseph to Shechem from "the vale of Hebron" took place, as in chapter xxxvii.

Soon after the loss of his son, Jacob himself seems to have moved to Shechem, where he had already bought a home (as we saw) in order to be nearer the flocks, and nearer his sons who were getting settled in life; perhaps, also, with a secret hope of yet finding Joseph, who had been so mysteriously lost in the wilds near Shechem. (xxxiii: 18-20.)

But the trouble that there occurred about his daughter Dinah (ch.

xxxiv) obliged him to leave the country (ver. 30); and he again moved southward, and came to Luz or Bethel once more (xxxv: 6, 7). Here "Deborah, Rebekah's nurse, died," (v. 8); which shows that she was now living with Jacob, having been taken by him from Hebron, when he moved north to Shechem, his mother Rebekah being then dead.

§ 21. Passing on still further southward, Jacob came to Bethlehem, where Benjamin was born, and his mother Rachel died (v. 16-20); then, after a stay "beyond the tower of Edar," (v. 21-26) he again reached Hebron (v. 27), about 20 years after leaving Haran; where about 5 years afterward his father Isaac died. (v. 28, 29.) For, Isaac's age being 180, Jacob, who was born when he was 60, must now be 120 years old, which makes Isaac's death to be 10 years before Jacob went to Egypt (xlvii: 9), *i. e.*, at the very time when Joseph stood before Pharaoh at 30 years of age (xli: 46), having been in Egypt 13 years. During those 13 years since Joseph was lost at Shechem, the events we have been reciting (from xxxiii: 19, to xxxv: 29), must evidently for the most part have taken place.

The funeral of Isaac brought together Jacob and Esau (xxxv: 29): and this leads the writer to go on and give the genealogy of Esau's descendants (Ch. xxxvi). But, having Jacob now back at Hebron, with most of the history disposed of except what relates to Joseph, the writer now feels ready to go back to Jacob's earlier residence here, when he sent off Joseph from Hebron to Shechem; beginning (here at Ch. xxxvii) that wonderful story of Joseph's life, which forms the finish and the crown of the book of Genesis. But, since quite a gap of time intervenes between the loss of Joseph in Shechem and the discovery of him in Egypt, the writer artistically allows one chapter (the xxxviii) to come in and fill the gap, with the story of Judah, which began about the time Joseph disappeared. This single episode does not unduly interrupt the history of Joseph, or draw attention from it: therefore it is left here in its order, although other intervening events have been disposed of first (in ch. 34-36), so as to be out of the way of Joseph's continuous biography.

Argument for This Order.

§ 22. Jacob upon coming from Haran, must have *soon* reached his father at Hebron. For,

(1) Nature calls for such a meeting of the family, which was indeed the very object of the journey (xxxi: 3, 13, 18, 30), "for to go to Isaac his father;" as Laban said to Jacob (30), "thou would'st needs be gone, because thou sore longedst after thy father's house." Says Scott: "It should not be concluded from the silence of Scripture, that Jacob had not before this (xxxv: 27) visited his father;" which *only recorded* visit is, in the order of narration, at least *twelve years* (probably 20) after the arrival in Canaan.

(2) The fulfillment of Jacob's vow (xxviii: 22), as recorded at xxxv: 1-7, 14, 15, must have been *soon* after his return to Canaan, on a *first* trip through Bethel to his father at Hebron; not ten (or twenty) years after, when the affairs at Ch. xxxiv had occurred. Especially is this plain from the statement (at xxxv: 9, 10), that this was "*when he came out of* Padan-aram," with reaffirmation of the change of name which had occurred just before (xxxii: 28). Particularly,

(3) The fact of Deborah's death, *with Jacob* at Bethel. (xxxv: 8), shows conclusively, that Jacob had already been with his father at Hebron, and had brought her thence away with him, probably on account of his mother Rebekah's death. Deborah naturally clung to the mother-boy Jacob, whom she had nursed in infancy, and whose wife Rachel needed her company.

§ 23. As therefore Jacob must have come and made some stay at Hebron *before* the recorded events of Ch. xxxiv, it was doubtless during that earlier residence there that Joseph was lost. For,

1. There is a gap of *many years* time at the close of Ch. xxxiii. concerning which nothing is said. All expositors are agreed, that there were at least 8 or 10 years from the arrival in Canaan to the opening of the chapter xxiv. Into this interval naturally falls the account of Joseph in the chapter xxvii. By this view is saved that forced crowding of events afterward, which results from retaining Ch. xxxvii in the order recorded; whereby all chapters, xxxiv-xxxvii, are pressed into a space of one or two years, after that long gap unaccounted for.

2. At the *return* to Hebron in the order of the record, the date is altogether too late for Joseph to be then only 17 years old, as stated. (xxxvii: 2.) In Ch. xxxiv, Dinah must have been at least 15 years old, probably more: and Joseph being probably older than she (as Scott observes), was at least 16. From that time, through chapter xxxiv and xxxv, (and we say into a second period of residence in Hebron), after Jacob's sons had been some time back in Shechem with their flocks, *must be some years;* (Scott, by the closest reckoning, tries to reduce it to two years); so that then Joseph must be at least 18 or 19 years, probably much more.

3. It seems from xxxvii: 29, 30, that Reuben yet felt his birth-right responsibility; which therefore he had not yet lost; as he afterward did. (xxxv: 22, comp. xlix: 4, 5, 10, with I Chron. v: 1, 2.) This goes to show, that much of chapters xxxiv to xxxvii belongs chronologically *after* chapter xxxvii. But chiefly,

4. The loss of Joseph near Shechem, when he was 17 years old, as recorded in Ch. xxxvii, must have occurred *before* the story of Dinah, recorded in Ch. xxxiv. For, the terrible slaughter by Jacob's sons of Shechem and his father and the male inhabitants of the town, with the plunder of all their wealth (v. 25-29), could not be before those sons, Simeon and Levi, who accomplished it, were at least 21 years old ;—

which would make Joseph as much as 17 already. Probably they were all much older than that, and Dinah much older than 15; Joseph having been sold *before* this *second* residence at Shechem. This slaughter and havoc there by his sons, so disgusted Jacob as well as the people thereabouts (xxxiv: 30), that Jacob left the country (as at xxxv: 6–8), proceeding by way of Bethel back to Hebron (v. 16–27).

§ 24. Now it was not possible, that on this return to Hebron, he could *immediately* send back these very murderous sons with the flocks to feed about Shechem, the very scene of their recent butchery. And especially, he could not (*immediately*, as the recorded order would require), send off his young beloved Joseph, to hunt them up in that country so aroused against them. Plainly, this feeding of flocks, this visit of Joseph, was in the *early* days after arrival at Shechem; when we are expressly told that "Jacob *came in peace to the city of Shechem*," (xxxiii: 18, Revision); in evident contrast with the warlike catastrophe that afterward drove and kept him and his family away from that region.

This proves beyond a doubt, that the story of Joseph's departure (in Ch. xxxvii) belongs back, before the story about Dinah (in Ch. xxxiv); and that there (probably at xxxiii: 19) comes in the visit of Jacob to his father Isaac (xxxv: 27), during which *first* stop at Hebron, Joseph was sent back to his brethren at Shechem, as the history proceeds to narrate (in Ch. xxxvii).

The reason of this inverted order in the narrative, I have sufficiently shown; it being a skilfully artistic arrangement, by which, when Shechem is once named, the subsequent events there disconnected with Joseph are related. The same plan being again followed when Bethel is once named, and when Hebron is once named and Esau; all interruptive affairs are thus disposed of beforehand, so that the story of Joseph, when once begun, can go on without any disturbing intermixture.

5. A fifth proof should be named. The death of Isaac, and the consequent discourse about Esau, (xxxv: 28 to xxxvi: 43), is certainly put out of its chronological order, by an *anticipation* of some years, as all expositors observe. And this evidently is done for the very object we have explained, that Hebron being once named (xxxv: 27), everything there may be so disposed of, as not to interrupt the story of Joseph when begun. All I do is, to extend this acknowledged anticipation back still farther to chapter 33.

6. If Gen. xlviii: 22, refers to the same land as xxxiii: 11 (as generally thought), then Jacob must have come back to live there a second time, recapturing the land, say, after the loss of Joseph,—just as here argued. "The Amorite" may mean *in general* the "Canaanites," including Shechemites, as at Gen. xv: 16.

Results.

§ 25. The principal result of this view is, that the birth of Benjamin (and the death of his mother Rachel) is thus brought *after* the sale of Joseph into Egypt; showing several things:

1. Why Joseph "was the son of his old-age" to Jacob, (xxxvii: 3); which he could hardly be called, if the younger Benjamin were already born. (See xliv: 20.)

2. Why "Israel loved Joseph more than all his brethren" (xxxvii: 3), notwithstanding xxxv: 18, which must be *afterward*. "His father called him (the last son) Benjamin," *i. e.*, "son of the right-hand," *marg.*, meaning "particularly dear and precious,—as some think, originally Beja*mim*, *i. e.*, "a son of days," or of old-age. —*Jamieson*. When Joseph was so singled out, it was as being the *only* son (as yet) of Jacob's beloved Rachel. Such specializing would hardly have been, if the infant Benjamin were already present.

3. Why Jacob said (v. 10), "Shall I and *thy mother* and thy brethren indeed come to bow down ourselves to thee?" He could not have thus spoken to Joseph of his *own* "mother," if she were already dead. Joseph's dream had in it *eleven* stars to make obeisance to him (v. 9), as meaning the *eleven children* (including Dinah, who was numbered with the heads of families, xlvi: 15); or else, as prophetic that there was to be "another son." (See xxx: 24.)

4. Why we are told of "Rachel weeping for her children; she refused to be comforted for her children, because they are not," (Jer. xxxi: 15; Mat. ii: 18). The living Rachel herself, it seems, literally began this weeping over her lost Joseph; (comp. Gen. xxxv: 18, *marg.*, "son of my sorrow" over Joseph.) She only mourned as her husband Jacob did, who also "refused to be comforted" (xxxvii: 34, 35), saying, "Joseph is not," (xlii: 36);—to Rachel "Joseph was not" *till she died* uttering those words.

5. Why Benjamin is called so *young*, as being a mere "lad" when he was taken to Egypt; (xliii: 8, 29, and xliv: 20, 22, 31, 32, 33, 34), "a child of his old age, *a little one*,"—just as Joseph at 17 years is called "a lad" (xxxvii: 2). It is probable that Benjamin was not older than 17 also; instead of being about 25, as the current view makes him, when he was thus called "a lad — a child, a little one."

(Note. The "inductive studies" of the Institute of Sacred Lit. in the S. S. Times, April 7, 1894, even says: "Benjamin was at least 30 years old" on meeting Joseph!)

6. Why Joseph was so moved at mention of Benjamin when (says Judah, xliii: 7), "He asked straightly concerning ourselves, and concerning our kindred, saying, 'Is your father yet alive,? have ye any

other brother?' (comp. xxx: 24), and we told him,"—doubtless mentioning that the mother died when the boy was born. How Joseph schemed to get a sight of the lad, his only own brother, *never yet seen*, now the sole memento left him of his long-desired mother!

How he sought assurance, that it was indeed his own mother's boy! (xliii: 29, 30.) "And he lifted up his eyes, and saw his brother Benjamin, *his mother's son*, and said, IS this your younger brother, of whom ye spake unto me? And he said, God be gracious unto thee, my son. And Joseph made haste, for his bowels did yearn upon his brother; and he sought where to weep, and he entered into his chamber, and wept there." At length (xlv: 14), "he fell upon his brother Benjamin's neck and wept!"

In view of all considerations, is not the arrangement here given worthy of thoughtful examination?

PERIOD A, B—DILUVIAN CHRONOLOGY.

PART I.

THE DIFFERING TEXTS.

§ 1. Diluvian Chronology has two periods, (*A*) *antediluvian*, and (*B*) *postdiluvian* (reaching to the birth of Abraham), as recorded in Genesis v and xi. We have three differing texts of these tables of chronology, the Hebrew of our English Bible, the Samaritan pentateuch, and the Septuagint or Greek version made 250 B. C. Josephus professes to give the old Hebrew as he had it; but it may be claimed, that as his numbers are about the same as those of the Septuagint, they are only copied therefrom. We take them as at least fairly representing the Septuagint. The three texts compared give us as follows:

§ 2. THE THREE TEXTS.

	A	Period.	B		Total.	
Present Hebrew	1656	+	292†		= 1948	
		350		650		300
Euseb. Samaritan *	1306	+	942		= 2248	
		950		50		1000
Jos. Septuagint	2256	+	992		= 3248	
		600		700		1300

---

* The 1306 of the Samaritan was written as the "1307th" year for the flood (as seen in Eusebius); the 53 years of Lamech being doubtless only the 53d year (or 52 complete), *i. e.*, 30 years taken from [1]82, as 20 are taken from Methuselah's [1]87, with Jared [1]60.

† With the age of Terah (Gen. xi: 32) alike in the Hebrew and the Lxx, the inspired statement of Stephen in Acts vii: 4 (see ver. 55), drawn doubtless from authentic tradition, requires the addition of 60 years to the chronology of Period B, making 352 years as Usher and others have put it. Gen. xi: 27, is explained as a reversal of the sons' names, Abraham being put first on account of his pre-eminence in the history to follow, though Haran was probably the first-born at "70 years" of his father; while Abraham was born 60 years later, or "75 years" before his father died at 205. (Compare ver. 32 with xii: 4.) The greater age of Haran is indicated by his previous death, with a son Lot to emigrate at an early date out of Chaldea. (xi: 31.) See § 58. note.

§ 3. We here learn the following facts:

(1) The tens and units agree in the present Heb. and the Sept. as represented by Jos., and substantially so in the Sam. Therefore, the changes made among them are *even hundreds* to or from the numbers of Josephus.

(2) The changes were made *purposely*, by even hundreds transferred from one side to the other of the births, adjusting both Periods A and B at once and applied to some two out of the three texts, Heb., Sam., Sep.

§ 4. (3) The Sam. is inconsistent as to birth ages in the Periods A and B, and in other respects. It shows its artificiality in the changed life-ages of Jared, Methusaleh, and Lamech, adjusting them all to die at the flood; and this can not have been the original text. Therefore, the only question is this: Is the present Heb. a diminution from Josephus as the original Heb., or is the Sep. represented by Josephus an enlargement from the present Hebrew as the original?

(4) Upon this question, testing the different totals obtained in the three texts as to the favorite jubilee reckoning of the Jews, we have as follows:

```
         A, B, + Period C =     Exodus A. M.
Heb....1948 )                 ( 2453 )           ( —3 dropped = 50 jubilees
Sam....2248 } + 505  =        } 2753 } + 49     } +40 to Josh. = 57 jubilees
Sep.....3248 )                ( 3753 )           ( = 76 jubilees and 29 over.
```

——Here we see that the Sep. reckoning is the only one free from the superstitious Jewish calculation of jubilees; and this gives a strong presumption in favor of the Sep. as the original text. (See afterward.)

§ 5. (5) If the Sep. is an enlargement upon the Heb. as the original text, then it became so at its formation, as early as 250 B. C. For, no copy of the Sep. has ever been found containing the Heb. numbers; and not only Josephus, as early as the first century, but also Demetrius, the Jewish historian (220 B. C.), as well as Eupolemus (174 B. C.), use the larger Sept. values alone.

(6) As a purposed change of the text made at that time there is no conceivable motive adequate to account for it. Is it suggested that all peoples have a tendency to magnify their antiquity? But in this case the lengthening made by Jews is not of their own nationality, but of pre-national times.

Is it suggested (as in the Bib. Sacra, April, 1890, p. 300), "that these changes were made by the Sep. translators or others for the sake of accommodating the Mosaic narrative to the imperative demands of the accepted Egyptian antiquity?" But when we remember that the fabulous Egyptian chronology, made 30,000 years before the flood, and over 4,000 down thence to the time of the Israelitish Exodus, we see that there is no possible imitation of this in the Septuagint.

§ 6. Moreover, to suppose such an imperative demand, is much more of an argument for its having been originally met in the Hebrew text by Moses himself, who was "learned in all the wisdom of the Egyptians"; especially when it is claimed (as it is by the writer cited) that Moses *could not* have meant to give the shorter reckoning of the Hebrew as a *bona fide chronology* in presence of the Egyptian claims to antiquity. If the Hebrew numbers were not meant as chronology, but only "as a conspectus of individual lives" and their length, as the writer urges,—then Moses could have selected and arranged those numbers to look like satisfying Egyptian demands, just as well as the Lxx could do it; and he would be the more likely originator of the larger numbers.

§ 7. Or, if the Lxx also viewed those numbers as not meant for chronology (as the writer also urges), then still they could not deliberately change them, whether to suit Egyptians, or merely "to make a more symmetrical division of individual lives" (the reason urged by the writer), without a belying of the individual lives given by the Hebrew text. A desire on the part of the Lxx translators to furnish more time for the play of Egyptian fables concerning their antiquity, or especially a mere wish to make the numbers look more symmetrical, could, by no possibility, be an adequate motive to constrain those 70 learned Jewish magnates to violate the Hebrew text before them, and purposely falsify the Scripture which all Jews (down to the New Testament times) so sedulously guarded.

(7) If the Sep. is thus an enlargement upon the Heb., then the Sam. is also a modification made upon the Heb.; and as such it is utterly inexplicable. For, the Sam. enlarges the Heb. in Period B, but *diminishes* it in Period A, the result being a net increase of only 300, instead of the 1300 excess of the Sep. For so slight a result as an enlargement of time there could be no motive. And to suppose the change made (as does the writer in the Bib. Sacra, p. 300) merely to render the numbers in Period A more symmetrical, while Period B is thus put in still more unsymmetrical contrast with it, offers no adequate motive at all for such proposed mutilation of Scripture.

§ 8. If the Sam. manipulator merely thought it important enough to mutilate by reducing Jared, Methusaleh, and Lamech, so as to have a regular diminution of life and age of parentage down to the flood, why did he proceed in Period B to *do the very opposite*, by enlarging the ages of parentage after the flood to 100 years more than those before, when by leaving the Hebrew here untouched he would have his desired decrease all the way through? We repeat, the Sam. text is utterly inexplicable on the supposition that the Hebrew was the original text.

CHAPTER I.

Is the Hebrew Corrupt?

§ 9. (8) But if, on the contrary, the present Heb. is a diminution made from Jos. (or a Sep. value) as the original text, then it was not made until about the second century, or after the time of Josephus. For he professes to be giving the numbers from *his Hebrew* Bible, (see in his preface to the Antiq.); and he has them in the enlarged form of the Sep. This is seen at Antiq. I, iii: 4, and vi: 5. Thus, 2256+992; Nahor's 129 being corrupted to 120, and the 2 years after the flood corrupted to 12; while the present Hebrew total 292 here is a corruption from Jos.' own true total "992," as seen from his items added up. Neither Jos. nor any writer as early as he has the diminished total of the present Heb., though great efforts have been made, by corruptions of his text, to have him so appear.

"Josephus' total after (as well as before) the flood has been corrupted so as to agree with the present Heb. so confusing Jos. that chronologists can not agree on him. It was all done before the time of Eusebius, who cites him as having to the death of Moses 'near 3,000 years,' instead of the correct 'near 4,000.'" *Jackson*, p. 119. For Jos. says that the Old Testament down to Nehemiah (over 1,000 years later) "contains the history of 5,000 years." *Antiq. Pref. 3, Vs. Ap., 1, 1.*) See Restor. Jos., § 71.

§ 10. At Antiq. 10, viii: 5, the interpolation is evident, leaving out the "2 years after the flood" (Gen. xi: 10), which Josephus is careful to put in (see his 3, vi: 5). Thus it reads as if "1062½"+505+290= "1857½" back to the flood (corrupted to 1957½)+1656= "3513½ to creation; whereas, Jos. would have put it '1062½'+505+992= 2559½+2256=4815½. There is like interpolation at Ant. 8, iii: 1, where we are given "1022" (corrupt 1020)+Ab. 75+60+290="1447" (corrupt 1440) to the flood+1656="3103" corrupt 3102) to the creation. In the interpolation, not only is the "2 years after the flood" left out, but the 60 years (of Usher) before Abraham's birth are put in, which may go to indicate when this corrupt figuring was imposed upon Josephus. Plainly a mighty effort has been made by corruptors to make Jos. seem to endorse the present Heb. text. But this attempt to set Jos. in confusion and contradiction of himself is obviously exposed. So the present Hebrew numbers can not be found as early as Josephus.

§ 11. (9) If the present Heb. is a diminution made from Jos. (or a Sep. value) as the original text, and gotten up (say) within a century after his day, then we can see an *adequate motive* to account for the purposed change made in the Heb. text. For the Jews, who mostly possessed and controlled the Hebrew, were then very bitter against the Christians, and, in order to disprove the claims of Jesus as the Messiah appointed to come "in the last days, they may have been tempted to the desperate step of lessening the Biblical age of the world so as to plead that "the last days" of it were not yet arrived. (And may they not have excused themselves for such mutilation by some such theory as that lately gotten up, that those numbers were not really meant for chronology, and so might be adjusted differently without much harm)? They were early accused of making such corruptions, and for this very purpose, and may not the complaint be true?

§ 12. Here note these particulars:

(a.) It was the Jews, who in the second century mostly possessed and controlled the Hebrew Scriptures. "Few Christians then understood the Hebrew. So it was easy to corrupt it. And most Hebrew copies were lost in the destruction of Jerusalem and the destruction in the reign of Hadrian." (*Jackson*.) In the early centuries the Christians used and depended upon the Sep., which was, therefore, slighted by the Jews, who watched to see if it was not corrupted by the Christians. "Even Jews would have detected and condemned it had it been the Sep. corrupted." (*id*.) "Since the destruction of Jerusalem the Jews condemn and reject the Sep. as a corruption and falsification of the word of God, and the Talmud designates the origin of the Sep. as a disastrous day." (*Seyffarth, p. 131*.)

§ 13. (b) It was a theory very current in the early Christian church, that the world was to last a *great week*, or seven of the 1000-year days of God, (Hab. xc: 4; II Pet. iii: 8); and that in "the last days" of that world's week, according to the prophets, Messiah would appear. And, as by the Septuagint chronology, they had the age of the world in the time of Herod as about 5500 years, they judged this to be in the very midst of the sixth day (or Friday of time) *i. e.*, in the last days of the world's week. This the early Christians urged as an argument for Christ as the true Messiah, he having thus appeared at the fitting time in the world's history. Rom. v: 6. (*See authorities given by Jackson, p. 97*.)

§ 14. We see how prominent was this view, by the testimony of the "Gospel of Nicodemus," one of the purest and most valuable of the apocraphal books; which we are told was "of very great antiquity," and being "in use for public reading in some of the churches two hundred years after the apostles," must have existed long before that. It says, ch. xiv: 5, "The angel said to Seth, thou canst not by any means obtain it [the blessing] till the last day and times, namely, till five thousand and five hundred years be past; then will Christ come on earth," etc. The same is repeated at ch. xxii: 11, and again at ver. 13;

after which follows a computation of the Old Testament dates to make out the 5500 years at the birth of Christ. (See § 78.)

This reckoning of 5500 A. M. at the nativity formed the basis of the chronology of Julius Africanus (A. D. 200), and all the other early chroniclers of the church. Of course, this reckoning and this claim as to "the last days" must have provoked the Jewish leaders, who were so bitter against the Christians, and would naturally tempt them to make the figures of their original Hebrew show a more recent origin of the world, as only 4,000 years old or less; so that they could plead, that the last days had not come and Messiah was not yet due. *

§ 15. (c) We know that the Jews did in those days *purposely corrupt their chronology* of the time back to the captivity, in order to adjust the "seventy weeks" prophecy of Daniel to their own wishes for *a Messiah not yet due*, in opposition to the Christian claims. In A. D. 130, Rabbi Akiba in behalf of the Jewish people devised the modern Jewish chronology, still used by the Jews of our day; wherein the time is put as "seventy years captivity+352 years to the Christian era+69 years to A. D. 70=the 491st year (10 jubilees) to the destruction of Jerusalem." This makes the 490 years or "70 weeks" of Daniel reach from the close of the 70 years captivity to 70 years after the destruction of Jerusalem, *i. e.*, to A. D. 140, just after the devising of this scheme,—or later, according as the 70 weeks were started from any point *after* the captivity. "This view was promoted by the false Christ whom the Jews then got up, about A. D. 128." (*Jackson*.) Or rather, the false Christ grew out of this chronological figuring. (See Period F, § 53, note.)

§ 16. Here was a very adroit scheme of Jewish chronology (still existent before our eyes), gotten up evidently on purpose to postpone Messiah's coming, to the overthrow of the Christian claim concerning Jesus of Nazareth:—a scheme which did not scruple to drop out near 200 years from the true chronology of the captivity, which we all know ended 537 B. C., instead of the 352 B. C., where they assign it. Since

---

* So in the "General Epistle of Barnabas," companion of Paul, supposed by many to belong properly in the New Testament canon, we read (ch. xiii: 4-6): "Consider, my children, what that signifies. He finished them [His works] in six days. The meaning of it is this: That in six thousand years the Lord God will bring all things to an end. For with him a thousand years are one day. * * * When His Son shall come * * * then he shall gloriously rest in that seventh day." Ver. 9, 10, 'The Sabbaths, saith He, which ye now keep, are not acceptable unto me, but those which I have made; when, resting from all things, I shall begin the 8th day, that is, the beginning of the other world. For which cause we observe the 8th day with gladness, in which Jesus rose from the dead." (How general this tradition then was, concerning 6,000 years, see *Coteler, Annot. in loco, Edit. Oxon., p. 90*.)

the Jews of that day did thus fabricate a false chronology in their attempt to defeat Christianity; the only question is, Did they go further, and corrupt the numbers of Genesis for the same purpose? Did they drop out from 1300 to 1500 years from the Hebrew text (then in their control, in order to reduce the world's age below 4000, so as to destroy the argument of Christians concerning "the last days."

§ 17. (d) It is a grave charge to make against them. But the charge was freely made in those early times. "Justin Martyr (A. D. 142) mentions several instances of their altering and erasing prophesies concerning the death of Christ in the Septuagint. * * * Epiphanius (A. D. 380) *in De Mensur*, *p. 171*, says that Aquila (pupil of Rabbi Akaba) perverted the Heb. text to invalidate the prophesies concerning Christ," etc. (*Jackson*.) "Origin (*Cont. C. I., 40*), Justin Martyr, (*Dial. c. Tryph., 68, 71*), Epiphanius, Eusebius, Jerome, Augustine, Julian of Toledo, Syncellus, and many others, declare that the true chronology of the pentateuch was preserved in the Sep., but shortened by the Jews after the destruction of Jerusalem." (Seyffarth, p. 137.)

"The Jews in Spain openly assailed the Christian church, A. D. 680, with the reproach that Christ having been born 1500 years too early, was therefore a false Messiah; whilst they maintained that the true Messiah would come 1500 years later, *i. e.*, in the sixth thousand years after the creation." (*Id., p. 135*.)

§ 18. "Jerome asserts again and again (A. D. 360), that the Hebrew text had been corrupted by the Jews; *e. g.*, at Gal. iii: 10, 13. Augustine (A. D. 400), *Civit. Dei., xv: 11*, says: 'The Christians believe that the truth is contained in these [the Sep. Scriptures], not in those of the Jews: * * * that it is incredible that the seventy interpreters could have erred, or could have lied, as they had nothing to gain by it; but that on the contrary the Jews had made certain alterations in their books, in order thus to diminish the authority of ours.'" (*Seyffarth, p, 138*, the Latin given. Also *Jackson*.) Syncellus says (p. 84): "I concur entirely in the opinion, that this shortening was a criminal act of the Jews."—"Augustine himself lays the blame to a first copier of the Septuagint, in order to make the ages at puberty agree." (*Jackson*.)

§ 19. This idea of Augustine is the only early suggestion we find, of a possible corruption by the Sep. And Augustine could not have seen Josephus' numbers, cited from the Hebrew just as in the Lxx; or he would not have made such a suggestion. And as to the modern suggestion, that the Lxx themselves expanded the original chronology 1500 years to harmonize it with the Egyptian antiquity—we have already seen (here at § 5) that neither this nor the theory just named is reasonable, or furnishes an adequate motive for such corruption at that time. *

We will not presume to decide the question, whether the present Hebrew numbers in Gen. v, xi, are a corruption introduced by the Jews, as above charged. But we must say, that an *adequate motive* is seen for such corruption,—while no motive can be discovered for the Sep. numbers as a corruption, since they were in existence long before Christianity and the controversies arising from it.

---

* § 20. Take some later opinions:
"Abraham Ecchelensis (*Hist. Orient. Sup., p. 175*), a learned Syrian Maronite, charges the Jews with having corrupted the chronology of their Scriptures, upon the testimonies of their most ancient rabbis," etc. (*Jackson*.)

"Abulfeda says: 'The Jews diminished the age of the world 1475 years, in order to make themselves living *in the midst* of the 7000 years agreed by all, not in *the last times*. The Greek version is approved by the most accurate chronologists." (*Seyffarth, p. 144*. The Latin is given.)

"Abul-pharagius, another learned Mohammedan, says: 'According to the Hebrew, from creation to the Messiah is 4220 years, but by the Sep. in the hands of almost all Christians it is 5586. Which diminution of the Hebrew is ascribed to the Jewish doctors, because by the law, the prophets, and the ancient rabbis, Christ was to come in *the last times*. So they reduced the patriarchs, bringing Jesus in the 5th milleniad, about the midst of the world's years, which all give as 7000, saying the time of Messiah is not yet arrived. But the Sept. reckoning makes it the 6th milleniad, and the proper time for Messiah.'" (*Seyffarth, p. 144*. The Latin is given.)

"There is extant also a modern edition of the Heb. Bible, with a German-Rabbinical interpretation, in which Daniel's seventy weeks are wanting." (*Id.*, p. 126.)

"Luther and others showed in many places, *e. g.*, Isa. ix: 6, that the rabbis did, in A. D. 800, falsify the Hebrew text, for the purpose of discrediting or obliterating certain prophesies in respect to Christ." (*Id., p. 170.*)

"The Hebrew was corrupted by the later Jews themselves, and so the Christians were imposed upon. The true Mosaic chronology was divinely preserved in the Greek translation, established centuries before these corruptions were introduced. It was also preserved in Josephus, who says he followed the Hebrew copies. The variations were made to confound the time of Christ's coming. But by a good Providence the truth was preserved. So Josephus has been corrupted in many places to agree with the present Hebrew; and the new Greek translations of Aquila (A. D. 128), Theodotian (185), Symmachus (200), vary much from the Sep. The change (in leaving out Cainan) was made between A. D. 100 and 120, before Aquila was employed to get up the new translation." (*Chron. Antiq. by John Jackson, folio, London. 1752.*) See Period D, Appendix D, § 100.

CHAPTER II.

Process of Corruption.

§ 21. (10) If the present Hebrew is a diminution made from Jos. (or a Sep. value) as the original text, and gotten up (say) within a century after his day,—then we can see how the Samaritan copy got its peculiar values, which are inexplicable with the theory that the Sep. is the corrupted text. (See here, § 7.) The Samaritan was used as a medium for corrupting the Hebrew, by a process traceable as follows:

If the Hebrew text is corrupt, then the Samaritan is also corrupt. (See here, § 4.) And the corruption of the Samaritan copy probably preceded that of the old Hebrew copy, preparing the way for it. For, we find the Samaritan chronology existent before we have any traces of the Hebrew reckoning. The Jewish "Book of Jubilees" is a work written about the year A. D. 100, as all are agreed.* It is a Pharisaic "Targum of those days in the spirit of the New Testament Judaism." It wonderfully exalts all the legal niceties of ritualism, teaching that they were first ordinances in heaven, whence they were imparted to Moses. And it carefully dates every event of Genesis by a system of fifty Jubilees as reaching from creation to Joshua's entering Canaan; thus making Jubilee Chronology to antedate the Mosaic institution of Jubilees, and indeed to have been prearranged "in the councils of heaven," even "according to the weeks of the Jubilees to eternity." (See its ch. i: 22-24.)

---

* § 22. "BOOK OF JUBILEES. The editor of the Ethiopic texts and German translator of this book, Prof. Dillman, has proved to the satisfaction of scholars in general, that the book is a production of the first Christian century. Ewald shows that the book presupposes and cites those parts of the book of Enoch which date up to about the birth of Christ, while it, in turn, has been used and quoted by the Test. of the Twelve Pat., a work similar in spirit and a product of the early part of the second century. This will decide the end of the first century after Christ as the date for the composition of the Book of Jubilees. By Christian authors the work is not quoted until later. Epiphanius, Jerome and Rufinus are the first to mention it, while Cedrenus, Syncellus, and other Byzantine writers quote from it at length. But the testimony of the Test. xii, Pat. is decisive as to the *terminus ad quem*. Rönsch confidently claims that it was written before the destruction of Jerusalem.

"As the book is undoubtedly the work of a Palestinian Jew and written in Hebrew, it can fairly be condsidered as an outgrowth of that school and spirit of Judaism, which we in the New Testament find arrayed in opposition to Christianity and its work. The book, can best be described by calling it a haggadic commentary on certain portions of Genesis and the opening chapters of Exodus, and it is thus the oldest

This Book of Jubilees has the time "1307 years" of the Samaritan Pentateuch as the period before the flood, saying (v: 20) that Noah entered the ark at "the 6th year of the 5th week of the 27th Jubilee," *i. e.*, at 1307 years. So, then, the present corrupted text of the Samaritan copy was in existence at that time, about A. D. 100. Already had the Sep. number (of Jos.) "2256 years" before the flood, been lowered 900 years, by transferring 100 years from the time before to the time after parentage of each patriarch; and lowered also by 20 years more taken from Methusaleh's, and 30 years more taken from Lamech's age at parentage, in order to make a regular decrease in the age of parentage throughout. And thus had the 1306 years (called 1307th year) been obtained, or a reduction of 950 years. This, with a loss of 50 years from the 992 of the Sep. (as in Jos.) after the flood, gave a reduction of 1000 years; which lessened the Sep. from about 5500 to only about 4500 at the time of Herod, and plainly answered a purpose of argument against the Christian claim as to "the last days." The Samaritan corruption thus seems to have been *the first attempt* in that direction, made some time in the first century of the Christian era.*

§ 24. But, as found in the Jewish Book of Jubilees, it was a later attempt. For this book adds a large reduction of the period after the flood to that already made in the period before. The corruption of the Samaritan copy had not ventured to meddle seriously with the time after the flood, leaving it as 942 (as found also in some copies of the Lxx, see Euseb.), and thinking the loss of 1000 years sufficient for its purpose. But the writer of the Book of Jubilees, to make still further reductions, and at the same time to accommodate his Jubilee

---

of the Midrashim, and a representative example of the manner in which the learned contemporaries of Christ made use of the Biblical books for their own peculiar purpose and object. It is a sample of an exegetical Targum of those days in the spirit of New Testament Judaism. * * * One scholar advocates a Samaritan origin, another an Essene; but all agree as to its thoroughly Jewish origin, and in general its representative character, while Rönsch even thinks that he detects an anti-Christian tendency. * * * The center of its orthodoxy is the law, and its paraphernalia, and all means lawful and unlawful, are put into requisition to exalt the importance of that law and to increase its authority. Outwardly the leading feature is the chronological system of the book, namely, its division of all ancient history of the Israelites according to the sacred periods of Jubilees of forty-nine years; and the time between the creation and the entrance of Israel into Canaan is counted as fifty Jubilees, or 2450 years." (*Prof. of Prof. Schodde to the English Trans. in Bib. Sacra*, 1885, Oct., p. 629.)

*One form of the Samaritan reckoning (reported in a note to Jerome's Euseb.), reduced the period before the flood down as low as "1070 years"—probably by dropping all the 12 hundreds to give the 1056 year down to Noah's 500th year, and then adding 25 to Seth's age at parentage (as in Jerome's list), so making 1056th+25=) 1070.

theory, called the time just fifty Jubilees from creation to Joshua's entering Canaan (when he supposed the Jewish Jubilee practically to begin). This required him to have the Samaritan 1307th year+600th after the flood+505 to the Exodus+40 to Joshua=2451st year or 50 Jubilees. (But by mistake, putting Abraham's entering Canaan at 40 Jubilees, so as to have the two migrations just 70 weeks or 490 years apart, he has 1307th+580th+525+40=2451st year as before.)

§ 25. This further reduction of (942—600th—) 343 years more after the flood (distributed variously upon the ten generations), increased the Samaritan loss from 1000 up to 1343, giving that much more advantage in the argument against the Christians. And so the matter stood at the writing of the Book of Jubilees, (say 100 A. D.) But when the Jewish Rabbi Akiba (about A. D. 130) started the present Jewish Chronology, wherein we find the first mention of the present Hebrew values of Gen. v, xi, and wherein the chronology from the captivity to the Christian era is reduced from 537 to 352 years, as we have seen—the object in this whole reckoning was evidently to get as small a world-age as possible, seemingly for the purpose of denying "the last days" alleged by the Christians.

§ 26. Not satisfied, therefore, with the Samaritan reduction of 1,000 (made mostly by whole 100's in Period A (before the flood)—and seeing that the further reduction in the Book of Jubilees, not being by even 100's, could not creditably be applied to the Scripture text—they concluded not to follow the Samaritan plan, of taking 100 years from every parent in Period A, but not Period B (which seemed inconsistent and irregular); but proceeded to take 100 years from each parent *in both periods*, except in the case of Methusaleh, Lamech, and Noah, where this could not be done without disturbing the other numbers which give the life-length of those men.

§ 27. This left them 1556+292 instead of the Sep. 2256+992 (as in Jos.), a reduction of 700 years upon each period (a very systematic thing), and gave them an advantage of 1400 years loss in the argument with the Christians (in place of the 1343 years given in the Book of Jubilees.) However, when the corruption of the period (D) from the Exodus to the temple became soon established as "the 480th year" (instead of the true value, the 580 years, as we have shown elsewhere), then this by offset allowed Jared (in Period A) to retain his original 162 (not 62), so as to have no age at parentage go below 65, which was deemed a proper thing. Thus the whole loss was kept at 1400, but was now only 600 in Period A, and 700 in Period B, with 100 in Period D (while some copies of the Lxx by insertion of Cainan, etc., had the whole variation 1500 or even more). And thus it came to pass, that "all eastern copies of the Heb. (earliest made?) have 1556, but all western copies have 1656, we are told by an author of good credit." (*Jackson.*) See Period D, § 83.

§ 28. We can thus clearly see the steps by which the Samaritan and then the Hebrew corruption came in, within the first and then within the second century; until Eusebius (A. D. 320) sets forth the completed corruption in full. All this upon the supposition, that the Septuagint numbers (as in Jos.) agreed with the original Hebrew text. No such consistent and natural process of corruption can we find on the opposite supposition, that our present Hebrew is the original. Hence the presumption is strongly in favor of the Septuagint as correct.

CHAPTER III.

Is the Septuagint Correct?

§ 29. (11) It is worthy of note, that when the new Hebrew text reduced Jos. 2256 to 1656, the reduction by 600 was the same as Noah's age at the flood: so that the manipulator of the corruption was merely *making the 1656 years of Jos. at the birth of Noah reach instead to the flood.* And this may be what settled down the change to 1656, instead of 1556 as at first proposed: it was leaving unchanged *a familiar total before the flood*, only applied somewhat differently. In like manner, when the Samaritan copy reduced Jos. 2256 to 1306, the reduction by 950 years was the same as Noah's total age: so that the manipulator of the corruption was merely *making the 1656 of Jos. at the birth of Noah reach instead to the death of Noah*—a well known total retained, but differently applied. Both facts are curious; and do they not serve to show, that both cases were corruptions from the original Sep. reckoning?

§ 30. There are other presumptions in favor of the Septuagint. Jared, Methusaleh, and Lamech are alike in Josephus and the Hebrew, and these numbers must be correct. But these look as if giving the ages at puberty, as about one-fifth the whole ages, which is reasonable; and the presumption is that all would be about the same, as Jos. has them. Adam, of course, is older at the birth of Seth, there being children before him. Also the agreement of the Samaritan with the Septuagint in Period B after the flood, looks in favor of the Sep., as seen in the process of change above shown.*

---

* § 31. We have used the 1656+992 of Jos. as fairly representing the Sep. values, in supposed accordance with the old Hebrew text. But the following variations are found in the Sep. text itself; each of which has to be considered by itself, in determining what were the original figures:

§ 32. (12) Another fact strongly favors the Septuagint as the genuine original reckoning. We have seen how popular it was with the Jews, to conform their chronology to Jubilee periods of 49 years and seventy-week periods of 10 Jubilees or 490 years. They often strained a point in trying to make such cycles fit the history. So we find them making Jubilee reckoning *before* there were any Jubilees, from the giving of the Law back to the creation. Thus, the Samaritan copy, which we have seen as the first form of corruption, has just 57 Jubilees from creation to possession of Canaan: namely, 1307th+942 +75+430=2753+40 to Joshua =2793 years +49=just 57 Jubilees, to the first year of another Jubilee. (See ¿ 4.)

¿ 33. Probably the Samaritans reckoned 11 more Jubilees to Solomon's temple, and 10 more to the second temple, or (21×49=) 1029 years from Joshua down to the dedication of the second temple as in B. C. 513, where Jos. has it), with 2 more Jubilees down to B. C. 415, as the date when *their* temple was built on Mt. Gerizim by Sanballat, for Manasseh in the reign of Darius Nothus, (Jos. II, viii); at which time probably the Samaritan copy of the Pentateuch was originated for the uses of that temple. (*Prideaux's Connection*, Vol. I. p. 424.) Thus the Samaritans reckoned just (57+23=) 80 Jubilees or 3920 years A. M. from creation to the building of their temple. And this even calculation by Jubilees is doubtless what determined the numbers in the corruption of the Samaritan Pentateuch, with its exact number of Jubilees at Joshua's entering Canaan. This shows the artificial character of the reckoning as a sure corruption.

	A	B
Josephus,	2256	992
	+6 Lamech	−50 Nahor.
(*In Jackson*),	2262 (*Dem.*)	942 (*Sam.*)
	−20 Methu.	
Euseb. LXX,	2242	942
		+130 Cainan.
Demetrius,	2242 +	1072−2=3212+2=1656.
	2262 +	1072="3334" +290=" 3624."
		+100 Nahor
Vatican LXX,	2242	1172
Bib. Sac., Apl., '76.	2262	1172
		−130
J. Jackson,	2256	1072 (only 6 less than Dem.)
(Origen.	1656)	1072 (Africanus.)
Origen. Hexap., & Euseb.		942 (Aquila, &c., left out the 130.)
Theophilus, (198 A. D.)		936 (Euseb. & Jerome ")

§ 34. Then followed the Book of Jubilees itself (A. D. 100), carrying out the Jubilee scheme still more fully, as we saw; with that interval from creation to Joshua's entering Canaan put as just 50 Jubilees, instead of 57. And next, the Hebrew text, as we have it, is found introduced in the current Jewish Chronology (devised about A. D. 130), with the same 50 Jubilees, but reckoned now to the Exodus, no longer to Joshua. (Here § 4.)

§ 35. For, this present Hebrew text has 1656+292+75+430=2453 years to the Exodus; (which Usher increases to 2513, by 60 years—see § 2, note—put in at the birth of Abraham, as required by Acts vii: 4). This 2453 at the Exodus is 3 years over 50 Jubilees, or 2450 years; and this makes the first Jubilee observed (49 years after) to come at the beginning of Joshua's 7th year, about the time when it is usually understood to have been actually held; that is in connection with the *first Sabbatic year* in the promised land. The *artificiality* of this scheme, with just 50 Jubilee periods worked in before any Jubilee reckoning was known, is evidence that the Hebrew text before and after the flood has been "doctored" to give this result.

And this is no less apparent when we find the Modern Jewish Chronology treating the present Hebrew text as giving them just 2450 years, or fifty Jubilees exact, to the Exodus itself, in the view that there began the first actual Jubilee period. They make it out by discarding the 2 years mentioned at Gen. xi: 10, and then treating the number at Ex. xii: 40, as the 430th year; so that they have 1656+290+505th=2450 years, or 2451st year, the beginning of the 51st Jubilee period at the Exodus.*

§ 37. Thus the artificial Jubilee reckonings found both in the Samaritan and in the present Hebrew text, are evidence (seemingly convincing) against their either of them being the original and genuine account. On the other hand, the Septuagint, in any form, is not subject to this objection. As given in Josephus, it has 2256+992+505=3753+49=76 Jubilee periods *and 29 years over;* and none of the variations in the Sep. will give even Jubilees, either to the Exodus or to

---

* § 36. Even Eusebius (as late as A. D. 320) follows this fanciful scheme of pre-dated Jubilees: but, strangely, takes 50 years to a Jubilee! Thus he gives the Hebrew text =2453 to the Exodus + the 47th year to the 7th of Joshua = the 2500th year, or the beginning of "the 51st Jubilee:" making this (505+46=551 years, or) the 452d "year of Abraham." Then he makes just 30 more of these Jubilees, or 1500 years to the end of Daniels' 70 weeks (A. D. 34), calling that (2500+1500=) 4000 A. M., or the end of 80 Jubilees from the creation, and the year (551+1500=) "2051 of Abraham." Such a *fabulous machine-scheme* is made out of our present Hebrew text, by the very author who first introduces it fully to the Christian church!

Joshua.* This freedom of the Sept. reckoning from all the artificial Jubilee theories found in the Samaritan and Hebrew texts,—with the real Jubilee of the Mosaic law left to take care of itself as applying only after its establishment,—this is a convincing proof in favor of the Septuagint Chronology.

CHAPTER IV.

Net Result.

§ 38. We are not going to give our *ipse dixit*, that the Septuagint represents the original Hebrew text of Gen. v, xi: because the present is eminently a case of reasoning from combined probabilities, and every reader must judge for himself what the balance of probabilities is. We will only say, that to us the argument seems as strong, at least, for the Septuagint as for the present Hebrew.

§ 39. The one great objection, perhaps the only real objection, against accepting at once the Septuagint chronology as correct, is the fear that this would weaken our hold upon our Hebrew Bible as the accurate text of God's Word, handed down to us with scrupulous care and fidelity by the Jews themselves. We know that they did most sedulously guard against the corruption of the Hebrew in the earlier days, and until long after the Septuagint version came in. And we are anxious to preserve intact this argument for the validity of the Old Testament as we have it.

§ 40. But we know that there are *some* corruptions in the Hebrew text.† And may we not safely take the ground, that the Jews were the best of custodians for the Scriptures, *until* they were cast off for their rejection of Christ; but that then they became so embittered against the truth, that they may have even corrupted *numbers* which they thought against them: but only where it could be done by change of a single figure (as by an even hundred), without altering the structure of a sentence or the count of the words, and without daring to go further and modify any essential truth. This at least we know, that, in God's all-wise Providence, even this was not permitted to occur, until the Septuagint version had been prepared, and had received a divine sanction through Christ and his apostles,—so as to preserve the text, and to be

---

* J. Schwartz (in the Bib. Sacra., Jan., 1888), tries to make it do so by taking it as 2262+1040+60+Ab'm 99+430=3921+49=80 Jubilees and 1 over. But this (especially the 99 for Ab.) is a monstrous perversion of the Septuagint.

† Comp. "8 years" in II Chron. xxxvi: 9, with "18 years" in II Ki. xxiv: 8. In some cases, the Heb. is corrected by the Sept. See Ezek. xlv: 5. Revis., marg.

a sure corrector of any corruption that might thereafter creep in. See what Jackson says on this point (here at § 20, note).

§ 41. The Septuagint has its imperfections, we know, especially in some parts. But on the whole it was a faithful translation; and it is conceded that the Pentateuch is the most exactly rendered portion of the whole. Philo, the learned Jew, says of it, in the first century, "The Sept. translation was made with such care and exactness, that there was not the least variation in it from the sacred Hebrew original, either by additions, omissions, or otherwise." Josephus also bears witness to its excellence. And our divine Lord and his inspired apostles made use of it as indeed the word of God. So that it must not be decried.* Doubtless the Septuagint has been furnished by God to help us to the right knowledge of the original Scriptures.

§ 42. In all this discussion, we have used only the argument of textual criticism, and have made no reference to the argument of science and common sense. The science of archæology wants all the time of the Septuagint back to the flood, to accommodate the early traditions of Egypt and other ancient civilizations. The science of paleontology wants all the time of the Septuagint back to the creation, to explain the human fossils that point out the antiquity of man. And commonsense promptly decides against the probability, that Noah was living in the times of Abraham, and Shem was living in the times of Jacob, as the Hebrew text requires, with nothing said about them or their dying in those late days.

§ 43. "Mark the absurdity of regarding Noah as living so long in Abraham's life, and no notice taken of it! Of the earth's so soon becoming so populous as it was! Think of Shem living 109 years after the establishment of circumcision and the Abrahamic covenant! and with such settled idolatry fled from in the life-time of Noah!" (*Jackson.*) Prof. Green, of Princeton, points out the impossibility of accepting such a chronology. (*Bib. Sacra, Apl., 1890, p. 303.*) We verily believe, that, were it not for the prejudice arising from the fear of conceding any corruption in the Hebrew text, as we just now explained, there would be at once a general acceptance of the Septuagint Chronology in Gen. v, xi, as the correct report of the Hebrew original.

---

*Augustine says: "the very highest respect is due to the translators of the Lxx. who, as the better informed Christians maintain, translated under such an influence of the Holy Spirit, that all were of one and the same mind."

"Julius Pomeranius, the Catholic bishop of Toledo, did not hesitate, A. D. 685, to demonstrate, in spite of the already authorized vulgate, that between the creation and Christ's advent 6,000 years had intervened, and that especially the chronology of the Septuagint was the work of the Holy Spirit." (*Seyffarth, p. 138.*) "The learned Morinus contends for the integrity of the Sept. He shows how the Bab. and Jeru. Talmuds extol the Sept., mentioning the very few differences, but none on the early chronology." (Jackson.)

PART II.

THE CHRONOLOGY OF GEN. V, XI.

§ 44. In an essay accompanying this (see Part III),* we show the possibility that the primeval man was a race physically human, before the spiritually human Adam began. We do this in the interest of the Bible Chronology; in order that it may not be deemed necessary to quarrel with the Scripture datings, for the purpose of satisfying a supposed scientific demand for a greater antiquity of man. Some Bible scholars feel anxious to forestall objections in this direction, and have thought to defend the book from dreaded assault, by belittling beforehand its teaching as to dates. For some time there has been a fashion of treating Bible datings as unreliable and of little account. And especially, in order to make way for a greater allowable antiquity of Adam, the Scripture Chronological tables of the period from Adam to Abraham, as contained in Gen. v and xi, have been urgently called in question. These tables proceed as follows:

Gen. v: 3. "And Adam lived a hundred and thirty years, and begat a son in his own likeness, after his image, and called his name Seth. And the days of Adam after he begat Seth were eight hundred years; and he begat sons and daughters. And all the days that Adam lived were nine hundred and thirty years, and he died. And Seth lived a hundred and five years, and begat Enos. And Seth lived after he begat Enos eight hundred and seven years, and begat sons and daughters. And all the days of Seth were nine hundred and twelve years, and he died. And Enos lived ninety years, and begat Cainan." And so on, through the *ten* names to the flood, and the *ten* other names to (and including) Abram. Thus we have as follows the Bible's

---

*Prof. G. Frederick Wright, D. D., LL. D., editor of the Bibliotheca Sacra, June 29, 1893, wrote thus of these two Essays: "I have taken pains to read over, in connection with your table of contents, the two Mss. which you sent me, and which I see are two chapters of your great work. Permit me to say, that I have the highest admiration of your faithfulness in pursuing through so many years the intricate lines of investigation which you have been following, and an equal admiration for the clearness of your style, and the logical character of your arrangement of material. The two Mss. which I have in hand ought to be published in the Bibliotheca, and I can say to you positively, that if you will let them remain in my hands, I will work them into the January and April numbers."

§ 45. First Chronological Table.

1. Adam was 130 years old, when to Adam was born Seth.
   + 800 = 930.
2. Seth was 105 years old, when to Seth was born Enos.
   + 807 = 912.
3. Enos was 90 years old, when to Enos was born Cainan.
   + 815 = 905.
4. Cainan was 70 years old, when to Cainan was born Mahalael.
   + 840 = 910.
5. Mahalael was 65 years old, when to Mahalael was born Jared.
   + 830 = 895.
6. Jared was 162 years old, when to Jared was born Enoch.
   + 800 = 962.
7. Enoch was 65 years old, when to Enoch was born Methusaleh.
   + 300 = 365.
8. Methu. was 187 years old, when to Methu. was born Lamech.
   + 782 = 969.
9. Lamech was 182 years old, when to Lamech was born Noah.
   + 595 = 777.
10. Noah was 500 years old, when to Noah was born Shem, etc.
    + 450 = 950.
    Noah + 100

1656 years at the flood.

This Chronological table *contains* a genealogical list (on the right hand): "To Adam was born Seth, to Seth was born Enos," etc. Such genealogies are frequent in Scripture, but except here they are without any Chronology given with them. Take for example at Mat. i: 7, where we learn that,—To Solomon was born Rehoboam, to Rehoboam was born Abijah, to Abijah was born Asa, to Asa was born Jehoshaphat, to Jehoshaphat was born Joram, to Joram was born Uzziah, to Uzziah was born Jotham, etc. Here we know, that Uzziah was the great-great-grandson of Joram (II Chron. xxi: 16, to xxvi: 1). So that, there are *three generations omitted* in this list; and we thus learn, that in a mere genealogical list "begat" is not always followed by the immediate son, but sometimes indicates only a *descendant* born to the before-named person.

§ 46. Such an *omission of names* is thus seen to be a liability in any *mere genealogical list* found in Scripture. For illustration: In the above genealogical list contained in the Chronological table of Gen. v.—"To Adam was born Seth, to Seth was born Enos," etc., there might possibly be names omitted; Seth (for example) being not the son, but (say) the great grandson of Adam; and Enos being not the son but the descendant of Seth, and so on. But this would have *no effect on the Chronology* of the table containing the names. Suppose that when Adam was 70 years old, a *son* Alvah, was born, and when that son Alvah was 60 years old *his son* Seth was born; in that case a name (Alvah) is omitted in the genealogy; but this does not change the *chronological fact* given that "Adam was 130 years old when to Adam was born Seth." All the variation is, that in such case Seth is born to Adam, not as a *son*, but as a *grandson* or descendant. And so at every step in the table.

Omission of names in a genealogy can not affect the interval of time between any two names given consecutively. Omission of names does not change date numbers.

The interval between Adam's birth and Seth's birth is given as "130 years," and the interval between Seth's birth and Enos' birth is given as "105 years," making 235 years of Adam at Enos' birth; and no insertion of omitted names will change this length of time. The Chronological Table given here, as is not the case with other mere genealogical lists, *fixes the duration* of the genealogy contained in it. Yet, evident as this is, attempts have been made to invalidate the chronology.

§ 47. "Some have supposed, that along with the patriarchs named their *races* and peoples are meant to be included; Rosenmuller, Freidreich, and others think that from these orally transmitted genealogies many names had fallen out. Hensler holds that the expression 'year' denotes among the patriarchs lesser spaces of time. To the first supposition is opposed the definite characterizing of single persons; to the second the fact that in the same manner the son always follows the father; to the third the constant signification of the year as tropical." (Langè on Gen. v: 4.)

Such have been the vain endeavors to change the lengths of time as given in Scripture. But the more recent attempts have sought to open the way for lengthening the antiquity of man, by *breaking down the Bible Chronology* (particularly of Gen. v, xi) *as being no definite chronology at all.*

Two notable examples of such endeavors have appeared in the Bibliotheca Sacra: the earlier in April, 1873, p. 323, by Prof. Gardiner of Middletown, Conn., which we will call theory A; the later in April, 1890, p. 285, by Prof. Green, of Princeton, N. J., which we will call theory B.

§ 48. *The Non-Chronology Theories.*

I. Theory A gives the purpose of the sacred writer as not chronological, but simply this:

"It was sought to record two facts in one—the age in each case of commencing paternity, and the name of the particular son by whom the line was continued. Thus Seth, *e. g.*, might have begun to be a father at 105, but might have actually begotten Enos at any reasonable time during the 807 years which he afterward lived; so that the true meaning of the text would be shown by a paraphrase running in this wise: ' Seth lived 105 years, and begat children, among whom was Enos; and Seth lived after his beginning to beget children 807 years, and begat both sons and daughters; and all the days of Seth were 912 years, and he died.'" (P. 324.)

That is, the language of Genesis is supposed to mean: " Adam was 130 years old when to Adam was born "— not Seth, as it says, but— "some unnamed elder brother of Seth!" And so on through.

§ 49. The writer concludes, that the sum of the ages before paternity (1056 years to Noah) is only the *minimum* length of time; while the actual length of time is an undetermined quantity, the sum of any different ages of the several parents, each taken somewhere between the age of first parentage and "a reasonable time" (say 100 years) before death (except in Enoch's case) as the end of parentage.

Thus, the total ages of all but Noah being 7625, take out eight 100's and we have 6825 years+600 years of Noah=7425 as the *maximum* number of years possible before the flood; which, with the *minimum* 1656 (the sum of the birth ages given) leave us a range of (7425— 1656=)5769 years;—"by which length of time the chronology, on this theory, is uncertain and variable," says the writer.

In the same way he works out a possible variation of "some 1500 to 2000 years" above the minumum or accepted chronology from Shem to Abram. This gives him a possible enlargement of the Bible chronology of (say 5769+2000=) some 7700 years,—using the Hebrew text.

But now notice the insuperable difficulties of this scheme:

§ 50. (1) He imagines the purpose of the sacred writer to be, not to give chronology, but to give "the age *in each case* of *commencing* paternity." And he gives Seth (at the second step) as illustration. Why did he not give us Adam (at the first step)? That will upset his whole theory! Adam was the father of Cain, and of Abel, and of Cain's wife (?) and of an indefinite number of people, before Seth was born. So the very first step is not a case of " commencing paternity "; which proves that the writer had no such purpose as alleged,—and the whole scheme is nipped in the bud without further words. How irrational to suppose an exact *minimum* dating carefully given, and also a *maximum* dating, but the real date suppressed! And how intolerable the claim, that when Scripture reads, " And Seth lived *after he begat Enos* 807 years,"—it means, " And Seth lived *after his beginning to beget children* (long before Enos) 807 years "!

(2) The theory well owns, that the purpose of the sacred writer must be " in each case " to give " the name of the particular son by

whom the line was continued." But it has to be conceded, that the particular son Seth was *born at the very date given* (130 years of Adam), as pre-asserted at Gen. iv: 25, 26; and that to Noah a particular son named was *born at the very date given* (500 years of Noah), as made sure by Gen. xi: 10. The cases, at the beginning of both lists, prove the method of the whole series, and show (what the language itself requires) that in every case the particular son is *named* as being born at the particular time stated. There could be *no object* in specifying the time, except to show the date when that individual was born.

(3) No case can be found in Scripture to warrant the theory. When a *date* is given with the birth of a son (or descendant), it always is and must be the date of that very mentioned person's birth. So Gen. xxi: 5, and xxv: 26, etc. Nor is Gen. v: 32, an exception. "And Noah was 500 years old; and Noah begat Shem, Ham and Japheth;" *i. e.*, one of the three *named* was born at the date named, and the other names are mentioned on account of their importance in peopling the new world. Again, Gen. xi: 26, "Terah lived seventy years, and begat Abram, Nahor, and Haran;" where the names are probably inverted, because of Abram's prominence in the history, though the Samaritan text gives Abram's birth as the particular one meant at Terah's 70 years. *In no case is the birth-date given of a person un-named*, as the theory wrongly alleges.

§ 51. (4) The great fault of the theory is, that while conceding ten definite dates limited to ten definite generations, it denies all definite dating results; thus leaving *no adequate motive* for giving the dates. The chronology of this distinct Chronological Table is thus annulled, as if it were a mere genealogical list of names, which it is not. No wonder it has been thought that a new attempt must be made; namely,

II. Theory B. This theory cuts loose from all limit of generations, supposing not one but any number of generations for each of the ten dates given. In other words, it does not confine the un-named births (supposed after each given date) to the single parent named, but imagines them as successive generations extending on indefinitely any number of years; till the last member of that race (or dynasty) is taken as the next name given in the list, wherewith to begin a new race. It is as if the record read thus: "And Adam lived 130 years, and begat (an ancestor of) Seth; and Seth lived 105 years, and begat (an ancestor of) Enos," etc.

And thus the language of Genesis is interpreted as if meaning: "Adam was 130 years old when to Adam was born"—not the descendant Seth, as it says, but—" some un-named son who was an ancestor to Seth!" And so on through. Notice that the difficulties here are still insuperable.

§ 52. (1) The chronology is thus broken up completely. The very purpose of the writing as an evident Chronological Table is ignored and denied, and it is treated as a *mere genealogical* list like those in other parts of Scripture, which it plainly is not. We have already shown (above), that the supposition or assertion of *omitted names* in a Chronological Table with definite dates, will not and can not affect those dates. The ancestor's ages will remain, as given, whether it be the name of a son, or of a grand-son, or of any more remote descendant, assigned to that date.

There is no getting round this fundamental defect of the theory. The "begat" indicates *the birth of the person named* after it; and the date of that birth being given, it matters not how many un-named generations intervene. The *chronology* is fixed and unchanged. No such anomaly is known in Scripture, or in reason, as a dating given to an *un-named ancestor's* birth. The chronology here added to the genealogy forbids any such fast-and-loose play upon omissions.

§ 53. (2) This theory *takes away all purpose* on the part of the sacred writer in giving the birth-dates he has so carefully arranged. The author of the theory thus describes what he considers *the only design* of the statements in Genesis:

"They merely afford us a conspectus of individual lives. And for this reason doubtless they are recorded. They exhibit in these selected examples the original term of human life. They show what it was in the ages before the flood. They show how it was afterward gradually narrowed down. But in order do to this it was not necessary that every individual should be named in the line from Adam to Noah and from Noah to Abraham, nor anything approaching it. A series of specimen lives, with the appropriate numbers attached, was all that was required. And, so far as appears, this is all that has been furnished us." (Page 297.)

Now, if this had been the sole design, the account in Genesis would certainly have run simply somewhat thus: " And Adam lived 930 years, and he died. And his descendant Seth lived 912 years, and he died," etc. There is no possible reason for putting in besides, at every stage, a *double date*, before and after the birth of each successor, —except by this means to give the *successive dates* or chronology of the whole series. Mere "specimen lives" are given, we are told. How was Seth's life made a *specimen life* by putting the *next specimen* (Enos) as beginning at Seth's 105th year? And so through. It is plainly a consecutive interlocked series. The theory before us rules out entirely all chronological intent on the part of the sacred writer, and so makes utterly idle and senseless *two-thirds* of all the numbers so carefully given.

§ 54. On the other hand, our current reasonable view of the passage adds to that simple design of giving life-lengths the higher purpose of giving dates and lengths of duration, which required the assertion also of the *age of parentage* in each case. And then, in the first table (ch. v), were inserted the *ages after parentage*, to be for us an admirable proof through all time (by addition) that there is no error or corruption by mistake in any of the numbers.

This *proof-purpose* is so evident that all scholars now are by this means aware that variations here in the Septuagint and Samaritan texts can not be mistakes, but must have come from designed change. Could there be any method devised to show more conclusively than does this multiplying and interlocking of dates that the purpose of the historian was strictly chronological? and that too with uncommon exactness of reckoning?

If this be not chronology then there can be no chronology. No mode of speech could be contrived to give successive dates to Bible generations if those tables in Genesis be denied as such. It surely is undesirable to reduce the carefully elaborated reckonings of Gen. v and xi to a mere jargon of senseless and purposeless verbiage, as the theory proposes to do. No reverent reader wishes to regard this, or any portion of God's inspired word, as such a comparatively useless mass of inflated speech. A straining of interpretation, so far-fetched and forced, against the obvious meaning, would open the door to an *explaining away* of almost anything in Scripture.

§ 55. (3) The theory has no support in any of the surroundings of the Scripture in question. The author of the theory thinks the birth-ages are not meant to be added together, because the writer of Genesis has not himself added them up. So, the birth-dates of Abram, Isaac, and Jacob as "sojourners in Canaan," (viz., 100—75, 60, and 130, in Gen. xii: 4, and xxi: 5, and xxv: 26, and xlvii: 9), are nowhere summed up; yet we just as certainly know that the amount was 215 years from Abram's reaching to Jacob's leaving Canaan. Revelation was not given to do all our thinking for us, but it always leaves enough untold to task our study, and lead us to "search the Scriptures." But the theory tells us: "So far as the biblical records go we are *without any data whatever*, which can be brought into comparison with these genealogies" (of Genesis) for the purpose of testing their continuity and completeness. (P. 295.) On the contrary, see Jude 14, "And Enoch also, the seventh from Adam, prophesied." This certainly means "*the seventh individual or generation* from Adam, not the seventh dynasty or race.

There is really but one sum total of years in the Old Testament, the "430 years" of Ex. xii: 40; where the sum *had* to be given, as there were no items given from which to compute it; and this shows how certain was the Scripture purpose to give a *complete chronology*. The "480th year" found in I Kings vi: 1, is no doubt an interpolation, as all the facts concerning it go to prove. (See here Period D, § 1, 21.) Paul in Acts xiii: 17-22, as well as the Book of Judges, have supplied the lack by a statement of the items. The full giving of all needed items in Genesis, according to Bible usage, precluded the giving of totals there.

The genealogy given at Ex. vi: 16-20, is cited as favoring the theory before us; but it is decidedly against it. There the plain intent was not chronology, but mere genealogy; and therefore only the life-lengths were given, (137, 133, 137), which can furnish no dating; so that the total covering the period had to be given (as at xii: 40). But at Gen. v, xi, no total being furnished, the successive items or birth-datings had to be inserted in addition to the life-lengths, in order to give the chronology. In Exodus there are no such birth-dates, and so no chronology. In Genesis the given birth dates make the genealogy into a complete chronological table, needing no total given. Nothing could demonstrate more plainly than this comparison the complete difference between the chronology in Genesis and the mere genealogies found elsewhere. Thus we see the futility of trying to rule out chronology from Gen. v, xi, because it is not found in other genealogies.

§ 56. (4) The objections 2 and 3 to the other theory, A, are just as forcible against this. (Read them over.)

(5) The theory is contradicted by facts and circumstances named in the account. There are, indeed, births to Adam *before* that of Seth, which shows it to be no purpose of these birth-dates to give the age of beginning paternity; so that they have no purpose whatever in this theory, and such previous births omitted can not affect the chronology as we have seen. But the birth of Seth was certainly the birth of a *son*, and not of a remote descendant of that name. For beforehand (at iv: 25) we learn that he was born to Eve herself who herself also named him "Seth," the *appointed* seed in place of her own son Abel. The same is shown (at ver. 26) concerning the next descendant Enos, who was *named* by Seth himself as his own "son," not a remote descendant. And again Shem was the immediate son of Noah; and Peleg was the immediate son of Eber, for another son was "his brother" (x: 25). Moreover, at every step in ch. v, xi, the *after*-life of each parent is expressly said to be "after" the birth of *the persons named*, as being a son, not a remote successor. Everything indicates that the individuals are consecutive.

§ 57. It is urged, that these lists are too *artificial* to be an exact account of all the names or generations included; for, it is said, there are just *ten* steps in each list, with triple names at the close of each. But when you take Shem and his brothers as the last step, the first list (to the flood) has 11 steps, and the second list (after Shem and the flood) has but 9 steps (in the Hebrew) including Abram and his brothers. So that, the alleged artificiality is wanting; and Peleg, "the divider," does not artificially *divide* the list in the middle, as claimed. "In the number *ten* there is in truth a symbolical significancy; but a symbolical number is not on that account a mythical [or an unreliable] number," says Lange concerning the ten antediluvians. Such trifling objections can not overturn the clearly marked chronology of these Scripture tables.

The author of theory B thinks, that the Septuagint version made in the 3d century B. C. purposely changed the numbers from the Hebrew text, yet had no idea of those numbers as containing any chronology in them. But, to show that such an absence of chronology from the views then held concerning the subject could not exist, we cite the Jewish historians Demetrius (B. C. 220) and Eupolemus (B. C. 174); both of whom use that longer reckoning of the Lxx (so soon after its issue in that version), and both of whom employ it as giving the chronology or age of the world down to their day, viz., "5147 years from creation to Ptolemy Soter, B. C. 290." (*Chron. Antiq.*, by *John Jackson*, 1752.)

§ 58. THE RESULT.

We have thus shown, that the non-chronology theories of Gen. v, xi, both theory A and theory B, are untenable. The grand error of both theories is in detaching the birth-dates given from the offspring to whom they are applied, for which no Scripture and no rational excuse can be found. Theory A transfers the given birth-date to *an elder brother* of the person named; theory B transfers the given birth-date to *a remote ancestor* of the person named. As both these devices are unscriptural and irrational, the result is, that we are shut up to the Bible Chronology as to the antiquity of Adam and Eve in Eden.

The Hebrew, the Septuagint, and the Samaritan text, all give different lengths of time for the two periods, the antediluvian and the postdiluvian, contained in the two chapters. The birth of Abraham being, by the Usher reckoning, B. C. 1996, or by the later, more reliable reckoning, B. C. 2096, we have the values as follows:

	Hebrew.	Samaritan.	Septuagint.
Birth Abram, B. C.	2096	2096	2096
Period B.	352	942	1232
The Flood, B. C.	2448	3038	3328
Period A.	1656	1307	2262
The Creation, B. C.	4104	4345	5590

Gen. xi: 10–26, adds up 292 years; and some, therefore, put this as the interval to the birth of Abraham, instead of the 352 or 60 years more here given. But the Scripture is definite and certain here, as elsewhere, generally, in its chronology. Gen. xi: 32, through xii: 4, in the revision, reads thus: "And the days of Terah were two hundred and five years; and Terah died in Haran. Now the Lord said unto

Abram, Get thee out of thy country. * * * So ABRAM WENT, as the Lord had spoken unto him; and Lot went with him; and Abram was seventy-five years old when he departed out of Haran," and came to Canaan. ("Now the Lord HAD said unto Abram," etc., xii: 1, is an error of the King James version.) See § 2, note.

We are expressly told that Abram was seventy-five years old, *when his father had died aged 205;* so that Abram was born when his father Terah was 130 years old. And this 130 years of Terah gives the 352 years after the flood, not the 292. The New Testament asserts the same date. Acts vii: 4. "From thence [Haran] *when his father was dead,* he removed him [Abram] to this land." So that this date is certain. And Gen. xi: 26, does not contradict this; for the three sons of Terah, viz., Abram, Nahor and Haran, were certainly *not all born at once,* at Terah's 70 years; and Abram is named first, not because firstborn, but because most prominent in the history.

Haran was probably born first, as he died first; and Abram was doubtless born last, at Terah's 130 years, as just now found. The only other similar case, of a father and three sons named, is treated by the writer just this way. Gen. v: 32: "And Noah was 500 years old; and Noah begat Shem, Ham and Japheth." Here Shem is named first, because the most prominent in the history, although he was not first-born of the three, since Noah was 502 years old (not 500) at his birth, as we learn from vii: 6, and xi: 10. How careful is Scripture thus to give us exact and sure datings in every case, even when to a casual view there might seem to be ambiguity.

§ 59. We are persuaded that all ancient history can be brought within the duration thus given by the Bible, if not in the Hebrew, at least in the Septuagint copy, with its 3328 years B. C. back to the flood. Or, if the flood were not universal, then we should have 5590 years back to the creation, or 4104 even in the Hebrew text. The question between the Hebrew and the Septuagint texts, as to which is correct, is by no means decided, the evidence in favor of the Septuagint being at least equal to that on the other side. (See Part I, § 29.)

Some archæologists have ascribed to the ancient Egyptian civilization a very great antiquity; but later research has inclined to a more sober view. "Egyptian history involves the date of the earliest historical epoch of man. * * * The epoch of Menes is the first point in the chronology of the history of ancient Egypt, and has been placed by Lepsius B. C. 3892, by Bunsen 3643, by Poole 2717, by Nolan 2673 B. C." (*Chambers' Cyc.*) "With Menes, the first known human king of Egypt, the historical times of Egypt commenced, according to that ingenuous and profound writer Gorres, 2712 years before the Christian era." (*Anthon's Clas. Dic.*)

"We have the Eponyon Canon, and also a 'synchronistic history' of Assyria and Babylon covering about B. C. 1450–850 * * * The earliest Assyrian ruler known to us is in B. C. 1850. About 2100 B. C. an energetic native ruler gained the chief power, and made Babylon the seat of his government. * * * B. C. 2500 or even 3000 is probably well within the truth as the time of the beginning of Shemitic dominion in Mesopotamia." (*Dic. of Relig. Knowl.*)

The Hebrew Bible has the confounding of language at Babel as about 2300 B. C.; the Septuagint has it about 2800 B. C. "Ninus and Semiramis are to be considered as mere inventions of Greek writers. The earliest known king of Assyria is Bel-lush, about 1273 B. C." (*Chambers' Cyc.*)

§ 60. We thus see, that the Bible Chronology will amply cover all the demands of authentic history, as really known or to be known; so that there is no necessity or excuse for discarding the chronology of Gen. v and xi.

PART III.

PRIMEVAL MAN.

Reprint from the Bibliotheca Sacra, Jan., 1894.

§ 61. The Hebrew Bible fixes the placing of Adam in Eden at about 4000 years before the Christian era. The current Usher chronology has it 4004 years; but the most reliable reckoning of the Hebrew increases it to 4104 years. So that 6000 years from Adam expire in A. D. 1897. This expiration, within a few years from now, of *the six week days* of human history (since "one day is with the Lord as a thousand years," 2 Pet. iii: 8), is drawing some attention to the speedy opening of the seventh thousand years, or *Sabbatic day* of human history, as a supposed *millennial epoch* described in Revelation xx: 1-7.

But in a different quarter there is an awakened interest in the scientific question: How are we to reconcile so short a period of human existence as the six thousand years of Hebrew chronology, now about expiring, with the accumulating geologic facts, which go to show, by human fossils and relics of human handiwork, that man has existed on the earth much more than six thousand years? The Septuagint, or earliest Greek version of the Old Testament, translated from the Hebrew about 200 B. C., allows some fifteen hundred years more than the six thousand; but this is thought not sufficient for the geologic demands. What more can be done about it?

In order to *forestall* this alleged difficulty of science, some biblical scholars are trying to invalidate the early chronology of the Bible, from Adam to Abraham, as given in Genesis v and xi;* so as, by having *no Bible chronology* of early times, to allow science full sweep for speculation as to the antiquity of man. (Part II.)

---

* See the Bibliotheca Sacra for April, 1873, pp. 323-331; April, 1890, pp. 285-303.

§ 62. The present writer is fully convinced that these endeavors to do away with the Bible chronology can not succeed; and, further, does not entertain the apprehension that any greater antiquity for man than the Bible chronology allows, will be *positively proved* by science; so that he does not feel that need of "hedging" (to use a term current in worldly business), in behalf of the Bible, which is stirring many scholars. For we believe that the geologists of our day are somewhat infatuated with the idea *that they know the rate* with which nature's changes proceeded in prehistoric times. Whereas, we have no witnesses (except God) to testify at what an amazing pace vast developments might leap forward in the young gush of nature under new conditions,—such developments as require ages under the settled environment of the present.

Nevertheless we are ready, in our life-long research of Scripture, to lend a helping hand to those that feel it needful to be prepared against any emergency, with *time enough* on hand to allow modern science full sweep in its venturesome theorizing. It can do no harm to be fore-armed, even though we expect modern science to grow more sober and modest as it increases in age; it may finally withdraw its challenge against God's testimony as to the time of his own handiwork, at least in primeval eras, where there is no other witness to speak. Yet we are the more willing to aid in discovering time enough for every exigency, in harmony with God's word, in order to check (if possible) the present tendency to undervalue and undermine the chronnology of the Bible, which we consider one of the main bulwarks of its strength.

Our Method.

§ 63. What, then, is our method of finding time enough for all geologic emergencies without impairing in the least the Bible chronology? We find the ample time desired in the very place where reverent geology has all along been finding it—not within the Adamic limit of Bible chronology, but before that Adamic limit (at the garden of Eden) begins, in the *six unmeasured days* of creation. It is now universally allowed that there is time enough in those six untimed periods to meet all the demands of geology. Each "day" may be thousands of years in length; and the "sixth day" may be as long as any day before it. And the last half of the sixth day, wherein *man was being created*, from his physical manhood on to his full spiritual manhood in Eden, may have occupied many thousands of years, with successive generations of incipient, decaying, *physical men*, before the completed *spiritual Adam* emerged (for aught the Bible contains), if science should insist on claiming human fossils so old as that.

In short, our claim is, that Gen. i: 27, may cover any amount of time that the discovered facts of human palæontology may require.

§ 64. All advocates of the evolution theory will at once accept this view. And they are welcome to find, if they can, their needed "missing links" among the fossils of that palæolithic age of unfinished physical man which we here concede to have possibly existed. But we ourselves reject the idea of a long *evolutionary process*, and hold to immediate creation, in only two steps; first, the physical or animal man; and second, the spiritual or godlike man—with an undefined length of time between—as recorded in Genesis (i: 27; ii. 7).

It was all in "the sixth day" of creation. But the human *body* or physical being may have been "created" at mid-day; and the inbreathing of the higher divine *spirit*, whereby the individual Adam became "a living soul" complete, may have been at the close of the day; with possibly many generations of time and physical propagation between, as intimated at the start. (See i: 27, 28.)

That man at first was *mortal*, like other creatures, giving opportunity for human fossils in that pre-Eden era, is rendered quite plausible by the fact, that it was not till *after* the completed Adam appeared (ii: 7), that an Eden-enclosure was fitted up for him (ver. 8-15), and a "tree of life" furnished to him, as if to guard him from outside perils and to keep him from a mortality before inevitable. When he sinned, he lost the "tree of life" which had saved him from death, and fell back to the outside reign of mortality.

Of course, any attempt to explain the particulars of such an unaccustomed view must be of the nature of hypothesis. And while we venture to name a few points of conjecture, and our reasons for them, we want to be understood as only theorizing, not giving positive opinions or doctrines to be maintained either by ourselves or others. Mere Scripture theory here serves to offset the mere geologic theory calling for it. Let us try, then, to answer hypothetically two or three questions that will at once be asked.

§ 65. Unity of the Race.

1. If a race of men, physically such, existed for generations long before the perfected spiritual man Adam, what became of that race, when "the first man Adam"—the first complete man—began? Must they not still survive? and does not this necessitate a denial of *the unity of the human race?* By no means, we answer. If God so chose, he could readily bring about an extinction of all else of that race at about the close of the sixth day, when he used the individual Adam for development into a new race. And this could occur as simply and as naturally as in previous extinctions of species, which all geology teaches, whether at the "evenings" following the "mornings" of creation, or at other points of time.

In A. D. 1655, the French scholar Peyrerius broached the theory of

"Preadamite Man." But that view made the preadamites to be our still surviving human race complete as we are now; while Adam and his family were regarded as merely the selected Jewish race, preserved afterward in part from the flood, which was looked upon as only a limited disaster confined to the Jewish or Adamic family. Such a crude theory we of course utterly repudiate. Our hypothesis is, on the contrary, that of an *extinct* prehistoric race, physically but not spiritually human, and only namable as preadamite man in the sense, that they were the unfinished race of men—the bodily mold for our humanity; which *mold was broken* (so to speak), in the common fate of other lost fossil species, when the consummated perfect Adam was reached.*

§ 66. There is nothing contrary to reason or to science in the claim of such a loss of an imperfect human species. Indeed, the indications of geology suggest *two stages* of advancement in the most ancient human fossils discovered. Says Professor G. F. Wright, in the *Bibliotheca Sacra:*† "Between the polished-stone period (or Neolithic, according to Lubbock's classification) and the Palæolithic period, or the period in which flint implements show no signs of having been ground, there is a wide separation, which no student of the subject can fail to recognize as of great significance. It is the evidence of the great antiquity of the Palæolithic period that now attracts the principal attention of students of this subject." Moreover, the certainty that there was some cataclysm or crisis extinguishing species between the earlier, or Palæolithic, and the later, or Neolithic, age of human remains, appears from the geologic fact mentioned by the same writer, thus:—

"The explorations by a committee of scientific men—of whom Mr. Evans and Sir John Lubbock are members—of, among others, Kent's cavern, in Torquay, England, fully substantiate the evidence that had been before adduced in proof of the fact that the cave was inhabited by men of the Palæolithic period, at a time when the mammoth (*elephas*

---

* If any one, accepting our hypothesis in general, should proceed to imagine that some at least of the primeval imperfect race may have survived, and furnished the much-inquired-after *wife of Cain* in the "land of Nod" (Gen. iv: 16, 17), as well as the "daughters of men" put in contrast with the Adamic "sons of God," producing "giants" bodily, and *monsters* morally (as told in vi: 1-4):—such a speculation is of no practical account, since the *universal* flood (vii: 21-23) soon swept away all races except a remnant from Adam and Eve. Not until scientific research shall have positively found some human race actually without a conscience or spirit-soul, can any question be raised against the presumption of *universal extinction* for all humanity save the family of Noah.

† April, 1873, p. 382.

primigenius), the wooly rhinoceros, the cave bear, the cave hyena, the reindeer, and many other *extinct* gigantic mammalia, abounded in England. These remains are separated from later species and more recent marks of man's presence above them by a continuous layer of stalagmite, from one to three feet thick; and bones of existing species are conspicuous for their absence from the lower deposit."

§ 67. Now, since various other species of animals became extinct after man in some condition was present, as seen by the Palæolithic fossils; there is no reason known why the then-existent species of animal man may not also have become extinct, between the Palæolithic and the Neolithic age, that is, at the end of the "sixth day," being succeeded by the now-existent and newly created or perfected human race of Adam, the fossils of which are those found in the new, or Neolithic, age of geology. Our view of the "six days" of creation as *actual days* of "light" followed by *actual nights* of "darkness" (their length being undefined), will corroborate this view, of darkness (and consequent crisis in nature) as following "the sixth day."

Nor is there wanting in the Bible narrative some intimation of a possible cataclysm or crisis in creation at the close of the sixth day, as well as of the previous days. *After* the full perfecting of Adam (at ii:7), and the establishing of Adam in the Eden fitted up for him (at ii: 8-17), we are next told (at ver. 18-20), "And the Lord God said, It is not good that man should be alone; I will make him a helpmeet for him. And out of the ground the Lord God formed every beast of the field, and every fowl of the air, and brought them unto Adam, to see what he would call them. * * * And Adam gave names to all cattle. * * * But for Adam there was not found an helpmeet for him." Here are two singular points given, which need to be accounted for.

§ 68. (1) An *interval of time* between the existence and action of the complete Adam, on the one hand, and the strange originating of Eve, on the other hand. Whereas, the earlier account (at i: 27, 28) represents the creation of male and female as if simultaneous, with an immediate direction for propagating the race. This seeming discrepancy is at once adjusted, if we suppose that the sexes of the unperfected man at once existed and propagated as in chapter i., which is according to the teachings of natural science; but that after a time, at the close of the sixth day, some crisis obliterated the unperfected race, except that the physical form of one drowned individual was providentially rescued and used for perfecting a new and complete humanity, as in the second chapter.

In this view, chap. i: 26-28, is a first exhibit of the divine *plan* and its execution *summed up as a whole*,—so as to complete the "six days" and bring out the Sabbath institution (ii: 1-3), while chap. ii. 4-25, is a second exhibit of the executed plan, with fuller details (especially of the sixth day's work); the creation of man being shown in its *two stages* at ver. 7, and the new and strange production of woman being shown afterward (as a necessity of the race extinction), coming in the "deep sleep" that naturally closed the sixth day of creation.*

This view is not affected, whether we consider the two chapters as two different *documents* used by the writer (Moses), or as merely two recitals,—one in general, the other in detail—prepared by one and the same writer. But such a view as presented by our theory throws light on the peculiar and non-scientific creation of Eve, which has always puzzled students of the Bible. Only *a single human body* was recovered from the extinct human race, as the man-form which God had "formed"—through undefined lapse of time—"from the dust of the ground"—this being the record of a first stage given at ver. 7. And this one human form, when perfected into Adam, seems to have contained the elements of both sexes: so that woman came forth by separation, not by simultaneous double creation, as at the start (in chap. i). Perhaps the anomalous re-creation of Adam required this anomalous non-scientific evolution of sex.*

§ 69. (2) A second difficulty in the account is the fact that at ii: 19, *in the midst* of divine planning as to a needed "helpmeet" for man, (begun at ver. 18 and continued to the close of ver. 20), we have the statement: "And out of the ground the Lord God formed every beast of the field," etc.,—as if here came in the creation of animals, *after* the completed formation of man in ver. 7. This looks like a contradiction of chap. i, which finishes the creation of animals before the creation of man. But the Samaritan Pentateuch has a different reading,— "the Lord God ONCE MORE formed every beast," etc. So also, the Septuagint has "ἔτι," still or *yet further formed*. As if there had been a crisis or wasting of animals, now followed by a new furnishing of species here at the close of the sixth day. However, this is not decisive; for, instead of the Samaritan reading, we may suppose that our Revisers should have translated the Hebrew as a *pluperfect*, "had formed," as in ver. 8.

The striking feature here is, that the interposed arraying of all the animals in sight of Adam, for him to inspect and to name, was evi-

---

* (Gen. ii: 2, says: "And on the SEVENTH day God ended his work which he had made." The Samaritan copy avoids this seeming discrepancy by reading here "on the SIXTH day." But may it not rather be true, that *the work of creation* ended with the sixth day at ii: 7, with *the work of providence* going on the seventh day through chap. ii: (as it still goes on); so that, the furnishing of the Eden residence, the instructions given to Adam, and the providing of a helpmeet (which items finish up that chapter), were indeed a providential ending on the seventh day of the created work of the sixth day? If so, man's first day of life being the seventh day of creation, the first day of Adam and Eve together was the eighth day, or *the first day* of a new week.

dently meant to convince Adam that there was no creature to be found as a fit companion to him. This review and naming of creatures is begun by God's statement, "It is not good that the man should be alone; I will make him an helpmeet for him." And it closes with this statement, "Adam gave names to all * * * but for Adam there was *not found* an helpmeet for him." Whereupon, God proceeds at once to the formation of Eve. In view of this account, how plausible the idea that God, having chosen for completion but one individual from a perished race, thought best to impress upon this perfected individual the fact that he was the sole survivor of his kind, and that only Sovereign Power could give him a suitable mate, as he saw that all other creatures had. This then is a rational ground for the hypothesis of *a perished race*, as here presented. *

§ 70. FURTHER QUERIES.

2. Another question may be asked. Is not our theory inconsistent with I Cor. xv: 45 (Revision), "And so it is written, THE FIRST MAN Adam became a living soul?" We reply: He who when finished "BECAME a living soul," was indeed "the first man Adam" COMPLETE. The Bible was given for the use and benefit of our present historical human race; and it knows nothing and cares nothing about pre-existent races. Our theory does not pretend to be Scripture teaching; it is extra-biblical, and only asks to be received as *not forbidden* by the Scriptures. As to Gen. v: 1, 2, it is certainly true, that God called their name Adam IN THE DAY WHEN THEY WERE CREATED;" namely, in the sixth day wherein *both stages* of their creation were completed.

If any one should deem our theory too great a modification of the current literal understanding of Adam and Eve's creation, we would simply suggest—that the other scheme, for lengthening the antiquity of man by destroying the Chronology of Genesis, looks far more like a wresting of Scripture, and a rending of its plain import in chaps. v and xi, than anything here proposed concerning the account of double formation in chaps. i, ii.

3. There is a still further question: Since the primeval man is here treated as a mere unfinished or animal race, before the first complete man Adam existed, could the primeval creature be rightly called "man"? No, we answer, not in the biblical sense, as denoting the present race of morally accountable beings, possessed of a spirit from God as well as a body from the dust. But for the uses of geology, and

---

* "Adam was created, and his wife in his side, and (afterward) he showed her to him." Book of Jubilees, A. D. 100. "That is, she was created at the same time with Adam, but in and within him, and it was only afterward that she became a separate creature."—Professor Schodde, in Bibliotheca Sacra (January, 1886), p. 58.

in the discussion of fossils as indicating the age of races and of species, the title "man" applies simply to the physical creature of that structure, with no great capacity required. And in the sense of words as used by modern science, no higher than *the highest animal* nature is requisite to express the geological status of man. For, animal intelligence in its fullest development greatly resembles human thought.

§ 71. Indeed, many of our most distinguished scientists are agnostics and sceptics, denying that man has any higher or spirit nature, or that he is anything more than the highest species of the animal races. Of course, all such thinkers must regard the unfinished primeval man that we speak of as being full manhood complete; with no new creation or new nature given to Adam, but only an evolution of primeval faculty. With such unbelievers we can have no contention. If *they* have not been able to find out that they have a spirit-soul, and insist on ranking themselves as merely the highest grade of animals, they put their origin just where we put it—in the times of the earliest human-like fossils; and our theory remains unimpaired.

We simply add to their materialistic view our spiritualistic biblical doctrine; declaring, as in Job (xxxii: 8), "BUT THERE IS A SPIRIT IN MAN, and the breath of the Almighty hath given them understanding." And we see this higher bestowment announced in Gen. ii: 7, as *the second stage* of human creation:—"AND (*God*) *breathed* into his nostrils *the breath* of life, and man BECAME a living soul" in God's image, no longer merely human but also divine. The perfect man is *later* than the first formed physical humanity; and, according to the theory here broached, there may have been a long interval between.

Our view is exactly the scientific view;[*] only we carry the development a step farther on, and insist that ever since Adam (if not always before) man has a soul as well as a body, a spirit-substance as well as a matter-substance. And we are sure that whatever physical humanity may have existed before Adam, it was with the finished Adam and Eve of the Bible that accountable *human spirits* began.

---

[*] Prof. Agissiz suggested this very view. See Bib. Sacra, Jan., 1868, p. 197.

PART IV.

HISTORY AND PROPHECY.

CHAPTER I.

AGE OF THE WORLD.

1. By the Hebrew.

§ 72. By the chronology of the Hebrew Bible we have as follows:

Pre-diluvian   (A)=1656 yrs. (Usher same.)
Post-diluvian   (B)= 352 yrs. (Usher same.)

Total to birth Ab.=2008
Birth of Abram (C § 17) 2096 B. C. (Usher 100.)

Total   (A—E.)=4104 B. C. (Usher 4004.)
From 6000 yrs.=1897 A. D.

FOUR VIEWS COMPARED.

	Usher.	Clinton.	Elliott.	Good-enough.
Diluvian	2008	2008	2008	2008
To the Exodus	505	505	505	505
To 4th Solomon	480th	612	580th	580
To 2nd Darius	492	493	516	491
To A. D.	520	520	520	520
Total B. C.	4004	4138	4128	4104
From	6000 yrs	6000	6000	6000
A. D.	1977	1863	1873	1897

Here are given the most approved views of the Hebrew reckoning.* Which is right? All agree down to the Exodus, and after the 2d of Darius; the only divergence is in the two periods preceding and following the 4th of Solomon. After the 4th of Solomon Usher is nearest right, though he has a year too much (having all thrown back a year by Nebuchadnezzar's destruction of Jerusalem, put at B. C. 588 instead of the correct 587.) We have shown that Solomon began building the temple in the spring of B. C. 1011, a sabbatic year ending the next September, and that he dedicated it 8½ years afterward, at the blowing of the jubilee trumpet in September of B. C. 1003. Usher has

---

* That of Archbishop Usher set forth A. D. 1650; that of Clinton, of Oxford, A. D. 1845, in his *Fas. Rom.* and *Fas. Hel.*, and that of Elliott still later.

the dedication at the beginning of the sabbatic, Oct., B. C. 1004, and the founding in the 4th of Solomon he puts 8½ years before in the spring of B. C. 1012. (Josephus in his "War" has it B. C. 1011, varying to 1010 in his "Antiquities.")

§ 73. But the interval thence back to the Exodus is evidently more correct as given by Elliott, viz., 579 years (rather 580 years), just as St. Paul makes it in Ac. xiii: 18, 22 (see D § 1), which is given as "480th year" in our present copies of 1 Ki. vi: 1, as Usher uses it. We have elsewhere shown (D § 63), how the true 580 years by mistake got interpreted into 612 (in Josephus) as Clinton puts it, and how it finally got abridged into "480th," as used by Usher. This present reading (480th) may be not so much a corruption as a misunderstood text. It may mean "The 480th year of *recorded reigns*," with 100 years of odious and ignored foreign oppressions left out. (D § 73.)

So then, Elliott's chronology is correct, with the exception of the period between the two temples. This 516 years is 25 years more than the correct 491. And it is plain to see how he gets this error. He puts 70 years of captivity between Nebuchadnezzar's destruction of Jerusalem and the Cyrus decree for rebuilding,* whereas there were certainly not over 51 years (B. C. 587-536). Here is an excess of 19 years, carrying his capture of Samaria from B. C. 720 to 739. Then by merely adding the reigns in Judah, without allowing for 6 years of joint reign (the certainty of which we have shown, Period E, § 23), he has Solomon's death six years more too early, or (19+6=) 25 excess in all, making 516 instead of 491.

§ 74. We thus see that most certainly the Hebrew chronology of the Bible has not 4004 years, as in Usher, but 4104 years at the beginning of the Christian era. Whence it follows that the 6000th year of the world's history will come, according to the Hebrew Scripture, in A. D. 1896-7. For 4104+1896=6000 A. M. (With Solomon given but 39 years alone, as in Josephus, the 6000 years run out in A. D. 1897, giving him full 40 years, it is 1896.)

2. By the Septuagint.

§ 75. By the Greek chronology of the Lxx, we have,

	Lxx. of Euseb.	Of Josephus.	Corrected.	Vatican.
Antediluvian (A) =	2242 yrs.	2256	2262	2242
Post-diluvian (B) =	942 yrs.	992	-1132	1172
Total to birth Ab. =	3184	3248	3394	3414
Birth of Abra. (C, § 17) =	2096 B. C.	2096 B. C.	2096 B. C.	2096 B. C.
Total, B. C.	5280	5344	5490	5510
From	7000	7000	7000	7000
	A. D. 1720	1656	1510	1490 A. D.

* The very error ascribed to Josephus (Rest. of Jos., § 36.)

Here Josephus corrected will have for A 2262 of Demetrius; and will have for B 1132, made up of his 992—his extra 50 on Nahor + 130 for Cainan (in agreement with Luke iii: 36) + 60 before Abraham's birth (which we adopt from Usher, as required by Ac. vii: 4) = total 1132. The Vatican Lxx above, with its 2242 enlarged to 2262, gives B. C. 5510, and has its 7000 ending A. D. 1490.

§ 76. JEWISH CHRONOLOGY. The modern Jewish Chronology is a fabrication, giving no true idea of the age of the world. It goes thus: To the flood 1656, to Abraham's birth 290, to the Exodus 505, to the temple 480th year, to its destruction 410, then the captivity 70, then 40 to the Seleucic era, then 311 to the Christian era = total 3761 B. C. Hence, the year 1893 A. D. they call (3761 + 1893) 5654 A. M.*

Look at the progress of Jewish corruption in their chronology. Josephus gives their original view, drawn from the numbers of the Lxx, which he claims to get from his "*Hebrew* Scriptures." (*Pref. to Antiq.*, § 2, *and Ap. I. 10, etc.*), viz.: that the scriptures "contain in them the history of 5000 years," *i. e.*, from the creation to the time of Nehemiah with whom the Old Testament ends. Philo confirms the same view; and, down to that New Testament age and afterward, we find no trace of any other or shorter reckoning (like our modern Hebrew) known by anybody either among Jews or Christians.

§ 77. But presently, the *theory* came in, that the 5000 years reached down to the Maccabees, put as B. C. 161, with the previous Persian period (of which they were very ignorant) reduced to suit this reckoning. This made them have (5000 + 161 =) 5161 years B. C. Then, when the Christians claimed full 5500 years as properly completed down to the last days of the Messiah (as the Friday morning of the World's Week), the Jews, in order to oppose their claim, and to argue that the world was not so old, and the time for Messiah had not yet arrived, boldly dropped 1400 years (by single hundreds changed in periods A and B, so it is claimed), reducing their 5161 to 3761 B. C. (See § 27.)

This modern Jewish chronology was originated by Rabbi Akiba in A. D. 130; and it has (70+40+311+69=)490 years, *i. e.*, the "seventy weeks" of Daniel, reaching from the Nebuchadnezzar to the Titus

---

* Some give the 290 as 292, then the 505, then the 480th as full 480. Then the 410 + 70 = 480 also; then the 40 + 311 = 351 is put as 352 or 40 + 312 (*i. e.*, 246 to Aristobulus' royalty + 106) to the Christian era. (See in *Prideaux*, yr. 486; and *Hales*, and *Jewish Calendar*, Montreal.) Nicholas' Chron. of Hist. gives the total as 3760½ years B. C. Hales says the Rabbi's have 3740 to 3616. The Talmud Chron. Table (London, 5636) gives Titus' triumph in A. M. 3828, which—69 = 3759 yrs. B. C.

destruction of Jerusalem. And moreover, their new A. M. (3761+69=) 3830 for the latter event, enabled them to claim yet (4000—3830=) 170 years before the Messiah was likely to come after even 4000 years of the world's age. See here unfolded the spuriousness of the later Jewish figuring, and the probability that that people, in their hostility to the Christian Messiah, are responsible for the clashing between the Hebrew and the Greek chronology.

The End of 6000 Years.

§ 78. The current belief of the early Christian church, that the world's week of duration was to last 6000 years, when a *Sabbatic* 1000 years would be ushered in, grew in part out of Rev. xx: 4-7, where the "thousand years" *millennium* is described. It was corroborated by II Pet. iii: 8, where, speaking of "the day of judgment," the apostle assures us that "one day is with the Lord as a thousand years, and a thousand years as one day." Also Psa. xc: 4, "A thousand years in thy sight are but as yesterday when it is past." (See § 13.)

The Creation Week was thus regarded as a type of the creation's duration, and God's rest on the 7th day as a type of Messiah's reign, when "the stone which the builders refused" should become "the head of the corner." "THIS IS THE DAY (they said) *which the Lord hath made; we* will rejoice and be glad in it." (Psa. cxviii: 22-24.) There may be something in this view of thousand-year periods in history; and with all of us an interest attaches to the date when 6000 years expire, although we may not be able to determine just what event in human development belongs at that point.

§ 79. Notice that, by the Septuagint chronology, with the two earlier dates for the end of 7000 years (as given here at § 75), viz., A. D. 1490 (or 70) and 1510, we have a suggestion of the thousand-year theory of the early church (as above) in a somewhat modified form. Having the birth of Christ (as they did) at about 5500 years from the Creation (as if on Friday morning of the World's Week),—let us, instead of putting the consummation at 6000 years (as they thought, *i. e.*, as if at Friday night of the World's Week)—let us put it at 7500 (*i. e.*, as if on the *Sunday morning* of a new, resurrection World-Age). Then 7000 years or about A. D. 1500 bring us down to the Saturday night of Creation, when the *evening* of a Millenial Sunday commences with the discovery of a "new world" and the "reformation" of the old; to be followed after about 500 years by the dawn of the Lord's Day morning of Creation. This is the new Sabbath of a renewed earth, overtopping (for an indefinite time) the old Sabbatarian reckoning; as was typified by our Lord's resurrection on the 8th day, following the finished week and buried Sabbath of the law.

§ 80. In this view, the period from Egypt to the Temple (about A. M. 4000 to 4500) was the "evening" preceding the Hebrew day of royalty. And the period from the Exile to the Christian Era (about 5500) was the evening preceding the gospel morning, which reached to A. D. 500. And the period from popery begun to popery fully fixed (about 6000 to 6500 or A. D. 500 to 1000) was the evening of a "dark age" continuing 500 years more (to about 7000 or A. D. 1500.) While the period from the Reformation (7000 to 7500 or A. D. 1500 to 2000) is the "evening" of a millenial "morning," to dawn at 7500 A. M. (or about A. D. 2000, and to continue through "a thousand years of indeterminate length."

Notice how many grand events centered around the epoch 1500 A. D. here pointed out as the world's Saturday evening:—The discovery of the "new world," A. D. 1492 and the years following (so close to the 1490-1 of the Vatican Lxx noted above;)—the establishment of the inquisition in Spain (A. D. 1481) and the birth of Luther (A. D. 1483) to begin the reformation;—and just before, the invention of printing (A. D. 1447), and the end of the eastern Roman empire (A. D. 1453), in preparation for those other great events. The present 500 years (from A. D. 1500 to 2000) are certainly the *advancing* eve of a more resplendent day now near at hand.

§ 81. There is a modification of the 6000-year idea, which it may be well to mention.

Suppose a "thousand years" prophetic to be purposely ambiguous, because it was not *for them* in those early days "to know the times and the seasons;" and suppose the expression is found (as the end approaches) to mean *twenty-five jubilee periods*, or two and-a-half times the "seventy weeks" of Daniel, *i. e.*, (490×2½=49×25=) 1225 years. If this be the length of each day of the world's week, then the six days will be out in (1225×6=) 7350 A. M., instead of 6000 years. Now, if the Period B (after the flood) in Josephus be corrected from his "992 years" to 1102 years by adding the 50 years more to Nahor which are found in the Vatican copy of the Lxx (see here, Part I. § 31, note) and also adding the 60 years' correction before Abraham's birth which we adopt from Usher, (see Part I. § 2, note),—then we shall have from Josephus corrected (Cainan not being inserted), Period A, 2256 years + Period B, 1102 years + 2096 B. C. for Abraham's birth = total 5454 B. C. which taken from the whole 7350 years (composing the six world days) = 1897 A. D.,—the same as reached by the 6 times 1000 years of the Hebrew chronology.

§ 82. Two of these world days, or 50 jubilees, or 2450 years, minus one jubilee, are 2401 years; which is the *square* of the jubilee period, 49 years, or the 4th power of the sacred number 7. Singularly enough, the interval between A. D. 1897, and the time when Daniel had the vision pointing to it (in chap. vii: ver. 25), viz. B. C. 554,* is just two of these world-day periods of 1225, *i. e.*, 2450 years (or exactly *one-third* of the world's time) from B. C. 554 to A. D. 1897.†

Another curious fact is, that this 1225 years *solar* equals 1260 years *lunar*, each lunar year being taken roughly as 355 days (which Schwartz informs us was the reckoning of the Romans in their old lunar calendar).‡ So that (1260−1225 =) 35 years, or a loss of one whole Jewish "generation" (See period D, ₴ 10, notes), left just (1225 +35=) 35 generations in the interval, or (6 times 35=) 210 generations in 6 such intervals, *i. e.* (210 times 35 =) 7350 years of history in all.

₴ 83. Thus the "1260 days" of Scripture (or "42 months," or "time, times, and a half,") may designate 1260 *lunar* years, as equal the 1225 solar years before us (or 25 Jubilee periods): each of these 1225 year intervals being a world-day of human history *shortened*,—as Christ said (Matt. xxiv: 22), "for the elect's sake those days shall be shortened."

These world-days (and half days) will date thus:

	B. C. 5454	——	Creation.
1.	—— ——	4842	——Cainan 12 years old.
	B. C. 4229	——	Enoch 103 years old.
2.	——	3617	——Noah 182 years old.
	B. C. 3004	——	Arphaxad 57 years old.
3.	——	2392	——Nahor 13 years old.
	B. C. 1779	——	Jacob died 1791.
4.	——	1167	——End of Abdon.
	B. C. 554	——	Daniel's vision, 1 Belshazzar.
5.	——A. D.	58	——Nero's 4th year.
	A. D. 672	——	Romanism Latinized.
6.	——	1283	——Wicliffe born.
	A. D. 1897	——	End of the world-week.

7350 = total world-age. ÷ 6 days =1225 yrs. each.

Is it not possible, that the Hebrew text before Abraham is, as to dates, a corruption from the Septuagint (as here given), providentially ordered on purpose that men might not *too soon* come "to know the times and the seasons" of the coming kingdom?

---

* The date of the vision is given (Dan. vii: 1) as "the 1st year of Belshazzar," whose 17 years ended at the capture of Babylon, B. C. 538. Hence that 1st year was B. C. 554.
Clinton makes the vision of chap. viii to be B. C. 553. "Belshazzar's accession according to Ptolemy's Canon being 555," soon after which in his 1st year the previous vision of chap. vii took place.

†The "Book of Jubilees" (A. D. 100) uses this very two-day period, or "2450 years," so figuring as to make it cover the interval from creation to Joshua, which it calls a period of "fifty jubilees." (See here, Part I, § 24, 34.)

‡ With exact lunations 354 d.+336, the 1260 lunar years=1223 solar years.

CHAPTER II.

PROPHETIC DATINGS.

§ 84. Christ told his disciples (Acts i: 7): "It is not for you to know the times and the seasons which the Father hath put in his own power." We are warned by this not to look in Scripture for exact dates of future events, especially as to the coming of "the kingdom" here inquired about. Yet we know for certain, that there are *some* important datings given long beforehand, such as the "seventy weeks" of Daniel, made sufficiently plain to serve as a general guide when the event approached. (See Isa. vii: 8, etc.) We are expressly instructed to watch "the signs of the times" foretold; and Bible numbers may in some cases have been furnished, not to be understood then (I Pet. i: 2), but to be developed as time advances. There are certainly prophetic times given in the Word of God.

In the "seventy weeks," and in some other cases, a day stood for a year, as we are expressly informed (Ezek. iv: 6; Num. xiv: 34); and many think a large part of the prophetic dates are thus intended, especially the apocalyptic numbers 1260, 1290, 1335, 2300, 666, etc. Much can be said in favor of this view. One strong argument for it is, the seeming *pettiness* of foretelling an event centuries distant without giving its date; yet taking pains to specify the exact number of *days* for its continuance—a number which can not be verified as days, even after the occurrence, as in case of the "2300." Of what possible use can such a prophesy be to anybody? and what could be the intent in giving it? But without adopting the year-day theory, we shall find in past history some striking illustrations of its application, which are remarkable coincidences, to say the least. Take a few examples.

§ 85. In regard to the ending of 6000 years at A. D. 1897 (see here, previous chapter), it is worthy of note that the prophetic number given by Daniel in closing his visions (xii: 11), viz.: "1290 days," if interpreted as usual upon the year-day theory as meaning 1290 years, will reach back from A. D. 1897 to A. D. 607, the very time when the Romish hierarchy was fully established. And the "1260" which he gives at ver. 7, and also at vii: 25 (as "time, times, and a half" for the "little horn" of Rome=3½ years of 360 days each=1260 days or years, or "42 months" of 30 days each,—so at Rev. xi: 2, 3, and xii: 6, 14, and xiii: 5),—these 1260 extend from that same A. D. 607-10 down to 1866-70, when the Romish hierarchy began to end by being shorn of its temporal power!

The Roman Emperor Phocas ascended the throne November 23, A. D. 602. In the 5th year of his reign, August 1, A. D. 607 ("indic. xi" beginning) is dated his decree making Boniface III, the Bishop of

Rome (who had commenced the 18th of February, before) to be *Pope* and "head of all the churches,") " Papa—*caput esse omnium ecclesiarum*"), both east and west, including the church of Constantinople (the Emperor's capital) as well as of Rome (the seat of the Pope.) This was but the carrying out and enforcement of a previous similar decree of the emperor Justinian dated in A. D. 533. Pope Boniface III lived but three months more, dying November 10, A. D. 607; so that, it was Boniface IV that enjoyed the first papal supremacy, under the emperor Phocas who died in A. D. 610, having in 608 donated to his papal protegè the Roman Vatican, thenceforward dedicated to the Virgin Mary and all the saints. Thus was the Romish church supremacy fully established in A. D. 607-610.*

§ 86. And after 1,260 years, in A. D. 1867-70, that supremacy received its consuming stroke by the loss of its temporal power, just as it was putting on its latest airs as anti-Christ, asserting the Papal infallibility. In 1866-7 several Romish countries succumbed to their foes, and a rebellion in Rome had to be put down by French troops. In 1869 the Pope gathered an immense council, which on July 18th, 1870, proclaimed him infallible. The very next day the war of France against Prussia was proclaimed. The fall of Napoleon III and the proclamation of the Republic followed. On the 21st of August the French troops evacuated Rome, and September 20th, A. D. 1870, Victor Emanuel entered Rome with the Italian troops, from which time the Pope's temporal power was at an end.

Thus did the supremacy of the Romish Papacy, arising in A. D. 607-10, finish its 1260 years in A. D. 1867-70 with the loss of its temporal power, wherewith it was able to "wear out the saints of the Most High * * * until a time and times and the dividing of time,"(1260 yrs. Dan. vii: 25), in the last days following the fourth great empire (the Roman world, ver. 23, 24.) † What further awaits it, at the end of the "1290" (of Dan. xii: 11), viz: at A. D. 1897-1900, where ends the

---

* The 1st year of the emperor Phocas, A. D. 603, was just 666 years after Rome first conquered Jerusalem through Pompey in B. C. 64. And in Rev. xiii: 18, this "666" is given as "the number of the beast" —the second or ecclesiastical development of the Roman beast (ver. 11). Is not this *Roman hierarchy* here numbered by the *date* of the emperor (Phocas) who gave it supremacy?—a date of the interval before him during which the Romans had held sway over God's people. Did not the Roman hierarchy thus have a *date-number* 666, as well as a "number of the *name*" 666 as expressed by the letters of the Roman designation " Lateinos "?

† Scott's Commentary (as early as 1812) following Faber, gave the rise of Popery by the decree of Phocas as A. D. 606, saying: "Probably at the end of 1260 years from A. D. 606 [in A. D. 1866] the glowing events predicted will begin to receive a remarkable fulfillment." (*Com. on Dan. vii: 25.*)

6,000 years from Creation, remains to be seen. But there is another side to these prophetic numberings, which is worthy of close consideration.

§ 87. Daniel's vision of the Papal "horn" in the 7th chapter, as just cited (ver. 8, 20, 25), was followed by another vision in the 8th chapter (ver. 1), a vision of the Down-Treading "horn" (ver. 9-14.) Many have supposed this to mean the same power as in the previous chapter; but the fourth or Roman kingdom is left out entirely from this vision, and the *down-treading* horn comes out from one of the four divisions of the Greek Kingdom (ver. 8, 9, 21-23.) Its primary reference may have been to Antiochus Epiphanes coming out of the Macedonian division, and in B. C. 168-5 overpowering Jerusalem with a brief literal fulfillment of the abominations here depicted. The Maccabees at that time so understood Daniel's prophecy (see I Mac. i: 57, 62, etc.) and so did Josephus afterward (Antiq. 10, xi: 7, and 12, vii: 6.)

But Daniel's vision plainly had a much further reach, as is evident from the explanation of it given by the angel (ver. 17), "Understand, O son of man, for *at the time of the end* shall be the vision." (See ver. 19-23.) "Shut thou up the vision, for it shall be *for many days*" (ver. 26). At a later date, that same Gabriel came to make Daniel "understand the matter and consider *the vision*" (ix: 21-23), which evidently meant the vision now before us in the 8th chapter, for the angel now tells about the very taking away of the sacrifice and setting up of abomination (ix: 27), which that vision relates (viii: 11-13). And in this angel-explanation of the down-treading "horn" is put (at ix: 23-27) the full exhibit of the "seventy weeks" that were to intervene before the finished work of "Messiah the Prince." Moreover, in chapter 9 (ver. 21), it was the same "Gabriel * * * seen in the vision at the beginning," viz: at chapter viii: 16, who explains the whole two chapters (though years apart) as pertaining to the same vision.

§ 88. Those "seventy weeks," or 70 times 7 days of years=490 years, are universally thus expounded upon the year-day theory, as reaching from the Ezra decree (B. C. 457) to Christ's finished announcement to the Gentiles (A. D. 34), he being "cut off in the midst of the week ending the seventy, viz., in A. D. 30. This goes to confirm the year-day theory. And thus the division reaches down to the time of Christ, at least. Christ himself cited this "abomination of desolation spoken of by Daniel the prophet," applying it to the Roman army (Mat. xxiv: 15, Mark xiii: 14). We are certain, therefore, by the testimony of our Lord, that the *down-treading* "horn" of Daniel was meant to include more than the literal *days* of Antiochus Epiphanes. It, doubtless, was intended as a picture of down-treading and oppression to God's people, and especially to the Jews (his original people), down to "the time of the end," as the vision itself declares (viii: 17), when Daniel himself by resurrection should "stand in his lot *at the end of the days*." (xii: 2, 12.)

"Trodden Under Foot."

§ 89. What, then, have been the signal indignities offered to Jerusalem and the sanctuary or temple of the Jews, which might well be viewed in the vision as "the place of his sanctuary cast down" (ix: 11), and "the abomination of desolation" set up, and "both the sanctuary and the host (or people of God) trodden under foot," (viii: 13, and ix: 27, and xii:11)? We answer: The depredations of Antiochus showed such a typical disaster and its cure: the later Roman invasion and destruction of Jerusalem and the temple was a more complete fulfilment of the casting down part of the vision. But beyond and above all, the still later seizing of Jerusalem by the Mohammedans, and the rearing of a Moslem pagoda, the Mosque of Omar, on the very site of the temple, there remaining to desecrate holy ground to this day,—this is the crowning or "overspreading of abominations" to the Jewish "sanctuary," "making it desolate (he says) even until the consummation, and that determined shall be poured upon the desolate" (ix: 27), as we see it to-day.

The learned Faber, and after him Dr. Scott in his commentary, has fully and ably shown, how clearly that down-treading vision of Daniel depicts the Mohammedan power: and the British Commentary of Fausset and others concur in this view. Arising in Arabia, the southeastern division of the third (the Greek or Macedonian) Empire, the bloody Moslem sword swept "toward the south (Africa), and toward the east (Asia), and toward the pleasant land" of the Jews (viii: 9); and with a professed commission from God himself "the *place* of his sanctuary was cast down" (ver. 11), and a Mohammedan mosque was "set up" in its place, as an "abomination of desolation" (ver. 13) to all after ages. It was in A. D. 637 that these Moslem hordes got possession of Jerusalem, and marked the site for the mosque of Omar on the ruins of the Jewish temple. (See *Chambers' Cyc.* and all authorities.) That mosque then built has ever since stood as the sign of the down-treading of both Judaism and Christianity by the Mohammedan "horn."

§ 90. And what was to be the length of this *treading-down* by the Mohammedan "horn"? After Daniel's vision of the 8th and 9th chapters, an angel came to make him understand "the vision" (x: 14), which he was told related to "what shall befall *thy people* in the latter days." This shows, both that the time of the vision reached to *remote ages*, and that even there it had some relation to the *literal Jews* (Daniel's own people), and to their own Jerusalem and the place of their sanctuary, as profaned by the Moslem mosque. In this last explanation the angel gives particulars reaching down even to the final resurrection of the dead (xii: 2), and then at ver. 7 (Revision) the duration of the closing part of the vision (the treading-down portion or Moslem profanation) is given. The angel "lifted up his right hand and his left hand to heaven, and sware by Him that liveth forever, that it shall be for *a time, times and a half*, and when he shall have made an end of breaking in pieces the power of the holy people, all these things shall be finished." That is, the *treading-down* shall end at the end of the days, when God's people shall seem to be completely *scattered and forsaken*. The same duration of the treading-down is given by John in the Revelation (xi: 2), evidently cited from Daniel. "The court which is without the temple * * * is given unto the Gentiles, and the holy city shall they *tread under foot* forty and two months," *i. e.*, 1260 days or years, the same as the 3½ "times" or years of years.

Now mark that these 1260 years of the Moslem profanation or completed *treading under foot*, carry us from A. D. 637, when the mosque of Omar was established at Jerusalem then captured by the armies of Mohammed, down exactly to A. D. 1897, when 6000 years of the world's history expire, according to the Hebrew chronology of the Bible. This certainly is a most striking coincidence, concerning the meaning of which every one must judge for himself. Does it mean that then about A. D. 1897, the Mohammedan power, already so weakened in the hands of the Turks, is to lose completely its hold upon Jerusalem, and even the mosque of Omar is to fall or to become consecrated to the use of the true Israel of God? Things as strange as that have happened in our day.

§ 91. But another striking point occurs in this closing chapter of Daniel. As soon as he was told of his "time, times and a half," or 1260 years, he was still more definitely instructed thus (ver. 11): "And from the time that the daily sacrifice shall be taken away, and the abomination that maketh desolate set up, there shall be a thousand two hundred and *ninety* days," or years. These 30 more years are given, evidently back to an earlier date, *i. e.*, from another starting point specified—not the *treading-down* but the *end of sacrifice*. In other words, these 1290 years carry us back from A. D. 1897 to A. D. 607, just 30 years before the A. D. 637, when the mosque of Omar was founded in Jerusalem. And what occurred then? The crushing of the true spiritual daily sacrifice by *the rise* of Mohammedanism as well as Popery, both at that time.

Mohammed was born "about A. D. 570;" he first proclaimed his system at "about 40 years of age," *i. e.*, about A. D. 610. So says Chambers' Cyc., and all authorities agree. The "Hegira" or flight from Mecca, from which the Mohammedan calendar dates its years, was July 16, A. D. 622, which was "ten, thirteen or fifteen years (according to the different traditions) after his assuming the sacred office." (*Chambers Cyc.*) The 13 years makes his work begin A. D. 609; the 15 years makes it begin A. D. 607. We may safely say, therefore, that Mohammedanism arose from A. D. 607 to 610, and Daniel's 1290 years for its existence carry us to the point A. D. 1897 to 1900.

§ 92. But why is this 1290 reckoning added to the 1260 reckoning above? It would seem that the angel, after telling Daniel the length of Moslem possession or treading-down of the holy city *literally*, wished to notify him that there was a higher sense in which spiritually the Moslem sway was to be dated from its *rise*, when it did in reality begin to "take away the daily sacrifice" or true worship of God, and to "set up the abomination of desolation" or false worship, even in "the place of the sanctuary," or the regions held before that by the Christian church, the true Israel, the real Jerusalem, the spiritual temple of God. And this Christian or New Testament notation of the time was added, no doubt, in order to connect the more Judaic reckoning as to the literal Jerusalem with the Papal reckoning which pertained to the Christain church or spiritual Israel.

For, let it be here well noted, that the Mohammedan power and the Papal both arose together, as twin monsters of religious error and persecution, treading down the true church of God. Mohammed set forth his system from A. D. 607 to 610, as we have seen; and the Papacy began its universal supremacy in A. D. 607 with the decree of the Emperor Phocas, more fully carried out to his death in A. D. 610. Thence the 1260 years, as given for the Papacy particularly in Dan. vii: 25, and in Rev. xii: 6, 14, and xiii: 5, reach to A. D. 1867 to 1870, as we saw, when the Pope's temporal power was taken away, as the beginning of the end. And the 30 years extra, here added at the end in case of the Pope (instead of the Moslem 30 coming at the beginning), carry us to the "consummation" or end of 6000 years at A. D. 1897 to 1900.

The prophesying of the "two witnesses clothed in sackcloth" (Rev. xi: 3), understood as the Word of God experienced in the true church (*i. e.*, "the Spirit and the Bride saying Come," xxii: 17), may not only reach through the 1260 years of complete Roman Supremacy (A. D. 606-10 to 1866-70), but may also cover a preliminary 1260 years of Bible Apostacy, from A. D. 254, when the Novation reform was suppressed, (Neander, Vol. I, p. 237, 246, 248), to A. D. 1514, when Tetzel's Popish indulgences led to Luther's reformation. (See my essay on "Antichrist and the Two Witnesses.")

§ 93. Thus do the prophetic numbers, both of Daniel and of John, wonderfully combine in the harmony of history, concerning the two great opposing religious powers of Christendom. Mormonism and the like are but forms of the Moslem heresy; and all church hierarchy and formalism is but an offshoot of Popery. These all must share the same fate, as one common Antichrist or man of sin, "whom the Lord shall consume with the spirit of his mouth (as he is already doing), and (presently) shall destroy with the brightness of his coming." (II Thes. ii: 8.)

THE "2300 DAYS" OR YEARS.

§ 94. There is another aspect of these prophetic numbers, which calls for our special notice. In Daniel's downtreading vision of the 8th chapter, its full length is given as "2300 days" or years (ver. 14); and the "70 weeks" or 490 years are said to be "determined." (Heb. *cut off*), as if those 70 weeks began the 2300 as years. If then we date both from B. C. 457 (where the 70 weeks certainly begin), the 2300 years will reach to A. D. 1844. And what was to take place then, at the close of the 2300-year vision? The Angel says: "Then shall the sanctuary be cleansed," *i. e.*, from the down-treading and abomination which took away the daily sacrifice or true worship. This would seem to mean, that "the sanctuary" or region of God's earlier worship would then be cleansed, or begin to be cleansed, from the Mohammedan "abomination" of oppression which had *trodden down* the true daily sacrifice, or worship of God.

And that very thing did take place in A. D. 1844. A DECREE OF RELIGIOUS TOLERATION was wrung from the Ottoman government, the Turkish Pasha at Constantinople, giving liberty of worship throughout his Mahomedan dominions, including Palestine and Jerusalem; so that, from that time the daily sacrifice of true worship (till then completely trodden down) is set up, and the old sanctuary of Jewish and Christian service in and about "the holy city" is so far cleansed from the "abomination" of Moslem despotism. The edict was dated March 21, A. D. 1844. Then *was* "the sanctuary (in a measure) cleansed," as the beginning of the end, which is soon to sweep away the Moslem and the Papal powers together. Prophetic students just before that event noticed this pointing of the 2300 to that year, and thought *something* was coming then. Whatever folly may be thought to have attended the Miller excitement of 1843, there was at least this one true idea connected with it. Something biblical did then occur, as we see, a striking omen of the end.

§ 95. We have seen (at § 87) that the 70 weeks of chapter 9 and the 2300 days or years of chapter 8 begin together as one vision, at B. C. 457. The selection of so late a date, at the Ezra-Nehemiah decree of Artaxerxes, as the first starting point for the whole vision (both of the 70 weeks and of the 2300 days), is at first a matter of surprise. But a little thought shows us the probable reason. The question was (viii: 13), "How long shall be the vision concerning the daily sacrifice, and the transgression of desolation, to give both the sanctuary and the host to be trodden under foot?" So then, "the daily sacrifice" and "the transgression" against it were the two things covered by the vision and its "2300" years,—the literal continuance of the daily sacrifice being covered by its first part, the " 70 weeks,"—and the transgression against it occupying the rest of the 2300 years, particularly the last " 1260 years " of it. This last part, Christ calls "the times of the Gentiles," (Luke xxi: 24); and Paul refers to the same. (Rom. xi: 25.)

Now "the daily sacrifice " probably was not fully re-established till the coming of Ezra to Jerusalem. For, although Jeshua began it in B. C. 537, (see Ezra iii: 3, 4), yet it was at once interrupted for 21 years till the dedication of the temple in B. C. 516, (see vi: 15-18); and then a great gap of decline followed (at vii: 1) for 59 years (or 80 years in all) till in B. C. 457 Ezra came (followed by Nehemiah), with a decree "to *restore* and *build* Jerusalem." Ezra chiefly restored things in a religious and civil way, reinstating the sacrifices, etc. (vii: 17, and ix: 5); while Nehemiah soon added the material building up. This date, then, the 7th of Artaxerxes, was the real era of a fully restored daily sacrifice, and well selected as the date beginning its continuance and its subsequent suppression.

§ 96. Since the 1260 years of Mohammedan power over Jerusalem (from A. D. 637) reach " an end " at A. D. 1897, and the 2300 years (from B. C. 457) reach to the beginning of the " sanctuary cleansed " in A. D. 1844, as we have seen,—it seems there are (1897—1844=) 53 years of cleansing between. That is, the total 2300 (from B. C. 457 to A. D. 1844), applies also to the interval 53 years later (from B. C. 404 to A. D. 1897). And as there were 53 years of wall-building and preparation at the beginning, so there are also 53 years of preparing the end, viz., from A. D. 1844 to 1897. And the 70 weeks or 490 years beginning the 2300 thus also apply 53 years later, from B. C. 404 to A. D. 87. *

These 53 years are 7½ weeks of years; and it will be noticed, that the 70 weeks are divided into 7 weeks and 1 week in addition to 62 weeks, "the midst" or half of the 1 week being put at the end of all (Dan: ix: 27), or,—by equivalence—after the first 7 weeks, making 7½ weeks or 53 years (from B. C. 457 to 404) as the full time of decree and preparation. So that the 62 weeks (or the 434th year) before " Messiah the Prince," extends from the crucifixion in A. D. 30 back to B. C. 404.

§ 97. And why was that year B. C. 404 thus marked? Probably as the date of Malachi and the close of the Old Testament, or as a close of preparation and wall building both for the city and for the

---

* An intermediate reckoning of the 2300 is that of Dr. Hales, viz., from B. C. 421 to A. D. 70 and to A. D. 1880.

book.* In like manner, the "70 weeks" dated again from that time to A. D. 87, may give us the date of John's book of Revelation and the closing of the New Testament Canon; as indicated at Dan. ix: 24, where we are told that the 70 weeks are "to seal up vision and prophecy." A. D. 87 will answer as the date of Revelation, since we only know from Ireneus that it was in the reign of Domitian, A. D. 81-96. And such a *double reckoning* of the 490 and 2300 is scriptural, as seen in the case of the 70 years' captivity and other intervals. †

§ 98. But the most singular thing about these numbers is yet to be named. Not only did the down-treading vision of Daniel 8th and 9th point out a 70 weeks or 490 years "cut off" at the beginning of the 2300, but also a 1260 years cut-off at the end, as the special portion of Moslem down-treading. The 1260 solar years reach back from A. D. 1897 to the beginning of Moslem down-treading in A. D. 637; but at the same time, 1260 Mohammedan or lunar years are ($\frac{354}{365.25}$ of 1260=) 1222½ solar years, from A. D. 1844 back to A. D. 622, the era of "the Hegira," whence Mohammedans number their years. So that, as 1260 of their years reach from the Moslem Era to 1844, therefore the year A. D. 1844 was the very Mohammedan year "1260," when the decree of toleration was issued, and the "treading-down" of the sanctuary began to have a let-up, in accordance with Daniel's prophecy concerning "time, times, and half a time." Is not this a wonderful coincidence between prophecy and history? Who can deny that this offers some argument in favor of the year-day theory?

These remarkable coincidences we have given, not as any dogmatic assertion of the year-day theory, but simply as facts worthy of the thoughtful consideration of mankind.

---

* Many think that Malachi prophesied during Nehemiah's reformation, after his second coming to Jerusalem (Neh. xiii: 6, 7), say about B. C. 425; because Malachi's earlier chapters preached a like reformation. But if so, yet the life and the book of Malachi did not *end* till afterward; as indicated by the "7 weeks" of restoration cut off from the 70 weeks of Daniel. "Re-establishing the holy law and the holy city was a work effected by Ezra and Nehemiah, with the aid of Malachi, in a period of about half a century, ending with the death of Malachi and Nehemiah in the last ten years of the 5th century B. C., that is, the 'seven weeks.'" (*British Com. of Faussett et al.*)

† If the 53 years from B. C. 404 back to 457 be put with the 97 years thence back to B. C. 553-4 when Daniel had the vision, there are just 150 years after the vision to B. C. 404, its final starting point for the 490 and the 2300. So that, the 150+the 2300=the 2450, or *two of the world-days* from B. C. 554 to A. D. 1897. (See in Chap. I.)

RESTORATION OF JOSEPHUS.

§ 1. In the study of the Holy Scriptures there is no greater outward help than the works of Josephus. Living and writing in the very time of the apostles, and going over in detail, as he does, the whole biblical and Jewish history from Adam to the destruction of Jerusalem by Titus, his books throw a flood of light and confirmation over the contents of the Bible. For, Josephus is a remarkably faithful and painstaking historian. (See the citations in commendation of Josephus from various authors, ancient and modern, in Bib. Chron., Period D, § 100.)

§ 2. Josephus is particularly full and exact in regard to dates and intervals of time; and his figures, when rightly construed, furnish the best vindication we have of the Bible History and Chronology, as the true record of the early career of mankind. But alas! the present copies of Josephus are sadly disfigured with evident corruptions of his text in the matter of *time intervals;* which have resulted from the attempts of critics to accommodate his numbers to their diverse theories. Not comprehending certain Jewish modes of speaking about time intervals, as expressed by Josephus, scholars have greatly mistaken his meaning, and by their side notes and conjectural emendations have brought in corruptions and interpolations, which render his originally beautiful system of chronology so confused and contradictory as to be utterly incomprehensible in its mutilated form.

"Among early Christians Josephus' chronology was in the highest repute. He was a consummate chronologist, an illustrious historian, a profound antiquarian: but his text, especially the dates, we find greatly mangled. The younger Spanheim in his chronology has devoted an entire chapter to errors, anachronisms and inconsistencies in Josephus, mostly from mistakes of transcribers and theorists. He says the recovery of the genuine computation is very difficult and hazardous." (*Hales.*)

§ 3. Hales undertook a "Restoration of Josephus," but his method and results are as unsatisfactory as those that went before. We in our turn have searched out the source of all this error and confusion, and we think we have found a key that unlocks the whole mystery and reveals to us Josephus' chronological system, beautiful and harmonious, and almost entirely in conformity with the sacred Scriptures, giving them a wonderful confirmation. To exhibit this key we must begin with Josephus' Maccabean history. (See O. T. Chron., Period F.)

PART I.

THE PRIMARY MISTAKE.

§ 4. The dating of Josephus is so nearly correct, both in New Testament and in Old Testament times, that we see his error to be chiefly in passing from one to the other. We learn the state of the case by the following:

CITATIONS FROM JOSEPHUS.

1. "After the term of the seventy years' captivity under the Babylonians, Cyrus, king of Persia, sent the Jews from Babylon to their own land, and gave them leave to rebuild their temple; at which time Jesus, the son of Jozedek, took the high priesthood over the captives, when they were returned home. Now he and his posterity, who were in all fifteen, until King Antiochus Eupator, were under a democratical government for four hundred and fourteen years; and then—the fore-named Antiochus and Lysias, the general of his army, deprived Onias, who was also named Menelaus, of the high-priesthood, and slew him at Berea, and put Jacemus into the place of the high-priest." (Antiq. 20, x: 1.) "This was in the hundred and fiftieth year of the Seleucidæ [B. C. 163] * * * It was the seventh year" Sabbatic. (Antiq. 12, ix: 3, 5, 7.)

2. "Aristobulus changed the government into a kingdom, and was the first to put a diadem upon his head, four hundred seventy and one years and three months after our people came down into this country, when they were set free from the Babylonish slavery." (War. 1, iii: 1.) "When their father Hyrcanus was dead, the elder son Aristobulus intended to change the government into a kingdom, for so he resolved to do; he, first of all, put a diadem on his head, four hundred and eighty [seventy] and one years and three months after the people had been delivered from the Babylonish slavery, and were returned to their own country again." (Antiq. 13, xi: 1.) This was B. C. 106.

3. "Now the breast-plate, and this sardonyx [on the high-priest] left off shining two hundred years before I composed this book, God having been displeased at the transgression of his laws." (Antiq. 3, viii: 9.) "This very year is the 13th year of Cæsar Domitian and the 56th year of my own life." (Antiq. 20, xi: 3.) I was born to Matthias in the first year of the reign of Caius Cæsar." (Jos. Life, § 1.)

4. "This desolation [by Antiochus] came to pass according to the prophecy of Daniel, which was given four hundred and eight years before; for he declared that the Macedonians would dissolve that worship [for some time]." (Antiq. 12, vii: 6.)

See further in Period F, § 3.

JOSEPHUS' 57 YEARS EXCESS.

§ 5. The Jews originally reckoned downward from the finished captivity the same correct interval which is given us by Ptolemy's Canon. This will appear as follows:

The original Jewish Chronology may be discovered from the Priest Record of Josephus (Antiq. xx: 10), whose principal numbers he evidently borrowed from some previous official document. It was there he learned of the "414 years" downward from the finished captivity; but he misunderstood by 57 years the *terminus ad quem* where that 414 was intended to end. He applied it as reaching only down to the deposition of Menelaus from the high priesthood by Antiochus Eupator, in B. C. 163 (See Period F, § 9); and he so made that Priest Record to read, as seen in Citation 1 (here at § 4). But in this he was unwittingly misrepresenting the intent of the number "414," which, as given before Josephus in the Priest Record document, was meant to terminate at the change of government when Aristobulus "put on a diadem" in B. C. 106, or 57 years later than where Josephus put the terminus. He thus carelessly introduced an *error of 57 years excess* in his chronology; which increases that much all his intervals of time that reach back from the later times to the captivity or beyond.

This is the simple explanation of that which has confounded all chronologists in regard to Josephus, and which has thrown all his simple and harmonious system into the utmost jargon of absurd and inconsistent datings, according to the teachings of many learned men. In order to clear up the fog concerning this excess, the reasons for it, and the exact amount of it (about which there has been such dispute and bewilderment), let us examine, first

§ 6. (I.) The *certainty* that Josephus made the mistake of just 57 years as above explained, and the *cause* of it.

It is certain, to begin with, that the "414" is assigned by Josephus to B. C. 163 (see in Period F, § 9), and that this is altogether too early a date for 414 years from the finished captivity to terminate. Now we will show that it was at B. C. 106 (instead of 163) that those 414 years were *at first* intended to end.

This very Priest Record, that gives the 414 years, says that

"Judas, who was also called Aristobulus,—kept the priesthood together with the royal authority; for this Judas was the first to put on a diadem for his one year;" after which "the *royal* authority" was kept up by his successors. (See what his second successor says of himself and of his father as kings, Ant. 14, III, 2.) Elsewhere Josephus tells us (Antiq. 13, xi: 1), how "Aristobulus resolved to change the government into a kingdom, and so he first of all put a diadem on his head." And in his other work (War. 1, III, 1), Josephus says: "Aristobulus changed the government into a kingdom, and was the first that put a diadem upon his head, * * * after our people came down into this country when they were set free from the Babylonish slavery."

The *time* when Aristobulus thus took the crown, we have (in Period F), learned from the reckoning of Josephus to have been in B. C. 106; at which time also the priest's oracular "breastplate left off shining," as Josephus tells us, 200 years before his writing, "God having been displeased at the transgression of his laws."

§ 7. Now that very Priest Record, which thus makes that memorable epoch, and clearly explains the year's reign of Aristobulus as the era of democracy ended and royal government begun, asserts that "the Jews were under a democratical government 414 years" downward from the finished captivity, and then—" (See Citation 1 here, p. 3). And what then? It must have meant to say— "and then the democratical government ended, and the royal authority was assumed by Aristobulus," with the cessation of the priestly oracle. As Josephus himself says (Ant. 11, iv: 8), "the high priests were at the head of their affairs, until the posterity of the Asmoneans (the Maccabees) set up kingly government."

This is the only consistent story that the original Priest Record could have told. And this was the exact truth of history. For it was just 414 years from B. C. 520 (the year 2 of Darius, when the decree of restoration after the captivity went into effect, down to B. C. 106, when Aristobulus put on the diadem of royalty. Eusebius uses this 414 years of the Priest Record just as we put it here; for he says, (Hist. B. 1, p. 178.) "Aristobulus took the diadem in the year 484 after the Bablonish captivity," *i. e.*, (484-70=) "414 years" after its close, just as the original Priest Record had it, not as Josephus wrongly makes it, (414+57=) "471 years," (See citation 2, here §4.)

§ 8. But this accurate account of the original Priest Record which Josephus had before him, was so loosely worded, or somehow so mistaken by Josephus, that he gives the *terminus ad quem* quite different from its intent. He has got it to read (20 x: 1) "The Jews were under democratical government 414 years" downwards; "AND THEN

—(not democracy ended, but)—then" the high-priest Menelaus was deposed by Eupator. The mistake of Josephus is obvious, which thus thrust 57 extra years into his chronology. Plainly, the numbers given were those of a document, which he was *editing* in that closing chapter of his Antiquities; and it shows a mixture of the previous reckoning and of his own mistaken application of it.

§ 9. But how *could* Josephus make such a large mistake in the chronology of these inter-testimental times? The error was caused or facilitated by the general ignorance prevalent among the Jews, and evident in Josephus as well as in Christian writers afterward, concerning the pre-Seleucic history. The true inter-testimental interval of time in the dark age between Xerxes and Alexander the Great was lost. (Had Josephus seen the Greek historians, as he had the Babylonian and Tyrian, the early Olympic dates would have set him right.) Josephus shows how ignorant he was of the Persian history, by his meager and mixed account of this long period (Book xi). This is his one weak spot. When with Nehemiah he reached the end of the Bible record, he was all afloat, until he got to the Seleucic era in B. C. 312. Hales, like others, seems to have no idea of the cause or occasion of error, only intimating by the word "present" that there may have been some corrupting of the text. But the fact that all Josephus' reckoning is based upon this error, forbids such a supposition.

§ 10. (II.) Having thus shown the *cause* of error,—inter-testamental ignorance,—let us now note the probable *occasion* of it. The Jews were of course greatly interested in the "seventy weeks" of Daniel, which seemed to fix distinctly beforehand the time of their expected Messiah, or deliverer from foreign oppression, as they interpreted it. They, therefore, early began to figure upon the application of the "three-score and two weeks," (434 days taken as years, Dan. ix: 25), and of the "seven weeks" (49 years), as well as the "one week" (7 years) and the whole "70 weeks" (490 years).

In their ignorance of the Persian history, the Jews of that day estimated the decree of Cyrus in his 1st year (Ezra i: 1) as 20 years before the renewal of it by Darius in his 2nd year, (Ezra iv: 24). This is shown by Prideaux, who (at the year 486) says: "The Jews have a tradition, (*Abraham Zacutus in Juchasin. David Gang in Zemach David. Sedar Olam Zuta, etc.*); and from that tradition they reckon thus: Darius the Median reigned 1 year, Cyrus 3 years Cambyses 16 years, and Darius 32 years;—and they tell us that the kingdom of the Persians ceased also the same year, and that the whole dominion of the Persian empire was only these 52 years," from Cyrus to the end of Darius. This very reckoning is found in the modern Jewish chronology, still followed by that people. (See in my treatise on Diluvian

Chronology, Period A. B.) Here Cyrus 3 years + Cambyses 16 years make 20 years to 2d Darius, *i. e.*, 52-32 (See here, at § 30). *

§ 11. As they found their Priest Record giving them "414 years" from the restoration at 2d Darius down to Aristobulus (B. C. 520 to 106), reckoning as here shown from Darius back to Cyrus, they would have the Cyrus decree 20 years earlier as (414+20=) 434 years before Aristobulus (as if in B. C. 540). And this 434 years was just the "62 weeks" "from the going forth of the commandment to restore and to build," as issued by Cyrus. (Dan. ix: 25.) This, of course, fired the Jewish heart, and led many to fancy (at first) that the time of Messiah was arrived, and that Aristobulus in assuming royalty was the promised "king of the Jews," who was to deliver them from all foreign foes. Or, it may have been this enthusiastic figuring that led Aristobulus to "put on the diadem," and also led to the 20 years calculation from Cyrus to Darius.†

§ 12. But Aristobulus was forthwith himself cut off, with no great deliverance following from his assumption of the crown; and faith as to his being a Messiah must have soon died out.‡ New figuring of the "weeks" had to be made. And the thought arose, that the same calculation that had been made upon "Judas who was also called Aristobulus" (as the Priest Record expresses it), would better apply to the other Judas before, Judas Maccabeus; who did indeed arise as a signal deliverer of the Jews from the foreign tyrants; and who became fully recognized as their sovereign when Menelaus the high priest was deposed and killed.

§ 13. The irregular substitution in the high-priesthood of the ineligible Alcimus by a foreign invading king, Ant. Eupator, so soon after the awful three years' profanation of Jerusalem and the temple by his father, Ant. Epiphanes, and the wonderful restoration wrought by Judas Maccabeus, as a redeemer of Zion; all this made a deep impression ever after on the Jewish mind, and seemed, when looked back

---

* In accordance with this, is Josephus' reckoning of the reigns before Cyrus back to the destruction of Jerusalem (Vs. Ap, I, 20): "Nebuchadnezzar (43—18=) 25+ Evil-merodach 2 yrs. [Antiq. 1½] + Neriglassar 4+ Labo. 9 mo. + Nabonedus [Baltazar] 17th" =47 years from B. C. 587 to B. C. 540 as the 1st year of Cyrus (or 50 years from B. C. 590.) The same reckoning is given at Antiq. 10 xi: 1, 2, much corrupted.

† As to the other "seven weeks" of Daniel's vision, they may have thought of them as reaching on after the accession of Aristobulus; or else, as reaching back from the 1st Cyrus 49 years to the *siege* of Jerusalem at the end of B. C 590, —since the Jews were accustomed to reckon the captivity from B. C. 590 to 520. (See here, § 30.)

‡ To him Gamaliel may refer, when he says (Acts v: 36): "For before these days rose up Theudas boasting himself to be somebody,

upon, as a fulfillment, in part at least, of Daniel's seventy weeks,—more so than the assumption of royalty by Judas Aristobulus, where their first attempt at fixing those seventy weeks had fastened. And so, the ending of the 414 years at Aristobulus was transferred to Judas Maccabeus, fifty-seven years earlier; which carried the 62 weeks or 434 years to the 1st Cyrus back too far, making the 2nd of Darius to be thus (163+414=) 577 B. C. or 57 years too early.

This could be done notwithstanding the previour correct dating of the *original* Priest Record, on account of the prevalent ignorance that came in concerning those Persian times intervening, as we have pointed out. And so, Josephus got the Priest Record corrupted to the form of statement which he has in it; the *cause* being ignorance of the Persian period, and the *occasion* being the speculations of Jewish Rabbis concerning the "seventy weeks." (See Appendix B, § 75.)

§ 14. We have now thoroughly learned, that Josephus' estimate of the interval between the Maccabees and the captivity was overdrawn by just the 57 years between B. C. 106 and 163; and that therefore 57 years must be taken from all his datings that reach over that interval, in order to have his true Old Testament Chronology without this excess. Thus, he calls the time from Aristobulus (B. C. 106) "471 years" back to the decree of the 2d Darius, or his B. C. 577, (see in citation 2, here at § 4), which is 57 years more than the correct 414 years to B. C. 520. This clinches our reckoning beyond all dispute.

And we thus find that Josephus has the 2d Darius or B. C. 520 *right*, when his unwitting excess of 57 years is dropped. So of all his Old Testament dates. What has been considered by many as his jumbled and senseless method of reckoning, now becomes, under the unlocking wrought by this magic key, a beautiful system of correct and scriptural chronology. And the Bible has a most wonderful backing and confirmation in the datings of Josephus, when once they are simply and accurately understood.*

§ 15. As Josephus has the Priest Record's "414 years," reaching from the 2d Darius down to "the 150th Seleucic year," or B. C. 163

---

* * * who was slain * * * and brought to naught." The name Theudas was very likely the same as Thaddeus, as Olshausen remarks; and this latter was only another name for Judas, as we see in the case of our Lord's disciple. (Mark iii: 18.) So that "Judas" Aristobulus may very possibly be the "Theudas" referred to. (See further in my treatise on the Seventy Weeks.)

* Jacob Schwartz, a learned librarian of New York, having examined this 57-year and 70-week exposition here given, says of it: "It is a wonderful discovery and throws a flood of light upon the subject" of Josephus' chronology. (See his letter.)

(when Menelaus was slain),—so he has 7 years less or 407 years reaching down to "the 143d Seleucic year," or B. C. 170 (when Antiochus Epiphanes captured Jerusalem). This 407 reached also from the B. C. 163 back to the "9 Darius," where Josephus puts the finished dedication of the second temple, after "seven years" from its beginning in 2d Darius. (Antiq. 11, iv: 7, see here §32.) Thus, Josephus has the captivity ended there at 9 Darius, viz., at (B. C. 163 + 407=) his 570 B. C.; from which deducting his excess of 57 years we have B. C. 513 as Josephus' *correct* date for the 9 Darius. In the same manner all his Old Testament dates are rectified, and are found to agree with scripture all the way back to the accession of David.

We are now prepared to apply this result to Josephus' system of chronology.

JOSEPHUS' CHRONOLOGY IN THE WAR.

§ 16. The main outline of Josephus' Old Testament chronology is found in a compact form, clear and intelligible, at the close of his first work, the "Jewish War," namely, at 6, iv: 8, and 6, x: 1. We will first give the two citations and then will unfold in tabular form the numbers there presented in the light of what we have already learned.

1. "One can not but wonder at the accuracy of the period; for the same month and day were now observed, wherein the holy house was burnt formerly by the Babylonians. Now the number of years that passed from its first foundation [establishment] which was laid by King Solomon till this its destruction, which happened in the second year of the reign of Vespasian, are collected to be one thousand one hundred and thirty, besides seven months and fifteen days. And from the second building of it, which was done [finished] by Haggai in the second year of King Cyrus [corrupt for Darius] till its destruction under Vespasian, there were six hundred and thirty-nine years and forty-five days." (*War. 6, iv: 8.*)

2. "And thus was Jerusalem taken, in the second year of the reign of Vespasian, on the 8th day of the month Gorpieus (Elul). It had been taken five times before. * * * The King of Babylon conquered it and made it desolate, one thousand four hundred and sixty-eight years and six months after it was built (by Melchizedek). However, David, the king of the Jews ejected the Canaanites and settled his own people therein. It was demolished entirely by the Babylonians four hundred and seventy-seven years and six months after

him [corrupted from 470½].* And from King David, who was the first of the Jews who reigned therein, to the destruction under Titus, were one thousand one hundred and seventy-nine years." (*War* 6, x: 1.)

§ 17. JOSEPHUS' INTERVALS.

War 6, x: 1.				*War 6, iv: 8.*	
Melchiz.	"2177" [½]	Melchiz.	"2177" [½]	1st Temp.	"1130½"
David,	"1179" [½]	Captivity,	"1468½"	2d Temp.,	"639"

Mel. to Da.	998	Titus,	709	Tem. to Tem.,	491½
75 Abram	—18	David,	"1179" [½]	Cyrus,	20

Ab. to Da.	980	Da. to Cap.	"470½"	Temp. to Cy.,	471½
Temple,	42		(not 477½)		

Ab. to Tem. "1022"

David, "1179" [½] (6, x: 1.)
1st Temp., "1130½" (6, iv: 8.)

Interval, 49 years †

§ 18. JOSEPHUS' DATES.

(*War, 6, x: 1.*)

Fall of Jeru.,	Fall,	A. D.	70	B. C.	
Captivity,	Fall,	B. C.	570—57=	513	"639"
Captivity,	Fall,	"	640	583	70 } "1179" [½]
David,	Spring,	"	1110	1053	"470½" }
Temple,	Spring,	"	1068	1011	42
Exodus,	Spring,	"	1660	1603	"592" } "1022"
75 Abram,	Spring,	"	2090	2033	"430" } (Antiq. 8, iii: 1.)
Melchiz.	Spring,	"	2108	2051	18

"2177" [½]
—709

"1468½"

---

* This is conceded by Schwartz and by critics generally.

† The 49 would be 50 if reckoned back from the dedication at the Jubilee, with but 490 years after it, instead of the 491. Josephus here, in the War, reckons the temple as built from 2 years to 9 years of Solomon (not from 3 to 10), understanding the "4th of Solomon," and the "11th of Solomon" in I Ki. vi: 1,38, to include one year of reign with his father.

		(*War. 6, iv: 8.*)			
Titus,	Fall,	A. D.	70	B. C.	
				—————	"639"
2d Temp.,	Fall,	B. C.	570—57=	513	27
Cyrus,	Fall,	"	597	" 540	491½ 464½ "1030½"
1st Temp.	Spring,	"	1061	" 1004	
				—————	7
Founded,	Spring,	"	1068	" 1011	
				—————	"1022" (Ant. 8, iii: 1.)
75 Abram,	Spring,	"	2090	" 2033	
				—————	18
Melchiz.	Spring,	"	2108	" 2051	
					"2177"[½]
	(See Appendix C, § 80.)				

§ 19. REMARKS.

Josephus (Antiq. 11, iv: 7) puts the building of the 2d temple as from 2d to 9th Darius, which was B. C. 520 to 513 (his B. C. 577 to 570). So here he has *an excess* of (570—513=)57 years between his own time and the 2d temple; and all his dates B. C. have to be lowered 57 years.

When the 57 years excess is taken from all Josephus' Old Testament numbers, everything is clear and correct. And it is wonderful, that all his dates back to David are thus found to be the accurate Scriptural dates, as seen in our Bible Chronology; namely, B. C. 513 for 9th Darius, 520 for 2d Darius, 583 for 23d Nebuchadnezzar, 1004 for 11th Solomon, 1011 for 4th Solomon, 1013 for Solomon alone, and 1053 for 1st David.*

§ 20. In the War reckoning above, Josephus gives ("1130"—"639" =) 491 years from Solomon's finished temple to the end of 70 years captivity. And we have found the Bible Chronology to have 580 years from Solomon's temple begun, or 587 from the temple finished, back to the Exodus. The two values added together give (491 + 587 =) 1078 years from the Exodus to the end of captivity (B. C. 1591 to 513); and this is the very value ("612" + "466" =) 1078 given by the PRIEST

---

* This true reckoning of Josephus is traceable in many authors following him. For instance, the "Gospel of Nicodemus" (written say 200 A. D.) seems to build upon Josephus dates. For, one copy of it (in my N. T. Apocrapha) has Josephus' "510 from Moses to David + 500 from David to the captivity;" resembling Josephus' 470 + 43 = 513 to Cyrus. Another copy of it (in Ante-Nicene Fathers, Edinburgh,) has Josephus' 470 from Abram *through* Moses + "511" to David (Jos. 510) + "464" to 19 Neb. (Jos. 466) = 1445,—about the same as Josephus' (430 + 592 + 424th =) 1446th; while it puts that 19 Neb. at 636 B. C., nearly the same as Josephus' 644 B. C. (with his 57 years excess included). (See Appendix D, § 82.)

Record in Josephus' Antiquities (20, x: 1), taken as a *continuous dating* of the high priesthoods from the official archives of the Jews. This proves the accuracy of our Bible Chronology as here given, and the correctness of our interpretation of Josephus in harmony with it; and this links together the Priest Record (in the antiquities) with Josephus' chronology in the War, forming a key to unlock all the mysteries of his dating. (See § 40.)

PART II.

Jewish Datings Expounded.

Let us now examine the respective dates given in this Chronology of Josephus.

JOSEPHUS' PECULIAR METHOD.

§ 21. One reason why Josephus' numbers have been misunderstood is, that his critics have not noticed a peculiarity of his method, in naming events and giving their dates. He has a way of looking at an epoch as progressive and cumulant, covering a series of years rather than a single point. So that, he commonly *names the chief event* distinguishing an epoch, while at the same time he *gives the date number marking the close* or culmination of the epoch. In a word, he is apt to date to *the finished event* rather than to the single noted item of that event. Take *three* examples of this peculiarity in his chronology, as we have here given it from the War.

§ 22. (1) THE FINISHED TEMPLE. Josephus (in citation 1, § 4) *names* "its foundation [establishment] which was laid by King Solomon;" but to this he attaches the *date* of finishing the temple, 7 years later. For he gives that later date ("1130 years" ago) as 49 years after David's accession to the throne ("1179 years" ago, in citation 2). From which it is plain that he reckons 40 years of David, and 2 of Solomon to the founding, (Solomon's "4th year" being understood as including a joint year with David, see I Chron. xxiii: 1), and 7 more to the finishing of the temple (1 Ki. vi: 1, 38), total 49 years. This makes it certain that Josephus *dates to the finished temple*, although it is the *founding* of the temple that he *names* in giving the date. Here is a very clear case determining the *peculiar method* of Josephus; and it is a neglect of this as a key to Josephus' chronology, that has led to the confusion of his annotators concerning his reckoning.

§ 23. (2) THE FINISHED CAPTURING. Josephus (in citation 2) *names* Jerusalem as "conquered and made desolate" and "demolished" by Babylon, which plainly points to "the 19 Nebuchadnezzar" when the city was destroyed; but to this *naming* of the most notable event of that epoch he attaches *the date* of "the 23 Neb.," 4 years later (Jer. lii: 30), when Babylon *finished its capturing* and completely "made desolate" the land, so *finishing the epoch named.* That Josephus is actually dating to 23 Neb. (instead of the 19 Neb. of destruction referred to) is evident; for he gives it as ("2177"— "1468"=) 709 years ago, viz., (A. D. 70 from 709 yrs.=) his B. C. 640, or (counting out his 57 excess=) the correct B. C. 583, which is 23 Neb. as in the Scripture. And here again is a plain example of his method, *naming* the most notable event, but *dating* to the finished epoch.

§ 24. (3) THE FINISHED CAPTIVITY. Josephus treats the second temple as he does the first; and he dates to the finished *captivity as he* does to the finished *capturing.* He follows the old Jewish tradition of a *delay* after Ezra vi: 15, with "7 years" for finishing the temple (as in the case of Solomon), so that the dedicating was not complete till "the 9 Darius," as he says (Antiq. 11, iv: 7). Thus, while he dates the *finished capturing* at B. C. 583 (by means of his "709"), he puts in the next 70 years as a *finished captivity* at B. C. 513 (by means of his "639"). And so we see, that Josephus consistently carries out his peculiar method (of *finality dating*) at all these epochs. * Such systemized chronal numbering (with the accompanying *double reckoning*, (see § 29), suited the Jewish mind. And when we put this peculiarity along with the 57 years excess of Josephus, we have most of the mysteries of his Chronology cleared up.

THE "70 YEARS" CAPTIVITY.

§ 25. In getting at the captivity reckoning of Josephus, there are three parties concerned, viz., the original Priest Record, the continuator of the Priest Record, and Josephus himself.

(1.) The *original Priest Record* of the Jews ended the 70 years captivity at 9 Darius, *the Jubilee year.* For thus it gives the correct Scripture dating, viz., "612+466"=1078 years (22 Jubilee periods) from the Exodus in B. C. 1591 to the 9 Darius in B. C. 513; that is, 1078 minus (580 + 8 of the first temple, or) 588=490 years (10 Jubilee intervals) from temple to temple, B. C. 1003 to 513, the traditional Jubilee years for both dedications complete. Moreover, Josephus in the War gives this same 490 years from B. C. 1003 to 513. (See § 18.)

§ 26. (2) But *the continuator* of the Priest Record, who (about B. C. 100) appended to it the "414 years" down to B. C. 106, began them at B. C. 520, the 2 Darius, supposing the previous "466" to end there (instead of beginning 407 years from 9 Darius, as he might have

---

* See an example at § 86, and § 53, and § 35, note.

done). This makes an apparent excess of 7 years in the Priest Record taken as a continuous whole; viz., 612+466+414"=1492, instead of the correct "612+466"+407=1485 years from the Exodus in B. C. 1591 to the royalty in B. C. 106. (For this correct 1591, see Period D, § 7.)

Thus the 466 was treated as reaching from 2 Darius back to 25 (instead of 32) years of Solomon's temple. But when the continuator construed the Priest Record's "612 years" of high-priests as reaching to the death of Zadok as at 20 years (instead of 32) after the founding of Solomon's temple in B. C. 1011,—he thus had (20+466=) 486 years after that founding, to B. C. 525 for the death of Jozadek; which was 5 years before the second temple began in B. C. 520, where the continuator put the 70 years' captivity as ending. By this means the continuator had ("612"—20=)592 years from the Exodus to the 4th of Solomon, as Demetrius had already (in B. C. 220) reckoned it. The 466 thus became (466+5=) 471 to 2 Darius and (+20=) 491 from 4 Sol. (as at § 17 18); which in the Antiq. are 470 and 490. (See § 51.) But he thus had the Priest Record distorted twelve years; viz., the five years which would carry that record to the 2 Darius, *plus* the seven years more which it actually reached to the 9 Darius. And this twelve years deficiency was offset by the twelve years excess which the continuator allowed at the 4th of Solomon, ("592"+20=612, instead of the original "580"+32=612. See D, § 62).

And so, the method of reckoning the seventy years captivity became changed (about 100 B. C.), from the original counting of it as from B. C. 583 to 513, to the new counting of it as from B. C. 590 to 520; that is, it was now put as reaching from the *beginning* of the siege in the 16 Neb. to the *beginning* of the temple in the 2 Darius, instead of the previous putting, from the *finished* capturing in the 23 Neb. to the *finished* temple as dedicated in the 9 Darius.

§ 27. (3) *Josephus' Chronology*, given in his first work, the Jewish War, ollows the original Priest Record's reckoning of the seventy years captivity, as ending at the 9 Darius: but he uses after the Exodus the "592" of the continuator (and of Demetrius), instead of the Priest Record's correct 580 (*i. e.* 580+32+466=1078). And he retains the established tradition of 490 years from dedication to dedication in the Jubilee years B. C. 1003 to 513 (*i. e.*, 491 from B. C. 1004)—which was really in the Priest Record (though he saw it not therein). By this combination, Josephus has twelve years longer chronology than the Priest Record's correct reckoning: viz. (592+8 temp. +490=) 1090 years from B. C. 1603 to 513, instead of the true (580+8 temp. +490=)1078 years from B. C. 1591 to 513. And in the War he uses, not the "414 years" of the Priest Record, but this value reduced seven years (to correct the continuator's change from 9 to 2 Darius), viz., 407 years from B. C. 513 to 106.

Thus, leaving out his 57 years excess (in changing 106 to 163), we have Josephus' Chronology as follows: B. C. 106+407=B. C. 513+70= B. C. 583+421=B. C. 1004+7=B. C. 1011. And all these are the very dates which Josephus correctly gives, as we see at § 18. His only error (besides the 57) is the twelve excess of his 592 over the true 580 back to the Exodus.

§ 28. We have in Josephus' Antiquities the plain evidence that he followed an established Jewish tradition, putting the seventy years captivity from the 23 Neb. to the 9 Darius, *i. e.*, from B. C. 583 to 513, —and that in this he was no doubt following the original reckoning of the Priest Record.

(1) As to the 9 Darius, B. C. 513, Josephus says (Antiq. 11, iv: 7): "Now the temple was built in seven years' time; and in the 9th year of the reign of Darius, on the 23d day of the 12th month, which is by us called Adar, the priests and Levites, and the other multitude of the Israelites offered sacrifices, as *the renovation of their former posterity after their captivity*, and because they had now the temple rebuilt." This language shows that this year was regarded as the date of full "restoration" from "captivity" and of the reinstated high-priesthood, with a now fully established "democratical government." And in accordance with this, Josephus gives "639 years" back to the restored temple (War, 6, iv: 8), *i. e.*, 639—70 A. D.=570 B. C., minus Josephus' excess 57=B. C. 513 or 9 Darius. This 9 Darius began in Dec. B. C. 514; so that the finishing of the temple is put in "Adar" (or March) of B. C. 513. There must have been an established tradition that, after Ezra vi: 15, the dedicating was delayed (as in the case of Solomon) to reach the Jubilee year.

§ 29. (2) As to the 23 Nebuchadnezzar, B. C. 583. This is given in Jer. lii: 26, 30, as the date when the capturing of the Jews by Babylon was finished. And Josephus (Antiq. 10, ix: 7) recites it thus: "On the 5th year [four full years] after the destruction of Jerusalem, which was the 23d [beginning] of the reign of Neb., he made an *expedition against Coelosyria, and made war against the Ammonites and Moabites*, and fell upon Egypt, * * * and he took those Jews that were captives, and led them away to Babylon." (See Jer. xliv: 14, 30.) No doubt captives were taken at this time from Judea as well as from Egypt. (So say Scott, Fausset, and other expositors.) It is at this point that Josephus makes comparison and gives the interval back to the finished capturing of the ten tribes. And from this finish of the capturing in B. C. 583, he evidently begins his seventy years for the captivity down to B. C. 513. (See Appendix E, § 87.)

We have thus made it plain, that Josephus reckoned the seventy years, like the original Priest Record, from B. C. 583 to 513. And we have seen just now, how the continuator of the Priest Record changed the reckoning seven year, to end at 2 Darius in B. C. 520, with the seventy years before at B. C. 590, the beginning of the siege in 8 Zedekiah (Jer. xxxvii: 5, and xxxix: 1). Thus (about B. C. 100), there had come to be among the Jews these two reckonings of the captivity—one from *finished* capturing to finished dedication, the other from siege *begun* to temple begun.* Such *double reckoning* of epochs was a favorite method with the Jews, as pointed out elsewhere. (See § 24, etc.) The exacter dating, from destruction to reconstruction of the temple, was between these two reckonings, viz., from B. C. 587 to 516.

§ 30. We have seen (at § 10) how, before B. C. 100, there had come in a reckoning of the Cyrus decree as twenty years before the Darius decree of B. C. 520. This brought 1 Cyrus in B. C. 540, or 50 years after the beginning of the siege in B. C. 590. Thus the double-dating of the captivity went as follows:

```
                                        B. C.   Interval.
                                                1st  2nd
16 Neb. begin. of siege.............    590   ⎫
                                       — 7    ⎪
23 Neb. completed capturing..........   583   ⎪  70 ⎫
                                       —43    ⎬     ⎪
  1 Cyrus.........................      540   ⎪     ⎬ 70
                                       —20    ⎪     ⎪
Decree of 2 Darius...................   520   ⎪     ⎪
                                       — 7    ⎭     ⎭
Dedication of 9 Darius...............   513
```

Josephus in the war ends the 70 years at the original Priest Record's B. C. 513 (the terminus of his "639," or 407 years before B. C. 106.) Eusebius, following Josephus, ends the 70 years at the B. C. 520 of the Priest Record continuator, with the 414 instead of the 407 from B. C.

---

* Besides these two reckonings of the seventy years in his systemized chronology, Josephus was aware of one or two other reckonings of the 70. Thus in Antiq. 11, i: 1, he gives "the 70th year" before Cyrus, as recognized by Daniel (ix: 2, and Jer. xxv: 1, 11, 12); which, with his 1st Cyrus put at B. C. 540, will begin the captivity at the 1st instead of the 4th Jehoiakim (B. C. 609 instead of 606), when Josiah was slain, and Jehoahaz was captured by Pharaoh Necho of Egypt. (II Ki. xxiii: 29, 34; II Chron. 36: 3, 4; Antiq. 10, v: 1, 2.) In this victory of Necho (recorded by Heroditus) on the way to the Euphrates, some captives from Josiah, fleeing away, may have got carried to Babylonia; so that Josephus there mentions Jeremiah's prophesy of the captivity (10, v: 1).

Josephus thus had just fifty years from Cyrus back to Nebuchadnezzar's devastation, reckoned as B. C. 590 to 540 (and by some Jews from B. C. 583 to 533). He seems even to have had correctly the fifty years from B. C. 587 to 537. For he says expressly (Vs. Ap. i: 21): "Nebuchadnezzar laid our temple desolate; and so it lay in that state of obscurity *for fifty years;* but in the 2d year of the reign of Cyrus its foundations were laid," etc. (For the "2d year." See Ezra iii: 8, 10. He thus understood B. C. 537 as "the 70th" year from B. C. 606. See Period F, § 15.)

106. For Eusebius says (Hist. B. I., p. 178), "Aristobulus took the diadem in the year 484, after the Babylonish captivity;" that is 414 + 70, from B. C. 106 to 520, and then to 590 B. C., as the beginning of captivity. (See § 24.) This shows that neither the "414" nor the "639" of Josephus went back to 1 Cyrus (as many allege); a point which we proceed to discuss.

THE PRIEST RECORD'S "414 YEARS."

§ 31. We have all the way argued that, while the original Priest Record's "466 years" reached down to the end of captivity as at the 9 Darius, on the other hand, the continuator of the Priest Record (and Josephus) applied the added "414 years" as from the 2 Darius, changing from the original by these 7 years. On the contrary most writers have claimed that the "414 years" were reckoned *from 1 Cyrus*, not from 2 Darius; and by this means they have been kept from seeing the secret of Josephus' chronology in his 57 years excess, as we have exhibited it. It becomes necessary, therefore, for us here to set forth clearly the state of the case. Cyrus or Darius? That is the question.

The only clear argument for 1 Cyrus as the starting point of the "414 years" in citation 1 here at § 4 (from Ant. 20, x: 1), is the "408 years" in citation 4 (from Ant. 12, vii: 6). The argument is this: The "414" must be from 1 Cyrus to 150 Seleucic (or B. C. 163), because the "408" (as 408th or 407 full years) is put from 3 Cyrus (Dan. x: 1 with xi: 31) to 145 Seleucic (or B. C. 168), *i. e.*, from the vision of Daniel to the desolation by Antiochus.

§ 32. But this makes the "408 years" mean the 408th year, or only 407 full years; and as such it may be only a reflection of the 407 years which Josephus himself puts from 9 Darius to 150 Seleucic, *i. e.*, the 414 minus the 7 from 2 to 9 Darius (see § 15). He is speaking of the "desolation" wrought by Antiochus, which he begins with his capturing of Jerusalem in "143 Seleucic" (Ant. 12, v: 3), 7 years before his terminus of the "414" years" in "150 Seleucic" (Ant. 12, ix: 3, 5, 7). So that he naturally names the "desolation" as the 408th year, or 407 years (*i. e.*, the 414 minus the 7 from 143 to 150 Seleucic), looking back to the same 2 Darius, when the rebuilding decree (as Josephus understood it) set forward the 70 week prophecy of Daniel, as a "going forth of the commandment to restore." (Dan. ix: 25.) He may be dating not so much from the *vision* as from "the *prophecy* of Daniel, which was given (or was going forth) the 408th year before" Antiochus' "desolation" of Jerusalem began. (See F, § 9, note.)

§ 33. Or, the "408 years" may be a corruption for 428. As we have shown (here § 11), that Josephus regarded the "414 years" back to 2 Darius as giving 434 years (or "sixty-two weeks") back to 1

Cyrus, therefore, from Daniel's "vision" 2 years later to the "desolation" 5 years earlier, would be 7 years less than 534, or the 528th year. The middle figure 2 may have dropped out accidentally; or some editor, supposing Josephus' 414 went to 1 Cyrus (as so many have thought), may have made this change as a supposed correction of Josephus' number. At any rate, the "408" is no insuperable objection to our view.

§ 34. On the other hand, in offset to that undecisive argument, we have given *positive* proofs, that the "414" and the "408th" (or 407), both being reckoned back to the *close* of captivity, and differing only 7 years, *must* refer to 2 Darius and to 9 Darius, *two dates which Josephus himself carefully distinguishes*. It must be so, because *there are no other two dates seven years apart to which he can refer*. To maintain (as does Schwartz), that Josephus, while following the Priest Record as *his own*, yet in the war changes its "414" years to 407, using *both as referring to 1 Cyrus!*—this is a charge of absurdity on Josephus' part too gross to be believed.

Josephus makes up his full chronology in the War. (See § 16.) And he reckons it thus: From the fall of Jerusalem in A. D. 70, he has the "107th" year to Herod's accession in B. C. 37, and then "126 years" to the death of Menelaus in B. C. 163. (See F, § 5): and then "407 years" to the "9 Darius" in his B. C. 570, or (deducting his 57 years in excess) in B. C. 513. Thus he has (107th+126+407=) his "639" years back to the time when "the second building of the temple was *done*," (War, 6, iv: 8), not back to 1 Cyrus, *when no temple was built*. This is positive proof that "the second year of Cyrus" found there in the present text is a corruption for "second year of Darius, meaning built from 2 Darius onward." It was "done by (or under) Haggai," he says; and neither does he nor the Scripture recognize Haggai as present till the time of Darius. (Antiq. 11, i: to iv: 7; Ezra v: 1; Hag. i: 1.)

§ 35. Thus certain is it, that Josephus in the War lays out his full Old Testament chronology, from Darius (not Cyrus) as his starting point. And in his later work, the Antiquities, he only uses the "414 years" of the Priest Record instead of the 407, reaching 2 Darius instead of 9 Darius, or (B. C. 163+414=) 577, instead of (B. C. 163+407 =) 570, *i. e.*, (minus his 57 excess=) B. C. 520 instead of 513. The language giving the "414 years" (see citation 1, p. 3), indicates Darius, though at first glance it looks as if pointing to Cyrus (as so many think). His expression "at which time" has a wide import, covering the whole period from the Cyrus to the Darius decree; and he expressly dates the "414 years of *democratical government*" from the time when "Jesus the son of Jozedek took the high-priesthood over the captives *when they were returned home*," by which last expression Josephus means the time of Darius.

For, there was *no settled "government"* till then for them to be under, and Josephus knows nothing of the high-priest Jesus till then. In this part of his history he does not follow our canonical Ezra, but the whole of Ezra ii: 1, to iv: 6, he transfers till after "the 2d Darius" at Ezra v: 1 (viz., at his Antiq. 11, iii: 1, through ch. iv). Until which 2d of Darius he has no mention of "Jesus," or "Jeshua" (viz., at ch. iii: 1, and iv: 1. Thus, the seeming start of the "414 years" from Cyrus, turns out to be, by Josephus' own account, a start from Darius, where alone he recognizes "Jesus," or "Jeshua," as "taking the high-priesthood over the captives *when they were returned home*." *

§ 36. Moreover, the very fact that 70 years are given between Nebuchadnezzar's desolating and the "639" or 407 of the War (the 649 or "414" of the Antiquities), proves that these latter datings are to Darius and not to Cyrus. Josephus says: "2177"—"1468"=709 years *minus* the "639"=70 years. (War, 6, x: 1.) But he expressly asserts (Ap. I, 21), that there were but "fifty years" between the desolation by Neb. and Cyrus. In Book 11 of the Antiquities (see the caption dating) but 50 of the 70 years are put before Cyrus; how then could Book 20 (ch. x) of the same work mean to give the whole 70 years crowded into the 50 years space? Josephus has no such mixed-up absurdities as are thus ascribed to him by Schwartz and others. †

The proof seems unmistakable; and, on the whole, we feel well assured that the two datings of Josephus, both to the end of the captivity, yet 7 years different, refer not both to 1 Cyrus, but the one to 2 Darius and the other to 9 Darius.

The Priest Record's "466 Years."

§ 37. We have all the way argued that the original Priest Record's "466 years" reached down to the 9 Darius, or B. C. 513. But this could not be with the language now found in the Priest Record, which reads thus (Antiq. 20, x: 1): "Eighteen high-priests took the high-priesthood at Jerusalem, one in succession to another, from the days of King Solomon until Nebuchadnezzar, king of Babylon, made an expedition against that city, and burned the temple, and removed our nation into Babylon, and then took Jozedek, the high-priest captive;

---

* Josephus (in Antiq. 11, iv: 7) says, "the temple was built in seven years time," being finished "in the 9th year of Darius." Yet (in Vs. Ap. i: 21) he says: "In the reign of Cyrus its foundations were laid, and it was *finished again* in the 2d year of Darius," *i. e., finished in the 2d to 9th of Darius*. This shows clearly Josephus' peculiar method of cumulant or finality dating (see § 21), and proves unmistakably that when (in the War, 6, iv: 8) we read, "The second building of the temple *was done* in the 2d year of Cyrus [Darius] the king,"—the meaning is "it was done in the 2d to 9th year of Darius."

† See Appendix F. § 89.

the time of these high-priests was four hundred and sixty-six years (six months and ten days), *while the Jews were still under the regal government*. But after the term of 70 years captivity under the Babylonians, Cyrus sent the Jews from Babylon, and Jesus, the son of Jozedek, took the high-priesthood over the captives when they were returned home."

§ 38. Our idea is, that the original Priest Record went no farther than this: and that, when the subsequent part was appended (about B. C. 100), some change was made in joining the two parts together, in order to fit the addition to the closing portion of the original above; particularly in the clause we have *italicised*. So that, in our view; the original read somewhat thus: "— four hundred sixty-six years, *until the Jews were established under a democratical government*, after the term of seventy years captivity. But Cyrus," etc. We have already shown (§ 35), that the re-establishment of high-priesthood under "a democratical government is here assigned as under Darius. And we now add, that when the continuator had so stated in what he has appended,—to avoid a repetition of the same expression "under a democratical government," he struck that clause from the original reading and substituted the present text, which agrees with the continuator's idea of the original intent.

§ 39. Now look over the original as thus restored. It expressly starts the priesthood of the "466 years" as being "from the days of king Solomon," which seems to exclude a large part of Solomon's reign; and it ends the "466 years" with the changed "democratical government," as a *marked epoch* proper for beginning a new numbering; while the "70 years captivity" are included as a finish of the "466 years" period; at whose beginning "the government was regal," as previously declared by the original Priest Record itself. Moreover, it includes "18 high-priests," which necessitates the numbering of "Jeshua son of Jozedek" with the rest. (For Josephus gives the list, at Antiq. 10, viii: 6, and he has after Zadock, who closes the previous period, only 17 high-priests before Jeshua, even including Azariah after Hilkiah, from I Chron. vi: 13, 14, whom he has omitted.)

§ 40. But here it will be asked, did not the *original* Priest Record have this "466 years" thus ending at 2 (not 9) Darius, just as the continuator naturally understood it to mean, as we concede? In reply we say: Our reason for thinking 9 Darius (not 2 Darius) to have been originally intended, is (1) that thus it gives the right scriptural interval of time. We are assured that the Bible is correct in giving (as it does) a total of 1078 years from the Exodus to the 9 Darius (as B. C. 1591 to 513). And the presumption is, that the original official Priest Record of the Jews has that same correct biblical interval, when it gives a total of (612+466=)1078 also. We so think (2) because the total 1078 of the

Priest Record is plainly meant for a Jubilee interval; it being just 22 times 49, or 22 Jubilee periods, doubtless meant to reach from the Exodus Jubilee (B. C. 1591) to the Jubilee of 9 Darius (B. C. 513) just after the second temple was built; (as 12 Jubilee periods ended in B. C. 1003, just after the first temple was built.)

§ 41. Scripture does not tell us about Jozedek being carried to Babylon. And when Josephus mentions it (at Antiq. 10, viii: 6) in his catalogue of priests, he merely speaks of him as "the son of Seriah" (who was then high-priest, see II Ki. xxv: 18), probably a boy, "carried captive to Babylon" he says, not telling when. And (at Antiq. 20, x: 1) we merely read: "The king of Babylon made an expedition against the city, and burned the temple, and removed our nation into Babylon, and then took Jozedek captive"; *and then*, *i. e.*, at the very end of all. Here is a *catalogue* of Neb.'s doings, and the "then" evidently means, not at the expedition, not at the temple burning, but at the completion of all, the *taking captive*, which Josephus treats as accomplished fully at 23 Neb., as we saw before (§ 23). The truth may be, that the original records thus treated his capture as closing up their disasters, (as Josephus says, Antiq. 10; ix: 7, "the end of the nation"), with the capturing of the *boy* Jozedek, the heir to official authority being thus gone at last; though left as an unnoticed youth before, just as the "daughters of Zedekiah" were left. (Antiq. 10, ix: 4.) Thus treating the capture of Jozedek, the original Priest Record would naturally add the 70 years captivity down to the Jubilee at B. C. 513, as the epoch of full deliverance, according to tradition.

§ 42. But it is plain that the continuator of the Priest Record took it as reaching only to 2 Darius; and Josephus may have looked upon the "466 years" as not including the captivity, but as ending at the destruction of Jerusalem. Viewed in that light, the "466 years" reach back, by correct scripture reckoning agreeing with his, to the accession of David exactly, *i. e.*, from B. C. 587 to 1053. This makes the Priest Record as a whole to be *not continuous* chronology, but having a *gap* at the captivity and an overlap upon the "612." And if the gap and the overlap be alike, each 74 yrs., *i. e.*, from B. C. 513 to 587, and from 32 years after to 42 years before the founding of Solomon's temple, then the correct scriptural chronology is still in the Priest Record; and it simply furnishes a specimen of that *double reckoning* so popular with the Jews. (See § 24, 29, etc.)

That is, "the 466 years, while reaching as we have argued from Zadok's death to 9 Darius (B. C. 979 to 513), reached also from David's accession to 19 Neb. (B. C. 1053 to 587). And the language of the Priest Record is somewhat mixed, as if (purposely) to fit in part the one, in part the other reckoning.

(NOTE. That the later placing of the "466" as *continuous* after the whole "612" is included in the reckoning, is evident from the express statement, that it reached "from the days of King Solomon" (Antiq. 20, x: 1), not from King David). This view of the original "466 years" as a scripturally correct but two-fold dating, is certainly more rational than the current theories, that make this ancient and seemingly official Record of priesthoods to be entirely discordant with correct Bible chronology.

§ 43. Schwartz thinks the "466 years" end at 19 Neb., but reach back only to the capture of Jerusalem by David after 7 years of reign, rather than to his accession. This violates all the Bible chronology by 7 years, making the accession of David B. C. 1060, the founding of the temple B. C. 1018, with 431 years (instead of 424) thence to B. C. 587. We think it more likely that this original document was biblically right.

Josephus, using his peculiar method of *finality* reckoning (see § 21), preferred to say "470 years" to the finished capturing B. C. 583, instead of the "466 years" to the destruction of the city, B. C. 587. * And this "470 years" is the interval that he uses in his Chronology in the War, as we have seen. This is still correct reckoning, though carried to a different point. Then adding the 70 years captivity, he has (470 + 70 =) 540 years to 9 Darius, and leaving off David's reign he has (540—40 =) 500 years from the (joint) accession of Solomon in B. C. 1013, or (500—9 =) 491 years from 9 years of Solomon at B. C. 1004 (*i. e.*, 490 years or 10 Jubilee periods between the two temple dedications.) Thus all his chronology harmonizes.

THE PRIEST RECORD'S "612 YEARS."

§ 44. We have all the way argued, that the original Priest Record's "612 years" extend to the death of Zadok, 32 years after the founding of the temple; leaving 580 years back to the Exodus, which we show to be the true Scripture reckoning. (See Period D.) But Josephus, taking the 612 as reaching but 20 years after the founding of the temple, put 592 (instead of 580) back to the Exodus. The manner of his making this mistake, we show in our "Origin of the '480th year' reading." (D, § 69). Schwartz and others think the whole "612 years" were put between the Exodus and the founding of the temple. What are the facts in the case?

---

* The original and correct double reckoning of Scripture, was the Priest Record's "466½ years" (instead of Josephus' 470½), reaching (1) from 1st David to 19th Neb. (B. C. 1053 to 587), and fifty years later reaching (2) from 11 Solomon to 1st Cyrus (B. C. 1003 to 537); with the same 466½ years also (3) from the death of the high-priest Zadok to the full accession of Jeshua, son of Jozedek to the high-priesthood, (B. C. 979 to 513). But Josephus, following the current idea of 1st Cyrus (as 20 yrs. before 2d Darius) expressed the double reckoning with his enlarged "470½ years," as shown above.

§ 45. The "612" is expressly given in the Priest Record as "the number of years during the rule of these" 13 high-priests, inclusive of Zadok as serving "*in that temple* which Solomon erected." The 13 beginning with Aaron could not be made out without including Zadok. (See Antiq. 5, xi: 5); and his service continued long into Solomon's reign, being "IN the temple" as the Record declares, not ending when the temple was founded. "It is not known when he died, but his successor was his son Ahimaaz, who enjoyed the high-priesthood under Rehoboam." (So says Calmet.) There were 20 years of building (I Kings ix: 10); and Josephus then ends the 612, giving the 20 less, or "592 years," as his interval before the temple, several times repeated. Only once (in another work, Vs. Ap. II, 2) does he forget himself, and fail to deduct the 20 years. Everywhere else he gives 592 before the temple, which he evidently considers as consistent with the "612." See the many proofs of his 592 at Appendix G, § 90.

To suppose, as Schwartz does, that Josephus, while explicitly teaching 592 years, both in Antiq. 8 (iii: 1) and in Antiq. 10 (viii: 5), straightway, in the same Antiq. 20 (x: 1) teaches as his own number (says Schwartz) 612 years for the same interval,—is to accuse Josephus of an inconsistency and stupidity altogether unbelievable.

§ 46. In order to make out the theory, that in the War Josephus has 612 years back to the Exodus, contrary to his reckoning in the Antiquities, Schwartz interprets his reckoning of "2177 years" back to Melchizedek's building of Jerusalem as meaning back to Abraham's arrival in Canaan! He thus says: The 2177 years—430 to the Exodus and—612 to the temple = 1135 years + 44 = his "1179 years" to the accession of David. But this makes 44 years before the temple, while Josephus plainly makes but 42 (see § 18). Moreover, this makes the "1179" reach back to the *accession* of David, while Schwartz' own theory claims that it reaches only to David's capture of Jerusalem! Mark how contradictory of himself this makes Josephus to be. His chronology in the War expressly *gives 49 years* from the completion of the temple back through David's reign, as the epoch from which his numbers are dated. This settles his whole reckoning, and makes it simply impossible for him to intend any other starting point.

Schwartz himself (when pressed) has to concede this; but he is thus necessitated to claim that all these numbers in the War are "a blunder" of Josephus! falsifying his real chronology here intended, by 7 years' deficiency in all the numbers, and by 3 years more deficiency in most of them. To start thus an entire *reconstruction* of Josephus (not a "restoration"), by asserting that he was such a gross bungler and "blunderer" as this, is a theory we can by no means accept. Josephus has no *system of chronology*, unless it is here in the War, where he carefully brings together the combined numbers that constitute it as one whole system. And the capture of Jerusalem by David as an epoch is here completely ruled out.

§ 47. As for Melchizedek, we know that he was already well fixed as "king of Salem" before Abraham's arrival in Canaan, (Gen. xiv: 18); so that, the notion that not till then he began to build the city, is altogether too unlikely to be ascribed to Josephus, especially as he makes *no reference* to Abraham in this connection. And how could Josephus be reckoning 612 years to the temple, which would be (612—35 =) 577 to David's capture of Jerusalem,—when he so expressly gives it as only 557, *i. e.*, 42 years from the Exodus to 2 years of Joshua + his "515 years" thence to David's capture of Jerusalem? (Antiq. 7, iv: 2. See here, Appendix G, § 90.) Impossible!

It is true, *Josephus mentions* that David captured Jerusalem; but when he gives *the date*, he says only that it was "from King David, who was the first of the kings who reigned therein," (War, 6, x: 1). Though he *spoke of the place*, it was the *personality* of king and people in the Davidic line that *gave him the date;* and so it was at the end, "470 years" later. (See p. 13.) We dismiss the theory referred to, (that 1 David is *used* by Josephus blunderingly, while 8 David is *meant* by him)) as utterly out of the question.*

PART III.

Josephus' One Consistent System.

§ 48. We have now exhibited Josephus' system of chronology, as set forth in his earlier work, the "War." It is one consistent whole, without regard to any reckoning found in his later work, the "Antiquities;" which, however, we find carrying out the same chronology, with only the variation of one year at "the 4th of Solomon." At the same time, we have found this one unchanging chronology of Josephus to be based upon, and in agreement with, the Priest Record (of Antiq. 20, x: 1); which Record gives the correct Bible Chronology.

FROM TEMPLE TO TEMPLE.

The chief point of interest about Josephus' chronology is, that, by our showing, he has the same interval from temple to temple as scripture has; and particularly, he has the duration of the ten tribes of Israel, from the 1st of Jeroboam to the capture of Samaria, as the very same 254 years which the Bible figures demand. And thus his testimony confirms and establishes our Bible Chronology as correct.

---

* Appendix H, § 95.

§ 49. The certainty of the 254 years as the reckoning of Josephus, is seen both from the foregoing exhibit from the War, and also from express statements in the Antiquities.

1. In the War. The "1130 years" at 9 years of Solomon minus the "639 years" to the end of 70 years' captivity, give 491 years; which, taking out the 70, are 421 years from 9 years of Solomon to the beginning of 70 years captivity. These 421 years can only be made up thus: One year of Solomon being put as joint reign with his father, there are 30 more years of Solomon + the 254 of Israel + the 133 to the 19 Neb.=417 years + 4 years more=421 years to the 23 Neb., as the final capturing which Josephus makes the beginning of his 70 years. (§ 24.)

2. In the Antiquities, (10, iv: 2, 4) Josephus says: "The prophet who came to Jeroboam foretold (etc.) These predictions took effect after three hundred and sixty-one years," "when now Josiah was in the 18th year of his reign." Now, the 254 years + 23 more of Hezekiah + 55 of Manasseh + 2 of Ammon + 17 of Josiah=351 years, which is evidently the correct reading of the 361. For that 361 can in no way be made out, and the 260 (claimed by Schwartz in place of the 254) can by no means be got in.

§ 50. This is conclusive. And it proves that Josephus, like Scripture, has this 351 + (14 more of Josiah + 11 + 11 + 4 years more, or) 40 more, making the 391st year, or full 390 years, and 40 years, from the final capturing in 23 Neb., for "the burden" of Israel and of Judah respectively, as at Ezek. iv: 5, 6. (See Period E, § 45.) And it proves that Josephus had the duration of the temple as (37 more of Solomon + the 254 + the 133 to 19 Neb. =424 years, not 430 (or 431) as Schwartz claims.

§ 51. We have seen, that, while Josephus in the War has Solomon's *dedication* rightly after 10 years of his *sole* reign (which is 11 years in all), yet he there has the temple *built* from 2 years to 9 years of the sole reign (which is 3 to 10 years in all). But in the later written Antiquities he seems plainly to put the *building* of the temple one year later (from B. C. 1010 to 1003 instead of B. C. 1011 to 1004), *i. e.*, from 3 years to 10 years of the sole reign; thus having the completion and the dedication of the temple both in the same autumn, after 10 years of Solomon's sole reign, and after 7½ (no longer 8½) from the founding. This leaves Josephus but 490 years (instead of 491 in the War) from one temple's building to the other temple's building, with 50 years (instead of 49) back to the beginning of David. The only change thus made in the numbers of the War, is "1130" reduced to 1129. (See Period D, § 41.)

§ 52. Let us look further at the Antiquities, and see how Josephus adheres to his one consistent chronology of the War. He says (at

Antiq. 10, viii: 4): "The kings of David's race thus ended their lives, being in number 21, until the last king, who *altogether* reigned 514 years 6 months and 10 days; *of whom Saul*, who was their first king, retained the government 20 years, though he was not of the same tribe as the rest.* And (at Antiq. 11, iv: 8) he says: "Before their captivity and the dissolution of their polity, they at first had kingly government, from Saul or David, for 532 years 6 months and 19 days; but before these kings such rulers governed them as were called judges."

In both these passages, Josephus evidently reckons Jehoiachin "the last king" till "he ended his life" in Babylon, 22 years after the 23 Neb., *i. e.*, in B. C. 561, which was "the 37th year" of his reign (or captivity beginning B. C. 598). (Jer. lii: 31 34.) And so, in the second of the two passages, Josephus says: These 22 years + the "470 years" back to 1 David + Saul 40 years = "532 years" for the kings. Here Josephus shows a vestige of the correct "40 years" for Saul, as rightly given by Paul (in Acts xiii: 21). But in the first of the two citations, Josephus gives his own reckoning of Saul as "20 years." This will reduce his total "532" to 512, and how does he get the other two years? Whiston, in a note at Antiq. 6, xiv: 9, interprets his "2 years" for Saul as "twenty and two," and thus would account for these extra 2 years. The "514" may be a corruption for 512. †

Josephus' "470 Years."

§ 54. We have seen (§ 10) how, in Josephus' day, the Cyrus decree had come to be regarded as twenty years before the 2 Darius, *i. e.*, as if in B. C. 540; which divided Josephus' seventy years captivity into

---

* Notice Josephus' peculiar *style* of speaking; "Kings of David's line" are the subject, yet the predicate "reigned 514 years" includes Saul's 20 years; ("of whom Saul," is his expression).

† § 53. Everybody knows that in Josephus' day there were current two estimates of Saul's reign, he making it 20 or 22, and Paul calling it 40; and in the "532," we see Josephus falling into the latter view. (See § 92.)

Schwartz objects to our inclusion of Jehoiachin's captivity in Josephus' period of the kings, because it is given at the *mention* of Zedekiah's overthrow. He seems unaware of Josephus' peculiarity of method, his fondness for *mentioning* an epoch by its most striking event, while he carries down the *time* interval to its finished results. (See § 21.) Thus, he mentions the fall of Jerusalem and the Jews at 19 Neb., but he carries the time interval (his "1468" and his "470" in the War) down to the finished capturing in 23 Neb. So, he mentions the end of the reigning kings, but he carries the interval of kings down till all had "ended their lives," as he himself expresses it. (Ant. 10, viii: 4.)

Schwartz himself, trying to figure out the amount without Jehoiachin, gets 534 years instead of the "532." So that theory will not work.

forty-three years before Cyrus and twenty-seven years after him.
(§ 30.) When, with this forty-three years from 23 Neb. to Cyrus,
Josephus put also forty-three years (instead of the forty-two) from the
accession of David to the founding of the temple, as shown above
(§ 51), he thus had a new *double reckoning* (not only at the captivity as
before seen, but also) from temple to temple. For with the 427 years
from 4 Sol. to 23 Neb. (B. C. 1010 to 583), he had forty-three years
more (making 470) back to 1 David (B. C. 1053), and also forty-three
years more (making 470) forward to 1 Cyrus (B. C. 540), as follows:

B. C. Intervals.

```
1 David,      1053
                — 43  ⎫
4 Solomon,    1010    ⎬  470 years of Jerusalem.
                —427  ⎭
23 Neb'zar,    583    ⎫  470 years of the temple.
                — 43  ⎭
1 Cyrus,       540
```

This double reckoning (so popular, see § 24, 29, 42), was doubtless
one reason for changing from 42 to 43 years at the 4th of Solomon.
But this second reckoning of the 470 years (for the temple), is a peculiarity of Josephus' Antiquities, which has more completely nonplussed chronologists generally than any other dating he has given.
The difficulty arises from the *ambiguousness* with which Josephus
assigns the terminus of the 470 years. We will try to unravel the
mystery.

§ 55. At Nebuchadnezzar's capture of Jerusalem (Antiq. 10, viii: 5)
Josephus thus writes: "Now the temple was burnt 470 years 6 months
and 10 days after it was built. It was then 1062 years 6 months and
10 days from the departure out of Egypt;"—that is, there was 1062½
—the 470½=) 592 years between the Exodus and the Temple, just as
he elsewhere puts it.

Here it does *look* as if the "470½ years" must end at the burning
of the temple in the 19th of Neb. (B. C. 587.) But that is simply impossible to be meant by Josephus. For, the caption-datings at the
head of these three books (8, 9, 10) are (163+157+180½ [182½]=) a
total of 500; and 3 years of Solomon + the 470 = 473 out of the 500,
leave but 27 years from their close to the end of Book 10; whereas we
know that the last 50 years of this Book's "180½ years" extend from
Neb.'s capturing to Cyrus. (See Ant. 10, ix: 7.) Therefore to consider
the terminus of the "470 years" as at the 19 Neb. is to leave but 27
years from that time to Cyrus, or (50—27 =) 23 years less than the
caption dating declares. The 19th Neb. *can not* be the terminus meant
for the "470 years." What then was the intent of Josephus' reckoning here?

§ 56. We just now showed that the temple's "470 years" as a *second reckoning* of Jerusalem's "470 years" correctly reaches by scripture from the "4th Solomon" *to the 1st Cyrus* (as reckoned by Josephus, 20 years before the 2d Darius, or 27 years before the temple's dedication as in the 9th Darius. So that, if the intended terminus of the temple's 470 years be indeed at Josephus' 1st Cyrus, then the remaining 27 years of the 500 given in the captions is a mistake of the caption writer; and they really carry us down to the 9 Darius, with the 470+20 = 490 years to the 2 Darius, or from temple to temple as shown above. The surplus 27 years plainly belongs in the next Book after the 1st of Cyrus. This will solve the riddle of the "470 years."

§ 57. We have seen that Josephus' favorite assignment for the captivity was from 23d Neb. to 9th Darius (B. C. 583 to 513). To the Jews these 70 years were a blank, a lost period which they disliked to count by itself. But in the midst of it was one bright spot, at the decree of Cyrus, put by Josephus as 43 years after the beginning and 27 years before the closing of these 70 years captivity (*i. e.*, at B. C. 540), which they looked upon as the era of *finished destruction* and dawning restoration: That era Josephus had in his eye, and his "470 years" dating should properly have been there (some pages later) at the close of this Book 10. For, his thought was of that finished destruction, that dawning restoration of THE TEMPLE. By some means his dating is out of place; and while he wrote "built" and "burnt," he really meant "built" and "ready to be rebuilt." Therefore, reading between the lines we interpret Josephus' language thus: "Now the temple was [and remained] burnt 470½ years after it was built," *till the edict for it to be rebuilt.*

§ 58. This we deem the solution of this great mystery in Josephus, and by it his whole system of chronology is preserved in harmonious truthfulness. For thus, we have his ("639"+7 =) 646 years back to 2d Darius (B. C. 520) + 20 = 666 years back to 1st Cyrus (as B. C. 540) + this "470 years" (for the 471 in the War) = 1136 years back to the building of Solomon's temple (put as from 1136 to 1129 years, or B. C 1010 to 1003)—in place of the 1137 to "1130 years" (or B. C. 1011-1004) given in the War.

With this harmonize all Josephus' computations. In the War he has this same number "470½ years," given as the interval from the finished capturing in 23d Neb. (B. C. 583) back to the beginning of David's reign (in B. C. 1053). And now here, he takes the two termini each 43 years later, viz., B. C. 1010 (after 40 years of David and 3 of Solomon), and B. C. 540 (after 43 years of captivity),—and he has these points also (B. C. 1010 and 540) just the same "470 years" apart. Such *double reckonings* of striking time intervals we have seen to be a favorite study of the Jewish scribes, and Josephus has them frequently. (See § 24, 29, 42, 54, 58.)

§ 59. The attempt of some scholars to make this "470 years" of Josephus mean so long from the death of David (instead of his accession) to the destruction of Jerusalem, is utterly impracticable. For, that contradicts Josephus' own fixing of it in all his War numbers, as shown fully above, as well as in the datings we have just cited. And it also contradicts Josephus' other "470 years" dating (of the temple) just now recited. As he says *the temple* which began *in 4th Solomon* went on 470 years (*till 19 Neb.* say these scholars),—how could he at the same time (in the War) be reckoning only 470 years *from 1st Solomon to 23d Neb?* This distance must be an excess of 7 years over the other, and must require 477 instead of 470 years. That very corruption of Josephus' number has crept into his text (at War, 6, x; 1), through just such attempts to reconstruct him as we are pointing out.

§ 60. The most futile attempt of all is to fasten upon Josephus himself the absurd 40 years corruption of his text, by which (at Antiq. 8, vii: 8) the reign of Solomon is increased to 80 years! with his age correspondingly enlarged. This, say the scholars, accounts for the large reckoning of Josephus' (470 years) given to the duration of the temple; and "Josephus always adds in those 40 years with all his numbers," says even so acute a chronologist as Jackson; from whom the sentiment is re-echoed down to this day. In order to have the 40 years just fill out the 470, Schwartz insists on 430 years as Josephus *previous* reckoning in the Priest Record; but how in the same work (the Antiquities) he could have both 470 and 430 for the duration of the temple, it is hard to explain. And great straining is used to make out the diverse medleys of Josephus reckoning which have been hereupon invented. It is pitiable to witness the tergiversations and distortions of chronology, which have thus been wrought out and (alas!) imposed upon Josephus, as if parts of his system, which on the contrary is so beautiful and consistent.

§ 61. The 40 years corruption of Solomon is so gross and monstrous, so abhorrent to all Josephus' numbers, as we have shown, that it is a wonder for a critical scholar to be deceived thereby. After framing so plain and so consistent a system of Old Testament dating as Josephus shows in his earlier work (the War), how is it possible for any thoughful man to imagine, that in his later, riper work (the Antiquities) Josephus deliberately repudiated and upset the whole, by so absurd and unscriptural a notion as "80 years" for Solomon's reign? and especially when he so repeatedly employs in the Antiquities the very reckoning of the War, as we have seen? It is entirely impossible to believe the careful Josephus guilty of such consummate folly; and we *must* find some other origin of the 40 year corruption, rather than to ascribe it to Josephus himself. A very slight inspection of his work betrays the source of the corruption.

The Caption Datings.

§ 62. Look at the captions over the several books of Josephus' Antiquities. They include in each case a statement of the *number of years* covered by the book. These numbers are plainly the work of some editor, not of Josephus himself; for they in many cases mistake Josephus' reckoning, as we proceed to show. In our examination we shall find that this erroneous editing of the captions was the origin of the 40 years corruption in the reign of Solomon.

§ 63. The caption numbers and Josephus' own reckonings proceed as follows:

Book.		Captions.		Josephus.	
1. Creation to death of Isaac.......		3833 years.		3533	
2. To the Exodus..................		220 "		220	
3. Rejection of that generation.....		2 ⎫ "		1 ⎫	
4. To death of Moses..............		38 ⎪ 548		39 ⎪ 549	
5. To death of Eli.................		476 ⎪		477 ⎪	
6. To death of Saul...............		32 ⎭		32 ⎭	
7. To death of David		40		40	
8. To death of Ahab..............	540½	+41 ⎫ Sol. ext.			27+513½
		122 ⎬ —6		116	
9. To capture of 10 tribes		157 + 20		177	
10. To 1 Cyrus		182½-[2]*		180½	
		Overlap,		27	
11. To death of Alexander the Great		253½--7=		⎧ 190 ⎫ 247	
				⎩ +57 ⎭	
12. To death of Judas Maccabeus ...	284	170 ⎫			44
13. To death of Alexandra..........		82 ⎬ +2=		286	
14. To death of Antigonus..........		32 ⎭			
15. Finishing the Temple...........	+⎧	18 ⎫		18 ⎫	
16. Death of Alex. and Arist........		12 ⎬		12 ⎬	
17. Banishment of Archelaus........		14 ⎭		14 ⎭	
18. Jews from Babylon.............	57	32 ⎫			
19. Fadus Procurator		3½ ⎬ +5=		62	
20. To Florus (and the War)		22 ⎭			
Back to Captivity		639		"639 yrs."	
				⎧ + 27	
Back to 1 David.............		540½=		⎩ 513½	
		1179½		"1179[½]"	

---

* The "182½ years" at Book 10 is evidently a misprint for the correct 180½ as Schwartz also concedes.

THE MANIPULATION.

§ 64. Note the many variations between the caption numbers and Josephus' own dating. In inserting those caption numbers, the editor (or manipulator) forgot the 5 years omitted after Florus; and argued that Josephus' "639 years" reached from Titus to 1 Cyrus instead of the proper 9 Darius (just the mistake continually made); and therefore, that the books 11-20 covering that period must contain 639 years. And the headings of these books do so add up. Whereas, Josephus has "639 years" to 9 Darius (B. C. 513)+27 to 1 Cyrus (as B. C. 540)=666 years in those books, leaving but 513½ years in his books 7-10, which carry us back (666+513½=) "1179 [½] years" to 1 David. (§ 17.) But the manipulator finds left a full (" 1179[½]"— "639"=)540 ½ years (instead of Josephus' 513½ years left), to be got in some way into the four books back from 10 to 7. He must contrive a way to make out this excess of 27 years, in order to reach the total "1179[½]" years of Josephus at the beginning of David. What does he devise?

§ 65. At book 10 he has lost 27 years of his material (from 9 Darius to 1 Cyrus), and proceeding backward to books 9 and 8 he loses 14 more. This he does by taking a random remark of Josephus (at Ant. 9, xiv: 1,—never used by him as chronology),—that the reigns in Israel *add up* "240½ years"; and using this 240 as the reckoning of Josephus,—instead of the 260 of added reigns in Judah, correctly reduced by 6 to 254 in Josephus, on account of overlaps,—the manipulator has an added loss of (20—6=) 14, put with the other loss 27, making a total loss of 41 years which he finds he has accumulated, or 40 years loss when Solomon is given 40 *solus* instead of Josephus' 39. And thereupon, as he has now reached the farthest book backward, where the accumulated error must somehow be got rid of (to make out the total "1130½" to the temple and "1179[½]" to 1 David),—the manipulator grows desperate, and—dumps the whole loss into a 40-year surplus built for it upon Solomon!

§ 66. Calling Solomon "80" is giving him an excess of 41; for Josephus has but 39 to Solomon *solus*, 1 of his 40 years being given to joint reign with his father. And thus we see, that this "80 years" corruption originates with the very editor who invents the caption numbers. That astute manipulator rolls up the 40 years' deficiency, book by book, as he numbers backward; so that when reaching his limit at Solomon, he feels necessitated to *assume* for him a longer reign,—not having the wit to see how his deficiency has arisen. And so he increases this caption number from 123 to "163," and brackets in a needed [80] of reign, which in time becomes fixed as the real reading.

By this happy expedient of an 80-year Solomon, the manipulator recovers from all his losses, and Josephus is fixed out nicely! A clever dodge, perhaps. But, was ever a more shallow corruption? And yet, learned magnates to this day are ringing in our ears the wonderful dictum that *Josephus* himself put the reign of Solomon at 80 years! Let us hear it no more.*

§ 67. They tell us that Josephus "always adds in" the 80 years. And Jackson gives as a specimen Antiq. 9, xiv: 1, where we read: "The ten tribes were removed out of Samaria 947 years after their forefathers were come out of the land of Egypt and possessed this country, but 800 years after Joshua had been their leader; and 240 years, 7 months, and 7 days after they revolted from Rehoboam."† Jackson tries to make out the "947 years" thus: The "612" of the Priest Record +(80—3=) 77 of Solomon +260 as the added reigns of Judah=949 years. But (1) this does not give the number required. (2) not one of these items is a reckoning of Josephus, (3) what then becomes of the "240½ years" and the "800 years" after Joshua here given? Indeed, the whole attempt is monstrous.

This passage is plainly one of the interpolations thrust upon Josephus, to help out some one of the scores of theories concerning him. Very likely Josephus did make the remark about "240½ years" as the added reigns in Israel; but he made no use of it as *chronology*. He did not even use 260 of added reigns, in Judah, but correctly reduced them to 254 by overlaps, as we have proved. Some one has taken advantage of this 240 year remark here, to insert other numbers with it, whereby to make out a theory thus: Josephus' "592d" year to the temple+(Josephus' 39—3=) 36 more of Solomon+the "240" not thus used by Josephus=) 867 years from the Exodus. minus 40 of Moses and 27 of Joshua (from Africanus not Josephus who has 25)="800 years after Joshua." The "947" is a pure fabrication or misprint. (Or. see § 93.)

§ 68. Schwartz repeats the usual assertion, that Josephus includes 80 years of Solomon in all his reckonings, saying there are "at least 10 instances of this." But he enumerates only *five*, besides which we can find no others; and his number 5 is not a case from Josephus, but from the mutilating editor of the caption-datings, the very originator of the 80 year corruption. Moreover, his number four is only the duplicate of number three; so that he has in fact but 3 places cited from Josephus. One of these is the "476 years" considered above. The other two are disposed of here at § 52.

---

* See Appendix I, at §97.
† The Scripture numbers add 141½, but Josephus' numbers really add but 239½, since he drops a year each from Jehu and Jeroboam II.

Instead of Josephus " always adding in " the extra 40 for Solomon, no case can be proved of his adding it in. And the assumption that Josephus himself got up this 80 years enormity, in face of his beautiful, harmonious, and scriptural system of chronology everywhere apparent, is a monstrous absurdity, impossible of belief.* We repeat, there cannot be found in the " Antiquities " any departure (except one year of change at the 4th of Solomon) from the full and consistent plan of Old Testament dates laid out at the close of the " Jewish War," which we have exhibited above. (§ 17.)

Josephus' Whole Chronology.

§ 69. We have seen that Josephus (in the War) gives "1130½ years" from Titus back to the finished temple of Solomon, "and 1179" [½] back to the beginning of David's reign; with the 49 intervening years covering 40 of David and 9 of Solomon,—the founding of the temple being thus set as at 2 years of Solomon's *sole* reign (after 1 year with his father). Those two numbers (1130½ and 1179½) minus 57 of excess and minus A. D. 70, give 1004 B. C. and 1053 B. C. as Josephus' dates for the finished temple and the beginning of David. The building of the temple, thus assigned to B. C. 1011-1004, Josephus in his later work (the Antiquities) changes one year to B. C. 1010-1003; and this is the only change he anywhere makes in his chronology.

§ 70. The interval from the temple back to the Exodus, and thence back to Abraham, is given by Josephus (at Ant. 8, iii: 1) as "592 + 430 = 1022" (corrupt 1020) years "from Abraham's coming into Canaan " to the time when " Solomon began the temple in the fourth year of his reign." The "592" back to the Exodus is confirmed by other passages. (Ant. 10, viii: 5, etc. See my " Hist. of the 480th year reading " in I Ki. vi: 1, Appendix A.) The "612" of Josephus (found at Ant. 20, x: 1) is simply the Priest Record's duration of high-priesthood from Aaron to the death of Zadok, understood by Josephus as reaching 20 years after the founding of the temple, and so in agreement with his "592" back to the Exodus. (See the same Hist. of

---

*If anyone prefers (like Schwartz) to think that the author of the headings was rightly including the 5 years at the close, and also the 2 years of error he has seemingly lost, making his real total not the "639 years " of Josephus, as it now stands, but 646 (thought to reach back to 1 Cyrus); then this 646 taken from Josephus' "1179 years " leaves 533 years (not the proper 540) back to his date for David. And this will indicate that the writer of the caption-datings himself understood Josephus as reckoning from the 8th, not from the 1st of David (See §§ 43-47.) But this does not fasten such a reckoning on Josephus himself; it only suggests that this mistake concerning Josephus *arose very early*, even with the author of his headings,—it may be Clemens Alex. himself. (See Appendix J, § 101.)

mine.) Josephus once (Ap. ii: 2) speaks loosely of the period by the "612" number; but when trying to be exact he always puts it "592."

The 430 years from Abraham's arrival in Canaan to the Exodus, is confirmed by the numbers in the War (6, x: 1), thus: The "2177[½]" —"1130½" = 1047—7 and —592 — 448 from Melchizedek — 18 — 430 from Abraham's arrival. Then we have (+ 75 years back —) 505 from Abraham's birth to the Exodus, just as all writers have it. Thus, in his Antiquities, Josephus has

Founding of the Temple, B. C. 1010
                                  —592 years.
Exodus from Egypt,   B. C. 1602
                                  —505 years.
Birth of Abraham,   B. C. 2107

And in the War these dates are all one year earlier.

DILUVIAN CHRONOLOGY.

§ 71. The *post-diluvian* period, from the flood to the birth of Abraham, is given at Antiq. 1, vi: 5, and is much the same as the Septuagint and the Samaritan (not as our Hebrew) text. Thus: The "2 years (corrupt 12) after the flood" + 135 + [no Cainan] + 130 + 134 + 130 + 130 + 132 + Nahor 129 [corrupt 120] + Terah 70 = "992 years" [corrupt 292]. The corruption here is evident, and the reason of it,— an attempt to make Josephus agree with the Hebrew text, which has 700 less than Josephus, or "292." The Samaritan has 50 less than Josephus (at Nahor), *i. e.*, 942. The Septuagint has Josephus' "992," or (with Cainan) "1072" or "1122," or more, in different copies. (See my Diluvian Chron., Period A, B. §§ 58, 75.)

The *ante-diluvian* period, from Creation to the Flood, is given at Antiq. 1, iii: 4, and is much the same as the Septuagint (not as the Samaritan or the Hebrew) text. Thus: Adam 230 + 205 + 190 + 170 + 165 + 162 + 165 + 187 + 182 + Noah 600 = total "2256 years." Here a like corruption has been attempted, by insertion of [1656] in brackets, which is the Hebrew value, the Samaritan having but 1307. But the larger (or Lxx) values in both periods are obviously the true reckoning of Josephus. Of course, the heading of his Book I, with its "3833 years from the Creation to the death of Isaac," is not Josephus' number; but should be (2256 + 992 + Ab. 100 + Isaac 185 =) 3533 years.

The corruptions here attempted are introduced also at Ant. 8, iii: 1, and at 10, viii: 5. At the former place the corruption is introduced thus: Josephus' 1022 [corrupt 1020] back to Abraham's arrival + 75 to his birth + 60 of Terah (as in Usher) + Hebrew text 290 (with 2 at the flood lost) = "1447 years" [corrupt 1440] back to the flood as given. Then, the 1447 + Heb. text 1656 = "3103" [corrupt 2] back to creation, as given. At the latter place the corruption is introduced thus: Josephus' "1062½" back to the Exodus+505 to the birth of Abraham (without Usher's 60)+Heb. text 290 (with 2 at the flood lost) ="1857½" years [corrupt 1957½] back to the flood, as given. Then, 1857½+Heb. text 1656—"3513½ years," back to creation, as given. The diverse methods of corruption here apparent may indicate somewhat when the respective corruptions were made. (See our Chron., Period A, B, § 9, 10.)

§ 72. We thus have all Josephus' Old Testament chronology as follows:

Creation,	B. C. 5356	
		—2256 —Period A.
Flood,	B. C. 3100	
		— 992 —Period B.
Birth Abram,	B. C. 2108 *	
		— 505 —Period C.
Exodus,	B. C. 1603	
		— 592 —Period D.
4th Solomon,	B. C. 1011	
		— 491†—Period E.
2d Darius,	B. C. 520	
		— 520 —Period F.
Christian Era,	B. C. 0	

§ 73. We have now sufficiently examined all Josephus' Old Testament chronology, and we find it when freed from corruption and misunderstanding, a beautiful and harmonious system, accordant with Scripture, except in one or two small particulars easily explainable. (See interval D, "592" years, and the date of 1st Cyrus, B. C. 540.) We have prosecuted this study in the interest of the Holy Scriptures, which are greatly illucidated and corroborated by these authentic datings of the great Jewish author. Indeed, we believe that no branch of research will throw such light upon the Bible and show the accuracy of its history so clearly as will this Restored Chronology of Josephus. Therefore, in the hope of rearing a Bible bulwark against incoming tides of assault upon the historical and chronological verity of Scripture, we have pursued this labor of love. Let it demonstrate, as it must, the truthfulness of GOD'S WORD!

[Appendix A to J left in Ms.]

---

* This 2108 B. C. of Jos. for the birth of Abram is but 12 years more than the true Scriptural date (B. C. 2096) as we have shown it (Period A, B, § 17), and this arises from his 592 instead of 580 after the Exodus.

† In his later work, the Antiquities, Josephus has one year less at Solomon's temple (see § 51.) And his Priest Record (at Ant. 20, x: 1) if taken continuously would give 5 years less (*i. e.*, 7 years excess instead of Jos. 12), or a total of 5351 B. C. (viz., B. C. 106+"414"+ "466½"+"612"=1598 B. C. for the Exodus.) See § 26.

Supplementary Note.

As the great aim of all the foregoing work is to show the truthfulness of Scripture, and its consequent claim to our acceptance as the Word of God,—it was not possible to follow this line of thought, without awakening a kindred desire to justify the religious *contents of the Bible*, as indeed the Good Word of a Gracious God, worthy to be accepted and loved by all. This led to a thorough overhauling of theological thought as evolved simply from the Bible history; to discover, if possible, what little screw was loose in men's theories of doctrine, making them grate so harshly on the sensibilities of mankind.

The result was, another work on "Immortality and the Doom of Sin"; wherein it is shown, that the orthodox faith of Christendom, in a moderately Calvinistic (or rather Calv-arminian) form, commends itself to all minds as the Bible Truth,—with all appearance of over-harshness and severity removed,—when only the little false notion of *natural* inborn immortality is left out from the unwarranted *philosophizing* about Eden, and each person's eternity is left to the wise ordering of God. Immortality is thus brought to light in the Gospel, rather than philosophized out of Genesis. In fact, a *limited immortality*, meted out to individuals in righteousness and love as occasion requires, with opportunity for natural Decay in Sin where endless misery is not by stubbornness necessitated,—this is found the key, to unlock all doctrinal difficulty, and to exhibit the Bible as an inspired record, not only in itself absolutely truthful, but coming from a God infinitely lovable, and therefore a record eminently fit to be true.

No sooner was this work accomplished, than now the tide of sceptical and agnostic criticism from Germany strikes us, denying the truthfulness of all that has been held most true,—denying that even inspiration secures truth, or that there is any proof or any need of truthfulness in the Word of Christ or in the Word of God as given;—claiming, in short, that historic verity is of very little account in religion, and that Christianity can flourish and must be pushed (like other religions) on grounds of pious tradition and natural evolution. The sad eclipse of Faith foretokened by these wide-spread belittlings of Scripture, we have tried to ward off by a few clear and sharp-cut thrusts from the Sword of the Spirit,—such thrusts as seem lamentably wanting, though urgently called for by the times. And this finishes our three-fold work in behalf of *the inspired truthfulness of the original Scriptures*.

This last outbreak of Bible unbelief amply justifies our whole undertaking from the first; and shows that the church must begin back from the foundations, and demonstrate (as here attempted) the historical truthfulness of the Bible. Does not God at last show his hand in the hitherto hidden plan of our life-work, as a needed investigation for our times? "The Lord reigneth; let the earth rejoice!"

(PRIVATE REMARK. I regard as one of the tokens of divine Providence, that, from severe sickness, God has raised me so far as to be able to write this note, as a completion of the book. Thank God! for the faithful wife, a daughter of Mt. Holyoke, whose gentle hand and untiring devotion (in true Mary Lyon spirit) have kept me alive so long, to finish the work.)

SMITH B. GOODENOW,

Battle Creek, Iowa, May 16th, 1895.

THE END.

Another large work by the same author.

IMMORTALITY,

AND THE DOOM OF SIN.

Treated Rationally, Scripturally, Historically, and Psychologically.

Being an attempt to vindicate the Bible and the ways of God in every human destiny, as seen in orthodox Scripture doctrine; by the view that endless conscious being is only for intelligent accepters and rejecters of Christ.

IN TWELVE PARTS.

PART I.   Everlasting Punishment Attended With Everlasting Decay. (Chicago, 1873.)
PART II. The Pilgrim Faith Maintained. (Boston, 1884.)
PART III. The Crying Want of Our Times. (Set forth in sundry essays.)
PART IV. The Early Church on Retribution. ("Advance," 1874.)
PART V.   Psychology, or the Science of Spirit. (Compared with the science of matter.)
PART VI. Vital Theology. (More than moral theology.)
PART VII. The Eden Destiny. (Not eternalizing.)
PART VIII. New Testament View of the Fall. (Exposition of Rom. v: 12.)
PART IX. The Way to Endless Being.
PART X.   Is Christianity Universal?
PART XI. Is Gospel Judgment Universal?
PART XII. One Great Eternal Sin.

ALSO

SUNDRY ESSAYS, Showing the TRUTHFULNESS of the Bible as the WORD OF GOD.

www.ingramcontent.com/pod-product-compliance
Lightning Source LLC
Chambersburg PA
CBHW030350230426
43664CB00007BB/592